Reinforced
concrete
design

Other Macmillan titles of interest to civil engineers:

Reinforced concrete design

FIFTH EDITION

W. H. MOSLEY

FORMERLY NANYANG TECHNOLOGICAL UNIVERSITY, SINGAPORE
AND DEPARTMENT OF CIVIL ENGINEERING
UNIVERSITY OF LIVERPOOL

J. H. BUNGEY

DEPARTMENT OF CIVIL ENGINEERING
UNIVERSITY OF LIVERPOOL

R. HULSE

SCHOOL OF THE BUILT ENVIRONMENT
COVENTRY UNIVERSITY

First published 1976
Reprinted five times
Second edition 1982
Reprinted four times
Third edition 1987
Reprinted twice
Fourth edition 1990
Reprinted seven times
Fifth edition 1999
Published by
MACMILLAN PRESS LTD
Houndmills, Basingstoke, Hampshire RG21 6XS
and London
Companies and representatives throughout the world

ISBN 0-333-73956-6

A catalogue record for this book is available from the British Library.

This book is printed on paper suitable for recycling and made from
fully managed and sustained forest sources.

10   9   8   7   6   5   4   3   2   1
08   07 06 05 04 03 02 01 00 99

Printed in Great Britain by
Antony Rowe Ltd
Chippenham, Wiltshire

Contents

20 pages

Preface to Fifth Edition

The purpose of this book is to provide a straightforward introduction to the principles and methods of design for concrete structures. It is directed primarily at students and young designers who require an understanding of the basic theory and a concise guide to design procedures. Although the detailed design methods are generally according to British Standards, much of the theory and practice is of a fundamental nature and should, therefore, be useful to engineers in other countries. Limit state concepts are used and the calculations are in SI units throughout.

The subject matter has been arranged so that chapters 1 to 5 deal mostly with theory and analysis while the subsequent chapters cover the design and detailing of various types of member and structure. In order to include topics that are usually in an undergraduate course, there is a chapter on earth-retaining and water-retaining structures, and also a chapter on prestressed concrete.

Important equations that have been derived within the text are highlighted by an asterisk adjacent to the equation number.

In preparing the fifth edition of this book, the principal aim has been to update the text to incorporate changes and amendments introduced in the 1997 version of BS 8110 and to include new material such as corbel and pile cap design. A completely new chapter on composite construction has been added.

It should be mentioned that standard Codes of Practice such as BS 8110 are always liable to be revised, and readers should ensure that they are using the latest edition of any relevant standard.

Extracts from the British Standards are reproduced by permission of the British Standards Institution, 2 Park Street, London W1A 2BS, from whom complete copies can be obtained.

Finally, the authors wish to thank Ms S. De-Voisey who assisted in the preparation of the diagrams, Mrs F. Zimmermann who typed most of the draft and final copies of the original manuscript, and Dr E. A. Dickin and Mr C. Thomas for assistance in the preparation of some of the material in this edition.

Notation

Notation is generally in accordance with BS 8110, and the principal symbols are listed below. Other symbols are defined in the text where necessary. The symbols ε for strain and f for stress have been adopted throughout, with the general system of subscripts such that the first subscript refers to the material, c – concrete, s – steel, and the second subscript refers to the type of stress, c – compression, t – tension.

Notation for Chapters 1 to 12

A_s	Cross-sectional area of tension reinforcement
A'_s	Cross-sectional area of compression reinforcement
A_{sb}	Cross-sectional area of shear reinforcement in the form of bent-up bars
A_{sv}	Cross-sectional area of shear reinforcement in the form of links
a	Deflection
a_{cr}	Distance from surface crack position to point of zero strain
b	Width of section
b_v	Breadth of web or rib of a member
b_w	Breadth of web or rib of a member
d	Effective depth of tension reinforcement
d'	Depth to compression reinforcement
E_c	Static secant modulus of elasticity of concrete
E_s	Modulus of elasticity of steel
e	Eccentricity
F	Ultimate load
f_{cu}	Characteristic concrete cube strength
f_{pu}	Characteristic strength of prestressing tendons
f_s	Service stress or steel stress
f_y	Characteristic strength of reinforcement
f_{yv}	Characteristic strength of link reinforcement
G_k	Characteristic dead load
g_k	Characteristic dead load per unit length or area
h	Overall depth of section in plane of bending
h_f	Thickness of flange
I	Second moment of area
k_1	Average compressive stress in the concrete for a rectangular–parabolic stress block
k_2	A factor that relates the depth to the centroid of the rectangular–parabolic stress block and the depth of the neutral axis
l_a	Lever-arm factor $= z/d$
l_e	Effective height of a column or wall

M	Bending moment
M_u	Ultimate moment of resistance
N	Axial load
N_{bal}	Axial load on a column corresponding to the balanced condition
n	Ultimate load per unit area
P_0	Initial prestress force (chapter 12)
Q_k	Characteristic imposed load
q_k	Characteristic live load per unit length or area
$1/r_x$	Curvature of a beam at point x
r_{crit}	Critical steel ratio to control thermal cracks
s	Depth of equivalent rectangular stress block
s_{max}	Maximum likely crack spacing
s_v	Spacing of links along the member
T	Torsional moment
u	Perimeter
V	Shear force
W_k	Characteristic wind load
w_{max}	Maximum likely surface crack width
w_u	Ultimate load per unit length
x	Neutral axis depth
z	Lever arm
α_c	Coefficient of thermal expansion of mature concrete
α_e	Modular ratio
γ_f	Partial safety factor for load
γ_m	Partial safety factor for strength
ε_{sh}	Shrinkage strain
μ	Coefficient of friction
ν	Shear stress
ν_c	Ultimate shear stress in concrete
Φ	Bar size
ϕ	Creep coefficient

Notation for composite construction, Chapter 13

A	Area of steel section
A_{cv}	Area of concrete shear surface per unit length of beam
A_{sv}	Area of transverse reinforcement per unit length of beam
B	Breadth of steel flange
B_e	Total effective breadth of concrete flange
D	Depth of steel section
D_p	Overall depth of profiled steel sheet
D_s	Overall depth of concrete slab
d	Clear depth of steel web
d_s	Diameter of shear stud
h	Overall height of shear stud
I_s	Second moment of area of the steel beam about major axis
I_T	Second moment of area of the transformed section about neutral axis
k_1	Reduction factor to stud shear capacity for positive moments

k_2	Reduction factor to stud shear capacity based on the dimensions of the profiled steel decking
M_c	Moment capacity of composite section
M_s	Moment capacity of steel section
M_u	Ultimate design moment
N	Number of shear connectors in a group
N_f	Number of shear connectors for full shear connection
N_p	Number of shear connectors for partial shear connection
p_y	Design strength of structural steel
Q_e	Effective strength of shear stud
Q_k	Characteristic strength of shear stud
R_c	Resistance of concrete flange
R_{cx}	Resistance of concrete above neutral axis
R_s	Resistance of steel section
R_{sf}	Resistance of steel flange
R_{sx}	Resistance of steel flange above neutral axis
R_v	Resistance of clear web depth
R_w	Resistance of overall web depth $= R_s - 2R_{sf}$
R_{wx}	Resistance of web above neutral axis
S	Plastic modulus of steel section
s	Longitudinal spacing centre to centre of a group of shear connectors
t	Steel web thickness
Z	Elastic modulus of steel section
z	Lever arm
δ	Deflection
ε	Constant, equal to $(275/p_y)^{1/2}$
ν	Longitudinal shear per unit length
ν_p	Longitudinal shear contribution of profiled steel sheeting per unit length
ν_r	Longitudinal shear resistance of concrete flange per unit length

CHAPTER 1

Properties of reinforced concrete

CHAPTER INTRODUCTION

Reinforced concrete is a strong durable building material that can be formed into many varied shapes and sizes ranging from a simple rectangular column, to a slender curved dome or shell. Its utility and versatility are achieved by combining the best features of concrete and steel. Consider some of the widely differing properties of these two materials that are listed below.

	Concrete	Steel
strength in tension	poor	good
strength in compression	good	good, but slender bars will buckle
strength in shear	fair	good
durability	good	corrodes if unprotected
fire resistance	good	poor – suffers rapid loss of strength at high temperatures

It can be seen from this list that the materials are more or less complementary. Thus, when they are combined, the steel is able to provide the tensile strength and probably some of the shear strength while the concrete, strong in compression, protects the steel to give durability and fire resistance. This chapter can present only a brief introduction to the basic properties of concrete and its steel reinforcement. For a more comprehensive study, it is recommended that reference should be made to the specialised texts listed in Further Reading at the end of the book.

1.1   Composite action

The tensile strength of concrete is only about 10 per cent of the compressive strength. Because of this, nearly all reinforced concrete structures are designed on the assumption that the concrete does not resist any tensile forces. Reinforcement is designed to carry these tensile forces, which are transferred by bond between the interface of the two materials. If this bond is not adequate, the reinforcing bars will just slip within the concrete and there will not be a composite action. Thus members should be detailed so that the concrete can be well compacted around the reinforcement during construction. In addition, some bars are ribbed or twisted so that there is an extra mechanical grip.

In the analysis and design of the composite reinforced concrete section, it is assumed that there is a perfect bond, so that the strain in the reinforcement is identical to the strain in the adjacent concrete. This ensures that there is what is known as 'compatibility of strains' across the cross-section of the member.

The coefficients of thermal expansion for steel and for concrete are of the order of 10×10^{-6} per °C and $7\text{–}12 \times 10^{-6}$ per °C respectively. These values are sufficiently close that problems with bond seldom arise from differential expansion between the two materials over normal temperature ranges.

Figure 1.1 illustrates the behaviour of a simply supported beam subjected to bending and shows the position of steel reinforcement to resist the tensile forces, while the compression forces in the top of the beam are carried by the concrete.

Figure 1.1
Composite action

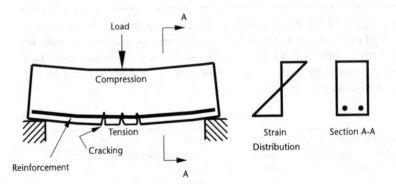

Wherever tension occurs it is likely that cracking of the concrete will take place. This cracking, however, does not detract from the safety of the structure provided there is good reinforcement bond to ensure that the cracks are restrained from opening so that the embedded steel continues to be protected from corrosion.

When the compressive or shearing forces exceed the strength of the concrete, then steel reinforcement must again be provided, but in these cases it is only required to supplement the load-carrying capacity of the concrete. For example, compression reinforcement is generally required in a column, where it takes the form of vertical bars spaced near the perimeter. To prevent these bars buckling, steel binders are used to assist the restraint provided by the surrounding concrete.

1.2 ▌ Stress–strain relations

The loads on a structure cause distortion of its members with resulting stresses and strains in the concrete and the steel reinforcement. To carry out the analysis and design of a member it is necessary to have a knowledge of the relationship between these stresses and strains. This knowledge is particularly important when dealing with reinforced concrete which is a composite material; for in this case the analysis of the stresses on a cross-section of a member must consider the equilibrium of the forces in the concrete and steel, and also the compatibility of the strains across the cross-section.

1.2.1 Concrete

Concrete is a very variable material, having a wide range of strengths and stress–strain curves. A typical curve for concrete in compression is shown in figure 1.2. As the load is applied, the ratio between the stresses and strains is approximately linear at first and the concrete behaves almost as an elastic material with virtually a full recovery of displacement if the load is removed. Eventually, the curve is no longer linear and the concrete behaves more and more as a plastic material. If the load were removed during the plastic range the recovery would no longer be complete and a permanent deformation would remain. The ultimate strain for most structural concretes tends to be a constant value of approximately 0.0035, irrespective of the strength of the concrete. The precise shape of the curve is very dependent on the length of time the load is applied, a factor which will be further discussed in section 1.4 on creep. Figure 1.2 is typical for a short-term loading.

Concrete generally increases its strength with age. This characteristic is illustrated by the graph in figure 1.3 which shows how the increase is rapid at first, becoming more gradual later. The precise relationship will depend upon the type of cement used. That

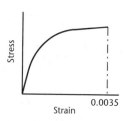

Figure 1.2
Stress–strain curve for concrete in compression

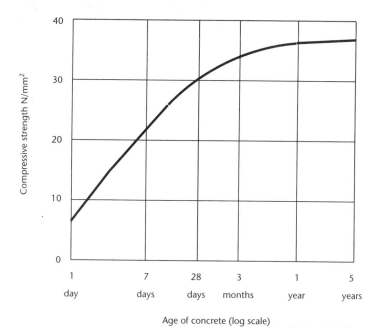

Figure 1.3
Increase of concrete strength with age. Typical curve for a grade C30 concrete made with a class 42.5 Portland cement

shown is for the typical variation of an adequately cured concrete made with commonly used class 42.5 Portland Cement. Some codes of practice allow the concrete strength used in design to be varied according to the age of the concrete when it supports the design load. BS 8110 does not permit the use of strengths greater than the 28-day value in calculations, but the Modulus of Elasticity may be modified to account for age as shown overleaf.

Modulus of elasticity of concrete

It is seen from the stress–strain curve for concrete that although elastic behaviour may be assumed for stresses below about one-third of the ultimate compressive strength, this relationship is not truly linear. Consequently it is necessary to define precisely what value is to be taken as the modulus of elasticity.

$$E = \frac{\text{stress}}{\text{strain}}$$

A number of alternative definitions exist, but the most commonly adopted is $E = E_c$ where E_c is known as the *secant* or *static modulus*. This is measured for a particular concrete by means of a static test in which a cylinder is loaded to just above one-third of the corresponding control cube stress and then cycled back to zero stress. This removes the effect of initial 'bedding-in' and minor stress redistributions in the concrete under load. Load is then reapplied and the behaviour will then be almost linear; the average slope of the line up to the specified stress is taken as the value for E_c. The test is described in detail in BS 1881 and the result is generally known as the *instantaneous static modulus of elasticity*.

The *dynamic modulus of elasticity*, E_{cq}, is sometimes referred to since this is much easier to measure in the laboratory and there is a fairly well-defined relationship between E_c and E_{cq}. The standard test is based on determining the resonant frequency of a laboratory prism specimen and is also described in BS 1881. It is also possible to obtain a good estimate of E_{cq} from ultrasonic measuring techniques, which may sometimes be used on site to assess the concrete in an actual structure. The standard test for E_{cq} is on an unstressed specimen. It can be seen from figure 1.4 that the value obtained represents the slope of the tangent at zero stress and E_{cq} is therefore higher than E_c. The relationship between the two moduli is given by

Static modulus $E_c = (1.25E_{cq} - 19)$ kN/mm^2

This equation is sufficiently accurate for normal design purposes.

Figure 1.4
Moduli of elasticity of concrete

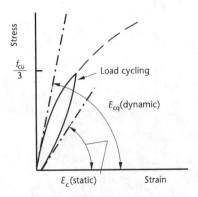

Load cycling

E_{cq}(dynamic)

E_c(static)   Strain

Table 1.1 Short-term modulus of elasticity of concrete

28-day characteristic cube strength $f_{cu, 28}$ (N/mm^2)	Static modulus $E_{c, 28}$ (kN/mm^2)	
	Typical range	Mean
25	19–31	25
30	20–32	26
40	22–34	28
50	24–36	30
60	26–38	32

The actual value of E for a concrete depends on many factors related to the mix, but a general relationship is considered to exist between the modulus of elasticity and the compressive cube strength. Ranges of E_c for various concrete grades which are suitable for design are shown in table 1.1. The magnitude of the modulus of elasticity is required when investigating the deflection and cracking of a structure. When considering short-term effects, member stiffnesses will be based on the static modulus E_c, as defined above. If long-term effects are being considered it can be shown that the effects of creep can be represented by modifying the value of E_c and this is discussed in section 6.3.2.

The elastic modulus at an age other than 28 days may be estimated from

$$E_{c, t} = E_{c, 28}(0.4 + 0.6 f_{cu, t} / f_{cu, 28})$$

1.2.2 Steel

Figure 1.5 shows typical stress–strain curves for (a) mild steel, and (b) high-yield steel. Mild steel behaves as an elastic material, with the strain proportional to the stress up to the yield, at which point there is a sudden increase in strain with no change in stress. After the yield point, mild steel becomes a plastic material and the strain increases rapidly up to the ultimate value. High-yield steel on the other hand, does not have a definite yield point but shows a more gradual change from an elastic to a plastic behaviour. Both materials have a similar slope of the elastic region with $E_s = 200$ kN/mm^2 approximately.

The specified strength used in design is based on the yield stress for mild steel, whereas for high-yield steel the strength is based on a specified proof stress. A 0.2 per cent proof stress is defined in figure 1.5 by the broken line drawn parallel to the linear part of the stress–strain curve.

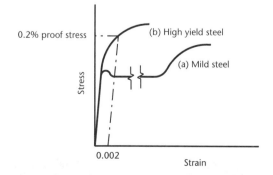

Figure 1.5
Stress–strain curves for steel

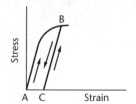

Figure 1.6
Strain hardening

Removal of the load within the plastic range would result in the stress–strain diagram following a line approximately parallel to the loading portion – see line BC in figure 1.6. The steel will be left with a permanent strain AC, which is known as 'slip'. If the steel is again loaded, the stress–strain diagram will follow the unloading curve until it almost reaches the original stress at B and then it will curve in the direction of the first loading. Thus, the proportional limit for the second loading is higher than for the initial loading. This action is referred to as 'strain hardening' or 'work hardening'.

The deformation of the steel is also dependent on the length of time the load is applied. Under a constant stress the strains will gradually increase – this phenomenon is known as 'creep' or 'relaxation'. The amount of creep that takes place over a period of time depends on the grade of steel and the magnitude of the stress. Creep of the steel is of little significance in normal reinforced concrete work, but it is an important factor in prestressed concrete where the prestressing steel is very highly stressed.

1.3 | Shrinkage and thermal movement

As concrete hardens there is a reduction in volume. This shrinkage is liable to cause cracking of the concrete, but it also has the beneficial effect of strengthening the bond between the concrete and the steel reinforcement. Shrinkage begins to take place as soon as the concrete is mixed, and is caused initially by the absorption of the water by the concrete and the aggregate. Further shrinkage is caused by evaporation of the water which rises to the concrete surface. During the setting process the hydration of the cement causes a great deal of heat to be generated, and as the concrete cools, further shrinkage takes place as a result of thermal contraction. Even after the concrete has hardened, shrinkage continues as drying out persists over many months, and any subsequent wetting and drying can also cause swelling and shrinkage. Thermal shrinkage may be reduced by restricting the temperature rise during hydration, which may be achieved by the following procedures.

1. Use a mix design with a low cement content.
2. Avoid rapid hardening and finely ground cement if possible.
3. Use cement replacements such as Ground Granulated Blast-furnace Slag (ggbs) or Pulverised Fuel Ash (pfa).
4. Keep aggregates and mixing water cool.
5. Use steel shuttering and cool with a water spray.
6. Strike the shuttering early to allow the heat of hydration to dissipate.

A low water–cement ratio will help to reduce drying shrinkage by keeping to a minimum the volume of moisture that can be lost.

If the change in volume of the concrete is allowed to take place freely without restraint, there will be no stress change within the concrete. Restraint of the shrinkage, on the other hand, will cause tensile strains and stresses. The restraint may be caused externally by fixity with adjoining members or friction against an earth surface, and internally by the action of the steel reinforcement. For a long wall or floor slab, the restraint from adjoining concrete may by reduced by using a system of constructing successive bays instead of alternate bays. This allows the free end of every bay to contract before the next bay is cast.

Day-to-day thermal expansion of the concrete can be greater than the movements caused by shrinkage. Thermal stresses and strains may be controlled by the correct positioning of movement or expansion joints in a structure. For example, the joints should be placed at an abrupt change in cross-section and they should, in general, pass completely through the structure in one plane.

When the tensile stresses caused by shrinkage or thermal movement exceed the strength of the concrete, cracking will occur. To control the crack widths, steel reinforcement must be provided close to the concrete surface; the codes of practice specify minimum quantities of reinforcement in a member for this purpose.

Calculation of stresses induced by shrinkage

(a) Shrinkage restrained by the reinforcement

The shrinkage stresses caused by reinforcement in an otherwise unrestrained member may be calculated quite simply. The member shown in figure 1.7 has a free shrinkage strain ε_{sh} if made of plain concrete, but this overall movement is reduced by the inclusion of reinforcement, giving a compressive strain ε_{sc} in the steel and causing an effective tensile strain ε_{ct} in the concrete. Thus

$$\varepsilon_{sh} = \varepsilon_{ct} + \varepsilon_{sc}$$
$$= \frac{f_{ct}}{E_c} + \frac{f_{sc}}{E_s} \tag{1.1}$$

where f_{ct} is the tensile stress in concrete area A_c and f_{sc} is the compressive stress in steel area A_s.

Equating forces in the concrete and steel for equilibrium gives

$$A_c f_{ct} = A_s f_{sc} \tag{1.2}$$

therefore

$$f_{ct} = \frac{A_s}{A_c} f_{sc}$$

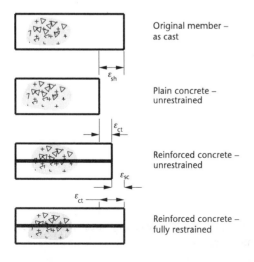

Original member –
as cast

Plain concrete –
unrestrained

Reinforced concrete –
unrestrained

Reinforced concrete –
fully restrained

Figure 1.7
Shrinkage strains

Substituting for f_{ct} in equation 1.1

$$\varepsilon_{sh} = f_{sc}\left(\frac{A_s}{A_c E_c} + \frac{1}{E_s}\right)$$

Thus if

$$\alpha_e = \frac{E_s}{E_c}$$

$$\varepsilon_{sh} = f_{sc}\left(\frac{\alpha_e A_s}{A_c E_s} + \frac{1}{E_s}\right)$$

$$= \frac{f_{sc}}{E_s}\left(\frac{\alpha_e A_s}{A_c} + 1\right)$$

Therefore steel stress

$$f_{sc} = \frac{\varepsilon_{sh} E_s}{1 + \frac{\alpha_e A_s}{A_c}} \tag{1.3}$$

EXAMPLE 1.1

Calculation of shrinkage stresses in concrete that is restrained by reinforcement only

A member contains 1.0 per cent reinforcement, and the free shrinkage strain ε_{sh} of the concrete is 200×10^{-6}. For steel, $E_s = 200$ kN/mm^2 and for concrete $E_c = 15$ kN/mm^2. Hence from equation 1.3:

$$\text{stress in reinforcement } f_{sc} = \frac{\varepsilon_{sh} E_s}{1 + \alpha_e \dfrac{A_s}{A_c}}$$

$$= \frac{200 \times 10^{-6} \times 200 \times 10^3}{1 + \dfrac{200}{15} \times 0.01}$$

$$= 35.3 \text{ N/mm}^2 \text{ compression}$$

$$\text{stress in concrete } f_{ct} = \frac{A_s}{A_c} f_{sc}$$

$$= 0.01 \times 35.3$$

$$= 0.35 \text{ N/mm}^2 \text{ tension}$$

The stresses produced in members free from external restraint are generally small as in the above example, and can be easily withstood both by the steel and the concrete.

(b) Shrinkage fully restrained

If the member is fully restrained, then the steel cannot be in compression since $\varepsilon_{sc} = 0$ and hence $f_{sc} = 0$ (figure 1.7). In this case the tensile strain induced in the concrete ε_{ct} must be equal to the free shrinkage strain ε_{sh}, and the corresponding stress will probably be high enough to cause cracking in immature concrete.

EXAMPLE 1.2

Calculation of fully restrained shrinkage stresses

If the member in example 1.1 were fully restrained, the stress in the concrete is given by

$$f_{ct} = \varepsilon_{ct} E_c$$

where

$$\varepsilon_{ct} = \varepsilon_{sh} = 200 \times 10^{-6}$$

then

$$f_{ct} = 200 \times 10^{-6} \times 15 \times 10^3$$
$$= 3.0 \text{ N/mm}^2$$

When cracking occurs, the uncracked lengths of concrete try to contract so that the embedded steel between cracks is in compression while the steel across the cracks is in tension. This feature is accompanied by localised bond breakdown, adjacent to each crack. The equilibrium of the concrete and reinforcement is shown in figure 1.8 and calculations may be developed to relate crack widths and spacings to properties of the cross-section; this is examined in more detail in chapter 6, which deals with serviceability requirements.

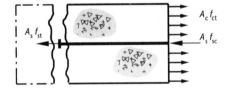

Figure 1.8
Shrinkage forces adjacent to a crack

Thermal movement

As the coefficients of thermal expansion of steel and concrete (α_s and α_c) are similar, differential movement between the steel and concrete will only be very small and is unlikely to cause cracking.

The differential thermal strain due to a temperature change T may be calculated as

$$T(\alpha_c - \alpha_s)$$

and should be added to the shrinkage strain ε_{sh} if significant.

The overall thermal contraction of concrete is, however, frequently effective in producing the first crack in a restrained member, since the required temperature changes could easily occur overnight in a newly cast member, even with good control of the heat generated during the hydration processes.

EXAMPLE 1.3

Thermal shrinkage

Find the fall in temperature required to cause cracking in a restrained member if ultimate tensile strength of the concrete $f_t = 2$ N/mm^2, $E_c = 16$ kN/mm^2 and $\alpha_c = \alpha_s = 10 \times 10^{-6}$ per °C. Ultimate tensile strain of concrete

$$\varepsilon_{ult} = \frac{f_t}{E_c} = \frac{2}{16 \times 10^3} = 125 \times 10^{-6}$$

Minimum temperature drop to cause cracking

$$= \frac{\varepsilon_{ult}}{\alpha_c} = \frac{125}{10} = 12.5°C$$

It should be noted that full restraint, as assumed in this example, is unlikely to occur in practice; thus the temperature change required to cause cracking is increased. A maximum 'restraint factor' of 0.5 is often used, with lower values where external restraint is likely to be small. The temperature drop required would then be given by the theoretical minimum divided by the 'restraint factor'.

1.4 Creep

Creep is the continuous deformation of a member under sustained load. It is a phenomenon associated with many materials, but it is particularly evident with concrete. The precise behaviour of a particular concrete depends on the aggregates and the mix design, but the general pattern is illustrated by considering a member subjected to axial compression. For such a member, a typical variation of deformation with time is shown by the curve in figure 1.9.

The characteristics of creep are

1. The final deformation of the member can be three to four times the short-term elastic deformation.

2. The deformation is roughly proportional to the intensity of loading and to the inverse of the concrete strength.

3. If the load is removed, only the instantaneous elastic deformation will recover – the plastic deformation will not.

4. There is a redistribution of load between the concrete and any steel present.

The redistribution of load is caused by the changes in compressive strains being transferred to the reinforcing steel. Thus the compressive stresses in the steel are increased so that the steel takes a larger proportion of the load.

The effects of creep are particularly important in beams, where the increased deflections may cause the opening of cracks, damage to finishes, and the non-alignment of mechanical equipment. Redistribution of stress between concrete and steel occurs primarily in the uncracked compressive areas and has little effect on the tension reinforcement other than reducing shrinkage stresses in some instances. The provision of reinforcement in the compressive zone of a flexural member, however, often helps to restrain the deflections due to creep.

Figure 1.9

Typical increase of deformation with time for concrete

1.5 Durability

Concrete structures, properly designed and constructed, are long lasting and should require little maintenance. The durability of concrete is influenced by

1. the exposure conditions
2. the concrete quality
3. the cover to the reinforcement
4. the width of any cracks.

Concrete can be exposed to a wide range of conditions such as the soil, sea water, stored chemicals or the atmosphere. The severity of the exposure governs the type of concrete mix required and the minimum cover to the reinforcing steel. Whatever the exposure, the concrete mix should be made from impervious and chemically inert aggregates. A dense, well-compacted concrete with a low water–cement ratio is all important and for some soil conditions it is advisable to use a sulfate-resisting cement.

Adequate cover is essential to prevent corrosive agents reaching the reinforcement through cracks and pervious concrete. The thickness of cover required depends on the severity of the exposure and the quality of the concrete (as shown in the table 6.1). The cover is also necessary to protect the reinforcement against a rapid rise in temperature and subsequent loss of strength during a fire. Information concerning this is given in Part 2 of BS 8110, while durability requirements with related design calculations to check and control crack widths and depths are described in chapter 6.

1.6 Specification of materials

1.6.1 Concrete

The selection of the type of concrete is frequently governed by the strength required, which in turn depends on the intensity of loading and the form and size of the structural members. For example, in the lower columns of a multi-storey building a higher-strength concrete may be chosen in preference to greatly increasing the size of the column section with a resultant loss in clear floor space.

The concrete strength is assessed by measuring the crushing strength of cubes or cylinders of concrete made from the mix. These are usually cured, and tested after twenty-eight days according to standard procedures. Concrete of a given strength is identified by its 'grade' – a grade C25 concrete has a characteristic cube crushing strength of 25 N/mm^2. Table 1.2 shows a list of commonly used grades and also the lowest grade appropriate for various types of construction.

Exposure conditions and durability can also affect the choice of the mix design and the grade of concrete. A structure subject to corrosive conditions in a chemical plant, for example, would require a denser and higher grade of concrete than, say, the interior members of a school or office block. Although Portland cement (PC) would be used in most structures, other cement types can also be used to advantage. Blast-furnace or sulfate-resisting cement may be used to resist chemical attack, low-heat cements in massive sections to reduce the heat of hydration, or rapid-hardening cement when a high early strength is required. In some circumstances it may be useful to replace some of the cement by materials such as Pulverised Fuel Ash or Ground Granulated Blastfurnace Slag which have slowly developing cementitious properties. These will reduce the heat

Table 1.2 Grades of concrete

Grade	Lowest grade for use as specified
C7.5	Plain concrete
C10	
C15	Reinforced concrete with lightweight aggregate
C20	
C25	Reinforced concrete with dense aggregate
C30	
C35	Concrete with post-tensioned tendons
C40	Concrete with pre-tensioned tendons
C50	
C60	

of hydration and may also lead to a smaller pore structure and increased durability. Generally, natural aggregates found locally are preferred; however, manufactured lightweight material may be used when self-weight is important, or a special dense aggregate when radiation shielding is required.

The concrete mix may either be classified as 'designed' or 'prescribed'. A 'designed mix' is one where the contractor is responsible for selecting the mix proportions to achieve the required strength and workability, whereas for a 'prescribed mix' the engineer specifies the mix proportions, and the contractor is responsible only for providing a properly mixed concrete containing the correct constituents in the prescribed proportions. Detailed requirements for mix specifications and compliance are given in BS 5328, together with details of cement types available.

1.6.2 Reinforcing steel

Table 1.3 lists the characteristic design strengths of several of the more common types of reinforcement. The nominal size of a bar is the diameter of an equivalent circular area.

Hot-rolled mild-steel bars usually have a smooth surface so that the bond with the concrete is by adhesion only. Mild-steel bars can readily be bent, so they are often used where small radius bends are necessary, such as for links in narrow beams or columns, but their availability and usage are becoming less common.

High-yield bars are manufactured either with a ribbed surface or in the form of a twisted square. Ribbed bars are usually described by the British Standards as type 2 bars

Table 1.3 Strength of reinforcement

Designation	Nominal sizes (mm)	Specified characteristic strength f_y (N/mm^2)
Hot-rolled mild steel (BS 4449)	All sizes	250
Hot-rolled high yield (BS 4449) Cold-worked high yield (BS 4461)	All sizes	460
Hard-drawn steel wire (BS 4482)	Up to and including 12	485

provided specified requirements are satisfied, and these are the bars most commonly used. Square twisted bars have inferior bond characteristics and are usually classified as type 1 bars, although these are more or less obsolete. All deformed bars have an additional mechanical bond with the concrete so that higher ultimate bond stresses may be specified as described in section 5.2. The bending of high-yield bars through a small radius is liable to cause tension cracking of the steel, and to avoid this the radius of the bend should not be less than three times the nominal bar size (see figure 5.6). The ductility of reinforcing steel is also classified for design purposes. All ribbed high-yield bars and all Grade 250 mild-steel bars may be assumed to be high ductility (Class H).

High-yield steel bars are only slightly more expensive than mild-steel bars. Therefore, because of their significant stress advantage, high-yield bars are the more economical. Nevertheless, mild-steel bars are sometimes preferred in water-retaining structures, where the maximum steel stresses are limited in order to reduce the tensile strains and cracking of the concrete.

Floor slabs, walls, shells and roads may be reinforced with a welded fabric of reinforcement, supplied in rolls and having a square or rectangular mesh. Hard-drawn steel wire is often used for this and can give large economies in the detailing of the reinforcement and also in site labour costs of handling and fixing. Prefabricated reinforcement bar assemblies are also becoming increasingly popular for similar reasons. Welded fabric mesh made of ribbed wire greater than 6 mm diameter may be Class H ductility, but plain or indented wire fabric may be assumed to be normal ductility (Class N).

The cross-sectional areas and perimeters of various sized bars, and the cross-sectional area per unit width of slabs are listed in the Appendix. Reinforcing bars in a member should either be straight or bent to standard shapes. These shapes must be fully dimensioned and listed in a schedule of the reinforcement which is used on site for the bending and fixing of the bars. Standard bar shapes and a method of scheduling are specified in BS 4466. The bar types as previously described are commonly identified by the following codes: R for mild steel; Y for high yield deformed steel, type 1; T for high yield deformed steel, type 2; this notation is generally used throughout this book.

Limit state design

The design of an engineering structure must ensure that (1) under the worst loading the structure is safe, and (2) during normal working conditions the deformation of the members does not detract from the appearance, durability or performance of the structure. Despite the difficulty in assessing the precise loading and variations in the strength of the concrete and steel, these requirements have to be met. Three basic methods using factors of safety to achieve safe, workable structures have been developed; they are

1. The permissible stress method in which ultimate strengths of the materials are divided by a factor of safety to provide design stresses which are usually within the elastic range.
2. The load factor method in which the working loads are multiplied by a factor of safety.
3. The limit state method which multiplies the working loads by partial factors of safety and also divides the materials' ultimate strengths by further partial factors of safety.

The permissible stress method has proved to be a simple and useful method but it does have some serious inconsistencies. Because it is based on an elastic stress distribution, it is not really applicable to a semi-plastic material such as concrete, nor is it suitable when the deformations are not proportional to the load, as in slender columns. It has also been found to be unsafe when dealing with the stability of structures subject to overturning forces (see example 2.2).

In the load factor method the ultimate strength of the materials should be used in the calculations. As this method does not apply factors of safety to the material stresses, it cannot directly take account of the variability of the materials, and also it cannot be used to calculate the deflections or cracking at working loads.

$\longrightarrow$

→

The limit state method of design overcomes many of the disadvantages of the previous two methods. This is done by applying partial factors of safety, both to the loads and to the material strengths, and the magnitude of the factors may be varied so that they may be used either with the plastic conditions in the ultimate state or with the more elastic stress range at working loads. This flexibility is particularly important if full benefits are to be obtained from development of improved concrete and steel properties.

2.1 | Limit states

The purpose of design is to achieve acceptable probabilities that a structure will not become unfit for its intended use – that is, that it will not reach a limit state. Thus, any way in which a structure may cease to be fit for use will constitute a limit state and the design aim is to avoid any such condition being reached during the expected life of the structure.

The two principal types of limit state are the ultimate limit state and the serviceability limit state.

(a) Ultimate limit state

This requires that the structure must be able to withstand, with an adequate factor of safety against collapse, the loads for which it is designed. The possibility of buckling or overturning must also be taken into account, as must the possibility of accidental damage as caused, for example, by an internal explosion.

(b) Serviceability limit states

Generally the most important serviceability limit states are

1. Deflection – the appearance or efficiency of any part of the structure must not be adversely affected by deflections.
2. Cracking – local damage due to cracking and spalling must not affect the appearance, efficiency or durability of the structure.
3. Durability – this must be considered in terms of the proposed life of the structure and its conditions of exposure.

Other limit states that may be reached include

4. Excessive vibration – which may cause discomfort or alarm as well as damage.
5. Fatigue – must be considered if cyclic loading is likely.
6. Fire resistance – this must be considered in terms of resistance to collapse, flame penetration and heat transfer.
7. Special circumstances – any special requirements of the structure which are not covered by any of the more common limit states, such as earthquake resistance, must be taken into account.

The relative importance of each limit state will vary according to the nature of the structure. The usual procedure is to decide which is the crucial limit state for a particular structure and base the design on this, although durability and fire resistance requirements may well influence initial member sizing and concrete grade selection. Checks must also be made to ensure that all other relevant limit states are satisfied by the results produced. Except in special cases, such as water-retaining structures, the ultimate limit state is generally critical for reinforced concrete although subsequent serviceability checks may affect some of the details of the design. Prestressed concrete design, however, is generally based on serviceability conditions with checks on the ultimate limit state.

In assessing a particular limit state for a structure it is necessary to consider all the possible variable parameters such as the loads, material strengths and constructional tolerances.

2.2 Characteristic material strengths and characteristic loads

2.2.1 Characteristic material strengths

The strengths of materials upon which design is based are those strengths below which results are unlikely to fall. These are called 'characteristic' strengths. It is assumed that for a given material, the distribution of strength will be approximately 'normal', so that a frequency distribution curve of a large number of sample results would be of the form shown in figure 2.1 The characteristic strength is taken as that value below which it is unlikely that more than 5 per cent of the results will fall. This is given by

$$f_k = f_m - 1.64s$$

where f_k = characteristic strength, f_m = mean strength, s = standard deviation.

The relationship between characteristic and mean values accounts for variations in results of test specimens and will, therefore, reflect the method and control of manufacture, quality of constituents, and nature of the material.

Figure 2.1
Normal frequency distribution of strengths

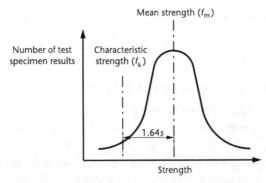

2.2.2 Characteristic loads

Ideally it should also be possible to assess loads statistically, in which case

characteristic load = mean load ± 1.64 standard deviations

In most cases it is the maximum loading on a structural member that is critical and the upper, positive value given by this expression is used, but the lower, minimum value may apply when considering stability or the behaviour of continuous members.

These characteristic values represent the limits within which at least 90 per cent of values will lie in practice. It is to be expected that not more than 5 per cent of cases will exceed the upper limit and not more than 5 per cent will fall below the lower limit. They are design values which take into account the accuracy with which the loads can be predicted.

Usually, however, there is insufficient statistical data to allow loading to be treated in this way, and in this case the standard loadings, given in BS 6399 Design Loads for Buildings, Part 1: Code of Practice for dead and imposed loads, should be used as representing characteristic values.

2.3 Partial factors of safety

Other possible variations such as constructional tolerances are allowed for by partial factors of safety applied to the strength of the materials and to the loadings. It should theoretically be possible to derive values for these from a mathematical assessment of the probability of reaching each limit state. Lack of adequate data, however, makes this unrealistic and in practice the values adopted are based on experience and simplified calculations.

2.3.1 Partial factors of safety for materials (γ_m)

$$\text{Design strength} = \frac{\text{characteristic strength } (f_k)}{\text{partial factor of safety } (\gamma_m)}$$

The following factors are considered when selecting a suitable value for γ_m

1. The strength of the material in an actual member. This strength will differ from that measured in a carefully prepared test specimen and it is particularly true for concrete where placing, compaction and curing are so important to the strength. Steel, on the other hand, is a relatively consistent material requiring a small partial factor of safety.
2. The severity of the limit state being considered. Thus, higher values are taken for the ultimate limit state than for the serviceability limit state.

Recommended values for γ_m are given in table 2.1 although it should be noted that for precast factory conditions it may be possible to reduce the value for concrete at the ultimate limit state.

Table 2.1 Partial factors of safety applied to materials (γ_m)

Limit state	Material	
	Concrete	Steel
Ultimate		
Flexure	1.5	1.05
Shear	1.25	1.05
Bond	1.4	
Serviceability	1.0	1.0

2.3.2 Partial factors of safety for loads (γ_f)

Errors and inaccuracies may be due to a number of causes:

1. design assumptions and inaccuracy of calculation
2. possible unusual load increases
3. unforeseen stress redistributions
4. constructional inaccuracies

These cannot be ignored, and are taken into account by applying a partial factor of safety (γ_f) on the loadings, so that

design load = characteristic load × partial factor of safety (γ_f)

The value of this factor should also take into account the importance of the limit state under consideration and reflect to some extent the accuracy with which different types of loading can be predicted, and the probability of particular load combinations occurring. Recommended values are given in table 2.2. It should be noted that design errors and constructional inaccuracies have similar effects and are thus sensibly grouped together. These factors will account adequately for normal conditions although gross errors in design or construction obviously cannot be catered for.

Table 2.2 Partial factors of safety for loadings

Load combination	Ultimate				Serviceability
	Dead (γ_G)	Imposed (γ_Q)	Earth & Water (γ_Q)	Wind (γ_W)	All ($\gamma_G, \gamma_Q, \gamma_W$)
Dead & Imposed (+ Earth & Water)	1.4 (or 1.0)	1.6 (or 0.0)	1.4	—	1.0
Dead & Wind (+ Earth & Water)	1.4 (or 1.0)	—	1.4	1.4	1.0
Dead & Imposed & Wind (+ Earth & Water)	1.2	1.2	1.2	1.2	1.0

The lower values in brackets applied to dead or imposed loads at the Ultimate Limit State should be used when *minimum* loading is critical.

2.4 Global factor of safety

The use of partial factors of safety on materials and loads offers considerable flexibility, which may be used to allow for special conditions such as very high standards of construction and control or, at the other extreme, where structural failure would be particularly disastrous.

The global factor of safety against a particular type of failure may be obtained by multiplying the appropriate partial factors of safety. For instance, a beam failure caused by yielding of tensile reinforcement would have a factor of

$$\gamma_m \times \gamma_f = 1.05 \times 1.4 = 1.47 \qquad \text{for dead loads only}$$

or

$$1.05 \times 1.6 = 1.68 \qquad \text{for live loads only}$$

Thus the practical case will have a value between these, depending on the relative loading proportions, and this can be compared with the value of 1.8 which has generally been used as the overall factor in the load factor design approach.

Similarly, failure by crushing of the concrete in the compression zone has a factor of $1.5 \times 1.6 = 2.40$ due to live loads only, which reflects the fact that such failure is generally without warning and may be very serious. Thus the basic values of partial factors chosen are such that under normal circumstances the global factor of safety is similar to that used in earlier design methods.

EXAMPLE 2.1

Determine the cross-sectional area of a mild steel cable which supports a total dead load of 3.0 kN and a live load of 2.0 kN as shown in figure 2.2.

The characteristic yield stress of the mild steel is 250 N/mm^2.

Carry out the calculations using

1. The load factor method with a load factor $= 1.8$.

2. A permissible stress design with a factor of safety of 1.8 on the yield stress.

3. A limit state design with the following factors of safety.

$\gamma_G = 1.4$ for the dead load, $\gamma_Q = 1.6$ for the live load, $\gamma_m = 1.05$, for the steel strength.

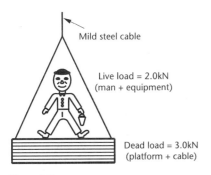

Figure 2.2
Diagram for example 2.1

(a) Load factor method

Design load = load factor (dead load + live load)

$$= 1.8(3.0 + 2.0) = 9.0\text{kN}$$

$$\text{Required cross-sectional area} = \frac{\text{design load}}{\text{yield stress}}$$

$$= \frac{9.0 \times 10^3}{250} = 36 \text{ mm}^2$$

(b) Permissible stress method

Design load $= 3.0 + 2.0 = 5.0$ kN

$$\text{Permissible stress} = \frac{\text{yield stress}}{\text{safety factor}}$$

$$= \frac{250}{1.8} = 139 \text{ N/mm}^2$$

$$\text{Required cross-sectional area} = \frac{\text{design load}}{\text{permissible stress}}$$

$$= \frac{5.0 \times 10^3}{139} = 36 \text{ mm}^2$$

(c) Limit state method

Design load $= \gamma_G \times$ dead load $+ \gamma_Q \times$ live load

$$= 1.4 \times 3.0 + 1.6 \times 2.0 = 7.4 \text{ kN}$$

$$\text{Design stress} = \frac{\text{characteristic yield stress}}{\gamma_m}$$

$$= \frac{250}{1.05} = 238 \text{ N/mm}^2$$

$$\text{Required cross-sectional area} = \frac{\text{design load}}{\text{design stress}}$$

$$= \frac{7.4 \times 10^3}{238}$$

$$= 31.1 \text{ mm}^2$$

These different design methods all give similar results for the cross-sectional area. Fewer calculations are required for the permissible stress and the load factor methods, so reducing the chances of an arithmetical error. The limit state method provides much better control over the factors of safety, which are applied to each of the variables. For convenience, the partial factors of safety in the example are the same as those recommended in BS 8110. Probably, in a practical design, higher factors of safety would be preferred for a single supporting cable, in view of the consequences of a failure.

EXAMPLE 2.2

Figure 2.3 shows a beam supported on foundations at A and B. The loads supported by the beam are its own uniformly distributed dead weight of 20 kN/m and a 170 kN live load concentrated at end C. Determine the weight of foundation required at A in order to resist uplift

1. by applying a factor of safety of 2.0 to the reaction calculated for the working loads
2. using a limit state approach with partial factors of safety of $\gamma_G = 1.4$ or 1.0 for the dead load and $\gamma_Q = 1.6$ for the live load.

Investigate the effect on these designs of a 7 per cent increase in the live load.

(a) Factor of safety on uplift = 2.0

Taking moments about B

$$\text{Uplift } R_a = \frac{(170 \times 2 - 20 \times 8 \times 2)}{6.0} = 3.33 \text{ kN}$$

Weight of foundation required = $3.33 \times$ safety factor

$$= 3.33 \times 2.0 = 6.7 \text{ kN}$$

With a 7 per cent increase in the live load

$$\text{Uplift } R_A = \frac{(1.07 \times 170 \times 2 - 20 \times 8 \times 2)}{6.0} = 7.3 \text{ kN}$$

Thus with a slight increase in the live load there is a significant increase in the uplift and the structure becomes unsafe.

(b) Limit state method

The arrangement of the loads for the maximum uplift at A is shown in figure 2.3b.

Design dead load over BC $= \gamma_G \times 20 \times 2$

$$= 1.4 \times 20 \times 2 = 56 \text{ kN}$$

Design dead load over AB $= \gamma_G \times 20 \times 6$

$$= 1.0 \times 20 \times 6 = 120 \text{ kN}$$

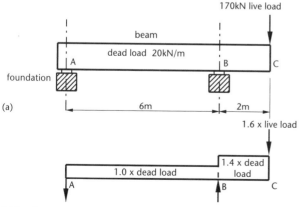

Figure 2.3
Uplift calculation example

(b) Loading arrangement for uplift at A at the ultimate limit state

Design live load $= \gamma_Q \times 170$

$$= 1.6 \times 170 = 272 \text{ kN}$$

Taking moments about B for the ultimate loads

$$\text{Uplift } R_A = \frac{(272 \times 2 + 56 \times 1 - 120 \times 3)}{6.0} = 40 \text{ kN}$$

Therefore weight of foundation required = 40 kN.

A 7 per cent increase in the live load will not endanger the structure, since the actual uplift will only be 7.3 kN as calculated previously. In fact in this case it would require an increase of 65 per cent in the live load before the uplift would exceed the weight of a 40 kN foundation.

CHAPTER 3

Analysis of the structure

CHAPTER INTRODUCTION

A reinforced concrete structure is a combination of beams, columns, slabs and walls, rigidly connected together to form a monolithic frame. Each individual member must be capable of resisting the forces acting on it, so that the determination of these forces is an essential part of the design process. The full analysis of a rigid concrete frame is rarely simple; but simplified calculations of adequate precision can often be made if the basic action of the structure is understood.

The analysis must begin with an evaluation of all the loads carried by the structure, including its own weight. Many of the loads are variable in magnitude and position, and all possible critical arrangements of loads must be considered. First the structure itself is rationalised into simplified forms that represent the load-carrying action of the prototype. The forces in each member can then be determined by one of the following methods.

1. Applying moment and shear coefficients.
2. Manual calculations.
3. Computer methods.

Tabulated coefficients are suitable for use only with simple, regular structures such as equal-span continuous beams carrying uniform loads. Manual calculations are possible for the vast majority of structures, but may be tedious for large or complicated ones. The computer can be an invaluable help in the analysis of even quite small frames, and for some calculations it is almost indispensable. However, the amount of output from a computer analysis is sometimes almost overwhelming; and then the results are most readily interpreted when they are presented diagrammatically by means of a graph plotter or other visual device.

Since the design of a reinforced concrete member is generally based on the ultimate limit state, the analysis is usually performed for loadings corresponding to that state. Prestressed concrete members, however, are normally designed for serviceability loadings, as discussed in chapter 12.

3.1 | Loads

The loads on a structure are divided into two types: 'dead' loads, and 'live' (or imposed) loads. Dead loads are those which are normally permanent and constant during the structure's life. Live loads, on the other hand, are transient and are variable in magnitude, as for example those due to wind or to human occupants. Recommendations for the loadings on buildings are given in the British Standards BS 6399: Part 1. Design loads for buildings, and Part 2. Wind loads. Bridge loadings are specified in BS 5400: Part 2. Specification for loads.

A table of values for some useful dead loads and imposed loads is given in the Appendix.

3.1.1 Dead loads

Dead loads include the weight of the structure itself, and all architectural components such as exterior cladding, partitions and ceilings. Equipment and static machinery, when permanent fixtures, are also often considered as part of the dead load. Once the sizes of all the structural members, and the details of the architectural requirements and permanent fixtures have been established, the dead loads can be calculated quite accurately; but first of all, preliminary design calculations are generally required to estimate the probable sizes and self-weights of the structural concrete elements.

For most reinforced concretes, a typical value for the self-weight is 24 kN per cubic metre, but a higher density should be taken for heavily reinforced or dense concretes. In the case of a building, the weights of any partitions should be calculated from the architects' drawings. A minimum partition imposed loading of 1.0 kN per square metre is usually specified, but this is only adequate for light-weight partitions.

Dead loads are generally calculated on a slightly conservative basis, so that a member will not need redesigning because of a small change in its dimensions. Over-estimation, however, should be done with care, since the dead load can often actually reduce some of the forces in parts of the structure as will be seen in the case of the hogging moments in the continuous beam of figure 3.1.

3.1.2 Imposed loads

These loads are more difficult to determine accurately. For many of them, it is only possible to make conservative estimates based on standard codes of practice or past experience. Examples of imposed loads on buildings are: the weights of its occupants, furniture, or machinery; the pressures of wind, the weight of snow, and of retained earth or water; and the forces caused by thermal expansion or shrinkage of the concrete.

A large building is unlikely to be carrying its full imposed load simultaneously on all its floors. For this reason the British Standard Code of Practice allows a reduction in the total imposed floor loads when the columns, walls or foundations are designed, for a building more than two storeys high. Similarly, the imposed load may be reduced when designing a beam span which supports a floor area greater than 40 square metres.

Although the wind load is an imposed load, it is kept in a separate category when its partial factors of safety are specified, and when the load combinations on the structure are being considered.

3.2 | Load combinations

3.2.1 Load Combinations for the Ultimate State

Various combinations of the characteristic values of dead load G_k, imposed load Q_k, wind load W_k and their partial factors of safety must be considered for the loading of the structure. The partial factors of safety specified by BS 8110 are discussed in chapter 2, and for the ultimate limit state the loading combinations to be considered are as follows.

1. Dead and imposed load

   $1.4G_k + 1.6Q_k$

2. Dead and wind load

   $1.0G_k + 1.4W_k$

3. Dead, imposed and wind load

   $1.2G_k + 1.2Q_k + 1.2W_k$

The imposed load can usually cover all or any part of the structure and, therefore, should be arranged to cause the most severe stresses. Load combination 1 should also be associated with a minimum design dead load of $1.0G_k$ applied to such parts of the structure as will give the most unfavourable condition,

For load combination 1, a three-span continuous beam would have the loading arrangement shown in figure 3.1, in order to cause the maximum sagging moment in the outer spans and the maximum possible hogging moment in the centre span. A study of the deflected shape of the beam would confirm this to be the case.

Figure 3.2 shows the arrangements of vertical loading on a multi-span continuous beam to cause (i) maximum sagging moments in alternate spans and maximum possible hogging moments in adjacent spans, and (ii) maximum hogging moments at support A.

As a simplification, BS 8110 allows the ultimate design moments at the supports to be calculated from one loading condition with all spans fully covered with the ultimate load $1.4G_k + 1.6Q_k$ as shown in part (iii) of figure 3.2.

Under load combination 2, dead and wind load, it is possible that a critical stability condition may occur if, on certain parts of a structure, the dead load is taken as $1.4G_k$. An example of this is illustrated in figure 3.3, depicting how the dead load of the cantilever section increases the overturning moment about support B.

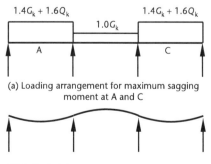

$1.4G_k + 1.6Q_k$ $1.0G_k$ $1.4G_k + 1.6Q_k$

A C

(a) Loading arrangement for maximum sagging
moment at A and C

(b) Deflected shape

Figure 3.1
Three-span beam

Figure 3.2
Multi-span beam loading
arrangements

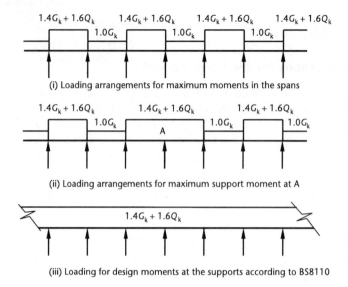

(i) Loading arrangements for maximum moments in the spans

(ii) Loading arrangements for maximum support moment at A

(iii) Loading for design moments at the supports according to BS8110

Figure 3.3
Load combination dead plus
wind

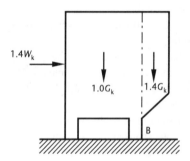

3.2.2 Load combinations for the serviceability limit state

A partial factor of safety of $\gamma_f = 1.0$ is usually applied to all load combinations at the serviceability limit state.

In considering deflections, the imposed load should be arranged to give the worst effects. The deflections calculated from the load combinations are the immediate deflections of a structure. Deflection increases due to the creep of the concrete should be based only on the dead load plus any part of the imposed load which is permanently on the structure, this being considered fully in chapter 6, which deals with serviceability requirements.

3.3 | Analysis of beams

To design a structure it is necessary to know the bending moments, torsional moments, shearing forces and axial forces in each member. An elastic analysis is generally used to determine the distribution of these forces within the structure; but because – to some extent – reinforced concrete is a plastic material, a limited redistribution of the elastic moments is sometimes allowed. A plastic yield-line theory may be used to calculate the moments in concrete slabs. The properties of the materials, such as Young's modulus, which are used in the structural analysis should be those associated with their characteristic strengths. The stiffnesses of the members can be calculated on the basis of any one of the following.

1. The entire concrete cross-section (ignoring the reinforcement).
2. The concrete cross-section plus the transformed area of reinforcement based on the modular ratio.
3. The compression area only of the concrete cross-section, plus the transformed area of reinforcement based on the modular ratio.

The concrete cross-section described in (1) is the simpler to calculate and would normally be chosen.

A structure should be analysed for each of the critical loading conditions which produce the maximum stresses at any particular section. This procedure will be illustrated in the examples for a continuous beam and a building frame. For these structures it is conventional to draw the bending-moment diagram on the tension side of the members.

Sign conventions

1. For the moment-distribution analyses anti-clockwise support moments are positive as, for example, in table 3.1 for the fixed end moments (FEM).
2. For subsequently calculating the moments along the span of a member, moments causing sagging are positive, while moments causing hogging are negative, as illustrated in figure 3.5.

3.3.1 Non-continuous beams

One-span, simply supported beams or slabs are statically determinate and the analysis for bending moment and shearing forces is readily performed manually. For the ultimate limit state we need only consider the maximum load of $1.4G_k + 1.6Q_k$ on the span.

EXAMPLE 3.1

Analysis of a non-continuous beam

The one-span simply supported beam shown in figure 3.4 carries a distributed dead load including self-weight of 25 kN/m, a permanent concentrated partition load of 30 kN at mid-span, and a distributed imposed load of 10 kN/m.

Figure 3.4 shows the values of ultimate load required in the calculations of the shearing forces and bending moments.

$$\text{Maximum shear force} \quad = \frac{42}{2} + \frac{204}{2} \quad = 123 \text{ kN}$$

$$\text{Maximum bending moment} = \frac{42 \times 4}{4} + \frac{204 \times 4}{8} = 144 \text{ kN m}$$

The analysis is completed by drawing the shearing-force and bending-moment diagrams which would later be used in the design and detailing of the shear and bending reinforcement.

Figure 3.4
Analysis of one-span beam

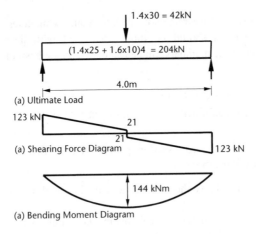

(a) Ultimate Load

(a) Shearing Force Diagram

(a) Bending Moment Diagram

3.3.2 Continuous beams

The methods of analysis for continuous beams may also be applied to continuous slabs which span in one direction. A continuous beam is considered to have no fixity with the supports so that the beam is free to rotate. This assumption is not strictly true for beams framing into columns and for that type of continuous beam it is more accurate to analyse them as part of a frame, as described in section 3.4. A simplified method of analysis that can be applied to slabs is described in chapter 8.

A continuous beam should be analysed for the loading arrangements which give the maximum stresses at each section, as described in section 3.2.1 and illustrated in figures 3.1 and 3.2. The analysis to calculate the bending moments can be carried out manually by moment distribution or equivalent methods, but tabulated shear and moment coefficients may be adequate for continuous beams having approximately equal spans and uniformly distributed loads.

Continuous beams – the general case

Having determined the moments at the supports by, say, moment distribution, it is necessary to calculate the moments in the spans and also the shear forces on the beam. For a uniformly distributed load, the equations for the shears and the maximum span moments can be derived from the following analysis.

Using the sign convention of figure 3.5 and taking moments about support B:

$$V_{AB}L - \frac{wL^2}{2} + M_{AB} - M_{BA} = 0$$

therefore

$$V_{AB} = \frac{wL}{2} - \frac{(M_{AB} - M_{BA})}{L} \tag{3.1}$$

and

$$V_{BA} = wL - V_{AB} \tag{3.2}$$

Maximum span moment M_{max} occurs at zero shear, and distance to zero shear

$$a_3 = \frac{V_{AB}}{w} \tag{3.3}$$

therefore

$$M_{max} = \frac{V_{AB}^2}{2w} + M_{AB} \tag{3.4}$$

The points of contraflexure occur at $M = 0$, that is

$$V_{AB}x - \frac{wx^2}{2} + M_{AB} = 0$$

where x is the distance from support A. Taking the roots of this equation gives

$$x = \frac{V_{AB} \pm \sqrt{(V_{AB}^2 + 2wM_{AB})}}{w}$$

so that

$$a_1 = \frac{V_{AB} - \sqrt{(V_{AB}^2 + 2wM_{AB})}}{w} \tag{3.5}$$

and

$$a_2 = L - \frac{V_{AB} + \sqrt{(V_{AB}^2 + 2wM_{AB})}}{w} \tag{3.6}$$

A similar analysis can be applied to beams that do not support a uniformly distributed load. In manual calculations it is usually not considered necessary to calculate the distances a_1, a_2 and a_3 which locate the points of contraflexure and maximum moment – a sketch of the bending moment is often adequate – but if a computer is performing the calculations these distances may as well be determined also.

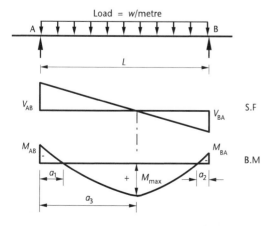

Figure 3.5
Shears and moments in a beam

EXAMPLE 3.2

Analysis of a continuous beam

The continuous beam shown in figure 3.6 has a constant cross-section and supports a uniformly distributed dead load including its self-weight of $G_k = 25$ kN/m and an imposed load $Q_k = 10$ kN/m.

Figure 3.6

Continuous beam loading arrangement

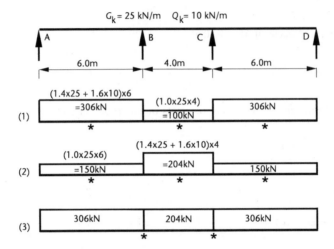

The critical loading arrangements for the ultimate limit state are shown in figure 3.6 where the 'stars' indicate the region of maximum moments, sagging or possible hogging. Table 3.1 is the moment distribution carried out for the first loading arrangement: similar calculations would be required for each of the remaining load cases. It should be noted that the reduced stiffness of $\frac{3}{4} I/L$ has been used for the end spans.

The shearing forces, the maximum span bending moments, and their positions along the beam, can be calculated using the formulae previously derived. Thus for the first loading arrangement and span AB, using the sign convention of figure 3.5:

$$\text{Shear } V_{AB} = \frac{\text{load}}{2} - \frac{(M_{AB} - M_{BA})}{L}$$

$$= \frac{306}{2} - \frac{131.8}{6.0} = 131.0 \text{ kN}$$

$$V_{BA} = \text{load} - V_{AB}$$

$$= 306 - 131.0 = 175.0 \text{ kN}$$

$$\text{Maximum moment, span AB} = \frac{V_{AB}{}^2}{2w} + M_{AB}$$

where $w = 306/6.0 = 51$ kN/m. Therefore

$$M_{max} = \frac{131.0^2}{2 \times 51} = 168.2 \text{ kN m}$$

$$\text{Distance from A, } a_3 = \frac{V_{AB}}{w} = \frac{131.0}{51} = 2.6 \text{ m}$$

Table 3.1 Moment distribution for the first loading case

	A		B		C	D
Stiffness (k)	$\dfrac{3}{4}\cdot\dfrac{l}{L}$ $\dfrac{3}{4}\cdot\dfrac{1}{6}=0.125$		$\dfrac{l}{L}$ $\dfrac{1}{4}=0.25$		$\dfrac{3}{4}\cdot\dfrac{l}{L}$ $=0.125$	
Distr. factors	$\dfrac{0.125}{0.125+0.25}$ $=1/3$		$\dfrac{0.25}{0.125+0.25}$ $=2/3$	2/3	1/3	
Load (kN)	306		100		306	
F.E.M.	0	$\dfrac{-306\times6}{8}$	$\pm\dfrac{100\times4}{12}$		$+\dfrac{306\times6}{8}$	0
=	0	-229.5	$+\ 33.3$	$-\ 33.3$	$+229.5$	0
Balance		$+\ 65.4$	$+130.8$	-130.8	$-\ 65.4$	
Carry over		$-\ 65.4$		$+\ 65.4$		
Balance		$+\ 21.8$	$+\ 43.6$	$-\ 43.6$	$-\ 21.8$	
Carry over			$-\ 21.8$	$+\ 21.8$		
Balance		$+\ 7.3$	$+\ 14.5$	$-\ 14.5$	$-\ 7.3$	
Carry over			$-\ 7.3$	$+\ 7.3$		
Balance		$+\ 2.4$	$+\ 4.9$	$-\ 4.9$	$-\ 2.4$	
Carry over			$-\ 2.4$	$+\ 2.4$		
Balance		$+\ 0.8$	$+\ 1.6$	$-\ 1.6$	$-\ 0.8$	
M (kN m)	0	-131.8	$+131.8$	-131.8	$+131.8$	0

The bending-moment diagrams for each of the loading arrangements are shown in figure 3.7 and the corresponding shearing-force diagrams are shown in figure 3.8. The individual bending-moment diagrams are combined in figure 3.9a to give the bending-moment design envelope. Similarly, figure 3.9b is the shearing-force design envelope. Such envelope diagrams are used in the detailed design of the beams, as described in chapter 7.

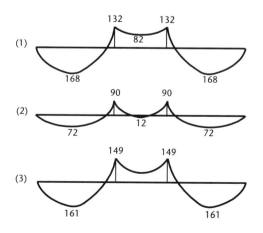

Figure 3.7
Bending moment diagrams
(kN m)

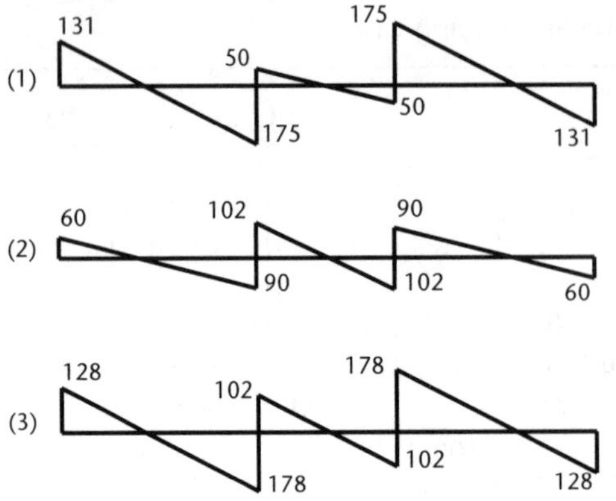

Figure 3.8
Shearing force diagrams (kN)

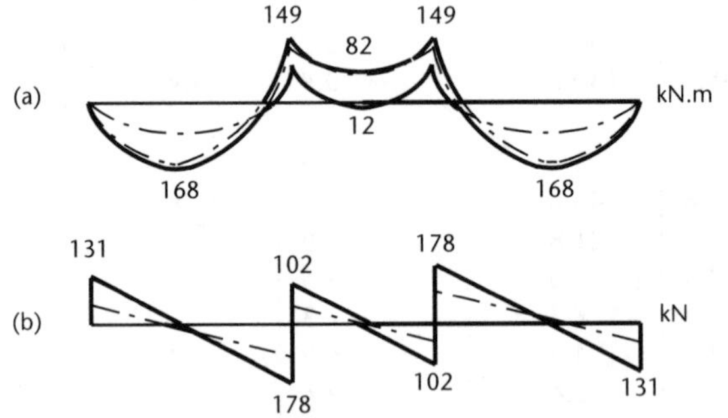

(1)

131
175
50
50
175
131

(2)

60
102
90
90
102
60

(3)

128
102
178
178
102
128

Figure 3.9
Bending-moment and
shearing-force envelopes

(a)

149   149
82
12
kN.m
168   168

(b)

131
102
178
kN
178
102
131

Continuous beams with approximately equal spans and uniform loading

The ultimate bending moments and shearing forces in continuous beams of three of more approximately equal spans can be obtained from BS 8110 provided that the spans differ by no more that 15 per cent of the longest span, that the loading is uniform, and that the characteristic live load does not exceed the characteristic dead load. The values from BS 8110 are shown in diagrammatic form in figure 3.10 for beams(equivalent simplified values for slabs are given in chapter 8).

The possibility of hogging moments in any of the spans should not be ignored, even it is not indicated by these coefficients. For example, a beam of three equal spans will have a hogging moment in the centre span if Q_k exceeds $G_k/16$.

Figure 3.10
Bending-moment and
shearing-force coefficients for
beams

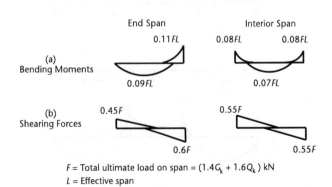

End Span

Interior Span

0.11*FL*   0.08*FL*   0.08*FL*

(a)
Bending Moments

0.09*FL*   0.07*FL*

(b)
Shearing Forces

0.45*F*   0.55*F*

0.6*F*   0.55*F*

F = Total ultimate load on span = $(1.4G_k + 1.6Q_k)$ kN
L = Effective span

3.4 | Analysis of frames

In situ reinforced concrete structures behave as rigid frames, and should be analysed as such. They can be analysed as a complete space frame or be divided into a series of plane frames. Bridge-deck types of structures can be analysed as an equivalent grillage, whilst some form of finite-element analysis can be utilised in solving complicated shear-wall buildings. All these methods lend themselves to solution by the computer, but many frames can be simplified for solution by hand calculations.

The general procedure for a building frame is to analyse the slabs as continuous members supported by the beams or structural walls, The slabs can be either one-way spanning or two-way spanning. The columns and main beams are considered as a series of rigid plane frames, which can be divided into two types: (1) braced frames supporting vertical loads only, (2) frames supporting vertical and lateral loads.

Type 1 frames are in buildings where none of the lateral loads, including wind, are transmitted to the columns and beams but are carried by shear walls or other forms of bracing. Type 2 frames are designed to carry the lateral loads, which cause bending, shearing and axial forces in the beams and columns. For both types of frame the axial forces due to the vertical loads in the columns can normally be calculated as if the beams and slabs were simply supported.

3.4.1 Braced frames supporting vertical loads only

A building frame can be analysed as a complete frame, or it can be simplified into a series of substitute frames for analysis. The frame shown in figure 3.11, for example, can be divided into any of the subframes shown in figure 3.12.

The substitute frame 1 in figure 3.12 consists of one complete floor beam with its connecting columns (which are assumed rigidly fixed at their remote ends). An analysis of this frame will give the bending moments and shearing forces in the beams and columns for the floor level considered.

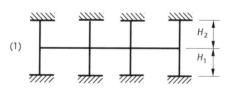

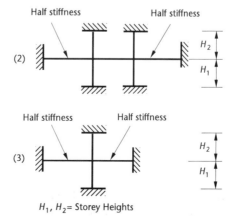

Figure 3.12
Substitute frames

H_1, H_2 = Storey Heights

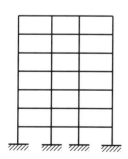

Figure 3.11
Building frame

Substitute frame 2 is a single span combined with its connecting columns and two adjacent spans, all fixed at their remote ends. This frame may be used to determine the bending moments and shearing forces in the central beam. Provided that the central span is greater than the two adjacent spans, the bending moments in the columns can also be found with this frame.

Substitute frame 3 can be used to find the moments in the columns only. It consists of a single junction, with the remote ends of the members fixed. This type of subframe would be used when the beams have been analysed as continuous over simple supports.

In frames 2 and 3, the assumption of fixed ends to the outer beams over-estimates their stiffnesses. These values are, therefore, halved to allow for the flexibility resulting from continuity.

The various critical loading arrangements to produce maximum stresses have to be considered. In general these loading arrangements for the ultimate limit state as specified by the code are:

1. Alternate spans loaded with total ultimate load $(1.4G_k + 1.6Q_k)$ and all other spans loaded with minimum dead load $(1.0G_k)$; this loading will give maximum span moments and maximum column moments.

2. All spans loaded with the total ultimate load $(1.4G_k + 1.6Q_k)$ to provide the design moments at the supports.

When considering the critical loading arrangements for a column, it is sometimes necessary to include the case of maximum moment and minimum possible axial load, in order to investigate the possibility of tension failure caused by the bending.

EXAMPLE 3.3

Analysis of a substitute frame

The substitute frame shown in figure 3.13 is part of the complete frame in figure 3.11. The characteristic loads carried by the beams are dead loads (including self-weight), $G_k = 25$ kN/m, and imposed load, $Q_k = 10$ kN/m, uniformly distributed along the beam.

Figure 3.13
Substitute frame

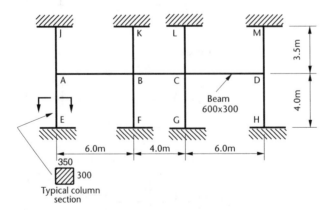

The analysis of the beam will be carried out by moment distribution: thus the member stiffnesses and their relevant distribution factors are first required.

Stiffnesses, k

Beam

$$I = \frac{0.3 \times 0.6^3}{12} = 5.4 \times 10^{-3} \ m^4$$

Spans AB and CD

$$k_{AB} = k_{CD} = \frac{5.4 \times 10^{-3}}{6.0} = 0.9 \times 10^{-3}$$

Span BC

$$k_{BC} = \frac{5.4 \times 10^{-3}}{4.0} = 1.35 \times 10^{-3}$$

Columns

$$I = \frac{0.3 \times 0.35^3}{12} = 1.07 \times 10^{-3} \ m^4$$

Upper

$$k_U = \frac{1.07 \times 10^{-3}}{3.5} = 0.31 \times 10^{-3}$$

Lower

$$k_L = \frac{1.07 \times 10^{-3}}{4.0} = 0.27 \times 10^{-3}$$

$$k_U + k_L = (0.31 + 0.27)10^{-3} = 0.58 \times 10^{-3}$$

Distribution factors

Joints A and D

$$\sum k = 0.9 + 0.58 = 1.48$$

$$D.F._{AB} = D.F._{DC} = \frac{0.9}{1.48} = 0.61$$

$$D.F._{cols} = \frac{0.58}{1.48} = 0.39$$

Joints B and C

$$\sum k = 0.9 + 1.35 + 0.58 = 2.83$$

$$D.F._{BA} = D.F._{CD} = \frac{0.9}{2.83} = 0.32$$

$$D.F._{BC} = D.F._{CB} = \frac{1.35}{2.83} = 0.48$$

$$D.F._{cols} = \frac{0.58}{2.83} = 0.20$$

The critical loading arrangements for the ultimate limit state are identical to those for the continuous beam in example 3.2, and they are illustrated in figure 3.6. The moment distribution for the first loading arrangement is shown in table 3.2 In the table, the distributions for each upper and lower column have been combined, since this simplifies the layout for the calculations.

Table 3.2 Moment distribution for the first loading case

	A		B			C			D	
D.F.s	Cols. (∑M) 0.39	AB 0.61	BA 0.32	Cols. (∑M) 0.20	BC 0.48	CB 0.48	Cols. (∑M) 0.20	CD 0.32	DC 0.61	Cols. (∑M) 0.39
Load kN		306			100			306		
F.E.M.		+153	−153		+33.3	−33.3		+153	−153	
Bal.	−59.7	−93.3	+38.3	+23.9	+57.5	−57.5	−23.9	−38.3	+93.3	+59.7
C.O.		+19.2	−46.6		−28.8	+28.8		+46.6	−19.2	
Bal.	−7.5	−11.7	+24.1	+15.1	+36.2	−36.2	−15.1	−24.1	+11.7	+7.5
C.O.		+12.0	−5.8		−18.1	+18.1		+5.8	−12.0	
Bal.	−4.7	−7.3	+7.6	+4.8	+11.5	−11.5	−4.8	−7.6	+7.3	+4.7
C.O.		+3.8	−3.6		−5.8	+5.8		+3.6	−3.8	
Bal.	−1.5	−2.3	+3.0	+1.9	+4.5	−4.5	−1.9	−3.0	+2.3	+1.5
M (kN m)	73.4	+73.4	136.0	45.7	90.3	90.3	45.7	136.0	73.4	73.4

The shearing forces and the maximum span moments can be calculated from the formulae of section 3.3.2. For the first loading arrangement and span AB:

$$\text{Shear } V_{AB} = \frac{\text{load}}{2} - \frac{(M_{AB} - M_{BA})}{L}$$

$$= \frac{306}{2} - \frac{(-73.4 + 136.0)}{6.0} = 143 \text{ kN}$$

$$V_{BA} = \text{load} - V_{AB}$$

$$= 306 - 143 = 163 \text{ kN}$$

$$\text{Maximum moment, span AB} = \frac{V_{AB}{}^2}{2w} + M_{AB}$$

$$= \frac{143^2}{2 \times 51} - 73.4 = 126 \text{ kN m}$$

$$\text{Distance from A, } a_3 = \frac{V_{AB}}{w}$$

$$= \frac{143}{51} = 2.8 \text{ m}$$

Figure 3.14 shows the bending moments in the beams for each loading arrangement: figure 3.15 shows the shearing forces. These diagrams have been combined in figure 3.16 to give the design envelopes for bending moments and shearing forces.

A comparison of the design envelopes of figure 3.16 and figure 3.9 will emphasise the advantages of considering the concrete beam as part of a frame, not as a continuous beam as in example 3.2. Not only is the analysis of a subframe more precise, but many moments and shears in the beam are smaller in magnitude.

The moment in each column is given by

$$M_{col} = \sum M_{col} \times \frac{k_{col}}{\sum k_{cols}}$$

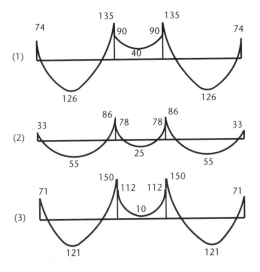

Figure 3.14
Beam bending-moment diagrams (kN m)

Figure 3.15
Beam shearing-force diagrams
(kN)

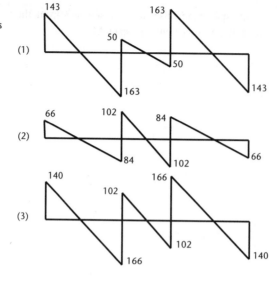

Figure 3.16
Bending-moment and
shearing-force envelopes

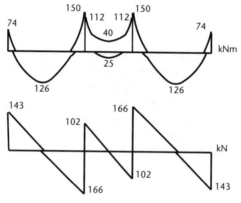

Figure 3.17
Column bending moments
(kN m)

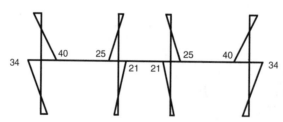

Thus, for the first loading arrangement and taking $\sum M_{col}$ from table 3.2 gives

$$\text{column moment } M_{AJ} = 74 \times \frac{0.31}{0.58} = 40 \text{ kN m}$$

$$M_{AE} = 74 \times \frac{0.27}{0.58} = 34 \text{ kN m}$$

$$M_{BK} = 46 \times \frac{0.31}{0.58} = 25 \text{ kN m}$$

$$M_{BF} = 46 \times \frac{0.27}{0.58} = 21 \text{ kN m}$$

This loading arrangement gives the maximum column moments, as plotted in figure 3.17.

EXAMPLE 3.4

Analysis of a substitute frame for a column

The substitute frame for this example, shown in figure 3.18, is taken from the building frame in figure 3.11. The loading to cause maximum column moments is shown in the figure for $G_k = 25$ kN/m and $Q_k = 10$ kN/m.

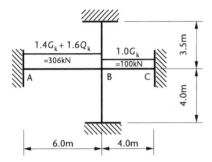

Figure 3.18
Substitute frame

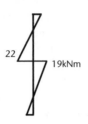

Figure 3.19
Column moments

The stiffnesses of these members are identical to those calculated in example 3.3, except that for this type of frame the beam stiffnesses are halved. Thus

$$k_{AB} = \frac{1}{2} \times 0.9 \times 10^{-3} = 0.45 \times 10^{-3}$$

$$k_{BC} = \frac{1}{2} \times 1.35 \times 10^{-3} = 0.675 \times 10^{-3}$$

upper column $k_U = 0.31 \times 10^{-3}$

lower column $k_L = 0.27 \times 10^{-3}$

$$\sum k = (0.45 + 0.675 + 0.31 + 0.27) \times 10^{-3}$$

$$= 1.705 \times 10^{-3}$$

fixed-end moment $M_{BA} = 306 \times \dfrac{6}{12} = 153$ kN m

fixed-end moment $M_{BC} = 100 \times \dfrac{4}{12} = 33.3$ kN m

Column moments are

upper column $M_U = (153 - 33.3) \times \dfrac{0.31}{1.705} = 22$ kN m

lower column $M_L = (153 - 33.3) \times \dfrac{0.27}{1.705} = 19$ kN m

The column moments are illustrated in figure 3.19. They should be compared with the corresponding moments for the internal column in figure 3.17.

In examples 3.3 and 3.4 the second moment of area of the beam was calculated as $bh^3/12$ for a rectangular section for simplicity, but where an *in situ* slab forms a flange to the beam, the second moment of area may be calculated for the T-section or L-section.

3.4.2 Frames supporting vertical and lateral loads

Lateral loads on a structure may be caused by wind pressures, by retained earth, or by seismic forces.

BS 8110 also specifies that all building structures should be capable of resisting a notional horizontal design ultimate load equal to 1.5 per cent of the characteristic dead weight of the structure. This load is to be distributed proportionally to act as point loads at each floor and roof level.

An unbraced frame subjected to wind forces must be analysed for all the three loading combinations described in section 3.2.1. The vertical-loading analysis can be carried out by the methods described previously for braced frames (see page 33). The analysis for the lateral loads should be kept separate and the forces may be calculated by an elastic analysis or by a simplified approximate method. For preliminary design calculations, and also for medium-size regular structures, a simplified analysis may well be adequate.

BS 8110 recommends that any simplified form of analysis should assume points of contraflexure at the mid-lengths of all the columns and beams. A suitable approximate analysis is the cantilever method. It assumes that:

1. Points of contraflexure are located at the mid-points of all columns and beams; and
2. The direct axial loads in the columns are in proportion to their distances from the centre of gravity of the frame. It is also usual to assume that all the columns in a storey are of equal cross-sectional area.

Application of this method is probably best illustrated by an example, as follows.

EXAMPLE 3.5

Simplified analysis for lateral loads – cantilever method

Figure 3.20 shows a building frame subjected to a characteristic wind load of 3.0 kN per metre height of the frame. This load is assumed to be transferred to the frame as a concentrated load at each floor level as indicated in the figure.

Figure 3.20
Frame with lateral load

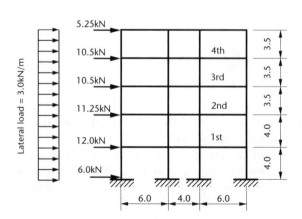

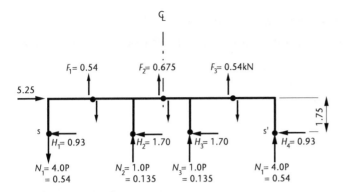

Figure 3.21
Subframes at the roof and
fourth floor

(a) Roof

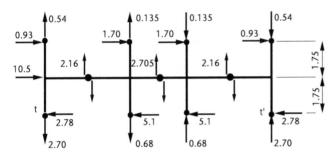

(b) 4th Floor

By inspection, there is tension in the two columns to the left and compression in the columns to the right; and by assumption 2 the axial forces in columns are proportional to their distances from the centre line of the frame. Thus

axial force in exterior column : axial force in interior column $= 4.0P : 1.0P$

The analysis of the frame continues by considering a section through the top-storey columns: the removal of the frame below this section gives the remainder shown in figure 3.21a. The forces in this subframe are calculated as follows.

(a) Axial forces in the columns
Taking moments about point s, $\sum M_s = 0$, therefore

$$5.25 \times 1.75 + P \times 6.0 - P \times 10.0 - 4P \times 16.0 = 0$$

and therefore

$$P = 0.135 \text{ kN}$$

thus

$$N_1 = -N_4 = 4.0P = 0.54 \text{ kN}$$
$$N_2 = -N_3 = 1.0P = 0.135 \text{ kN}$$

*(b) Vertical shearing forces **F** in the beams*
For each part of the subframe, $\sum F = 0$, therefore

$$F_1 = N_1 = 0.54 \text{ kN}$$
$$F_2 = N_1 + N_2 = 0.675 \text{ kN}$$

(c) Horizontal shearing forces H in the columns

Taking moments about the points of contraflexure of each beam, $\sum M = 0$, therefore

$$H_1 \times 1.75 - N_1 \times 3.0 = 0$$
$$H_1 = 0.93 \text{ kN}$$

and

$$(H_1 + H_2)1.75 - N_1 \times 8.0 - N_2 \times 2.0 = 0$$
$$H_2 = 1.70 \text{ kN}$$

The calculations of the equivalent forces for the fourth floor (figure 3.21b) follow a similar procedure as follows.

(d) Axial forces in the columns

For the frame above section tt', $\sum M_t = 0$, therefore

$$5.25(3 \times 1.75) + 10.5 \times 1.75 + P \times 6.0 - P \times 10.0 - 4P \times 16.0 = 0$$
$$P = 0.675 \text{ kN}$$

therefore

$$N_1 = 4.0P = 2.70 \text{ kN}$$
$$N_2 = 1.0P = 0.68 \text{ kN}$$

(e) Beam shears

$$F_1 = 2.70 - 0.54 = 2.16 \text{ kN}$$
$$F_2 = 2.70 + 0.68 - 0.54 - 0.135 = 2.705 \text{ kN}$$

(f) Column shears

$$H_1 \times 1.75 + 0.93 \times 1.75 - (2.70 - 0.54)3.0 = 0$$
$$H_1 = 2.78 \text{ kN}$$
$$H_2 = \tfrac{1}{2}(10.5 + 5.25) - 2.78 = 5.1 \text{ kN}$$

Values calculated for sections taken below the remaining floors are

third floor	$N_1 = 7.03$ kN	$N_2 = 1.76$ kN	
	$F_1 = 4.33$ kN	$F_2 = 5.41$ kN	
	$H_1 = 4.64$ kN	$H_2 = 8.49$ kN	
second floor	$N_1 = 14.14$ kN	$N_2 = 3.53$ kN	
	$F_1 = 7.11$ kN	$F_2 = 8.88$ kN	
	$H_1 = 6.61$ kN	$H_2 = 12.14$ kN	
first floor	$N_1 = 24.37$ kN	$N_2 = 6.09$ kN	
	$F_1 = 10.23$ kN	$F_2 = 12.79$ kN	
	$H_1 = 8.74$ kN	$H_2 = 16.01$ kN	

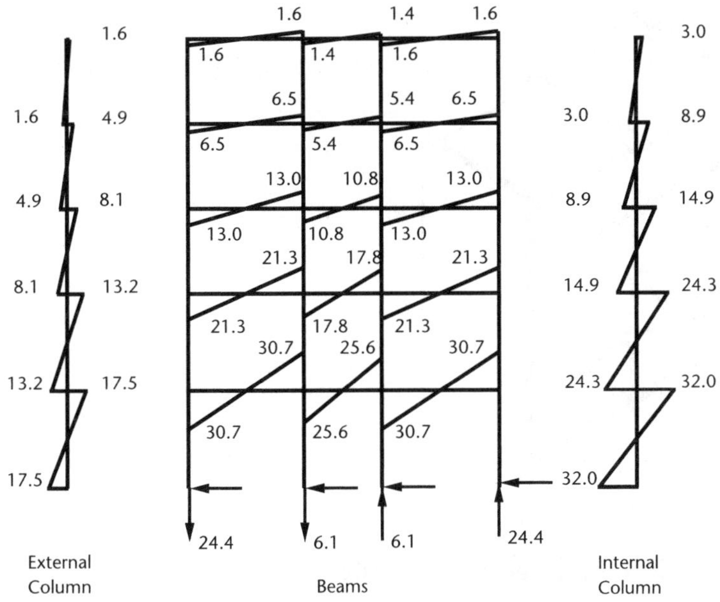

Figure 3.22
Moments (kN m) and
reactions (kN)

The bending moments in the beams and columns at their connections can be calculated from these results by the following formulae

beams $M_B = F \times \frac{1}{2}$ beam span

columns $M_C = H \times \frac{1}{2}$ storey height

so at the roof's external connection

$M_B = 0.54 \times \frac{1}{2} \times 6.0$
$\quad = 1.6 \text{ kN m}$
$M_C = 0.93 \times \frac{1}{2} \times 3.5$
$\quad = 1.6 \text{ kN m}$

As a check at each joint, $\sum M_B = \sum M_C$.

The bending moments due to characteristic wind loads in all the columns and beams of this structure are shown in figure 3.22.

3.5 Shear wall structures resisting horizontal loads

A reinforced concrete structure with shear walls is shown in figure 3.23. Shear walls are very effective in resisting horizontal loads such as F_Z in the figure which act in the direction of the plane of the walls. As the walls are relatively thin they offer little resistance to loads which are perpendicular to their plane.

The floor slabs which are supported by the walls also act as rigid diaphragms which transfer and distribute the horizontal forces into the shear walls. The shear walls act as vertical cantilevers transferring the horizontal loads to the structural foundations.

Figure 3.23
Shear wall structure

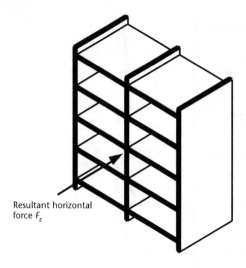

Resultant horizontal
force F_z

3.5.1 Symmetrical arrangement of walls

With a symmetrical arrangement of walls as shown in figure 3.24 the horizontal load is distributed in proportion to the relative stiffness k_i of each wall. The relative stiffnesses are given by the second moment of area of each wall about its major axis such that

$$k_i \approx h \times b^3$$

where h is the thickness of the wall and b is the length of the wall.

The force P_i distributed into each wall is then given by

$$P_i = F \times \frac{k_i}{\sum k}$$

EXAMPLE 3.6

Symmetrical arrangement of shear walls

A structure with a symmetrical arrangement of shear walls is shown in figure 3.24. Calculate the proportion of the 100 kN horizontal load carried by each of the walls.

Figure 3.24
Symmetrical arrangement of
shear walls

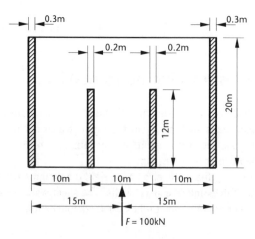

$F = 100\text{kN}$

Relative stiffnesses:

Walls A $k_A = 0.3 \times 20^3 = 2400$

Walls B $k_B = 0.2 \times 12^3 = 346$

$\sum k = 2(2400 + 346) = 5492$

Force in each wall:

$$P_A = \frac{k_B}{\sum k} \times F = \frac{2400}{5492} \times 100 = 43.7 \text{ kN}$$

$$P_B = \frac{k_b}{\sum k} \times F = \frac{346}{5492} \times 100 = 6.3 \text{ kN}$$

Check: $2(43.7 + 6.3) = 100 \text{ kN} = F$

3.5.2 Unsymmetrical arrangement of walls

With an unsymmetrical arrangement of shear walls, as shown in figure 3.25, there will also be a torsional force on the structure about the centre of rotation in addition to the direct forces caused by the translatory movement. The calculation procedure for this case is:

1. Determine the location of the centre of rotation by taking moments of the wall stiffnesses k about convenient axes. Such that

   $$\bar{x} = \frac{\sum (k_x x)}{\sum k_x} \quad \text{and} \quad \bar{y} = \frac{\sum (k_y y)}{\sum k_y}$$

   where k_x and k_y are the stiffnesses of the walls orientated in the x and y directions respectively.

2. Calculate the torsional moment M_t on the group of shear walls as

   $$M_t = F \times e$$

   where e is the eccentricity of the horizontal force F about the centre of rotation.

3. Calculate the force P_i in each wall as the sum of the direct component P_d and the torsional rotation component P_r

   $$P_i = P_d + P_r = F \times \frac{k_x}{\sum k_x} \pm M_t \times \frac{k_i r_i}{\sum (k_i r_i^2)}$$

   where r_i is the perpendicular distance between the axis of each wall and the centre of rotation.

EXAMPLE 3.7

Unsymmetrical layout of shear walls

Determine the distribution of the 100 kN horizontal force F into the shear walls A, B, C, D and E as shown in figure 3.25. The relative stiffness of each shear wall is shown in the figure in terms of multiples of k.

Figure 3.25
Unsymmetrical arrangement
of shear walls

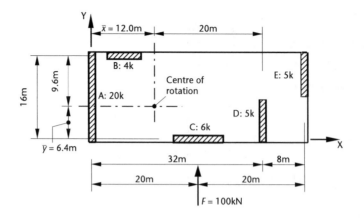

Centre of rotation

$$\sum k_x = 20 + 5 + 5 = 30$$

Taking moments for k_x about YY at wall A

$$\bar{x} = \frac{\sum(k_x x)}{\sum k} = \frac{20 \times 0 + 5 \times 32 + 5 \times 40}{30} = 12.0 \text{ metres}$$

$$\sum k_y = 6 + 4 = 10$$

Taking moments for k_y about XX at wall C

$$\bar{y} = \frac{\sum(k_y y)}{\sum k_y} = \frac{6 \times 0 + 4 \times 16}{10} = 6.4 \text{ metres}$$

The torsional moment M_t is

$$M_t = F \times (20 - \bar{x}) = 100 \times (20 - 12) = 800 \text{ kN m}$$

The remainder of these calculations are conveniently set out in tabular form:

Wall	k_x	k_y	r	kr	kr^2	P_d	P_r	P_i
A	20	0	12	240	2880	66.6	− 20.4	46.2
B	0	4	9.6	38.4	369	0	− 3.3	− 3.3
C	0	6	6.4	38.4	246	0	3.3	3.3
D	5	0	20	100	2000	16.7	8.5	25.2
E	5	0	28	140	3920	16.7	11.9	28.6
$\sum$	30	10			9415	100	0	100

As an example for wall A:

$$P_A = P_t + P_r = F \times \frac{k_A}{\sum k} - M_t \times \frac{k_A r_A}{\sum(k_i r_i^2)}$$

$$= 100 \times \frac{20}{30} - 800 \times \frac{20 \times 12}{9415}$$

$$= 66.6 - 20.4 = 46.2 \text{ kN}$$

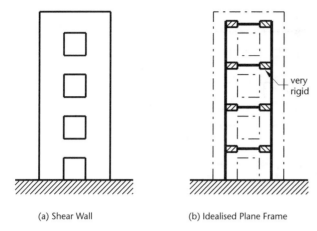

Figure 3.26
Shear wall with openings

(a) Shear Wall   (b) Idealised Plane Frame

3.5.3   Shear walls with openings

Shear walls with openings can be idealised into equivalent plane frames as shown in figure 3.26. In the plane frame the second moments of area I_c of the columns is equivalent to that of the wall on either side of the openings. The second moment of area I_b of the beams is equivalent to that part of the wall between the openings. The lengths of beam that extend beyond the openings as shown shaded in figure 3.26 are given very large stiffnesses so that their second moment of area would be, say, $100I_b$.

The equivalent plane frame would be analysed by computer with a plane frame program.

3.5.4   Shear walls combined with structural frames

For simplicity in the design of low- or medium-height structures, shear walls or a lift shaft are usually considered to resist all of the horizontal load. With higher-rise structures, for reasons of stiffness and economy it often becomes necessary to include the combined action of the shear walls and structural frames in the design

A method of analysing a structure with shear walls and structural frames as one equivalent linked-plane frame is illustrated by the example in figure 3.27. In the actual structure shown in plan there are four frames of type A and two frames of type B which include shear walls. In the linked frame shown in elevation the four frames of type A are lumped together into one frame whose member stiffnesses are multiplied by four. Similarly the two frames of type B are lumped together into one frame whose member stiffnesses are doubled. These two equivalent frames are then linked together by beams pinned at each end.

The two shear walls are represented by one column having the sectional properties of the sum of the two shear walls. For purposes of analysis this column is connected to the rest of its frame by beams with a very high bending stiffness, say, 1000 times that of the other beams so as to represent the width and rigidity of the shear wall.

The link beams transfer the loads axially between the two types of frames A and B so representing the rigid diaphragm action of the concrete floor slabs. These link beams pinned at their ends would be given a cross-sectional area of, say, 1000 times that of the other beams in the frame.

Figure 3.27
Idealised link frame for a
structure with shear walls and
structural frames

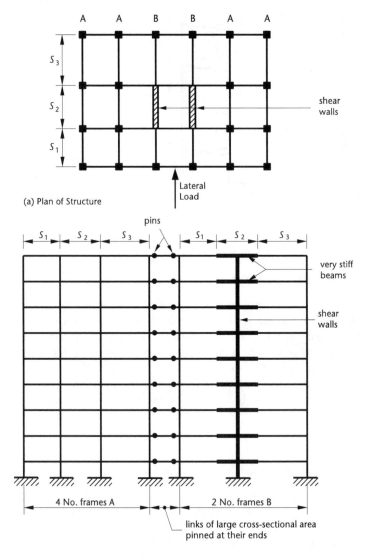

(a) Plan of Structure

(b) Elevation of Link-Frame Model

As all the beams in the structural frames are pressing against the rigid shear wall in the computer model the effects of axial shortening in these beams will be exaggerated, whereas this would normally be of secondary magnitude. To overcome this, the cross-sectional areas of all the beams in the model may be increased to, say, 1000 m^2 and this will virtually remove the effects of axial shortening in the beams.

In the computer output the member forces for frames type A would need to be divided by a factor of four and those for frames type B by a factor of two.

3.6 Redistribution of moments

A method of elastic analysis is generally used to calculate the forces in a concrete structure, despite the fact that the structure does not behave elastically near its ultimate load. The assumption of elastic behaviour is reasonably true for low stress levels; but as

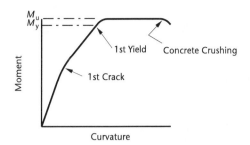

Figure 3.28
Typical moment/curvature
diagram

a section approaches its ultimate moment of resistance, plastic deformation will occur. This is recognised in BS 8110, by allowing redistribution of the elastic moments subject to certain limitations.

Reinforced concrete behaves in a manner midway between that of steel and concrete. The stress–strain curves for the two materials (figures 1.5 and 1.2) show the elastoplastic behaviour of steel and the plastic behaviour of concrete. The latter will fail at a relatively small compressive strain. The exact behaviour of a reinforced concrete section depends on the relative quantities and the individual properties of the two materials. However, such a section may be considered virtually elastic until the steel yields; and then plastic until the concrete fails in compression. Thus the plastic behaviour is limited by the concrete failure; or more specifically, the concrete failure limits the rotation that may take place at a section in bending. A typical moment–curvature diagram for a reinforced concrete member is shown in figure 3.28.

Thus, in an indeterminate structure, once a beam section develops its ultimate moment of resistance M_u, it then behaves as a plastic hinge resisting a constant moment of that value. Further loading must be taken by other parts of the structure, with the changes in moment elsewhere being just the same as if a real hinge existed. Provided rotation of a hinge does not cause crushing of the concrete, further hinges will be formed until a mechanism is produced. This requirement is considered in more detail in chapter 4.

EXAMPLE 3.8

Moment redistribution – single span fixed-end beam

The beam shown in figure 3.29 is subjected to an increasing uniformly distributed load.

$$\text{Elastic support moment} = \frac{wL^2}{12}$$

$$\text{Elastic span moment} \quad = \frac{wL^2}{24}$$

In the case where the ultimate bending strengths are equal at the span and at the supports, and where adequate rotation is possible, then the additional load w_a, which the member can sustain by plastic behaviour, can be found.

At collapse

$$M_u = \frac{wL^2}{12} = \frac{wL^2}{24} + \text{ additional mid-span moment } m_B$$

where $m_B = (w_aL^2)/8$ as for a simply supported beam with hinges at A and C.

Figure 3.29
Moment redistribution –
one-span beam

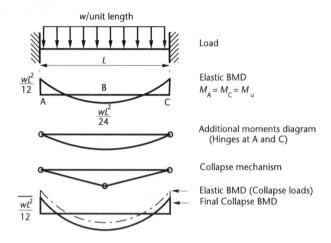

Thus $\dfrac{wL^2}{12} = \dfrac{wL^2}{24} + \dfrac{w_aL^2}{8}$

Hence $w_a = \dfrac{w}{3}$

where w is the load to cause the first plastic hinge, thus the beam may carry a load of $1.33w$ with redistribution.

From the design point of view, the elastic bending-moment diagram can be obtained for the required ultimate loading in the ordinary way. Some of these moments may then be reduced; but this will necessitate increasing others to maintain the static equilibrium of the structure. Usually it is the maximum support moments which are reduced, so economising in reinforcing steel and also reducing congestion at the columns. The requirements for applying moment redistribution are:

(a) Equilibrium between internal and external forces must be maintained, hence it is necessary to recalculate the span bending moments and the shear forces for the load case involved.

(b) At sections of largest moment the depth of neutral axis, x, is limited by

$x \not> (\beta_b - 0.4)d$

where $d =$ the effective depth, and

$\beta_b = \dfrac{\text{moment at section after redistribution}}{\text{moment at section before redistribution}}$

This rule effectively prevents any reduction of the moments in columns which are primarily compression members with large values of x, and this is dealt with more fully in chapter 4.

(c) The moment of resistance of any section should be at least 70 per cent of the moment from the elastic analysis, hence allowing up to 30 per cent redistribution. This requirement ensures that there can be no movement in the position of the points of contraflexure obtained from the elastic analysis as shown by figure 3.30. It thus also ensures that a sufficient length of tension reinforcement is provided to resist cracking at the serviceability limit state.

For unbraced structures over four storeys the redistribution is limited to 10 per cent, to prevent lateral instability.

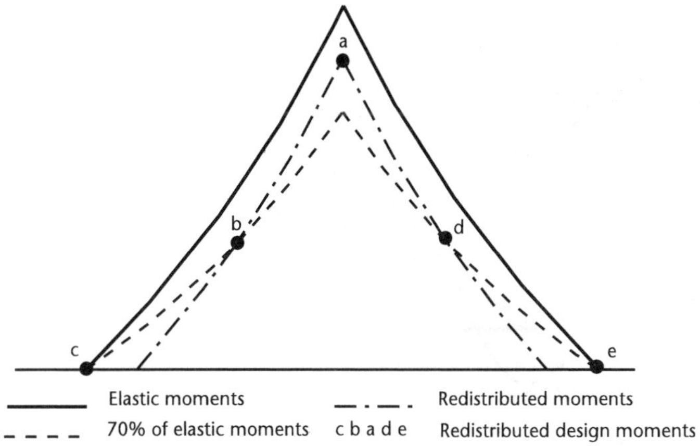

Figure 3.30
Redistribution of hogging
moments

Elastic moments ——— ·—· — Redistributed moments

– – – – 70% of elastic moments   c b a d e   Redistributed design moments

EXAMPLE 3.9

Moment redistribution

In example 3.3, figure 3.14 it is required to reduce the maximum support moment of $M_{BA} = 150$ kN m as much as possible, but without increasing the span moment above the present maximum value of 126 kN m.

Figure 3.31a duplicates the original bending-moment diagram (part 3 of figure 3.14) of example 3.3 while figure 3.31b shows the redistributed moments, with the span moment set at 126 kN m. The moment at support B can be calculated, using a rearrangement of equations 3.4 and 3.1. Thus

$$V_{AB} = \sqrt{[(M_{\text{max}} - M_{AB})2w]}$$

and

$$M_{BA} = \left(V_{AB} - \frac{wL}{2}\right)L + M_{AB}$$

For span AB, $w = 51$ kN/m, therefore

$$V_{AB} = \sqrt{[(126 + 70) \times 2 \times 51]}$$
$$= 141 \text{ kN}$$
$$M_{BA} = \left(141 - \frac{51 \times 6.0}{2}\right)6.0 - 70$$
$$= -142\text{kN m}$$

and

$$V_{BA} = 306 - 141$$
$$= 165 \text{ kN}$$

Reduction in $M_{BA} = 150 - 142$
$$= 8 \text{ kN m}$$
$$= \frac{8 \times 100}{150}$$
$$= 5.3 \text{ per cent}$$

Figure 3.31
Moments and shears with
redistribution

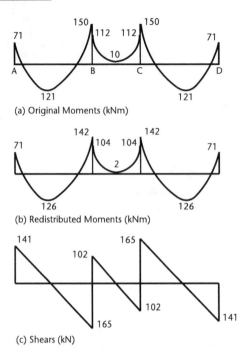

(a) Original Moments (kNm)

(b) Redistributed Moments (kNm)

(c) Shears (kN)

In order to ensure that the moments in the columns at joint B are not changed by the distribution, moment M_{BC} must also be reduced by 8 kN m. Therefore

$$M_{BC} = 112 - 8 = 104 \text{ kN m} \qquad \text{hogging}$$

Figure 3.31c shows the revised shearing-force diagram to accord with the redistributed moments.

This example illustrates how, with redistribution

1. the moments at a section of beam can be reduced without exceeding the maximum design moments at other sections;

2. the values of the column moments are not affected; and

3. the equilibrium between external loads and internal forces is maintained.

CHAPTER 4

Analysis of the section

CHAPTER INTRODUCTION

A satisfactory and economic design of a concrete structure rarely depends on a complex theoretical analysis. It is achieved more by deciding on a practical overall layout of the structure, careful attention to detail and sound constructional practice. Nevertheless the total design of a structure does depend on the analysis and design of the individual member sections.

Wherever possible the analysis should be kept simple, yet it should be based on the observed and tested behaviour of reinforced concrete members. The manipulation and juggling with equations should never be allowed to obscure the fundamental principles that unite the analysis. The three most important principles are

1. The stresses and strains are related by the material properties, including the stress–strain curves for concrete and steel.
2. The distribution of strains must be compatible with the distorted shape of the cross-section.
3. The resultant forces developed by the section must balance the applied loads for static equilibrium.

These principles are true irrespective of how the stresses and strains are distributed, or how the member is loaded, or whatever the shape of the cross-section.

This chapter describes and analyses the action of a member section under load. It derives the basic equations used in design and also those equations required for the preparation of design charts. Emphasis has been placed mostly on the analysis associated with the ultimate limit state but the behaviour of the section within the elastic range and the serviceability limit state has also been considered.

Section 4.7 deals with the redistribution of the moments from an elastic analysis of the structure, and the effect it has on the equations derived and the design procedure.

4.1 Stress–strain relations

Short-term stress–strain curves are presented in BS 8110. These curves are in an idealised form which can be used in the analysis of member sections.

4.1.1 Concrete

The behaviour of structural concrete (figure 4.1) is represented by a parabolic stress–strain relationship, up to a strain ε_0, from which point the strain increases while the stress remains constant. Strain ε_0 is specified as a function of the characteristic strength of the concrete (f_{cu}), as is also the tangent modulus at the origin. The ultimate design stress is given by

$$\frac{0.67f_{cu}}{\gamma_m} = \frac{0.67f_{cu}}{1.5} = 0.447f_{cu} \approx 0.45f_{cu}$$

where the factor of 0.67 allows for the difference between the bending strength and the cube crushing strength of the concrete, and $\gamma_m = 1.5$ is the usual partial safety factor for the strength of concrete when designing members cast *in situ*. The ultimate strain of 0.0035 is typical for all grades of concrete.

Figure 4.1
Short-term design stress–strain curve for concrete in compression

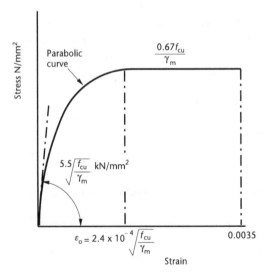

4.1.2 Reinforcing steel

The representative short-term design stress–strain curve for reinforcement is given in figure 4.2. The behaviour of the steel is identical in tension and compression, being linear in the elastic range up to the design yield stress of f_y/γ_m where f_y is the characteristic yield stress and γ_m is the partial factor of safety.

Within the elastic range, the relationship between the stress and strain is

$$\text{stress} = \text{elastic modulus} \times \text{strain}$$
$$= E_s \times \varepsilon_s \tag{4.1}$$

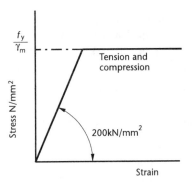

Figure 4.2
Short-term design stress–strain
curve for reinforcement

so that the design yield strain is

$$\varepsilon_y = \left(\frac{f_y}{\gamma_m}\right) \Big/ E_s$$

At the ultimate limit for $f_y = 460$ N/mm^2

$$\varepsilon_y = 460/(1.05 \times 200 \times 10^3)$$
$$= 0.00219$$

and for $f_y = 250$ N/mm^2

$$\varepsilon_y = 250/(1.05 \times 200 \times 10^3)$$
$$= 0.0019$$

4.2 | The distribution of strains and stresses across a section

The theory of bending for reinforced concrete assumes that the concrete will crack in the regions of tensile strains and that, after cracking, all the tension is carried by the reinforcement. It also assumes that plane sections of a structural member remain plane after straining, so that across the section there must be a linear distribution of strains.

Figure 4.3 shows the cross-section of a member subjected to bending, and the resultant strain diagram, together with three different types of stress distribution in the concrete.

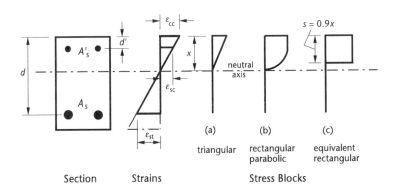

Figure 4.3
Section with strain diagrams
and stress blocks

1. The triangular stress distribution applies when the stresses are very nearly proportional to the strains, which generally occurs at the loading levels encountered under working conditions and is, therefore, used at the serviceability limit state.

2. The rectangular–parabolic stress block represents the distribution at failure when the compressive strains are within the plastic range and it is associated with the design for the ultimate limit state.

3. The equivalent rectangular stress block is a simplified alternative to the rectangular–parabolic distribution.

As there is compatability of strains between the reinforcement and the adjacent concrete, the steel strains ε_{st} in tension and ε_{sc} in compression can be determined from the strain diagram. The relationship between the depth of neutral axis (x) and the maximum concrete strain (ε_{cc}) and the steel strains is given by

$$\varepsilon_{st} = \varepsilon_{cc}\left(\frac{d-x}{x}\right) \tag{4.2}$$

and

$$\varepsilon_{sc} = \varepsilon_{cc}\left(\frac{x-d'}{x}\right) \tag{4.3}$$

where d is the effective depth of the beam and d' is the depth of the compression reinforcement.

Having determined the strains, we can evaluate the stresses in the reinforcement from the stress–strain curve of figure 4.2, together with the equations developed in section 4.1.2.

For analysis of a section with known steel strains, the depth of the neutral axis can be determined by rearranging equation 4.2 as

$$x = \frac{d}{1 + \dfrac{\varepsilon_{st}}{\varepsilon_{cc}}} \tag{4.4}$$

At the ultimate limit state the maximum compressive strain in the concrete is taken as

$$\varepsilon_{cc} = 0.0035$$

For steel with $f_y = 460$ N/mm^2 the yield strain is 0.00219. Inserting these values into equation 4.4:

$$x = \frac{d}{1 + \dfrac{0.00219}{0.0035}} = 0.615d$$

Hence, to ensure yielding of the tension steel at the ultimate limit state:

$$x \ngtr 0.615d$$

At the ultimate limit state it is important that member sections in flexure should be ductile and that failure should occur with the gradual yielding of the tension steel and not by a sudden catastrophic compression failure of the concrete. Also, yielding of the reinforcement enables the formation of plastic hinges so that redistribution of maximum moments can occur, resulting in a safer and more economical structure (see section 3.6). To be very certain of the tension steel yielding, the code of practice limits the depth of neutral axis so that

$$x \ngtr (\beta_b - 0.4)d$$

where

$$\beta_b = \frac{\text{moment at the section after redistribution}}{\text{moment at the section before redistribution}}$$

Thus with moment redistribution not greater than 10 per cent, and $\beta_b \geq 0.9$:

$$x \not> 0.5d$$

This limit will normally be adopted for ultimate state design, but larger degrees of moment redistribution will require a smaller limit to x to ensure that plastic hinges can form, providing adequate rotation at the critical sections (see section 4.7 and table 4.1).

4.3 Bending and the equivalent rectangular stress block

For the design of most reinforced concrete structures it is usual to commence the design for the conditions at the ultimate limit state, which is then followed by checks to ensure that the structure is adequate for the serviceability limit state without excessive deflection or cracking of the concrete. For this reason the analysis in this chapter will first consider the simplified rectangular stress block which can be used for the design at the ultimate limit state.

The rectangular stress block as shown in figure 4.4 may be used in preference to the more rigorous rectangular–parabolic stress block. This simplified stress distribution will facilitate the analysis and provide more manageable design equations, in particular when dealing with non-rectangular cross-sections.

It can be seen from the figure that the stress block does not extend to the neutral axis of the section but has a depth $s = 0.9x$. This will result in the centroid of the stress block being $s/2 = 0.45x$ from the top edge of the section, which is very nearly the same location as for the more precise rectangular–parabolic stress block; also the areas of the two types of stress block are approximately equal (see section 4.9). Thus the moment of resistance of the section will be similar using calculations based on either of the two stress blocks.

The design equations derived in sections 4.4 to 4.6 are for redistribution of moments being not greater than 10 per cent. When a greater moment redistribution is applied, reference should be made to section 4.7 which describes how to modify the design equations.

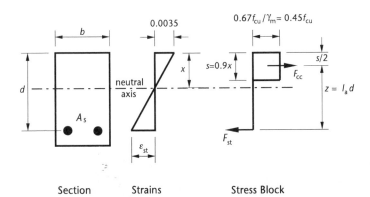

Figure 4.4
Singly reinforced section with rectangular stress block

4.4 Singly reinforced rectangular section in bending

Bending of the section will induce a resultant tensile force F_{st} in the reinforcing steel, and a resultant compressive force in the concrete F_{cc} which acts through the centroid of the effective area of concrete in compression, as shown in figure 4.4.

For equilibrium, the ultimate design moment, M, must be balanced by the moment of resistance of the section so that

$$M = F_{cc} \times z = F_{st} \times z \tag{4.5}$$

where z is the lever arm between the resultant forces F_{cc} and F_{st}.

$$F_{cc} = \text{stress} \times \text{area of action}$$
$$= 0.45 f_{cu} \times bs$$

and

$$z = d - s/2 \tag{4.6}$$

So that substituting in equation 4.5

$$M = 0.45 f_{cu} bs \times z$$

and replacing s from equation 4.6

$$M = 0.9 f_{cu} b (d - z) z \tag{4.7}$$

Rearranging and substituting $K = M/bd^2 f_{cu}$:

$$(z/d)^2 - (z/d) + K/0.9 = 0$$

Solving this quadratic equation:

$$z = d[0.5 + \sqrt{(0.25 - K/0.9)}] \tag{4.8*}$$

which is the equation in the code of practice BS 8110 for the lever arm, z, of a singly reinforced section.

In equation 4.5

$$F_{st} = (f_y/\gamma_m) A_s \quad \text{with} \quad \gamma_m = 1.05$$
$$= 0.95 f_y A_s$$

Hence

$$A_s = \frac{M}{0.95 f_y \times z} \tag{4.9*}$$

Equations 4.8 and 4.9 can be used to design the area of tension reinforcement in a concrete section to resist an ultimate moment, M.

Equation 4.8 for the lever arm z can be used to set up a table and draw a lever-arm curve as shown in figure 4.5, and the curve may be used to determine the lever arm, z, instead of solving the equation 4.8.

The upper limit of the lever-arm curve, $z = 0.95$, is specified by BS 8110. The lower limit of $z = 0.775d$ is when the depth of neutral axis $x = d/2$, which is the maximum value allowed by the code for a singly reinforced section in order to provide a ductile section which will have a gradual tension type failure as already described. With $z = 0.775d$ from equation 4.7:

$$M = 0.9 f_{cu} b(d - 0.775d) \times 0.775d$$

$K = M/bd^2 f_{cu}$	0.05	0.06	0.07	0.08	0.09	0.10	0.11	0.12	0.13	0.14	0.15	0.156
$l_a = z/d$	0.941	0.928	0.915	0.901	0.887	0.873	0.857	0.842	0.825	0.807	0.789	0.775

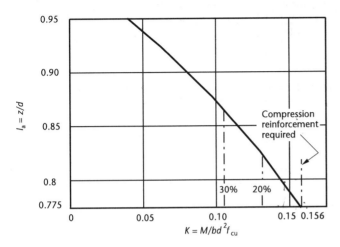

Figure 4.5
Lever-arm example

The % values on the K axis mark the limits for
singly reinforced sections with moment redistribution applied (see Section 4.7)

or

$$M = 0.156 f_{cu} bd^2 \qquad (4.10)^*$$

as marked on the lever-arm diagram. The coefficient 0.156 has actually been calculated
using the concrete stress as more precisely equal to $0.67 f_{cu}/\gamma_m = 0.447 f_{cu}$, instead of
$0.45 f_{cu}$.

When

$$\frac{M}{bd^2 f_{cu}} = K > 0.156$$

compression reinforcement is also required to supplement the moment of resistance of
the concrete.

EXAMPLE 4.1

Design of a singly reinforced rectangular section

The ultimate design moment to be resisted by the section in figure 4.6 is 185 kN m.
Determine the area of tension reinforcement (A_s) required given the characteristic material
strengths are $f_y = 460$ N/mm^2 and $f_{cu} = 30$ N/mm^2.

$$K = \frac{M}{bd^2 f_{cu}}$$

$$= \frac{185 \times 10^6}{260 \times 440^2 \times 30} = 0.122$$

$$< 0.156$$

therefore compression steel is not required.

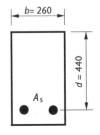

Figure 4.6
Design example – singly
reinforced section

Lever arm:

$$z = d\left\{0.5 + \sqrt{\left(0.25 - \frac{K}{0.9}\right)}\right\}$$

$$= 440\left\{0.5 + \sqrt{\left(0.25 - \frac{0.122}{0.9}\right)}\right\}$$

$$= 369 \text{ mm}$$

(Or alternatively, the value of $z = l_a d$ could be obtained from the lever-arm diagram, figure 4.5.)

$$A_s = \frac{M}{0.95 f_y z}$$

$$= \frac{185 \times 10^6}{0.95 \times 460 \times 369}$$

$$= 1147 \text{ mm}^2$$

Analysis equations for a singly reinforced section

The following equations may be used to calculate the moment of resistance of a given section with a known area of steel reinforcement.

For equilibrium of the compressive force in the concrete and the tensile force in the steel in figure 4.4:

$$F_{cc} = F_{st}$$

or

$$0.45 f_{cu} b \times s = 0.95 f_y A_s$$

Therefore depth of stress block is

$$s = \frac{0.95 f_y A_s}{0.45 f_{cu} b} \tag{4.11}$$

and

$$x = s/0.9$$

Therefore moment of resistance of the section is

$$M = F_{st} \times z$$

$$= 0.95 f_y A_s (d - s/2)$$

$$= 0.95 f_y A_s \left(d - \frac{0.95 f_y A_s}{0.9 f_{cu} b}\right) \tag{4.12}$$

These equations assume the tension reinforcement has yielded, which will be the case if $x \not> 0.615d$. If this is not the case, the problem would require solving by trying successive values of x until

$$F_{cc} = F_{st}$$

with the steel strains and hence stresses being determined from equations 4.2 and 4.1, to be used in equation instead of $0.95f_y$.

EXAMPLE 4.2

Analysis of singly reinforced rectangular section in bending

Determine the ultimate moment of resistance of the cross-section shown in figure 4.7 given that the characteristic strengths are $f_y = 460$ N/mm^2 for the reinforcement and $f_{cu} = 30$ N/mm^2 for the concrete.

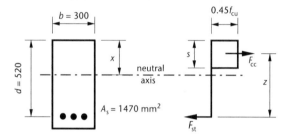

Figure 4.7
Analysis example – singly reinforced section

For equilibrium of the compressive and tensile forces on the section

$$F_{cc} = F_{st}$$

therefore

$$0.45f_{cu}bs = 0.95f_yA_s$$
$$0.45 \times 30 \times 300 \times s = 0.95 \times 460 \times 1470$$

therefore

$$s = 159 \text{ mm}$$

and

$$x = s/0.9 = 159/0.9$$
$$= 177 \text{ mm}$$

This value of x is less than the value of $0.615d$ derived from section 4.2, and therefore the steel has yielded and $f_{st} = 0.95f_y$ as assumed.

Moment of resistance of the section is

$$M = F_{st} \times z$$
$$= 0.95f_yA_s(d - s/2)$$
$$= 0.95 \times 460 \times 1470(520 - 145/2) \times 10^{-6}$$
$$= 287 \text{ kN m}$$

4.5 | Rectangular section with compression reinforcement at the ultimate limit state

(a) Derivation of basic equations

It should be noted that the equations in this section have been derived for the case where the reduction in moment at a section due to moment redistribution is not greater than 10 per cent. When this is not the case, reference should be made to section 4.7 which deals with the effect of moment redistribution.

From the section dealing with the analysis of a singly reinforced section when

$$M > 0.156 f_{cu} bd^2$$

the design ultimate moment exceeds the moment of resistance of the concrete and therefore compression reinforcement is required. For this condition the depth of neutral axis, $x \not> 0.5d$, the maximum value allowed by the code in order to ensure a tension failure with a ductile section.

Therefore

$$z = d - s/2 = d - 0.9x/2$$
$$= d - 0.9 \times 0.5d/2$$
$$= 0.775d$$

For equilibrium of the section in figure 4.8

$$F_{st} = F_{cc} + F_{sc}$$

so that with the reinforcement at yield

$$0.95 f_y A_s = 0.45 f_{cu} bs + 0.95 f_y A'_s$$

or with $s = 0.9 \times d/2 = 0.45d$

$$0.95 f_y A_s = 0.201 f_{cu} bd + 0.95 f_y A'_s \qquad (4.13)$$

Figure 4.8
Section with compression reinforcement

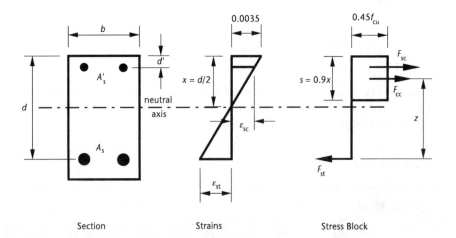

Section   Strains   Stress Block

and taking moments about the centroid of the tension steel, A_s

$$M = F_{cc} \times z + F_{sc}(d - d')$$
$$= 0.201 f_{cu} bd \times 0.775 d + 0.95 f_y A'_s(d - d')$$
$$= 0.156 f_{cu} bd^2 + 0.95 f_y A'_s(d - d') \tag{4.14}$$

From equation 4.14

$$A'_s = \frac{M - 0.156 f_{cu} bd^2}{0.95 f_y(d - d')} \tag{4.15}*$$

Multiplying both sides of equation 4.13 by $z = 0.775d$ and rearranging gives

$$A_s = \frac{0.156 f_{cu} bd^2}{0.95 f_y \times z} + A'_s \tag{4.16}*$$

with $z = 0.775d$.

Hence the areas of compression steel, A'_s, and tension steel, A_s, can be calculated from equations 4.15 and 4.16.

Substituting $K' = 0.156$ and $K = M/bd^2 f_{cu}$ into these equations would convert them into the same forms as in the code of practice, BS 8110, which are

$$A'_s = \frac{(K - K') f_{cu} bd^2}{0.95 f_y(d - d')} \tag{4.17}*$$

$$A_s = \frac{K' f_{cu} bd^2}{0.95 f_y z} + A'_s \tag{4.18}*$$

In this analysis it has been assumed that the compression steel has yielded so that the steel stress $f_{sc} = 0.95 f_y$. From the proportions of the strain distribution diagram:

$$\frac{\varepsilon_{sc}}{x - d'} = \frac{0.0035}{x} \tag{4.19}$$

so that

$$\frac{x - d'}{x} = \frac{\varepsilon_{sc}}{0.0035}$$

or

$$\frac{d'}{x} = 1 - \frac{\varepsilon_{sc}}{0.0035}$$

At yield with $f_y = 460$ N/mm^2, the steel strain $\varepsilon_{sc} = \varepsilon_y = 0.00219$. Therefore for yielding of the compression steel

$$\frac{d'}{x} \not> 1 - \frac{0.00219}{0.0035} \not> 0.37 \tag{4.20}*$$

or

$$\frac{d'}{d} \not> 0.185 \quad \text{with } x = \frac{d}{2} \tag{4.21}$$

The ratio of d'/d for the yielding of other grades of steel can be determined by using their yield strain in equation 4.19, but for values of f_y less than 460 N/mm^2, the application of equation 4.21 will provide an adequate safe check.

If $d'/d > 0.185$, then it is necessary to calculate the strain ε_{sc} from equation 4.19 and then determine f_{sc} from

$$f_{sc} = E_s \times \varepsilon_{sc} = 200\,000\varepsilon_{sc}$$

This value of stress for the compressive steel must then be used in the denominator of equation 4.15 in place of $0.95\,f_y$ in order to calculate the area A'_s of compression steel. The area of tension steel is calculated from a modified equation 4.16 such that

$$A_s = \frac{0.156 f_{cu} bd^2}{0.95 f_y z} + A'_s \times \frac{f_{sc}}{0.95 f_y}$$

(b) Design charts

The equations for the design charts are obtained by taking moments about the neutral axis. Thus

$$M = 0.45 f_{cu} 0.9x(x - 0.9x/2) + f_{sc} A'_s(x - d') + f_{st} A_s(d - x)$$

This equation and 4.13 may be written in the form

$$f_{st} \frac{A_s}{bd} = 0.405 f_{cu} \frac{x}{d} + f_{sc} \frac{A'_s}{bd}$$

$$\frac{M}{bd^2} = 0.405 f_{cu} \frac{x^2}{d^2}(1 - 0.45) + f_{sc} \frac{A'_s}{bd}\left(\frac{x}{d} - \frac{d'}{d}\right) + f_{st} \frac{A_s}{bd}\left(1 - \frac{x}{d}\right)$$

For specified ratios of A'_s/bd, x/d and d'/d, the two non-dimensional equations can be solved to give values for A_s/bd and M/bd^2 so that a set of design charts such as the one shown in figure 4.9 may be plotted. Before the equations can be solved, the steel stresses f_{st} and f_{sc} must be calculated for each value of x/d. This is achieved by first determining the relevant strains from the strain diagram (or by applying equations 4.2 and 4.3) and then by evaluating the stresses from the stress–strain curve of figure 4.2. Values of x/d below 0.5 apply when moments are redistributed.

Figure 4.9
Typical design chart for doubly reinforced beams

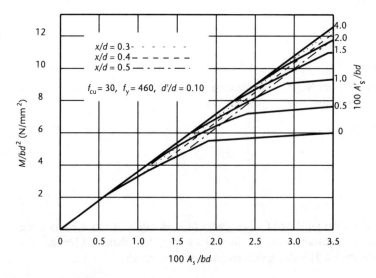

EXAMPLE 4.3

Design of a rectangular section with compression reinforcement
(moment redistribution factor $\beta_b \geq 0.9$)

The section shown in figure 4.10 is to resist an ultimate design moment of 285 kN m. The characteristic material strengths are $f_y = 460$ N/mm^2 and $f_{cu} = 30$ N/mm^2. Determine the areas of reinforcement required.

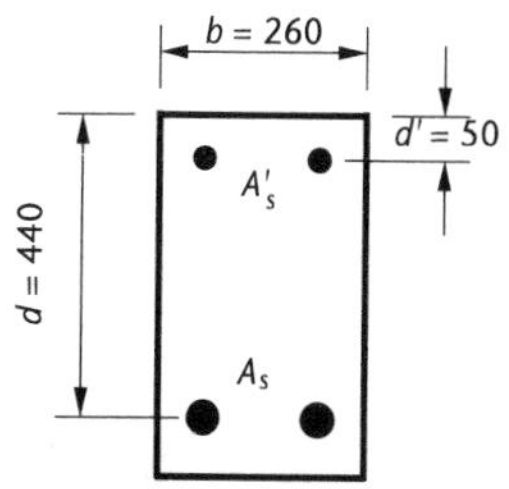

$$K = \frac{M}{bd^2 f_{cu}}$$

$$= \frac{285 \times 10^6}{260 \times 440^2 \times 30} = 0.189$$

$$> 0.156$$

therefore compression steel is required

$$d'/d = 50/440 = 0.11 < 0.185$$

as in equation 4.21 and the compression steel will have yielded.
Compression steel:

$$A'_s = \frac{(K - K')f_{cu}bd^2}{0.95 f_y (d - d')}$$

$$= \frac{(0.189 - 0.156)30 \times 260 \times 440^2}{0.95 \times 460(440 - 50)}$$

$$= 292 \text{ mm}^2$$

Tension steel:

$$A_s = \frac{K'f_{cu}bd^2}{0.95 f_y z} + A'_s$$

$$= \frac{0.156 \times 30 \times 260 \times 440^2}{0.95 \times 460(0.775 \times 440)} + 292$$

$$= 1581 + 292 = 1873 \text{ mm}^2$$

Figure 4.10
Design example with compression reinforcement, $\beta_b \geq 0.9$

b = 260

d = 440

d' = 50

A'_s

A_s

EXAMPLE 4.4

Analysis of a doubly reinforced rectangular section

Determine the ultimate moment of resistance of the cross-section shown in figure 4.11 given that the characteristic strengths are $f_y = 460$ N/mm^2 for the reinforcement and $f_{cu} = 30$ N/mm^2 for the concrete.

For equilibrium of the tensile and compressive forces on the section:

$$F_{st} = F_{cc} + F_{sc}$$

Assuming initially that the steel stresses f_{st} and f_{sc} are the design yield values, then

$$0.95 f_y A_s = 0.45 f_{cu} bs + 0.95 f_y A'_s$$

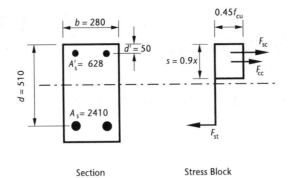

Figure 4.11
Analysis example, doubly
reinforced section

Therefore

$$s = \frac{0.95 f_y (A_s - A_s')}{0.45 f_{cu} b}$$

$$= \frac{0.95 \times 460(2410 - 628)}{0.45 \times 30 \times 280} = 206 \text{ mm}$$

$$x = s/0.9 = 229 \text{ mm}$$

$$x/d = 229/510 = 0.45 < 0.615$$

so the tension steel will have yielded. Also

$$d'/x = 50/229 = 0.22 < 0.37$$

so the compression steel will also have yielded, as assumed.

Taking moments about the tension steel

$$
\begin{aligned}
M &= F_{cc}(d - s/2) + F_{sc}(d - d') \\
&= 0.45 f_{cu} bs(d - s/2) + 0.95 f_y A_s'(d - d') \\
&= 0.45 \times 30 \times 280 \times 206(510 - 206/2) + 0.95 \times 460 \times 620(510 - 50) \\
&= 441 \times 10^6 \text{ N mm} = 441 \text{ kN m}
\end{aligned}
$$

If the depth of neutral axis was such that the compressive or tensile steel had not yielded, it would have been necessary to try successive values of x until

$$F_{st} = F_{cc} + F_{sc}$$

balances, with the steel strains and stresses being calculated from equations 4.2, 4.3 and 4.1. The steel stresses at balance would then be used to calculate the moment of resistance.

4.6　Flanged section in bending at the ultimate limit state

T-sections and L-sections which have their flanges in compression can both be designed or analysed in a similar manner, and the equations which are derived can be applied to either type of cross-section. As the flanges generally provide a large compressive area, it is usually unnecessary to consider the case where compression steel is required; if it should be required, the design would be based on the principles derived in section 4.6.3.

For the singly reinforced section it is necessary to consider two conditions:

1. the stress block lies within the compression flange, and
2. the stress block extends below the flange.

4.6.1 Flanged section the depth of the stress block lies within the flange, $s < h_f$ (figure 4.12)

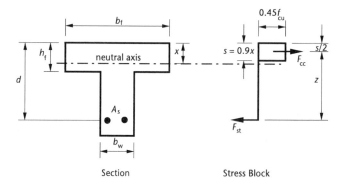

Figure 4.12
T-section, stress block within the flange, $s < h_f$

Section   Stress Block

For this depth of stress block, the beam can be considered as an equivalent rectangular section of breadth b_f equal to the flange width. This is because the non-rectangular section below the neutral axis is in tension and is, therefore, considered to be cracked and inactive. Thus $K = M/b_f d^2 f_{cu}$ can be calculated and the lever arm determined from the lever-arm curve of figure 4.5 or equation 4.8. The relation between the lever arm, z, and depth, x, of the neutral axis is given by

$$z = d - 0.5s$$

or

$$s = 2(d - z)$$

If s is less than the flange thickness (h_f), the stress block does lie within the flange as assumed and the area of reinforcement is given by

$$A_s = \frac{M}{0.95 f_y z}$$

The design of a T-section beam is described further in section 7.2.3 with a worked example.

EXAMPLE 4.5

Analysis of a flanged section

Determine the ultimate moment of resistance of the T-section shown in figure 4.13. The characteristic material strengths are $f_y = 460$ N/mm^2 and $f_{cu} = 30$ N/mm^2.

Assume initially that the stress block depth lies within the flange and the reinforcement is strained to the yield, so that $f_{st} = 0.95 f_y$.

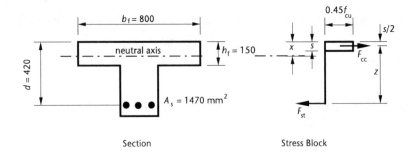

Section   Stress Block

For no resultant axial force on the sections

$$F_{cc} = F_{st}$$

therefore

$$0.45 f_{cu} b_f s = 0.95 f_y A_s$$

and solving for the depth of stress block

$$s = \frac{0.95 \times 460 \times 1470}{0.45 \times 30 \times 800}$$

$$= 59 \text{ mm}$$

$$x = s/0.9 = 66 \text{ mm}$$

Hence the stress block does lie within the flange and with this depth of neutral axis the steel will have yielded as assumed.

Lever arm:

$$z = d - s/2$$

$$= 420 - 59/2 = 390 \text{ mm}$$

Taking moments about the centroid of the reinforcement the moment of resistance is

$$M = F_{cc} \times z$$

$$= 0.45 f_{cu} b_f s z$$

$$= 0.45 \times 30 \times 800 \times 59 \times 390 \times 10^{-6}$$

$$= 249 \text{ kN m}$$

If in the analysis it had been found that $s > h_f$, then the procedure would then be similar to that in example 4.7.

4.6.2 Flanged section – the depth of the stress block extends below the flange, $s > h_f$

For the design of a flanged section, the procedure described in section 4.6.1 will check if the depth of the stress block extends below the flange. An alternative procedure is to calculate the moment of resistance, M_f, of the section with $s = h_f$, the depth of the flange (see equation 4.22 of example 4.6 following). Hence if the design moment, M, is such that

$$M > M_f$$

then the stress block must extend below the flange, and

$$s > h_f$$

In this case the design can be carried out by either:

(a) using an exact method to determine the depth of the neutral axis, as in example 4.6

or

(b) designing for the conservative condition of $x = d/2$ as described at the end of this section.

EXAMPLE 4.6

Design of a flanged section with the depth of the stress block below the flange

The T-section beam shown in figure 4.14 is required to resist an ultimate design moment of 180 kN m. The characteristic material strengths are $f_y = 460$ N/mm^2 and $f_{cu} = 30$ N/mm^2. Calculate the area of reinforcement required.

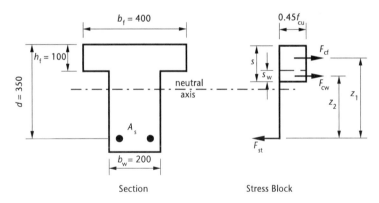

Figure 4.14
Design example of a T-section, $s > h_f$

Section   Stress Block

In the figure

F_{cf} is the force developed in the flange

F_{cw} is the force developed in the area of web in compression

Moment of resistance, M_f, of the flange is

$$M_f = F_{cf} \times z_1$$

or

$$M_f = 0.45 f_{cu} b_f h_f (d - h_f/2) \tag{4.22}*$$
$$= 0.45 \times 30 \times 400 \times 100(350 - 100/2) \times 10^{-6}$$
$$= 162 \text{ kN m} < 180 \text{ kN m, the design moment}$$

Therefore, the stress block must extend below the flange.

It is now necessary to determine the depth, s_w, of the web in compression, where $s_w = s - h_f$.

For equilibrium:

Applied moment

$$180 = F_{cf} \times z_1 + F_{cw} \times z_2$$

$$= 162 + 0.45 f_{cu} b_w s_w \times z_2$$

$$= 162 + 0.45 \times 30 \times 200 s_w (250 - s_w/2) \times 10^{-6}$$

$$= 162 + 2700 s_w (250 - s_w/2) \times 10^{-6}$$

This equation can be rearranged into

$$s_w{}^2 - 500 s_w + 13.33 \times 10^3 = 0$$

Solving this quadratic equation

$$s_w = 28 \text{ mm}$$

So that the depth of neutral axis

$$x = s/0.9 = (100 + 28)/0.9$$

$$= 142 \text{ mm}$$

As $x < d/2$, compression reinforcement is not required.
For the equilibrium of the section

$$F_{st} = F_{cf} + F_{cw}$$

or

$$0.95 f_y A_s = 0.45 f_{cu} b_f h_f + 0.45 f_{cu} b_w s_w$$
$$0.95 \times 460 \times A_s = 0.45 \times 30(400 \times 100 + 200 \times 28)$$

Therefore

$$A_s = \frac{616 \times 10^3}{0.95 \times 460}$$

$$= 1410 \text{ mm}^2$$

EXAMPLE 4.7

Analysis of a flanged section

Determine the ultimate moment of resistance of the T-beam section shown in figure 4.15 given $f_y = 460$ N/mm^2 and $f_{cu} = 30$ N/mm^2.
The compressive force in the flange is

$$F_{cf} = 0.45 f_{cu} b_f h_f$$

$$= 0.45 \times 30 \times 450 \times 150 \times 10^{-3}$$

$$= 911.2 \text{ kN}$$

Then tensile force in the reinforcing steel, assuming it has yielded, is

$$F_{st} = 0.95 f_y A_s$$

$$= 0.95 \times 460 \times 2410 \times 10^{-3}$$

$$= 1053.2 \text{ kN}$$

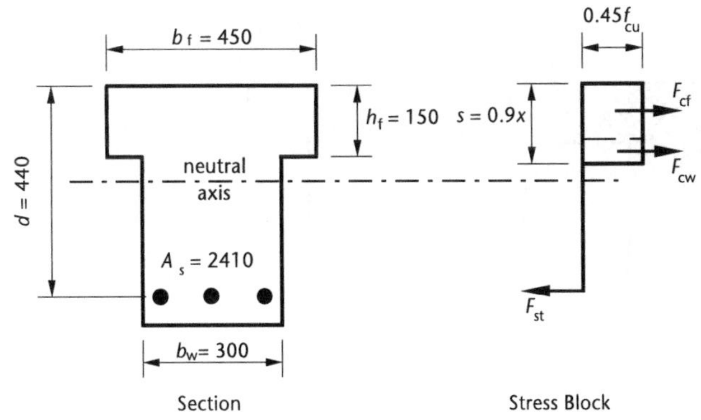

Figure 4.15
Analysis example of a
T-section, $s > h_f$

Therefore $F_{st} > F_{cc}$ so that $s > h_f$ and the force in the web is

$$F_{cw} = 0.45 f_{cu} b_w (s - h_f)$$
$$= 0.45 \times 30 \times 300 (s - 150) \times 10^{-3}$$
$$= 4.05 (s - 150)$$

For equilibrium

$$F_{cw} = F_{st} - F_{cf}$$

or

$$4.05 (s - 150) = 1053.2 - 911.2$$

Hence

$$s = 185 \text{ mm}$$
$$x = s/0.9 = 206 \text{ mm}$$

With this depth of neutral axis the reinforcement has yielded, as assumed, and

$$F_{cw} = 4.05 (185 - 150)$$
$$= 142 \text{ kN}$$

(If $F_{cf} > F_{st}$, the the stress block would not extend beyond the flange and the section would be analysed as in example 4.2 for a rectangular section of dimensions $b_f \times d$.)

Taking moments about the centroid of the reinforcement

$$M = F_{cf}(d - h_f/2) + F_{cw}(d - s/2 - h_f/2)$$
$$= [911.2(440 - 150/2) + 142(440 - 185/2 - 150/2)] \times 10^{-3}$$
$$= 371 \text{ kN m}$$

EXAMPLE 4.8

Design of a flanged section with depth of neutral axis $x = d/2$

A safe but conservative design for a flanged section with $s > h_f$ can be achieved by setting the depth of neutral axis to $x = d/2$, the maximum depth allowed in the code. Design equations can be derived for this condition as follows.

Depth of stress block, $s = 0.9x = 0.45d$

Figure 4.16
Flanged section with depth of
neutral axis $x = d/2$

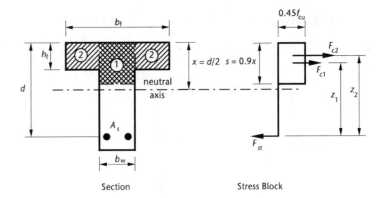

Section   Stress Block

Divide the flanged section within the depth of the stress block into areas 1 and 2 as shown in figure 4.16, so that

$$\text{Area } 1 = b_w \times s$$

$$= 0.45 b_w d$$

$$\text{Area } 2 = (b_f - b_w) \times h_f$$

and the compression forces developed by these areas are

$$F_{c1} = 0.45 f_{cu} \times 0.45 b_w d$$

$$= 0.2 f_{cu} b_w d$$

$$F_{c2} = 0.45 f_{cu} h_f (b_f - b_w)$$

Taking moments about F_{c2} at the centroid of the flange

$$M = F_{st}(d - h_f/2) - F_{c1}(s/2 - h_f/2)$$

$$= 0.95 f_y A_s (d - h_f/2) - 0.2 f_{cu} b_w d (0.45d - h_f)/2$$

Therefore

$$A_s = \frac{M + 0.1 f_{cu} b_w d (0.45d - h_f)}{0.95 f_y (d - 0.5 h_f)} \tag{4.23}*$$

This is the equation given in clause 3.4.4.5 of BS 8110. It should not be used when $h_f > 0.45d$.

Applying this equation to example 4.6:

$$A_s = \frac{180 \times 10^6 + 0.1 \times 30 \times 200 \times 350(0.45 \times 350 - 100)}{0.95 \times 460(350 - 100/2)}$$

$$= 1465 \text{ mm}^2 \text{ (compare with 1410 mm}^2 \text{ of example 4.6)}$$

Before using equation 4.23 for calculating A_s, it is necessary to confirm that compression reinforcement is not required. This is achieved by using equation 4.24 to check that the moment of resistance of the concrete, M_c, is greater than the design moment, M.

4.6.3 Flanged section with compression reinforcement

With $x = d/2$ in figure 4.16 and taking moments about A_s, the maximum resistance moment of the concrete is

$$M_c = F_{c1} \times z_1 + F_{c2} \times z_2$$
$$= 0.156 f_{cu} b_w d^2 + 0.45 f_{cu} (b_f - b_w)(d - h_f/2) \tag{4.24}$$

(Note that the value of 0.156 was derived previously for the rectangular section.)
  Dividing through by $f_{cu} b_f d^2$

$$\frac{M_c}{f_{cu} b_f d^2} = 0.156 \frac{b_w}{b_f} + 0.45 \frac{h_f}{d} \left(1 - \frac{b_w}{b_f}\right)\left(1 - \frac{h_f}{2d}\right) \tag{4.25}*$$

which is similar to the equation given in BS 8110.
  If the applied design moment, $M > M_c$, compression reinforcement is required. In which case the areas of steel can be calculated from

$$A_s' = \frac{M - M_c}{0.95 f_y (d - d')} \tag{4.26}$$

and considering the equilibrium of forces on the section

$$F_{st} = F_{c1} + F_{c2} + F_{sc}$$

so that

$$A_s = \frac{0.2 f_{cu} b_w d + 0.45 f_{cu} h_f (b_f - b_w)}{0.95 f_y} + A_s' \tag{4.27}$$

Again, $d'/x \not> 0.37$, otherwise the design compressive steel stress is less than $0.95 \, f_y$.
  When, because of moment redistribution, $\beta_b < 0.9$ the limiting depth of neutral axis is less than $d/2$ and these equations will require modification using the factors given in the table 4.1 of section 4.7 which deals with moment redistribution.

4.7 Moment redistribution and the design equations

The plastic behaviour of reinforced concrete at the ultimate limit state affects the distribution of moments in a structure. To allow for this, the moments derived from an elastic analysis may be redistributed based on the assumption that plastic hinges have formed at the sections with the largest moments. The formation of plastic hinges requires relatively large rotations with yielding of the tension reinforcement. To ensure large strains in the tension steel, the code of practice restricts the depth of the neutral axis of a section according to the reduction of the elastic moment so that

$$x \not> (\beta_b - 0.4)d \tag{4.28}*$$

where d is the effective depth and

$$\beta_b = \frac{\text{moment at section after redistribution}}{\text{moment at section before redistribution}} \leq 1.0$$

So, for the design of a section with compression reinforcement after moment redistribution the depth of neutral axis x will take the maximum value from equation 4.28.

Therefore the depth of the stress block is

$$s = 0.9(\beta_b - 0.4)d$$

and the level arm is

$$z = d - \frac{s}{2}$$
$$= d - 0.9(\beta_b - 0.4)d/2 \tag{4.29}$$

The moment of resistance of the concrete in compression is

$$M_c = F_{cc} \times z = 0.45 f_{cu} bs \times z$$
$$= 0.45 f_{cu} b \times 0.9(\beta_b - 0.4)d \times [d - 0.9(\beta_b - 0.4)d/2]$$

Therefore

$$\frac{M_c}{bd^2 f_{cu}} = 0.45 \times 0.9(\beta_b - 0.4)[1 - 0.45(\beta_b - 0.4)]$$
$$= 0.402(\beta_b - 0.4) - 0.18(\beta_b - 0.4)^2$$

So that rearranging

$$M_c = K'bd^2 f_{cu}$$

where $\quad K' = 0.402(\beta_b - 0.4) - 0.18(\beta_b - 0.4)^2 \tag{4.30}*$

This is the equation for K' given in BS 8110. (It should be noted that in calculating the coefficients 0.402 and 0.18, the more precise value of concrete stress $f_{cc} = 0.67 f_{cu}/1.5$ has been used and not the value 0.45 f_{cu}.)

When the ultimate design moment is such that

$$M > K'bd^2 f_{cu}$$

or $\quad K > K'$

then compression steel is required such that

$$A_s' = \frac{(K - K')f_{cu}bd^2}{0.95 f_y (d - d')} \tag{4.31}*$$

and

$$A_s = \frac{K' f_{cu} bd^2}{0.95 f_y z} + A_s' \tag{4.32}*$$

where $\quad K = \dfrac{M}{bd^2 f_{cu}} \tag{4.33}*$

These equations are identical in form to those derived previously for the design of a section with compression reinforcement for $\beta_b \geq 0.9$.

Table 4.1 shows the various design factors associated with the moment redistribution. If the value of d'/d for the section exceeds that shown in the table, the compression steel will not have yielded and the compressive stress will be less than $0.95 f_y$. In such cases, the compressive stress f_{sc} will be $E_s \varepsilon_{sc}$ where the strain ε_{sc} is obtained from the proportions of the strain diagram. This value of f_{sc} should replace $0.95 f_y$ in equation 4.31, and equation 4.32 becomes

$$A_s = \frac{K' f_{cu} bd^2}{0.95 f_y z} + A_s' \times \frac{f_{sc}}{0.95 f_y}$$

Table 4.1 Moment redistribution design factors

Redistribution (per cent)	β_b	x/d	z/d	K'	d'/d
≤ 10	≥ 0.9	0.5	0.775	0.156	0.185
15	0.85	0.45	0.797	0.144	0.168
10	0.8	0.4	0.82	0.132	0.150
25	0.75	0.35	0.842	0.199	0.131
30	0.7	0.3	0.865	0.104	0.112

It should be noted that for a singly reinforced section $(K < K')$, the lever arm z is calculated from equation 4.8.

For a section requiring compression steel, the lever arm can be calculated from equation 4.29 or by using the equation

$$z = d[0.5 + \sqrt{(0.25 - K'/0.9)}] \tag{4.34}$$

as given in BS 8110, and is similar to equation 4.8 but with K' replacing K.

EXAMPLE 4.9

Design of a section with moment redistribution applied and $\beta_b = 0.8$

The section shown in figure 4.17 is subject to an ultimate design moment of 228 kN m. The characteristic material strengths are $f_y = 460$ N/mm^2 and $f_{cu} = 30$ N/mm^2. Determine the areas of reinforcement required.

(A) From first principles

Limiting neutral axis depth $\quad x = (\beta_b - 0.4)d = (0.8 - 0.4)d$

$$= 0.4d = 176 \text{ mm}$$

Stress block depth $\qquad s = 0.9x = 0.36d$

Lever arm $\qquad\qquad z = d - s/2 = 0.82d$

Moment of resistance of the concrete

$\quad M_c = F_{cc} \times z = 0.45 f_{cu} bs \times z$

$\qquad\qquad = 0.45 \times 30 \times 260 \times 0.36 \times 0.82 \times 440^2 \times 10^{-6}$

$\qquad\qquad = 201 \text{ kN m}$

$\qquad\qquad < 228 \text{ kN m, the applied moment}$

therefore compression steel is required.

$\quad d'/x = 50/176 = 0.28$

$\qquad\quad < 0.37$

therefore the compression steel has yielded.

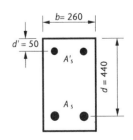

Figure 4.17
Design example with moment redistribution, $\beta_b = 0.8$

Compression steel:

$$A_s = \frac{M - M_c}{0.95 f_y (d - d')}$$

$$= \frac{(228 - 201) \times 10^6}{0.95 \times 460 (440 - 50)} = 158 \text{ mm}^2$$

Tension steel:

$$A_s = \frac{M_c}{0.95 f_y z} + A_s'$$

$$= \frac{201 \times 10^6}{0.95 \times 460 \times 0.82 \times 440} + 158$$

$$= 1275 + 158 = 1433 \text{ mm}^2$$

(B) Alternative solution applying equations from BS 8110

From equations 4.30 to 4.34:

$$K' = 0.402(\beta_b - 0.4) - 0.18(\beta_b - 0.4)^2$$

$$= 0.402(0.8 - 0.4) - 0.18(0.8 - 0.4)^2$$

$$= 0.132$$

$$K = \frac{M}{bd^2 f_{cu}}$$

$$= \frac{228 \times 10^6}{260 \times 440^2 \times 30}$$

$$= 0.151 > K'$$

therefore compression steel is required.

Compression steel:

$$A_s' = \frac{(K - K') f_{cu} b d^2}{0.95 f_y (d - d')}$$

$$= \frac{(0.151 - 0.132)30 \times 260 \times 440^2}{0.95 \times 460 (440 - 50)}$$

$$= 168 \text{ mm}^2$$

(The variation with the previous result is due to rounding-off errors in the arithmetic and the subtraction of two numbers of similar magnitude in the numerator.)

Tension steel:

$$z = d[0.5 + \sqrt{(0.25 - K'/0.9)}]$$

$$= d[0.5 + \sqrt{(0.25 - 0.132/0.9)}] = 0.82d$$

$$A_s = \frac{K' f_{cu} b d^2}{0.95 f_y z} + A_s'$$

$$= \frac{0.32 \times 30 \times 260 \times 440^2}{0.95 \times 460 \times 0.82 \times 440} + 168$$

$$= 1265 + 168 = 1433 \text{ mm}^2$$

4.8 Bending plus axial load at the ultimate limit state

The applied axial force may be tensile or compressive. In the analysis that follows, a compressive force is considered. For a tensile load the same basic principles of equilibrium, compatability of strains, and stress–strain relationships would apply, but it would be necessary to change the sign of the applied load (N) when we consider the equilibrium of forces on the cross-section. (The area of concrete in compression has not been reduced to allow for the concrete displaced by the compression steel. This could be taken into account by reducing the stress f_{sc} in the compression steel by an amount equal to $0.45 f_{cu}$.)

Figure 4.18 represents the cross-section of a member with typical strain and stress distributions for varying positions of the neutral axis. The cross-section is subject to a moment M and an axial compressive force N, and in the figure the direction of the moment is such as to cause compression on the upper part of the section and tension on the lower part.

Let

F_{cc} be the compressive force developed in the concrete and acting through the centroid of the stress block

F_{sc} be the compressive force in the reinforcement area A'_s and acting through its centroid

F_s be the tensile or compressive force in the reinforcement area A_s and acting through its centroid.

(i) Basic equations and design charts

The applied force (N) must be balanced by the forces developed within the cross-section, therefore

$$N = F_{cc} + F_{sc} + F_s$$

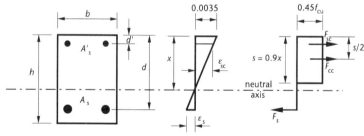

(a) $s = 0.9x < h$

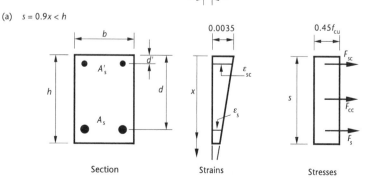

Section Strains Stresses

(b) $s = h:\ 0.9x > h$

Figure 4.18
Bending plus axial load with varying positions of the neutral axis

In this equation, F_s will be negative whenever the position of the neutral axis is such that the reinforcement A_s is in tension, as in figure 4.18a. Substituting into this equation the terms for the stresses and areas

$$N = 0.45 f_{cu} bs + f_{sc} A_s' + f_s A_s \qquad (4.35)*$$

where f_{sc} is the compressive stress in reinforcement A_s' and f_s is the tensile or compressive stress in reinforcement A_s.

The design moment M must be balanced by the moment of resistance of the forces developed within the cross-section. Hence, taking moments about the mid-depth of the section

$$M = F_{cc}\left(\frac{h}{2} - \frac{s}{2}\right) + F_{sc}\left(\frac{h}{2} - d'\right) + F_s\left(\frac{h}{2} - d\right)$$

or

$$M = 0.45 f_{cu} bs\left(\frac{h}{2} - \frac{s}{2}\right) + f_{sc} A_s'\left(\frac{h}{2} - d'\right) - f_s A_s\left(d - \frac{h}{2}\right) \qquad (4.36)*$$

When the depth of neutral axis is such that $0.9x \geq h$ as in part (b) of figure 4.18, then the whole concrete section is subject to a uniform compressive stress of $0.45 f_{cu}$. In this case, the concrete provides no contribution to the moment of resistance and the first term on the right side of the equation 4.36 disappears.

For a symmetrical arrangement of reinforcement ($A_s' = A_s = A_{sc}/2$ and $d' = h - d$), equations 4.35 and 4.36 can be rewritten in the following form

$$\frac{N}{bh} = \frac{0.45 f_{cu} s}{h} + f_{sc}\frac{A_s}{bh} + f_s\frac{A_s}{bh} \qquad (4.37)$$

$$\frac{M}{bh^2} = \frac{0.45 f_{cu} s}{h}\left(0.5 - \frac{s}{2h}\right) + \frac{f_{sc} A_s}{bh}\left(\frac{d}{h} - 0.5\right) - \frac{f_s A_s}{bh}\left(\frac{d}{h} - 0.5\right) \qquad (4.38)$$

In these equations the steel strains, and hence the stresses f_{sc} and f_s, vary with the depth of the neutral axis (x). Thus N/bh and M/bh^2 can be calculated for specified ratios of A_s/bh and x/h so that column design charts for a symmetrical arrangement of reinforcement such as the one shown in figure 4.19 can be plotted.

Figure 4.19
Typical column design chart

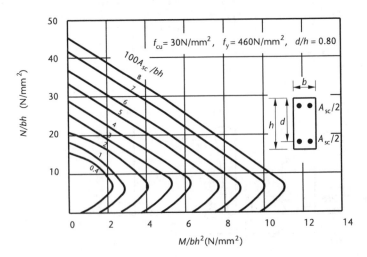

The direct solution of equations 4.37 and 4.38 for the design of column reinforcement would be very tedious and, therefore, a set of design charts for the usual case of symmetrical sections have been prepared by the British Standards Institution. Examples showing the design of column steel are given in chapter 9.

(ii) Modes of failure

The relative magnitude of the moment (M) and the axial load (N) governs whether the section will fail in tension or in compression. With large effective eccentricity ($e = M/N$) a tensile failure is likely, but with a small eccentricity a compressive failure is more likely. The magnitude of the eccentricity affects the position of the neutral axis and hence the strains and stresses in the reinforcement.

Let

ε_{sc} be the compressive strain in reinforcement A_s'
ε_s be the tensile or compressive strain in reinforcement A_s
ε_y be the tensile yield strain of steel as shown in the stress–strain curve of figure 4.2.

From the linear strain distribution of figure 4.18

$$\varepsilon_{sc} = 0.0035 \left(\frac{x - d'}{x} \right)$$

and   (4.39)*

$$\varepsilon_s = 0.0035 \left(\frac{d - x}{x} \right)$$

The steel stresses and strains are then related according to the stress–strain curve of figure 4.2.

Consider the following modes of failure of the section as shown on the interaction diagram of figure 4.20.

(a) Tension failure, $\varepsilon_s > \varepsilon_y$ This type of failure is associated with large eccentricities (e) and small depths of neutral axis (x). Failure begins with yielding of the tensile reinforcement, followed by crushing of the concrete as the tensile strains rapidly increase.

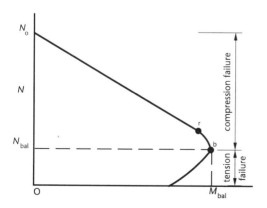

Figure 4.20
Bending plus axial load chart with modes of failure

(b) Balanced failure, $\varepsilon_s = \varepsilon_y$, point b on figure 4.20 When failure occurs with yielding of the tension steel and crushing of the concrete at the same instant it is described as a 'balanced' failure. With $\varepsilon_s = \varepsilon_y$ and from equation 4.39

$$x = x_{bal} = \frac{d}{1 + \dfrac{\varepsilon_y}{0.0035}}$$

For example, substituting the values of $\varepsilon_y = 0.00219$ for grade 460 steel

$$x_{bal} = 0.615d$$

Equations 4.35 and 4.36 become

$$N_{bal} = F_{cc} + F_{sc} - F_s$$

$$= 0.45 f_{cu} b \times 0.9 \times x_{bal} + f_{sc} A'_s - 0.95 f_y A_s \tag{4.40}$$

and $\qquad M_{bal} = F_{cc}\left(\dfrac{h}{2} - \dfrac{0.9 x_{bal}}{2}\right) + F_{sc}\left(\dfrac{h}{2} - d'\right) + F_s\left(d - \dfrac{h}{2}\right)$

where

$$f_{sc} \leq 0.95 f_y$$

At point b on the interaction diagram of figure 4.20, $N = N_{bal}$, $M = M_{bal}$ and $f_s = -0.95 f_y$. When the design load $N > N_{bal}$ the section will fail in compression, whilst if $N < N_{bal}$ there will be an initial tensile failure, with yielding of reinforcement A_s.

(c) Compression failure In this case $x > x_{bal}$ and $N > N_{bal}$. The change in slope at point r in figure 4.20 occurs when

$$\varepsilon_{sc} = \varepsilon_y$$

and from equation 4.39

$$x_r = 0.0035 d' / (0.0035 - \varepsilon_y)$$
$$= 2.67 d' \text{ for grade 460 steel}$$

Point r will occur in the tension failure zone of the interaction diagram if $x_r < x_{bal}$. When $x < d$

$$f_s \leq 0.95 f_y \text{ and tensile}$$

When $x = d$

$$f_s = 0$$

When $x > d$

$$f_s \leq 0.95 f_y \text{ and compressive}$$

When $x = 2.67d$, then from equation 4.39

$$\varepsilon_s = 0.00219$$
$$= \varepsilon_y \text{ for grade 460 steel}$$

At this stage, both layers of steel will have yielded and there will be zero moment of resistance with a symmetrical section, so that

$$N_0 = 0.45 f_{cu} bh + 0.95 f_y (A'_s + A_s)$$

Such M–N interaction diagrams can be constructed for any shape of cross-section which has an axis of symmetry by applying the basic equilibrium and strain compatibility equations with the stress–strain relations, as demonstrated in the following examples. These diagrams can be very useful for design purposes.

EXAMPLE 4.10

M–N interactive diagram for an unsymmetrical section

Construct the interaction diagram for the section shown in figure 4.21 with $f_{cu} = 30$ N/mm^2 and $f_y = 460$ N/mm^2. The bending causes maximum compression on the face adjacent to the steel area A'_s.

For a symmetrical cross-section, taking moments about the centre-line of the concrete section will give $M = 0$ with $N = N_0$ and both areas of steel at the yield stress. This is no longer true for unsymmetrical steel areas as $F_{sc} \neq F_s$ at yield therefore, theoretically, moments should be calculated about an axis referred to as the 'plastic centroid'. The ultimate axial load N_0 acting through the plastic centroid causes a uniform strain across the section with compression yielding of all the reinforcement, and thus there is zero moment of resistance. With uniform strain the neutral-axis depth, x, is at infinity.

The location of the plastic centroid is determined by taking moments of all the stress resultants about an arbitrary axis such as AA in figure 4.21 so that

$$
\begin{aligned}
\bar{x}_p &= \frac{\sum(F_{cc}h/2 + F_{sc}d' + F_s d)}{\sum(F_{cc} + F_{sc} + F_s)} \\
&= \frac{0.45 f_{cu} A_{cc} \times 450/2 + 0.95 f_y A'_s \times 60 + 0.95 f_y A_s \times 390}{0.45 f_{cu} A_{cc} + 0.95 f_y A'_s + 0.95 f_y A_s} \\
&= \frac{0.45 \times 30 \times 350 \times 450^2/2 + 0.95 \times 460(1610 \times 60 + 982 \times 390)}{0.45 \times 30 \times 350 \times 450 + 0.95 \times 460(1610 + 982)} \\
&= 211 \text{ mm from AA}
\end{aligned}
$$

The fundamental equation for calculating points on the interaction diagram with varying depths of neutral axis are

(i) Compatibility of strains (used in table 4.2, columns 2 and 3):

$$
\begin{aligned}
\varepsilon_{sc} &= 0.0035\left(\frac{x - d'}{x}\right) \\
\varepsilon_s &= 0.0035\left(\frac{d - x}{x}\right)
\end{aligned}
\tag{4.41}
$$

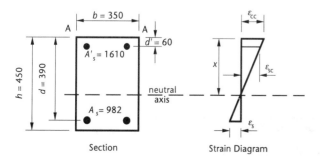

Section   Strain Diagram

Figure 4.21
Non-symmetrical section M–N interaction example

Table 4.2 *M–N interaction values for example 4.9*

(1) x	(2) ε_{sc}	(3) ε_{s}	(4) f_{sc}	(5) f_{s}	(6) N	(7) M
$d' = 60$	0	>0.00219	0	$-0.95 f_y$	-175	124
$2.67d' = 160$	0.00219	>0.00219	$0.95 f_y$	$-0.95 f_y$	955	278
$x_{bal} = 0.615d$	>0.00219	0.00219	$0.95 f_y$	$-0.95 f_y$	1295	288
$= 240$						
$d = 390$	>0.00219	0	$0.95 f_y$	0	2363	165
$2.67d = 1041$	>0.00219	>0.00219	$0.95 f_y$	$0.95 f_y$	3260	0

(ii) Stress–strain relations for the steel (table 4.2, columns 4 and 5):

$$\varepsilon \geq \varepsilon_y = 0.00219 \qquad f = 0.95 f_y$$
$$\varepsilon < \varepsilon_y \qquad f = E \times \varepsilon$$

(4.42)

(iii) Equilibrium (table 4.2, columns 6 and 7):

$$N = F_{cc} + F_{sc} + F_{s}$$
$$\text{or} \quad 0.9x < h \quad N = 0.45 f_{cu} b 0.9x + f_{sc} A'_s + f_s A_s$$
$$0.9x > h \quad N = 0.45 f_{cu} b h + f_{sc} A'_s + f_s A_s$$

Taking moments about the plastic centroid

$$0.9x < h \quad M = F_{cc}(\bar{x}_p - 0.9x/2) + F_{sc}(\bar{x}_p - d') - F_s(d - \bar{x}_p)$$
$$0.9x \geq h \quad M = F_{cc}(\bar{x}_p - h/2) + F_{sc}(\bar{x}_p - d') - F_s(d - \bar{x}_p)$$

F_s is negative when f_s is a tensile stress.

These equations have been applied to provide the values in table 4.2 for a range of key values of x. Then the *M–N* interaction diagram has been plotted in figure 4.22 from the values in table 4.2 as a series of straight lines. Of course, N and M could have been calculated for intermediate values of x to provide a more accurate curve.

Figure 4.22
M–N interaction diagram for a non-symmetrical section

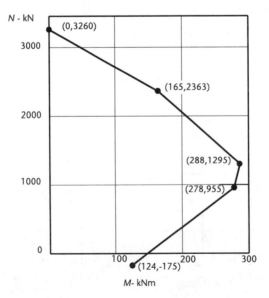

EXAMPLE 4.11

M–N interaction diagram for a non-rectangular section

Construct the interaction diagram for the equilateral triangular column section in figure 4.23 with $f_{cu} = 30$ N/mm^2 and $f_y = 460$ N/mm^2. The bending is about an axis parallel to the side AA and causes maximum compression on the corner adjacent to the steel area A'_s.

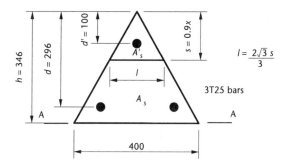

Figure 4.23
Non-rectangular section
M–N interaction diagram

For this triangular section, the plastic centroid is at the same location as the geometric centroid, since the moment of F_{sc} equals the moment of F_s about this axis when all the bars have yielded in compression.

The fundamental equations for strain compatibility and the steel's stress–strain relations are as presented in example 4.9 and are used again in this example. The equilibrium equations for the triangular section become

$$N = F_{cc} + F_{sc} + F_s$$

or $0.9x < h$ $\quad N = 0.45 f_{cu} sl/2 + f_{sc} A'_s + f_s A_s$

$0.9x > h$ $\quad N = 0.45 f_{cu} h \times 400/2 + f_{sc} A'_s + f_s A_s$

$0.9x < h$ $\quad M = F_{cc} 2(h - 0.9x)/3 + F_{sc}(2h/3 - d') - F_s(d - 2h/3)$

$0.9x \geq h$ $\quad M = F_{sc}(2h/3 - d') - F_s(d - 2h/3)$

F_s is negative when f_s is a tensile stress, and from the geometry of figure 4.23

$$l = \frac{2}{3} s\sqrt{3}$$

Table 4.3 has been calculated using the fundamental equations with the values of x shown. The interaction diagram is shown constructed in figure 4.24.

Table 4.3 *M–N interaction values for example 4.11*

x	ε_{sc}	ε_{st}	f_{sc} (N/mm^2)	f_s (N/mm^2)	N (kN)	M (kN m)
$d' = 100$	0	>0.00219	0	$-0.95 f_y$	-367	38.9
$x_{bal} = 0.615d$ $= 182$	0.0016	0.00219	315	$-0.95 f_y$	-66	73.7
$2.67d' = 267$	0.00219	0.00034	$0.95 f_y$	-76	590	64.7
$d = 296$	>0.00219	0	$0.95 f_y$	0	768	57.5
$2.67d = 790$	>0.00219	>0.00219	$0.95 f_y$	$0.95 f_y$	1578	0

Figure 4.24
M–N interaction diagram for a non-rectangular section

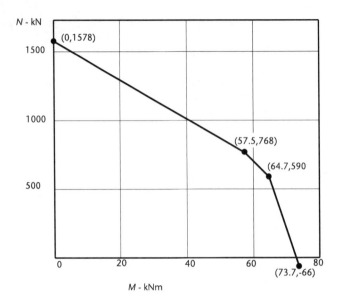

With a non-rectangular section, it could be advisable to construct a more accurate interaction diagram using other intermediate values of x. This would certainly be the case with, say, a flanged section where there is sudden change in breadth.

4.9 | The rectangular–parabolic stress block

A rectangular–parabolic stress block may be used to provide a more rigorous analysis of the reinforced concrete section. The stress block is similar in shape to the stress–strain curve for concrete in figure 4.1, having a maximum stress of $0.45 f_{cu}$ at the ultimate strain of 0.0035.

In figure 4.25

ε_0 = the concrete strain at the end of the parabolic section

w = the distance from the neutral axis to strain ε_0

x = depth of the neutral axis

k_1 = the mean concrete stress

k_2x = depth to the centroid of the stress block.

(a) To determine the mean concrete stress, k_1

From the strain diagram

$$\frac{x}{0.0035} = \frac{w}{\varepsilon_0}$$

therefore

$$w = \frac{x\varepsilon_0}{0.0035}$$

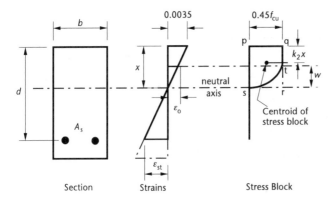

Figure 4.25
Section in bending with a
rectangular–parabolic stress
block

Substituting for $\varepsilon_0 = 2.4 \times 10^{-4}\sqrt{(f_{cu}/\gamma_m)}$ (see figure 4.1)

$$w = \frac{x\sqrt{f_{cu}}}{17.86} \text{ with } \gamma_m = 1.5 \tag{4.43}$$

For the stress block

$$k_1 = \frac{\text{area of stress block}}{x}$$

$$= \frac{\text{area pqrs} - \text{area rst}}{x}$$

Thus, using the area properties of a parabola as shown in figure 4.26, we have

$$k_1 = \frac{0.45 f_{cu} x - 0.45 f_{cu}.w/3}{x}$$

Substituting for w from equation 4.43 gives

$$k_1 = \left(0.45 - \frac{0.15\sqrt{f_{cu}}}{17.86}\right) f_{cu} \tag{4.44}*$$

(b) To determine the depth of the centroid $k_2 x$

k_2 is determined for a rectangular section by taking area moments of the stress block
about the neutral axis – see figures 4.25 and 4.26. Thus

$$(x - k_2 x) = \frac{\text{area pqrs} \times x/2 - \text{area rst} \times w/4}{\text{area of stress block}}$$

$$= \frac{(0.45 f_{cu} x)x/2 - (0.45 f_{cu} w/3)w/4}{k_1 x}$$

$$= \frac{0.45 f_{cu}(x^2/2 - w^2/12)}{k_1 x}$$

Substituting for w from equation 4.43

$$(x - k_2 x) = \frac{0.45 f_{cu} x^2}{k_1 x}\left[0.5 - \frac{f_{cu}}{3828}\right]$$

hence

$$k_2 = 1 - \frac{0.45 f_{cu}}{k_1}\left[0.5 - \frac{f_{cu}}{3828}\right] \tag{4.45}*$$

Figure 4.26
Properties of a parabola

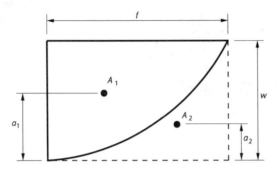

Areas: $A_1 = \dfrac{2\,wf}{3}$, $A_2 = \dfrac{wf}{3}$

Position of centroid : $a_1 = \dfrac{5\,w}{8}$, $a_2 = \dfrac{w}{4}$

Table 4.4 Values of k_1 and k_2 for different concrete grades

f_{cu} (N/mm²)	k_1 (N/mm²)	k_1/f_{cu}	k_2	$k_1/k_2 f_{cu}$
20	8.249	0.412	0.460	0.896
25	10.200	0.408	0.456	0.895
30	12.120	0.404	0.452	0.894
40	15.875	0.397	0.445	0.892
50	19.531	0.391	0.439	0.890
60	23.097	0.385	0.434	0.887
Typical values		0.4	0.45	0.89

Values of k_1 and k_2 for varying characteristic concrete strengths have been tabulated in table 4.4.

Once we know the properties of the stress block, the magnitude and position of the resultant compressive force in the concrete can be determined, and hence the moment of resistance of the section calculated using procedures similar to those for the rectangular stress block.

Using typical values from table 4.4, a comparison of the rectangular–parabolic and the rectangular stress blocks provides

(i)   Stress resultant, F_{cc}

rectangular–parabolic: $k_1 bx \approx 0.4 f_{cu} bx$

rectangular: $0.45 f_{cu} \times 0.9 bx \approx 0.4 f_{cu} bx$

(ii)   Lever arm, z

rectangular parabolic: $d - k_1 x \approx d - 0.45x$

rectangular: $d - \frac{1}{2} \times 0.9x = d - 0.45x$

So both stress blocks have almost the same moment of resistance, $F_{cc} \times z$, showing it is adequate to use the simpler rectangular stress block for design calculations.

4.10 ▍ The triangular stress block

The triangular stress block applies to elastic conditions during the serviceability limit state. In practice it is not generally used in design calculations except for liquid-retaining structures, or for the calculations of crack widths and deflections as described in chapter 6. With the triangular stress block, the cross-section can be considered as

(i)   cracked in the tension zone, or

(ii) uncracked with the concrete resisting a small amount of tension.

4.10.1 Cracked section

A cracked section is shown in figure 4.27 with a stress resultant F_{st} acting through the centroid of the steel and F_{cc} acting through the centroid of the triangular stress block.
  For equilibrium of the section

$$F_{cc} = F_{st}$$

or $0.5bxf_{cc} = A_s f_{st}$ (4.46)*

and the moment of resistance

$$M = F_{cc} \times z = F_{st} \times z$$

or $M = 0.5bxf_{cc}(d - x/3) = A_s f_{st}(d - x/3)$ (4.47)*

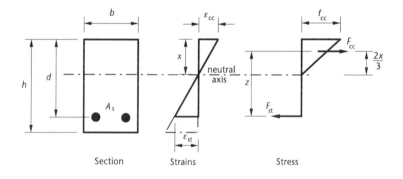

Figure 4.27
Triangular stress block –
cracked section

(i) Analysis of a specified section

The depth of the neutral axis, x, can be determined by converting the section into an 'equivalent' area of concrete as shown in figure 4.28, where $\alpha_e = E_s/E_c$, the modular ratio. Taking the area moments about the upper edge:

$$x = \frac{\sum(Ax)}{\sum A}$$

Therefore

$$x = \frac{bx \times x/2 + \alpha_e A_s d}{bx + \alpha_e A_s}$$

or

$$\tfrac{1}{2}bx^2 + \alpha_e A_s x - \alpha_e A_s d = 0$$

Figure 4.28
Equivalent transformed
section with the concrete
cracked

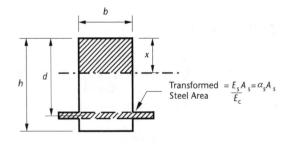

Solving this quadratic equation gives

$$x = \frac{-\alpha_e A_s \pm \sqrt{\left[(\alpha_e A_s)^2 + 2b\alpha_e A_s d\right]}}{b}$$

(4.48)*

Equation 4.48 may be solved using a chart such as the one shown in figure 4.29.
Equations 4.46 to 4.48 can be used to analyse a specified reinforced concrete section.

(ii) Design of steel area, A_s, with stresses f_{st} and f_{cc} specified

The depth of the neutral axis can also be expressed in terms of the strains and stresses of
the concrete and steel.

From the linear strain distribution of figure 4.27:

$$\frac{x}{d} = \frac{\varepsilon_{cc}}{\varepsilon_{cc} + \varepsilon_{st}} = \frac{f_{cc}/E_c}{f_{cc}/E_c + f_{st}/E_s}$$

Therefore

$$\frac{x}{d} = \frac{1}{1 + \frac{f_{st}}{\alpha_e f_{cc}}}$$

(4.49)*

Equations 4.47 and 4.49 may be used to design the area of tension steel required, at a
specified stress, in order to resist a given moment.

Figure 4.29
Neutral-axis depth for cracked
rectangular sections – elastic
behaviour

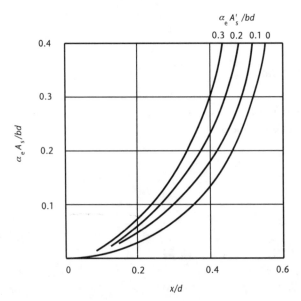

EXAMPLE 4.12

Analysis of a cracked section using a triangular stress block

For the section shown in figure 4.30, determine the concrete and steel stresses caused by a moment of 120 kN m, assuming a cracked section. Take $E_s/E_c = \alpha_e = 15$.

$$\alpha_e \frac{A_s}{bd} = \frac{15 \times 1470}{300 \times 460} = 0.16$$

Using the chart of figure 4.29 or equation 4.48 gives $x = 197$ mm.
From equation 4.47

$$M = \tfrac{1}{2}bx f_{cc}\left(d - \frac{x}{3}\right)$$

therefore

$$120 \times 10^6 = \tfrac{1}{2} \times 3000 \times 197 \times f_{cc}\left(460 - \frac{197}{3}\right)$$

therefore

$$f_{cc} = 10.3 \text{ N/mm}^2$$

From equation 4.46

$$f_{st}A_s = \tfrac{1}{2}bx f_{cc}$$

therefore

$$f_{st} = 300 \times 197 \times \frac{10.3}{2} \times \frac{1}{1470}$$

$$= 207 \text{ N/mm}^2$$

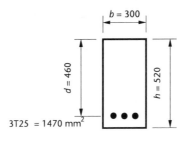

Figure 4.30
Analysis example with triangular stress block

$b = 300$

$d = 460$

$h = 520$

3T25 = 1470 mm²

4.10.2 Triangular stress block – uncracked section

The concrete may be considered to resist a small amount of tension. In this case a tensile stress resultant F_{ct} acts through the centroid of the triangular stress block in the tension zone as shown in figure 4.31.

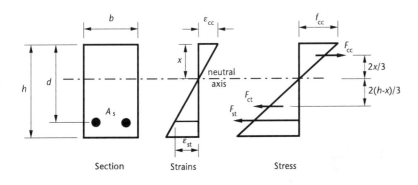

Figure 4.31
Triangular stress block – uncracked section

b

ε_{cc}

f_{cc}

x

neutral axis

F_{cc}

$2x/3$

$2(h-x)/3$

h

d

F_{ct}

F_{st}

A_s

ε_{st}

Section

Strains

Stress

For equilibrium of the section

$$F_{cc} = F_{ct} + F_{st}$$ (4.50)

where $F_{cc} = 0.5bx\,f_{cc}$

$F_{ct} = 0.5b(h-x)f_{ct}$

and $F_{st} = A_s \times f_{st}$

Taking moments about F_{cc}, the moment of resistance of the section is given by

$$M = F_{st} \times (d - x/3) + F_{ct} \times \left(\frac{2}{3}x + \frac{2}{3}(h-x)\right)$$ (4.51)*

The depth of the neutral axis, x, can be determined by taking area moments about the upper edge AA of the equivalent concrete section shown in figure 4.32, such that

$$x = \frac{\sum(Ax)}{\sum A}$$

$\alpha_e = \dfrac{E_s}{E_c}$ is termed the modular ratio

Therefore

$$x = \frac{bh \times h/2 + \alpha_e A_s \times d}{bh + \alpha_e A_s}$$

$$= \frac{h + 2\alpha_e rd}{2 + 2\alpha_e r}$$ (4.52)*

where $r = A_s/bh$

From the linear proportions of the strain diagram in figure 4.31:

$$\varepsilon_{cc} = \frac{x}{h-x} \times \varepsilon_{ct}$$

$$\varepsilon_{st} = \frac{d-x}{h-x} \times \varepsilon_{ct}$$ (4.53)

Therefore as stress $= E \times$ strain:

$$f_{ct} = E_c\varepsilon_{ct}$$

$$f_{cc} = \frac{x}{h-x} \times f_{ct}$$ (4.54)*

$$f_{st} = \frac{d-x}{h-x} \times \alpha_e f_{ct}$$

Hence if the maximum tensile strain or stress is specified, it is possible to calculate the corresponding concrete compressive and steel tensile stresses from equations 4.54.

Figure 4.32
Equivalent transformed section with the concrete uncracked

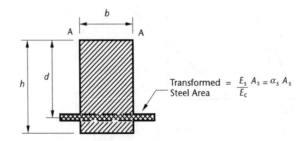

The equations derived can be used to analyse a given cross-section in order to determine the moment of resistance of the uncracked section, as for liquid-retaining structures. This is illustrated further by examples in chapter 11.

EXAMPLE 4.13

Analysis of an uncracked section

For the section shown in figure 4.30, calculate the serviceability moment of resistance with no cracking of the concrete, given $f_{ct} = 3$ N/mm^2, $E_c = 30$ kN/mm^2 and $E_s = 200$ kN/mm^2.

$$r = \frac{A_s}{bh} = \frac{1470}{300 \times 520} = 0.0094$$

$$\alpha_e = \frac{E_s}{E_c} = \frac{200}{30} = 6.67$$

$$x = \frac{h + 2\alpha_e rd}{2 + \alpha_e r}$$

$$= \frac{520 + 2 \times 6.67 \times 0.0094 \times 460}{2 + 2 \times 6.67 \times 0.0094} = 272 \text{ mm}$$

$$f_{st} = \left(\frac{d - x}{h - x}\right)\alpha_e f_{ct}$$

$$= \frac{(460 - 272)6.67 \times 3}{(520 - 272)} = 15.2 \text{ N/mm}^2$$

$$M = A_s f_{st}\left(d - \frac{x}{3}\right) + \frac{1}{2}b(h - x)f_{ct}\left(\frac{2}{3}x + \frac{2}{3}(h - x)\right)$$

$$= 1470 \times 15.2\left(460 - \frac{272}{3}\right)10^{-6} + \frac{1}{2} \times 300(520 - 272) \times 3$$

$$\times \left(\frac{2}{3} \times 272 + \frac{2}{3}(520 - 272)\right)10^{-6}$$

$$= 8.3 + 38.7 = 47 \text{ kN m}$$

CHAPTER 5

Shear, bond and torsion

CHAPTER INTRODUCTION

Reinforced concrete beams are designed to resist the shear forces resulting from the various combinations of ultimate loads once the primary longitudinal bending reinforcement has been determined. As discussed in this chapter, shear resistance is usually provided by the addition of shear links wherever the nominal shear capacity of the concrete itself proves inadequate.

All beams are designed to resist shear. Some beams are subject to torsional forces and can fail in shear as a result of forces arising from the application of torsional moments. This chapter also considers the theory of torsional behaviour and the determination of the reinforcing links and additional longitudinal steel necessary to provide adequate torsional resistance.

All types of reinforcement must be firmly anchored within the concrete section in order that the full tensile or compressive capacity of the reinforcement can be utilised. This is generally ensured by providing adequate anchorage of the reinforcing steel beyond the point where it is no longer needed. This is done by either calculation to ensure that the length of the embedded bar is sufficient to provide full bond between the concrete and the reinforcement, or by compliance with simple detailing rules.

This chapter therefore deals with the theory and derivation of the design equations for shear, bond and torsion. Some of the more practical factors governing the choice and arrangement of the reinforcement are dealt with in the chapters on member design, particularly chapter 7, which contains examples of the design and detailing of shear and torsion reinforcement in beams. Punching shear caused by concentrated loads on slabs is covered in section 8.2 of the chapter on slab design.

5.1 | Shear

Figure 5.1 represents the distribution of principal stresses across the span of a homogeneous concrete beam. The direction of the principal compressive stresses takes the form of an arch, while the tensile stresses have the curve of a catenary or suspended chain. Towards mid-span, where the shear is low and the bending stresses are dominant, the direction of the stresses tends to be parallel to the beam axis. Near the supports, where the shearing forces are greater, the principal stresses are inclined at a steeper angle, so that the tensile stresses are liable to cause diagonal cracking. If the diagonal tension exceeds the limited tensile strength of the concrete then shear reinforcement must be provided. This reinforcement is either in the form of (1) stirrups, or (2) inclined bars (used in conjunction with stirrups).

The shear in a reinforced concrete beam without shear reinforcement is carried by a combination of three main components. These are

(i)   concrete in the compression zone

(ii) dowelling action of tensile reinforcement

(iii) aggregate interlock across flexural cracks.

The actual behaviour is complex, and is difficult to analyse theoretically, but by applying the results from many experimental investigations, reasonable simplified procedures for analysis and design have been developed.

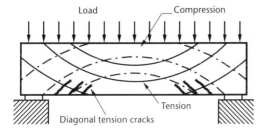

Figure 5.1
Principal stresses in a beam

5.1.1 Stirrups

In order to derive simplified equations the action of a reinforced concrete beam in shear is represented by an analogous truss in which the longitudinal reinforcement forms the bottom chord, the stirrups are the vertical members and the concrete acts as the diagonal and top chord compression members as indicated in figure 5.2. In the truss shown, the stirrups are spaced at a distance equal to the effective depth (d) of the beam so that the diagonal concrete compression members are at an angle of 45°, which more or less agrees with the experimental observations of the cracking of reinforced concrete beams close to their supports.

In the analogous truss, let

A_{sv} be the cross-sectional area of the two legs of the stirrup

f_{yv} be the characteristic strength of the stirrup reinforcement

V be the shear force due to the ultimate loads.

Figure 5.2
Stirrups and the analogous truss

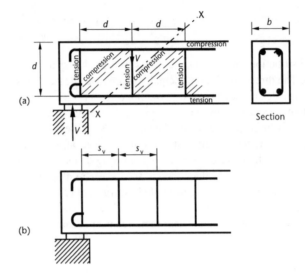

Using the method of sections it can be seen at section XX in the figure that at the ultimate limit state the force in the vertical stirrup member must equal the shear force V, that is

$$0.95f_{yv}A_{sv} = V$$

or

$$0.95f_{yv}A_{sv} = \nu\, bd \qquad (5.1)$$

where $\nu = V/bd$ is the average shear stress on the section.

When the stirrup spacing is less than the effective depth, a series of superimposed equivalent trusses may be considered, so that the force to be resisted by the stirrup is reduced proportionally. Thus if $s_v =$ the stirrup spacing, equation 5.1 becomes

$$0.95f_{yv}A_{sv} = \nu\, bd\left(\frac{s_v}{d}\right)$$

or

$$\frac{A_{sv}}{s_v} = \frac{\nu b}{0.95f_{yv}}$$

Since the concrete is also capable of resisting a limited amount of shear this equation is rewritten as

$$\frac{A_{sv}}{s_v} = \frac{b(\nu - \nu_c)}{0.95f_{yv}} \qquad (5.2)*$$

where ν_c is the ultimate shear stress that can be resisted by the concrete. Values of ν_c are given in table 5.1. It can be seen from the table that ν_c increases for shallow members and those with larger percentages of tensile reinforcement. The longitudinal tension bars contribute to the shear resistance by their dowelling action and they also help to prevent shear cracks from commencing at small tension cracks. To be effective, these tension bars should continue an effective depth, d, beyond the section, or at a support they should be adequately curtailed and anchored.

Close to supports, sections have an enhanced shear resistance owing in part to the induced compressive stresses from the concentrated reaction and the steeper angle of the failure plane, which would normally occur at angle of $30°$ to the horizontal for an

Table 5.1 Value of ultimate shear stress ν_c (N/mm²) for a concrete strength of $f_{cu} = 30$ N/mm²

$\dfrac{100A_s}{bd}$	Effective depth (mm)						
	150	175	200	225	250	300	≥ 400
≤ 0.15	0.46	0.44	0.43	0.41	0.40	0.38	0.36
0.25	0.54	0.52	0.50	0.49	0.48	0.46	0.42
0.50	0.68	0.66	0.64	0.62	0.59	0.57	0.53
0.75	0.76	0.75	0.72	0.70	0.69	0.64	0.61
1.00	0.86	0.83	0.80	0.78	0.75	0.72	0.67
1.50	0.98	0.95	0.91	0.88	0.86	0.83	0.76
2.00	1.08	1.04	1.01	0.97	0.95	0.91	0.85
≥ 3.00	1.23	1.19	1.15	1.11	1.08	1.04	0.97

For characteristic strengths other than 30 N/mm² the values in the table may be multiplied by $(f_{cu}/25)^{\frac{1}{3}} \div 1.06$. The value of f_{cu} should not be greater than 40 N/mm².

unreinforced section. Within a distance of $2d$ from a support or a concentrated load the design concrete shear stress ν_c may be increased to $\nu_c 2d/a_v$. The distance a_v is measured from the support or concentrated load to the section being designed. This enhancement is useful when designing beams with concentrated loads near to a support, or with corbels and pile caps as described in sections 7.6.1 and 10.7.

As a simplified approach for beams carrying mainly uniformly distributed loads, the critical section for design may be taken at a distance d from the face of the support using the value ν_c from table 5.1 in equation 5.2. The shear links required should then continue to the face of the support.

Large shearing forces are also liable to cause crushing of the concrete along the directions of the principal compressive stresses, and therefore at the face of a support the average shear stress should never exceed the lesser of $0.8\sqrt{f_{cu}}$ or 5 N/mm².

The areas and spacings of the stirrups can be calculated from equation 5.2. Rearrangement of the equation gives the shearing resistance for a given stirrup size and spacing thus:

$$\text{Shear resistance} = \nu\, bd = \left(\frac{A_{sv}}{s_v} \times 0.95 f_{yv} + b\nu_c\right) d \qquad (5.3)$$

Further information on the practical details and design examples are given in section 7.3 (Design for Shear).

5.1.2 Bent-up bars

To resist the shearing forces, bars may be bent up near the supports as shown in figure 5.3. The bent-up bars and the concrete in compression are considered to act as an analogous lattice girder and the shear resistance of the bars is determined by taking a section XX through the girder.

From the geometry of part (a) of the figure, the spacing of the bent-up bars is

$$s_b = (d - d')(\cot\alpha + \cot\beta)$$

and at the section XX the shear resistance of the single bar is

$$V = 0.95 f_{yv} A_{sb} \sin\alpha \qquad (5.4)$$

where A_{sb} is the cross-sectional area of the bent-up bar.

Figure 5.3
Bent-up bars

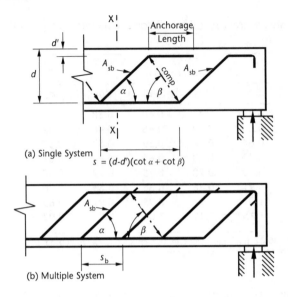

(a) Single System
$s = (d-d')(\cot \alpha + \cot \beta)$

(b) Multiple System

For a multiple system of bent-up bars, as in part (b) of the figure, the shear resistance is increased proportionately to the spacing s_b. Hence

$$V = 0.95 f_{yv} A_{sb} \sin \alpha \frac{(d - d')(\cot \alpha + \cot \beta)}{s_b} \tag{5.5}$$

The angles α and β should both be greater than, or equal to 45° and the code requires that the spacing s_b has a maximum value of 1.5d. With $\alpha = \beta = 45°$ and $s_b = (d - d')$, equation 5.5 becomes

$$V = 1.34 f_{yv} A_{sb} \tag{5.6}$$

and this arrangement is commonly referred to as a double system.

EXAMPLE 5.1

Shear resistance at a section

Determine the shear resistance of the beam shown in figure 5.4 which carries a uniformly distributed load. The characteristic strengths are: $f_{yv} = 250$ N/mm^2 for the stirrups, $f_{yv} = 460$ N/mm^2 for the bent-up bars and $f_{cu} = 30$ N/mm^2 for the concrete.

Figure 5.4
Beam with stirrups and
bent-up bars

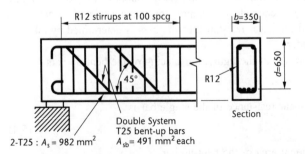

R12 stirrups at 100 spcg

$b=350$

$d=650$

R12

45°

Section

2-T25 : A_s = 982 mm^2

Double System
T25 bent-up bars
A_{sb}= 491 mm^2 each

$$\frac{100A_s}{bd} = \frac{100 \times 982}{350 \times 650} = 0.43$$

Thus, from table 5.1, $\nu_c = 0.5$ N/mm^2 by interpolation. Cross-sectional area of a size 12 bar $= 113$ mm^2.

Thus, for the stirrups, $A_{sv}/s_v = 2 \times 113/100 = 2.26$. The shear resistance of the stirrups plus the concrete is given by equation 5.3 as

$$V_s = \frac{A_{sv}}{s_v} \times 0.95 f_{yv} d + b\nu_c d$$
$$= 2.26 \times 0.95 \times 250 \times 650 + 350 \times 0.5 \times 650$$
$$= (349 + 114) \times 10^3 \text{ N } = 463 \times 10^3 \text{ N}$$

The bent-up bars are arranged in a double system. Hence the shear resistance of the bent-up bars is

$$V_b = 1.34 f_{yv} A_{sb}$$
$$= 1.34 \times 460 \times 491$$
$$= 302 \times 10^3 \text{ N}$$

Total shear resistance of the stirrups, concrete and bent-up bars is therefore

$$V = V_s + V_b = (463 + 303)10^3$$
$$= 765 \times 10^3 \text{ N}$$

It should be noted that the shear resistance of 349 kN provided by the stirrups is greater than the shear resistance of the bent-up bars, 303 kN, as required by BS 8110.

It should also be checked that at the face of the support V/bd does not exceed the lesser of $0.8 \sqrt{f_{cu}}$ or 5 N/mm^2.

5.2 | Anchorage bond

The reinforcing bar subject to direct tension shown in figure 5.5 must be firmly anchored if it is not to be pulled out of the concrete. Bars subjected to forces induced by flexure must similarly be anchored to develop their design stresses. The anchorage depends on the bond between the bar and the concrete, and the area of contact. Let

L = minimum anchorage length to prevent pull out

ϕ = bar size or nominal diameter

f_{bu} = ultimate anchorage bond stress

f_s = the direct tensile or compressive stress in the bar

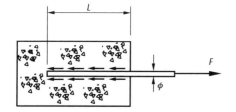

Figure 5.5
Anchorage bond

Table 5.2 Value of bond coefficient β

Bar type	β	
	Bars in tension	Bars in compression
Plain bars	0.28	0.35
Type 1: deformed bars	0.40	0.50
Type 2: deformed bars	0.50	0.63
Fabric	0.65	0.81

Considering the forces on the bar

tensile pull-out force = bar's cross-sectional area × direct stress

$$= \frac{\pi \phi^2}{4} f_s$$

anchorage force = contact area × anchorage bond stress

$$= (L\pi\phi) \times f_{bu}$$

therefore

$$(L\pi\phi) f_{bu} = \frac{\pi \phi^2}{4} \times f_s$$

hence

$$L = \frac{f_s}{4 f_{bu}} \phi$$

and when $f_s = 0.95 f_y$, the ultimate tensile or compressive stress, the anchorage length is

$$L = \frac{0.95 f_y}{4 f_{bu}} \phi \tag{5.7}*$$

The design ultimate anchorage bond stress, f_{bu}, is obtained from the equation

$$f_{bu} = \beta \sqrt{f_{cu}} \tag{5.8}$$

The coefficient β depends on the bar type and whether the bar is in tension or compression. Values of β are given in table 5.2.

Figure 5.6
Anchorage values for bends and hooks

(a) Anchorage value = 4r but not greater than 12ϕ

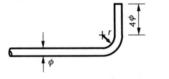

(b) Anchorage value = 8r but not greater than 24ϕ

For mild steel bars minimum $r = 2\phi$
For high yield bars minimum $r = 3\phi$ or
4ϕ for sizes 25mm and above

Equation 5.7 may be written as

anchorage length $L = K_A \phi$

Values of K_A corresponding to the anchorage of tension and compression bars for various grades of concrete and reinforcing bars have been tabulated in the Appendix.

Anchorage may also be provided by hooks or bends in the reinforcement; their anchorage values are indicated in figure 5.6. When a bent bar or hook is used, the bearing stress on the inside of the bend should be checked as described in section 7.3.2 and example 7.8.

EXAMPLE 5.2

Calculation of anchorage length

Determine the length of tension anchorage required for the 25 mm diameter plain mild steel reinforcing bars in the cantilever of figure 5.7. The characteristic material strengths are $f_{cu} = 30$ N/mm^2 and $f_y = 250$ N/mm^2.

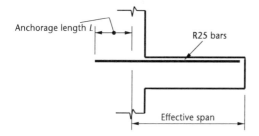

Figure 5.7
Anchorage for a cantilever beam

The ultimate anchorage bond stress, $f_{bu} = \beta\sqrt{f_{cu}} = 0.28\sqrt{30} = 1.5$ N/mm^2 (see table 5.2).

Anchorage length $L = \dfrac{0.95 f_y}{4 f_{bu}} \phi$

$$= \frac{0.95 \times 250}{4 \times 1.5} \times 25 = 39.6 \times 25$$

therefore $L = 990$ mm.

5.3 | Laps in reinforcement

Lapping of reinforcement is often necessary to transfer the forces from one bar to another. The rules for this are:

1. The laps should preferably be staggered and be away from sections with high stresses.
2. The minimum lap length should be not less than the greater of

$\qquad 15\phi$ or 300 mm for bars

$\qquad\qquad$ 250 mm for fabric

Figure 5.8
Lapping of reinforcing bars

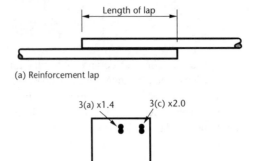

(a) Reinforcement lap

(b) Increased lap lengths

3. Tension laps should be equal to at least the design tension anchorage length, but in certain conditions this should be increased as shown in figure 5.8, according to the following rules.

   (a) At the top of a section and with minimum cover $< 2\phi$

      multiply by 1.4

   (b) At corners where minimum cover to either face $< 2\phi$ or clear spacing between adjacent laps <75 mm or 6ϕ

      multiply by 1.4

   (c) Where both (a) and (b) apply

      multiply by 2.0

   The concrete at the top of a member is generally less compacted and also tends to have a greater water content, resulting in a lower concrete strength. Also, at the corners of members there is less confinement of the reinforcement. For these reasons longer lap lengths are required at these locations.

4. Compression laps should be at least 25 per cent greater than the compression anchorage length.

5. Lap lengths for unequal size bars may be based on the smaller bar.

A table of minimum lap lengths is included in the Appendix.

5.4 | Analysis of section subject to torsional moments

Torsional moments produce shear stresses which result in principal tensile stresses inclined at approximately $45°$ to the longitudinal axis of the member. Diagonal cracking occurs when these tensile stresses exceed the tensile strength of the concrete. The cracks will form a spiral around the member as in figure 5.9.

Reinforcement in the form of closed links and longitudinal bars will carry the forces from increasing torsional moment after cracking, by a truss action with reinforcement as tension members and concrete as compressive struts between links. Failure will eventually occur by reinforcement yielding, coupled with crushing of the concrete along line AA as the cracks on the other faces open up.

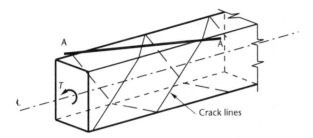

Figure 5.9
Torsional cracking

Crack lines

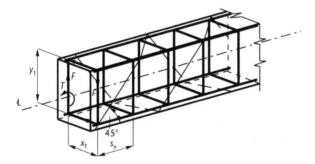

Figure 5.10
Torsional reinforcement

It is assumed that once the torsional shear stress on a section exceeds the value to cause cracking, tension reinforcement in the form of closed links must be provided to resist the full torsional moment (figure 5.10).

Tension force in link $F = \dfrac{A_{sv}}{2} \times 0.95 f_{yv}$

moment of force F about centre line $= F\dfrac{x_1}{2}$ for vertical leg

and $\hspace{4cm} = F\dfrac{y_1}{2}$ for horizontal leg

where A_{sv} = cross-sectional area of the two legs of a link. The total torsional moment provided by one closed link is, therefore, given by the sum of the moments due to each leg of the link about the centre line of the section, that is

$$T = F\dfrac{x_1}{2} \times 2 + F\dfrac{y_1}{2} \times 2$$

Where links are provided at a distance s_v apart, the torsional resistance of the system of links is obtained by multiplying the moments due to each leg in the above expressions by the number of legs crossing each crack. This number is given by y_1/s_v for vertical legs and x_1/s_v for horizontal legs if it is assumed that all cracks are approximately at 45°.

The total torsional resistance then becomes

$$T = \dfrac{A_{sv}}{2}(0.95 f_{yv})\dfrac{y_1}{s_v}\dfrac{x_1}{2} \times 2 + \dfrac{A_{sv}}{2}(0.95 f_{yv})\dfrac{x_1}{s_v}\dfrac{y_1}{2} \times 2$$

Hence $\quad T = \dfrac{A_{sv}}{s_v} x_1 y_1 (0.95 f_{yv}) \times 0.8$

The efficiency factor of 0.8 is included to allow for errors in assumptions made about the truss behaviour.

Hence closed links must be provided such that

$$\frac{A_{sv}}{s_v} \geq \frac{T}{0.8x_1y_1(0.95f_{yv})}$$

To ensure the proper action of these links, longitudinal bars evenly distributed round the inside perimeter of the links must be provided. This reinforcement which resists the longitudinal component of the diagonal tension forces should be such that the total quantity is equal to the same volume as the steel in the links, suitably adjusted to allow for differing strengths. This is given by

$$A_s \geq \frac{A_{sv}f_{yv}}{s_v f_y}(x_1 + y_1)$$

where f_y is the characteristic yield strength of longitudinal reinforcement.

The calculated amounts of torsional reinforcement must be provided in addition to the full bending and shear reinforcement requirements for the ultimate load combination corresponding to the torsional moment considered. Where longitudinal bending reinforcement is required, the additional torsional steel area may either be provided by increasing the size of bars provided, or by additional bars. A member which is designed for torsion plus bending or shear will require to be heavily reinforced.

The clear distance between longitudinal torsion bars must not exceed 300 mm, and a minimum of four bars must be used in each link. All torsion steel must also extend a distance at least equal to the largest member dimension past the point at which it is not required to resist torsion, to ensure that all possible cracks are adequately protected.

The torsional shear stress on a section can be determined by a variety of methods. BS 8110 recommends a plastic analysis such that, for a rectangular section

$$\nu_t = \frac{2T}{h_{min}^2(h_{max} - h_{min}/3)}$$

where h_{min} is the smaller dimension of the section, h_{max} is the larger dimension of the section, or

$$\nu_t = \frac{T}{2Ah_t} \quad \text{for a thin hollow section}$$

where h_t is the wall thickness and A is the area enclosed by the centre-line of the walls.

If the sum of wall thicknesses of a hollow section exceeds one-quarter of the overall dimension, this should be treated as solid.

A section having a T-, L- or I-shape should be divided into component rectangles to maximise the function $\sum(h_{min}^3 h_{max})$. The torsion shear stress on each rectangle should then be calculated by considering the rectangle as carrying a torsional moment of

$$T \times \left(\frac{h_{min}^3 h_{max}}{\sum(h_{min}^3 h_{max})}\right)$$

Torsion reinforcement will be required if the torsional shear stress ν_t exceeds the capacity of the concrete section. It has been found experimentally that this value is related approximately to the square root of the characteristic concrete cube strength, and the limiting value recommended by BS 8110 is

$$\nu_{tmin} = 0.067\sqrt{f_{cu}} \quad \text{but not more than 0.4 N/mm}^2$$

Torsion combined with bending and shear stress

Torsion is seldom present alone, and in most practical situations will be combined with shear and bending stresses.

(a) Shear stresses   Diagonal cracking starts on the side of a member where torsional and shear stresses are additive. The shear force has a negligible effect on ultimate torsional strength when $V < v_c bd$, the shear strength of the concrete section, but once diagonal cracks form, the torsional stiffness is reduced considerably.

To ensure that crushing of the concrete does not occur (figure 5.9) the sum of the shear and torsion stresses on a section should not be excessive so that

$$(v + v_t) \not> v_{tu}$$

where

$$v_{tu} = 0.8\sqrt{f_{cu}} \text{ or } 5 \text{ N mm}^2$$

Additionally in the case of small sections where y_1 is less than 550 mm

$$v_t \not> v_{tu}\frac{y_1}{550}$$

must be satisfied to prevent spalling of the corners.

The recommendations for reinforcement to resist a combination of shear and torsion are given in table 7.3.

(b) Bending stresses   When a bending moment is present, diagonal cracks will usually develop from the top of the flexural cracks. The flexural cracks themselves only slightly reduce the torsional stiffness, provided that the diagonal cracks do not develop. The final mode of failure will depend on the distribution and quantity of reinforcement present.

Figure 5.11 shows a typical ultimate moment and ultimate torsion interaction curve for a section. As can be seen, for moments up to approximately $0.8M_u$ the section can also resist the full ultimate torsion T_u. Hence no calculations for torsion are generally necessary for the ultimate limit state of reinforced concrete unless torsion has been included in the original analysis or is required for equilibrium.

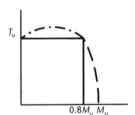

Figure 5.11
Combined bending and torsion

CHAPTER 6

Serviceability, durability and stability requirements

CHAPTER INTRODUCTION

The concept of serviceability limit states has been introduced in chapter 2, and for reinforced concrete structures these states are often satisfied by observing empircal rules which affect the detailing only. In some circumstances, however, it may be desired to estimate the behaviour of a member under working conditions, and mathematical methods of estimating deformations and cracking must be used. The design of water-retaining structures, and prestressed concrete, are both based primarily on the avoidance or limitation of cracking and these are considered separately in other chapters.

Where the foundations of a structure are in contact with the ground, the pressures developed will influence the amount of settlement that is likely to occur. To ensure that these movements are limited to acceptable values and are similar throughout a structure, the sizes of foundations necessary are based on the service loads for the structure.

Durability is necessary to ensure that a structure remains serviceable throughout its lifetime. This requirement will involve aspects of design, such as concrete mix selection and determination of cover to reinforcing bars, as well as selection of suitable materials for the exposure conditions which are expected. Good construction procedures including adequate curing are also essential if reinforced concrete is to be durable.

$\longrightarrow$

→

Simplified rules governing the selection of cover, member dimensions, and reinforcement detailing are given in sections 6.1 and 6.2, while more rigorous procedures for calculation of actual deflections and crack widths are described in sections 6.3 to 6.5. Durability and fire resistance are discussed in section 6.6.

The stability of a structure under accidental loadings, although an ultimate limit state analysis, will usually take the form of a check to ensure that empirical rules designed to give a reasonable minimum resistance against misuse or accident are satisfied. Like serviceability checks, this will often merely involve detailing of reinforcement and not affect the total quantity provided. Stability requirements are described in section 6.7.

6.1 | Detailing requirements

These are to ensure that a structure has satisfactory durability and serviceability performance under normal circumstances. BS 8110 recommends simple rules concerning the concrete mix and cover to reinforcement, minimum member dimensions, and limits to reinforcement quantities and spacings which must be taken into account at the member sizing and reinforcement detailing stages. Reinforcement detailing may also be affected by stability considerations as described in section 6.7, as well as rules concerning anchorage and lapping of bars which have been discussed in sections 5.2 and 5.3.

6.1.1 Minimum concrete mix and cover (exposure conditions)

These requirements are interrelated, and BS 8110 specifies minimum combinations of thickness of cover and mix characteristics for various exposure conditions. The mixes are expressed in terms of minimum cement content, maximum water/cement ratio and corresponding minimum strength grade. These basic requirements are given in table 6.1.

The nominal cover is that to all steel, and allows for a maximum fixing tolerance such that the actual cover does not fall below 5 mm less than that specified. Adjustments must be made to cement contents if different aggregate sizes are used, and details of these and other possible modifications are given in BS 5328.

6.1.2 Minimum member dimensions and cover (fire resistance)

BS 8110 also provides tabulated values of minimum dimensions and nominal covers for various types of concrete member which are necessary to permit the member to withstand fire for a specified period of time. These are summarised in tables 6.2 and 6.3.

6.1.3 Maximum spacing of reinforcement

The maximum clear spacings given in table 6.4 apply to bars in tension in beams when a maximum likely crack width of 0.3 mm is acceptable and the cover to reinforcement does not exceed 50 mm.

Table 6.1 Nominal cover and mix requirements for normal weight 20 mm maximum size aggregate concrete

Environment classification	Nominal cover to all reinforcement (mm)				
Mild: for example, protected against weather or aggressive conditions	25	20	20	20	20
Moderate: for example, sheltered from severe rain and freezing while wet; subject to condensation or continuously under water; in contact with non-aggressive soil	—	35	30	25	20
Severe: for example, exposed to severe rain; alternate wetting and drying; occasional freezing or severe condensation	—	—	40	30	25
Very Severe: for example exposed to sea water spray, de-icing salts, corrosive fumes or severe wet freezing	—	—	50*	40*	30
Most Severe: for example, frequently exposed to sea water spray, de-icing salts or in tidal zone to 1 m below low water	—	—	—	—	50
Abrasive: exposed to abrasive action (sea water and solids, flowing acid water, machinery or vehicles)	—	—	—	As above + cover loss allowance	
Maximum free water/cement ratio	0.65	0.60	0.55	0.50	0.45
Minimum cement content (kg/m^3)	275	300	325	350	400
Lowest concrete grade	C30	C35	C40	C45	C50

Note: *Entrained air required for wet freezing

Table 6.2 Nominal cover for fire resistance

Fire resistance (hours)	Nominal cover to all reinforcement (mm)						
	Beams		Floors		Ribs		Columns
	s.s.	cont.	s.s.	cont.	s.s.	cont.	
0.5	20	20	20	20	20	20	20
1.0	20	20	20	20	20	20	20
1.5	20	20	25	20	35	20	20
2.0	40	30	35	25	45*	35	25
3.0	60*	40	45*	35	55*	45*	25
4.0	70*	50*	55*	45*	65*	55*	25

*Additional measures necessary to reduce risk of spalling

Table 6.3 Minimum dimensions of RC members for fire resistance
(nominal cover requirements satisfied)

Fire resistance (hours)	Minimum dimensions (mm)					
	Beam width	Rib width	Floor thickness	Exposed column width	Wall thicknesses $\frac{A_s}{A_c}$	
					<0.4%	>1.0%
0.5	200	125	75	150	150	75
1.0	200	125	95	200	150	75
1.5	200	125	110	250	175	100
2.0	200	125	125	300		100
3.0	240	150	150	400		150
4.0	280	175	170	450		180

Table 6.4 Maximum clear spacings (mm) for tension bars in beams

f_y	% Moment redistribution						
	− 30	− 20	10	0	+ 10	+ 20	+ 30
250	210	240	270	300	300	300	300
460	115	130	145	160	180	195	210

It can be seen that the spacing is restricted according to the amount of moment redistribution applied. Any bar of diameter less than 0.45 times that of the largest bar in a section must be ignored when applying these spacings. Bars adjacent to corners of beams must not be more than one-half of the clear distance given in table 6.4 from the corner.

Rules for slabs permit greater spacings under specified conditions as follows:

    (a)   If $h \le 200$ mm with high yield steel ($f_y = 460$ N/mm^2)

or (b)   If $h \le 250$ mm with mild steel ($f_y = 250$ N/mm^2)

or (c)   If $100\, A_s/bd \le 0.3$ per cent

then the maximum clear spacing between bars should not exceed 750 mm or $3d$, whichever is smaller.

If none of these apply, the maximum spacing should be taken as that given in table 6.4, except that if the ratio $100A_s/bd$ is less than 1.0, the values from table 6.4 should be divided by that ratio. If the amount of moment redistribution is unknown when using table 6.4 for slabs, zero should be assumed for span moments and − 15 per cent for support moments.

6.1.4 Minimum spacing of reinforcement

To permit concrete flow around reinforcement during construction the minimum clear gap between bars, or groups of bars, should exceed ($h_{agg} + 5$ mm) horizontally and ($2h_{agg}/3$) vertically, where h_{agg} is the maximum size of the coarse aggregate. The gaps should be vertically in line and must also exceed the bar diameter, or in the case of 'bundled bars' the diameter of a bar of equivalent total cross-sectional area.

6.1.5   Minimum areas of reinforcement

For most purposes, thermal and shrinkage cracking may be controlled within acceptable limits by the use of minimum reinforcement quantities specified by BS 8110, although requirements of water-retaining structures will be more stringent (see chapter 11). The principal requirements are summarised in table 6.5, although other requirements include 0.15 per cent traverse reinforcement in the top surfaces of flanges in flanged beams and 0.25 per cent (high-yield) or 0.30 per cent (mild steel) anti-crack steel in plain walls (bar diameter $\not< 6$ mm or one-quarter diameter of vertical compressive bars). Requirements for shear links and column binders are given in sections 7.3 and 9.3 respectively. It should be noted that at least four bars with a diameter not less than 12 mm are required in rectangular columns and six in circular columns.

6.1.6   Maximum areas of reinforcement

These are determined largely from the practical need to achieve adequate compaction of the concrete around reinforcement. The limits specified by BS 8110 are as follows.

(a) For a slab or beam, longitudinal steel

$$\frac{100A_s}{bh} \quad \text{or} \quad \frac{100A_{sc}}{bh} \quad \text{not greater than 4 per cent each}$$

Where bars are lapped, the sum of the bar sizes in a layer must not be greater than 40 per cent of the section breadth.

Table 6.5   Minimum reinforcement areas

		Mild steel $(f_y = 250\ N/mm^2)$	High-yield steel $(f_y = 460\ N/mm^2)$
Tension reinforcement			
(1) Pure tension	$100A_s/A_c$	$=0.8\%$	0.45%
(2) Flexure			
(a) rectangular section	$100A_s/A_c$		
(both ways in solid slabs)		$=0.24\%$	0.13%
(b) flanged – web in tension			
$b_w/b \geq 0.4$	$100A_s/b_wh$		
$b_w/b < 0.4$	$100A_s/b_wh$	$=0.32\%$	0.18%
– flange in tension			
T-beam	$100A_s/b_wh$	$=0.48\%$	0.26%
L-beam	$100A_s/b_wh$	$=0.36\%$	0.20%
Compression reinforcement			
(1) General	$100A_{sc}/A_{cc}$		
(2) Rect. column or wall	$100A_{sc}/A_c$	$=0.4\%$	0.4%
(3) Flanged beam			
flange in compression	$100A_{sc}/bh_f$		
web in compression	$100A_{sc}/b_wh$	$=0.2\%$	0.2%
(4) Rectangular beam	$100A_{sc}/A_c$		

(b) For a column

$$\frac{100A_s}{bh}$$ not greater than 6 per cent if cast vertically

not greater than 8 per cent if cast horizontally

not greater than 10 per cent at laps in either case

6.1.7   Side face reinforcement in beams

Where beams exceed 750 mm in depth, longitudinal bars should be provided near side faces at a spacing $\not> 250$ mm over a distance $2h/3$ from the tension face. These bars, which may be used in calculating the moment of resistance, must have a diameter $> \sqrt{(s_b b/f_y)}$ where s_b is the bar spacing and b the breadth of the section (or 500 mm if less), as indicated in figure 6.1.

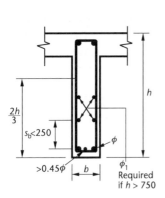
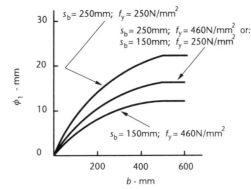

Figure 6.1
Side face reinforcement in beams

6.2 | Span–effective depth ratios

BS 8110 specifies a set of basic span–effective depth ratios to control deflections which are given in table 6.6 for rectangular sections and for flanged beams with spans less than 10 m. Where the web width of a flanged beam $b_w > 0.3b$, linear interpolation should be used between the values for a flanged beam and a rectangular section. Ratios for spans >10 m are factored as in example 6.1 when it is necessary to control the increase in deflections after the application of partitions or finishes (except for cantilevers). Table 6.6 can otherwise be used.

The basic ratios given in table 6.6 are modified in particular cases according to

(a)   The service stress in the tension steel and the value of M/bd^2, as shown in table 6.7, which is also presented in the form of a chart in figure 8.5.

(b)   The area of compression steel as in table 6.8.

The area of tension reinforcement provided is related to the value of M/bd^2, thus lower values of service stress and M/bd^2 will result in smaller depths of neutral axis x. This effect will reduce deflections due to creep, as there will be less of the section subject to compressive stresses. Compression reinforcement restrains creep deflections in a similar manner and also reduces the effects of shrinkage.

Table 6.6 Basic span–effective depth ratios

	Rectangular section	Flanged ($b_w \leq 0.3b$)
Cantilever	7	5.6
Simply supported	20	16.0
Continuous	26	20.8

Table 6.7 Tension reinforcement modification factors

Reinforcement service stress	(N/mm²)	M/bd^2								
		0.50	0.75	1.0	1.5	2.0	3.0	4.0	5.0	6.0
	100	2.0	2.0	2.0	1.86	1.63	1.36	1.19	1.08	1.01
($f_y = 250$)	167	2.0	2.0	1.91	1.63	1.44	1.21	1.08	0.99	0.92
	200	2.0	1.95	1.76	1.51	1.35	1.14	1.02	0.94	0.88
($f_y = 460$)	307	1.56	1.41	1.30	1.14	1.04	0.91	0.84	0.79	0.76

Table 6.8 Compression reinforcement modification factors

$\dfrac{100A'_{s,\,prov}}{bd}$	Factor
0.00	1.00
0.15	1.05
0.25	1.08
0.35	1.10
0.50	1.14
0.75	1.20
1.0	1.25
1.5	1.33
2.0	1.40
2.5	1.45
≥ 3.0	1.50

The service stress in the reinforcement f_s is usually a function of the yield stress f_y, as indicated in the table. The values shown are $2/3f_y$, but may be factored by the ratio $A_{s,req}/A_{s,prov}$ as well as an allowance for moment redistribution $1/\beta_b$ if known (see section 8.3). The reinforcement areas A_s and A'_s are measured at the centre of span, or at the support for a cantilever, and the value of A'_s used with table 6.8 should include all bars located in the compression zone.

The use of these factors is illustrated by example 6.1. It should be noted that the basic ratios given in table 6.6 are for uniformly distributed loadings, and procedures for making adjustments to the basic ratios to allow for other loading patterns are given in section 6.3.4 and illustrated by example 6.3.

EXAMPLE 6.1

Span–effective depth ratio check

A rectangular continuous beam spans 12 m with a mid-span ultimate moment of 400 kN m. If the breadth is 300 mm, check the acceptability of an effective depth of 600 mm when high yield reinforcement $f_y = 460$ N/mm^2 is used. Two 16 mm bars are located within the compressive zone.

Basic span–effective depth ratio (table 6.6) $= 26$.

To avoid damage to finishes, modified ratio $= 26 \times \dfrac{10}{12} = 21.7$

Tensile reinforcement modification factor:

$$\frac{M}{bd^2} = \frac{400 \times 10^6}{300 \times 600^2} = 3.7$$

thus, from table 6.7 for $f_y = 460$ N/mm^2, modification factor $= 0.86$.
Compression reinforcement modification factor:

$$\frac{100A'_s}{bd} = \frac{100 \times 402}{300 \times 600} = 0.22$$

thus from table 6.8, modification factor $= 1.07$.
Hence, modified span–effective depth ratio limit is equal to

$$21.7 \times 0.86 \times 1.07 = 20.0$$

Span–effective depth ratio provided $= \dfrac{12 \times 10^3}{600} = 20$

which is the same as the allowable upper limit, thus deflection requirements are likely to be satisfied.

6.3　Calculation of deflections

The general requirement is that neither the efficiency nor appearance of a structure is harmed by the deflections which will occur during its life. Deflections must thus be considered at various stages. The limitations necessary to satisfy the requirements will vary considerably according to the nature of the structure and its loadings, but for reinforced concrete the following may be regarded as reasonable guides.

1. The final deflection of horizontal members below the level of casting should not exceed span/250.

2. The deflection taking place after fixing of partitions or application of finishes should not exceed the lesser of 20 mm or span/500 to avoid damage.

Lateral deflections must not be ignored, especially on tall slender structures, and limitations in these cases must be judged by the engineer. It is important to realise that there are many factors which may have significant effects on deflections, and are difficult to allow for, thus any calculated value must be regarded as an estimate only. The most important of these effects are as follows

1. Support restraints must be estimated on the basis of simplified assumptions, which will have varying degrees of accuracy.

2. The precise loading and duration cannot be predicted and errors in dead loading may have significant effect.

3. A cracked member will behave differently to one that is uncracked – this may be a problem in lightly reinforced members where the working load may be close to the cracking limits.

4. The effect of floor screeds, finishes and partitions are very difficult to assess. Frequently these are neglected despite their 'stiffening' effect.

It may sometimes be possible to allow for these factors by averaging maximum and minimum estimated effects, and provided that this is done there are a number of calculation methods available which will give reasonable results. The method adopted by BS 8110 is very comprehensive, and is based on the calculation of curvatures of sections subjected to the appropriate moments, with allowance for creep and shrinkage effects where necessary. Deflections are then calculated from these curvatures.

The procedure for estimating deflections is rather lengthy and complex, involving the following stages which are illustrated in example 6.2.

1. Calculate the short-term curvature under total load; $C_{s.tot}$.

2. Calculate the short-term deflection from (1), and if the long-term deflection is required:

3. Calculate the short-term curvature due to permanent loads, $C_{s.perm}$.

4. Calculate the long-term curvature due to permanent loads, $C_{1.perm}$.

5. Calculate the curvature due to shrinkage, C_{shr}.

6. Estimate the total long-term curvature C_1 as

$$C_1 = C_{s.tot} - C_{s.perm} + C_{1.perm} + C_{shr}$$

7. Calculate the long-term deflection using the value from (6).

The curvatures in 1, 3 and 4 are taken as the larger value from considering the section as

(a) cracked

(b) uncracked.

As the concrete may have cracked under the total load, the additional short-term curvature $C_{s.temp}$ due to the temporary loading is obtained from

$$C_{s.temp} = C_{s.tot} - C_{s.perm}$$

in part (6) of the procedure and is not calculated directly.

If deflections are assumed to be small, elastic bending theory is based on the expression

$$M_x = EI \frac{d^2 y}{dx^2} \tag{6.1}$$

where M_x is the bending moment at a section distance x from the origin as shown in figure 6.2.

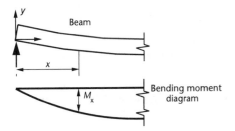

Figure 6.2
Curvature of a beam

For small deflections the term $\mathrm{d}^2y/\mathrm{d}x^2$ approximately equals the curvature, which is the reciprocal of the radius of curvature; thus

$$M_x = EI\frac{1}{r_x} \qquad (6.2)$$

where $1/r_x$ is the curvature at x.

Integrating expression 6.1 twice will yield values of displacements y of the member, thus if curvatures of a member are known, displacements can be deduced.

The analysis of deflections will use the partial factors of safety from tables 2.1 and 2.2 which effectively mean that materials properties are taken as the characteristic values, and that loadings are true working loads.

6.3.1   Calculation of curvatures – short term

The curvature of any section should be taken as the larger value obtained from considering the section to be either uncracked or cracked.

Uncracked section

The assumed elastic strain and stress distributions are shown in figure 6.3 and the upper limit to concrete stress at the level of tension reinforcement should be noted.

From equation 6.2

$$\text{curvature } \frac{1}{r} = \frac{M}{E_c I}$$

from the theory of bending

$$f_c = \frac{Mx}{I}$$

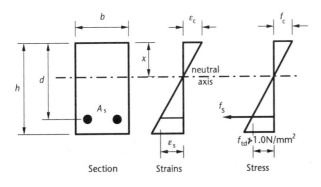

Figure 6.3
Uncracked section – strain and stress distribution

hence

$$\frac{1}{r} = \frac{f_c}{E_c}\frac{1}{x}$$

where M = applied moment at section considered

E_c = instantaneous static modulus of elasticity of concrete (for short-term deflections)

I = second moment of area of section

f_c = maximum compressive stress in the concrete

x = depth of neutral axis.

The above expression gives the instantaneous curvature of the uncracked section. If this is found to be greater than for a cracked section, the tensile stress f_{td} of the concrete at the level of tension reinforcement must be checked.

Cracked section

The recommended stress and strain distribution are given in figure 6.4 where the stiffening effect of the cracked concrete is taken into account by the tensile stress block shown.

$$\text{Curvature } \frac{1}{r} = \frac{f_c}{xE_c}$$

$$= \frac{f_s}{(d-x)E_s}$$

Hence it is necessary to analyse the section subjected to its applied moment M to obtain values of x and either f_c or f_s. This calculation is ideally suited to computer application, but if required to be solved manually must be performed on a trial and error basis.

Considering the section equilibrium by taking moments about the centre of compression

$$M = A_s f_s\left(d - \frac{x}{3}\right) + \frac{1}{3}bhf_{ct}(h - x) \tag{6.3}$$

and from the strain distribution

$$f_c = \frac{x}{(d-x)}\frac{E_c}{E_s}f_s \tag{6.4}$$

Figure 6.4
Cracked section – strain and stress distribution

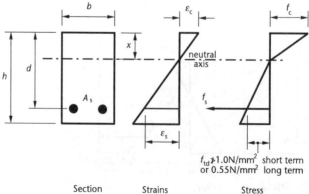

$f_{td} \not{\!\!} 1.0\,N/mm^2$ short term
or $0.55\,N/mm^2$ long term

Section　　　Strains　　　Stress

and equating tension and compression forces

$$\tfrac{1}{2}bxf_c = f_s A_s + \tfrac{1}{2}b(h-x)f_{ct} \tag{6.5}$$

where f_{ct} = maximum tensile stress allowed in the concrete = $\left(\dfrac{h-x}{d-x}\right)f_{td}$

$E_s = 200 \text{ kN/mm}^2$

E_c = instantaneous static modulus of elasticity of concrete (for short-term deflection)

The most convenient method of solving these expressions is to assume a neutral axis position; for this value of x evaluate f_s from equation 6.3 and using this value obtain two values of f_c from equations of 6.4 and 6.5. This should be repeated for two further trial values of x, and a plot of f_c from each expression is made against x. The intersection of the two curves will yield values of x and f_c with sufficient accuracy to permit the curvature to be calculated. This method is demonstrated in example 6.2.

6.3.2. Calculation of curvatures – long term

In calculating long-term curvatures it is necessary to take into account the effects of creep and shrinkage in addition to the reduced tensile resistance of the cracked concrete as indicated in figure 6.4.

Creep

This is allowed for by reducing the effective modulus of elasticity of the concrete to $E_{eff} = E_c/(1+\phi)$ where ϕ is a creep co-efficient, equal to the ratio of creep strain to initial elastic strain.

The value of ϕ, while being affected by aggregate properties, mix design and curing conditions, is governed also by the age at first loading, the duration of the load and the section dimensions. Figure 6.5 gives long-term values of ϕ, as suggested by BS 8110, and it may be assumed that about 40 percent, 60 per cent and 80 per cent of this will occur within 1 month, 6 months and 30 months under load respectively for constant relative humidity. The effective section thickness is taken as twice the cross-sectional area divided by the exposed perimeter, but is taken as 600 mm if drying is prevented by sealing or immersion of the concrete in water.

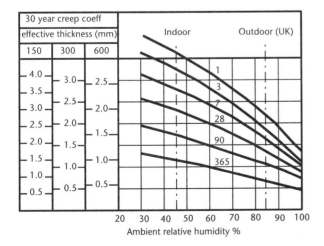

Figure 6.5
Creep coefficients

Shrinkage

Curvature due to shrinkage must be estimated and added to that due to applied moments, such that

$$\frac{1}{r_{cs}} = \frac{\varepsilon_{cs}\alpha_e S_s}{I}$$

where ε_{cs} is the free shrinkage strain, α_e is the modular ratio E_s/E_{eff}, and S_s is the first moment of area of the reinforcement about the centroid of the cracked or gross cross-section as appropriate.

Shrinkage is influenced by many features of the mix and construction procedures, but for most circumstances where aggregates do not have high shrinkage characteristics, values of ε_{cs} may be obtained from figure 6.6 which is based on BS 8110.

The total long-term curvature of a section subjected to a combination of permanent and non-permanent loads should be compounded as follows.

Total long-term curvature = long-term curvature due to permanent loads

+ short-term curvature due to non-permanent loads

+ shrinkage curvature

In this expression the short-term curvature due to the non-permanent loads is calculated as the curvature due to the total loads minus that due to the permanent loads. This is because the total loads may cause a cracked section and a larger curvature.

The net result is that the long-term curvature of a reinforced concrete member may be considerably greater than the instantaneous value, as illustrated in example 6.2.

6.3.3 Calculation of deflections from curvatures

Double integration of the expression 6.1

$$EI\frac{d^2y}{dx^2} = M_x$$

will yield an expression for the deflection. This may be illustrated by considering (figure 6.7) the case of a pin-ended beam subjected to constant moment M throughout its length, so that $M_x = M$.

$$EI\frac{d^2y}{dx^2} = M \qquad (6.6)$$

therefore

$$EI\frac{dy}{dx} = Mx + C$$

but if the slope is zero at mid-span where $x = L/2$, then

$$C = -\frac{ML}{2}$$

and

$$EI\frac{dy}{dx} = Mx - \frac{ML}{2}$$

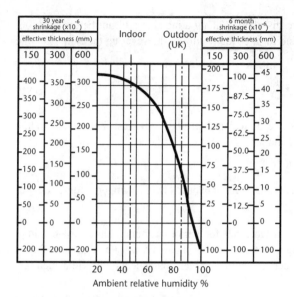

Figure 6.6
Drying shrinkage

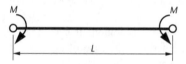

Figure 6.7
Pin-ended beam subjected to
a constant moment

Integrating again gives

$$EIy = \frac{Mx^2}{2} - \frac{MLx}{2} + D$$

but at left-hand end support when $x = 0$, $y = 0$. Hence

$$D = 0$$

thus

$$y = \frac{M}{EI}\left(\frac{x^2}{2} - \frac{Lx}{2}\right) \quad \text{at any section} \tag{6.7}$$

The maximum deflection in this case will occur at mid-span, where $x = L/2$, in which case

$$y_{max} = -\frac{M}{EI}\frac{L^2}{8} \tag{6.8}$$

but since at any uncracked section

$$\frac{M}{EI} = \frac{1}{r}$$

the maximum deflection may be expressed as

$$y_{max} = -\frac{1}{8}L^2\frac{1}{r}$$

In general, the bending-moment distribution along a member will not be constant, but will be a function of x. The basic form of the result will however be the same, and the deflection may be expressed as

$$\text{maximum deflection } a = KL^2 \frac{1}{r_b} \tag{6.9}*$$

where K = a constant, the value of which depends on the distribution of bending moments in the member

L = the effective span

$\dfrac{1}{r_b}$ = the mid-span curvature for beams, or the support curvature for cantilevers.

Typical values of K are given in table 6.9 for various common shapes of bending-moment diagrams. If the loading is complex, then a value of K must be estimated for the complete load since summing deflections of simpler components will yield incorrect results.

Although the derivation has been on the basis of an uncracked section, the final expression is in a form that will deal with a cracked section simply by the substitution of the appropriate curvature.

Since the expression involves the square of the span, it is important that the true effective span as defined in chapter 7 is used, particularly in the case of cantilevers. Deflections of cantilevers may also be increased by rotation of the supporting member, and this must be taken into account when the supporting structure is fairly flexible.

Table 6.9 Typical deflection coefficients

Loading	B.M. Diagram	K
M M		0.125
aL W	$WaL(1-a)$	$\dfrac{4a^2 - 8a + 1}{48a}$ (if a = 0.5 then K = 0.083)
w	$WL^2/8$	0.104
aL W	$-WaL$	End deflection = $\dfrac{a(3-a)}{6}$ (If a = 1 then K = 0.33)
aL w	$-Wa^2L^2/2$	End deflection = $\dfrac{a(4-a)}{12}$ (If a = 1 then K = 0.25)

EXAMPLE 6.2

Calculation of a deflection

Estimate short-term and long-term deflections for the simply supported beam shown in figure 6.8, which is assumed to be made of normal aggregates and props removed at twenty-eight days.

Concrete grade: C30
Instantaneous static modulus of elasticity $= 26$ kN/mm^2
Reinforcement: Hot-rolled high-yield f_y $= 460$ N/mm^2
Loading: Dead (permanent) $= 10$ kN/m u.d.l.
          Live (transitory) $= 5$ kN/m u.d.l.

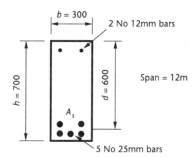

Figure 6.8
Deflection calculation
example

(a) Calculate design moments at mid-span

From table 2.1

$$\gamma_m = 1.0 \text{ for steel and concrete}$$

From table 2.2

$$\gamma_f = 1.0 \text{ for dead and live loads}$$

$$\text{Design moments} - \text{total} = \frac{15 \times 12^2}{8} = 270 \text{ kN m}$$

$$\text{Permanent} = \frac{10 \times 12^2}{8} = 180 \text{ kN m}$$

$$\text{Live} = \frac{5 \times 12^2}{8} = 90 \text{ kN m}$$

(b) Calculate short-term curvature – uncracked section – total load

$$\frac{1}{r_b} = \frac{M}{E_c I}$$

$$= \frac{270 \times 10^6}{26 \times 10^3 \times 300 \times 700^3/12} = 1.2 \times 10^{-6}/\text{mm}$$

(c) Calculate short-term curvature – cracked section – total load

Consider equations 6.3, 6.4 and 6.5. Assume $x = 100$ and substitute in equation 6.3, that is

$$M = A_s f_s \left(d - \frac{x}{3}\right) + \frac{1}{3} b h f_{ct}(h - x)$$

with

$$f_{ct} = \left(\frac{h-x}{d-x}\right) \times 1.0 = \frac{700-100}{600-100}$$
$$= 1.2 \text{ N/mm}^2$$

and

$$A_s = 2450 \text{ mm}^2$$

thus

$$f_s = \left(270 \times 10^6 - \frac{300 \times 700 \times 600 \times 1.2}{3}\right) \times \frac{1}{567 \times 2450}$$
$$= 158 \text{ N/mm}^2$$

From equation 6.4

$$f_c = f_{c1} = \frac{x}{(d-x)}\frac{E_c}{E_s}f_s$$
$$= \frac{100}{500} \times \frac{26}{200} \times 158$$
$$= 4.1 \text{ N/mm}^2$$

But f_c is also given by equation 6.5 as

$$f_c = f_{c2} = \frac{f_s A_s + \frac{1}{2}b(h-x)f_{ct}}{\frac{1}{2}bx}$$
$$= \frac{158 \times 2450 + 0.5 \times 300 \times 600 \times 1.2}{150 \times 100}$$
$$= 33.0 \text{ N/mm}^2$$

These values of f_c do not agree, therefore further depths of the neutral axis are tried giving the following results.

x	f_{c1}	f_{c2}
100	4.1	33.0
210	12.2	16.5
300	24.7	12.1

These values are plotted in figure 6.9a from which it is seen that $f_{c1} = f_{c2} = f_c$ $= 15 \text{ N/mm}^2$ approximately, at $x = 230$ mm. Hence

$$\frac{1}{r_b} = \frac{f_c}{xE_c}$$
$$= \frac{15}{230 \times 26 \times 10^3}$$
$$= 2.5 \times 10^{-6} \text{ /mm}$$

Since this curvature is greater than the uncracked value, it is not necessary to check the concrete tensile stress for that case, the cracked value of 2.5×10^{-6}/mm being used to determine the deflection.

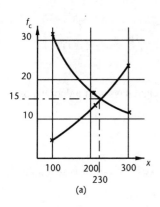

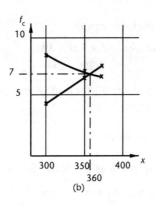

Figure 6.9
Calculation of neutral-axis depth

(a) (b)

(d) Calculate short-term deflection – total load

$$a = KL^2 \frac{1}{r_b}$$

where

$$\frac{1}{r_b} = 2.5 \times 10^{-6} \text{ /mm}$$

$$L = 12\text{m}$$

$$K = 0.104 \text{ for u.d.l. from table 6.9}$$

Hence mid-span short-term deflection

$$a = 0.104 \times 12^2 \times 10^6 \times 2.5 \times 10^{-6}$$
$$= 37 \text{ mm approximately}$$

(e) Calculate short-term curvature due to permanent loads

Permanent moment $= 180$ kN m

Thus, if section uncracked

$$\frac{1}{r_b} = \frac{180 \times 10^6}{26 \times 10^3 \times 300 \times 700^3/12} = 0.8 \times 10^{-6} \text{ /mm}$$

and if cracked, an approach similar to that used in (c) above gives $f_c = 9.7$ N/mm^2 at $x = 245$ mm. Hence

$$\frac{1}{r_b} = \frac{9.7}{245 \times 26 \times 10^3} = 1.5 \times 10^{-6} \text{ /mm}$$

(f) Calculate long-term curvature due to permanent loads

In this case, analysis is based on a reduced concrete tensile stress of 0.55 N/mm^2 at the level of reinforcement, thus

$$f_{ct} = \left(\frac{h-x}{d-x}\right) \times 0.55$$

and a reduced

$$E_{eff} = \frac{26}{1+\phi}$$

The effective section thickness equals

$$\frac{\text{twice cross-sectional area}}{\text{perimeter}} = \frac{2 \times 700 \times 300}{2(700 + 300)} = 210 \text{ mm}$$

thus the value of ϕ from figure 6.5 for loading at twenty-eight days with indoor exposure is approximately 2.75. Hence

$$E_{\text{eff}} = \frac{26}{1 + 2.75} = 6.93 \text{ kN/mm}^2$$

Thus, using the same approach as previously for the cracked analysis, it is found that

when $x = 300$ mm then $f_{c1} = 4.5$ N/mm^2, $f_{c2} = 8.1$ N/mm^2

$x = 350$ mm $\quad f_{c1} = 6.6$ N/mm^2, $f_{c2} = 7.1$ N/mm^2

$x = 370$ mm $\quad f_{c1} = 7.7$ N/mm^2, $f_{c2} = 6.8$ N/mm^2

Thus as can be seen from figure 6.9b, the solution lies at $x = 360$ mm when $f_c = 7.0$ N/mm^2. Therefore

$$\frac{1}{r_b} = \frac{7.0}{360 \times 6.93 \times 10^3} = 2.8 \times 10^{-6} \text{ /mm}$$

In this instance it is not necessary to evaluate the uncracked case since in part (e) it has been established that the permanent loads yield the higher instantaneous curvature when the section is cracked.

(g) Calculate shrinkage curvature

$$\frac{1}{r_{cs}} = \frac{\varepsilon_{cs} \alpha_e S_s}{I}$$

where $\quad \alpha_e = \dfrac{E_s}{E_{\text{eff}}} = \dfrac{200}{6.93} = 28.9$

And for a transformed cracked section (see figure 4.28)

$$I = \frac{bx^3}{12} + bx\left(\frac{x}{2}\right)^2 + \alpha_e A_s (d - x)^2$$

therefore with $x = 360$ mm from part (f)

$$I = (1.17 + 3.50 + 4.08) \times 10^9$$
$$= 8.75 \times 10^9 \text{ mm}^4$$

and $\quad S_s = A_s(d - x)$

$$= 2450 \times 240$$
$$= 588 \times 10^3 \text{ mm}^3$$

From figure 6.6 for indoor exposure, the long-term value

$$\varepsilon_{cs} \approx 390 \times 10^{-6}$$

Thus

$$\frac{1}{r_{cs}} = \frac{390 \times 10^{-6} \times 28.9 \times 588 \times 10^3}{8.75 \times 10^9}$$
$$\approx 0.8 \times 10^{-6} \text{ /mm}$$

(h) Calculate total long-term deflection

Short-term curvature, non-permanent loads = Short-term curvature, total loads

$$- \text{ Short-term curvature, permanent loads}$$

$$= 2.5 \times 10^{-6} - 1.5 \times 10^{-6}$$

$$= 1.0 \times 10^{-6}/\text{mm}$$

Long-term curvature, permanent loads = $2.8 \times 10^{-6}/\text{mm}$

Shrinkage curvature = $0.8 \times 10^{-6}/\text{mm}$

Therefore

$$\text{Total long-term curvature} \quad \frac{1}{r_b} = 4.6 \times 10^{-6}/\text{mm}$$

hence

$$\text{estimated total long-term deflection} = \frac{KL^2}{r_b}$$

$$= 0.104 \times 12^2 \times 10^6 \times 4.6 \times 10^{-6}$$

$$= 69 \text{ mm}$$

6.3.4 Basis of span–effective depth ratios

The calculation of deflections has been shown to be a tedious operation, however for general use rules based on limiting the span–effective depth ratio of a member are adequate to ensure that the deflections are not excessive. The application of this method is described in section 6.2.

The relationship between the deflection and the span–effective depth ratio of a member can be derived from equation 6.9; thus

$$\text{deflection } a = K \frac{1}{r_b} L^2$$

and for small deflections it can be seen from figure 6.10 that for unit length, s

$$\phi = \frac{1}{r_b} = \frac{\varepsilon_{cm} + \varepsilon_{rm}}{d}$$

where ε_{cm} = maximum compressive strain in the concrete

ε_{rm} = tensile strain in the reinforcement

K = a factor which depends on the pattern of loading.

Therefore

$$\frac{\text{span}}{\text{effective depth}} = \frac{L}{d} = \frac{a}{L} \frac{1}{K} \frac{1}{(\varepsilon_{cm} + \varepsilon_{rm})}$$

The strains in the concrete and tensile reinforcement depend on the areas of reinforcement provided and their stresses. Thus for a particular member section and a pattern of loading, it is possible to determine a span–effective depth ratio to satisfy a particular a/L or deflection/span limitation.

Figure 6.10
Curvature and strain
distribution

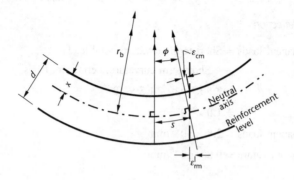

The modified span–effective depth ratios obtained in section 6.2 are based on limiting the total deflection to span/250 for a uniformly distributed loading. For spans of less than 10 m this should also ensure that the limits of span/500 or 20 mm after application of finishes are met but, for spans over 10 m where avoidance of damage to finishes may be important, the basic ratios of table 6.6 should be factored by 10/span.

For loading patterns other than uniformly distributed a revised ratio is given by changing the basic ratio in proportion to the relative values of K, as shown in example 6.3. Similarly, for limiting the deflection to span/β

$$\text{revised ratio} = \text{basic ratio} \times \frac{250}{\beta}$$

In cases where the basic ratio has been modified for spans greater than 10 m, maximum deflections are unlikely to exceed 20 mm after construction of partitions and finishes.

When another deflection limit is required, the ratios given should be multiplied by $\alpha/20$ where α is the proposed maximum deflection.

EXAMPLE 6.3

Adjustment of basic span to effective depth ratio

Determine the appropriate basic ratio for a cantilever beam supporting a uniform load and a concentrated point load at its tip as shown in figure 6.11.

Figure 6.11
Point load on cantilever
example

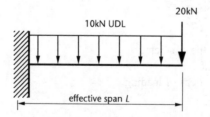

Basic ratio from table 6.6 = 7 for a u.d.l.

From table 6.9:

   K for cantilever with u.d.l. over full length = 0.25

   K for cantilever with point load at tip = 0.33

Thus, for the point load only, adjusted basic ratio equals

$$7 \times \frac{0.25}{0.33} = 5.3$$

An adjusted basic ratio to account for both loads can be obtained by factoring the moment due to the point load by the ratio of the K values as follows

$$M_{udl} = 10 \times L/2 = 5L$$
$$M_{point} = 20L$$

$$\text{Adjusted basic ratio} = \text{Basic ratio} \left(\frac{M_{udl} + M_{point} \times K_{udl}/K_{point}}{M_{udl} + M_{point}} \right)$$

$$= 7 \left(\frac{5 + 20 \times 0.25/0.33}{5 + 20} \right)$$

$$= 5.6$$

6.4 | Flexural cracking

Members subjected to bending generally exhibit a series of distributed flexural cracks, even at working load. These cracks are unobtrusive and harmless unless the widths become excessive, in which case appearance and durability suffer as the reinforcement is exposed to corrosion.

The actual width of cracks in a reinforced concrete structure will vary between wide limits, and cannot be precisely estimated, thus the limiting requirement to be satisfied is that the probability of the maximum width exceeding a satisfactory value is small. The maximum acceptable value suggested by BS 8110 is 0.3 mm at any position on the surface of the concrete in normal environments, although some other codes of practice recommend lower values for important members. Requirements for specialised cases such as water-retaining structures may be more stringent and these are given in chapter 11.

If calculations to estimate maximum crack widths are performed, they are based on 'working' loads with $\gamma_f = 1.0$ and material partial factors of safety of $\gamma_m = 1.0$ for steel and concrete. BS 8110 recommends that the effective modulus of elasticity of the concrete should be taken as half the instantaneous value as given in table 1.1, to allow for creep effects.

Prestressed concrete members are designed primarily on the basis of satisfying limitations which are different from those for reinforced concrete.

6.4.1 Mechanism of flexural cracking

This can be illustrated by considering the behaviour of a member subjected to a uniform moment.

A length of beam as shown in figure 6.12 will initially behave elastically throughout as the applied uniform moment M is increased. When the limiting tensile strain for the concrete is reached a crack will form, and the adjacent tensile zone will no longer be acted upon by direct tension forces. The curvature of the beam, however, causes further direct tension stresses to develop at some distance from the original crack to maintain

Figure 6.12
Bending of a length of beam

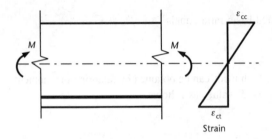

internal equilibrium. This in turn causes further cracks to form, and the process continues until the distance between cracks does not permit sufficient tensile stresses to develop to cause further cracking. These initial cracks are called 'primary cracks', and the average spacing in a region of constant moment has been shown experimentally to be approximately $1.67(h\text{-}x)$ and will be largely independent of reinforcement detailing.

As the applied moment is increased beyond this point, the development of cracks is governed to a large extent by the reinforcement. Tensile stresses in the concrete surrounding reinforcing bars are caused by bond as the strain in the reinforcement increases. These stresses increase with distance from the primary cracks and may eventually cause further cracks to form approximately midway between the primary cracks. This action may continue with increasing moment until the bond between concrete and steel is incapable of developing sufficient tension in the concrete to cause further cracking in the length between existing cracks. Since the development of the tensile stresses is caused directly by the presence of the reinforcing bars, the spacing of cracks will be influenced by the spacings of the reinforcement. If bars are sufficiently close for their 'zones of influence' to overlap then secondary cracks will join up across the member, while otherwise they will form only adjacent to the individual bars. It has been confirmed experimentally that the average spacing of cracks along a line parallel to, and at a distance a_{cr} from, a main reinforcing bar depends on the efficiency of bond, and may be taken as $1.67a_{cr}$ for deformed bars, or $2.0a_{cr}$ for plain round bars.

6.4.2 Estimation of crack widths

If the behaviour of the member in figure 6.13 is examined, it can be seen that the overall extension per unit length at depth y below the neutral axis is given by

$$\varepsilon_1 = \frac{y}{(d-x)}\varepsilon_s$$

where ε_s is the average strain in the main reinforcement over the length considered, and may be assumed to be equal to f_s/E_s where f_s is the steel stress at the cracked sections.

Figure 6.13
Bending strains

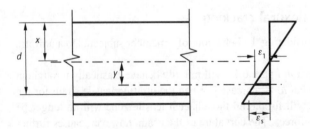

Hence assuming any tensile strain of concrete between cracks as small, since full bond is never developed

$$\varepsilon_1 = \frac{y}{(d-x)}\frac{f_s}{E_s}$$

$$= \sum w$$

where $\sum w$ = sum of crack widths per unit length at level y.

The actual width of individual cracks will depend on the number of cracks in this unit length, the average number being given by length/average spacing where average spacing, $s_{av} = 1.67a_{cr}$ for deformed bars; also $s_{av} \leq 1.67(h-x)$, the spacing of primary cracks. Thus

$$\text{average crack width } w_{av} = \frac{\sum w}{\text{av. number of cracks}}$$

$$= \varepsilon_1 s_{av}$$

The designer is concerned however with the maximum crack width, and it has been shown experimentally that if this is taken as twice the average value, the chance of this being exceeded is about 1 in 100, hence for deformed reinforcing bars, the maximum likely crack width w_{max} at any level defined by y in a member will thus be given by

$$w_{max} = \varepsilon_1 2s_{av}$$

$$= \varepsilon_1 3.33a_{cr}$$

provided that the limit of $w_{max} = \varepsilon_1 3.33(h-x)$ based on the primary cracks is not exceeded.

The positions on a member where the surface crack widths will be greatest depend on the relative values of strain (ε_1) and the distance to a point of zero strain (a_{cr}). Despite the effects of bond slip adjacent to cracks, and the steel strain across cracks, the crack width at the surface of a reinforcing bar is very small and may be assumed to be zero. This may therefore be taken as a point of zero strain for the purposes of measuring a_{cr}. The neutral axis of the beam will also have zero strain, and hence a_{cr} may also relate to this if appropriate.

Critical positions for maximum crack width will on a beam generally occur at the positions indicated in figure 6.14. These occur when the distance to points of zero strain, that is, reinforcement surface or neutral axis, are as large as possible. Positions 1 and 2 will have a maximum value of strain, while at position 3, although the strain is smaller, a_{cr} is considerably larger. The expression for w_{max} at any point may thus be expressed in the general form

maximum surface crack width at a point
  = constant × distance to the surface of the nearest reinforcing bar or neutral
    axis × apparent tensile strain in the concrete at the level considered

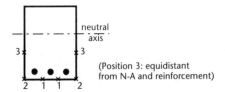

Figure 6.14
Critical crack positions

(Position 3: equidistant
from N-A and reinforcement)

The expression for maximum surface crack width given in BS 8110 is basically of this form, with the constant based on a probability of the calculated value being exceeded of somewhat greater than 1 in 100. The expression is given as

$$w_{max} = \frac{3a_{cr}\varepsilon_m}{1 + 2\left(\dfrac{a_{cr} - c_{min}}{h - x}\right)} \tag{6.10}*$$

where c_{min} is the minimum cover to the main reinforcement and ε_m is the average concrete strain and is based on ε_1 but allows for the stiffening effect of the cracked concrete in the tension zone ε_2. The value of ε_2 is given by an empirical expression

$$\varepsilon_2 = \frac{b_t(h - x)(a' - x)}{3E_s A_s(d - x)} \tag{6.11}*$$

and

$$\varepsilon_m = \varepsilon_1 - \varepsilon_2$$

where b_t is the width of section at centroid of tensile steel and a' the distance from compressive face to the point at which crack is calculated. This expression allows for variations of steel stress between cracks, and results in correspondingly reduced maximum crack width estimates. A negative value of ε_m indicates that the section is uncracked.

6.4.3 Analysis of section to determine crack width

Whatever formula is used, it is necessary to consider the apparent concrete strain at the appropriate position. This must be done by elastic analysis of the cracked section using half the instantaneous value of E_c to allow for creep effects as discussed in section 6.4.

The methods discussed in section 4.10.1 should be used to find the neutral axis position x and hence f_s the stress in the tensile reinforcement. Then

$$\varepsilon_1 = \frac{y}{(d - x)}\frac{f_s}{E_s}$$

hence ε_m may be obtained.

Figure 6.15
Crack width calculation example

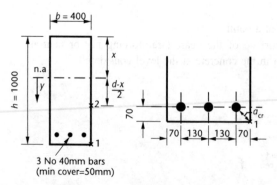

3 No 40mm bars
(min cover=50mm)

(a) Cross-section   (b) Detail of reinforcement position

EXAMPLE 6.4

Calculation of flexural crack widths

Estimate the maximum flexural crack widths for the beam section shown in figure 6.15a when subjected to a moment of 650 kN m.

Characteristic strengths of concrete $f_{cu} = 30$ N/mm^2
of steel f_y = 460 N/mm^2
Modulus of elasticity of steel E_s = 200 kN/mm^2

Calculate neutral axis position and steel stress.

From table 1.1, instantaneous modulus of elasticity $= 26$ kN/mm^2, therefore

$$E_c = \frac{26}{2} = 13 \text{ kN/mm}^2$$

Then from section 4.10.1 the neutral axis position is given by

$$\tfrac{1}{2}bx^2 + \frac{E_s}{E_c}A_s x - \frac{E_s}{E_c}A_s d = 0$$

In this case $A_s =$ area of three no. 40 mm bars $= 3770$ mm^2

$$d = 1000 - (20 + 50) = 930 \text{ mm}$$

thus

$$\tfrac{1}{2} \times 400 \times x^2 + \frac{200}{13} \times 3770 \times x - \frac{200}{13} \times 3770 \times 930 = 0$$

therefore

$$x = -\frac{290 \pm \sqrt{(290^2 + 4 \times 269\,700)}}{2}$$

$$= 394 \text{ mm}$$

(Alternatively charts may be used, as in figure 4.29 in which case

$$\alpha_e \frac{A_s}{bd} = \frac{200}{13}\frac{3770}{400 \times 930} = 0.156$$

taking $A_s' = 0$, $x/d = 0.42$ from charts and hence $x = 391$ mm.)
The stress in the reinforcement

$$f_s = \frac{M}{(d - x/3)A_s} = \frac{650 \times 10^6}{798 \times 3770}$$

$$= 216 \text{ N/mm}^2$$

thus

$$\varepsilon_1 = \frac{y}{536} \times \frac{216}{200 \times 10^3}$$

$$= y \times 2.04 \times 10^{-6}$$

and using equation 6.11

$$\varepsilon_m = \varepsilon_1 - \frac{b_t(h - x)(a' - x)}{3E_s A_s(d - x)}$$

The maximum crack width will occur either at position 1 or 2 indicated on figure 6.15; thus

Position	y	a_{cr}	a'	$\varepsilon_1 \times 10^{-3}$
1	606	$\sqrt{(70^2 + 70^2)} - 20 = 79$	1000	1.24
2	$\dfrac{536}{2} = 268$	$\sqrt{(70^2 + 268^2)} - 20 = 257$	662	0.55

Minimum cover, $c_{min} = 50$ mm; thus at position 1

$$\varepsilon_m = \left(1.24 - \frac{400(1000 - 394)(1000 - 394)}{3 \times 200 \times 3770(930 - 394)}\right) \times 10^{-3}$$

$$= 1.12 \times 10^{-3}$$

and equation 6.10 gives

$$w_{max} = \frac{3a_{cr}\varepsilon_m}{1 + 2\left(\dfrac{a_{cr} - c_{min}}{h - x}\right)}$$

$$= \frac{3 \times 79 \times 1.12 \times 10^{-3}}{1 + 2\left(\dfrac{79 - 50}{1000 - 394}\right)} = 0.24 \text{ mm}$$

and similarly at position 2

$$\varepsilon_m = \left[0.55 - \frac{400(1000 - 394)(662 - 394)}{3 \times 200 \times 3770(930 - 394)}\right] \times 10^{-3}$$

$$= 0.50 \times 10^{-3}$$

thus

$$w_{max} = \frac{3 \times 257 \times 0.50 \times 10^{-3}}{1 + 2\left(\dfrac{257 - 50}{606}\right)} = 0.23 \text{ mm}$$

The maximum crack width of 0.24 mm is therefore likely to occur at the bottom corners of the member, and the cracks are likely to be at an average spacing of $1.67a_{cr} = 1.67 \times 79 \approx 130$ mm at these positions. Cracks of similar width may occur on side faces at a spacing of approximately $1.67 \times 257 \approx 430$ mm.

6.4.4 Control of crack widths

It is apparent from the expressions derived above that there are two fundamental ways in which surface crack widths may be reduced.

1. Reduce the stress in the reinforcement (f_s).
2. Reduce the distance to the nearest bar (a_{cr}).

The use of steel at reduced stresses is generally uneconomical, and although this approach is used in the design of water-retaining structures where cracking must often be avoided altogether, it is generally easier to limit the bar cover and spacing and hence a_{cr}. Durability requirements limit the minimum value of cover; however bars should be as close to the concrete surface as is allowed. Reinforcement spacing may be reduced by keeping bar diameters as small as is reasonably possible.

Since the side face of a beam is often a critical crack-width position it is good practice to consider the provision of longitudinal steel in the side faces of beams of moderate depth. Recommendations regarding this, and spacing of main reinforcement, are given by BS 8110 and are discussed in section 6.1. If these recommendations are followed, it is not necessary to calculate crack widths except in unusual circumstances. Reinforcement detailing however, has been shown to have a large effect on flexural cracking, and must in practice be a compromise between the requirements of cracking, durability and constructional ease and costs.

6.5 | Thermal and shrinkage cracking

Thermal and shrinkage effects, and the stresses developed prior to cracking of the concrete were discussed in chapter 1. After cracking, the equilibrium of concrete adjacent to a crack is illustrated in figure 6.16.

Equating tension and compression forces

$$A_s f_{st} = A_c f_{ct} - A_s f_{sc}$$

or

$$f_{ct} = \frac{A_s}{A_c}(f_{st} + f_{sc})$$

If the condition is considered when steel and concrete simultaneously reach their limiting values in tension, that is, $f_{st} = f_y$ and $f_{ct} = f_t =$ tensile strength of concrete at appropriate age – usually taken as three days, then

$$r = \frac{A_s}{A_c} = \frac{f_t}{f_y + f_{sc}}$$

where r is the steel ratio.

The value of f_{sc} can be calculated but is generally very small and may be take as zero without introducing undue inaccuracy; hence the critical value of steel ratio

$$r_{crit} = \frac{A_s}{A_c} = \frac{f_t}{f_y} \quad \text{approximately} \tag{6.12}*$$

If the steel ratio is less than this value, the steel will yield in tension resulting in a few wide cracks, however if it is greater then more cracks will be formed when the tensile stress caused by bond between the steel and concrete exceeds the concrete tensile strength, that is

$$f_b s \sum u_s \geq f_t A_c$$

where f_b = average bond stress
$\quad\quad s$ = development length along a bar
$\quad\quad \sum u_s$ = sum of perimeters of reinforcement.

Figure 6.16
Forces adjacent to a crack

For a round bar

$$\frac{u_s}{A} = \frac{4\pi\Phi}{\pi\Phi^2} = \frac{4}{\Phi}$$

Hence, since

$$\sum u_s = \frac{A_s}{A} u_s \quad \text{for similar bars}$$

then

$$\sum u_s = \frac{4rA_c}{\Phi}$$

and thus

$$s \geq \frac{f_t\Phi}{4r f_b}$$

The maximum crack spacing is twice this value immediately prior to the formation of a new crack, when the development length on both sides is s_{min}, that is

$$s_{max} = \frac{f_t\Phi}{2r f_b} \tag{6.13}*$$

Crack spacing and hence width, therefore, is governed both by the reinforcement size and quantity for ratios above the critical value, which should be taken as a minimum requirement for controlled cracking. Empirical values for general use are given in section 6.1.

6.5.1 Crack width calculation

The expressions for crack spacing assume that the total thermal and shrinkage strains are sufficient to cause cracking, although in practice it is found that predicted cracks may not always occur. It is possible to estimate however the maximum crack width likely to occur by considering total concrete contraction in conjunction with the maximum likely crack spacing. For steel ratios greater than the critical value, and when the total contraction exceeds the ultimate tensile strain for the concrete (ε_{ult}), the tensile stress in the concrete increases from zero at a crack to a maximum value at mid-distance between cracks. Hence the mean tensile strain in the uncracked length is $\varepsilon_{ult}/2$ when a new crack is just about to form. The crack width is thus given by crack width = (total unit movement – concrete strain) × crack spacing with the maximum width corresponding to the maximum spacing of s_{max}

$$w_{max} = \left(\varepsilon_{sh} + T\alpha_c - \tfrac{1}{2}\varepsilon_{ult}\right)s_{max} \tag{6.14}$$

where ε_{sh} = shrinkage strain
T = fall in temperature from hydration peak
α_c = coefficient of thermal expansion of concrete.

In practice, variations in restraints cause large variations within members and between otherwise similar members, with 'full' restraint seldom occurring. The behaviour depends considerably on this and temperatures at the time of casting.

Allowance for these influences, and creep, can be made by the use of 'restraint factors' (see section 1.3) so that the equation for maximum crack width becomes

$$w_{max} = \left[R(\varepsilon_{sh} + T\alpha_c) - \tfrac{1}{2}\varepsilon_{ult}\right]s_{max} \tag{6.15}$$

where R = restraint factor (maximum value 0.5 for 'full' restraint). Further guidance concerning possible 'restraint factors' is given in Part 2 of BS 8110.

EXAMPLE 6.5

Calculation of shrinkage and thermal crack widths

A fully restrained section of reinforced concrete wall is 150 mm thick, and drying shrinkage strain of 50 microstrain (ε_{sh}) is anticipated together with a temperature drop (T) of 20°C after setting. Determine the minimum horizontal reinforcement to control cracking and estimate maximum crack widths and average spacing for a suitable reinforcement arrangement.

Three-day ultimate tensile strength of concrete (f_t) = ultimate average bond stress (f_b) = 1.5 N/mm^2

Modulus of elasticity of concrete (E_c) = 10 kN/mm^2

Coefficient of thermal expansion for mature concrete (α_c) = 12 microstrain/°C

Characteristic yield strength of reinforcement (f_y) = 460 N/mm^2

Modulus of elasticity of reinforcement (E_s) = 200 kN/mm^2

Critical steel ratio $r_{crit} = \dfrac{f_t}{f_y} = \dfrac{1.5}{460} = 0.33$ per cent from equation 6.12

$$= \frac{0.33}{100} \times 150 \times 1000$$

$$= 495 \text{ mm}^2/\text{m}$$

This could be conveniently provided as 10 mm bars at 300 mm centres in each face of the member (524 mm^2/m).

For this reinforcement, the maximum crack spacing is given by equation 6.13 as

$$s_{max} = \frac{f_t \Phi}{2\dfrac{A_s}{A_c} f_b} = \frac{1.5 \times 10}{2 \times \dfrac{524 \times 1.5}{150\,000}}$$

$$= 1430 \text{ mm}$$

Since the minimum spacing is given by one-half of this value, the average spacing will be $s_{av} = 0.75 \times 1430 = 1072$ mm.

The maximum crack width corresponds to s_{max} and is given by

$$w_{max} = s_{max}\left[R(\varepsilon_{sh} + T\alpha_c) - \tfrac{1}{2}\varepsilon_{ult}\right]$$

as given in equation 6.15 where ultimate tensile strain for the concrete

$$\varepsilon_{ult} = \frac{f_t}{E_c}$$

$$= \frac{1.5}{10 \times 10^3} = 150 \text{ microstrain}$$

therefore assuming $R = 0.5$

$$w_{max} = 1430 \left[0.5(50 + 20 \times 12) - \frac{150}{2} \right] \times 10^{-6} = 0.10 \text{ mm}$$

6.6 Other serviceability requirements

The two principal other serviceability considerations are those of durability and resistance to fire, although occasionally a situation arises in which some other factor may be of importance to ensure the proper performance of a structural member in service. This may include fatigue due to moving loads or machinery, or specific thermal and sound insulation properties. The methods of dealing with such requirements may range from the use of reduced working stresses in the materials, to the use of special concretes, for example light-weight aggregates for good thermal resistance.

6.6.1 Durability

Deterioration will generally be associated with water permeating the concrete, and the opportunities for this to occur should be minimised as far as possible by providing good architectural details with adequate drainage and protection to the concrete surface.

Permeability is the principal characteristic of the concrete which affects durability, although in some situations it is necessary to consider also physical and chemical effects which may cause the concrete to decay.

For reinforced concrete, a further important aspect of durability is the degree of protection which is given to the reinforcement. Carbonation by the atmosphere will, in time, destroy the alkalinity of the surface zone concrete, and if this reaches the level of the reinforcement will render the steel vulnerable to corrosion in the presence of moisture and oxygen.

If a concrete is made with a sound inert aggregate, deterioration will not occur in the absence of an external influence. Since concrete is a highly alkaline material, its resistance to other alkalis is good, but it is however very susceptible to attack by acids or substances which easily decompose to produce acids. Concrete made with Portland cement is thus not suitable for use in situations where it comes into contact with such materials, which include beer, milk and fats. Some neutral salts may also attack concrete, the two most notable being calcium chloride and soluble sulfates. These react with a minor constituent of the hydration products in different ways. The chloride must be in concentrated solution, when it has a solvent effect on the concrete in addition to its more widely recognised action in promoting the corrosion of the reinforcement, while sulfates need only be present in much smaller quantities to cause internal expansion of the concrete with consequent cracking and strength loss. Sulfates present the most commonly met chemical-attack problem for concrete since they may occur in groundwater and sewage. In such cases cements containing reduced proportions of the vulnerable tricalcium aluminate, such as Sulfate Resisting Portland Cement, should be used. The addition of Pulverised Fuel Ash (pfa) or ground granulated blast furnace slag (ggbfs) may also be beneficial. BS 5328 provides detailed guidance on concrete mix requirements for use in situations where sulfates are present. Both chlorides and sulfates are present in sea water, and because of this the chemical actions are different, resulting in reduced sulfate damage, although if the concrete is of poor quality, serious damage may occur from reactions of soluble magnesium salts with the hydrated compounds. Well-constructed Portland cement structures have nevertheless been found to endure for many years in sea water.

Physical attack of the concrete must also be considered. This may come from abrasion of attrition as may be caused by sand or shingle, and by alternate wetting and drying. The latter effect is particularly important in the case of marine structures near the water surface, and causes stresses to develop if the movements produced are restrained. It is also possible for crystal growth to occur from drying out of sea water in cracks and pores, and this may cause further internal stresses, leading to cracking. Alternate freezing and thawing is another major cause of physical damage, particularly in road and runway slabs and other situations where water in pores and cracks can freeze and expand thus leading to spalling. It has been found that the entrainment of a small percentage of air in the concrete in the form of small discrete bubbles offers the most effective protection against this form of attack. Although this reduces the strength of the concrete, it is recommended that 5.5 ± 1.5 per cent by volume of entrained air (for 20 mm maximum aggregate size) should be included in concrete subjected to regular wetting and drying combined with severe frost.

All these forms of attack may be minimised by the production of a dense, well-compacted concrete with low permeability, thus restricting damage to the surface zone of the member. Aggregates which are likely to react with the alkali matrix should be avoided or the alkali levels of the cement carefully limited. Similarly, those which exhibit unusually high shrinkage characteristics should also be avoided. If this is done, then permeability, and hence durability, is affected by

1. aggregate type and density

2. water–cement ratio

3. degree of hydration of cement

4. degree of compaction.

A low water–cement ratio is necessary to limit the voids due to hydration, which must be well advanced with the assistance of good curing techniques. BS 8110 recommends minimum curing periods taking account of cement type, concrete temperature and ambient conditions. Coupled with this is the need for non-porous aggregates which are hard enough to resist any attrition, and for thorough compaction. It is essential that the mix is designed to have adequate workability for the situation in which it is to be used, thus the cement content of the mix must be reasonably high.

BS 8110 specifies minimum cement contents for various exposure conditions, as well as minimum strength and maximum water cement ratio, related to minimum cover requirements as described in section 6.1.1.

The consequences of thermal effects on durability must not be overlooked, and very high cement contents should only be used in conjunction with a detailed cracking assessment. BS 5328 suggests that 550 kg/m^3 cement content should be regarded as an upper limit for general use.

Provided that such measures are taken, and that adequate cover of sound concrete is given to the reinforcement, deterioration of reinforced concrete is unlikely. Thus although the surface concrete may be affected, the reinforcing steel will remain protected by an alkaline concrete matrix which has not been carbonated by the atmosphere. Once this cover breaks down and water and possibly chemicals can reach the steel, rusting and consequent expansion lead rapidly to cracking and spalling of the cover concrete and severe damage – visually and sometimes structurally.

6.6.2 Fire resistance

Depending on the type of structure under consideration, it may be necessary to consider the fire resistance of the individual concrete members. Three conditions must be examined

1. effects on structural strength
2. flame penetration resistance ⎫ in the case of dividing members such as walls
3. heat transmission properties ⎭ and slabs

Concrete and steel in the form of reinforcement or prestressing tendons exhibit reduced strength after being subjected to high temperatures. Although concrete has low thermal conductivity, and thus good resistance to temperature rise, the strength begins to drop significantly at temperatures above 300°C and it has a tendency to spall at high temperatures. The extent of this spalling is governed by the type of aggregate, with siliceous materials being particularly susceptible while calcareous and light-weight aggregate concretes suffer very little. Reinforcement will retain about 50 per cent of its normal strength after reaching about 550°C, while for prestressing tendons the corresponding temperature is only 400°C.

Thus as the temperature rises the heat is transferred to the interior of a concrete member, with a thermal gradient established in the concrete. This gradient will be affected by the area and mass of the member in addition to the thermal properties of the concrete, and may lead to expansion and loss of strength. Dependent on the thickness and nature of cover, the steel will rise in temperature and lose strength, thus leading to deflections and eventual structural failure of the member if the steel temperature becomes excessive. Design must therefore be aimed at providing and maintaining sound cover of concrete as a protection, thus delaying the temperature rise in the steel. The presence of plaster, screeds and other non-combustible finishes assists the cover in protecting the reinforcement and may thus be allowed for in the design.

BS 8110 gives tabulated values of minimum dimensions and nominal covers for various types of concrete member which are necessary to permit the member to withstand fire for a specified period of time. Although these values, which have been summarised in tables 6.2 and 6.3 for reinforced concrete, do not take into account the influence of aggregate type, they may be considered adequate for most normal purposes. More detailed information concerning design for fire resistance is given in Part 2 of BS 8110 including concrete type, member type and details of finishes. The period that a member is required to survive, both in respect of strength in relation to working loads and the containment of fire, will depend upon the type and usage of the structure – and minimum requirements are generally specified by building regulations. Prestressed concrete beams must be considered separately in view of the increased vulnerability of the prestressing steel which may lose tension whilst subject to heat.

6.7 Stability

While it would be unreasonable to expect a structure to withstand extremes of accidental loading as may be caused by collision, explosion or similar happening, it is important that resulting damage should not be disproportionate to the cause. It follows therefore that a major structural collapse must not be allowed to be caused by a relatively minor mishap which may have a reasonably high probability of happening in the anticipated lifetime of the structure.

The possibilities of a structure buckling or overturning under the 'design' loads will have been considered as part of the ultimate limit state analysis. However, in some instances a structure will not have an adequate lateral strength even though it has been designed to resist the specific combinations of wind load and vertical load. This could be the case if there is an explosion or a slight earth tremor, since then the lateral loads are proportional to the mass of the structure. Therefore it is recommended that a structure should always be capable of resisting a lateral force not less than 1.5 per cent of the total characteristice load acting through the centroid of the structure above any level considered.

Damage and possible instability should also be guarded against wherever possible, for example vulnerable load-bearing members should be protected from collision by protective features such as banks or barriers.

6.7.1 Ties

In addition to these precautions, the general stability and robustness of a building structure can be increased by providing reinforcement acting as ties. These ties should act both vertically between roof and foundations, and horizontally around and across each floor, and all external vertical load-bearing members should be anchored to the floors and beams.

Vertical ties

Vertical ties should be provided by reinforcement, effectively continuous from roof to foundation by means of proper laps, running through all vertical load-bearing members. This steel should be capable of resisting a tensile force equal to the maximum design ultimate load carried by the column or wall from any one storey. This calculation uses a partial factor of safety $\gamma_f = 1.05$ applied to the dead load plus between $\frac{1}{3}$ and 1.0 to the imposed load according to the usage of the structure. In *in situ* concrete, this requirement is almost invariably satisfied by a normal design, but joint detailing may be affected in precast work.

Horizontal ties

Horizontal ties should be provided for all buildings, irrespective of height, in three ways (see figure 6.17)

1. peripheral ties
2. internal ties
3. column and wall ties.

The resistance of these ties when stressed to their characteristic strength is given in terms of a force F_t, where $F_t = 60$ kN or ($20 + 4 \times$ number of storeys in structure) kN, whichever is less. This expression takes into account the increased risk of an accident in a large building and the seriousness of the collapse of a tall structure.

(a) Peripheral ties

The peripheral tie must be provided, by reinforcement which is effectively continuous, around the perimeter of the building at each floor and roof level. This reinforcement must lie within 1.2 m from the outer edge and at its characteristic stress be capable of resisting a force of at least F_t.

Figure 6.17
Tie forces

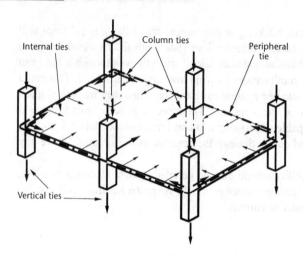

(b) Internal ties

Internal ties should also be provided at each floor in two perpendicular directions and be anchored at each end either to the peripheral tie or to the continuous column or wall ties.

These ties must be effectively continuous and they may either be spread evenly across a floor, or grouped at beams or walls as convenient. Where walls are used, the tie reinforcement must be concentrated in the bottom 0.5 m.

The resistance required is related to the span and loading. Internal ties must be capable of resisting a force of F_t kN per metre width or $[F_t(g_k + q_k)/7.5]L/5$ kN per metre width, if this is greater. In this expression, L is the greatest horizontal distance in the direction of the tie between the centres of vertical load-bearing members, or if smaller, $5\times$ the clear storey height measured to underside of the beams. The loading $(g_k + q_k)$ kN/m² is the average characteristic load on unit area of the floor considered. Internal ties parallel to cross-walls occurring in one direction only, on plan, need only resist the force F_t kN per metre width.

(c) Column and wall ties

Column and wall ties must be able to resist a force of at least 3 per cent of the total vertical ultimate load for which the member has been designed. Additionally, the resistance provided must not be less than the smaller of $2F_t$ or $F_t l_0/2.5$ kN where l_0 is the floor to ceiling height in metres. Wall ties are assessed on the basis of the above forces acting per metre length of the wall, while column ties are concentrated within 1 m either side of the column centre line. Particular care should be taken with corner columns to ensure they are tied in two perpendicular directions.

In considering the structure subjected to accidental loading it is assumed that no other forces are acting, thus reinforcement provided for any other purposes may also act as ties. Indeed, peripheral and internal ties may also be considered to be acting as column or wall ties.

As with vertical ties, the provision of horizontal ties for *in situ* construction will seldom affect the amount of reinforcement provided. Detailing of the reinforcement may however be affected, and particular attention must be paid to the manner in which internal ties are anchored to peripheral ties. The requirements for the full anchorage of ties are illustrated in figure 6.18. If these are not met, then the assumed stresses in the ties must be reduced appropriately.

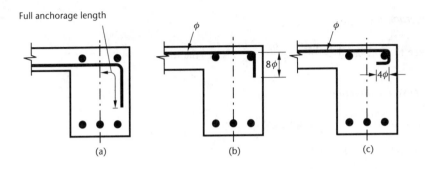

Figure 6.18
Anchorage requirements
for ties

Full anchorage length

(a)   (b)   (c)

Precast concrete construction however presents a more serious problem since the requirements of tie forces and simple easily constructed joints are not always compatible. Unless the required forces can be provided with the bars anchored by hooks and bends in the case of column and wall ties, an analysis of the structure must be performed to assess the remaining stability after a specified degree of structural damage.

EXAMPLE 6.6

Stability ties

Calculate the stability ties required in an eight-storey building to be used for office purposes of plan area shown in figure 6.19

Clear storey height under beams $= 2.9$ m
Floor to ceiling height (l_0) $= 3.4$ m
Characteristic deal load (g_k) $= 6$ kN/m^2
Characteristic live load (q_k) $= 3$ kN/m^2
Characteristic steel strength $(f_y) = 460$ N/mm^2
$F_t = (20 + 4 \times$ number of storeys$)$
$\quad = 20 + 4 \times 8 = 52$ kN < 60 kN

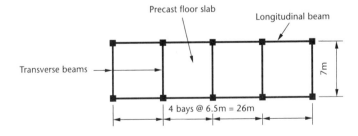

Precast floor slab
Longitudinal beam
Transverse beams
7 m
4 bays @ 6.5m = 26m

Figure 6.19
Stability tie example

(a) Peripheral ties

Force to be resisted $= F_t = 52$ kN

Bar area required $= \dfrac{52 \times 10^3}{460} = 113$ mm^2

This could be provided by one T12 bar.

(b) *Internal ties*

$$\text{Force to be resisted } = \frac{F_t(g_k + q_k)}{7.5} \times \frac{L}{5} \text{ kN per metre}$$

(1) *Transverse direction*

$$\text{Force } = \frac{52(6 + 3)}{7.5} \times \frac{7}{5} = 87.4 \text{ kN/m} > F_t$$

Force per bay $= 87.4 \times 6.5$

$$= 568.1 \text{ kN}$$

Therefore, bar area required in each transverse interior beam is

$$\frac{568.1 \times 10^3}{460} = 1235 \text{ mm}^2$$

This could be provided by 4T20 bars.

(2) *Longitudinal direction*

$$\text{Force } = \frac{52(6 + 3)}{7.5} \times \frac{6.5}{5} = 81.1 \text{ kN/m} > F_t$$

Therefore force along length of building $= 81.1 \times 7 = 567.7$ kN, hence bar area required in each longitudinal beam is

$$\frac{567.7 \times 10^3}{2 \times 460} = 617 \text{ mm}^2$$

This could be provided by 2T20 bars.

(3) *Column ties*

Force to be designed for is

$$\left(\frac{l_0}{2.5}\right)F_t = \left(\frac{3.4}{2.5}\right)52 = 70.7 \text{ kN} < 2F_t$$

or 3 per cent of ultimate floor load on a column is

$$8\left[\frac{3}{100}(1.4 \times 6 + 1.6 \times 3) \times 6.5 \times \frac{7}{2}\right] = 72 \text{ kN at ground level}$$

To allow for 3 per cent of column self-weight, take design force to be 75 kN, say, at each floor level.

$$\text{Area of ties required } = \frac{75 \times 10^3}{460} = 163 \text{ mm}^2$$

This would be provided by 1T20 and incorporated with the internal ties.

(c) *Vertical ties*

Taking one-third imposed load acting for office usage, the maximum column load from one storey is approximately equal to

$$(1.05 \times 1 + 1.05 \times 6) \times 3.5 \times 6.5 = 167.2 \text{ kN}$$

Therefore bar area required throughout each column is equal to

$$\frac{167.2 \times 10^3}{460} = 364 \text{ mm}^2$$

This would be provided by 4T12 bars.

6.7.2 Analysis of 'damaged' structure

This must be undertaken when a structure does not comply with the vertical-tie requirements, or when every precast floor or roof unit does not have sufficient anchorage to resist a force equal to F_t kN per metre width acting in the direction of the span. The analysis must show that each key load-bearing member, its connections, and the horizontal members which provide lateral support, are able to withstand a specified loading from any direction. If this cannot be satisfied, then the analysis must demonstrate that the removal of any single vertical load-bearing element, other than key members, at each storey in turn will not result in collapse of a significant part of the structure.

The minimum loading that may act from any direction on a key member is recommended as 34 kN/m^2 in BS 8110. The decision as to what loads should be considered acting is left to the engineer, but will generally be on the basis of permanent and realistic live-loading estimates, depending on the building usage. This method is attempting therefore to assess quantitatively the effects of exceptional loading such as explosion. The design 'pressure' must thus be regarded as a somewhat arbitrary value.

The 'pressure' method will generally be suitable for application to columns in precast framed structures; however, where precast load-bearing panel construction is being used an approach incorporating the removal of individual elements may be more appropriate. In this case, vertical loadings should be assessed as described, and the structure investigated to determine whether it is able to remain standing by a different structural action. This action may include parts of the damaged structure behaving as a cantilever or a catenary, and it may also be necessary to consider the strength of non-load-bearing partitions or cladding.

Whichever approach is adopted, such analyses are tedious, and the provision of effective tie forces within the structure should be regarded as the preferred solution both from the point of view of design and performance.

Continuity reinforcement and good detailing will greatly enhance the overall fire resistance of a structure with respect to collapse. A fire-damaged structure with reduced member strength may even be likened to a structure subjected to accidental overload, and analysed accordingly.

CHAPTER 7

Design of reinforced concrete beams

CHAPTER INTRODUCTION

Reinforced concrete beam design consists primarily of producing member details which will adequately resist the ultimate bending moments, shear forces and torsional moments. At the same time serviceability requirements must be considered to ensure that the member will behave satisfactorily under working loads. It is difficult to separate these two criteria, hence the design procedure consists of a series of interrelated steps and checks. These steps are shown in detail in the flow chart in figure 7.1, but may be condensed into three basic design stages

1. preliminary analysis and member sizing
2. detailed analysis and design of reinforcement
3. serviceability calculations.

Much of the material in this chapter depends on the theory and design specifications from the previous chapters. The loading and calculation of moments and shear forces should be carried out using the methods described in chapter 3. The equations used for calculating the areas of reinforcement have been derived in chapters 4 and 5.

Full details of serviceability requirements and calculations are given in chapter 6, but it is normal practice to make use of simple rules which are specified in the Code of Practice and are quite adequate for most situations. Typical of these are the span–effective depth ratios to ensure acceptable deflections, and the rules for maximum bar spacings and minimum quantities of reinforcement, which are to limit cracking, as described in chapter 6.

→

$\longrightarrow$

Design and detailing of the bending reinforcement must allow for factors such as anchorage bond between the steel and concrete. The area of the tensile bending reinforcement also affects the subsequent design of the shear and torsion reinforcement. Arrangement of reinforcement is constrained both by the requirements of the codes of practice for concrete structures and by practical considerations such as construction tolerances, clearance between bars and available bar sizes and length. Many of the requirements for correct detailing are illustrated in the examples which deal with the design of typical beams.

All calculations should be based on the effective span of a beam which is given as follows.

1. A simply supported beam – the smaller of the distances between the centres of bearings, or the clear distance between supports plus the effective depth.
2. A continuous beam – the distance between centres of supports.
3. A cantilever beam – the length to the face of the support plus half the effective depth, or the distance to the centre of the support if the beam is continuous.

7.1 | Preliminary analysis and member sizing

The layout and size of members are very often controlled by architectural details, and clearances for machinery and equipment. The engineer must either check that the beam sizes are adequate to carry the loading, or alternatively, decide on sizes that are adequate. The preliminary analysis need only provide the maximum moments and shears in order to ascertain reasonable dimensions. Beam dimensions required are

1. cover to the reinforcement
2. breadth (b)
3. effective depth (d)
4. overall depth (h)

Adequate concrete cover is required to protect the reinforcement from corrosion and damage. The necessary cover depends on the grade of concrete, the exposure of the beam, and the required fire resistance. Table 6.1 gives the nominal cover which should be provided to all reinforcement, including links. This cover should additionally never be less than the bar size, and it may also need to be increased to meet the fire resistance requirements of the Code of Practice.

The strength of a beam is affected considerably more by its depth than its breadth. A suitable breadth may be a third to half of the depth; but it may be much less for a deep beam and at other times wide shallow beams are used to conserve headroom. The beam should not be too narrow; if it is much less than 200 mm wide there may be difficulty in providing adequate side cover and space for the reinforcing bars.

Suitable dimensions for b and d can be decided by a few trial calculations as follows.

1. For no compression reinforcement

$$M/bd^2 f_{cu} \leq 0.156$$

Figure 7.1
Beam design flow chart

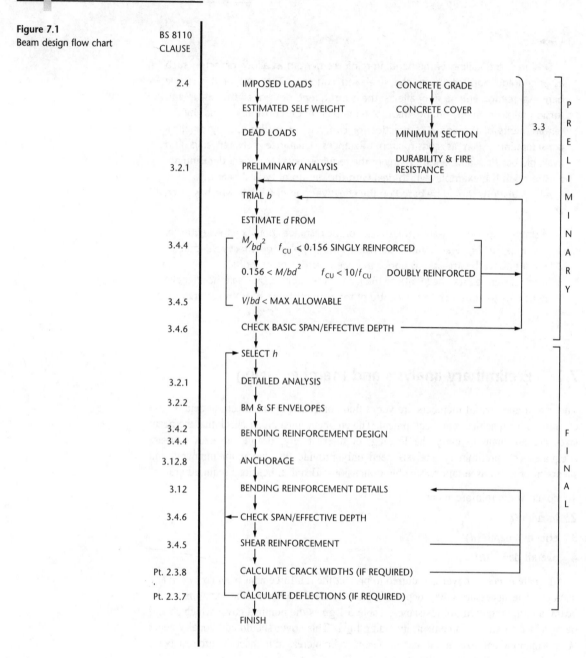

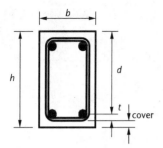

Figure 7.2
Beam dimensions

With compression reinforcement it can be shown that

$$M/bd^2 f_{cu} < 10/f_{cu}$$

if the area of bending reinforcement is not to be excessive.

2. Shear stress $\nu = V/bd$ and ν should never exceed $0.8\sqrt{f_{cu}}$ or 5 N/mm², whichever is the lesser. To avoid congested shear reinforcement, ν should preferably be somewhat closer to half (or less) of the maximum allowed.

3. The span–effective depth ratio for spans not exceeding 10 m should be within the basic values given below

    Cantilever beam   7

    Simply supported beam   20

    Continuous beam   26

    which are modified according to M/bd^2 and the service stress in the tension reinforcement as described in chapter 6. For spans greater than 10 m, the basic ratios are multiplied by 10/span.

4. The overall depth of the beam is given by

    $$h = d + \text{Cover} + t$$

    where t = estimated distance from the outside of the link to the centre of the tension bars (see figure 7.2). For example, with nominal sized 12 mm links and one layer of 32 mm tension bars, $t = 28$ mm approximately. It will, in fact, be slightly larger than this with deformed bars as they have a larger overall dimension than the nominal bar size.

EXAMPLE 7.1

Beam sizing

A concrete lintel with an effective span of 4.0 m supports a 230 mm brick wall as shown in figure 7.3. The loads on the lintel are $G_k = 100$ kN and $Q_k = 40$ kN. Determine suitable dimensions for the lintel if grade 30 concrete is used.

The beam breadth b will match the wall thickness so that

$$b = 230 \text{ mm}$$

Allowing, say, 14 kN for the weight of the beam, gives the ultimate load

$$F = 1.4 \times 114 + 1.6 \times 40$$
$$= 224 \text{ kN}$$

Figure 7.3
Beam sizing example

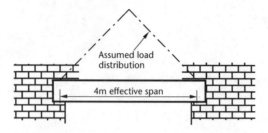

Therefore maximum shear

$$V = 112 \text{ kN}$$

Assuming a triangular load distribution for the preliminary analysis, we have

$$
\begin{aligned}
M &= \frac{F \times \text{span}}{6} \\
&= \frac{224 \times 4.0}{6} \\
&= 149 \text{ kN m}
\end{aligned}
$$

For such a relatively minor beam the case with no compression steel should be considered

$$\frac{M}{bd^2 f_{cu}} < 0.156$$

therefore

$$\frac{149 \times 10^6}{230 \times d^2 \times 30} < 0.156$$

$$d > 372 \text{ mm}$$

For mild conditions of exposure the cover $= 25$ mm (table 6.1). So for 10 mm links and, say, 32 mm bars

$$
\begin{aligned}
\text{overall depth } h &= d + 25 + 10 + 32/2 \\
&= d + 51
\end{aligned}
$$

Therefore make $h = 525$ mm as an integer number of brick courses. So that

$$
\begin{aligned}
d &= 525 - 51 \\
&= 474 \text{ mm}
\end{aligned}
$$

$$
\begin{aligned}
\text{shear stress } \nu &= \frac{V}{bd} \\
&= \frac{112 \times 10^3}{230 \times 474} \\
&= 1.03 \text{ N/mm}^2
\end{aligned}
$$

For grade 30 concrete, maximum ν allowed $= 0.8\sqrt{30} = 4.38$ N/mm^2. Therefore

$$\nu < \frac{4.38}{2}$$

$$\text{Basic span--effective depth} = \frac{4000}{474}$$

$$= 8.4 < 20$$

A beam size of 230 mm by 525 mm deep would be suitable.

Weight of beam $= 0.23 \times 0.525 \times 4.0 \times 24 = 11.6$ kN

which is sufficiently close to the assumed value.

7.2 Design for bending

The calculation of main bending reinforcement is performed using the equations and charts derived in chapter 4. In the case of rectangular sections which require only tension steel, the lever-arm curve method is probably the simplest. Where compression steel is required, either design charts or a manual approach with the simplified design formulae may be used. When design charts are not applicable, as in the case of non-rectangular sections, the formulae based on the equivalent rectangular stress block will simplify calculations considerably.

The type of reinforcing steel to be used must be decided initially since this, in conjunction with the chosen concrete grade, will affect the areas required and also influence bond calculations. In most circumstances one of the available types of high-yield bars will be used unless cracking is critical, as for example in water-retaining structures, when mild steel may be preferred. Areas of reinforcement are calculated at the sections with maximum moments, and suitable bar sizes selected. (Tables of bar areas are given in the Appendix.) This permits anchorage calculations to be performed and details of bar arrangement to be produced, taking into account the guidance given by the codes of practice.

An excessive amount of reinforcement usually indicates that a member is undersized and it may also cause difficulty in fixing the bars and pouring the concrete. Therefore the code stipulates A_s/bh should not exceed 4.0 per cent. On the other hand too little reinforcement is also undesirable therefore A_s/bh should not be less than 0.24 per cent for mild steel or 0.13 per cent for high-yield steel.

To avoid excessive deflections it is also necessary to check the span to effective depth ratio as outlined in chapter 6.

7.2.1 Singly reinforced rectangular section

A beam section needs reinforcement only in the tensile zone when M/bd^2f_{cu} is not greater than 0.156. This is not true if the moments at a section have been reduced by more than 10 per cent as a result of a redistribution of the elastic moments, and in this case reference should be made to equations 7.2 and 7.6 in order to decide whether or not compression steel is necessary.

The singly reinforced section considered is shown in figure 7.4 and it is subjected to a sagging moment M at the ultimate limit state. The design calculations for the longitudinal steel can be summarised as follows.

1. Calculate $K = M/bd^2f_{cu}$
2. Determine the lever-arm, z, from the curve of figure 7.5 or from the equation

$$z = d\left[0.5 + \sqrt{(0.25 - K/0.9)}\right] \tag{7.1}$$

Figure 7.4
Singly reinforced section with
rectangular stress block

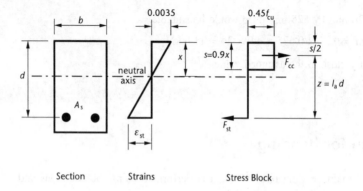

Section   Strains   Stress Block

3. The area of tension steel is given by

$$A_s = \frac{M}{0.95 f_y z}$$

4. Select suitable bar sizes.

5. Check that the area of steel actually provided is within the limits required by the code, that is

$$100 \frac{A_s}{bh} \le 4.0$$

and

$$100 \frac{A_s}{bh} \ge 0.13 \text{ for high-yield or } 0.24 \text{ for mild steel}$$

$K = M/bd^2 f_{cu}$	0.05	0.06	0.07	0.08	0.09	0.10	0.11	0.12	0.13	0.14	0.15	0.156
$l_a = z/d$	0.941	0.928	0.915	0.901	0.887	0.873	0.857	0.842	0.825	0.807	0.789	0.775

Figure 7.5
Lever-arm curve

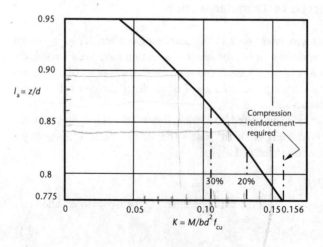

The percentage values on the K-axis mark the limits for singly reinforced sections with moment redistribution applied (see section 4.7)

EXAMPLE 7.2

Design of tension reinforcement for a rectangular section

The beam section shown in figure 7.6 has characteristic material strengths of $f_{cu} = 30$ N/mm^2 for the concrete and $f_y = 460$ N/mm^2 for the steel. The design moment at the ultimate limit state is 165 kN m which causes sagging of the beam

$$K = \frac{M}{bd^2 f_{cu}} = \frac{165 \times 10^6}{230 \times 490^2 \times 30} = 0.1$$

This is less than 0.156 therefore compression steel is not required.
    From the lever-arm curve of figure 7.5 $l_a = 0.87$, therefore

    lever arm $z = l_a d = 0.87 \times 490 = 426$ mm

and

$$A_s = \frac{M}{0.95 f_y z} = \frac{165 \times 10^6}{0.95 \times 460 \times 426} = 886 \text{ mm}^2$$

Provide two T25 bars, area $= 982$ mm^2. For the steel provided

$$\frac{100 A_s}{bh} = \frac{100 \times 982}{230 \times 550} = 0.78$$

and

$$0.13 < \frac{100 A_s}{bh} < 4.0$$

therefore the steel percentage is within the limits specified by the code.

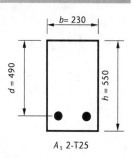

Figure 7.6
Singly reinforced beam example

7.2.2 Rectangular section with compression reinforcement

As shown in figure 7.7, compression steel is required whenever the concrete in compression is unable, by itself, to develop the necessary moment of resistance. Design charts such as the one in figure 4.9 may be used to determine the steel areas but the simplified equations based on the equivalent rectangular stress block are quick to apply.
    The maximum moment of resistance that can be developed by the concrete occurs with the neutral axis at the maximum depth allowed by the code of practice. This limiting depth is given as

$$x = (\beta_b - 0.4)d \not> 0.5d \qquad (7.2)$$

where $\beta_b = \dfrac{\text{moment at the section after redistribution}}{\text{moment at the section before redistribution}}$

This reduction is due to the designer redistributing the moments from an elastic analysis of the structure, as described in sections 3.6 and 4.7.
    With x less than $d/2$ the stress in the compression steel may be considerably less than the yield, therefore, the design procedure is somewhat different if β_b is less than 0.9.

It should also be noted that, in order to maintain the limitation on the depth of neutral axis as specified in equation 7.2, the areas of compression and tension reinforcement required and provided should meet the following requirement

$$\left(A'_{s.prov} - A'_{s.req}\right) \geq \left(A_{s.prov} - A_{s.req}\right) \tag{7.3}$$

This is to ensure a gradual tension type failure with yielding of the tension reinforcement as explained in chapter 4.

Moment redistribution factor $\beta_b \geq 0.9$ and $d'/d \not> 0.185$

If d'/d is not greater than 0.185, as is usually the case, the proportions of the strain diagram will ensure that the compression steel will have yielded.

Compression reinforcement is required if

$$M > 0.156 f_{cu} b d^2$$

and the design equations as given in section 4.5 are

1. Area of compression steel

$$A'_s = \frac{(M - 0.156 f_{cu}\, bd^2)}{0.95 f_y (d - d')} \tag{7.4}$$

2. Area of tension steel

$$A_s = \frac{0.156 f_{cu}\, bd^2}{0.95 f_y z} + A'_s \tag{7.5}$$

with lever arm $z = 0.775d$

If d'/d is greater than 0.185 the stress in the compression steel should be determined as outlined in part (2) of example 7.4.

Moment redistribution factor $\beta_b < 0.9$

The limiting depth of the neutral axis can be calculated from equation 7.2 and compression steel is required if

$$M > 0.45 f_{cu}\, bs\left(d - \frac{s}{2}\right) \tag{7.6}$$

where s = depth of stress block = $0.9x$.

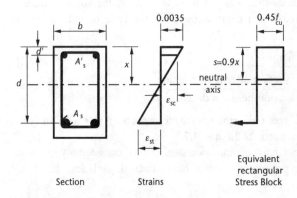

Figure 7.7
Beam doubly reinforced to resist a sagging moment

Section   Strains   Equivalent rectangular Stress Block

The design procedure is

1. Calculate $K = M/bd^2 f_{cu}$.

2. Calculate $K' = 0.402(\beta_b - 0.4) - 0.18(\beta_b - 0.4)^2$.

   If $K < K'$, compression steel is not required so proceed as for a singly reinforced section as in example 7.2.

   If $K > K'$, compression steel is required.

3. Calculate $x = (\beta_b - 0.4)d$

   If $d'/x < 0.37$, the compression steel has yielded and $f_{sc} = 0.95 f_y$.

   If $d'/x > 0.37$, calculate the steel compressive strain ε_{sc} and hence the stress f_{sc} as in example 7.4.

4. Calculate the area of compression steel from

$$A'_s = \frac{(K - K')f_{cu}bd^2}{f_{sc}(d - d')} \tag{7.7}$$

5. Calculate the area of tension steel from

$$A_s = \frac{K'f_{cu}bd^2}{0.95 f_y z} + A'_s \frac{f_{sc}}{0.95 f_y} \tag{7.8}$$

   where $z = d - 0.9x/2$.

Links should be provided to give lateral restraint to the outer layer of compression steel according to the following rules.

1. The links should pass round the corner bars and each alternate bar.

2. The link size should be at least one-quarter the size of the largest compression bar.

3. The spacing of the links should not be greater than twelve times the size of the smallest compression bar.

4. No compression bar should be more than 150 mm from a restrained bar.

EXAMPLE 7.3

Design of tension and compression reinforcement, $\beta_b > 0.9$

The beam section shown in figure 7.8 has characteristic material strengths of $f_{cu} = 30$ N/mm^2 and $f_y = 460$ N/mm^2. The ultimate moment is 165 kN m, causing hogging of the beam.

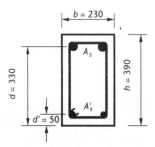

Figure 7.8
Beam doubly reinforced to resist a hogging moment

$$\frac{M}{bd^2 f_{cu}} = \frac{165 \times 10^6}{230 \times 330^2 \times 30}$$

$$= 0.22 > 0.156$$

so that compression steel is required, and

$$d'/d = 50/330 = 0.15 < 0.185$$

therefore

$$f_{sc} = 0.95 f_y$$

From equation 7.4

$$\text{Compression steel } A'_s = \frac{(M - 0.156 f_{cu} bd^2)}{0.95 f_y (d - d')}$$

$$= \frac{(165 \times 10^6 - 0.156 \times 30 \times 230 \times 330^2)}{0.95 \times 460 (330 - 50)}$$

$$= 391 \text{ mm}^2$$

And from equation 7.5

$$\text{tension steel } A_s = \frac{0.156 f_{cu} bd^2}{0.95 f_y z} + A'_s$$

$$= \frac{0.156 \times 30 \times 230 \times 330^2}{0.95 \times 460 \times 0.775 \times 330} + 391$$

$$= 1049 + 391 = 1440 \text{ mm}^2$$

Provide two T20 bars for A'_s, area $= 628$ mm^2 and two T32 bars for A_s, area $= 1610$ mm^2, so that for the areas of steel required and provided in equation 7.3

$$628 - 391 > 1610 - 1440$$

Also

$$\frac{100 A'_s}{bh} = \frac{100 \times 628}{230 \times 390} = 0.70$$

$$\frac{100 A_s}{bh} = \frac{100 \times 1610}{230 \times 390} = 1.79$$

therefore the bar areas are within the limits specified by the code.

The minimum link size $= 20/4 = 5$ mm, say 8 mm links, and the maximum link spacing $= 12 \times 20 = 240$ mm, centres. The link size and spacing may be governed by the shear calculations. Figure 7.8 shows the arrangement of the reinforcement to resist a hogging moment.

EXAMPLE 7.4

Design of tension and compression reinforcement, $\beta_b = 0.7$

The beam section shown in figure 7.9 has characteristic material strengths of $f_{cu} = 30$ N/mm^2 and $f_y = 460$ N/mm^2. The ultimate moment is 370 kN m, causing hogging of the beam.

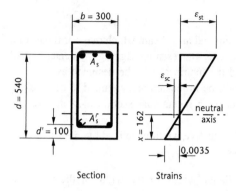

Figure 7.9
Beam doubly reinforced to
resist a hogging moment

As the moment reduction factor $\beta_b = 0.7$, the limiting depth of the neutral axis is

$$x = (\beta_b - 0.4)d$$

$$= (0.7 - 0.4)540 = 162 \text{ mm}$$

$$K = M/bd^2 f_{cu} = 370 \times 10^6/(300 \times 540^2 \times 30) = 0.141$$

$$K' = 0.402(\beta_b - 0.4) - 0.18(\beta_b - 0.4)^2$$

$$= 0.104$$

$K > K'$ therefore compression steel is required

$$d'/x = 100/162 = 0.62 > 0.37$$

therefore $f_{sc} < 0.95 f_y$

1.   Steel compressive strain $\varepsilon_{sc} = \dfrac{0.0035(x - d')}{x}$

$$= \frac{0.0035(162 - 100)}{162} = 0.00134$$

2.   From the relevant equation of section 4.1.2

     Steel compressive stress $= E_s \varepsilon_{sc}$

$$= 200\,000 \times 0.00134 = 268 \text{ N/mm}^2$$

3.   Compression steel $A'_s = \dfrac{(K - K')f_{cu}\, bd^2}{f_{sc}(d - d')}$

$$= \frac{(0.141 - 0.104)30 \times 300 \times 540^2}{268(540 - 100)} = 823 \text{ mm}^2$$

4.   Tension steel $A_s = \dfrac{K' f_{cu} bd^2}{0.95 f_y z} + A'_s \dfrac{f_{sc}}{0.95 f_y}$

$$= \frac{0.104 \times 30 \times 300 \times 540^2}{0.95 \times 460(540 - 0.9 \times 162/2)} + 823 \times \frac{268}{0.95 \times 460}$$

$$= 1337 + 505 = 1842 \text{ mm}^2$$

Provide two T25 bars for A'_s, area $= 982$ mm^2 and two T32 plus one T25 bars for A_s, area $= 2101$ mm^2, which also meet the requirements of equation 7.3.

These areas lie within the maximum and minimum limits specified by the code. To restrain the compression steel, at least 8 mm links at 300 mm centres should be provided.

7.2.3 T-beams

Figure 7.10 shows sections through a T-beam and an L-beam which may form part of a concrete beam and slab floor. When the beams are resisting sagging moments, part of the slab acts as a compression flange and the members may be designed as T- or L-beams. With hogging moments the slab will be in tension and assumed to be cracked, therefore the beam must then be designed as a rectangular section of width b_w and overall depth h.

When the slab does act as the flange its effective width is defined by empirical rules which are specified in BS 8110 as follows.

1. T-section – the lesser of the actual flange width, or the width of the web plus one-fifth of the distance between zero moments.

2. L-section – the lesser of the actual flange width or the width of the web plus one-tenth of the distance between zero moments.

As a simple rule, the distance between the points of zero moment may be taken as 0.7 times the effective span for a continuous beam.

Since the slab acts as a large compression area, the stress block for the T- or L-section usually falls within the slab thickness. For this position of the stress block, the section may be designed as an equivalent rectangular section of breadth b_f.

Transverse reinforcement should be placed across the top of the flange to prevent cracking. The area of this reinforcement should not be less than 0.15 per cent of the longitudinal cross-section of the flange.

Design procedure

1. Calculate $M/b_f d^2 f_{cu}$ and determine l_a from the lever-arm curve of figure 7.5.

   Lever arm $z = l_a d$ or from equation 7.1

2. If $d - z < h_f/2$ the stress block falls within the flange depth, and the design may proceed as for a rectangular section, breadth b_f.

3. Provide transverse steel in the top of the flange

   Area $= 0.15 h_f \times 1000/100 = 1.5 h_f$ mm² per metre length of the beam

On the very few occasions that the neutral axis does fall below the flange, reference should be made to the methods described in section 4.6.2 for a full analysis.

Figure 7.10
T-beam and L-beam

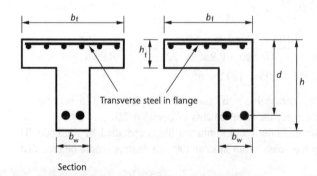

Section

EXAMPLE 7.5

Design of reinforcement for a T-section

The beam section shown in figure 7.11 has characteristic material strengths of $f_{cu} = 30$ N/mm^2 and $f_y = 460$ N/mm^2. The design moment at the ultimate limit state is 190 kN m, causing sagging.

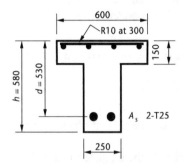

Figure 7.11
T-beam

$$\frac{M}{b_f d^2 f_{cu}} = \frac{190 \times 10^6}{600 \times 530^2 \times 30}$$

$$= 0.038$$

From the lever-arm curve, figure 7.5, $l_a = 0.95$, therefore

lever arm $z = l_a d$

$$= 0.95 \times 530 = 503 \text{ mm}$$

$$d - z = 530 - 503$$

$$= 27 \text{ mm} < h_f/2$$

Thus the stress block lies within the flange

$$A_s = \frac{M}{0.95 f_y z} = \frac{190 \times 10^6}{0.95 \times 460 \times 503}$$

$$= 865 \text{ mm}^2$$

Provide two T25 bars, area $= 982$ mm^2. For these bars

$$\frac{100 A_s}{b_w h} = \frac{100 \times 982}{250 \times 580}$$

$$= 0.68 \text{ per cent}$$

Thus the steel percentage is greater than the minimum specified by the code.

Transverse steel in the flange $= 1.5 h_f = 1.5 \times 150$

$$= 225 \text{ mm}^2/\text{m}$$

Provide R10 bars at 300 mm centres $= 262$ mm^2/m.

7.2.4 Anchorage bond

From section 5.2 the anchorage bond stress, f_{bu}, for a reinforcing bar is given by the following equation:

$$f_{bu} = \frac{f_s}{4L}\Phi$$

where f_s = the direct tensile or compressive stress in the bar
   L = the length of embedment beyond the section considered
   Φ = the bar size.

This stress should not exceed the ultimate anchorage bond stress given by

$$f_{bu} = \beta\sqrt{f_{cu}}$$

where the coefficient β is given in table 5.2.

The required anchorage length should be measured from the point at which the bar is assumed to be stressed

The Appendix lists the anchorage lengths appropriate to the ultimate stress, $0.95f_y$, for various grades of concrete and steel. The effective anchorage lengths for hooks and bends in reinforcing bars are detailed in figure 5.6.

The anchorage of a bar is more effective in a compression zone of a member than in a tension zone and this should be considered when detailing the reinforcement. Anchorage requirements are also important when detailing the curtailment of bars as described in the following section.

7.2.5 Curtailment of bars

As the magnitude of the bending moment on a beam decreases along its length, so may the area of bending reinforcement be reduced by curtailing bars as they are no longer required. Figure 7.12 illustrates the curtailment of bars in the span and at an internal support of a continuous beam. The bending-moment envelope diagram is divided into sections as shown, in proportion to the area and effective depth of each bar.

Figure 7.12
Curtailment of reinforcement

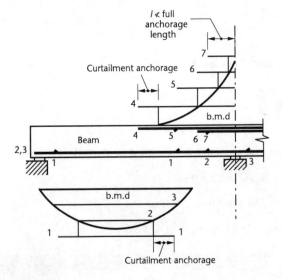

Each curtailed bar should extend beyond the point at which it is no longer needed so that it is well anchored into the concrete. The rules for curtailing such bars, other than at a simple end support, are as follows.

1. The curtailment anchorage should not be less than twelve times the bar size or the effective depth of the beam, whichever is the greater.

2. A bar should not be stopped in a tension zone unless

   (i)   the shear capacity is twice the actual shear present

   (ii) the continuing bars have twice the area required to resist the moment at that section, or

   (iii) the curtailment anchorage is increased to a full anchorage bond length based on a stress of $0.95 f_y$.

Thus in figure 7.12, bar 4 is curtailed in a compression zone and the curtailment anchorage would be the greater of twelve bar diameters or the effective depth. Bars 1 and 5, though, are curtailed in a tension zone and a full anchorage bond length would be required, unless the conditions of rules 2(i) or 2(ii) apply, in which case the curtailment anchorage would be twelve bar diameters or the effective depth.

It is most important that all bars should have at least a full anchorage bond length beyond the section of maximum moment. This is relevant to bars such as no. 7 in figure 7.12 and also to bars in a cantilever or at an end support framing into a column. The anchorage length should be based on the design stress of a bar as described in sections 5.2 and 7.2.4.

The curtailment of bars should be staggered wherever possible in order to avoid sudden changes in cross-section with resulting stress concentrations and possible cracking. This curtailment can often be achieved whilst using bars of equal length, as illustrated in figure 7.13.

At a simply supported end of a member, the reinforcing bars should extend over the supports so that the beam is sure to be reinforced in this region of high shears and bearing stresses. Therefore, each tension bar should be anchored according to one of the two rules shown diagrammatically in figure 7.14. No bend or hook should begin before the centre of the support for rule 1 nor before $d/2$ from the face of the support for rule 2.

Where the loads on a beam are substantially uniformly distributed, simplified rules for curtailment may be used. These rules only apply to continuous beams if the characteristic imposed load does not exceed the characteristic dead load and the spans are equal. Figure 7.15 shows the rules in a diagrammatic form.

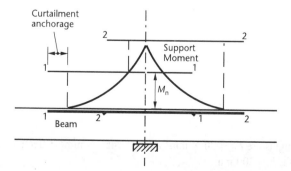

Figure 7.13
Staggering the curtailment of bars

Figure 7.14
Alternative anchorage lengths
at a simple support

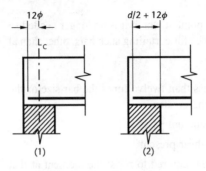

Figure 7.15
Simplified rules for curtailment
of bars in beams

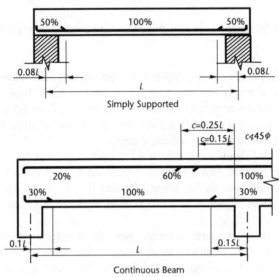

Simply Supported

Continuous Beam

7.2.6 Span–effective depth ratios

As already described in section 7.1, it is necessary to check the span–effective depth ratios to ensure that the deflections are not excessive. This is unlikely to be a problem with beams except perhaps for cantilevers or long span beams. These requirements are fully described and explained in chapter 6, dealing with Serviceability.

7.2.7 Bending-reinforcement example

The following example describes the calculations for designing the bending reinforcement for a simply supported beam. It brings together many of the items from the previous sections. The shear reinforcement for this beam is designed later in example 7.7.

EXAMPLE 7.6

Design of a beam – bending reinforcement

The beam shown in figure 7.16 supports the following uniformly distributed loads

dead load g_k = 40 kN/m, including self-weight

imposed load q_k = 12 kN/m

The characteristic material strengths are f_{cu} = 30 N/mm^2 and f_y = 460 N/mm^2. Effective depth, d = 550 mm and breadth, b = 300 mm.

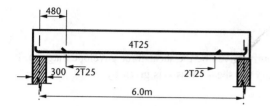

Figure 7.16
One-span beam-bending
reinforcement

(a) Analysis

Ultimate load $w_u = (1.4g_k + 1.6q_k)$ kN/metre

$$= (1.4 \times 40 + 1.6 \times 12) = 75.2 \text{ kN/metre}$$

therefore

maximum design moment $M = \dfrac{w_u L^2}{8}$

$$= \dfrac{75.2 \times 6.0^2}{8} = 338 \text{ kN m}$$

(b) Bending reinforcement

$K = \dfrac{M}{bd^2 f_{cu}}$

$$= \dfrac{338 \times 10^6}{300 \times 550^2 \times 30} = 0.124$$

From the lever-arm curve, figure 7.5, $l_a = 0.83$. Therefore

effective depth $z = l_a d = 0.83 \times 550 \times 456$ mm

$A_s = \dfrac{M}{0.95 f_y z}$

$$= \dfrac{338 \times 10^6}{0.95 \times 460 \times 456} = 1696 \text{ mm}^2$$

Provide four T25 bars, area $= 1960 \text{ mm}^2$

(c) Curtailment at support

A 90° bend with radius 4Φ beyond the support centre-line will provide an equivalent
anchorage, length 16Φ which meets the requirements of the code.

(d) Span–effective depth ratio

$M/bd^2 = 338 \times 10^6/(300 \times 550^2) = 3.72$

Basic ratio $= 20$. From table 6.7, modification factor $= 0.86$ by interpolation. Therefore

maximum $\dfrac{\text{span}}{d} = 20 \times 0.86 = 17.2$

actual $\dfrac{\text{span}}{d} = \dfrac{6000}{550} = 10.9$

7.3　Design for shear

The distribution of shear along a beam is given by the shear-force envelope diagram. If V is the shear force at a section, then the shear stress ν is given by

$$\nu = V/bd$$

The shear stress must never exceed the lesser of $0.8\sqrt{f_{cu}}$ of 5 N/mm^2.

Shear reinforcement will take the form of vertical stirrups or a combination of stirrups and bent-up bars.

7.3.1　Vertical stirrups

The usual form of stirrup is a closed link. This helps to make a rigid cage of the beam reinforcement and is essential if there is any compression steel present. An alternative is the open link as shown in figure 7.17; this may have a closing piece if lateral support is required, and offers advantages for *in situ* steel fixing.

All of the tension reinforcement must be enclosed by links, and if compression steel is not present, hanger bars are required to anchor the links in the compression zone (see figure 7.18). The minimum spacing of links is determined by the requirements of placing and compacting the concrete, and should not normally be less than about 80 mm. Maximum spacing of links longitudinally along the span should not exceed $0.75\,d$. At right angles to the span the spacing of the vertical legs should not exceed d, and all tension bars should be within 150 mm of a vertical leg. Because of these requirements (or if there are large shears), it may often be convenient to provide multiple links as illustrated in figure 7.17.

The choice of steel type is often governed by the fact that mild steel may be bent to a smaller radius than high-yield steel. This is particularly important in narrow members to allow correct positioning of tension reinforcement as shown in figure 7.18.

The advantages of mild steel links are further increased by the need to provide anchorage for the vertical leg of a stirrup within the compression zone. Although high-yield reinforcement has better bond characteristics, anchorage lengths are greater than for mild steel bars of comparable size if the steel is to act at its full design stress. This factor is of particular importance if 'open' links are to be used.

Figure 7.17
Types of shear link

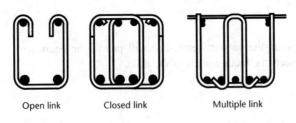

Open link　　　Closed link　　　Multiple link

Figure 7.18
Bending of links

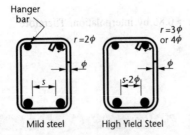

Mild steel　　　High Yield Steel

The size and spacing of the stirrups, according to the equations derived in section 5.1.1 should be such that

$$\frac{A_{sv}}{s_v} \geq \frac{b(\nu - \nu_c)}{0.95 f_{yv}}$$

where A_{sv} = cross-sectional area of the legs of a stirrup
  s_v = spacing of the stirrups
  b = breadth of the beam
  ν = V/bd
  ν_c = the ultimate shear stress from table 5.1
  f_{yv} = characteristic strength of the link reinforcement.

Values of A_{sv}/s_v for various stirrup sizes and spacing are tabulated in the Appendix. The calculation for A_{sv}/s_v is carried out at the critical section, usually distance d from the face of the support. Since the shear force diminishes along the beam, similar calculations can be repeated so that a greater spacing or a smaller stirrup size may be used.

If ν is less than ν_c nominal links must still be provided unless the beam is a very minor one and $\nu < \nu_c/2$. The nominal links should be provided such that

$$A_{sv}/s_v = 0.4b/0.95 f_{yv}$$

Even when shear steel is required, there is a section at which the shear resistance of the concrete plus the nominal stirrups equals the shear force from the envelope diagram. At this section the stirrups necessary to resist shear can stop and be replaced by the nominal stirrups. The shear resistance V_n of the concrete plus the nominal stirrups is given by

$$V_n = (0.4 + \nu_c)bd$$

or

$$V_n = \left(\frac{A_{sv}}{s_v} 0.95 f_{yv} + b\nu_c\right)d$$

for the link spacing provided (see equation 5.3). Once this value of V_n has been calculated it may be marked on the shear-force envelope to show the limits for the shear reinforcement, as shown in figure 7.19.

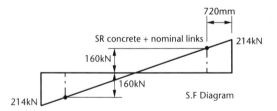

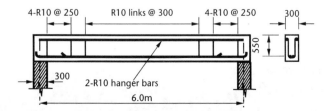

Figure 7.19
Non-continuous beam-shear reinforcement

EXAMPLE 7.7

Design of shear reinforcement for a beam

Shear reinforcement is to be designed for the one-span beam of example 7.6, as shown in figures 7.16 and 7.19. The characteristic strength of the mild steel links is $f_{yv} = 250$ N/mm^2.

(a) Check maximum shear stress

Total load on span, $F = w_u \times$ span $= 75.2 \times 6.0$

$$= 451 \text{ kN}$$

At face of support

shear $V_s = F/2 - w_u \times$ support width/2

$$= 451/2 - 75.2 \times 0.15 = 214 \text{ kN}$$

shear stress, $\nu = \dfrac{V_s}{bd} = \dfrac{214 \times 10^3}{300 \times 550}$

$$= 1.3 \text{ N/mm}^2 < 0.8\sqrt{f_{cu}}$$

(b) Shear links

Distance d from face of support

shear $V_d = V_s - w_u d$

$$= 214 - 75.2 \times 0.55 = 173 \text{ kN}$$

shear stress $\nu = \dfrac{173 \times 10^3}{300 \times 550} = 1.05 \text{ N/mm}^2$

Only two 25 mm bars extend a distance d past the critical section. Therefore for determining ν_c

$$\frac{100 A_s}{bd} = \frac{100 \times 982}{300 \times 550} = 0.59$$

From table 5.1, $\nu_c = 0.56$ N/mm^2

$$\frac{A_{sv}}{s_v} = \frac{b(\nu - \nu_c)}{0.95 f_{yv}} = \frac{300(1.05 - 0.56)}{0.95 \times 250} = 0.62$$

Provide R10 links at 250 mm centres

$$\frac{A_{sv}}{s_v} = \frac{2 \times 78.5}{250} = 0.63$$

(c) Nominal links

For mild steel links

$$\frac{A_{sv}}{s_v} = \frac{0.4b}{0.95 f_{yv}} = \frac{0.4 \times 300}{0.95 \times 250} = 0.51$$

Provide R10 links at 300 mm centres

$$\frac{A_{sv}}{s_v} = \frac{2 \times 78.5}{300} = 0.52$$

(d) Extent of shear links

Shear resistance of nominal links + concrete is

$$V_n = \left(\frac{A_{sv}}{s_v} 0.95 f_{yv} + b\nu_c\right) d$$
$$= (0.52 \times 0.95 \times 250 + 300 \times 0.56)\, 550$$
$$= 160 \text{ kN}$$

Shear reinforcement is required over a distance s given by

$$s = \frac{V_s - V_n}{w_u} = \frac{214 - 160}{75.2} = 0.72 \text{ metres from the face of the support}$$

Number of R10 links at 250 mm required at each end of the beam is

$$1 + (s/250) = 1 + (720/250) = 4$$

7.3.2 Bent-up bars

In regions of high shear forces it may be found that the use of links to carry the full force will cause steel congestion and lead to constructional problems. In these situations, consideration should be given to 'bending up' main reinforcement which is no longer required to resist bending forces. At least 50 per cent of the shear resistance provided by the steel should be in the form of links.

For a 'double system' of bent-up bars at 45° and spaced $(d - d')$ apart, as described in section 5.1.2, the shear resistance is

$$V = 1.34 f_y A_{sb}$$

where A_{sb} is the cross-sectional area of a bent-up bar. Values of V for different bar sizes are given in table 7.1.

Bent-up bars must be fully anchored past the point at which they are acting as tension members, as indicated in figure 5.3. To guard against possible crushing of the concrete it may also be necessary to check the bearing stress inside the bends of a bar. This stress is given by

$$\text{Bearing stress} = \frac{F_{bt}}{r\Phi}$$

where F_{bt} is the tensile force in the bar, r is the internal radius of the bend, and Φ is the bar size. This stress should not exceed

$$\frac{2f_{cu}}{1 + 2\Phi/a_b}$$

Table 7.1 Shear resistance in kN of bent-up bars, 'double system'

f_y (N/mm²)	Bar size Φ					
	12	16	20	25	32	40
250	38	67	105	164	269	422
460	70	123	193	302	495	776

where a_b is the centre to centre distance between bars perpendicular to the plane of the bend, but for a bar adjacent to the face of a member

$$a_b = \Phi + \text{side cover}$$

EXAMPLE 7.8

Bearing stresses inside a bend

Determine the inside radius required for the 25 mm bent-up bar shown in figure 7.20, so that the ultimate bearing stress is not exceeded. The bar has a side cover of 50 mm. Assume the bar is at the ultimate tensile stress of $0.95 f_y$ and the characteristic material strengths are $f_y = 460$ N/mm^2 and $f_{cu} = 30$ N/mm^2.

$$a_b = \Phi + \text{cover} = 25 + 50 = 75 \text{ mm}$$

therefore

$$\frac{2 f_{cu}}{1 + 2\Phi/a_b} = \frac{2 \times 30}{1 + 2 \times 25/75} = 36 \text{ N/mm}^2$$

$$\frac{F_{bt}}{r\Phi} = \frac{0.95 \times 460 \times A_s}{r \times 25} = \frac{0.95 \times 460 \times 491}{25r}$$

$$= \frac{8582}{r}$$

thus

$$\frac{8582}{r} \leq 36$$

or

$$r \geq \frac{8582}{36} = 238 \text{ mm or } 9.5\Phi$$

Figure 7.20
Radius of bend for bent-up bar

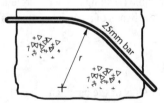

7.4 | Bar spacing

There are limitations on the minimum and maximum spacing of the reinforcing bars. In the case of minimum values this is governed by constructional requirements to allow for the access of poker vibrators and the flow of concrete to obtain a well-compacted and dense concrete. The maximum limitations on spacings are to prevent excessive cracking caused by shrinkage of the concrete and thermal expansion and contraction of the member. These serviceability requirements are dealt with in chapter 6.

7.5 | Continuous beams

Beams, slabs and columns of a cast *in situ* structure all act together to form a continuous load-bearing structure. The reinforcement in a continuous beam must be designed and detailed to maintain this continuity by connecting adjacent spans and tying together the beam and its supporting columns. There must also be transverse reinforcement to unite the slab and the beam.

The bending-moment envelope is generally a series of sagging moments in the spans and hogging moments at the supports as in figure 7.21, but occasionally the hogging moments may extend completely over the span. Where the sagging moments occur the beam and slab act together, and the beam can be designed as a T-section. At the supports, the beam must be designed as a rectangular section – this is because the hogging moments cause tension in the slab.

The moment of resistance of the concrete T-beam section is somewhat greater than that of the rectangular concrete section at the supports. Hence it is often advantageous to redistribute the support moments as described in chapter 3. By this means the design support moments can be reduced and the design span moments possibly increased.

Design of the beam follows the procedures and rules set out in the previous sections. Other factors which have to be considered in the detailed design are as follows.

1. At an exterior column the beam reinforcing bars which resist the design moments must have an anchorage bond length within the column.

2. A minimum area of transverse reinforcement must be placed in the top of the slab, across the effective flange width as described in section 7.2.3.

3. Reinforcement in the top of the slab must pass over the beam steel and still have the necessary cover. This must be considered when detailing the beam reinforcement and when deciding the effective depth of the beam at the support sections.

4. The column and beam reinforcement must be carefully detailed so that the bars can pass through the junctions without interference.

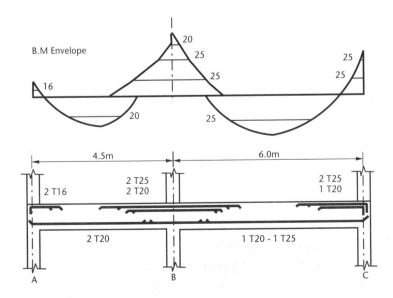

Figure 7.21
Arrangement of bending reinforcement

Figure 7.22
Arrangement of shear
reinforcement

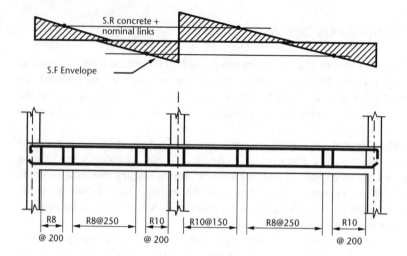

Figure 7.21 illustrates a typical arrangement of the bending reinforcement for a two-span continuous beam. The reinforcement has been arranged with reference to the bending-moment envelope and in accordance with the rules for anchorage and curtailment described in sections 7.2.4 and 7.2.5. The bending-moment envelope has been divided into sectors equivalent to the moment of resistance of each reinforcing bar. This establishes the cut-off points beyond which the bars must extend at least a curtailment anchorage length. It should be noted that at the external columns the reinforcement has been bent down to give a full anchorage bond length.

The shear-force envelope and the arrangement of the shear reinforcement for the same continuous beam are shown in figure 7.22. On the shear-force envelope the resistance of the concrete plus the nominal stirrups has been marked and this shows the lengths of the beam which need shear reinforcement. When designing the shear reinforcement, reference should be made to the arrangement of bending reinforcement to ensure that the longitudinal tension bars used to establish ν_c extend at least an effective depth beyond the section being considered.

EXAMPLE 7.9

Design of a continuous beam

The beam is 300 mm wide by 660 deep with three equal 5.0 m spans. In the transverse direction, the beams are at 4.0 m centres with a 180 mm thick slab, as shown in figure 7.24.

The live load q_k on the beam is 50 kN/m and the dead load g_k, including self-weight, is 85 kN/m.

Characteristic material strengths are $f_{cu} = 30$ N/mm^2, $f_y = 460$ N/mm^2 for the longitudinal steel and $f_{yv} = 250$ N/mm^2 for the links. For a mild exposure the minimum concrete cover is to be 25 mm.

For each span

ultimate load $w_u = (1.4g_k + 1.6q_k)$ kN/metre

$$= (1.4 \times 85 + 1.6 \times 50) = 199 \text{ kN/metre}$$

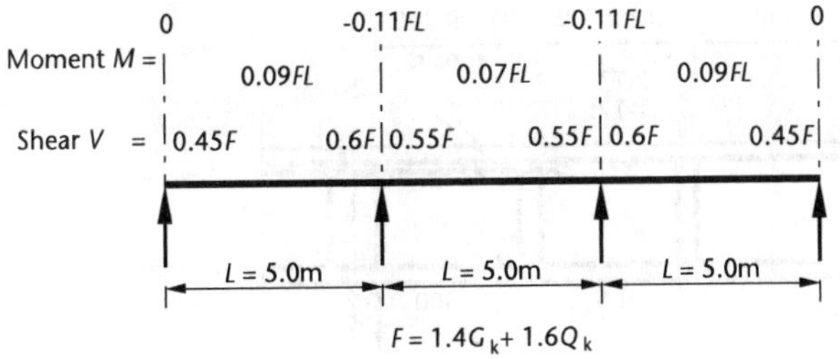

Figure 7.23
Continuous beam with
ultimate bending moment
and shear-force coefficients

Total ultimate load on a span is

$$F = 199 \times 5.0 = 995 \text{ kN}$$

As the loading is uniformly distributed, $q_k \not> g_k$, and the spans are equal, the coefficients shown in figure 7.23 have been used to calculate the design moment and shears.

Bending

(a) Mid-span of 1st and 3rd spans – design as a T-section

Moment $M = 0.09FL$

$$= 0.09 \times 995 \times 5 = 448 \text{ kN m}$$

Effective width of flange $= b_w + 0.7L/5$

$$= 300 + \frac{0.7 \times 5000}{5} = 1000 \text{ mm}$$

therefore

$$\frac{M}{bd^2 f_{cu}} = \frac{448 \times 10^6}{1000 \times 600^2 \times 30} = 0.041$$

From the lever-arm curve, $l_a = 0.95$, therefore

$$z = 0.95 \times 600 = 570 \text{ mm}$$

and

$$d - z = 600 - 570 = 30 < h_f/2$$

so that the stress block must lie within the 180 mm thick flange. Therefore

$$A_s = \frac{M}{0.95 f_y z}$$

$$= \frac{448 \times 10^6}{0.95 \times 460 \times 570} = 1799 \text{ mm}^2$$

Provide two T32 plus one T20 bar, area $= 1924$ mm^2 (bottom steel).

(b) Interior supports – design as a rectangular section

$$M = 0.11FL = 0.11 \times 995 \times 5 = 547 \text{ kN m hogging}$$

$$\frac{M}{bd^2 f_{cu}} = \frac{547 \times 10^6}{300 \times 580^2 \times 30} = 0.18 > 0.156$$

Thus, compression steel is required.

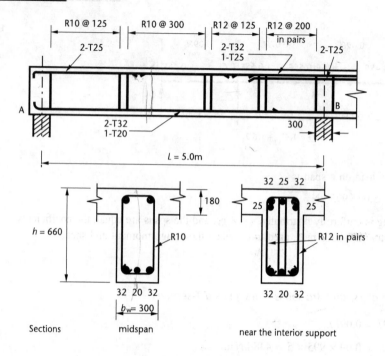

Figure 7.24
End-span reinforcement
details

$$A'_s = \frac{M - 0.156 f_{cu}bd^2}{0.95 f_y(d - d')}$$

$$= \frac{547 \times 10^6 - 0.156 \times 30 \times 300 \times 580^2}{0.95 \times 460(580 - 50)}$$

$$= 322 \text{ mm}^2$$

This area of steel will be provided by extending the span reinforcement beyond the supports.

$$A_s = \frac{0.156 f_{cu}bd^2}{0.95 f_y z} + A'_s$$

$$= \frac{0.156 \times 30 \times 300 \times 580^2}{0.95 \times 460 \times 0.775 \times 580} + 322$$

$$= 2727 \text{ mm}^2$$

Provide two T32 plus three T25 bars, area $= 3080 \text{ mm}^2$ (top steel).

(c) Mid-span of 2nd span – design as a T-section

$$M = 0.07FL$$

$$= 0.07 \times 995 \times 5 = 348 \text{ kN m}$$

Using the lever-arm curve, it is found that $l_a = 0.95$

$$A_s = \frac{M}{0.95 f_y z} = \frac{348 \times 10^6}{0.95 \times 460(0.95 \times 600)}$$

$$= 1397 \text{ mm}^2$$

Provide one T32 plus two T20 bars, area $= 1432 \text{ mm}^2$ (bottom steel).

Shear

(a) Check maximum shear stress

Maximum shear at face of support is

$$V_s = 0.6F - w_u \times \text{support width}/2$$
$$= 0.6 \times 995 - 199 \times 0.15 = 567 \text{ kN}$$
$$\nu = \frac{V_s}{bd} = \frac{567 \times 10^3}{300 \times 580}$$
$$= 3.26 \text{ N/mm}^2 < 0.8\sqrt{f_{cu}}$$

(b) Nominal links

$$\frac{A_{sv}}{s_v} = \frac{0.4b}{0.95 f_{yv}}$$
$$= \frac{0.4 \times 300}{0.95 \times 250} = 0.51$$

Provide R10 links at 300 mm centres, $A_{sv}/s_v = 0.52$

(c) End supports

Shear distance, d, from support face is

$$V_d = 0.45F - w_u(d + \text{support width}/2)$$
$$= 0.45 \times 995 - 199(0.6 + 0.15)$$
$$= 299 \text{ kN}$$
$$\nu = \frac{V_d}{bd} = \frac{299 \times 10^3}{300 \times 600} = 1.66 \text{ N/mm}^2$$
$$\frac{100A_s}{bd} = \frac{100 \times 1924}{300 \times 600} = 1.07$$

Therefore from table 5.1

$$\nu_c = 0.68 \text{ N/mm}^2$$
$$\frac{A_s}{s_v} = \frac{b(\nu - \nu_c)}{0.95 f_{yv}} = \frac{300(1.66 - 0.68)}{0.95 \times 250} = 1.24$$

Provide R10 links at 125 mm centres, $A_{sv}/s_v = 1.26$.

Shear resistance of nominal links + concrete is

$$V_n = \left(\frac{A_{sv}}{s_v} 0.95 f_{yv} + b\nu_c\right) d$$
$$= (0.52 \times 0.95 \times 250 + 300 \times 0.68) 600 = 196 \text{ kN}$$

Shear reinforcement other than the nominal is required over a distance

$$s = \frac{V_d - V_n}{w_u} + d$$
$$= \frac{299 - 196}{199} + 0.6 = 1.1 \text{ m}$$

from the face of the support.

(d) First and third spans interior supports

Distance d from support face

$$V_d = 0.6 \times 995 - 199(0.58 + 0.15)$$
$$= 452 \text{ kN}$$

$$\nu = \frac{452 \times 10^3}{300 \times 580} = 2.60 \text{ N/mm}^2$$

$$\frac{100A_s}{bd} = \frac{100 \times 3080}{300 \times 580} = 1.77$$

therefore from table 5.1

$$\nu_c = 0.81$$

$$\frac{A_{sv}}{s_v} = \frac{300(2.6 - 0.81)}{0.95 \times 250} = 2.26$$

Provide R12 links in pairs at 200 mm centres, $A_{sv}/s_v = 2.26$. Using V_n from part (c) as a conservative value, shear links are required over a distance

$$s = \frac{V_d - V_n}{w_u} + d = \frac{452 - 196}{199} + 0.58 = 1.87 \text{ m}$$

A similar calculation would show that single R12 links at 125 mm centres would be adequate 1.0 m from the support face.

(e) Second span

Distance d from support face

$$V_d = 0.55 \times 995 - 199(0.58 + 0.15) = 402 \text{ kN}$$

Calculations would show that R10 links in pairs at 150 mm centres would be adequate.

7.6 | Cantilever beams and corbels

The moments, shears and deflections for a cantilever beam are substantially greater than those for an equivalently loaded span that is supported at both its ends. Also the moments in a cantilever can never be redistributed to other parts of the structure – the beam must always be capable of resisting the full static moment. Because of these factors and the problems that often occur with increased deflections due to creep, the design and detailing of a cantilever beam should be done with care.

When the loads are uniformly distributed the reinforcement may be arranged as shown in figure 7.25. The provision of additional steel in the compressive zone of the beam can help to restrain the increased deflections caused by creep.

7.6.1 Design of corbels

Short cantilevers such as corbels may be designed as a strut and tie system as illustrated in figure 7.26. In the figure the vertical load N at point B is balanced by the vertical component of the compressive force F_c in the inclined concrete strut BC whilst the tensile force F_t in the steel tie AB maintains horizontal equilibrium.

At least a full
anchorage length

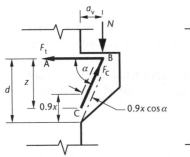

Figure 7.25
Cantilever reinforcement
details

Curtailment of bars

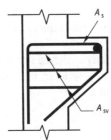

Figure 7.26
Concrete corbel

(a) Strut and Tie System   (b) Reinforcement Details

(a) Tension steel

The force in the concrete strut is given in terms of its stress by

$$F_c = 0.45 f_{cu} b \times 0.9 x \cos \alpha \tag{7.9}$$

where b is the breadth of the corbel.
   x is the depth of the neutral axis as shown in figure 7.26
   α is the angle of inclination of the strut BC.

Resolving vertically at B

$$N = F_c \sin \alpha = (0.45 f_{cu} b \times 0.9 x \cos \alpha) \sin \alpha$$

In this equation the terms $\cos \alpha$ and $\sin \alpha$ can be written in terms of the lever arm z at the root of the corbel as shown in figure 7.26. This results in a quadratic equation in z which can be rearranged and solved to give

$$z = d \left(0.5 + \sqrt{0.25 - (1 + k) k a_v^2 / d^2} \right) / (1 + k) \tag{7.10}$$

where $k = N / 0.9 f_{cu} b a_v$
and a_v is the distance between the load N and the face of the support.

The depth x of the neutral axis is given by

$$x = (d - z) / 0.45$$

Resolving horizontally at B the force F_t in the steel tie is

$$F_t = F_c \cos \alpha = N \cos \alpha / \sin \alpha$$

or $F_t = N \cot \alpha$ (7.11)

The code requires that F_t must not be less than one-half of the vertical load N, and the area of tension steel required is given by

$$A_s = F_t / f_{st}$$

The tension steel will have yielded if $x < 0.615d$ and in this case

$$A_s = F_t / 0.95 f_y$$

If $x > 0.615d$ then the steel will not have yielded and the stress f_{st} in the steel must be determined by considering the compatibility of strains using equations 4.1 and 4.2 in section 4.2.

The tension steel must be fully anchored into the support, and at the front edge of the corbel it should be anchored by welding to a transverse bar of equal strength or by bending the bars back to form a loop.

(b) Shear reinforcement

Shear reinforcement is provided in the form of horizontal links as shown in figure 7.26. The links should be placed in the top two-thirds of the effective depth at the root of the corbel.

The area of shear reinforcement is calculated using the procedures described in chapter 5. As the corbel is loaded close to the support the design concrete shear stress is increased to $2d\nu_c / a_v$. The total area of shear reinforcement required is given by

$$\sum A_{sv} = \frac{a_v b (\nu - 2d\nu_c / a_v)}{0.95 f_{yv}}$$

where

$(\nu - 2d\nu_c / a_v)$ must not be less than 0.4 N/mm^2

Also $\sum A_{sv}$ must not be less than one-half of the area A_s of the main tension reinforcement.

EXAMPLE 7.10

Design of a corbel

Design the reinforcement for the corbel shown in figure 7.27. The corbel has a breadth $b = 300$ mm and supports an ultimate load of $N = 600$ kN at a distance $a_v = 200$ mm from the face of the column. The main tension reinforcement has an effective depth of $d = 550$ mm. The characteristic material strengths are $f_{cu} = 30$ N/mm^2, $f_y = 460$ N/mm^2 and $f_{yv} = 460$ N/mm^2.

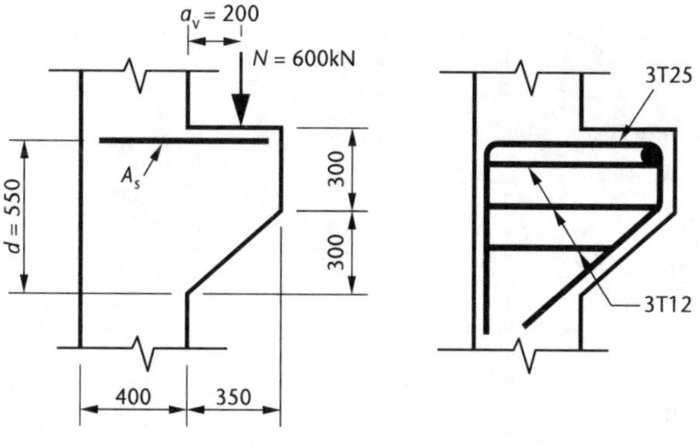

Figure 7.27
Corbel design

(a) Corbel Dimensions   (b) Reinforcement Details

(a) Tension reinforcement

Lever arm $z = d\left(0.5 + \sqrt{0.25 - (1 + k)ka_v^2/d^2}\right)\Big/(1 + k)$

where $k = \dfrac{N}{0.9 f_{cu} ba_v} = \dfrac{600 \times 10^3}{0.9 \times 30 \times 300 \times 200} = 0.37$

Therefore $z = 550\left(0.5 + \sqrt{0.25 - (1 + 0.37) \times 0.37 \times 200^2/550^2}\right)\Big/(1 + 0.37)$

$$= 372 \text{ mm} = 0.68d$$

Depth of neutral axis $x = (d - z)/0.45 = (550 - 372)/0.45$

$$= 396 \text{ mm} = 0.72d$$

As $x/d > 0.615$ the tension steel A_s has not yielded

From the proportions of the strain diagram and equation 4.2

Steel strain $\epsilon_{st} = \epsilon_{cc}\left(\dfrac{d - x}{x}\right) = 0.0035\left(\dfrac{550 - 396}{396}\right)$

$$= 0.00136 < \epsilon_y = 0.00219$$

Steel stress $f_{st} = E_s \epsilon_{st} = 200\,000 \times 0.00136 = 272 \text{ N/mm}^2$

Tensile force $F_t = N \cot \alpha = Na_v/z = 600 \times 220/372$

$$= 355 \text{ kN} > 0.5\,N = 300 \text{ kN}$$

Area of tension steel $A_s = F_t/f_{st} = 355 \times 10^3/272$

$$= 1305 \text{ mm}^2$$

Provide three T25 bars, area $= 1470 \text{ mm}^2$

As a check:

Compressive force $F_c = 0.45 f_{cu} b \times 0.9x \cos \alpha$

where $\alpha = \tan^{-1}(z/a_v) = \tan^{-1}(372/200) = 61.7°$

Therefore

$F_c = 0.45 \times 30 \times 300 \times 0.9 \times 396 \cos 61.7° \times 10^{-3}$

$$= 684 \text{ kN}$$

Resolving vertically

$$F_c \sin \alpha = 684 \times \sin 61.7°$$
$$= 602 \text{ kN} \approx N \quad \text{OK}$$

(b) Shear reinforcement

$$\nu = N/bd = 600 \times 10^3/(300 \times 550)$$
$$= 3.64 \text{ N/mm}^2$$

$$\frac{100A_s}{bd} = \frac{100 \times 1470}{300 \times 550} = 0.89$$

Interpolating from table 5.1, $\nu_c = 0.64 \text{ N/mm}^2$

$$\sum A_{sv} = \frac{a_v b(\nu - 2d\nu_c/a_v)}{0.95 f_{yv}} = \frac{200 \times 300(3.64 - 2 \times 550 \times 0.64/200)}{0.95 \times 460}$$
$$= \frac{200 \times 300 \times 0.12}{0.95 \times 460}$$

Because $0.12 < 0.4$

$$\sum A_{sv} = \frac{200 \times 300 \times 0.4}{0.95 \times 460}$$
$$= 55 \text{ mm}^2 < 0.5A_s$$

Therefore minimum $A_{sv} = 0.5A_s = 0.5 \times 1305 = 653 \text{ mm}^2$
Provide three T12 links $A_{sv} = 679 \text{ mm}^2$ (for two legs) at 150 mm spacing in the top two-thirds of the effective depth.

7.7 Design for torsion

The method for designing a beam to resist torsion is described in the Code of Practice. It consists of calculations to determine an additional area of longitudinal and link reinforcement required to resist the torsional shear forces. The requirements for torsion have also been described in section 5.4. The procedure for a rectangular section is as follows.

1. Determine A_s and A_{sv} to resist the bending moments and shear forces by the usual procedures.

2. Calculate the torsional shear stress

$$\nu_t = \frac{2T}{h_{min}^2(h_{max} - h_{min}/3)}$$

where T = torsional moment due to the ultimate loads
h_{min} = the smaller dimension of the beam section
h_{max} = the larger dimension of the beam section.

3. If $\nu_t > \nu_{t.min}$ in table 7.2, then torsional reinforcement is required. Refer to table 7.3 for the reinforcement requirements with a combination of torsion and shear stress ν.

Table 7.2 Ultimate torsion shear stresses (N/mm²)

	Concrete grade		
	25	30	40 or more
$\nu_{t.min}$	0.33	0.37	0.40
ν_{tu}	4.00	4.38	5.00

Table 7.3 Reinforcement for shear and torsion

	$\nu_t \leq \nu_{t.min}$	$\nu_t > \nu_{t.min}$
$\nu \leq \nu_c + 0.4$	Nominal shear reinforcement, no torsion reinforcement.	Designed torsion reinforcement only, but not less than nominal shear reinforcement
$\nu > \nu_c + 0.4$	Designed shear reinforcement, no torsion reinforcement	Designed shear and torsion reinforcement

4. $\nu + \nu_t$ must not be greater than ν_{tu} in table 7.2 where ν is the shear stress due to the shear force. Also for sections with $y_1 < 550$ mm

$$\nu_t \not> \frac{\nu_{tu}y_1}{550}$$

where y_1 is the larger centre-to-centre dimension of a link.

5. Calculate the additional shear reinforcement required from

$$\frac{A_{sv}}{s_v} = \frac{T}{0.8x_1y_1(0.95f_{yv})}$$

where x_1 is the smaller centre-to-centre dimension of the link. This value of A_{sv}/s_v is added to the value from step 1, and a suitable link size and spacing is chosen, but

$$s_v < 200 \text{ mm or } x_1$$

The links should be of the closed type shown in figure 7.28.

6. Calculate the additional area of longitudinal steel

$$A_s = \frac{A_{sv}}{s_v}\left(\frac{f_{yv}}{f_y}\right)(x_1 + y_1)$$

where A_{sv}/s_v is the value from step 5 and f_y is the characteristic strength of the longitudinal steel. A_s should be distributed evenly around the inside perimeter of the links. At least four corner bars should be used and the clear distance between bars should not exceed 300 mm.

EXAMPLE 7.11

Design of torsional reinforcement

The rectangular section of figure 7.28 resists a bending moment of 170 kN m, a shear of 160 kN and a torsional moment of 10 kN m. The characteristic material strengths are $f_{cu} = 30$ N/mm², $f_y = 460$ N/mm² and $f_{yv} = 250$ N/mm².

Figure 7.28
Torsion example

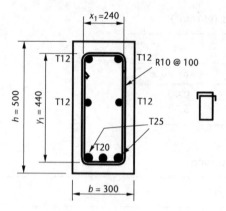

1. Calculations for bending and shear would give

    $$A_s = 1000 \text{ mm}^2$$

    and

    $$\frac{A_{sv}}{s_v} = 0.73$$

2. Torsional shear stress

    $$
    \begin{aligned}
    \nu_t &= \frac{2T}{h_{min}^2(h_{max} - h_{min}/3)} \\
    &= \frac{2 \times 10 \times 10^6}{300^2(500 - 300/3)} \\
    &= 0.56 \text{ N/mm}^2
    \end{aligned}
    $$

3. $0.56 > 0.37$ from table 7.2. Therefore torsional reinforcement is required.

4. ν_{tu} from table 7.2 = 4.38 N/mm²,

    $$
    \begin{aligned}
    \nu &= \frac{V}{bd} \\
    &= \frac{160 \times 10^3}{300 \times 450} = 1.19 \text{ N/mm}^2
    \end{aligned}
    $$

    therefore

    $$\nu + \nu_t = 1.19 + 0.56 = 1.75 \text{ N/mm}^2$$

    and

    $$
    \begin{aligned}
    \frac{\nu_{tu}y_1}{550} &= \frac{4.38 \times 440}{550} \\
    &= 3.5
    \end{aligned}
    $$

    so that $\nu_t < \nu_{tu}y_1/550$ as required.

5. Additional $\dfrac{A_{sv}}{s_v} = \dfrac{T}{0.8x_1y_1(0.95f_{yv})}$

    $$
    \begin{aligned}
    &= \frac{10.0 \times 10^6}{0.8 \times 240 \times 440 \times 0.95 \times 250} \\
    &= 0.50
    \end{aligned}
    $$

therefore

$$\text{Total } \frac{A_{sv}}{s_v} = 0.73 + 0.50 = 1.23$$

Provide R10 links at 100 mm centres

$$\frac{A_{sv}}{s_v} = 1.57$$

The links are of the closed type with their ends fully anchored.

6. Additional longitudinal steel

$$A_s = \left(\frac{A_{sv}}{s_v}\right)\left(\frac{f_{yv}}{f_y}\right)(x_1 + y_1)$$

$$= 0.50 \times \frac{250}{460}(240 + 440) = 185 \text{ mm}^2$$

therefore

total steel area $= 1000 + 185 = 1185 \text{ mm}^2$

Provide the longitudinal steel shown in figure 7.28.

7. The torsional reinforcement should extend at least h_{max} beyond where it is required to resist the torsion.

Design of reinforced concrete slabs

8.1 Simplified analysis

BS 8110 permits the use of a simplified load arrangement for all slabs of maximum ultimate design load throughout all spans or panels provided that the following conditions are met:

(a) In a one-way slab, the area of each bay $\not< 30$ m^2 (see figure 8.1).

(b) Live load $q_k \not> 1.25$ Dead load g_k

(c) Live load $q_k \not> 5$ kN/m^2 excluding partitions.

If analysis is based on this single load case, all support moments (except at a cantilever) should be reduced by 20 per cent and span moments increased accordingly. No further redistribution is then permitted, but special attention must be given to cases where a span or panel is adjacent to a cantilever of significant length. In this situation the condition where the cantilever is fully loaded and the span unloaded must be examined to determine possible hogging moments in the span.

Tabulated bending moment and shear force coefficients for use with approximately equal spans and when these conditions are satisfied are given in section 8.5.2 for one-way spanning slabs.

8.2 Shear in slabs

The shear resistance of a solid slab may be calculated by the procedures given in chapter 5. Experimental work has indicated that, compared with beams, shallow slabs fail at slightly higher shear stresses and this is incorporated into the values of design ultimate shear stress ν_c given in table 5.1.

The shear stress at a section in a solid slab is given by

$$\nu = \frac{V}{bd}$$

where V is the shear force due to the ultimate load, d is the effective depth of the slab and b is the width of section considered. Calculations are usually based on a strip of slab 1 m wide.

The code requires that for a solid slab

1. $\nu \not> $ the lesser of $0.8\sqrt{f_{cu}}$ or 5 N/mm^2.

2. $\nu \not> \nu_c$ for a slab thickness less than 200 mm.

3. If $\nu > \nu_c$, shear reinforcement must be provided in slabs more than 200 mm thick.

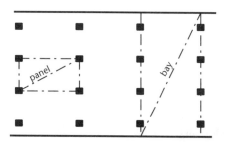

Figure 8.1
Slab definitions

If shear reinforcement is required, then nominal steel, as for beams, should be provided when $\nu < (\nu_c + 0.4)$ and 'designed' reinforcement provided for higher values of ν. Since shear stresses in slabs due to distributed loads are generally small, shear reinforcement will seldom be required for such loads. Localised 'punching' actions due to heavy concentrated loads may, however, cause more critical conditions as shown in the following sections. Practical difficulties concerned with bending and fixing of shear reinforcement lead to the recommendation that it should not be used in slabs which are less than 200 mm deep.

8.2.1 Punching shear – analysis

A concentrated load (N) on a slab causes shearing stresses on a section around the load; this effect is referred to as punching shear. The initial critical section for shear is shown in figure 8.2 and the shearing stress is given by

$$\nu = \frac{N}{\text{Perimeter of the section } \times d} = \frac{N}{(2a + 2b + 12d)d}$$

where a and b are the plan dimensions of the concentrated load. No shear reinforcement is required if the punching shear stress, $\nu < \nu_c$. The value of ν_c in table 5.1 depends on the percentage of reinforcement $100A_s/bd$ which should be calculated as an average of the area of tensile reinforcement in the two directions and should include all the reinforcement crossing the critical section and extending a further distance equal to at least d on either side.

Checks must also be undertaken to ensure that the stress ν calculated for the perimeter at the face of the loaded area is less than the smaller of $0.8\sqrt{f_{cu}}$ or 5 N/mm².

Figure 8.2
Punching shear

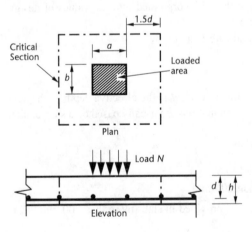

EXAMPLE 8.1

Punching shear

A slab 175 mm thick, $d = 145$ mm, is constructed with grade 30 concrete and is reinforced with 12 mm bars at 150 mm centres one way and 10 mm bars at 200 mm centres in the other direction. Determine the maximum load that can be carried on an area, 300×400 mm, without exceeding the ultimate shear stress.

For 12 mm bars at 150 mm centres

$$\frac{110A_s}{bd} = \frac{100 \times 754}{1000 \times 145} = 0.52$$

and for 10 mm bars at 200 mm centres

$$\frac{100A_s}{bd} = \frac{100 \times 393}{1000 \times 145} = 0.27$$

Average $\quad \dfrac{100A_s}{bd} = 0.395$

From table 5.1, $\nu_c = 0.62$ N/mm^2 for grade 30 concrete

$$\text{Punching shear perimeter} = (2a + 2b + 12d)$$
$$= 600 + 800 + 12 \times 145 = 3140 \text{ mm}$$
$$\text{Maximum load} = \nu_c \times \text{perimeter} \times d$$
$$= 0.62 \times 3140 \times 145$$
$$= 282 \times 10^3 \text{ N}$$

At the face of the loaded area, the shear stress

$$\nu = \frac{N}{(2a + 2b)d}$$
$$= \frac{282 \times 10^3}{(600 + 800)145}$$
$$= 1.39 \text{ N/mm}^2$$

which is less than $0.8\sqrt{f_{cu}}$ and 5 N/mm^2.

8.2.2 Punching shear – reinforcement design

If reinforcement is required for the initial critical section shown in figure 8.2, this steel should be located within the failure zone lying between the face of the loaded area and the perimeter checked. The amount of reinforcement required is given by

$$\sum A_{sv} \sin \alpha \geq \frac{(\nu - \nu_c)ud}{0.95 f_{yv}} \quad \text{where} \quad \nu \leq 1.6\nu_c$$

or $\quad \displaystyle\sum A_{sv} \sin \alpha \geq \frac{5(0.7\nu - \nu_c)ud}{0.95 f_{yv}} \quad \text{where} \quad 1.6\nu_c < \nu \leq 2\nu_c$

in either case

$$\sum A_{sv} \sin \alpha > \frac{0.4ud}{0.95 f_{yv}}$$

where $\quad \alpha = $ angle between shear reinforcement and the plane of the slab
$\qquad u = $ length of the outer perimeter of the zone.

The reinforcement should be distributed evenly around the zone on at least two perimeters not greater than $0.75d$ apart and with the first perimeter containing not less than 40 per cent of A_{sv}, located approximately $0.5d$ from the face of the loaded area as shown in figure 8.3. The spacing of shear reinforcement around a perimeter should not

Figure 8.3
Provision of shear
reinforcement

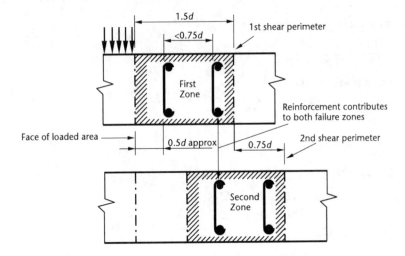

Figure 8.3
Provision of shear
reinforcement

exceed $1.5d$. It will then be necessary to check a second perimeter taken a distance $0.75d$ further away from the face of the load than the initial critical section, as shown in figure 8.4. The failure zone associated with this perimeter is $1.5d$ wide and shear reinforcement within the zone which has been provided to reinforce previous zones may be included when designing reinforcement for the zone. The design procedure continues by checking successive zones until a perimeter is obtained which does not require reinforcing.

Similar procedures must be applied to the regions of flat slabs which are close to supporting columns, but allowances must be made for the effects of moment transfer from the columns as described in section 8.7.

EXAMPLE 8.2

Design of punching shear reinforcement

A 260 mm thick slab of grade 30 concrete is reinforced by 12 mm high-yield bars at 200 mm centres in each direction. The slab is subject to a mild environment and must be able to support a localised concentrated load of 650 kN over a square area of 300 mm side. Determine the shear reinforcement required for $f_{yv} = 250$ N/mm^2.

For mild exposure, nominal cover required by grade 30 concrete is 25 mm, thus average effective depth allowing for 8 mm links is equal to

$$260 - (25 + 8 + 12) = 215 \text{ mm}$$

Figure 8.4
Punching shear reinforcement zone

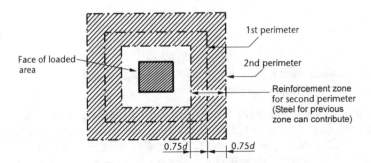

(a) Check shear stress at face of loaded area

Perimeter $u = 4 \times 300 = 1200$ mm

thus $v = \dfrac{V}{ud} = \dfrac{650 \times 10^3}{1200 \times 215}$

$\qquad\qquad = 2.52$ N/mm^2

which is less than $0.8\sqrt{f_{cu}}$ and 5 N/mm^2.

(b) Check first critical shear perimeter at 1.5d from load face

Perimeter side $= 300 + 2 \times 1.5 \times 215 = 945$ mm

and perimeter $u = 4 \times 945 = 3780$ mm.

Shear stress $v = \dfrac{V}{ud} = \dfrac{650 \times 10^3}{3780 \times 215} = 0.80$ N/mm^2

$\dfrac{100A_s}{bd} = \dfrac{100 \times 566}{1000 \times 215} = 0.26$

From table 5.1 $v_c = 0.50$ for grade 30 concrete. As $v_c > v \leq 1.6v_c$, shear reinforcement is required and for vertical links

$A_{sv} = \dfrac{(v - v_c)ud}{0.95f_{yv}}$

$(v - v_c) = 0.3$ N/mm^2 is less than the minimum 0.4 N/mm^2 required, thus take $(v - v_c) = 0.4$ and

$A_{sv} = \dfrac{0.4 \times 3780 \times 215}{0.95 \times 250}$

$\qquad = 1369$ mm^2

Total number of 8 mm links required $= \dfrac{A_{sv}}{2\pi\Phi^2/4}$

$\qquad\qquad\qquad\qquad\qquad\qquad = \dfrac{1369}{2 \times 50.3} = 14$

The links must be distributed evenly between two perimeters within the failure zone. The spacing between the legs of the links must not be greater than $1.5d = 1.5 \times 215 \approx 320$ mm.

Position the links on two perimeters 110 mm and 270 mm from the face of the load. The lengths of these perimeters are

$\qquad\qquad u_1 = 4 \times 520 = 2080$ mm

and $\qquad u_2 = 4 \times 840 = 3360$ mm

Number of links on perimeter, $u_1 = 14 \times \dfrac{2080}{(2080 + 3360)} = 6$

Number of links on perimeter, $u_2 = 14 - 6 = 8$

Spacing of legs of the links $= (2080 + 3360)/(2 \times 14)$

$\qquad\qquad\qquad\qquad\qquad \approx 200$ mm $< 1.5d = 322$ mm

(c) Check second shear perimeter at $(1.5 + 0.75)d$ from load face

Perimeter side $= 300 + 2 \times 2.25 \times 215 = 1268$ mm

and perimeter $u = 4 \times 1268 = 5072$ mm

Thus $\nu = \dfrac{V}{ud} = \dfrac{650 \times 10^3}{5072 \times 215} = 0.60$ N/mm^2

As $\nu_c < \nu \leq 1.6\nu_c$, nominal reinforcement is still required within the failure zone associated with the second perimeter.

$$A_{sv} = \frac{0.4 \times 5072 \times 215}{0.95 \times 250} = 1837 \text{ mm}^2$$

for 8mm links $\dfrac{1837}{2 \times 50.3} = 19$ are required

In part (b), on the perimeter at 270 mm from the load face 8 links are already provided, thus at least 11 further links are required. These could be provided at 430 mm from the load face by similar links at approximately 200 mm centres.

(d) Check third shear perimeter at $(1.5 + 1.5)d$ from the load face

Perimeter side $= 300 + 2 \times 3 \times 215 = 1590$ mm

and perimeter $u = 4 \times 1590 = 6360$ mm

Thus $\nu = \dfrac{V}{ud} = \dfrac{650 \times 10^3}{6360 \times 215} = 0.48$ N/mm^2

As this is less than ν_c no further reinforcement is required. It should be noted, however, that wherever links are required, top steel must also be provided in the slab at 200 mm centres to ensure proper fixing and anchorage of the shear links.

8.3 Span–effective depth ratios

Excessive deflections of slab will cause damage to the ceiling, floor finishes and other architectural details. To avoid this, limits are set on the span–depth ratios. These limits are exactly the same as those for beams as described in section 6.2. As a slab is usually a slender member the restrictions on the span–depth ratio become more important and this can often control the depth of slab required. In terms of the span–effective depth ratio the depth of the slab is given by

$$\text{minimum effective depth} = \frac{\text{span}}{\text{basic ratio} \times \text{modification factors}}$$

The modification factor is based on the area of tension steel in the shorter span when a slab is singly reinforced at mid-span but if a slab has both top and bottom steel at mid-span the modification factors for the areas of tension and compression steel, as given in tables 6.7 and 6.8, are used. For convenience, the factors for tension steel have been plotted in the form of a graph in figure 8.5.

It can be seen from the figure that a lower service stress gives a higher modification factor and hence a smaller depth of slab would be required. The service stress may be reduced by providing an area of tension reinforcement greater than that required to resist

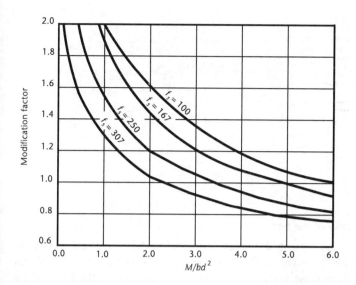

Figure 8.5
Modification factors for span–effective depth ratio

the design moment, or alternatively mild steel reinforcement with its lower service stress may be used.

The span–depth ratios may be checked using the service stress appropriate to the characteristic stress of the reinforcement, as given in table 6.7. Thus a service stress of 307 N/mm^2 would be used when f_y is 460 N/mm^2. However, if a more accurate assessment of the limiting span–depth ratio is required the service stress f_s can be calculated from

$$f_s = \frac{2}{3} f_y \frac{A_{s.req}}{A_{s.prov}} \times \frac{1}{\beta_b}$$

where $A_{s.req}$ = the area of reinforcement required at mid-span
      $A_{s.prov}$ = the area of reinforcement provided at mid-span
      β_b = the ratio of the mid-span moments after and before any redistribution.

The second part of example 8.3 illustrates the calculations to determine the service stress, and how the provision of extra reinforcement reduces the depth of slab required.

8.4 | Reinforcement details

To resist cracking of the concrete, codes of practice specify details such as the minimum area of reinforcement required in a section and limits to the maximum and minimum spacing of bars. Some of these rules are as follows:

(a) Minimum areas of reinforcement

$$\text{minimum area} = \frac{0.13bh}{100} \text{ for high yield steel}$$

or

$$= \frac{0.24bh}{100} \text{ for mild steel}$$

in both directions.

Figure 8.6
Anchorage at simple supports
for a slab

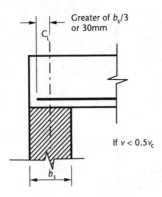

(b) Maximum spacing of the bars

These requirements are described in detail in section 6.1.3 and are similar to beams except that for thin slabs, or if the tensile steel percentage is small, spacings may be increased from those given in table 6.4 to a maximum of the lesser of $3d$ or 750 mm.

(c) Reinforcement in the flange of a T- or L-beam

When the slab forms the flange of a T- or L-beam the area of reinforcement in the flange and at right angles to the beam should not be less than 0.15 per cent of the longitudinal cross-section of the flange.

(d) Curtailment and anchorage of reinforcement

The general rules for curtailment of bars in a flexural member were discussed in section 7.2.5. Simplified rules for curtailment in different types of slabs are illustrated in the subsequent sections of this chapter. At a simply supported end the bars should be anchored as specified in figure 7.14 or figure 8.6.

8.5 | Solid slabs spanning in one direction

The slabs are designed as if they consist of a series of beams of 1 m breadth. The main steel is in the direction of the span and secondary or distribution steel is required in the transverse direction. The main steel should form the outer layer of reinforcement to give it the maximum lever arm.

The calculations for bending reinforcement follow a similar procedure to that used in beam design. The lever-arm curve of figure 7.5 is used to determine the lever arm (z) and the area of tension reinforcement is then given by

$$A_s = \frac{M_u}{0.95 f_y z}$$

For solid slabs spanning one way the simplified rules for curtailing bars as shown in figure 8.7 may be used provided the loads are substantially uniformly distributed. With a continuous slab it is also necessary that the spans are approximately equal and the simplified single load case analysis has been used.

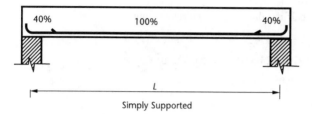

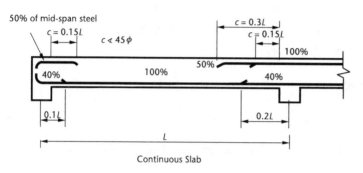

Figure 8.7
Simplified rules for curtailment of bars in slab spanning in one direction

8.5.1 Single-span solid slab

The effective span of the slab is taken as the lesser of: (a) the centre-to-centre distance of the bearings, or (b) the clear distance between supports plus the effective depth of the slab. The basic span–effective depth ratio for this type of slab is 20:1.

EXAMPLE 8.3

Design of a simply supported slab

The slab shown in figure 8.8 is to be designed to carry a live load of 3.0 kN/m^2, plus floor finishes and ceiling loads of 1.0 kN/m^2. The characteristic material strengths are $f_{cu} = 30$ N/mm^2 and $f_y = 460$ N/mm^2. Basic span-effective depth ratio = 20

$$\text{minimum effective depth } d = \frac{\text{span}}{20 \times \text{modification factor (m.f.)}}$$

$$= \frac{4500}{20 \times \text{m.f.}} = \frac{225}{\text{m.f.}}$$

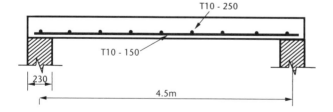

Figure 8.8
Simply supported slab example

1. *Solution using high-yield reinforcement*

Estimating the modification factor to be of the order of 1.3 for a lightly reinforced slab. Try effective depth $d = 180$ mm. For a mild exposure the cover = 25 mm.

Allowing, say, 5 mm as half the diameter of the reinforcing bar

overall depth of slab $h = 180 + 25 + 5 = 210$ mm

self-weight of slab $= 210 \times 24 \times 10^{-3} = 5.0$ kN/m^2

total dead load $= 1.0 + 5.0 = 6.0$ kN/m^2

For a 1 m width of slab

$$\text{ultimate load} = (1.4g_k + 1.6q_k)4.5$$
$$= (1.4 \times 6.0 + 1.6 \times 3.0)4.5 = 59.4 \text{ kN}$$

$M = 59.4 \times 4.5/8 = 33.4$ kN m

Span–effective depth ratio

$$\frac{M}{bd^2} = \frac{33.4 \times 10^6}{1000 \times 180^2} = 1.03$$

From table 6.7, for $f_s = 307$ N/mm^2 the span–effective depth modification factor $= 1.29$. Therefore

$$\text{limiting} \ \frac{\text{span}}{\text{effective depth}} = 20 \times 1.29 = 25.8$$

$$\text{actual} \ \frac{\text{span}}{\text{effective depth}} = \frac{4500}{180} = 25.0$$

Thus $d = 180$ mm is adequate.

Bending reinforcement

$$\frac{M}{bd^2 f_{cu}} = \frac{33.4 \times 10^6}{1000 \times 180^2 \times 30} = 0.034$$

From the lever arm curve of figure 7.5, $l_a = 0.95$. Therefore

lever arm $z = l_a d = 0.95 \times 180 = 171$ mm

$$A_s = \frac{M}{0.95 f_y z} = \frac{33.4 \times 10^6}{0.95 \times 460 \times 171}$$
$$= 447 \text{ mm}^2/\text{m}$$

Provide T10 bars at 150 mm centres, $A_s = 523$ mm^2/m.

Shear

At the face of the support

$$\text{Shear } V = \frac{59.4}{2} \left(\frac{2.25 - 0.5 \times 0.23}{2.25} \right) = 28.2 \text{ kN}$$

$$\text{Shear stress, } v = \frac{V}{bd} = \frac{28.2 \times 10^3}{1000 \times 180} = 0.16 \text{ N/mm}^2 < 0.8\sqrt{f_{cu}}$$

$$\frac{100A_s}{bd} = \frac{100 \times 523}{1000 \times 180} = 0.29$$

from table 5.1 $v_c = 0.51$ N/mm^2 and since at distance d from the support $v < v_c$ no further shear checks or reinforcement are required.

End anchorage (figure 8.6)

$$\nu = 0.16 < \nu_c/2$$

therefore

$$\text{anchorage length} \geq 30 \text{ mm} \quad \text{or} \quad \frac{\text{end bearing}}{3}$$

$$\text{end bearing} = 230 \text{ mm}$$

therefore

$$\text{anchorage length} = \frac{230}{3}$$

$$= 77 \text{ mm}$$

beyond the centre line of the support.

Distribution Steel

$$\text{Area of transverse high-yield reinforcement} = \frac{0.13bh}{100}$$

$$= \frac{0.13 \times 1000 \times 210}{100}$$

$$= 273 \text{ mm}^2/\text{m}$$

Provide T10 at 250 mm centres, $A_s = 314 \text{ mm}^2/\text{m}$.

2. Solution using mild steel reinforcement

The second part of this example illustrates how a smaller depth of slab is adequate provided it is reinforced so that there is a low service stress in the steel and therefore a high modification factor for the span–effective depth ratio. Try a thickness of slab, $h = 170$ mm and $d = 140$ mm.

$$\text{Self-weight of slab} = 0.17 \times 24 = 4.08 \text{ kN/m}^2$$

$$\text{total dead load} = 5.08 \text{ kN/m}^2$$

$$\text{ultimate load} = (1.4g_k + 1.6q_k)4.5$$

$$= (1.4 \times 5.08 + 1.6 \times 3.0)4.5$$

$$= 53.6 \text{ kN}$$

Bending

$$M = 53.6 \times \frac{4.5}{8} = 30.2 \text{ kN m}$$

$$\frac{M}{bd^2 f_{cu}} = \frac{30.2 \times 10^6}{1000 \times 140^2 \times 30} = 0.051$$

From the lever-arm curve, figure 7.5, $l_a = 0.94$. Therefore using mild steel bars

$$A_s = \frac{M}{0.95 f_y z} = \frac{30.2 \times 10^6}{0.95 \times 250 \times 0.94 \times 140}$$

$$= 966 \text{ mm}^2/\text{m}$$

Provide R12 at 100 mm centres, $A_s = 1130 \text{ mm}^2/\text{m}$.

Span–effective depth ratio

$$\frac{M}{bd^2} = \frac{30.2 \times 10^6}{1000 \times 140^2}$$

$$= 1.54$$

Service stress f_s is given by the equation of section 8.3 as

$$f_s = \frac{2}{3}f_y \times \frac{A_{s.req}}{A_{s.prov}} \times \frac{1}{\beta_b}$$

$$= \frac{2}{3} \times 250 \times \frac{966}{1130} \times 1$$

$$= 142 \text{ N/mm}^2$$

From figure 8.5, for $M/bd^2 = 1.54$, span–effective depth modification factor $= 1.69$. Therefore

$$\text{limiting } \frac{\text{span}}{\text{effective depth}} = 20 \times 1.69 = 33.8$$

$$\text{actual } \frac{\text{span}}{\text{effective depth}} = \frac{4500}{140} = 32.1$$

Therefore $d = 140$ mm is adequate.

8.5.2 Continuous solid slab spanning in one direction

For a continuous slab, bottom reinforcement is required within the span and top reinforcement over the supports. The effective span is the distance between the centre lines of supports and the basic span–effective depth ratio is 26:1.

If the conditions of section 8.1 are met for the single load case analysis, bending moment and shear force coefficients as shown in table 8.1 may be used.

The coefficients in the table include an allowance for a 20 per cent reduction in support moments due to the effects of moment redistribution.

Table 8.1 Ultimate bending moment and shear force coefficients in one-way spanning slabs

| | End support/slab connection | | | | | | |
| | Simple | | Continuous | | | | |
	At outer support	Near middle of end span	At outer support	Near middle of end span	At first interior support	Middle interior spans	Interior supports
Moment	0	0.086*Fl*	−0.04*Fl*	0.075*Fl*	−0.086*Fl*	0.063*Fl*	−0.063*Fl*
Shear	0.4*F*	—	0.46*F*	—	0.6*F*	—	0.5*F*

Note: F is the total design ultimate load $(1.4G_k + 1.6Q_k)$; *l* is the effective span.

EXAMPLE 8.4

Design of a continuous solid slab

The four-span slab shown in figure 8.9 supports a live load of 3.0 kN/m², plus floor finishes and a ceiling load of 1.0 kN/m². The characteristic material strengths are $f_{cu} = 30$ N/mm² and $f_y = 460$ N/mm².

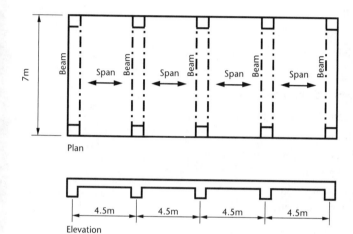

Figure 8.9
Continuous slab

Basic span – effective depth ratio = 26

$$\frac{\text{span}}{26} = \frac{4500}{26} = 173 \text{ mm}$$

Try effective depth $d = 140$ mm, and with a mild exposure overall depth, $h = 170$ mm.

$$\text{self-weight of slab} = 170 \times 24 \times 10^{-3}$$
$$= 4.08 \text{ kN/m}^2$$
$$\text{total dead weight} = 1.0 + 4.08$$
$$= 5.08 \text{ kN/m}^2$$
$$\text{ultimate load } F \text{ per span} = (1.4g_k + 1.6q_k)4.5$$
$$= (1.4 \times 5.08 + 1.6 \times 3.0)4.5$$
$$= 53.6 \text{ kN per metre width}$$

Bending

Since the bay size > 30m², the spans are equal and $q_k \not> 1.25g_k$ the moment coefficients shown in table 8.1 may be used. Thus, assuming that the end support is simply supported, from table 8.1 for the first span:

$$M = 0.086FL = 0.086 \times 53.6 \times 4.5 = 20.8 \text{ kN m}$$

Span–effective depth ratio

$$\frac{M}{bd^2} = \frac{20.8 \times 10^6}{1000 \times 140^2}$$
$$= 1.06$$

From table 6.7, span–depth modification factor $= 1.28$. Therefore

$$\text{limiting } \frac{\text{span}}{\text{effective depth}} = 26 \times 1.28 = 33.3$$

$$\text{actual } \frac{\text{span}}{\text{effective depth}} = \frac{4500}{140} = 32.1$$

Thus $d = 140$ mm is adequate.

Bending reinforcement

$$\frac{M}{bd^2 f_{cu}} = \frac{20.8 \times 10^6}{1000 \times 140^2 \times 30}$$

$$= 0.035$$

From the lever-arm curve, figure 7.5, $l_a = 0.95$. Therefore

$$\text{lever arm } z = l_a d = 0.95 \times 140 = 133 \text{ mm}$$

$$A_s = \frac{M}{0.95 f_y z}$$

$$= \frac{20.8 \times 10^6}{0.95 \times 460 \times 133}$$

$$= 357 \text{ mm}^2 \text{ per metre}$$

Provide T10 at 200 mm centres, $A_s = 393$ mm^2/m.

Similar calculations for the supports and the interior span give the steel areas shown in figure 8.10.

Over the interior support beams $100 A_s / b h_f > 0.15$ for the reinforcement provided and therefore extra steel is not required for the flange of the T-beam.

At the end supports there is a monolithic connection between the slab and the beam, therefore top steel should be provided to resist any negative moment. The area of this steel should not be less than half the area of steel at mid-span. In fact to provide the 0.15 per cent of steel for the flange of the L-beam, T10 bars at 300 mm centres have been specified.

The layout of the reinforcement in figure 8.10 is according to the simplified rules for the curtailment of bars in slabs as illustrated in figure 8.7.

$$\text{Transverse reinforcement} = \frac{0.13 bh}{100}$$

$$= \frac{0.13 \times 1000 \times 170}{100}$$

$$= 221 \text{ mm}^2\text{/m}$$

Provide T10 at 350 mm centres top and bottom, wherever there is main reinforcement.

Figure 8.10
Reinforcement in continuous slab

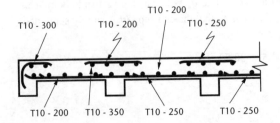

8.6 | Solid slabs spanning in two directions

When a slab is supported on all four of its sides it effectively spans in both directions, and it is sometimes more economical to design the slab on this basis. The amount of bending in each direction will depend on the ratio of the two spans and the conditions of restraint at each support.

If the slab is square and the restraints are similar along the four sides then the load will span equally in both directions. If the slab is rectangular then more than one-half of the load will be carried in the stiffer, shorter direction and less in the longer direction. If one span is much longer than the other, a large proportion of the load will be carried in the short direction and the slab may as well be designed as spanning in only one direction.

Moments in each direction of span are generally calculated using coefficients which are tabulated in the codes of practice. Areas of reinforcement to resist the moments are determined independently for each direction of span. The slab is reinforced with bars in both directions parallel to the spans with the steel for the shorter span placed furthest from the neutral axis to give it greater effective depth.

The span–effective depth ratios are based on the shorter span and the percentage of reinforcement in that direction.

With a uniformly distributed load the loads on the supporting beams may generally be apportioned as shown in figure 8.11.

8.6.1 Simply supported slab spanning in two directions

A slab simply supported on its four sides will deflect about both axes under load and the corners will tend to lift and curl up from the supports, causing torsional moments. When no provision has been made to prevent this lifting or to resist the torsion then the moment coefficients of table 8.2 may be used and the maximum moments are given by

$$m_{sx} = \alpha_{sx} n l_x^2 \quad \text{in direction of span } l_x$$

and

$$m_{sy} = \alpha_{sy} n l_x^2 \quad \text{in direction of span } l_y$$

where m_{sx} and m_{sy} are the moments at mid-span on strips of unit width with spans l_x and l_y respectively, and

$n = (1.4g_k + 1.6q_k)$, that is, the total ultimate load per unit area

l_y = the length of the longer side

l_x = the length of the shorter side

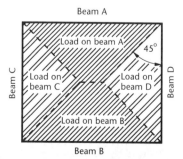

Figure 8.11
Loads carried by supporting beams

Table 8.2 Bending-moment coefficients for slabs spanning in two directions at right angles, simply supported on four sides

l_y/l_x	1.0	1.1	1.2	1.3	1.4	1.5	1.75	2.0
α_{sx}	0.062	0.074	0.084	0.093	0.099	0.104	0.113	0.118
α_{sy}	0.062	0.061	0.059	0.055	0.051	0.046	0.037	0.029

The area of reinforcement in directions l_x and l_y respectively are

$$A_{sx} = \frac{m_{sx}}{0.95 f_y z} \quad \text{per metre width}$$

and

$$A_{sy} = \frac{m_{sy}}{0.95 f_y z} \quad \text{per metre width}$$

The slab should be reinforced uniformly across the full width, in each direction.

The effective depth d used in calculating A_{sy} should be less than that for A_{sx} because of the different depths of the two layers of reinforcement.

At least 40 per cent of the mid-span reinforcement should extend to the supports and the remaining 60 per cent should extend to within $0.1l_x$ or $0.1l_y$ of the appropriate support.

EXAMPLE 8.5

Design the reinforcement for a simply supported slab 220 mm thick and spanning in two directions

The effective span in each direction is 4.5 m and 6.3 m and the slab supports a live load of 10 kN/m². The characteristic material strengths are $f_{cu} = 30$ N/mm² and $f_y = 460$ N/mm².

$$l_y/l_x = 6.3/4.5 = 1.4$$

From table 8.2, $\alpha_{sx} = 0.099$ and $\alpha_{sy} = 0.051$.

$$\text{Self-weight of slab} = 220 \times 24 \times 10^{-3} = 5.3 \text{ kN/m}^2$$

$$\text{ultimate load } n = 1.4 g_k + 1.6 q_k$$

$$= 1.4 \times 5.3 + 1.6 \times 10.0 = 23.4 \text{ kN/m}^2$$

Bending – short span

With mild exposure conditions take $d = 185$ mm.

$$m_{sx} = \alpha_{sx} n l_x^{\,2} = 0.099 \times 23.4 \times 4.5^2$$

$$= 46.9 \text{ kN m}$$

$$\frac{m_{sx}}{bd^2 f_{cu}} = \frac{46.9 \times 10^6}{1000 \times 185^2 \times 30} = 0.046$$

From the lever-arm curve, figure 7.5, $l_a = 0.95$. Therefore

lever arm $z = 0.95 \times 185 = 176$ mm

and

$$A_s = \frac{m_{sx}}{0.95 f_y z} = \frac{46.9 \times 10^6}{0.95 \times 460 \times 176}$$
$$= 610 \text{ mm}^2/\text{m}$$

Provide T12 at 175 mm centres, $A_S = 646 \text{ mm}^2/\text{m}$.

Span–effective depth ratio

$$\frac{m_{sx}}{bd^2} = \frac{46.9 \times 10^6}{1000 \times 185^2} = 1.37$$

$$\text{Service stress } f_s = \frac{2}{3} f_y \frac{A_{s.req}}{A_{s.prov}} = \frac{2}{3} \times 460 \times \frac{610}{646} = 290 \text{ N/mm}^2$$

From table 6.7 the modification factor $= 1.23$.

$$\text{limiting } \frac{\text{span}}{\text{effective depth}} = 20 \times 1.23 = 24.6$$

$$\text{actual } \frac{\text{span}}{\text{effective depth}} = \frac{4500}{185} = 24.3$$

Thus $d = 185$ mm is adequate.

Bending – long span

$$m_{sy} = \alpha_{sy} n l_x^2 = 0.051 \times 23.4 \times 4.5^2$$
$$= 24.2 \text{ kN m}$$

Since the reinforcement for this span will have a reduced effective depth, take $z = 176 - 12 = 164$ mm. Therefore

$$A_s = \frac{m_{sy}}{0.95 f_y z} = \frac{24.2 \times 10^6}{0.95 \times 460 \times 164} = 338 \text{ mm}^2/\text{m}$$

Provide T10 at 200 mm centres, $A_s = 393 \text{ mm}^2/\text{m}$

$$\frac{100 A_s}{bh} = \frac{100 \times 393}{1000 \times 220} = 0.18$$

which is greater than 0.13, the minimum for transverse steel.

The arrangement of the reinforcement is shown in figure 8.12.

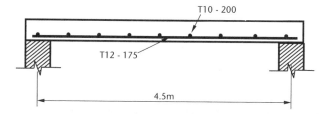

T10 - 200

T12 - 175

4.5m

Figure 8.12
Simply supported slab
spanning in two directions

8.6.2 Restrained slab spanning in two directions

When the slabs have fixity at the supports and reinforcement is added to resist torsion and to prevent the corners of the slab from lifting then the maximum moments per unit width are given by

$$m_{sx} = \beta_{sx} n l_x^2 \text{ in direction of span } l_x$$

and

$$m_{sy} = \beta_{sy} n l_x^2 \text{ in direction of span } l_y$$

where β_{sx} and β_{sy} are the moment coefficients given in table 3.14 of BS 8110 for the specified end conditions, and $n = (1.4g_k + 1.6q_k)$, the total ultimate load per unit area.

The slab is divided into middle and edge strips as shown in figure 8.13 and reinforcement is required in the middle strips to resist m_{sx} and m_{sy}. The arrangement this reinforcement should take is illustrated in figure 8.7. In the edge strips only nominal reinforcement is necessary, such that $100A_s/bh = 0.13$ for high-yield steel or 0.24 for mild steel.

In addition, torsion reinforcement is provided at discontinuous corners and it should

1. consist of top and bottom mats, each having bars in both directions of span

2. extend from the edges a minimum distance $l_x/5$

3. at a corner where the slab is discontinuous in both directions have an area of steel in each of the four layers equal to three-quarters of the area required for the maximum mid-span moment

4. at a corner where the slab is discontinuous in one direction only, have an area of torsion reinforcement only half of that specified in rule 3.

Torsion reinforcement is not, however, necessary at any corner where the slab is continuous in both directions.

Where $l_y/l_x > 2$, the slabs should be designed as spanning in one direction only.

Shear force coefficients are also given in BS 8110 for cases where torsion corner reinforcement is provided, and these are based on a simplified distribution of load to supporting beams which may be used in preference to the distribution shown in figure 8.11.

Figure 8.13
Division of slabs into middle and edge strips

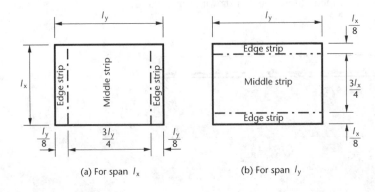

(a) For span l_x (b) For span l_y

EXAMPLE 8.6

Moments in a continuous two-way slab

The panel considered is an edge panel, as shown in figure 8.14 and the uniformly distributed load, $n = (1.4g_k + 1.6q_k) = 10 \text{ kN/m}^2$.

The moment coefficients are taken from case 3 of table 3.14 of BS 8110.

$$\frac{l_y}{l_x} = \frac{6.0}{5.0} = 1.2$$

Positive moments at mid-span

$$m_{sx} = \beta_{sx}nl_x^2 = 0.042 \times 10 \times 5^2$$
$$= 10.5 \text{ kN m in direction } l_x$$
$$m_{sy} = \beta_{sy}nl_x^2 = 0.028 \times 10 \times 5^2$$
$$= 7.0 \text{ kN m in direction } l_y$$

Negative moments

Support ad, $m_x = 0.056 \times 10 \times 5^2 = 14 \text{ kN m}$

Supports ab and dc, $m_y = 0.037 \times 10 \times 5^2 = 9.3 \text{ kN m}$

The moments calculated are for a metre width of slab.

The design of reinforcement to resist these moments would follow the usual procedure. Torsion reinforcement, according to rule 4 is required at corners b and c. A check would also be required on the span–effective depth ratio of the slab.

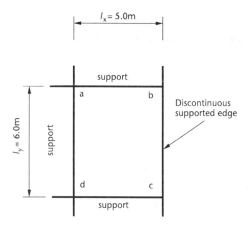

Figure 8.14
Continuous panel spanning in two directions

8.7 | Flat slab floors

A flat slab floor is a reinforced concrete slab supported directly by concrete columns without the use of intermediary beams. The slab may be of constant thickness throughout or in the area of the column it may be thickened as a drop panel. The column may also be of constant section or it may be flared to form a column head or capital. These various forms of construction are illustrated in figure 8.15.

Figure 8.15
Drop panels and column
heads

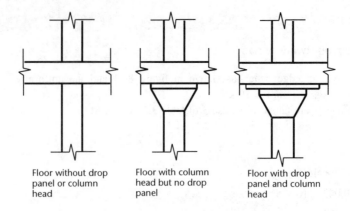

Floor without drop
panel or column
head

Floor with column
head but no drop
panel

Floor with drop
panel and column
head

The drop panels are effective in reducing the shearing stresses where the column is liable to punch through the slab, and they also provide an increased moment of resistance where the negative moments are greatest.

The flat slab floor has many advantages over the beam and slab floor. The simplified formwork and the reduced storey heights make it more economical. Windows can extend up to the underside of the slab, and there are no beams to obstruct the light and the circulation of air. The absence of sharp corners gives greater fire resistance as there is less danger of the concrete spalling and exposing the reinforcement. Deflection requirements will generally govern slab thicknesses which should not be less than 125 mm.

The analysis of a flat slab structure may be carried out by dividing the structure into a series of equivalent frames. The moments in these frames may be determined by

(a) a method of frame analysis such as moment distribution, or the stiffness method on a computer

or (b) a simplified method using the moment and shear coefficients of table 8.1 subject to the following requirements:

(i) the lateral stability is not dependent on the slab-column connections

(ii) the conditions for using the single load case described in section 8.1 are satisfied

(iii) there are at least three rows of panels of approximately equal span in the direction being considered

(iv) the moments at the supports as given in table 8.1 may be reduced by $0.15Fh_c$ where F is the total ultimate load on the slab $(1.4g_k + 1.6q_k)$ and h_c is the effective diameter of a column or column head.

Interior panels of the flat slab should be divided as shown in figure 8.16 into column and middle strips. Drop panels should be ignored if their smaller dimension is less than the one-third of the smaller panel dimension l_x. If a panel is not square, strip widths in both directions are based on l_x.

Moments determined from a structural analysis or the coefficients of table 8.1 are distributed between the strips as shown in table 8.3.

Reinforcement designed to resist these slab moments may be detailed according to the simplified rules for slabs, and satisfying normal spacing limits. This should be

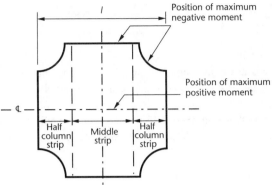

Figure 8.16
Flat slab divided into strips

Position of maximum negative moment

Position of maximum positive moment

Half column strip

Middle strip

Half column strip

Width of half column strip = $l/4$ with no drops
or = half drop width when drops are used

spread across the respective strip, but steel to resist negative moments in column strips should have two-thirds of the area located in the central half strip width. If the column strip is narrower because of drops, the moments resisted by the column and middle strips should be adjusted proportionally as illustrated in example 8.7.

Column moments can be calculated from the analysis of the equivalent frame.

Particular care is needed over the transfer of moments to edge columns. This is to ensure that there is adequate moment capacity within the slab adjacent to the column since moments will only be able to be transferred to the edge column by a strip of slab considerably narrower than the normal internal panel column strip width.

The reinforcement for a flat slab should be arranged according to the rules illustrated in figure 8.7.

An important feature in the design of the slabs are the calculations for punching shear at the head of the columns and at the change in depth of the slab, if drop panels are used. The design for shear should take the procedure described in the previous section on punching shear except that BS 8110 requires that the design shear force be increased above the calculated value by 15 per cent for internal columns and up to 40 per cent for edge columns to allow for the effects of moment transfer. If spans are not approximately equal, reference should be made to BS 8110. In this respect it can be advantageous to use mild steel in the design, as the resulting higher percentages of reinforcement will allow a correspondingly higher ultimate concrete shear stress.

The usual span–effective depth ratios may be used if the slabs have drop panels of widths at least equal to one-third of the respective span, otherwise the ratios should be multiplied by a factor of 0.9.

Reference should be made to codes of practice for further detailed information describing the requirements for the analysis and design of flat slabs.

Table 8.3   Division of moments between strips

	Column strip	Middle strip
Negative moment	75%	25%
Positive moment	55%	45%

EXAMPLE 8.7

Design of a flat slab

Design a flat slab that has columns at 6.5 m centres in each direction and supports an imposed load of 4 kN/m^2. The characteristic material strengths are $f_{cu} = 30$ N/mm^2 and $f_y = 460$ N/mm^2 for the reinforcement.

It is decided to use a floor slab as shown in figure 8.17 with 250 mm overall depth of slab, and drop panels 2.5 m square by 100 mm deep. The column heads are to be made 1.4 m diameter.

Figure 8.17
Flat slab example

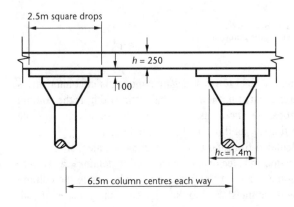

Permanent load

$$\text{Weight of slab} = 0.25 \times 24 \times 6.5^2 \quad = 253.5 \text{ kN}$$
$$\text{Weight of drop} = 0.1 \times 24 \times 2.5^2 \quad = 15.0 \text{ kN}$$
$$\text{Total} \quad = 268.5 \text{ kN}$$

Imposed load

$$\text{Total} = 4 \times 6.5^2 = 169.0 \text{ kN}$$

Therefore

$$\text{ultimate load on the floor, } F = 1.4 \times 268.5 + 1.6 \times 169.0$$
$$= 646 \text{ kN per panel}$$

and equivalent distributed load, $n = \dfrac{646}{6.5^2} = 15.3$ kN/m^2

The effective span, $L = 6.5$ m.

A concrete cover of 25 mm has been allowed, and where there are two equal layers of reinforcement the effective depth has been taken as the mean depth of the two layers in calculating the reinforcement areas.

The drop dimension is greater than one-third of the panel dimension, therefore the column strip is taken as the width of the drop panel (2.5 m).

Since the live load is less than 1.25 of the dead load, and is not greater than 5kN/m^2 the single load case may be used. From tables 8.1 and 8.3:

Bending reinforcement

1. Centre of interior span

Positive moment $= 0.063Fl$

$$= 0.063 \times 646 \times 6.5 = 265 \text{ kN m}$$

The width of the middle strip is $(6.5 - 2.5) = 4$ m which is greater than half the panel dimension. Therefore the proportion of this moment taken by the middle strip, using the coefficients given in table 8.3, is given by

$$0.45 \times \frac{4}{6.5/2} = 0.55$$

Thus middle strip positive moment $= 0.55 \times 265 = 146$ kN m.

The column strip positive moment $= (1 - 0.55) \times 265 = 119$ kN m.

(a) For the middle strip

$$\frac{M}{bd^2 f_{cu}} = \frac{146 \times 10^6}{4000 \times 205^2 \times 30} = 0.029$$

From the lever-arm curve (figure 7.5), $l_a = 0.95$, therefore

$$A_s = \frac{M}{0.95 f_y l_a d}$$

$$= \frac{146 \times 10^6}{0.95 \times 460 \times 0.95 \times 205} = 1716 \text{ mm}^2 \text{ bottom steel}$$

Thus provide sixteen T12 bars $(A_s = 1810 \text{ mm}^2)$ each way in the span, distributed evenly across the 4 m width of the middle strip [spacing $= 250$ m $< 3d$ $(= 615$ mm$)$].

(b) The column strip moments will require $1716 \times 119/146 = 1399 \text{ mm}^2$ bottom steel which can be provided as thirteen T12 bars $(A_s = 1470 \text{ mm}^2)$ in the span distributed evenly at 200 mm centres across the 2.5 m width of the column strip.

2. Interior support

Negative moment $= -0.063Fl$

$$= -0.063 \times 646 \times 6.5 = -265 \text{ kN m}$$

This moment may be reduced by $0.15Fh_c = 0.15 \times 646 \times 1.4 = 136$ kN m.

Hence the net negative moment $= 265 - 136 = 129$ kN m

and this is also divided into

$$\text{middle strip} = 0.25 \times \frac{4 \times 129}{6.5/2} = 0.31 \times 129 = 40 \text{ kN m}$$

and   column strip $= 0.69 \times 129 = 89$ kN m

(a) For the middle strip

$$A_s = \frac{M}{0.95 f_y l_a d} = \frac{40 \times 10^6}{0.95 \times 460 \times 0.95 \times 205} = 470 \text{ mm}^2$$

Provide eight evenly spaced T12 bars as top steel at 500 mm centres $(A_s = 905 \text{ mm}^2)$. Note that more reinforcement than necessary for strength criteria has been provided to ensure that the bar spacing does not exceed $3\times$ the slab effective depth.

Figure 8.18
Details of bending
reinforcement

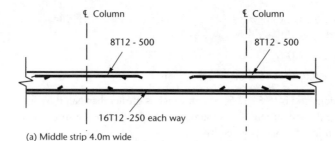

(a) Middle strip 4.0m wide

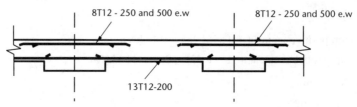

(b) Column strip 2.5m wide

(b) For the column strip

$$A_s = \frac{M}{0.95 f_y l_a d} = \frac{89 \times 10^6}{0.95 \times 460 \times 0.95 \times 305} = 703 \text{ mm}^2$$

Provide eight T12 bars as top steel ($A_s = 905$ mm^2). Six of these bars should be placed at approximately 250 mm centres within the centre half of the column strip. The bending reinforcement requirements are summarised in figure 8.18.

Punching shear

1. At the column head

Perimeter $u = \pi \times$ diameter of column head

$$= \pi \times 1400 = 4398 \text{ mm}$$

Shear force $V = F - \frac{\pi}{4} 1.4^2 n = 646 - \frac{\pi}{4} 1.4^2 \times 15.3$

$$= 622 \text{ kN}$$

To allow for the effects of moment transfer, V is increased by 15 per cent thus

$$\nu = \frac{1.15V}{ud} = \frac{1.15 \times 622 \times 10^3}{4398 \times 305} = 0.53 \text{ N/mm}^2$$

which is less than $0.8\sqrt{f_{cu}}$ and 5 N/mm^2.

2. The critical section for shear is 1.5 × effective depth = 1.5 × 305 = 458 mm from the column face, thus the length of the perimeter $u = 4(1400 + 2 \times 458) = 9264$ mm.

Ultimate shear force $= 646 - (1.4 + 2 \times 0.458)^2 \times 15.3 = 564$ kN

thus shear stress

$$\nu = \frac{1.15 \times 564 \times 10^3}{9264 \times 305} = 0.23 \text{ N/mm}^2$$

By inspection of table 5.1, $\nu < \nu_c$, therefore the section is adequate in punching shear.

3. At the dropped panel the critical section is $2.5 + 2 \times 1.5 \times 0.205 = 3.115$ m square with a perimeter $u = 4 \times 3115 = 12\,460$ mm.

Calculated shear $V = 646 - 3.115^2 \times 15.3 = 498$ kN

thus shear stress

$$v = \frac{1.15 \times 498 \times 10^3}{12460 \times 205} = 0.22 \text{ N/mm}^2$$

which is also less than v_c thus the section is adequate in punching shear.

Span–effective depth ratios

At the centre of the span

$$\frac{M}{bd^2} = \frac{146 \times 10^6}{4000 \times 205^2} = 0.87$$

From table 6.7, for a service stress $f_s = 307$ N/mm^2 the modification factor is 1.35. Therefore

$$\text{limiting } \frac{\text{span}}{\text{effective depth}} = 26 \times 1.35 = 35.1$$

$$\text{actual } \frac{\text{span}}{\text{effective depth}} = \frac{6500}{205} = 31.7$$

Hence the slab effective depth is acceptable. To take care of stability requirements, extra reinforcement may be necessary in the column strips to act as a tie between each pair of columns – see section 6.7.

8.8   Ribbed, waffle and hollow block floors

Typical ribbed, waffle and hollow block floor slabs are shown in figure 8.19. Ribbed slabs, which are two-way spanning and are constructed with ribs in both directions of span, as shown in figure 8.19(b), are termed *waffle slabs*. Ribbed floors are formed using temporary or permanent shuttering systems while the hollow block floor is generally constructed with blocks made of clay tile or with concrete containing a light-weight aggregate. If the blocks are suitably manufactured and have an adequate strength they can be considered to contribute to the strength of the slab in the design calculations, but in many designs no such allowance is made.

The principal advantage of these floors is the reduction in weight achieved by removing part of the concrete below the neutral axis and, in the case of the hollow block floor, replacing it with a lighter form of construction. Ribbed and hollow block floors are economical for buildings where there are long spans, over about 5 m, and light or moderate live loads, such as in hospital wards or apartment buildings. They would not be suitable for structures having a heavy loading, such as warehouses and garages.

Near to the supports the hollow blocks are stopped off and the slab is made solid. This is done to achieve a greater shear strength, and if the slab is supported by a monolithic concrete beam the solid section acts as the flange of a T-section. The ribs should be checked for shear at their junction with the solid slab. It is good practice to stagger the joints of the hollow blocks in adjacent rows so that, as they are stopped off, there is no

Figure 8.19
Ribbed, waffle slab and hollow
block floors

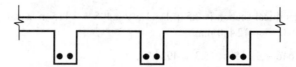

(a) Section through a ribbed floor

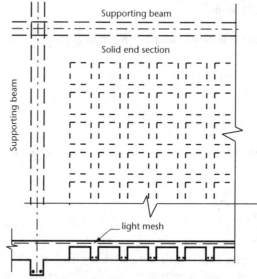

(b) Partial plan of and section through a waffle slab

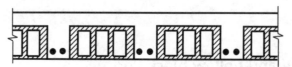

(c) Section through a hollow block floor

abrupt change in cross-section extending across the slab. The slabs are usually made solid under partitions and concentrated loads.

During construction the hollow tiles should be well soaked in water prior to placing the concrete, otherwise shrinkage cracking of the top concrete flange is liable to occur.

The thickness of the concrete flange or topping should not be less than

1. 30 mm for slabs with permanent blocks which are capable of contributing to the structural strength as specified in BS 8110, and where there is a clear distance between ribs of not more than 500 mm

2. 25 mm when the blocks described in (1) are jointed with a cement–sand mortar

3. 40 mm or one-tenth of the clear distance between ribs, whichever is the greater, for all other slabs with permanent blocks.

4. 50 mm or one-tenth of the clear distance between ribs, whichever is the greater, for slabs without permanent blocks.

The rib width will be governed by cover, bar spacing and fire resistance (section 6.1).

With *in situ* construction, the ribs should be spaced no further apart than 1.5 m and their depth below the flange should not be greater than four times their width.

The shear stress is calculated as

$$\nu = \frac{V}{b_w d}$$

where b_w is the breadth of the rib. If hollow blocks are used this breadth may be increased by the wall thickness of the block on one side of the rib. When ν exceeds ν_c shear reinforcement is required, and ν must be less than $0.8\sqrt{f_{cu}}$ and 5 N/mm^2.

Span–effective depth ratios are limited to the values for a flanged beam based on the shorter span but the web width used in determining the ratio from table 6.6 may include the thickness of the two adjacent block-walls.

At least 50 per cent of the total tensile reinforcement in the span should continue to the supports and be anchored. In some instances the slabs are supported by steel beams and are designed as simply supported even though the topping may be continuous. Reinforcement should be provided over the supports to prevent cracking in these cases. It is recommended that the area of this top steel should not be less than one-quarter of the area of steel required in the middle of the span and it should extend at least 0.15 of the clear span into the adjoining spans.

A light reinforcing mesh in the topping flange can give added strength and durability to the slab, particularly if there are concentrated or moving loads, or if cracking due to shrinkage or thermal movements is likely. An area of 0.12 per cent of the topping flange is recommended.

Waffle slabs are designed as ribbed slabs and their design moments in each direction are obtained from the moment coefficients which are tabulated in BS 8110 for two-way spanning slabs.

EXAMPLE 8.8

Design of a ribbed floor

The ribbed floor is constructed with permanent fibreglass moulds; it is continuous over several equal spans of 5.0 m. The characteristic material strengths are $f_{cu} = 30$ N/mm^2 and $f_y = 460$ N/mm^2.

An effective section as shown in figure 8.20 is to be tried. The characteristic dead load including self-weight and finishes is 4.5 kN/m^2 and the characteristic live load is 2.5 kN/m^2.

The calculations are for an interior span for which the moments and shears can be determined by using the coefficients in table 8.1. Considering a 0.4 m width of floor as supported by each rib

$$\text{Ultimate load} = 0.4(1.4g_k + 1.6q_k)$$

$$= 0.4(1.4 \times 4.5 + 1.6 \times 2.5)$$

$$= 4.12 \text{ kN/m}$$

ultimate load on the span $F = 4.12 \times 5.0 = 20.6$ kN

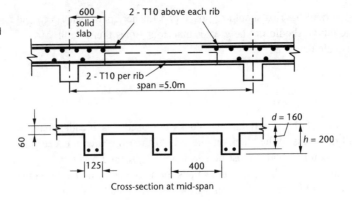

Figure 8.20
Ribbed slab (examples 8.8 and 8.9)

Cross-section at mid-span

Bending

1. At mid-span: design as a T-section

$$M = 0.063FL = 0.063 \times 20.6 \times 5.0 = 6.49 \text{ kN m}$$

$$\frac{M}{bd^2 f_{cu}} = \frac{6.49 \times 10^6}{400 \times 160^2 \times 30} = 0.021$$

From the lever-arm curve, figure 7.5, $l_a = 0.95$. Thus the neutral axis lies within the flange and

$$A_s = \frac{M}{0.95 f_y z} = \frac{6.49 \times 10^6}{0.95 \times 460 \times 0.95 \times 160}$$

$$= 98 \text{ mm}^2$$

Provide two T10 bars in the ribs, $A_s = 157 \text{ mm}^2$.

2. At a support: design as a rectangular section for the solid slab

$$M = 0.063FL = 0.063 \times 20.6 \times 5.0 = 6.49 \text{ kN m as in 1}$$

and

$$A_s = 98 \text{ mm}^2 \text{ as at mid-span}$$

Provide two T10 bars in each 0.4 m width of slab, $A_s = 157 \text{ mm}^2$.

3. At the section where the ribs terminate: this occurs 0.6 m from the centre line of the support and the moment may be hogging so that the 125 mm ribs must provide the concrete area required to develop the design moment. The maximum moment of resistance of the concrete ribs is

$$M_u = 0.156 f_{cu} bd^2 = 0.156 \times 30 \times 125 \times 160^2 \times 10^{-6}$$

$$= 15.0 \text{ kN m}$$

which must be greater than the moment at this section, therefore compression steel is not required.

Span–effective depth ratio

At mid-span $\quad M/bd^2 = \dfrac{6.49 \times 10^6}{400 \times 160^2} = 0.63$

and $\qquad f_s = \dfrac{2}{3} f_y \dfrac{A_{s.req}}{A_{s.prov}} = \dfrac{2}{3} \times 460 \times \dfrac{98}{157} = 191 \text{ N/mm}^2$

From table 6.7, with $f_s = 191$ N/mm^2, the modification factor $= 1.98$. For a T-section with web width $0.31\times$ flange width the basic ratio is 20.8 from table 6.6.

limiting $\dfrac{\text{span}}{\text{effective depth}} = 20.8 \times 1.98 = 41.2$

actual $\dfrac{\text{span}}{\text{effective depth}} = \dfrac{5000}{160} = 31.3$

Thus $d = 160$ mm is adequate.

Shear

Maximum shear in the rib 0.6 m from the support centre line

$= 0.5F - 0.6 \times 4.12 = 0.5 \times 20.6 - 2.5 = 7.8$ kN

Therefore

shear stress $= \dfrac{V}{bd} = \dfrac{7800}{125 \times 160} = 0.39$ N/mm^2

$\dfrac{100A_s}{bd} = \dfrac{100 \times 157}{125 \times 160} = 0.79$

From table 5.1, $\nu_c = 0.79$ N/mm^2; therefore the section is adequate in shear, and since $\nu < \nu_c$ no links are required provided that the bars in the ribs are securely located during construction.

EXAMPLE 8.9

Design of a waffle slab

Design a waffle slab for an internal panel of a floor system, each panel spanning 6.0 m in each direction. The characteristic material strengths are $f_{cu} = 30$ N/mm^2 and $f_y = 460$ N/mm^2. The section as used in example 8.8, figure 8.20 is to be tried with characteristic dead load including self-weight of 6.0 kN/m^2 and characteristic live load of 2.5 kN/m^2

Design ultimate load $= (1.4g_k + 1.6q_k)$

$= (1.4 \times 6.0) + (1.6 \times 2.5) = 12.4$ kN/m^2

As the slab has the same span in each direction the moment coefficients, β_{sx}, are taken from case 1 of table 3.14 of BS 8110 with $l_x/l_y = 1.0$. Calculations are given for a single 0.4 m wide beam section and in both directions of span. Hence:

Bending

1. At mid-span: design as a T section.

Positive moment at mid-span $= m_{sx} = \beta_{sx}nl_x{}^2$

$= 0.024 \times 12.4 \times 6^2 = 10.72$ kN m/m

Moment carried by each rib $= 0.4 \times 10.72 = 4.29$ kN m

$\dfrac{M}{bd^2f_{cu}} = \dfrac{4.29 \times 10^6}{400 \times 160^2 \times 30} = 0.014$

From the lever-arm curve, figure 7.5, $l_a = 0.95$. Thus the neutral axis lies within the flange and

$$A_s = \frac{M}{0.95 f_y z} = \frac{4.29 \times 10^6}{0.95 \times 460 \times 0.95 \times 160} = 65 \text{ mm}^2$$

Provide two T10 bars in each rib at the bottom of the beam, $A_s = 157 \text{ mm}^2$. Note that although one T10 bar would be adequate, two have been provided to reduce the service stress in the steel. This will lead to a higher modification factor in the span–effective depth ratio calculations thus ensuring that the span–effective depth ratio of the slab is kept within acceptable limits.

2. At a support: design as a rectangular section for the solid slab.

$$\text{Negative moment at support } m_{sx} = \beta_{sx} n l_x^2 = 0.031 \times 12.4 \times 6^2$$
$$= 13.84 \text{ kN m/m}$$

Moment carried by each 0.4 m width $= 0.4 \times 13.84 = 5.54$ kN m

$$\frac{M}{bd^2 f_{cu}} = \frac{5.54 \times 10^6}{400 \times 160^2 \times 30} = 0.018$$

From the lever-arm curve, figure 7.5, $l_a = 0.95$. Thus

$$A_s = \frac{M}{0.95 f_y z} = \frac{5.54 \times 10^6}{0.95 \times 460 \times 0.95 \times 160} = 83 \text{ mm}^2$$

Provide two T10 bars in each 0.4 m width of slab, $A_s = 157 \text{ mm}^2$.

3. At the section where the ribs terminate: the maximum hogging moment of resistance of the concrete ribs is 15.0 kN m, as in the previous example. This is greater than the moment at this section, therefore compression steel is not required.

Span–effective depth ratio

At mid-span $\dfrac{M}{bd^2} = \dfrac{4.29 \times 10^6}{400 \times 160^2} = 0.42$ and

$$f_s = \frac{2}{3} f_y \frac{A_{s.req}}{A_{s.prov}} = \frac{2}{3} \times 460 \times \frac{65}{157} = 127 \text{ N/mm}^2$$

and from table 6.7 with $f_s = 127 \text{ N/mm}^2$, the modification factor $= 2.00$. For a T-section with web width $0.31\times$ flange width the basic ratio is 20.8 from table 6.6

$$\text{limiting } \frac{\text{span}}{\text{effective depth}} = 20.8 \times 2.0 = 41.6$$

$$\text{actual } \frac{\text{span}}{\text{effective depth}} = \frac{6000}{160} = 37.5$$

Thus $d = 160$ mm is adequate.

Shear

From table 3.15 of BS 8110 the shear force coefficient for a continuous edge support is 0.33. Hence, for one rib, the shear at the support

$$V_{sx} = \beta_{vx} n l_x \times b = 0.33 \times 12.4 \times 6 \times 0.4 = 9.82 \text{ kN}$$

Maximum shear in the rib 0.6 m from the centre-line is

$$V = 9.82 - 0.6 \times 12.4 \times 0.4 = 6.8 \text{ kN}$$

Therefore

$$\text{shear stress} = \frac{V}{bd} = \frac{6800}{125 \times 160} = 0.34$$

$$\frac{100A_s}{bd} = \frac{100 \times 157}{125 \times 160} = 0.79$$

From table 5.1, $\nu_c = 0.78$ N/mm^2 ; therefore the section is adequate in shear, and since $\nu < \nu_c$ no links are required provided that the bars in the ribs are securely located during construction.

Reinforcement in the topping flange

Light reinforcing mesh should be provided in the top of the flange.

$$\text{Area required} = 0.12 \times b \times h/100 = 0.12 \times 1000 \times 60/100 = 72 \text{ mm}^2/\text{m}$$

Provided D98 mesh (see table A5), $A_s = 98$ mm^2/m.

8.9 Stair slabs

The usual form of stairs can be classified into two types: (1) those spanning horizontally in the transverse direction, and (2) those spanning longitudinally.

8.9.1 Stairs spanning horizontally

Stairs of this type may be supported on both sides or they can be cantilevered from a supporting wall.

Figure 8.21 shows a stair supported on one side by a wall and on the other by a stringer beam. Each step is usually designed as having a breadth b and an effective depth of $d = D/2$ as shown in the figure; a more rigorous analysis of the section is rarely justified. Distribution steel in the longitudinal direction is placed above the main reinforcement.

Details of a cantilevered stair are shown in figure 8.22. The effective depth of the member is taken as the mean effective depth of the section and the main reinforcement must be placed in the top of the stairs and anchored into the support. A light mesh of reinforcement is placed in the bottom face to resist shrinkage cracking.

8.9.2 Stair slab spanning longitudinally

The stair slab may span into landings which span at right angles to the stairs as in figure 8.23 or it may span between supporting beams as in figure 8.24 of the example.

The dead load is calculated along the slope length of the stairs but the live load is based on the plan area. Loads common to two spans which intersect at right angles and surround an open well may be assumed to be divided equally between the spans. The effective span (l) is measured horizontally between the centres of the supports and the thickness of the waist (h) is taken as the slab thickness. Span–effective depth ratios may be increased by 15 per cent provided that the stair flight occupies at least 60 per cent of the span.

Figure 8.21
Stairs spanning horizontally

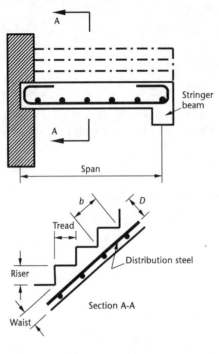

Figure 8.22
Cantilever stairs

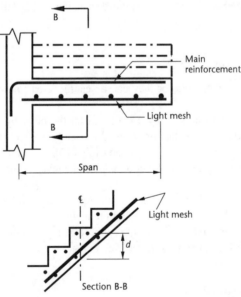

Stair slabs which are continuous and constructed monolithically with their supporting slabs or beams can be designed for a bending moment of say $Fl/10$, where F is the total ultimate load. But in many instances the stairs are precast or constructed after the main structure, pockets with dowels being left in the supporting beams to receive the stairs, and with no appreciable end restraint the design moment should be $Fl/8$.

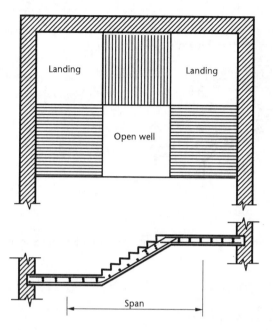

Figure 8.23
Stairs spanning into landings

Landing		Landing
	Open well	

Span

EXAMPLE 8.10

Design of a stair slab

The stairs are of the type shown in figure 8.24 spanning longitudinally and set into pockets in the two supporting beams. The effective span is 3 m and the rise of the stairs is 1.5 m, with 260 mm treads and 150 mm risers. The live load is 3.0 kN/m^2 and the characteristic material strengths are $f_{cu} = 30$ N/mm^2 and $f_y = 250$ N/mm^2.

Try a 125 mm thick waist, effective depth, $d = 90$ mm.

Slope length of stairs $= \sqrt{(3^2 + 1.5^2)} = 3.35$ m

Considering a 1 m width of stairs

$$\text{weight of waist plus steps} = (0.125 \times 3.35 + 0.26 \times 1.5/2)24$$
$$= 14.7 \text{ kN}$$
$$\text{Live load} = 3.0 \times 3 = 9.0 \text{ kN}$$
$$\text{Ultimate load } F = 1.4 \times 14.7 + 1.6 \times 9.0 = 35.0 \text{ kN}$$

With no effective end restraint

$$M = \frac{Fl}{8} = \frac{35.0 \times 3.0}{8}$$
$$= 13.1 \text{ kN m}$$

Check span to effective depth ratio:

$$\frac{M}{bd^2} = \frac{13.1 \times 10^6}{1000 \times 90^2} = 1.62$$

for simply supported span, basic ratio from table 6.6 = 20 and modification factor from table 6.7 for a service stress of 167 N/mm^2 is 1.58.

Figure 8.24
Stairs supported by beams

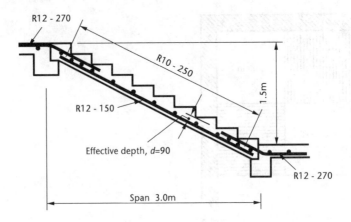

Since the stair flight occupies more than 60 per cent of the span, a further increase of 15 per cent is permitted, thus

$$\text{limiting } \frac{\text{span}}{\text{effective depth}} = 20 \times 1.58 \times 1.15 = 36.3$$

$$\text{actual } \frac{\text{span}}{\text{effective depth}} = \frac{3000}{90} = 33.3$$

$$\frac{M}{bd^2 f_{cu}} = \frac{13.1 \times 10^6}{1000 \times 90^2 \times 30} = 0.054$$

Therefore from the lever-arm curve of figure 7.5, $l_a = 0.93$

$$A_s = \frac{M}{0.95 f_y l_a d}$$
$$= \frac{13.1 \times 10^6}{0.95 \times 250 \times 0.93 \times 90}$$
$$= 659 \text{ mm}^2/\text{m}$$

Provide R12 bars at 150 mm centres, area 754 mm²/m.

$$\text{Transverse distribution steel} = \frac{0.24 bh}{100} = \frac{0.24 \times 1000 \times 125}{100}$$
$$= 300 \text{ mm}^2/\text{m}$$

Provide R10 bars at 250 mm centres, area = 314 mm²/m.

Continuity bars at the top and bottom of the span should be provided and about 50 per cent of the main steel would be reasonable, while satisfying maximum spacing limits of $3d = 270$ mm.

8.10 Yield line and strip methods

For cases which are more complex as a result of shape, support conditions, the presence of openings, or loading conditions it may be worth while adopting an ultimate analysis method. The two principal approaches are the yield line method, which is particularly suitable for slabs with a complex shape or concentrated loading, and the strip method which is valuable where the slab contains openings.

These methods have been the subject of research, and are well documented although they are of a relatively specialised nature. A brief introduction is included here to illustrate the general principles and features of the methods, which are particularly valuable in assisting an understanding of failure mechanisms.

8.10.1 Yield line method

The capacity of reinforced concrete to sustain plastic deformation has been described in section 3.4. For an under-reinforced section the capacity to develop curvatures between the first yield of reinforcement and failure due to crushing of concrete is considerable. For a slab which is subjected to increasing load, cracking and reinforcement yield will first occur in the most highly stressed zone. This will then act as a plastic hinge as subsequent loads are distributed to other regions of the slab. Cracks will develop to form a pattern of 'yield lines' until a mechanism is formed and collapse is indicated by increasing deflections under constant load.

It is assumed that a pattern of yield lines can be superimposed on the slab, which will cause a collapse mechanism, and that the regions between yield lines remain rigid and uncracked. Figure 8.25 shows the yield line mechanism which will occur for the simple case of a fixed ended slab spanning in one direction with a uniform load. Rotation along the yield lines will occur at a constant moment equal to the ultimate moment of resistance of the section, and will absorb energy. This can be equated to the energy expended by the applied load undergoing a compatible displacement and is known as the virtual work method.

Considerable care must be taken over the selection of likely yield line patterns, since the method will give an 'upper bound' solution, that is, either a correct or unsafe solution. Yield lines will form at right angles to bending moments which have reached the ultimate moment of resistance of the slab, and the following rules may be helpful.

1. Yield lines are usually straight and end at a slab boundary.
2. Yield lines will lie along axes of rotation, or pass through their points of intersection.
3. Axes of rotation lie along supported edges, pass over columns or cut unsupported edges.

In simple cases the alternative patterns to be considered will be readily determined on the basis of common sense, while for more complex cases differential calculus may be

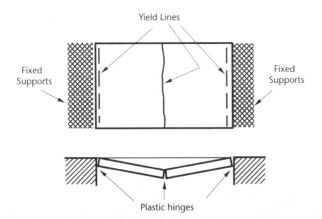

Yield Lines

Fixed
Supports

Fixed
Supports

Plastic hinges

Figure 8.25
Development of yield lines

Figure 8.26
Examples of yield-line patterns

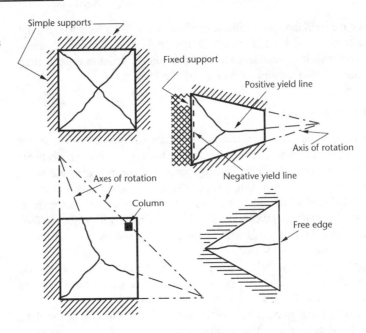

used. The danger of missing the critical layout of yield lines, and thus obtaining an incorrect solution, means that the method can only be used with confidence by experienced designers.

A number of typical patterns are shown in figure 8.26.

A yield line caused by a sagging moment is generally referred to as a 'positive' yield line and represented by a full line, while a hogging moment causing cracking on the top surface of the slab causes a 'negative' yield line shown by a broken line.

The basic approach of the method is illustrated for the simple case of a one-way spanning slab in example 8.11.

EXAMPLE 8.11

Simply supported, one-way spanning rectangular slab

The slab shown in figure 8.27 is subject to a uniformly distributed load w per unit area. Longitudinal reinforcement is provided as indicated giving a uniform ultimate moment of resistance m per unit width.

The maximum moment will occur at midspan and a positive yield line can thus be superimposed as shown. If this is considered to be subject to a small displacement Δ, then

external work done = area × load × average distance moved for each rigid

half of the slab

$$= \left(\alpha L \times \frac{L}{2} \right) \times w \times \frac{\Delta}{2}$$

therefore

$$\text{total} = \frac{1}{2} \alpha L^2 w \Delta$$

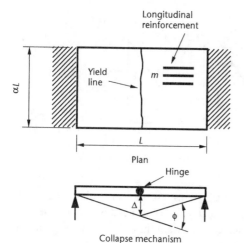

Figure 8.27
One-way spanning slab

Internal energy absorbed by rotation along the yield line is

$$\text{moment} \times \text{rotation} \times \text{length} = m\phi\alpha L$$

where

$$\phi \approx 2\left(\frac{\Delta}{0.5L}\right) = \frac{4\Delta}{L}$$

hence   internal energy $= 4m\alpha\Delta$

Thus equating internal energy absorbed with external work done

$$4m\alpha\Delta = \frac{1}{2}\alpha L^2 w\Delta$$

or

$$m = \frac{wL^2}{8} \quad \text{as anticipated}$$

Since the displacement Δ is eliminated, this will generally be set to unity in calculations of this type.

In the simple case of example 8.11 the yield line crossed the reinforcement at right angles and transverse steel was not involved in bending calculations. Generally, a yield line will lie at an angle θ to the orthogonal to the main reinforcement and will thus also cross transverse steel. The ultimate moment of resistance developed is not easy to define, but Johansen's stepped yield criteria is the most popular approach. This assumes that an inclined yield line consists of a number of steps, each orthogonal to a reinforcing bar as shown in figure 8.28.

If the ultimate moments of resistance provided by main and transverse steel are m_1 and m_2 per unit width, it follows that for equilibrium of the vectors shown, the ultimate moment of resistance normal to the yield line m_n per unit length is given by

$$m_n L = m_1 L \cos\theta \times \cos\theta + m_2 L \sin\theta \times \sin\theta$$

hence $m_n = m_1 \cos^2\theta + m_2 \sin^2\theta$

In the extreme cases of $\theta = 0$, this reduces to $m_n = m_1$, and when $m_1 = m_2 = m$, then $m_n = m$ for any value of θ. This latter case of an orthotropically reinforced slab (reinforcement mutually perpendicular) with equal moments of resistance is said to be isotropically reinforced.

Figure 8.28
Stepped yield line

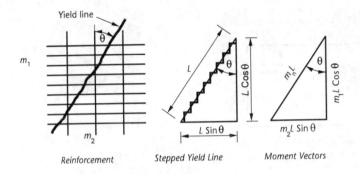

Reinforcement   Stepped Yield Line   Moment Vectors

When applying this approach to complex situations it is often difficult to calculate the lengths and rotations of the yield lines, and a simple vector notation can be used. The total moment component m_n can be resolved vectorially in the x and y directions and since internal energy dissipation along a yield line is given by moment × rotation × length it follows that the energy dissipated by rotation of yield lines bounding any rigid area is given by

$$m_x l_x \phi_x + m_y l_y \phi_y$$

where m_x and m_y are yield moments in directions x and y, l_x and l_y are projections of yield lines along each axis, and ϕ_x and ϕ_y are rotations about the axes. This is illustrated in example 8.12.

EXAMPLE 8.12

Slab simply supported on three sides

The slab shown in figure 8.29 supports a uniformly distributed load of w per unit area.

Internal energy absorbed (E) for unit displacement at points X and Y

Area A

$$E_A = m_x l_x \phi_x + m_y l_y \phi_y$$

where $\phi_x = 0$; hence

$$E_A = m_1 \alpha L \times \frac{1}{\beta L} = m_1 \frac{\alpha}{\beta}$$

Figure 8.29
Slab supported on three sides

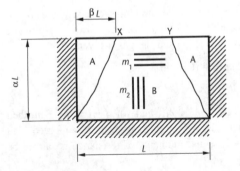

Area B

$$E_B = m_x l_x \phi_x + m_y l_y \phi_y$$

where $\phi_y = 0$; hence

$$E_B = 2m_2 \beta L \times \frac{1}{\alpha L} = 2m_2 \frac{\beta}{\alpha}$$

hence total for all rigid areas is

$$2E_A + E_B = \frac{2}{\alpha\beta}(m_1\alpha^2 + m_2\beta^2)$$

External work done can also be calculated for each region separately

$$W_A = \frac{1}{2}(\alpha L \times \beta L)w \times \frac{1}{3} = \frac{1}{6}w\alpha\beta L^2$$

$$W_B = \left[\frac{1}{6}w\alpha\beta L^2 + \alpha L\left(\frac{L}{2} - \beta L\right)w \times \frac{1}{2}\right] \times 2$$

therefore

$$\text{total} = 2W_A + W_B$$
$$= \frac{1}{6}\alpha(3 - 2\beta)L^2 w$$

Hence equating internal and external work, the maximum u.d.l. that the slab can sustain is given by

$$w_{max} = \frac{2}{\alpha\beta}(m_1\alpha^2 + m_2\beta^2) \times \frac{6}{\alpha(3 - 2\beta)L^2}$$
$$= \frac{12(m_1\alpha^2 + m_2\beta^2)}{\alpha^2 L^2(3\beta - 2\beta^2)}$$

It is clear that the result will vary according to the value of β. The maximum value of w may be obtained by trial and error using several values of β, or alternatively, by differentiation, let $m_2 = \mu m_1$, then

$$w = \frac{12m_1(\alpha^2 + \mu\beta^2)}{\alpha^2 L^2(3\beta - 2\beta^2)}$$

and

$$\frac{d(m_1/w)}{d\beta} = 0 \text{ will give the critical values of } \beta$$

hence

$$3\mu\beta^2 + 4\alpha^2\beta - 3\alpha^2 = 0$$

and

$$\beta = \frac{\alpha^2}{\mu}\left[\pm\sqrt{\left(\frac{4}{9} + \frac{\mu}{\alpha^2}\right)} - \frac{2}{3}\right]$$

A negative value is impossible, hence the critical value of β for use in the analysis is given by the positive root.

8.10.2 Hillerborg strip method

This is based on the 'lower bound' concept of plastic theory which suggests that if a stress distribution throughout a structure can be found which satisfies all equilibrium conditions without violating yield criteria, then the structure is safe for the corresponding system of external loads. Although safe, the structure will not necessarily be serviceable or economic, hence considerable skill is required on the part of the engineer in selecting a suitable distribution of bending moments on which the design can be based. Detailed analysis of a slab designed on this basis is not necessary, but the designer's structural sense and 'feel' for the way loads are transmitted to the supports are of prime importance.

Although this method for design of slabs was proposed by Hillerborg in the 1950s, developments by Wood and Armer in the 1960s have produced its currently used form. The method can be applied to slabs of any shape, and assumes that at failure the load will be carried by bending in either the x or y direction separately with no twisting action. Hence the title of 'strip method'.

Considering a rectangular slab simply supported on four sides and carrying a uniformly distributed load, the load may be expected to be distributed to the supports in the manner shown in figure 8.30.

Judgement will be required to determine the angle α, but it can be seen that if $\alpha = 90°$ the slab will be assumed to be one-way spanning and, although safe, is unlikely to be serviceable because of cracking near the supports along the y-axis. Hillerborg suggests that for such a slab, α should be 45°. The load diagram causing bending moments along typical strips spanning each direction is also shown. It will be seen that the alternative pattern, suggested by Wood and Armer in figure 8.31 will simplify the design, and in this case five strips in each direction may be conveniently used as shown. Each of these will be designed in bending for its particular loading, as if it were one-way spanning using the methods of section 8.5. Reinforcement will be arranged uniformly across each strip, to produce an overall pattern of reinforcement bands in two directions. Support reactions can also be obtained very simply from each strip.

The approach is particularly suitable for slabs with openings, in which case strengthened bands can be provided round the openings with the remainder of the slab divided into strips as appropriate. A typical pattern of this type is shown in figure 8.32.

Figure 8.30
Assumed load distribution

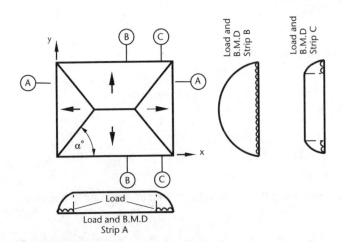

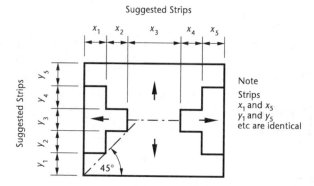

Suggested Strips

Note
Strips
x_1 and x_5
y_1 and y_5
etc are identical

Figure 8.31
Load distribution according to
Wood & Armer

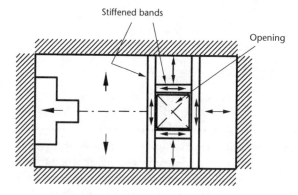

Stiffened bands

Opening

Figure 8.32
Strong bands around
openings

CHAPTER 9

Column design

CHAPTER INTRODUCTION

The columns in a structure carry the loads from the beams and slabs down to the foundations, and therefore they are primarily compression members, although they may also have to resist bending forces due to the continuity of the structure. The analysis of a section subjected to an axial load plus bending is dealt with in chapter 4, where it is noted that a direct solution of the equations which determine the areas of reinforcement can be very laborious and impractical. Therefore, design charts or some form of electronic computer are often employed to facilitate the routine design of column sections.

Design of columns is governed by the ultimate limit state; deflections and cracking during service conditions are not usually a problem, but nevertheless correct detailing of the reinforcement and adequate cover are important.

This chapter considers all aspects of column design. Consideration is given to the loading cases used to determine the worst combinations of axial load combined with bending moments and the detailing rules used to determine the quantity and location of the necessary reinforcing steel are outlined. The possible failure modes of a column are considered and rules are given for determining whether or not a column should be considered as short or slender. If, indeed, a column is classified as slender then the approach to design is more complex as, in addition to moments arising from primary loading, the additional moments arising from the eccentricity of axial loading as the column tends to buckle must be considered.

Although in many practical cases design charts will be used to determine the size and amount of reinforcement in a column, an understanding of the fundamental principles of column behaviour will facilitate the design of non-standard situations where the use of charts is not appropriate. Such cases include the provision of non-symmetrically located reinforcement and the design of non-rectangular sections. Both of these non-standard cases are considered in this chapter.

Consideration is also given to situations of biaxial bending such as may occur in a corner column within a building which supports beams spanning in different directions. Finally a brief description is given of the approach to design of axially loaded wall systems which may be considered as columns of unit length.

Many of the principles used in this chapter for the design of a column can also be applied in a similar manner to other types of members which also resist an axial load plus a bending moment.

9.1   Loading and moments

The loading arrangements and the analysis of a structural frame have been described with examples in chapter 3. In the analysis it was necessary to classify the column into one of the following types.

1. a braced column – where the lateral loads are resisted by walls or some other form of bracing, and

2 an unbraced column – where the lateral loads are resisted by the bending action of the columns.

With a braced column the axial forces and moments are caused by the dead and imposed load only, whereas with an unbraced column the loading arrangements which include the effects of the lateral loads must also be considered.

For a braced column the critical arrangement of the ultimate load is usually that which causes the largest moment in the column, together with a large axial load. As an example, figure 9.1 shows a building frame with the critical loading arrangement for the design of its centre column at the first-floor level and also the left-hand column at all floor levels. When the moments in columns are large and particularly with unbraced columns, it may also be necessary to check the case of maximum moment combined with the minimum axial load.

Table 9.1   Reduction of total imposed floor loads on columns, walls and foundations

No. of floors carried by member	Reduction of imposed load on all floors above the member
1	0 per cent
2	10
3	20
4	30
5 to 10	40
over 10	50

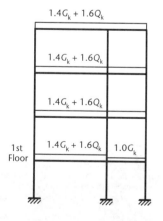

Figure 9.1
A critical loading arrangement

The axial forces due to the vertical loading may be calculated as though the beams and slabs are simply supported. In some structures it is unlikely that all the floors of a building will carry the full imposed load at the same instant, therefore, a reduction is usually allowed in the total imposed load when designing columns and foundations in buildings which are two or more storeys high, as shown by table 9.1.

9.2 | Column classification and failure modes

(1) Classification

A column is classified as short if both l_{ex}/h and l_{ey}/b are:

less than 15 for a braced column

less than 10 for an unbraced column

The effective heights l_{ex} and l_{ey} are relative to the XX and YY axis, h is the overall depth of the section in the plane of bending about the XX axis, that is h is the dimension perpendicular to the XX axis.

(2) Effective height l_e of a column

The effective heights are specified as

$$l_e = \beta l_0$$

l_0 is the clear distance between the column end restraints

and β is a coefficient which depends on the degree of end restraints as specified in table 9.2.

The application of these coefficients is illustrated for the braced column shown in figure 9.2.

Table 9.2

	β for braced columns				β for unbraced columns		
End condition at top	End condition at bottom			End condition at top	End condition at bottom		
	1	2	3		1	2	3
1	0.75	0.80	0.90	1	1.2	1.3	1.6
2	0.80	0.85	0.95	2	1.3	1.5	1.8
3	0.90	0.95	1.00	3	1.6	1.8	—
				4	2.2	—	—

End conditions. The four end conditions are as follows:

(a) *Condition 1*. The end of the column is connected monolithically to beams on either side which are at least as deep as the overall dimension of the column in the plane considered. Where the column is connected to a foundation structure, this should be of a form specifically designed to carry moment.

(b) *Condition 2*. The end of the column is connected monolithically to beams or slabs on either side which are shallower than the overall dimension of the column in the plane considered.

(c) *Condition 3*. The end of the column is connected to members which, while not specifically designed to provide restraint to rotation of the column will, nevertheless, provide some nominal restraint.

(d) *Condition 4*. The end of the column is unrestrained against both lateral movement and rotation (for example, the free end of a cantilever column in an unbraced structure).

EXAMPLE 9.1

Short or slender column

Determine if the braced column shown in figure 9.2 is short or slender.

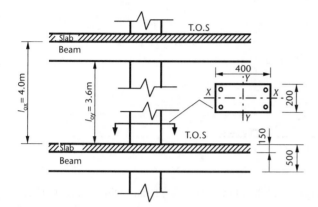

Figure 9.2
Column end condition details

For end condition 1 of table 9.2, top and bottom

$$\frac{l_{ey}}{b} = \frac{\beta_y l_{0y}}{b} = 0.75 \times \frac{3600}{400} = 6.75 < 15$$

For end condition 2, top and bottom

$$\frac{l_{ex}}{h} = \frac{\beta_x l_{0x}}{h} = 0.85 \times \frac{4000}{200} = 17 > 15$$

Therefore the column should be considered as slender.

(3) Failure modes

Short columns usually fail by crushing but a slender column is liable to fail by buckling. The end moments on a slender column cause it to deflect sideways and thus bring into play an additional moment Ne_{add} as illustrated in figure 9.3. The moment Ne_{add} causes a further lateral deflection and, if the axial load (N) exceeds a critical value, this deflection and the additional moment become self-propagating until the column buckles. Euler derived the critical load for a pin-ended strut as

$$N_{crit} = \frac{\pi^2 EI}{l^2}$$

The crushing load N_{uz} of a truly axially loaded column may be taken as

$$N_{uz} = 0.45 f_{cu} A_c + 0.95 f_y A_{sc}$$

where A_c is the area of the concrete and A_{sc} is the area of the longitudinal steel.

Values of N_{crit}/N_{uz} and l/h have been calculated and plotted in figure 9.4 for a typical column cross-section.

The ratio of N_{crit}/N_{uz} in the figure determines the type of failure of the column. With l/h less than, say, 15 the load will probably cause crushing, N_{uz} is much less than N_{crit},

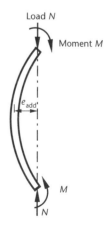

Load N

Moment M

e_{add}

M

N

Figure 9.3
Slender column with lateral deflection

Figure 9.4
Column failure modes

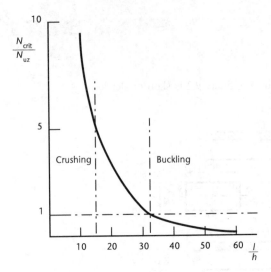

the load that causes buckling – and therefore a buckling failure will not occur. This is not true with higher values of l/h and so a buckling failure is possible, depending on such factors as the initial curvature of the column and the actual eccentricity of the load. When l/h is greater than 32 then N_{crit} is less than N_{uz} and in this case a buckling failure will occur for the column considered.

The mode of failure of a column can be one of the following.

1. Material failure with negligible lateral deflection, which usually occurs with short columns but can also occur when there are large end moments on a column with an intermediate slenderness ratio.

2. Material failure intensified by the lateral deflection and the additional moment. This type of failure is typical of intermediate columns.

3. Instability failure which occurs with slender columns and is liable to be preceded by excessive deflections.

9.3 Reinforcement details

The rules governing the minimum amounts of reinforcement in a load bearing column are as follows.

Longitudinal steel

1. A minimum of four bars is required in a rectangular column and six bars in a circular column. The size of the bars should be not less than 12 mm.

2.

$$\frac{100A_s}{A_{col}} \not< 0.4$$

3.

$$\frac{100A_s}{A_{col}} \not> 6.0 \text{ in a vertically cast column}$$

or

$$\frac{100A_s}{A_{col}} \not> 8.0 \text{ in a horizontally cast column}$$

but at laps

$$\frac{100A_s}{A_{col}} \not> 10.0 \text{ for both types of columns}$$

where A_s is the total area of longitudinal steel and A_{col} is the cross-sectional area of the column.

Links

1. Minimum size = $1/4 \times$ size of the largest compression bar but not less than 6 mm.
2. Maximum spacing = $12 \times$ size of the smallest compression bar.
3. The links should be arranged so that every corner bar and alternate bar or group in an outer layer of longitudinal steel is supported by a link passing round the bar and having an included angle not greater than 135°.
4. All other bars or groups not restrained by a link should be within 150 mm of a restrained bar.
5. In circular columns a circular link passing around a circular arrangement of longitudinal bars is adequate.

Although links are popular in the United Kingdom, helical reinforcement is popular in the USA and provides added strength in addition to added protection against seismic loading. Sizing and spacing of helical reinforcement should be similar to links.

Figure 9.5 shows possible arrangements of reinforcing bars at the junction of two columns and a floor. In figure 9.5a the reinforcement in the lower column is cranked so that it will fit within the smaller column above. The crank in the reinforcement should, if possible, commence above the soffit of the beam so that the moment of resistance of the column is not reduced. For the same reason, the bars in the upper column should be the ones cranked when both columns are of the same size as in figure 9.5b. Links should be provided at the points where the bars are cranked in order to resist buckling due to

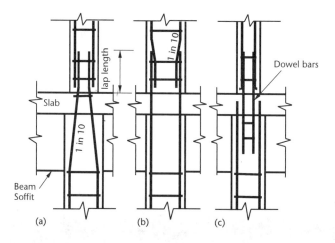

Figure 9.5
Details of splices in column reinforcement

horizontal components of force in the inclined lengths of bar. Separate dowel bars as in figure 9.5c may also be used to provide continuity between the two lengths of column. The column–beam junction should be detailed so that there is adequate space for both the column steel and the beam steel. Careful attention to detail on this point will greatly assist the fixing of the steel during construction.

9.4 Design of short columns

Short columns are divided into three categories according to the degree of eccentricity of the loading as described in the following sections.

9.4.1 Short braced axially loaded columns

This type of column can occur in precast concrete construction when there is no continuity between the members. Also it can be considered to occur when the columns support a symmetrical and very rigid structure.

When the load is perfectly axial the ultimate axial resistance is

$$N = 0.45 f_{cu} A_c + 0.95 f_y A_{sc}$$

where A_c is the net area of the concrete and A_{sc} is the area of the longitudinal reinforcement.

Perfect conditions never exist and to allow for a small eccentricity the ultimate load should be calculated from

$$N = 0.4 f_{cu} A_c + 0.80 f_y A_{sc} \qquad (9.1)*$$

For a rectangular column and to allow for the area of concrete displaced by the longitudinal reinforcement this equation may be modified to

$$N = 0.4 f_{cu} b h + A_{sc}(0.80 f_y - 0.4 f_{cu}) \qquad (9.2)$$

EXAMPLE 9.2

Axially loaded column

Design the longitudinal reinforcement for a 300 mm square column which supports an axial load of 1700 kN at the ultimate limit state. The characteristic material strengths are $f_y = 460$ N/mm^2 for the reinforcement and $f_{cu} = 30$ N/mm^2 for the concrete.

From equation 9.2

$$1700 \times 10^3 = 0.4 \times 30 \times 300^2 + A_{sc}(0.80 \times 460 - 0.4 \times 30)$$

therefore

$$A_{sc} = \frac{(1700 - 1080)10^3}{356}$$
$$= 1741 \text{ mm}^2$$

Provide four T25 bars, area $= 1960$ mm^2.

9.4.2 Short braced columns supporting an approximately symmetrical arrangement of beams

The moments of these columns will be small and due primarily to unsymmetrical arrangements of the live load. Provided the beam spans do not differ by more than 15 per cent of the longer, and the loading on the beams is uniformly distributed, the column may be designed to support the axial load only. The ultimate load that can be supported should then be taken as

$$N = 0.35f_{cu}A_c + 0.70f_yA_{sc} \qquad (9.3)*$$

To take account of the area of concrete displaced by the reinforcement the equation for a rectangular section may be written as

$$N = 0.35f_{cu}bh + (0.70f_y - 0.35f_{cu})A_{sc}$$

9.4.3 Short columns resisting moments and axial forces

The area of longitudinal steel for these columns is determined by:

1. using design charts or constructing M–N interaction diagrams as in section 4.8
2. a solution of the basic design equations, or
3. an approximate method.

Design charts are usually used for columns having a rectangular or circular cross-section and a symmetrical arrangement of reinforcement, but interaction diagrams can be constructed for any arrangement of cross-section as illustrated in examples 4.10 and 4.11. The basic equations or the approximate method can be used when an unsymmetrical arrangement of reinforcement is required, or when the cross-section is non-rectangular as described in section 9.5.

Whichever design method is used, a column should not be designed for a moment less than $N \times e_{min}$, where e_{min} has the lesser value of $h/20$ or 20 mm. This is to allow for tolerances in construction. The dimension h is the overall size of the column cross-section in the plane of bending.

9.4.3.1 Design charts and interaction diagrams

The design of a section subjected to bending plus axial load should be in accordance with the principles described in section 4.8, which deals with the analysis of the cross-section. The basic equations derived for a rectangular section as shown in figure 9.6 and with a rectangular stress block are

$$N = F_{cc} + F_{sc} + F_s \qquad (9.4)$$
$$= 0.45f_{cu}bs + f_{sc}A'_s + f_sA_s$$
$$M = F_{cc}\left(\frac{h}{2} - \frac{s}{2}\right) + F_{sc}\left(\frac{h}{2} - d'\right) - F_s\left(d - \frac{h}{2}\right) \qquad (9.5)$$

$\quad s \qquad$ = the depth of the stress block $= 0.9x$
$\quad A'_s \qquad$ = the area of longitudinal reinforcement in the more highly compressed face
$\quad A_s \qquad$ = the area of reinforcement in the other face
$\quad f_{sc} \qquad$ = the stress in reinforcement A'_s
$\quad f_s \qquad$ = the stress in reinforcement A_s, negative when tensile.

Figure 9.6
Column section

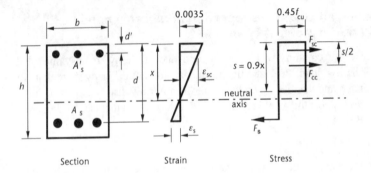

Figure 9.7
Column design chart

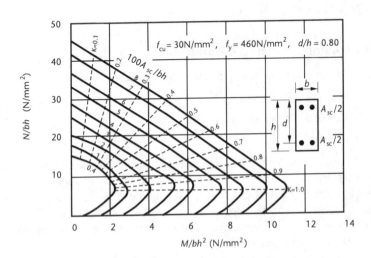

These equations are not suitable for direct solution and the design of a column with symmetrical reinforcement in each face is best carried out using design charts similar to those published in Part 3 of BS 8110. An example of one of these charts is shown in figure 9.7.

EXAMPLE 9.3

Column design using design charts

Figure 9.8 shows a frame of a heavily loaded industrial structure for which the centre columns along line PQ are to be designed in this example. The frames at 4 m centres, are braced against lateral forces, and support the following floor loads:

$$\text{dead load } g_k = 10 \text{ kN/m}^2$$
$$\text{live load } q_k = 15 \text{ kN/m}^2$$

Characteristic material strengths are $f_{cu} = 30 \text{ N/mm}^2$ for the concrete and $f_y = 460 \text{ N/mm}^2$ for the steel.

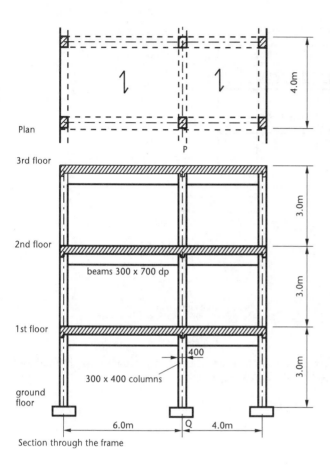

Plan

3rd floor

2nd floor

beams 300 x 700 dp

1st floor

400

300 x 400 columns

ground
floor

6.0m | Q | 4.0m

Section through the frame

4.0m

3.0m

3.0m

3.0m

P

Figure 9.8
Columns in an industrial
structure

Maximum ultimate load at each floor $= 4.0(1.4g_k + 1.6q_k)$ per metre

$$= 4(1.4 \times 10 + 1.6 \times 15)$$

$$= 152 \text{ kN/m}$$

Minimum ultimate load at each floor $= 4.0 \times 1.0g_k$

$$= 4.0 \times 10 = 40 \text{ kN per metre length of beam}$$

Consider first the design of the centre column at the underside (u.s.) of the first floor. The critical arrangement of load which will cause the maximum moment in the column is shown in figure 9.9a.

Column loads

second and third floors $= 2 \times 152 \times 10/2 \qquad = 1520 \text{ kN}$

first floor $= 152 \times 6/2 + 40 \times 4/2 = 536$

Column self-weight, say $2 \times 14 \qquad \underline{\quad 28 \quad}$

$$N = 2084 \text{ kN}$$

Similar arrangements of load will give the axial load in the column at the underside (u.s.) and top side (t.s.) of each floor level and these values of (N) are shown in table 9.3.

Figure 9.9

Substitute frames for column design example

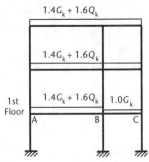

(a) Critical loading arrangement for centre columns at 1st floor

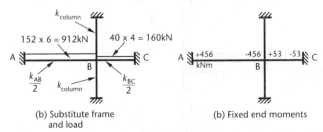

(b) Substitute frame and load

(b) Fixed end moments

The moments on the column are not large and therefore equation 9.3 may be used for a preliminary sizing. Trying a 300×400 column

$$N = 0.35 f_{cu} bh + 0.70 f_y A_{sc}$$

$$2084 \times 10^3 = 0.35 \times 30 \times 300 \times 400 + 0.70 \times 460 \times A_{sc}$$

from which

$$A_{sc} = 2559 \text{ mm}^2 \text{ and } 100 A_{sc}/bh = 2.13$$

This provides an adequate cross-section and a 300×400 column is to be used.

Column moments

The loading arrangement and the substitute frame for determining the column moments at the first and second floors are shown in figure 9.9b. Member stiffnesses are

$$\frac{k_{AB}}{2} = \frac{1}{2} \frac{bh^3}{12 L_{AB}} = \frac{1}{2} \times \frac{0.3 \times 0.7^3}{12 \times 6} = 0.71 \times 10^{-3}$$

$$\frac{k_{BC}}{2} = \frac{1}{2} \times \frac{0.3 \times 0.7^3}{12 \times 4} = 1.07 \times 10^{-3}$$

$$k_{col} = \frac{0.3 \times 0.4^3}{12 \times 3.0} = 0.53 \times 10^{-3}$$

therefore

$$\sum k = (0.71 + 1.07 + 2 \times 0.53)10^{-3} = 2.84 \times 10^{-3}$$

and

$$\text{distribution factor for the column} = \frac{k_{col}}{\sum k} = \frac{0.53}{2.84} = 0.19$$

Fixed end moments at B are

$$\text{F.E.M.}_{\text{BA}} = \frac{152 \times 6^2}{12} = 456 \text{ kN m}$$

$$\text{F.E.M.}_{\text{BC}} = \frac{40 \times 4^2}{12} = 53 \text{ kN m}$$

Thus

column moment $M = 0.19(456 - 53) = 76.6$ kN m

At the 3rd floor

$$\sum k = (0.71 + 1.07 + 0.53)10^{-3}$$
$$= 2.31 \times 10^{-3}$$

and

column moment $M = \dfrac{0.53}{2.31}(456 - 53) = 92.5$ kN m

The areas of reinforcement in table 9.3 are determined by using the design chart of figure 9.7. Sections through the column are shown in figure 9.10.

Cover for the reinforcement is taken as 50 mm and $d/h = 320/400 = 0.8$. The minimum area of reinforcement allowed in the section is given by

$A_{\text{sc}} = 0.004bh = 0.004 \times 300 \times 400 = 480 \text{ mm}^2$

and the maximum area is

$A_{\text{sc}} = 0.06 \times 300 \times 400 = 7200 \text{ mm}^2$

or at laps

$A_{\text{sc}} = 0.1 \times 300 \times 400 = 12000 \text{ mm}^2$

and the reinforcement provided is within these limits.

A smaller column section could have been used above the first floor but this would have involved changes in formwork and also increased areas of reinforcement. For simplicity in this example no reduction was taken in the total live load although this is permitted with some structures, as shown by table 9.1.

Table 9.3

Floor	N	M	$\dfrac{N}{bh}$	$\dfrac{M}{bh^2}$	$\dfrac{100A_{\text{sc}}}{bh}$	A_{sc}
	(kN)	(kN m)				(mm²)
3rd u.s.	536	92.5	4.47	1.93	0.4	480
2nd t.s.	774	76.6	6.45	1.60	0.4	480
	+536					
2nd u.s.	1310	76.6	10.92	1.60	0.4	480
1st t.s.	1548	76.6	12.9	1.60	0.9	1080
	+536					
1st u.s.	2084	76.6	17.37	1.60	2.1	2520
Foundation	2098	38.3	17.48	0.80	1.6	1920

Figure 9.10
Column sections in design example

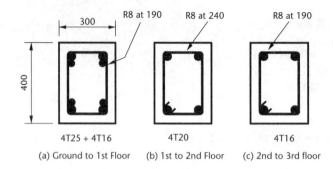

4T25 + 4T16   4T20   4T16

(a) Ground to 1st Floor   (b) 1st to 2nd Floor   (c) 2nd to 3rd floor

9.4.3.2 Design equations for a non-symmetrical section

The symmetrical arrangement of the reinforcement with $A'_s = A_s$ is justifiable for the columns of a building where the axial loads are the dominant forces and where any moments due to the wind can be acting in either direction. But some members are required to resist axial forces combined with large bending moments so that it is not economical to have equal areas of steel in both faces, and in these cases the usual design charts cannot be applied. A rigorous design for a rectangular section as shown in figure 9.11 involves the following iterative procedure.

1. Select a depth of neutral axis, x
2. Determine the steel strains ε_{sc} and ε_s from the strain distribution.
3. Determine the steel stresses f_{sc} and f_s from the equations relating to the stress–strain curve for the reinforcing bars (see section 4.1.2).
4. Taking moments about the centroid of A_s

$$N\left(e + \frac{h}{2} - d_2\right) = 0.45 f_{cu}bs(d - s/2) + f_{sc}A'_s(d - d') \tag{9.6}$$

where $s = 0.9x$. This equation can be solved to give a value for A'_s.

5. A_s is then determined from the equilibrium of the axial forces, that is

$$N = 0.45 f_{cu}bs + f_{sc}A'_s + f_sA_s \tag{9.7}$$

Figure 9.11
Column with unsymmetrical arrangement of reinforcement

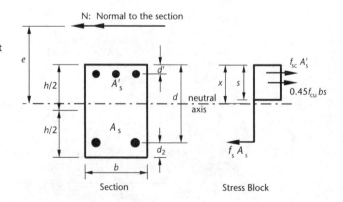

Section   Stress Block

6. Further values of x may be selected and steps 1 to 5 repeated until a minimum value for $A'_s + A_s$ is obtained.

The term f_{sc} in the equations may be modified to $(f_{sc} - 0.45f_{cu})$ to allow for the area of concrete displaced by the reinforcement A'_s. Stress f_s has a negative sign whenever it is tensile.

EXAMPLE 9.4

Column section with an unsymmetrical arrangement of reinforcement

The column section shown in figure 9.12 resists an axial load of 1100 kN and a moment of 230 kN m at the ultimate limit state. Determine the areas of reinforcement required if the characteristic material strengths are $f_y = 460$ N/mm^2 and $f_{cu} = 30$ N/mm^2.

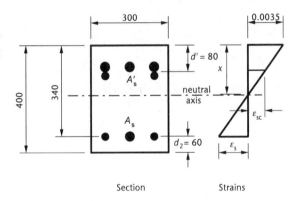

Section   Strains

Figure 9.12
Unsymmetrical column design example

1. Select a depth of neutral axis, $x = 190$ mm.

2. From the strain diagram

$$\text{steel strain } \varepsilon_{sc} = \frac{0.0035}{x}(x - d')$$

$$= \frac{0.0035}{190}(190 - 80) = 0.00203$$

and

$$\text{steel strain } \varepsilon_s = \frac{0.0035}{x}(d - x)$$

$$= \frac{0.0035}{190}(340 - 190) = 0.00276$$

3. From the stress–strain curve and the relevant equations of section 4.1.2

yield strain, $\varepsilon_y = 0.00219$ for grade 460 steel

$$\varepsilon_s > 0.00219$$

therefore $f_s = 460/1.05 = 438$ N/mm^2 tension

$$\varepsilon_{sc} < 0.00219$$

therefore $f_{sc} = E_s \varepsilon_{sc}$

$$= 200 \times 10^3 \times 0.00203 = 406 \text{ N/mm}^2$$

4. In equation 9.6

$$N\left(e + \frac{h}{2} - d_2\right) = 0.45 f_{cu} bs(d - s/2) + f_{sc}A'_s(d - d')$$

$$e = \frac{M}{N} = \frac{230 \times 10^6}{1100 \times 10^3} = 209 \text{ mm}$$

$$s = 0.9x = 0.9 \times 190$$
$$= 171 \text{ mm}$$

To allow for the area of concrete displaced

$$f_{sc} \text{ becomes } 406 - 0.45 f_{cu} = 406 - 0.45 \times 30 = 393 \text{ N/mm}^2$$

and from equation 9.6

$$A'_s = \frac{1100 \times 10^3 (209 + 140) - 0.45 \times 30 \times 300 \times 171(340 - 171/2)}{393(340 - 80)}$$

$$= 2032 \text{ mm}^2$$

5. From equation 9.7

$$N = 0.45 f_{cu} bs + f_{sc}A'_s + f_s A_s$$

$$A_s = \frac{(0.45 \times 30 \times 300 \times 171) + (393 \times 2032) - (1100 \times 10^3)}{438}$$

$$= 893 \text{ mm}^2$$

Thus

$$A'_s + A_s = 2925 \text{ mm}^2 \text{ for } x = 190 \text{ mm}$$

6. Values of $A'_s + A_s$ calculated for other depths of neutral axis, x, are plotted in figure 9.13. From this figure the minimum area of reinforcement required occurs with $x \approx 210$ mm. Using this depth of neutral axis, steps 2 to 5 are repeated giving

$$\varepsilon_{sc} = \varepsilon_s = 0.00217 \ngtr 0.00219$$
$$f_{sc} = E_s \varepsilon_{sc}$$
$$= 200 \times 10^3 \times 0.00217 = 434 \text{ N/mm}^2$$

and $f_s = 434$ N/mm^2 tension

so that

$$A'_s = 1796 \text{ mm}^2 \text{ and } A_s = 968 \text{ mm}^2$$

Figure 9.13
Design chart for unsymmetrical column example

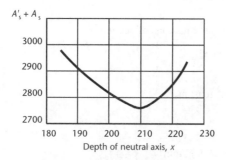

$A'_s + A_s$

3000

2900

2800

2700

180   190   200   210   220   230

Depth of neutral axis, x

(Alternatively separate values of A'_s and A_s as calculated for each value of x could also have been plotted against x and their values read from the graph at $x = 210$ mm.) This area would be provided with

A'_s = three T25 plus two T20 bars = 2098 mm^2

and

A_s = one T25 plus two T20 bars = 1119 mm^2

With a symmetrical arrangement of reinforcement the area would be $A'_s + A_s = 2950$ mm^2 or 7 per cent greater than the area with an unsymmetrical arrangement, and including no allowance for the area of concrete displaced by the steel.

These types of iterative calculations are readily programmed for solution by a small microcomputer, which could find the optimum steel areas without the necessity of plotting a graph.

9.4.3.3 Simplified design method

As an alternative to the previous rigorous method of design an approximate method may be used when the eccentricity of loading, e is not less than $(h/2 - d_2)$.

The moment M and the axial force N are replaced by an increased moment M_a where

$$M_a = M + N\left(\frac{h}{2} - d_2\right) \tag{9.8}$$

plus a compressive force N acting through the tensile steel A_s as shown in figure 9.14. Hence the design of the reinforcement is carried out in two parts.

1. The member is designed as a doubly reinforced section to resist M_a acting by itself. The equations for calculating the areas of reinforcement to resist M_a are given in section 4.5 as

$$M_a = 0.156f_{cu}bd^2 + 0.95f_yA'_s(d - d') \tag{9.9}$$
$$0.95f_yA_s = 0.201f_{cu}bd + 0.95f_yA'_s \tag{9.10}$$

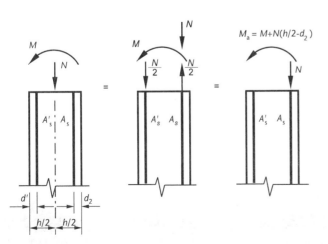

Figure 9.14
Simplified design method

2. The area of A_s calculated in the first part is reduced by the amount $N/0.95f_y$.

This preliminary design method is probably most useful for non-rectangular column sections as shown in example 9.7, but the procedure is first demonstrated with a rectangular cross-section in the following example.

EXAMPLE 9.5

Column design by the simplified method

Calculate the area of steel required in the 300×400 column of figure 9.12. $N = 1100$ kN, $M = 230$ kN m, $f_{cu} = 30$ N/mm^2 and $f_y = 460$ N/mm^2.

$$\text{Eccentricity } e = \frac{230 \times 10^6}{1100 \times 10^3} = 209 \text{ mm} > \left(\frac{h}{2} - d_2 \right)$$

1. Increased moment

$$M_a = M + N\left(\frac{h}{2} - d_2 \right)$$

$$= 230 + 1100(200 - 60)10^{-3} = 384 \text{ kN m}$$

The area of steel to resist this moment can be calculated using the formulae 9.9 and 9.10 for the design of a beam with compressive reinforcement, that is

$$M_a = 0.156f_{cu}bd^2 + 0.95f_yA'_s(d - d')$$

and

$$0.95f_yA_s = 0.201f_{cu}bd + 0.95f_yA'_s$$

therefore

$$384 \times 10^6 = 0.156 \times 30 \times 300 \times 340^2 + 0.95 \times 460A'_s(340 - 80)$$

so that

$$A'_s = 1950 \text{ mm}^2$$

and

$$0.95 \times 460A_s = 0.201 \times 30 \times 300 \times 340 + 0.95 \times 460 \times 1950$$

$$A_s = 3358 \text{ mm}^2$$

2. Reducing this area by $N/0.95f_y$

$$A_s = 3358 - \frac{1100 \times 10^3}{0.95 \times 460}$$

$$= 841 \text{ mm}^2$$

This compares with $A'_s = 1796$ mm^2 and $A_s = 968$ mm^2 with the design method of example 9.4. (To give a truer comparison the stress in the compressive reinforcement should have been modified to allow for the area of concrete displaced, as was done in example 9.4.)

9.5 | Non-rectangular sections

Design charts are not usually available for columns of other than a rectangular or a circular cross-section. Therefore the design of a non-rectangular section entails either (1) an iterative solution of design equations, (2) a simplified form of design, or (3) construction of M–N interaction diagrams.

9.5.1 Design equations

For a non-rectangular section it is much simpler to consider the equivalent rectangular stress-block. Determination of the reinforcement areas follows the same procedure as described for a rectangular column in section 9.4.3.2, namely

1. Select a depth of neutral axis.
2. Determine the corresponding steel strains.
3. Determine the steel stresses.
4. Take moments about A_s so that with reference to figure 9.15.

$$N\left(e+\frac{h}{2}-d_2\right) = 0.45f_{cu}A_{cc}(d-\bar{x}) + f_{sc}A'_s(d-d')$$

Solve this equation to give A'_s.
5. For no resultant force on the section

$$N = 0.45f_{cu}A_{cc} + f_{sc}A'_s + f_sA_s$$

Solve this equation to give A_s.
6. Repeat the previous steps for different values of x to find a minimum $(A'_s + A_s)$.

In steps 4 and 5

A_{cc} is the area of concrete in compression shown shaded
$\bar{x}$ is the distance from the centroid of A_{cc} to the extreme fibre in compression
f_s the stress in reinforcement A_s is negative if tensile.

The calculation for a particular cross-section would be very similar to that described in example 9.4 except when using the design equations it would be necessary to determine A_{cc} and $\bar{x}$ for each position of the neutral axis.

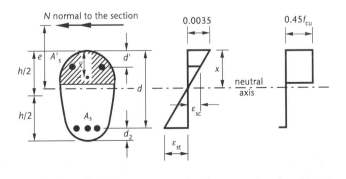

Section   Strains   Stress Block

Figure 9.15
Non-rectangular column section

9.5.2 Simplified preliminary design method

The procedure is similar to that described for a column with a rectangular section as described in section 9.4.3.3 and figure 9.14.

The column is designed to resist a moment M_a only, where

$$M_a = M + N\left(\frac{h}{2} - d_2\right) \tag{9.11}$$

The steel area required to resist this moment can be calculated from

$$M_a = 0.45f_{cu}A_{cc}(d - \bar{x}) + 0.95f_yA_s'(d - d') \tag{9.12}$$

and

$$0.95f_yA_s = 0.45f_{cu}A_{cc} + 0.95f_yA_s' \tag{9.13}$$

where A_{cc} is the area of concrete in compression with $x = d/2$, and $\bar{x}$ is the distance from the centroid of A_{cc} to the extreme fibre in compression.

The area of tension reinforcement A_s as given by equation 9.13 is then reduced by an amount equal to $N/0.95f_y$.

This method should not be used if the eccentricity, e, is less than $(h/2 - d_2)$.

9.5.3 *M–N* interaction diagram

These diagrams can be constructed using the method described in section 4.8 with examples 4.10 and 4.11. They are particularly useful for a column in a multi-storey building where the moments and associated axial forces change at each storey.

The diagrams can be constructed after carrying out the approximate design procedure in section 9.5.2 to obtain suitable arrangements of reinforcing bars.

EXAMPLE 9.6

Design of a non-rectangular column section

Design the reinforcement for the non-rectangular section shown in figure 9.16 given $M = 320$ kN m, $N = 1200$ kN at the ultimate limit state and the characteristic material strengths are $f_{cu} = 30$ N/mm^2 and $f_y = 460$ N/mm^2.

$$e = \frac{M}{N} = \frac{320 \times 10^6}{1200 \times 10^3} = 267 \text{ mm} > \left(\frac{h}{2} - d_2\right)$$

Increased moment $M_a = M + N\left(\frac{h}{2} - d_2\right)$

$$= 320 + 1200(200 - 80)10^{-3}$$

$$= 464 \text{ kN m}$$

With $x = d/2 = 160$ mm, $s = 0.9x = 144$ mm and the width (b_1) of the section at the limit of the stress block

$$b_1 = 300 + \frac{200(400 - 144)}{400} = 428 \text{ mm}$$

$$A_{cc} = \frac{x(b + b_1)}{2} = \frac{144(500 + 428)}{2} = 66\,816 \text{ mm}^2$$

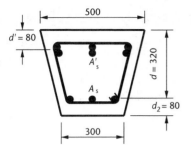

Figure 9.16
Non-rectangular section
example

The depth of the centroid of the trapezium is given by

$$\bar{x} = \frac{s(b + 2b_1)}{3(b + b_1)}$$

$$= 144\frac{(500 + 2 \times 428)}{3(500 + 428)} = 70.1 \text{ mm}$$

Therefore substituting in equation 9.12

$$464 \times 10^6 = 0.45 \times 30 \times 66\,816(320 - 70.1) + 0.95 \times 460A'_s(320 - 80)$$

hence

$$A'_s = 2275 \text{ mm}^2$$

Provide three T32 plus two T16 bars, area $= 2812$ mm^2.
   From equation 9.13

$$0.95f_yA_s = 0.45 \times 30 \times 66\,816 + 0.95 \times 460 \times 2275$$

therefore

$$A_s = 4339 \text{ mm}^2$$

Reducing A_s by $N/0.95f_y$ gives

$$A_s = 4339 - \frac{1200 \times 10^3}{0.95 \times 460}$$

$$= 1593 \text{ mm}^2$$

Provide one T16 plus two T32 bars, area $= 1811$ mm^2.
   The total area of reinforcement provided $= 4623$ mm^2 which is less than the 6 per cent
allowed.
   An M–N interaction diagram could now be constructed for this steel arrangement, as in
section 4.8, to provide a more rigorous design.

9.6 | Biaxial bending short columns

For most columns, biaxial bending will not govern the design. The loading patterns
necessary to cause biaxial bending in a building's internal and edge columns will not
usually cause large moments in both directions. Corner columns may have to resist
significant bending about both axes, but the axial loads are usually small and a design
similar to the adjacent edge columns is generally adequate.

Figure 9.17
Section with biaxial bending

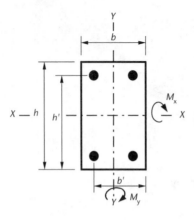

Table 9.4 Values of coefficient β for biaxal bending

$\dfrac{N}{bh\,f_{cu}}$	0	0.1	0.2	0.3	0.4	0.5	≥ 0.6
β	1.00	0.88	0.77	0.65	0.53	0.42	0.30

A design for biaxial bending based on a rigorous analysis of the cross-section and the strain and stress distributions would be according to the fundamental principles of chapter 4, otherwise a simplified method as described in BS 8110 may be used.

This method specifies that a column subjected to an ultimate load N and moments M_x and M_y about the xx and yy axes respectively may be designed for single axis bending but with an increased moment and subject to the following conditions:

(a) if $\dfrac{M_x}{h'} \geq \dfrac{M_y}{b'}$

then increased single axis design moment is

$$M'_x = M_x + \beta \frac{h'}{b'} \times M_y$$

(b) if $\dfrac{M_x}{h'} < \dfrac{M_y}{b'}$

then increased single axis design moment is

$$M'_y = M_y + \beta \frac{b'}{h'} \times M_x$$

The dimensions h' and b' are defined in figure 9.17 and the coefficient β is specified in table 9.4

EXAMPLE 9.7

Design of a column for biaxial bending

The column section shown in figure 9.18 is to be designed to resist an ultimate axial load of 1200 kN plus moments of $M_{xx} = 75$ kN m and $M_{yy} = 80$ kN m. The characteristic material strengths are $f_{cu} = 30$ N/mm^2 and $f_y = 460$ N/mm^2.

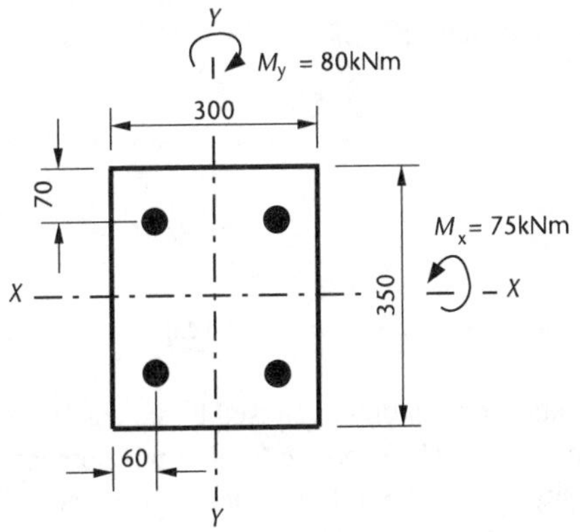

Figure 9.18
Biaxial bending example

$$\frac{M_x}{h'} = \frac{75}{(350 - 70)} = 0.268$$

$$\frac{M_y}{b'} = \frac{80}{(300 - 60)} = 0.333$$

$$M_x/h' < M_y/b'$$

therefore increased single axis design moment is

$$M'_y = M_y + \beta \frac{b'}{h'} \times M_x$$

$$N/bhf_{cu} = 1200 \times 10^3/(300 \times 350 \times 30) = 0.38$$

From table 9.4, $\beta = 0.55$

$$M'_y = 80 + 0.55 \times \frac{240}{280} \times 75 = 115.4 \text{ kN m}$$

$$N/bh = 1200 \times 10^3/(350 \times 300) = 11.4$$

$$M/bh^2 = 115.4 \times 10^6/(350 \times 300^2) = 3.66$$

From the design chart of figure 9.7

$$100A_{sc}/bh \approx 2.6$$

Therefore required $A_{sc} = 2730$ mm^2.
    Provide four T32 bars.

9.7 Design of slender columns

As specified in section 9.2, a column is classified as slender if the slenderness ratio about either axis is

> 15 for a braced column

or   > 10 for an unbraced column

There is a general restriction on the maximum slenderness of

$$l_0 \not> 60b'$$

and for an unbraced column

$$l_0 \not> 100\frac{b'^2}{h'}$$

where l_0 is the clear distance between end restraints and b' and h' are respectively the smaller and larger dimensions of the column section.

A slender column must be designed for an additional moment caused by its curvature at ultimate conditions. The expressions given in BS 8110 for the additional moments were derived by studying the moment-curvature behaviour for a member subject to bending plus axial load. The equations for calculating the design moments are only applicable to columns of a rectangular or circular section and with symmetrical reinforcement.

A slender column should be designed for an ultimate axial load (N) plus an increased moment given by

$$\begin{aligned} M_t &= M_i + M_{add} \\ &= M_i + Na_u \end{aligned} \tag{9.14}$$

where M_i is the initial moment in the column
M_{add} is the moment caused by the deflection of the column
a_u is the deflection of the column

The deflection of a rectangular or circular column is given by

$$a_u = \beta_a K h \tag{9.15}$$

The coefficient β_a is calculated from the equation

$$\beta_a = \frac{1}{2000}\left(\frac{l_e}{b'}\right)^2 \tag{9.16}$$

with b' being generally the smaller dimension of the column section except when biaxial bending is considered.

In equation 9.15 the coefficient K is a reduction factor to allow for the fact that the deflection must be less when there is a large proportion of the column section in compression. The value for K is given by the equation

$$K = \frac{N_{uz} - N}{N_{uz} - N_{bal}} \le 1.0 \tag{9.17}$$

where N_{uz} is the ultimate axial load such that

$$N_{uz} = 0.45f_{cu}A_c + 0.95f_yA_{sc}$$

and N_{bal} is the axial at balanced failure defined in section 4.8 and may be taken as

$$N_{bal} = 0.25f_{cu}A_c$$

for symmetrically reinforced rectangular sections.

In order to calculate K, the area A_{sc} of the columns reinforcement must be known and hence a trial and error approach is necessary, taking an initial conservative value of $K = 1.0$. Values of K are also marked on the column design charts as shown in figure 9.7.

9.7.1 Braced slender column

Typical bending moment diagrams for a braced column are shown in figure 9.19. The maximum additional moment M_{add} occurs near the mid-height of the column and at this location the initial moment is taken as

$$M_i = 0.4M_1 + 0.6M_2 \geq 0.4M_2 \tag{9.18}$$

where M_1 is the smaller initial end moment due to the design ultimate loads and M_2 is the corresponding larger initial end moment.

For the usual case with double curvature of a braced column, M_1 should be taken as negative and M_2 as positive. From figure 9.19, the final design moment should never be taken as less than

M_2

$M_i + M_{add}$

$M_1 + M_{add}/2$

or $N \times e_{min}$ with $e_{min} \not> h/20$ or 20 mm

Equations 9.14 to 9.18 can be used to calculate the additional moment and combined with the appropriate initial moment to design a slender column with single axis bending about either axis, provided that the ratio of the lengths of the sides is always less than 3 and the slenderness ratio l_e/h for a column bent about its major axis does not exceed 20. Where these conditions do not apply and the column is bent about its major axis, the effect of biaxial bending should be considered with zero initial moment about the minor axis and additional moments about both axes.

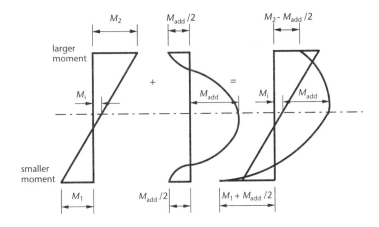

Figure 9.19
Braced slender column design moments

EXAMPLE 9.8

Design of a slender column

A braced column of 300×450 cross-section resists at the ultimate limit state an axial load of 1700 kN and end moments of 70 kN m and 10 kN m causing double curvature about the minor axis XX as shown in figure 9.20. The column's effective heights are $l_{ex} = 6.75$ m and $l_{ey} = 8.0$ m and the characteristic material strengths $f_{cu} = 30$ N/mm² and $f_y = 460$ N/mm².

Figure 9.20
Slender column example

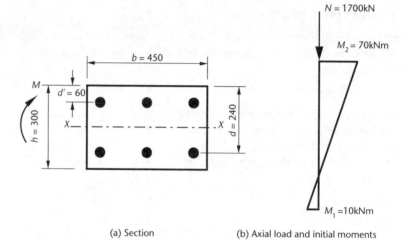

(a) Section (b) Axial load and initial moments

Slenderness ratios are

$$l_{ex}/h = 6.75/0.3 = 22.5 > 15$$
$$l_{ey}/b = 8.0/0.45 = 17.8 > 15$$

Therefore the column is slender.
As the column is bent in double curvature

$$M_1 = -10 \text{ kN m}$$

and

$$M_i = 0.4M_1 + 0.6M_2$$
$$= 0.4 \times (-10) + 0.6 \times 70 = 38 \text{ kN m}$$

and M_i is therefore greater than $0.4M_2$.
The additional moment induced by deflection of the column is

$$M_{add} = \frac{Nh}{2000} \left(\frac{l_e}{b'}\right)^2 K$$

$$= \frac{1700 \times 300}{2000} \left(\frac{6750}{300}\right)^2 \times 1.0 \times 10^3$$

$$= 129 \text{ kN m}$$

with $K = 1.0$ for the initial value.
For the first iteration the total moment is

$$M_t = M_i + M_{add}$$
$$= 38 + 129 = 167 \text{ kN m}$$

$$N/bh = \frac{1700 \times 10^3}{450 \times 300} = 12.6$$

$$M/bh^2 = \frac{167 \times 10^6}{450 \times 300^2} = 4.12$$

From the design chart of figure 9.7

$$100A_{sc}/bh = 3.0$$

and

$$K = 0.67$$

This new value for K is used to recalculate M_{add} and hence M_t for the second iteration. The design chart is again used to determine $100A_{sc}/bh$ and a new K is shown in table 9.5. The iterations are continued until the value of K in columns (1) and (5) of the table are in reasonable agreement, which in this design occurs after two iterations. So that the steel area required is

$$A_{sc} = 2.1bh/100$$
$$= 2.1 \times 450 \times 300/100 = 2835 \text{ mm}^2$$

As a check on the final value of K interpolated from the design chart:

$$N_{bal} = 0.25f_{cu}bd$$
$$= 0.25 \times 30 \times 450 \times 240 \times 10^{-3}$$
$$= 810 \text{ kN}$$
$$N_{uz} = 0.45f_{cu}bh + 0.95f_yA_{sc}$$
$$= (0.45 \times 30 \times 450 \times 300 + 0.95 \times 460 \times 2835)10^{-3}$$
$$= 3061 \text{ kN}$$
$$K = \frac{N_{uz} - N}{N_{uz} - N_{bal}}$$
$$= \frac{3061 - 1700}{3061 - 810}$$
$$= 0.6$$

which agrees with the final value in column 5 of the table.

Table 9.5

(1) K	(2) M_t	(3) M/bh^2	(4) $100A_{sc}/bh$	(5) K
1.0	167	4.12	3.0	0.67
0.67	124	3.0	2.1	0.6

9.7.2 Unbraced slender columns

The sway of an unbraced structure causes larger additional moments in the columns. Figure 9.21 shows how these additional moments are added to the initial moments at the ends of the columns. The additional moment calculated from equations 9.14 to 9.17 is added to the initial moment in the column at the end with the stiffer joint. At the other end of the column the additional moment may be reduced in proportion to the ratio of the stiffnesses of the two joints.

Figure 9.21
Unbraced slender column
design moments

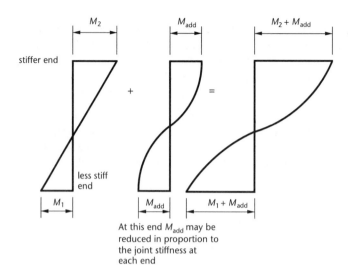

At this end M_{add} may be
reduced in proportion to
the joint stiffness at
each end

9.8 Walls

Walls may take the form of non-structural dividing elements in which case their thickness will often reflect sound insulation and fire-resistance requirements. Nominal reinforcement will be used to control cracking in such cases. More commonly, reinforced concrete walls will form part of a structural frame and will be designed for vertical and horizontal forces and moments obtained by normal analysis methods. In this situation a wall is defined as being a vertical load-bearing member whose length is not less than four times its thickness.

Where several walls are connected monolithically so that they behave as a unit, they are described as a wall system. Sometimes horizontal forces on a structure are resisted by more than one wall or system of walls, in which case the distribution of forces between the walls or systems will be assumed to be in proportion to their stiffnesses (see section 3.5).

It is normal practice to consider a wall as a series of vertical strips when designing vertical reinforcement. Each strip is then designed as a column subject to the appropriate vertical load and transverse moments at its top and bottom. Slenderness effects must be considered where necessary, as for columns. If a wall is subject predominantly to lateral bending, the design and detailing will be undertaken as if it were a slab, but the wall thickness will usually be governed by slenderness limitations, fire-resistance requirements and construction practicalities.

Reinforcement detailing

For a wall designed either as a series of columns or as a slab, the area of vertical reinforcement should lie between $0.004A_c$ and $0.04A_c$ and this will normally be divided between each face.

If the area of vertical steel is less than $0.02A_c$ then horizontal bars should be provided and should have a diameter of not less than one-quarter of that of the vertical bars, with a minimum size of 6 mm. The minimum area of these horizontal bars should be $0.003A_c$

or $0.0025A_c$ for mild steel and high-yield steel respectively. The horizontal bars should lie between the vertical bars and the concrete surface and should be evenly spaced.

If the area of vertical steel exceeds $0.02A_c$ then every vertical compression bar should be enclosed by a link of at least 6 mm diameter or one-quarter of the size of the largest compression bar. The horizontal or vertical link spacing must not be greater than twice the wall thickness in any direction and in the vertical direction must not exceed 16 times the bar size.

CHAPTER 10

Foundations

CHAPTER INTRODUCTION

A building is generally composed of a superstructure above the ground and a substructure which forms the foundations below ground. The foundations transfer and spread the loads from a structure's columns and walls into the ground. The safe bearing capacity of the soil must not be exceeded otherwise excessive settlement may occur, resulting in damage to the building and its service facilities, such as the water or gas mains. Foundation failure can also affect the overall stability of a structure so that it is liable to slide, to lift vertically or even overturn.

The earth under the foundations is the most variable of all the materials that are considered in the design and construction of an engineering structure. Under one small building the soil may vary from a soft clay to a dense rock. Also the nature and properties of the soil will change with the seasons and the weather. For example Keuper Marl, a relatively common soil, is hard like a rock when dry but when wet it can change into an almost liquid state.

It is important to have an engineering survey made of the soil under a proposed structure so that variations in the strata and the soil properties can be determined. Drill holes or trial pits should be sunk, in situ tests such as the penetration test performed and samples of the soil taken to be tested in the laboratory. From the information gained it is possible to recommend safe earth bearing pressures and, if necessary, calculate possible settlements of the structure. Representatives values of the safe bearing pressures for typical soils are listed in table 10.1.

In the design of foundations, the areas of the bases in contact with the ground should be such that the bearing pressures will not be exceeded. Settlement takes place during the working life of the structure, therefore the design loading to be considered when calculating the base areas should be those that apply to the serviceability limit state, and typical values that can be taken are

1. dead plus imposed load $= 1.0G_k + 1.0Q_k$
2. dead plus wind load $= 1.0G_k + 1.0W_k$
3. dead plus imposed plus wind load $= 1.0G_k + 0.8Q_k + 0.8W_k$

These partial factors of safety are suggested as it is highly unlikely that the maximum imposed load and the worst wind load will occur simultaneously.

Table 10.1 Typical allowable bearing values

Rock or soil	Typical bearing value (kN/m²)
Massive igneous bedrock	10 000
Sandstone	2000 to 4000
Shales and mudstone	600 to 2000
Gravel, sand and gravel, compact	600
Medium dense sand	100 to 300
Loose fine sand	less than 100
Hard clay	300 to 600
Medium clay	100 to 300
Soft clay	less than 75

Where the foundations are subject to a vertical and a horizontal load the following rule can be applied.

$$\frac{V}{P_v} + \frac{H}{P_h} < 1.0$$

where V = the vertical load
 H = the horizontal load
 P_v = the allowable vertical load
 P_h = the allowable horizontal load

The allowable horizontal load would take account of the passive resistance of the ground in contact with the vertical face of the foundation plus the friction and cohesion along the base.

The calculations to determine the structural strength of the foundations, that is the thickness of the bases and the areas of reinforcement, should be based on the loadings and the resultant ground pressures corresponding to the ultimate limit state.

With some structures, such as the type shown in figure 10.1, it may be necessary to check the possibility of uplift on the foundations and the stability of the structure when it is subjected to lateral loads. To ensure adequate safety, the stability calculations should also be for the loading arrangements associated with the ultimate limit state. The critical loading arrangement is usually the combination of maximum lateral load with minimum dead load and no live load, that is $1.4W_k + 1.0G_k$. Minimum dead load can

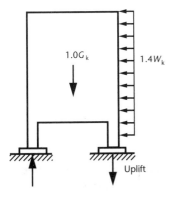

Figure 10.1
Uplift on footing

Figure 10.2
Pressure distributions under
footings

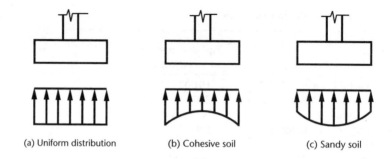

(a) Uniform distribution　　　　(b) Cohesive soil　　　　(c) Sandy soil

sometimes occur during erection when many of the interior finishes and fixtures may not
have been installed.

For most designs a linear distribution of soil pressures across the base of the footing
is assumed as shown in figure 10.2a. This assumption must be based on the soil acting as
an elastic material and the footing having infinite rigidity. In fact, not only do most soils
exhibit some plastic behaviour and all footings have a finite stiffness, but also the
distribution of soil pressure varies with time. The actual distribution of bearing pressure
at any moment may take the form shown in figure 10.2b or c, depending on the type of
soil and the stiffness of the base and the structure. But as the behaviour of foundations
involves many uncertainties regarding the action of the ground and the loading, it is
usually unrealistic to consider an analysis which is too sophisticated.

Foundations should be constructed so that the underside of the bases are below frost
level. As the concrete is subjected to more severe exposure conditions a larger nominal
cover to the reinforcement is required. It is recommended that the minimum cover
should be not less than 75mm when the concrete is cast against the ground, or less than
50 mm when the concrete is cast against a layer of blinding concrete. A concrete grade
of at least $f_{cu} = 35$ N/mm^2 is required to meet the serviceability requirements of
BS8110; see table 6.1.

10.1　Pad footings

The footing for a single column may be made square in plan, but where there is a large
moment acting about one axis it may be more economical to have a rectangular base.

Assuming there is a linear distribution the bearing pressures across the base will take
one of the three forms shown in figure 10.3, according to the relative magnitudes of the
axial load N and the moment M acting on the base.

1. In figure 10.3a there is no moment and the pressure is uniform

$$p = \frac{N}{BD} \qquad\qquad (10.1)*$$

2. With a moment M acting as shown, the pressures are given by the equation for axial
load plus bending. This is provided there is positive contact between the base and
the ground along the complete length D of the footing, as in figure 10.3b so that

$$p = \frac{N}{BD} \pm \frac{My}{I}$$

where I is the second moment of area of the base about the axis of bending and y is
the distance from the axis to where the pressure is being calculated.

Breadth of footing = B, Eccentricity (e) = M/N

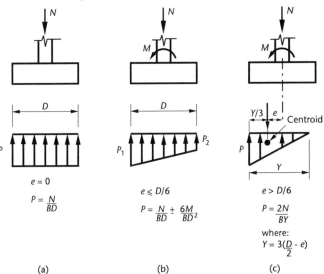

Figure 10.3
Pad footing – pressure
distributions

Substituting for $I = BD^3/12$ and $y = D/2$, the maximum pressure is

$$p_1 = \frac{N}{BD} + \frac{6M}{BD^2} \qquad (10.2)^*$$

and the minimum pressure is

$$p_2 = \frac{N}{BD} - \frac{6M}{BD^2} \qquad (10.3)^*$$

There is positive contact along the base if p_2 from equation 10.3 is positive. When pressure p_2 just equals zero

$$\frac{N}{BD} - \frac{6M}{BD^2} = 0$$

or

$$\frac{M}{N} = \frac{D}{6}$$

So that for p_2 to always be positive, M/N – or the effective eccentricity, e – must never be greater than $D/6$. In these cases the eccentricity of loading is said to lie within the 'middle third' of the base.

3. When the eccentricity, e, is greater than $D/6$ there is no longer a positive pressure along the length D and the pressure diagram is triangular as shown in figure 10.3c. Balancing the downward load and the upward pressures.

$$\tfrac{1}{2}pBY = N$$

therefore

$$\text{maximum pressure } p = \frac{2N}{BY}$$

where Y is the length of positive contact. The centroid of the pressure diagram must coincide with the eccentricity of loading in order for the load and reaction to be equal and opposite.

Thus

$$\frac{Y}{3} = \frac{D}{2} - e$$

or

$$Y = 3\left(\frac{D}{2} - e\right)$$

therefore in this case of $e > D/6$

$$\text{maximum pressure } p = \frac{2N}{3B(D/2 - e)} \qquad (10.4)*$$

A typical arrangement of the reinforcement in a pad footing is shown in figure 10.4. With a square base the reinforcement to resist bending should be distributed uniformly across the full width of the footing. For a rectangular base the reinforcement in the short direction should be distributed with a closer spacing in the region under and near the column, to allow for the fact that the transverse moments must be greater nearer the column. If the footing should be subjected to a large overturning moment so that there is only partial bearing, or if there is a resultant uplift force, then reinforcement may also be required in the top face.

Dowels or starter bars should extend from the footing into the column in order to provide continuity to the reinforcement. These dowels should be embedded into the footing and extend into the columns a full lap length. Sometimes a 75mm length of the column is constructed in the same concrete pour as the footing so as to form a 'kicker' or support for the column shutters. In these cases the dowel lap length should be measured from the top of the kicker.

The critical sections through the base for checking shear, punching shear and bending are shown in figure 10.5. The shearing force and bending moments are caused by the ultimate loads from the column and the weight of the base should not be included in these calculations

The thickness of the base is often governed by the requirements for shear resistance.

Figure 10.4
Pad footings – reinforcement details

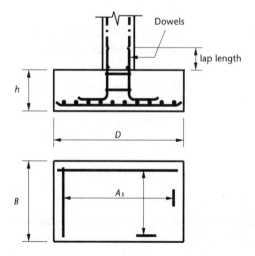

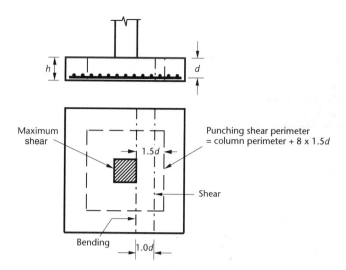

Figure 10.5
Critical sections for design

The principal steps in the design calculations are as follows.

1. Calculate the plan size of the footing using the permissible bearing pressure and the critical loading arrangement for the serviceability limit state.
2. Calculate the bearing pressures associated with the critical loading arrangement at the ultimate limit state.
3. Assume a suitable value for the thickness (h) and effective depth (d). Check that the shear stress at the column face is less than 5 N/mm^2 or $0.8\sqrt{f_{cu}}$, whichever is the smaller.
4. Check the thickness for punching shear, assuming a probable value for the ultimate shear stress, ν_c from table 5.1.
5. Determine the reinforcement required to resist bending.
6. Make a final check of the punching shear, having established ν_c precisely.
7. Check the shear stress at the critical sections.
8. Where applicable, foundations and structure should be checked for overall stability at the ultimate limit state.

Reinforcement to resist bending in the bottom of the base should extend at least a full tension anchorage length beyond the critical section for bending.

EXAMPLE 10.1

Design of a pad footing

The footing (figure 10.6) is required to resist characteristic axial loads of 1000 kN dead and 350 kN imposed from a 400 mm square column. The safe bearing pressure on the soil is 200 kN/m^2 and the characteristic material strengths are $f_{cu} = 35$ N/mm^2 and $f_y = 460$ N/mm^2.

Assume a footing weight of 150 kN so that the total dead load is 1150 kN.

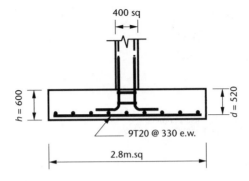

(a) For the serviceability limit state

Total design axial load $= 1.0G_k + 1.0Q_k$

$= 1150 + 350 = 1500$ kN

required base area $= \dfrac{1500}{200} = 7.5$ m^2

Provide a base 2.8 m square, area $= 7.8$ m^2.

(b) For the ultimate limit state

Column design axial load $= 1.4G_k + 1.6Q_k$

$= 1.4 \times 1000 + 1.6 \times 350 = 1960$ kN

earth pressure $= \dfrac{1960}{2.8^2} = 250$ kN/m^2

(c) Assume a 600 mm thick footing and with the footing constructed on a blinding layer of concrete the minimum cover is taken as 50 mm. Therefore take mean effective depth $d = 520$ mm.

At the column face

shear stress, $\nu_c = N/(\text{column perimeter} \times d)$

$= 1960 \times 10^3/(1600 \times 520)$

$= 2.36$ N/mm$^2 < 0.8\sqrt{f_{cu}}$

(d) Punching shear – see figure 10.5

critical perimeter $= \text{column perimeter} + 8 \times 1.5d$

$= 4 \times 400 + 12 \times 520 = 7840$ mm

area within perimeter $= (400 + 3d)^2$

$= (400 + 1560)^2 = 3.84 \times 10^6$ mm^2

therefore

punching shear force $V = 250(2.8^2 - 3.84) = 1000$ kN

punching shear stress $\nu = \dfrac{V}{\text{Perimeter} \times d}$

$= \dfrac{1000 \times 10^3}{7840 \times 520} = 0.25$ N/mm^2

From table 5.1 this ultimate shear stress is not excessive, therefore $h = 600$ mm will be suitable.

(e) Bending reinforcement – see figure 10.7a

At the column face which is the critical section

$$M = (250 \times 2.8 \times 1.2) \times \frac{1.2}{2} = 504 \text{ kN m}$$

for the concrete

$$M_u = 0.156 f_{cu} b d^2$$
$$= 0.156 \times 35 \times 2800 \times 520^2 \times 10^{-6}$$
$$= 4133 \text{ kN m} > 504$$

$$A_s = \frac{M}{0.95 f_y z}$$

From the lever-arm curve, figure 7.5, $l_a = 0.95$. Therefore

$$A_s = \frac{504 \times 10^6}{0.95 \times 460(0.95 \times 520)} = 2335 \text{ mm}^2$$

Provide nine T20 bars at 330 mm centres, $A_s = 2830 \text{ mm}^2$. Therefore

$$\frac{100 A_s}{bh} = \frac{100 \times 2830}{2800 \times 600} = 0.17 > 0.13 \text{ as required}$$

Maximum spacing = 750 mm. Therefore the reinforcement provided meets the requirements specified by the code for minimum area and maximum bar spacing in a slab.

(f) Final check of punching shear

From table 5.1, for $f_{cu} = 35$ and $100 A_s / bd = 0.19$

ultimate shear stress, $v_c = 0.4 \text{ N/mm}^2$

punching shear stress was 0.25 N/mm², therefore a 600 mm thick pad is adequate.

(g) Shear stress – see figure 10.7b

At the critical section for shear, $1.0d$ from the column face

$$V = 250 \times 2.8 \times 0.68 = 476 \text{ kN}$$

$$v = \frac{V}{bd} = \frac{476 \times 10^3}{2800 \times 520}$$
$$= 0.33 \text{ N/mm}^2 < 0.4$$

Therefore the section is adequate in shear.

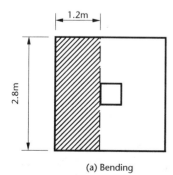

2.8m

1.2m

(a) Bending

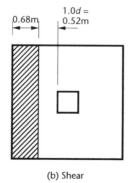

0.68m

1.0d = 0.52m

(b) Shear

Figure 10.7
Critical sections

Instead of assuming a footing weight of 150 kN at the start of this example it is possible to allow for the weight of the footing by using a net safe bearing pressure p_{net} where

$$p_{net} = 200 - h \times \text{unit weight of concrete}$$
$$= 200 - 0.6 \times 24 = 185.6 \text{ kN/m}^2$$

$$\text{Required base area} = \frac{1.0 \times \text{column load}}{p_{net}}$$
$$= \frac{1000 + 350}{185.6}$$
$$= 7.3 \text{m}^2$$

It should be noted that the self-weight of the footing or its effect must be included in the calculations at serviceability for determining the area of the base but at the ultimate limit state the self-weight should not be included.

10.2 Combined footings

Where two columns are close together it is sometimes necessary or convenient to combine their footings to form a continuous base. The dimensions of the footing should be chosen so that the resultant load passes through the centroid of the base area. This may be assumed to give a uniform bearing pressure under the footing and help to prevent differential settlement. For most structures the ratios of dead and imposed loads carried by each column are similar so that if the resultant passes through the centroid for the serviceability limit state then this will also be true – or very nearly – at the ultimate limit state, and hence in these cases a uniform pressure distribution may be considered for both limit states.

The shape of the footing may be rectangular or trapezoidal as shown in figure 10.8. The trapezoidal base has the disadvantage of detailing and cutting varying lengths of reinforcing bars; it is used where there is a large variation in the loads carried by the two columns and there are limitations on the length of the footing. Sometimes in order to strengthen the base and economise on concrete a beam is incorporated between the two columns so that the base is designed as an inverted T-section.

The proportions of the footing depend on many factors. If it is too long, there will be large longitudinal moments on the lengths projecting beyond the columns, whereas a short base will have a larger span moment between the columns and the greater width will cause large transverse moments. The thickness of the footing must be such that the shear stresses are not excessive.

Figure 10.8
Combined bases

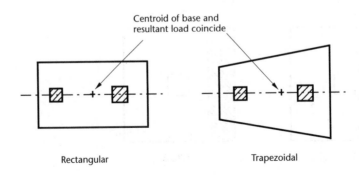

Rectangular   Trapezoidal

EXAMPLE 10.2

Design of a combined footing

The footing supports two columns 300 mm square and 400 mm square with characteristic dead and imposed loads as shown in figure 10.9. The safe bearing pressure is 300 kN/m^2 and the characteristic material strengths are $f_{cu} = 35$ N/mm^2 and $f_y = 460$ N/mm^2.

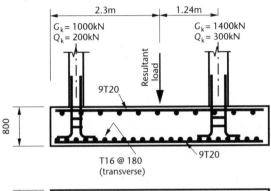

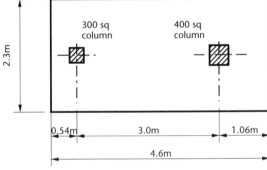

Figure 10.9
Combined footing example

1. Base area: allow, say, 250 kN for the self-weight of the footing. At the serviceability limit state

    total load $= 250 + 1000 + 200 + 1400 + 300 = 3150$ kN

    area of base required $= \dfrac{3150}{300} = 10.5$ m^2

    provide a rectangular base, 4.6 m × 2.3 m, area $= 10.58$ m^2.

2. Resultant of column loads and centroid of base: taking moments about the centre line of the 400 mm square column

    $$\bar{x} = \frac{1200 \times 3}{1200 + 1700} = 1.24 \text{ m}$$

    The base is centred on this position of the resultant of the column loads as shown in figure 10.9.

3. Bearing pressure at the ultimate limit state:

    column loads $= 1.4 \times 1000 + 1.6 \times 200 + 1.4 \times 1400 + 1.6 \times 300$

    $= 1720 + 2440 = 4160$ kN

therefore

$$\text{earth pressure} = \frac{4160}{4.6 \times 2.3} = 393 \text{ kN/m}^2$$

4. Assuming an 800 mm thick base with $d = 740$ mm for the longitudinal bars and with a mean $d = 730$ mm for punching shear calculations:

At the column face

shear stress, $\nu_c = N/\text{column perimeter} \times d$

For 300 mm square column

$$\nu_c = 1720 \times 10^3/(1200 \times 730) = 1.47 \text{ N/mm}^2 < 0.8\sqrt{f_{cu}}$$

For 400 mm square column

$$\nu_c = 2440 \times 10^3/(1600 \times 730) = 2.09 \text{ N/mm}^2 < 0.8\sqrt{f_{cu}}$$

5. Longitudinal moments and shear forces: the shear-force and bending-moment diagrams at the ultimate limit state and for a net upward pressure of 393 kN/m^2 are shown in figure 10.10.

6. Shear: punching shear cannot be checked, since the critical perimeter $1.5d$ from the column face lies outside the base area. The critical section for shear is taken $1.0d$ from the column face. Therefore with $d = 730$ mm

$$V = 1482 - 393 \times 2.3(0.74 + 0.2)$$
$$= 632 \text{ kN}$$

thus

$$\text{shear stress } \nu = \frac{V}{bd} = \frac{632 \times 10^3}{2300 \times 730}$$

$$= 0.38 \text{ N/mm}^2 \text{ which from table 5.1 is just satisfactory for grade 35 concrete}$$

Figure 10.10
Shear-force and
bending-moment diagrams

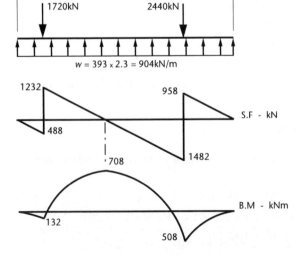

7. Longitudinal bending

(i) Mid-span between the columns

$$A_s = \frac{M}{0.95 f_y z} = \frac{708 \times 10^6}{0.95 \times 460 \times 0.95 \times 740}$$

$$= 2302 \text{ mm}^2$$

Provide nine T20 at 270 mm centres, area $= 2830 \text{ mm}^2$, top.

(ii) At the face of the 400 mm square column

$$M = 393 \times 2.3 \times \frac{(1.06 - 0.2)^2}{2}$$

$$= 334 \text{ kN m}$$

$$A_s = \frac{M}{0.95 f_y z} = \frac{334 \times 10^6}{0.95 \times 460 \times 0.95 \times 740}$$

$$= 1087 \text{ mm}^2$$

but

$$\text{minimum } A_s = \frac{0.13 bh}{100} = \frac{0.13 \times 2300 \times 800}{100}$$

$$= 2392 \text{ mm}^2$$

Provide nine T20 at 270 mm centres, $A_s = 2830 \text{ mm}^2$, bottom.

8. Transverse bending

$$M = 393 \times \frac{1.15^2}{2} = 260 \text{ kN m/m}$$

$$A_s = \frac{M}{0.95 f_y z} = \frac{260 \times 10^6}{0.95 \times 460 \times 0.95 \times 720}$$

$$= 870 \text{ mm}^2/\text{m}$$

but

$$\text{minimum } A_s = \frac{0.13 bh}{100} = \frac{0.13 \times 1000 \times 800}{100}$$

$$= 1040 \text{ mm}^2/\text{m}$$

Provide T16 bars at 180 mm centres, areas $= 1117 \text{ mm}^2$ per metre.

The transverse reinforcement should be placed at closer centres under the columns to allow for greater moments in those regions.

10.3 Strap footings

Strap footings, as shown in figure 10.11, are used where the base for an exterior column must not project beyond the property line. A strap beam is constructed between the exterior footing and the adjacent interior footing – the purpose of the strap is to restrain the overturning force due to the eccentric load on the exterior footing.

Figure 10.11
Strap footing with shearing
force and bending moments
for the strap beam

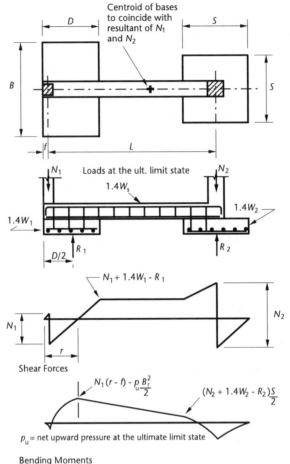

Loads at the ult. limit state

Shear Forces

p_u = net upward pressure at the ultimate limit state

Bending Moments

The base areas of the footings are proportioned so that the bearing pressures are uniform and equal under both bases. Thus it is necessary that the resultant of the loads on the two footings should pass through the centroid of the areas of the two bases. The strap beam between the footings should not bear against the soil, hence the ground directly under the beam should be loosened and left uncompacted.

To achieve suitable sizes for the footings several trial designs may be necessary. With reference to figure 10.11 the principal steps in the design are as follows.

1. Choose a trial D for the rectangular outer footing and assume weights W_1 and W_2 for the footings and W_s for the strap beam.

2. Take moments about the centre line of the inner column in order to determine the reaction R_1 under the outer footing. The loadings should be those required for the serviceability limit state. Thus

$$(R_1 - W_1)\left(L + f - \frac{D}{2}\right) - N_1 L - W_s \frac{L}{2} = 0 \qquad (10.5)$$

and solve for R_1.

The width B of the outer footing is then given by

$$B = \frac{R_1}{pD}$$

where p is the safe bearing pressure.

3. Equate the vertical loads and reactions to determine the reaction R_2 under the inner footing. Thus

$$R_1 + R_2 - (N_1 + N_2 + W_1 + W_2 + W_s) = 0 \qquad (10.6)$$

and solve for R_2. The size S of the square inner footing is then given by

$$S = \sqrt{\frac{R_2}{p}}$$

4. Check that the resultant of all the loads on the footings passes through the centroid of the areas of the two bases. If the resultant is too far away from the centroid then steps 1 to 4 must be repeated until there is adequate agreement.

5. Apply the loading associated with the ultimate limit state. Accordingly, revise equations 10.5 and 10.6 to determine the new values for R_1 and R_2. Hence calculate the bearing pressure p_u for this limit state. It may be assumed that the bearing pressures for this case are also equal and uniform, provided the ratios of dead load to imposed load are similar for both columns.

6. Design the inner footing as a square base with bending in both directions.

7. Design the outer footing as a base with bending in one direction and supported by the strap beam.

8. Design the strap beam. The maximum bending moment on the beam occurs at the point of zero shear as shown in figure 10.11. The shear on the beam is virtually constant, the slight decrease being caused by the beam's self-weight. The stirrups should be placed at a constant spacing but they should extend into the footings over the supports so as to give a monolithic foundation. The main tension steel is required at the top of the beam but reinforcement should also be provided in the bottom of the beam so as to cater for any differential settlement or downward loads on the beam.

10.4 | Strip footings

Strip footings are used under walls or under a line of closely-spaced columns. Even were it possible to have individual bases, it is often simpler and more economic to excavate and construct the formwork for a continuous base.

On the sloping site the foundations should be constructed on a horizontal bearing and stepped where necessary. At the steps the footings should be lapped as shown in figure 10.12.

The footings are analysed and designed as an inverted continuous beam subjected to the ground bearing pressures. With a thick rigid footing and a firm soil, a linear distribution of bearing pressure is considered. If the columns are equally spaced and equally loaded the pressure is uniformly distributed but if the loading is not symmetrical then the base is subjected to an eccentric load and the bearing pressure varies as shown in figure 10.13.

Figure 10.12
Stepped footing on a slope

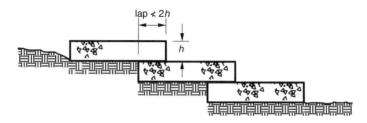

Figure 10.13
Linear pressure distribution
under a rigid strip footing

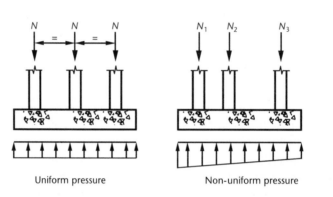

Uniform pressure   Non-uniform pressure

The bearing pressures will not be linear when the footing is not very rigid and the soil is soft and compressible. In these cases the bending-moment diagram would be quite unlike that for a continuous beam with firmly held supports and the moments could be quite large, particularly if the loading is unsymmetrical. For a large foundation it may be necessary to have a more detailed investigation of the soil pressures under the base in order to determine the bending moments and shearing forces.

Reinforcement is required in the bottom of the base to resist the transverse bending moments in addition to the reinforcement required for the longitudinal bending. Footings which support heavily loaded columns often require stirrups and bent-up bars to resist the shearing forces.

EXAMPLE 10.3

Design of a strip footing

Design a strip footing to carry 400 mm square columns equally spaced at 3.5 m centres. On each column the characteristic loads are 1000 kN dead and 350 kN imposed. The safe bearing pressure is 200 kN/m^2 and the characteristic material strengths are $f_{cu} = 35$ N/mm^2 and $f_y = 460$ N/mm^2.

1. Try a thickness of footing $= 800$ with $d = 740$ mm for the longitudinal reinforcement

$$\text{Net bearing pressure, } p_{net} = 200 - 24h$$
$$= 200 - 24 \times 0.8$$
$$= 180.8 \text{ kN/m}^2$$
$$\text{Width of footing required} = \frac{1000 + 350}{180.8 \times 3.5}$$
$$= 2.13 \text{ m}$$

Provide a strip footing 2.2 m wide.

At the ultimate limit state

column load $= 1.4 \times 1000 + 1.6 \times 350 = 1960$ kN

$$\text{bearing pressure} = \frac{1960}{2.2 \times 3.5}$$

$$= 255 \text{ kN/m}^2$$

2. *Punching shear* at column face

$$\nu_c = N/\text{column perimeter} \times d$$

$$= 1960 \times 10^3 / 1600 \times 740$$

$$= 1.7 \text{ N/mm}^2 < 0.8\sqrt{f_{cu}}$$

By inspection, the normal shear on a section at the column face will be significantly less severe.

3. *Longitudinal reinforcement*

Using the moment and shear coefficients for an equal-span continuous beam (figure 3.10), for an interior span

$$\text{moment at the columns} = 255 \times 2.2 \times 3.5^2 \times 0.08$$

$$= 550 \text{ kN m}$$

therefore

$$A_s = \frac{550 \times 10^6}{0.95 \times 460 \times 0.95 \times 740} = 1790 \text{ mm}^2$$

$$\text{minimum } A_s = \frac{0.13bh}{100} = 0.13 \times 2200 \times \frac{800}{100} = 2288 \text{ mm}^2$$

Provide eight T20 at 300 mm centres, area $= 2510$ mm^2, bottom steel (figure 10.14).

In the span

$$M = 255 \times 2.2 \times 3.5^2 \times 0.07$$

$$= 481 \text{ kN m}$$

therefore

$$A_s = \frac{481 \times 10^6}{0.95 \times 460 \times 0.95 \times 740} = 1566 \text{ mm}^2$$

Provide eight T20 bars at 300 mm centres, area $= 2510$ mm^2, top steel (figure 10.14).

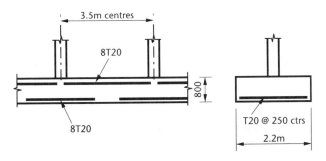

Figure 10.14
Strip footing with bending reinforcement

4. *Transverse reinforcement*

$$M = 255 \times \frac{1.1^2}{2} = 155 \text{ kN m/m}$$

$$A_s = \frac{155 \times 10^6}{0.95 \times 460 \times 0.95 \times 720} = 519 \text{ mm}^2/\text{m}$$

$$\text{minimum } A_s = \frac{0.13bh}{100} = 0.13 \times 1000 \times \frac{800}{100} = 1040 \text{ mm}^2$$

Provide T20 bars at 250 mm centres, area $= 1260$ mm^2/m, bottom steel.

5. *Normal shear* will govern as the punching shear perimeter is outside the footing.

1.0d from column face

$$V = 255 \times 2.2(3.5 \times 0.55 - 0.74 - 0.2) = 553 \text{ kN}$$

(The coefficient of 0.55 is from figure 3.10.)

$$\text{Shear stress } \nu = \frac{553 \times 10^3}{2200 \times 740} = 0.34 \text{ N/mm}^2$$

Allowable ultimate shear stress $= 0.38$ N/mm^2, from table 5.1 for $f_{cu} = 35$ N/mm^2.

10.5 | Raft foundations

A raft foundation transmits the loads to the ground by means of a reinforced concrete slab that is continuous over the base of the structure. The raft is able to span over any areas of weaker soil and it spreads the loads over a wide area. Heavily loaded structures are often provided with one continuous base in preference to many closely spaced, separate footings. Also where settlement is a problem, because of mining subsidence, it is common practice to use a raft foundation in conjunction with a more flexible superstructure.

The simplest type of raft is a flat slab of uniform thickness supporting the columns. Where punching shears are large the columns may be provided with a pedestal at their base as shown in figure 10.15. The pedestal serves a similar function to the drop panel in a flat slab floor. Other, more heavily loaded rafts require the foundation to be strengthened by beams to form a ribbed construction. The beams may be downstanding, projecting below the slab or they may be upstanding as shown in the figure. Downstanding beams have the disadvantage of disturbing the ground below the slab and the excavated trenches are often a nuisance during construction, while upstanding beams interrupt the clear floor area above the slab. To overcome this a second slab is sometimes cast on top of the beams, so forming a cellular raft.

Figure 10.15
Raft foundations

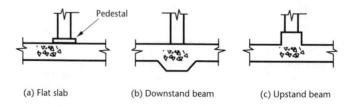

(a) Flat slab   (b) Downstand beam   (c) Upstand beam

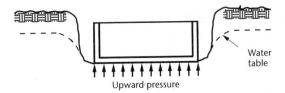

Figure 10.16
Raft foundation subject to
uplift

Rafts having a uniform slab, and without strengthening beams, are generally analysed and designed as an inverted flat slab floor subjected to the earth bearing pressures. With regular column spacing and equal column loading, the coefficients tabulated in section 8.7 for flat slab floors are used to calculate the bending moments in the raft. The slab must be checked for punching shear around the columns and around pedestals, if they are used.

A raft with strengthening beams is designed as an inverted beam and slab floor. The slab is designed to span in two directions where there are supporting beams on all four sides. The beams are often subjected to high shearing forces which need to be resisted by a combination of stirrups and bent-up bars.

Raft foundations which are below the level of the water table as in figure 10.16 should be checked to ensure that they are able to resist the uplift forces due to the hydrostatic pressure. This may be critical during construction before the weight of the superstructure is in place, and it may be necessary to provide extra weight to the raft and lower the water table by pumping. An alternative method is to anchor the slab down with short tension piles.

10.6 Piled foundations

Piles are used where the soil conditions are poor and it is uneconomical, or not possible, to provide adequate spread foundations. The piles must extend down to firm soil so that the load is carried by either (1) end bearing, (2) friction, or (3) a combination of both end bearing and friction. Concrete piles may be precast and driven into the ground, or they may be the cast *in situ* type which are bored or excavated.

A soils survey of a proposed site should be carried out to determine the depth to firm soil and the properties of the soil. This information will provide a guide to the lengths of pile required and the probable safe load capacity of the piles. On a large contract the safe loads are often determined from full-scale load tests on typical piles or groups of piles. With driven piles the safe load can be calculated from equations which relate the resistance of the pile to the measured set per blow and the driving force.

The load-carrying capacity of a group of piles is not necessarily a multiple of that for a single pile – it is often considerably less. For a large group of closely spaced friction piles the reduction can be of the order of one-third. In contrast, the load capacity of a group of end bearing piles on a thick stratum of rock or compact sand gravel is substantially the sum total of the resistance of each individual pile. Figure 10.17 shows the bulbs of pressure under piles and illustrates why the settlement of a group of piles is dependent on the soil properties at a greater depth.

The minimum spacing of piles, centre to centre, should not be less than (1) the pile perimeter – for friction piles, or (2) twice the least width of the pile – for end bearing piles. Bored piles are sometimes enlarged at their base so that they have a larger bearing area or a greater resistance to uplift.

Figure 10.17
Bulbs of pressure

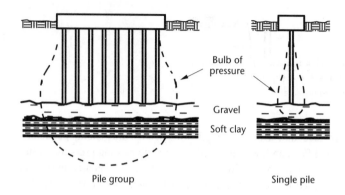

Pile group   Single pile

A pile is designed as a short column unless it is slender and the surrounding soil is too weak to provide restraint. Precast piles must also be designed to resist the bending moments caused by lifting and stacking, and the head of the pile must be reinforced to withstand the impact of the driving hammer.

It is very difficult if not impossible to determine the true distribution of load of a pile group, therefore, in general, it is more realistic to use methods that are simple but logical. A vertical load on a group of vertical piles with an axis of symmetry is considered to be distributed according to the following equation, which is similar in form to that for an eccentric load on a pad foundation:

$$P_n = \frac{N}{n} \pm \frac{Ne_{xx}}{I_{xx}} y_n \pm \frac{Ne_{yy}}{I_{yy}} x_n$$

where P_n is the axial load on an individual pile

N is the vertical load on the pile group

n is the number of piles

e_{xx} and e_{yy} are the eccentricities of the load N about the centroidal axes XX and YY of the pile group

I_{xx} and I_{yy} are the second moments of area of the pile group about axes XX and YY

x_n and y_n are the distances of the individual pile from axes YY and XX, respectively.

EXAMPLE 10.4

Loads in a pile group

Determine the distribution between the individual piles of a 1000 kN vertical load acting at position A of the group of vertical piles shown in figure 10.18.

Centroid of the pile group: taking moments about line TT

$$\bar{y} = \frac{\sum y}{n}$$

$$= \frac{2.0 + 2.0 + 3.0 + 3.0}{6} = 1.67 \text{ m}$$

where n is the number of piles. Therefore the eccentricities of the load about the XX and YY centroidal axis are

$$e_{xx} = 2.0 - 1.67 = 0.33 \text{ m}$$

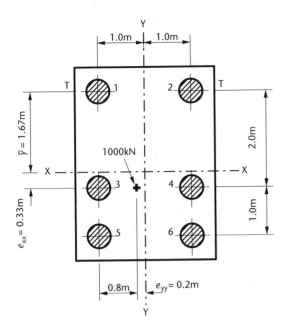

Figure 10.18
Pile loading example

and

$e_{yy} = 0.2$ m

$I_{xx} = \sum y_n^2$ with respect to the centroidal axis XX

$\qquad = 2 \times 1.67^2 + 2 \times 0.33^2 + 2 \times 1.33^2$

$\qquad = 9.33$

similarly

$I_{yy} = \sum x_n^2$

$\qquad = 3 \times 1.0^2 + 3 \times 1.0^2 = 6.0$

Therefore

$$P_n = \frac{N}{n} \pm \frac{Ne_{xx}}{I_{xx}} y_n \pm \frac{Ne_{yy}}{I_{yy}} x_n$$

$$\qquad = \frac{1000}{6} \pm \frac{1000 \times 0.33}{9.33} y_n \pm \frac{1000 \times 0.2}{6.0} x_n$$

$$\qquad = 166.7 \pm 35.4 y_n \pm 33.3 x_n$$

Therefore, substituting for y_n and x_n

$P_1 = 166.7 - 35.4 \times 1.67 + 33.3 \times 1.0 = 140.9$ kN

$P_2 = 166.7 - 35.4 \times 1.67 - 33.3 \times 1.0 = 74.3$ kN

$P_3 = 166.7 + 35.4 \times 0.33 + 33.3 \times 1.0 = 211.7$ kN

$P_4 = 166.7 + 35.4 \times 0.33 - 33.3 \times 1.0 = 145.1$ kN

$P_5 = 166.7 + 35.4 \times 1.33 + 33.3 \times 1.0 = 247.1$ kN

$P_6 = 166.7 + 35.4 \times 1.33 - 33.3 \times 1.0 = \underline{180.5}$ kN

$\qquad\qquad\qquad$ Total $\quad$ 999.6 $\approx$ 1000 kN

Figure 10.19
Forces in raking piles

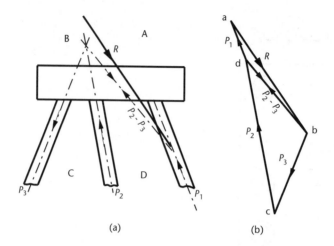

(a) (b)

When a pile group is unsymmetrical about both co-ordinate axes it is necessary to consider the theory of bending about the principal axes which is dealt with in most textbooks on strength of materials. In this case the formulae for the pile loads are

$$P_n = \frac{N}{n} \pm Ay_n \pm Bx_n$$

where

$$A = \frac{N\left(e_{xx}\sum x_n{}^2 - e_{yy}\sum x_n y_n\right)}{\sum x_n{}^2 \sum y_n{}^2 - \left(\sum x_n y_n\right)^2}$$

and

$$B = \frac{N\left(e_{yy}\sum y_n{}^2 - e_{xx}\sum x_n y_n\right)}{\sum x_n{}^2 \sum y_n{}^2 - \left(\sum x_n y_n\right)^2}$$

Note that e_{xx} is the eccentricity about the XX axis, while e_{yy} is the eccentricity about the YY axis, as in figure 10.18.

Piled foundations are sometimes required to resist horizontal forces in addition to the vertical loads. If the horizontal forces are small they can often be resisted by the passive pressure of the soil against vertical piles, otherwise if the forces are not small then raking piles must be provided as shown in figure 10.19a.

To determine the load in each pile either a static method or an elastic method is available. The static method is simply a graphical analysis using Bow's notation as illustrated in figure 10.19b. This method assumes that the piles are pinned at their ends so that the induced loads are axial. The elastic method takes into account the displacements and rotations of the piles which may be considered pinned or fixed at their ends. The pile foundation is analysed in a similar manner to a plane frame or space frame and available computer programs are commonly used.

10.7 Design of pile caps

The pile cap must be rigid and capable of transferring the column loads to the piles and should have sufficient thickness for anchorage of the column dowels and the pile reinforcement. Two methods of design are common: design using beam theory or design using a truss analogy approach. In the former case the pile cap is treated as an inverted beam and is designed for the usual conditions of bending and shear. The truss analogy method is used to determine the reinforcement requirements where the span to depth ratio is less than 2 such that beam theory is not appropriate.

10.7.1 The truss analogy method

In the truss analogy the force from the supported column is assumed to be transmitted by a triangular truss action with concrete providing the compressive members of the truss and steel reinforcement providing the tensile tie force as shown in the two pile cap in figure 10.20a. The upper node of the truss is located at the centre of the loaded area and the lower nodes at the intersection of the tensile reinforcement with the centre-lines of the piles. Where the piles are spaced at a distance greater than three times the pile diameter only the reinforcement within a distance of 1.5 times the pile diameter from the centre of the pile should be considered as effective in providing the tensile resistance within the truss.

From the geometry of the force diagram in figure 10.20b:

$$\frac{T}{N/2} = \frac{l}{d}$$

therefore

$$T = \frac{Nl}{2d}$$

Hence

$$\text{required area of reinforcement} = \frac{T}{0.95 f_y} = \frac{N \times l}{2d \times 0.95 f_y} \tag{10.7}$$

Where the pile cap is supported on a four-pile group, as shown in figure 10.21, the load can be considered to be transmitted equally by parallel pairs of trusses, such as AB and CD, and equation 10.7 can be modified to give:

$$\text{Required area of reinforcement in each truss} = \frac{T/2}{0.95 f_y} = \frac{N \times l}{4d \times 0.95 f_y} \tag{10.8}$$

and this reinforcement should be provided in both directions in the bottom face of the pile-cap.

The truss theory may be extended to give the tensile force in pile caps with other configurations of pile groups. Table 10.2 gives the force for some common cases.

Figure 10.20.
Truss model for a two pile cap

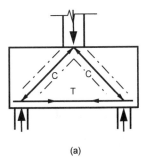

(a)

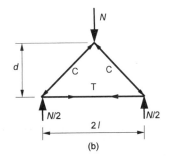

(b)

Figure 10.21
Four pile cap

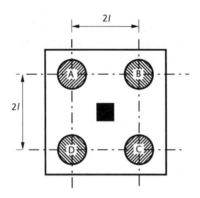

Table 10.2   Tension forces in pile cap

Number of Piles	Group Arrangement	Tensile Force
2	A ⬤ ■ ⬤ B $2l$	$T_{AB} = \dfrac{Nl}{2d}$
3	(triangular arrangement) $2l$, $2l$, A, C, B	$T_{AB} = T_{BC} = T_{AC} = \dfrac{2Nl}{9d}$
4	A ⬤ ⬤ B $2l$ ■ D ⬤ ⬤ C $2l$	$T_{AB} = T_{BC} = T_{CD} = T_{AD} = \dfrac{Nl}{4d}$

10.7.2 Design for shear

The shear capacity of a pile cap should be checked at the critical section taken to be 20 per cent of the pile diameter inside the face of the pile, as shown in figure 10.22. In determining the shear resistance, shear enhancement may be considered such that the shear capacity of the concrete may be increased to $2d/a_v \times v_c$ where a_v is the distance from the face of the column to the critical section. Where the spacing of the piles is less than or equal to three times the pile diameter, this enhancement may be applied across the whole of the critical section; otherwise it may only be applied to strips of width of three times the pile diameter located central to each pile.

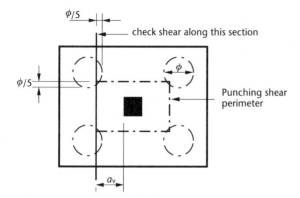

Figure 10.22
Critical sections for shear checks

10.7.3   Design for punching shear

Where the spacing of the piles exceeds three times the pile diameter then the pile cap should be checked for punching shear using the method outlined in section 8.2.2 for slabs. The critical perimeter for punching shear is as shown in figure 10.22. The design shear stress should be checked at the face of the column to ensure that it does not exceed the lesser of $0.8\sqrt{f_{cu}}$ N/mm^2 or 5 N/mm^2.

10.7.4   Reinforcement detailing

As for all members, normal detailing requirements must be checked. These include maximum and minimum steel areas, bar spacings, cover to reinforcement and anchorage lengths of the tension steel. The main tension reinforcement should continue past each pile and should be bent up vertically to provide a full anchorage length beyond the centre-line of each pile. In orthogonal directions in the top and bottom faces of the pile cap a minimum steel area of $0.0013bh$ for grade 460 reinforcement or $0.0024bh$ for grade 250 reinforcement should be provided. It is normal to provide fully lapped horizontal links of size not less than 12 mm and at spacings of no greater than 250 mm, as shown in figure 10.23b. The piles should be cut off so that they do not extend into the pile cap beyond the lower mat of reinforcing bars otherwise the punching shear strength may be reduced.

10.7.5   Sizing of the pile cap

In determining a suitable depth of pile cap table 10.3 may be used as a guide when there are up to six piles in the pile group.

Table 10.3   Depth of pile cap

Pile size (mm)	300	350	400	450	500	550	600	750
Cap depth (mm)	700	800	900	1000	1100	1200	1400	1800

EXAMPLE 10.5

Design of a pile cap

A group of four piles supports a 500 mm square column which transmits an ultimate axial load of 5000 kN. The piles are 450 mm diameter and are spaced at 1350 mm centres as shown. Design the pile cap for $f_{cu} = 30$ N/mm² and $f_y = 460$ N/mm².

Figure 10.23
Pile-cap design example

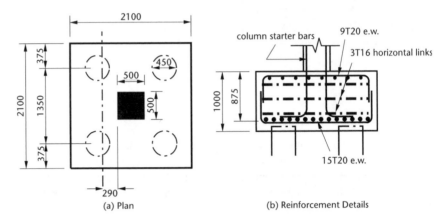

(a) Plan

(b) Reinforcement Details

(a) Dimensions of pile cap

Try an overall depth of 1000 mm and an average effective depth of 875 mm. Allow the pile to extend 375 mm either side to give a 2100 mm square cap.

(b) Design of main tension reinforcement

From equation 10.8, the required area of reinforcement in each truss is

$$A_s = \frac{T/2}{0.95 f_y} = \frac{N \times l}{4d \times 0.95 f_y} = \frac{5000 \times 10^3 \times (1350/2)}{4 \times 875 \times 0.95 \times 460} = 2207 \text{ mm}^2$$

The total area of reinforcement required in each direction $2 \times A_s = 2 \times 2207 = 4414$ mm². As the piles are spaced at three times the pile diameter this reinforcement may be distributed uniformly across the section. Hence provide fifteen T20 bars, area = 4710 mm², at 140 mm centres in both directions:

$$\frac{100 A_s}{bh} = \frac{100 \times 4710}{2100 \times 1000} = 0.22 \quad (> 0.13)$$

(c) Check for shear

$$\text{Percentage of steel provided} = \frac{100 A_s}{bd} = \frac{100 \times 4710}{2100 \times 875} = 0.26$$

Thus from table 5.1 the allowable shear stress, $\nu_c = 0.43$ N/mm²

$$\text{Enhanced shear stress} = 2d/a_v \times \nu_c = 2 \times \frac{875}{290} \times 0.43 = 2.59 \text{ N/mm}^2$$

Shear stress along critical section

$$\nu = \frac{(5000/2) \times 10^3}{2100 \times 875} = 1.36 \text{ N/mm}^2 \quad (< \nu_c = 2.59 \text{ N/mm}^2)$$

(d) Check for punching shear

As the pile spacing is at three times the pile diameter no punching shear check is necessary. The shear at the column face is given by

$$\nu = \frac{N}{ud}$$
$$= \frac{5000 \times 10^3}{(4 \times 500) \times 875}$$
$$= 2.86 \text{ N/mm}^2 \qquad (< 0.8\sqrt{f_{cu}} = 4.38 \text{ N/mm}^2)$$

CHAPTER 11

Water-retaining structures and retaining walls

CHAPTER INTRODUCTION

The design of both water-retaining structures and retaining walls is based on analysis and design techniques which have been discussed in previous chapters. Because of their specialised nature, however, design is often governed by factors which may be regarded as secondary in normal reinforced concrete work. Such structures are relatively common, in one form or another, and hence justify coverage in some detail.

The retention of liquid within water-retaining structures is obviously of importance and detailed consideration must be given to the control of cracking both as a result of loading and due to temperature and shrinkage effects. Detailed design must therefore address not only ultimate strength considerations but, equally importantly, serviceability considerations of cracking. Such design considerations must include the amount and distribution of the reinforcing steel together with the provision, and type, of movement joints which will control the development of cracks. This chapter therefore considers the design of water-retaining structures, in particular the calculations and practical considerations necessary for the control of cracking.

Retaining wall structures are used to resist earth and hydrostatic loading. There are a number of differing types, some of the more common forms of which are described. Walls must be designed to be stable with adequate resistance to overturning and sliding, allowable ground bearing pressures beneath the base of the wall must not be exceeded and all parts of the wall must be of adequate structural strength. All these aspects of design are outlined and illustrated with a detailed design example of a cantilever type retaining wall.

11.1 Water-retaining structures

This category includes those which are required to contain, or exclude, any non-aggressive aqueous liquid. Since water is that most commonly involved, however, the rather loose title is frequently used to describe such structures. Common structures of this type include water towers and reservoirs, storage tanks including sewage disposal and treatment systems, and floors and walls of basements and other underground constructions where it is necessary to prevent ingress of groundwater.

As it is important to restrain cracking so that leakages do not take place the design is generally governed by the requirements of the serviceability limit state, but stability considerations are particularly important and design must take careful account of the construction methods to be used. British Standard Code of Practice BS 8007 offers guidance on the design and construction of this category of structure, and is based on a limit state philosophy as embodied in BS 8110.

Elastic design methods have traditionally been used, and these are also summarised in this chapter although not included in BS 8007.

Code of Practice BS 8007 recommends modifications to the detailed Limit State design requirements of BS 8110, with the principal features being:

(a) Use of $\gamma_f = 1.4$ for liquid loads.

(b) Use of concrete grade C35A (this has a maximum water/cement ratio of 0.55 and minimum cement content of 325 kg/m^3 – that is, durability performance comparable to grade C40).

(c) Exposure classification of internal members and both faces of members exposed to liquid on at least one face is severe, giving minimum cover of 40 mm. If a more severe exposure condition exists, BS 8110 durability requirements may dominate.

(d) Maximum crack width limited to 0.2 mm unless the aesthetic appearance is critical, when 0.1 mm is required to avoid staining of the concrete.

(e) Maximum bar spacing of 300 mm.

(f) Anchorage bond stresses for straight horizontal bars in sections subjected to direct tension must be reduced to 70 per cent of the usual values.

(g) At least 75 mm blinding concrete is required below ground slabs.

Design procedures are aimed primarily at providing appropriate combinations of movement joints and reinforcement to limit crack widths to the required values.

11.1.1 Design and construction problems

To ensure a watertight structure the concrete must be adequately reinforced in sections where tension may occur. For this reason it is important to be able to envisage the deflected shape of the structure and its individual elements. Tensile stresses due to any direct tensile forces as well as those due to bending must be included in the design calculations.

Continuity reinforcement to prevent cracking must be provided at corners and at member junctions. This reinforcement must extend well beyond where it is required to resist the tensile stresses, particularly when these stresses occur on the face in contact with the liquid.

The design should consider the cases where the structure is full of liquid (allowing for blocked outlets) and also when it is empty. The structure when empty must have the strength to withstand the active pressure of any retained earth. Since the passive resistance of the earth is never certain to be acting, it should generally be ignored when designing for the structure full.

Cracking may occur not only from flexure and shrinkage, but also from subsidence and in some areas earthquakes. Careful attention must thus be given to geological aspects of a proposed site and in particular to the possibilities of differential settlement. It may sometimes be necessary to provide movement joints to cater for this, in addition to expansion and contraction joints required to allow for thermal and shrinkage movements. Flexural cracking can be controlled by careful design and detailing and is discussed in chapter 6, while shrinkage and thermal effects can be reduced considerably by careful attention to the construction factors listed in section 1.3.

With a thick section, the heat generated by hydration cannot readily be dissipated, and the resulting temperature rise in the body of the concrete may be considerable. In addition to the normal precautions, it may be necessary to use low-heat cements and to restrict the size of pours, for example. Experimental work has shown that in walls and slabs greater than 500 mm in thickness, the outer 250 mm on each face may be regarded as the surface zone and the remainder as core. Minimum reinforcement quantities to control thermal and shrinkage cracking should thus be based on a maximum member thickness of 500 mm.

The bottom surface zone for ground slabs should be only 100 mm. Temperature rises due to hydration must be averaged to allow for the core temperature.

The importance of good curing cannot be overemphasised, but it is important to remember that good compaction on site is just as vital, if not more critical, in producing an impermeable concrete. It is essential, therefore, that the concrete mix used is sufficiently workable to enable easy handling during construction, with no tendency to segregation. An increased water content combined with a higher cement content will help to achieve this, while a longer mixing time, and the use of natural aggregates in preference to crushed stone are also helpful. Wall thicknesses of at least 200 mm are recommended to assist compaction.

Formwork must also be carefully constructed to avoid grout leakage at joints and consequent areas of concrete vulnerable to water penetration. Particular care must also be given to the use of formwork ties. Through ties should not be used, as these offer a potential leakage path. The choice of surface finish should take account of possible staining of exposed surfaces.

Flotation, particularly during construction, is a major problem in many underground tanks and basements. To overcome this it may be necessary to dewater the site, increase the dead weight of the structure, use anchor piles or provide for temporary flooding of the structure. In any case, the construction sequence must be carefully studied, and specified at the design stage to ensure a minimum factor of safety of 1.1 against flotation.

When filling a tank or reservoir for the first time, this should be done slowly. This permits stress redistributions to occur, and this, coupled with creep effects, will greatly reduce the extent of cracking. An initial watertightness test is likely to be specified, and a recommended procedure is given by BS 8007. Access provision will be required for inspection, cleaning and testing and this must take account of safety and ventilation requirements.

11.2 ⏸ Joints in water-retaining structures

All concrete structures must inevitably contain construction joints, although the need for joints to accommodate movement in water-retaining structures is governed by the likelihood of, and need to restrict, unacceptable cracking principally due to shrinkage and thermal movements. Frequently it may be possible to combine the two categories of joint.

The principal characteristics of joints are that they must be watertight and, in the case of movement joints, must also permit the repeated required movements to take place as freely as possible. Waterbars will generally be incorporated, either the surface type in slabs, or commonly the centre bulb type in walls. These must be effectively held in position during concreting, while allowing good compaction of the concrete to be still possible. Such waterbars must furthermore be able to accommodate anticipated movement without tearing, and withstand considerable water pressures.

All movement joints must be sealed with a flexible compound which effectively is watertight and also prevents dust and grit from entering and thus blocking the joint. Jointing materials must be durable under the conditions of exposure to which they may be subjected, but routine replacement is likely to be necessary.

11.2.1　Construction joints

Construction joints (figure 11.1) cannot be avoided, and the aim must be to ensure reinforcement continuity with good bonding between the new concrete and old. Such requirements, of course, apply to any reinforced concrete construction but especial care must be taken in this instance if leakage is to be avoided. Laitance must always be removed to expose coarse aggregate and a sound irregular concrete surface. The new concrete is then poured either directly against this surface, or alternatively a thin layer of grout may be applied before casting. If well constructed, such joints should be completely watertight. Waterbars are not usually necessary; however, it is sometimes preferred to seal the joint on the water-retaining surface as an additional precaution.

Wherever possible the construction should be arranged so that the joints are either all horizontal or all vertical. In some instances long lengths of walls or slab are constructed in alternate lengths as shown in figure 11.2, so that when the intermediate pours are made later the older concrete in the earlier pours will have already taken up some of the shrinkage movement. But on the other hand some engineers prefer to construct successive lengths, arguing that this will mean there is only one restrained edge and the other edge of the slab is free to contract without cracking.

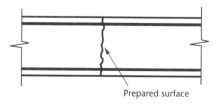
Prepared surface

Figure 11.1
Construction joint

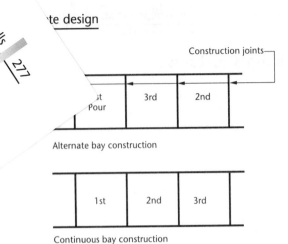

Construction joints

1st
Pour | 3rd | 2nd

Alternate bay construction

1st | 2nd | 3rd

Continuous bay construction

11.2.2 Movement joints

Movement joints are provided to reduce the likelihood of unwanted thermal or shrinkage stress concentrations. They ensure there is only a partially restrained condition during contraction of the immature concrete.

Joints to accommodate contraction may be of two types, 'partial' or 'complete', depending upon the extent of contraction anticipated and the degree of restraint that can be tolerated. 'Partial' contraction joints are the simplest to provide, and consist of a deliberate discontinuity of the concrete, but without an initial gap, as shown in figure 11.3. Care must be taken to prevent excessive adhesion of the concrete surfaces when the second slab is cast against the first, and a waterbar may be desirable as a precaution in addition to the joint sealer. Reinforcement is continuous across the joint to provide some shear transfer, but at the same time this reduces the effective freedom of movement of the adjacent concrete sections. Such joints thus provide only limited relief from constraint and they must always be separated by at least one movement joint with complete discontinuity of concrete and steel.

An example of a 'complete' contraction joint which fulfils this requirement is shown in figure 11.4a. In this case both steel and concrete are discontinuous, but if any shear must be transferred then a shear key is required, as shown. In this type of joint a waterbar is considered to be essential, although there is no initial gap between the concrete surfaces.

Figure 11.3
Partial contraction joint

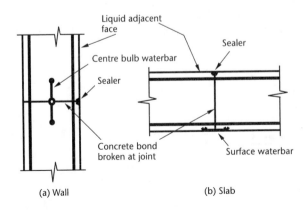

Liquid adjacent face

Centre bulb waterbar

Sealer

Sealer

Concrete bond broken at joint

Surface waterbar

(a) Wall   (b) Slab

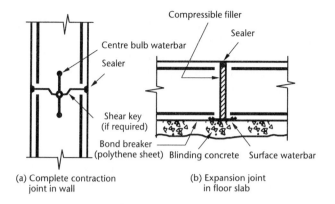

Figure 11.4
Complete movement joints

(a) Complete contraction joint in wall

(b) Expansion joint in floor slab

Where expansion of the concrete is considered possible, joints must be provided which permit this to take place freely without the development of compressive stresses in the concrete. Expansion joints must, therefore, not only provide complete discontinuity of concrete and steel reinforcement, but also must have an initial gap to accommodate such movement. Contraction can also of course be catered for by this type of joint. Figure 11.4b shows a common expansion joint detail, where in addition to a sealer and special waterbar, the joint is filled with a non-absorbent compressible filler. Shear can obviously not be transmitted by this joint, but if it is essential that provision for shear transfer be made, a special joint involving sliding concrete surfaces must be designed. Water pressure on the joint materials may also cause problems if the gap is wide, and this must be considered.

Occasionally, a structure may be designed on the basis that one part is to be free to move relative to another, for example in a circular tank on a flat base, the walls may be designed as independent of the base. In such cases special sliding joints are sometimes used. The essential requirement is that the two concrete surfaces are absolutely plane and smooth and that bond is broken between the surfaces such as by painting or the use of building paper, or that a suitable flexible rubber pad is used. Figure 11.5 shows a typical detail for such a joint, which must always be effectively sealed.

Provision of movement joints

The need for movement joints will depend to a considerable extent on the nature of the structure and the usage to which it is put. For instance an elevated structure may be subjected to few restraints, while an underground structure may be massive and restrained. On the other hand, temperature and moisture variations may be greater in exposed structures than those which are buried. If warm liquids are involved, then this must be reflected in the provision of adequate joints.

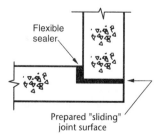

Figure 11.5
Typical sliding joint between slab and wall

The type of member, and construction sequence, will also be an important consideration. Floor slabs will generally be cast on a separating layer of polythene or some similar material laid on the blinding concrete, and in this case joints should be complete contraction or expansion joints. Alternatively, the slab may be cast directly on to the blinding and reinforced to limit cracking on the basis of full restraint as described in chapter 1.

Walls may similarly be designed as fully restrained, or alternatively contraction joints provided at spacings indicated by table 11.1.

Expansion joints must be provided if necessary. In some instances roofs must be separated from the walls by sliding joints. If the roof is to be designed as unrestrained then great care must be taken to minimise the restraints to thermal movement during construction. If significant restraints cannot be avoided, reinforcement must be designed to limit the likely cracking. Where roof and wall are monolithic, joints in the roof should correspond to those in the wall, which in turn may be related to those in the floor slab.

If design of a member is based on the fully restrained condition, it is assumed that cracking will be controlled by the reinforcement; therefore the critical steel ratio r_{crit} which is discussed in section 6.5 must be exceeded. The reinforcement is then detailed to limit the maximum likely crack width to the required value, using appropriate values of likely temperature change and concrete properties recommended by the code of practice. In this instance greatest benefit is obtained from closely spaced small diameter bars.

Alternatively, if proper movement joints are provided so that cracks are concentrated at the joints, reinforcement may be designed on the basis of only partial restraint as indicated in table 11.1, but bar spacing should not exceed 300 mm, or the section thickness.

11.3 Reinforcement details

Reinforcement should be placed near the surface of the concrete but with a minimum cover of 40 mm. Minimum steel areas in each of two directions at right angles depend on the joint arrangement as discussed above, but these will frequently need to be exceeded to limit thermal crack widths.

The critical steel ratio r_{crit}, is given by f_{ct}/f_y as in equation 6.12 of section 6.5, and typically has the following values for grade C35A concrete:

High-yield bars ($f_y = 460$ N/mm^2), $r_{crit} = 0.0035$

Mild steel bars ($f_y = 250$ N/mm^2), $r_{crit} = 0.0064$

In walls less than 200 mm thick or ground slabs less than 300 mm thick steel areas should be provided in one layer, but in thicker members two equal layers should be provided. Spacing should not exceed 300 mm or the section thickness.

Limitation of crack widths means that under service conditions the reinforcement is likely to be acting at stresses below those normally existing in reinforced concrete members. This reduces the advantages of increased strengths usually associated with high-yield steel. It will be noted however that minimum thermal crack control quantities are considerably reduced if deformed bars are used, because of their improved bond characteristics. The choice between high-yield and mild steel is, therefore, not well-defined and is often a matter of personal preference of the engineer.

Table 11.1 Design options for control of thermal contraction and restrained shrinkage

Option	Type of construction and method of control	Movement joint spacing	Steel ratio (see note)	Comments
1	Continuous: for full restraint	No joints, but expansion joints at wide spacings may be desirable in walls and roofs that are not protected from solar heat gain or where the contained liquid is subjected to a substantial temperature range	Minimum of r_{crit}	Use small size bars at close spacing to avoid high steel ratios well in excess of r_{crit}
2	Semicontinuous: for partial restraint	(a) Complete contraction joints, ≤ 15 m (b) Alternate partial and complete contraction joints (by interpolating), ≤ 11.25 m (c) Partial joints, ≤ 7.5 m	Minimum of r_{crit}	Use small size bars but less steel than in option 1
3	Close movement joint spacing; for freedom of movement	(a) Complete joints, in metres $$\leq 4.8 + \frac{w}{\varepsilon}$$ (b) Alternate partial and complete joints, in metres $$\leq 0.5 s_{max} + 2.4 + \frac{w}{\varepsilon}$$ (c) Partial joints $$\leq s_{max} + \frac{w}{\varepsilon}$$	Minimum of 2/3 r_{crit}	Restrict the joint spacing for options 3(b) and 3(c) In these expressions s_{max} = maximum likely crack spacing (metres) w = allowable crack width (mm) ε = strain in concrete

Note: In options 1 and 2 the steel ratio will generally exceed r_{crit} to restrict the crack widths to acceptable values. In option 3 the steel ratio of $\frac{2}{3} r_{crit}$ will be adequate. Evaluation of joint spacings for option 3 is illustrated in example 11.1.

11.4 Design methods

The design of water-retaining structures may be carried out using either

1. a limit state design, as recommended by BS 8007, or

2. an elastic design, which is not covered by the British Code of Practice.

A limit state design is based on both the ultimate and serviceability limit states, using the methods described in the previous chapters. As the restraint of cracking is of prime importance with these structures, the simplified rules for minimum steel areas and maximum spacing are no longer adequate. It is necessary to check the concrete strains and crack widths, using the methods described in chapters 1 and 6. The calculations tend to be lengthy and depend on factors such as the degree of restraint, shrinkage and creep which are difficult to assess accurately.

Elastic design is the traditional method which will possibly continue to be used for many structures. It is relatively simple and easy to apply. It could be used in conjunction with limit state methods when there are special circumstances, such as when stability calculations are necessary, or when the structure has an irregular layout, so that the critical loading patterns for the ultimate limit state should be considered. Even though a structure has been designed by the elastic method it may still be necessary to calculate the possible movement and crack widths.

11.4.1 Limit state design

The application of limit state techniques to water-retaining structures is based on the recommendations of BS 8110 subject to modifications contained in BS 8007. The principal steps are:

1. Ultimate limit state design calculations

2. Serviceability limit state design calculations with either
    (a) Calculation of crack widths
 or (b) 'Deemed to satisfy' requirements for applied loading effects on the mature concrete. These are based on maximum service stresses in the reinforcement and analysis involves the triangular stress block of section 4.10.

If a water-retaining structure is to be constructed in prestressed concrete, the category of prestressed member to be adopted as described in chapter 12 will be determined on the basis of the exposure conditions. Once the appropriate category has been established, each member will be designed in the way described in chapter 12. Special provisions for cyclindrical structures which are prestressed vertically and circumferentially are given in BS 8007.

For the ultimate limit state the procedures followed are exactly the same as for any other reinforced concrete structure. The partial factor of safety on imposed loading due to contained liquid should be taken as 1.4 for strength calculations to reflect the degree of accuracy with which hydrostatic loading may be predicted. Calculations for the analysis of the structure subject to the most severe load combinations will then proceed in the usual way.

Serviceability design will involve the classification of each member according to its crack-width category as described in section 11.1. External members not in contact with the liquid can be designed using the criteria discussed in other chapters for normal reinforced concrete work.

The maximum likely crack widths may be calculated using the methods given in section 1.3 and chapter 6 and then checked for compliance with the allowable values. Alternatively, reinforcement stresses due to bending or direct tension may be calculated and checked for compliance with the demand to satisfy limits as illustrated in example 11.1.

Serviceability calculations will be required to consider three specific cases:

1. *Flexural tension in mature concrete.* This may result from both dead and imposed loads.

2. *Direct tension in mature concrete.* This may be caused by hydrostatic loadings.

3. *Direct tension in immature concrete.* This is caused by restrained thermal and shrinkage movement.

Flexural tension in mature concrete

The design surface crack width may be calculated from equation 6.10 in section 6.4.2 such that

$$w_{max} = \frac{3a_{cr}\varepsilon_m}{1 + 2\left(\dfrac{a - c_{min}}{h - x}\right)} \qquad (6.10)*$$

where a_{cr} is the distance from the point at which the crack width is being calculated to a point of zero concrete strain (which is commonly taken as the surface of the nearest longitudinal reinforcing bar) as illustrated in figure 11.6. c_{min} is the minimum cover to main reinforcement, ε_m is the average concrete strain and is based on ε_1, the apparent strain, but allows for the stiffening effect of the cracked concrete in the tension zone by the relationship $\varepsilon_m = \varepsilon_1 - \varepsilon_2$. The value of ε_2 is given by an empirical expression such that

$$\varepsilon_2 = \frac{b_t(h - x)(a' - x)}{3E_sA_s(d - x)}$$

for a limiting design surface crack width of 0.2 mm, as in equation 6.11 or

$$\varepsilon_2 = \frac{1.5b_t(h - x)(a' - x)}{3E_sA_s(d - x)} \qquad (11.1)*$$

for a limiting design surface crack width of 0.1 mm. In these expressions b_t is the width of the section at the centroid of the tensile steel and a' is the distance from the compressive face to the point at which the crack is calculated. A negative value of ε_m indicates that the section is uncracked.

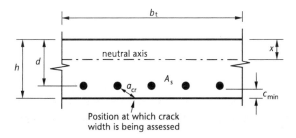

Figure 11.6
Position of calculated crack width

Table 11.2 Allowable steel stresses in direct or flexural tension for serviceability limit states

	Allowable stress	
Design crack width (mm)	Plain bars ($f_y = 250$ N/mm^2) (N/mm^2)	Deformed bars ($f_y = 460$ N/mm^2) (N/mm^2)
0.1	85	100
0.2	115	130

As an alternative to such calculations of crack widths, table 11.2 offers maximum service stresses for the reinforcement and if these values can be shown to be satisfied it may be assumed that maximum likely crack widths in the mature concrete will be below the limiting values. This requires an elastic analysis of the member under working conditions using the equations for the triangular stress block as derived in section 4.10 and illustrated in example 11.1. It should be noted however that this 'deemed to satisfy' approach may be more difficult to satisfy than crack width limits.

Direct tension in mature concrete

The maximum likely surface crack width due to direct tension may be calculated from

$$w_{max} = 3a_{cr}\varepsilon_m \tag{11.2}*$$

where a_{cr} is the distance to the surface of the nearest reinforcing bar and the average concrete strain ε_m is given by $\varepsilon_m = \varepsilon_1 - \varepsilon_2$

where $\quad \varepsilon_2 = \dfrac{2b_t h}{3E_s A_s}$ for a 0.2 mm design surface crack width limit $\tag{11.3}*$

or $\quad \varepsilon_2 = \dfrac{b_t h}{E_s A_s}$ for a 0.1mm design surface crack width limit $\tag{11.4}*$

In these expressions ε_1 is the apparent concrete tensile strain and b_t is the width of the section at the centroid of the tensile steel. This is illustrated in example 11.2.

Service stresses in the reinforcement may alternatively be calculated for comparison with the 'deemed to satisfy' stresses given in table 11.2.

Combined flexural and direct tension in mature concrete

Where flexural tension and direct tension are combined, the strains due to each must be added together in calculating crack widths in the mature concrete. Usually one of these will dominate as illustrated in example 11.3.

Direct tension in immature concrete

Calculations of crack widths are based on the procedures described in section 6.5 with some simplifications often used. Provided the critical steel ratio r_{crit} is exceeded, thermal cracking is taken to have a maximum spacing

$$s_{max} = \frac{f_{ct}}{f_b} \times \frac{\Phi}{2r}$$ (6.13)*

where r = steel ratio A_s/A_c
  Φ = bar diameter
  f_{ct} = 3 day tensile strength – taken as 1.6 N/mm² for grade C35A concrete
  f_b = average bond strength between concrete and steel – taken as 1.6 N/mm² for plain round bars, or 2.4 N/mm² for deformed type 2 bars, with grade C35A concrete.

The critical steel ratio r_{crit} will have a value of 0.0035 when f_y = 460 N/mm², or 0.0064 when f_y = 250 N/mm² as described in section 11.3.

If restraint factors are not used, the width of a fully developed crack may be taken generally as

$$w_{max} = s_{max}\left(\varepsilon_{sh} + T\frac{\alpha_c}{2} - (100 \times 10^{-6})\right)$$

$$= s_{max}\varepsilon_{th}$$

This is based on equation 6.14 where ε_{sh} is the drying shrinkage strain and α_c is the coefficient of thermal expansion of the mature concrete. A factor of 0.5 allows for creep effects. In practice the drying shrinkage strain may be of the order of $100 \times 10^{-6}\mu s$, hence a simplified expression

$$w_{max} = s_{max}T\frac{\alpha_c}{2}$$ (11.5)*

is suggested as adequate, where $T°C$ is the relevant temperature change.

Temperature rises due to hydration of the concrete ($T_1°C$) in walls may be expected to be of the order of 20°C in winter and 30°C in summer but should be increased for high cement contents, rapid hardening cement, thick members or timber shutters in summer. Values for ground floor slabs may be about 5°C less as illustrated in table 11.3.

Table 11.3 Typical design values of T_1 for P.C. concrete in the U.K.

Section thickness (mm)	Walls and slabs with steel formwork			Walls with 18 mm plywood formwork			Slabs on ground or plywood formwork		
	Cement content (kg/m³)			Cement content (kg/m³)			Cement content (kg/m³)		
	325	350	400	325	350	400	325	350	400
	°C	°C	°C	°C	°C	°C	°C	°C	°C
300	20*	20*	20*	23	25	31	15	17	21
500	20	22	27	32	35	43	25	28	34
700	28	32	39	38	42	49	—	—	—
1000	38	42	49	42	47	56	—	—	—

*15°C for slabs.
Note: These values assume a placing temperature of 20°C with a mean daily temperature of 15°C, and the formwork is not removed until the temperature peak has passed. No allowance has been made for solar gain in slabs.

Additional seasonal temperature falls may also be directly substituted into the above expression since the effects of concrete maturity are offset by a smaller ratio of tensile to bond strength and other effects. These should be included as $T_2°C$ in calculations for continuous construction so that $T = T_1 + T_2$.

The final details of reinforcement to be provided must be co-ordinated with the joint spacing arrangement. This is a complicated procedure since a wide range of possibilities exists, but some alternative combinations based on control of thermal and shrinkage effects are suggested in table 11.1 and are illustrated in example 11.1. Particular care must be taken to ensure that joints do not interfere with intended structural actions. Reinforcement provided to resist thermal and shrinkage cracking in the immature concrete may form part or the whole of the reinforcement required to resist direct or flexural cracking in the mature concrete.

It will be seen that small-sized, closely spaced bars are best when joint spacing is large; however, since crack spacing is related to bar diameter, large bars should be used when closer joints are combined with less steel. Although table 11.1 offers a general guide, flexural effects may dominate and it is recommended that the engineer consults specialist literature when undertaking a major design on this basis.

EXAMPLE 11.1

Limit state design of a water-retaining section

The wall section shown in figure 11.7 is subject to a moment of 14.6 kN m under working loads which may be considered as purely hydrostatic. The moment acts so that there is tension in the face adjacent to the liquid. A grade C35A concrete with mild steel bars are specified and appearance is not critical. 18 mm plywood formwork is to be used.

Minimum cover = 40 mm, therefore assume $d = 150$ mm.

Figure 11.7
Wall section

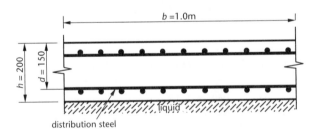

distribution steel

(a) Ultimate limit state

Ultimate moment $M = 14.6 \times 1.4 = 20.44$ kN m

$$\frac{M}{bd^2 f_{cu}} = \frac{20.44 \times 10^6}{1000 \times 150^2 \times 35} = 0.026$$

therefore lever-arm factor, $l_a = 0.95$ hence

$$A_{st} = \frac{20.44 \times 10^6}{0.95 \times 250 \times 0.95 \times 150} = 604 \text{ mm}^2/\text{m}$$

This could be provided by 12 mm bars at 150 mm centres, area = 754 mm^2/m.

(b) Serviceability limit state

Flexural tension in mature concrete

Using the 'deemed to satisfy' conditions, check the service stress in the reinforcement assuming a cracked section and an estimated $E_c = 27$ kN/mm^2.

Modular ratio $\alpha_e = \dfrac{E_s}{E_c/2} = \dfrac{200}{27/2} = 14.8$ (includes allowance for creep)

therefore

$$\alpha_e \frac{A_s}{bd} = \frac{14.8 \times 754}{1000 \times 150} = 0.074$$

and from figure 4.29, $x \approx 0.31d = 0.31 \times 150 = 46$ mm, therefore the reinforcement tensile stress is given by equation 4.47 as

$$f_s = \frac{M}{A_s\left(d - \dfrac{x}{3}\right)} = \frac{14.6 \times 10^6}{754\left(150 - \dfrac{46}{3}\right)} = 144 \text{ N/mm}^2$$

This is greater than the 115 N/mm^2 allowable from table 11.2 and the steel area must be increased if 'deemed to satisfy' requirements are to be met.

$$\text{Minimum } A_s = \frac{144}{115} \times 754 = 944 \text{ mm}^2/\text{m}$$

which may be provided as 12 mm bars at 110 mm centres, area 1028 mm^2/m, and exceeds the ultimate limit state requirement for the liquid-adjacent face.

Direct tension in immature concrete

To control thermal and shrinkage cracking, the critical steel ratio $r_{crit} = 0.0064$ from section 11.3 for plain bars and grade C35A concrete. Thus

minimum steel area to control cracking $= A_s = 0.0064A_c$

$= 0.0064 \times 1000 \times 200 = 1280 \text{ mm}^2/\text{m}$

and maximum crack spacing $s_{max} = \dfrac{f_{ct}}{f_b} \times \dfrac{\Phi}{2r}$ from equation 6.13.

For grade C35A concrete and plain bars, $f_{ct} = 1.6$ N/mm^2 and $f_b = 1.6$ N/mm^2, thus for 12 mm bars

$$s_{max} = \frac{1.6 \times 12}{1.6 \times 2 \times \dfrac{1280}{200 \times 1000}} = 937 \text{ mm}$$

The temperature fall from the hydration peak T_1, assuming summer concreting (ambient temperature 15°C), is taken as 23°C from table 11.3. Assuming a typical value of $\alpha_c = 10 \times 10^{-6}/°C$

$$w_{max} = s_{max} \frac{\alpha_c}{2} T_1$$

$$= 937 \times \frac{10 \times 10^{-6}}{2} \times 23 = 0.11 \text{ mm}$$

from equation 11.5. This satisfies the 0.2 mm limit.

Reinforcement and joint detailing

Since the wall is 200 mm thick, reinforcement must be provided in two layers with at least $1/2\,r_{crit} = 640$ mm^2/m in each face. (12 mm bars at 175 mm centres, area $= 646$ mm^2/m.) Thermal effects may thus be considered adequately covered if 12 mm bars are provided at 110 mm centres in the liquid-adjacent face as required by flexural requirements, and at 175 mm centres in the other face. Alternatively 10 mm bars also at 110 mm centres (area $= 722$ mm^2/m) may be more convenient in the liquid-remote face.

Continuous construction will be required in the direction subject to the bending moment. Thus seasonal temperature effects on thermal crack widths should be checked.

For the proposed reinforcement arrangement,

$$s_{max} = \frac{1.6 \times 1.2}{1.6 \times \dfrac{2 \times (1028 + 646)}{200 \times 1000}} = 717 \text{ mm}$$

and assuming $T_2 = 25°$C, equation 11.5 gives

$$w_{max} = s_{max}\frac{\alpha_c}{2}(T_1 + T_2) = 717 \times \frac{10}{2} \times 10^{-6}(23 + 25)$$
$$= 0.17 \text{ mm}$$

which still satisfies the 0.2 mm limit.

Transverse reinforcement requirements will depend on jointing arrangements. If there are no structural actions in that direction, options are defined in table 11.1 range from continuous construction to close joint spacings with steel reduced to $2/3\,r_{crit}$ which is the equivalent of 10 mm bars at 185 mm centres in each face (853 mm^2/m total).

If continuous construction is to be used, crack widths including seasonal temperature changes should be checked and it will be found that a total steel area of at least 1440 mm^2/m is required to satisfy the 0.2 mm limit.

If option 3 of table 11.1 is adopted, the alternatives are:

(a) Complete joints at $4.8 + \dfrac{w}{\varepsilon}$ metres

where $w =$ allowable crack width $= 0.2 \times 10^{-3}$ m

and $\varepsilon =$ thermal strain $= \dfrac{\alpha_c}{2}T_1 = \dfrac{10}{2} \times 10^{-6} \times 23 = 115 \times 10^{-6}$ m

thus spacing must be less than $4.8 + \dfrac{0.2 \times 10^{-3}}{115 \times 10^{-6}}$

$$= 4.8 + 1.74 = 6.54 \text{ m centres.}$$

(b) Alternate partial and complete joints at $\leq 0.5s_{max} + 2.4 + \dfrac{w}{\varepsilon}$ metres

In this calculation s_{max} should correspond to a steel area of 853 mm^2/m and 10 mm bars and will thus be

$$= 937 \times \frac{1280}{853} \times \frac{10}{12} \times 10^{-3} = 1.173 \text{ m}$$

thus spacing must be less than $\dfrac{1.173}{2} + 2.4 + 1.74 = 4.73$ m centres.

(c) Partial joints at $\leq s_{max} + \dfrac{w}{\varepsilon}$

thus spacing must be less than $1.173 + 1.74 = 2.91$ m centres.

EXAMPLE 11.2

Limit state design of section subject to direct tension only

A wall is subject only to a direct tensile working force of 265 kN/m due to hydrostatic loads. Determine a suitable thickness and reinforcement arrangement using high-yield bars $f_y = 460$ N/mm^2, and grade C35A concrete for a 0.1 mm maximum crack width.

(a) Ultimate limit state

Ultimate tensile force $= 265 \times 1.4 = 371$ kN/m

thus $\quad A_s = \dfrac{371 \times 10^3}{0.95 \times 460} = 849$ mm^2/m

(b) Serviceability limit state

Critical steel ratio to control thermal cracking from equation 6.12

$$r_{crit} = \frac{f_{ct}}{f_y} = \frac{1.6}{460} = 0.0035 \text{ as in section } 11.3$$

thus for continuous construction, maximum allowable section thickness for this steel area is given by

$$\frac{849}{1000h} = 0.0035$$

hence maximum $h = 243$ mm.
    Try $h = 150$ (note that this is less than the 200 mm generally recommended but it is used to illustrate procedures).

Direct tension in mature concrete

Maximum crack width $= 0.1$ mm $= 3a_{cr}\varepsilon_m$ thus for a 150 mm thick section, with 16 mm bars at 100 mm centres in one layer

$$A_s = 2010 \text{ mm}^2/\text{m}$$

and

$$\text{strain } \varepsilon_1 = \frac{\text{tension force}}{E_s A_s} = \frac{265 \times 10^3}{200 \times 10^3 \times 2010} = 0.00066$$

and from equation 11.4

$$\varepsilon_2 = \frac{b_t h}{E_s A_s} = \frac{1000 \times 150}{200 \times 10^3 \times 2010} = 0.00037$$

hence

$$\varepsilon_m = \varepsilon_1 - \varepsilon_2 = 0.00066 - 0.00037 = 0.00029$$

Since from equation 11.2 $w_{max} = 3a_{cr}\varepsilon_m$

$$\text{maximum allowable } a_{cr} = \frac{0.1}{3 \times 0.00029} = 115 \text{ mm}$$

For 16 mm bars in one layer at 100 mm centres at mid-section

$$a_{cr} = \sqrt{\left\{\left(\frac{100}{2}\right)^2 + \left(\frac{150}{2}\right)^2\right\}} - 8 = 82 \text{ mm}$$

which is less than 115 mm (see example 6.4).
   Therefore crack width is less than 0.1 mm as required.

Direct tension in immature concrete

To control thermal and shrinkage cracking

$$\text{steel ratio } r = \frac{A_s}{bh}$$

$$= \frac{2010}{1000 \times 150} = 0.013 \quad (> r_{crit})$$

thus from equation 6.13

$$s_{max} = \frac{f_{ct}\Phi}{f_b 2r} \text{ where } f_{ct}/f_b = 0.67 \text{ for high-yield bars}$$

$$= \frac{0.67 \times 16}{2 \times 0.013} = 412 \text{ mm}$$

Thus for continuous construction with $T_1 = 20°C$, $T_2 = 20°C$ and $\alpha_c = 10 \times 10^{-6}/°C$, equation 11.5 gives

$$w_{max} = s_{max}\frac{\alpha_c}{2}(T_1 + T_2)$$

$$= 412 \times \frac{10 \times 10^{-6}}{2}(20 + 20) = 0.08 \text{ mm} \quad (< 0.1 \text{ mm})$$

hence a 150 mm thick section with 16 mm bars at 100 mm centres in one central layer is acceptable.
   Note: If a thicker section is used, thermal cracking will probably dominate since ε_m in the direct tension calculation decreases while s_{max} increases. If the thickness exceeds 200 mm, steel should be provided in two equal layers.

EXAMPLE 11.3

Design of a water-retaining structure by the limit state method

A cross-section of a long rectangular tank which is to be designed is shown in figure 11.8. The floor slab spans on to supporting beams at B and C. A grade C35A concrete and plain mild steel bars are to be used (1 m³ of water weighs 9.81 kN). Aesthetic appearance is critical hence maximum crack width is 0.1 mm. It may be assumed that $\alpha_c = 10\mu s/°C$ and $E_c = 27$ kN/mm².

   For the walls: $h = 200$ mm and $d = 150$ mm with $T_1 = 20°C$ and $T_2 = 20°C$
   For the slab: $h = 300$ mm and $d = 250$ mm with $T_1 = 15°C$ and $T_2 = 15°C$

The design of the floor slab in this example illustrates the calculation of crack widths in the mature concrete.

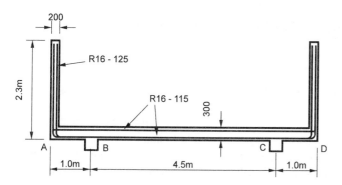

Figure 11.8
Water tank showing position
of main reinforcement

(i) Walls

Maximum water pressure at base of wall $= 9.81 \times 2.0 = 19.62$ kN/m². For the effective span of the cantilever and considering a 1 m length of wall, the serviceability moment

$$M = \frac{1}{2} \times 19.62 \times 2.0 \left(\frac{2.0}{3} + \frac{0.15}{2} \right) = 14.6 \text{ kN m}$$

(a) Ultimate limit state

This has been considered in example 11.1 giving a minimum requirement of 604 mm²/m. (12 mm bars at 150 mm centres gives area $= 754$ mm²/m)

(b) Serviceability limit state

Flexural tension in mature concrete

Check the service stress in the reinforcement as in example 11.1 giving 144 N/mm². For 0.1 mm crack width limit this stress must be limited to 85 N/mm² as in table 11.2.

Thus

$$\text{minimum } A_s = \frac{144}{85} \times 754 = 1277 \text{ mm}^2/\text{m}$$

Try 16 mm bars at 150 mm centres, area $= 1340$ mm²/m which exceeds ultimate limit state requirements.

Direct tension in immature concrete

To control thermal and shrinkage cracking, equation 6.12 gives

$$\text{critical steel ratio } r_{\text{crit}} = \frac{f_{\text{ct}}}{f_y} = \frac{1.6}{250} = 0.0064$$

thus

$$\text{minimum steel area} = 0.0064bh = 0.0064 \times 1000 \times 200 = 1280 \text{ mm}^2/\text{m}$$

If 16 mm bars at 150 mm centres are provided in each face

$$r = \frac{2 \times 1340}{1000 \times 200} = 0.0134 \text{ and for plain bars } f_{\text{ct}} = f_{\text{b}}$$

then

$$s_{\max} = \frac{f_{\text{ct}}}{f_{\text{b}}} \times \frac{\Phi}{2r} = \frac{1.0 \times 16}{2 \times 0.0134} = 597 \text{ mm from equation 6.13}$$

giving a maximum crack width of

$$w_{max} = s_{max} \frac{\alpha_c}{2}(T_1 + T_2) \quad \text{from equation 11.5}$$

$$= 597 \times \frac{10 \times 10^{-6}}{2}(20 + 20) = 0.12 \text{ mm}$$

Since this exceeds the 0.1 mm allowable, close 16 mm steel to 125 mm centres in each face giving $w_{max} = 0.10$ mm which is just acceptable. Continuous construction is required vertically. Similar steel should be provided transversely assuming continuous construction along the length of the tank, or alternatively joints should be provided as illustrated in example 11.1.

(ii) Floors

The serviceability bending moment diagram is shown drawn on the tension side of the structure in figure 11.9.

Weight of slab + water $= 0.3 \times 24 + 9.81 \times 2 = 26.8 \text{ kN/m}^2$
Weight of wall $= 2.3 \times 0.2 \times 24 = 11.0 \text{ kN/m}^2$

Considering 1 m breadth of slab; at the supporting beam

$$M = 14.6 + 11.0(1.0 - 0.1) + 26.8 \times 0.8^2/2 = 33.1 \text{ kN m hogging}$$

and at mid-span between B and C

$$M = 26.8 \times 4.5^2/8 - 33.1 = 34.7 \text{ kN m sagging}$$

The slab will also carry a direct tension force of

$$\frac{1}{2} \times 19.6 \times 2.0 = 19.62 \text{ kN/m}$$

which must be allowed for in the design. The critical section for bending is at mid-span.

(a) Ultimate limit state

$$\text{Ultimate moment} = 1.4 \times 34.7 = 48.6 \text{ kN m/m}$$

$$\frac{M}{bd^2 f_{cu}} = \frac{48.6 \times 10^6}{1000 \times 250^2 \times 35} = 0.022, \text{ thus } l_a = 0.95$$

and

$$A_s = \frac{48.6 \times 10^6}{0.95 \times 250 \times 0.95 \times 250} = 861 \text{ mm}^2/\text{m}$$

Figure 11.9
Bending-moment diagram
(kN m)

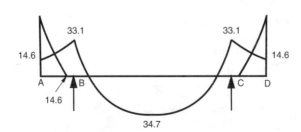

(b) Serviceability limit state

Flexural and direct tension in mature concrete

Try 16 mm bars at 125 mm centres, area $= 1610 \text{ mm}^2/\text{m}$, as for walls then

$$a_{cr} = \sqrt{\left\{ \left(\frac{125}{2} \right)^2 + 50^2 \right\}} - 8 = 72 \text{ mm}$$

and $\dfrac{\alpha_e A_s}{bd} = \dfrac{14.7 \times 1610}{1000 \times 250} = 0.095$

hence $x/d = 0.34$ from figure 4.29 and $x = 85$ mm, thus equation 4.47 gives the bending stress in steel

$$f_s = \frac{M}{\left(d - \dfrac{x}{3} \right) A_s} = \frac{34.7 \times 10^6}{\left(250 - \dfrac{85}{3} \right) 1610}$$

thus $f_s = 97.2 \text{ N/mm}^2$

and flexural strain $= \dfrac{(h-x)\, f_s}{(d-x)\, E_s} = \dfrac{215}{165} \times \dfrac{97.2}{200 \times 10^3} = 0.63 \times 10^{-3}.$

Direct tensile strain $= \dfrac{\text{tension force}}{A_s E_s} = \dfrac{19.62 \times 10^3}{1610 \times 2 \times 200 \times 10^3} = 0.03 \times 10^{-3}.$

Thus it is clear that flexural strain dominates, and total strain

$$\varepsilon_1 = (0.63 + 0.03) \times 10^{-3} = 0.66 \times 10^{-3}$$

For 0.1 mm crack width limit

$$\varepsilon_m = (\varepsilon_1 - \varepsilon_2) \text{ where } \varepsilon_2 = \frac{1.5 b_t (h-x)(a'-x)}{3 E_s A_s (d-x)} \text{ according to equation 11.1}$$

then $\varepsilon_2 = \dfrac{1.5 \times 1000(300-85)(300-85)}{3 \times 200 \times 10^3 \times 1610(250-85)} = 0.43 \times 10^{-3}$

thus $\varepsilon_m = (0.66 - 0.43) \times 10^{-3} = 0.23 \times 10^{-3}$

and equation 6.10 gives

$$w_{max} = \frac{3 a_{cr} \varepsilon_m}{1 + 2\left(\dfrac{a_{cr} - c_{min}}{h - x} \right)} = \frac{3 \times 72 \times 0.23 \times 10^{-3}}{1 + 2\left(\dfrac{72 - 40}{300 - 85} \right)}$$

$$= 0.038 \text{ mm}$$

which is acceptable.

Direct tension in immature concrete

To control thermal and shrinkage cracking the critical steel ratio $r_{crit} = 0.0064$, thus minimum $A_s = 0.0064\, A_c$. Therefore

$$A_s = 0.0064 \times 1000 \times 300 = 1920 \text{ mm}^2/\text{m}$$

thus proposed 16 mm at 125 mm centres in each face, area $= 3220 \text{ mm}^2/\text{m}$, satisfies this requirement.

$$r = \frac{A_s}{A_c} = \frac{3220}{1000 \times 300} = 0.0107$$

then $\quad s_{max} = \dfrac{f_{ct}}{f_b} \times \dfrac{\Phi}{2r} = \dfrac{1.0 \times 16}{2 \times 0.0107} = 748$ mm from equation 6.13

with equation 11.5 giving a maximum crack width

$$\begin{aligned} w_{max} &= s_{max} \frac{\alpha_c}{2}(T_1 + T_2) \\ &= 748 \times \frac{10}{2} \times 10^{-6}(15 + 15) \\ &= 0.11 \text{ mm} \end{aligned}$$

This just exceeds the allowable limit, and since continuous construction is required in the direction of the span 16 mm bar spacing should be reduced to 115 mm centres in both faces, area $= 3500$mm^2/m. The design of the slab is thus governed by thermal cracking requirements, and hogging moments at A and B are adequately covered. Similar reinforcement will be required transversely unless closely spaced joints are provided according to table 11.1.

11.4.2 Elastic design

This method is based on working loads, and permissible stresses in the concrete and steel which are considered to be acting within the elastic range. Hence the design assumes a triangular stress block as analysed in section 4.10. The ratio (α_e) of the modulus of elasticity of steel to that of concrete is taken as 15.

Calculations are performed on the basis of two criteria: strength, and resistance to cracking, with exposure class related to allowable crack widths.

Strength calculations assume a cracked section. Low permissible steel stresses are specified in order to limit the width of cracks and thus reduce the chance of leakage and corrosion of the reinforcement.

The analysis for resistance to cracking assumes a limiting tensile stress in the concrete and is based on an uncracked concrete section. The governing factor in such an analysis is inevitably the permissible tensile stress in the concrete, with the steel and concrete stresses being related by the compatibility of strains across the section.

Reference should be made to previous editions of this book for a more detailed treatment of this design approach.

11.5 | Retaining walls

Such walls are usually required to resist a combination of earth and hydrostatic loadings. The fundamental requirement is that the wall is capable of holding the retained material in place without undue movement arising from deflection, overturning or sliding. Detailed guidance concerning design, detailing and construction is given in BS 8002 which should be consulted when designing structures of this type.

11.5.1 Types of retaining wall

Concrete retaining walls may be considered in terms of three basic categories: (1) gravity, (2) counterfort, and (3) cantilever. Within these groups many common

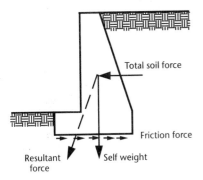

Figure 11.10
Gravity wall

variations exist, for example cantilever walls may have additional supporting ties into the retained material.

The structural action of each type is fundamentally different, but the techniques used in analysis, design and detailing are those normally used for concrete structures.

(i) Gravity walls

These are usually constructed of mass concrete, with reinforcement included in the faces to restrict thermal and shrinkage cracking. As illustrated in figure 11.10, reliance is placed on self-weight to satisfy stability requirements, both in respect of overturning and sliding. They may typically support retained heights up to about 3 m.

It is generally taken as a requirement that under working conditions the resultant of the self-weight and overturning forces must lie within the middle third at the interface of the base and soil. This ensures that uplift is avoided at this interface, as described in section 10.1. Friction effects which resist sliding are thus maintained across the entire base.

Bending, shear, and deflections of such walls are usually insignificant in view of the large effective depth of the section. Distribution steel to control thermal cracking is necessary however, and great care must be taken to reduce hydration temperatures by mix design, construction procedure and curing techniques.

(ii) Counterfort walls

This type of construction will probably be used where the overall height of wall is too large to be constructed economically either in mass concrete or as a cantilever.

The basis of design of counterfort walls is that the earth pressures act on a thin wall which spans horizontally between the massive counterforts (figure 11.11). These must be sufficiently large to provide the necessary dead load for stability requirements, possibly with the aid of the weight of backfill on an enlarged base. The counterforts must be designed with reinforcement to act as cantilevers to resist the considerable bending moments that are concentrated at these points.

The spacing of counterforts will be governed by the above factors, coupled with the need to maintain a satisfactory span–depth ratio on the wall slab, which must be designed for bending as a continuous slab. The advantage of this form of construction is that the volume of concrete involved is considerably reduced, thereby removing many of the problems of large pours, and reducing the quantities of excavation. Balanced against this must be considered the generally increased shuttering complication and the probable need for increased reinforcement.

Figure 11.11
Counterfort wall

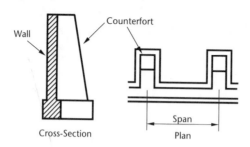

(iii) Cantilever walls

These are designed as vertical cantilevers spanning from a large rigid base which often relies on the weight of backfill on the base to provide stability. Two forms of this construction are illustrated in figure 11.12. In both cases, stability calculations follow similar procedures to those for gravity walls to ensure that the resultant force lies within the middle third of the base and that overturning and sliding requirements are met. They are typically economic up to heights of about 8 m.

11.5.2 Analysis and design

The design of retaining walls may be split into three fundamental stages: (1) Stability analysis – ultimate limit state, (2) Bearing pressure analysis – serviceability limit state, and (3) Member design and detailing – ultimate and serviceability limit states. BS 8002 requires design to allow for a minimum surcharge surface load of 10 kN/m² as well as unplanned excavation in front of the wall of not less than 0.5 m depth (and 10 per cent of retained height for cantilever walls). Allowance must also be made for imposed loads acting on the surface of the retained soil (these are often considered as equivalent surcharge loads). It may also be necessary in both analysis and design to consider a range of possible moisture and compaction conditions for the retained soil.

(i) Stability analysis

Under the action of the loads corresponding to the ultimate limit state, a retaining wall must be stable in terms of resistance to overturning and sliding. This is demonstrated by the simple case of a gravity wall as shown in figure 11.13.

Figure 11.12
Cantilever walls

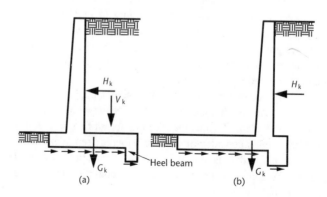

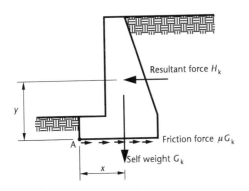

Resultant force H_k

y

Friction force μG_k

A

Self weight G_k

x

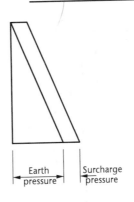

Earth pressure

Surcharge pressure

Figure 11.13
Forces and pressures on a gravity wall

The critical conditions for stability are when a maximum horizontal force acts with a minimum vertical load. To guard against a stability failure, it is usual to apply conservative factors of safety to the force and loads. The values given in table 2.2 are appropriate to strength calculations but a value of $\gamma_f = 1.6$ or higher should be used for stability calculations.

If this force is predominantly hydrostatic and well defined, a factor of 1.4 may be used. A partial factor of safety of $\gamma_f = 1.0$ is usually applied to the dead load G_k.

For resistance to overturning, moments would normally be taken about the toe of the base, point A on figure 11.13, thus the requirement is that

$$1.0G_k x \geq \gamma_f H_k y \tag{11.6}$$

Resistance to sliding is provided by friction between the underside of the base and the ground, and thus is also related to total self-weight G_k. Resistance provided by the passive earth pressure on the front face of the base may make some contribution, but since this material is often backfilled against the face, this resistance cannot be guaranteed and is usually ignored. Thus, if the coefficient of friction between base and soil is μ, the total friction force will be given by μG_k for the length of wall of weight G_k; and the requirement is that

$$1.0\mu G_k \geq \gamma_f H_k \tag{11.7}$$

where H_k is the horizontal force on this length of wall.

If this criterion is not met, a heel beam may be used, and the force due to the passive earth pressure over the face area of the heel may be included in resisting the sliding force. The partial load factor γ_f on the heel beam resisting force should be taken as 1.0 to give the worst condition. To ensure the proper action of a heel beam, the front face must be cast directly against sound, undisturbed material, and it is important that this is not overlooked during construction. Note that if a heel beam is provided, the force acting on the back of the wall must be calculated to include active pressures on the back of the heel beam, as shown in example 11.4.

In considering cantilever walls, a considerable amount of backfill is often placed on top of the base, and this is taken into account in the stability analysis. The forces acting in this case are shown in figure 11.14. In addition to G_k and H_k there is an additional vertical load V_k due to the material above the base acting a distance q from the toe. The worst condition for stability will be when this is at a minimum; therefore a partial load factor $\gamma_f = 1.0$ is appropriate. The stability requirements then become

$$1.0G_k x + 1.0V_k q \geq \gamma_f H_k y \quad \text{for overturning} \tag{11.8}$$
$$\mu(1.0G_k + 1.0V_k) \geq \gamma_f H_k \quad \text{for sliding} \tag{11.9}$$

Figure 11.14
Forces on a cantilever wall

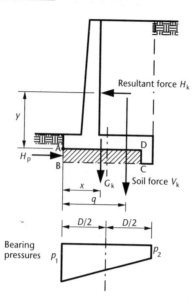

When a heel beam is provided the additional passive resistance of the earth H_p must be included in equation 11.9, together with the weight of soil in area ABCD below the wall (see figure 11.14). Sliding resistance is then calculated at the level of plane BC. BS 8002 also suggests that sliding checks should consider the inclined plane AC.

Stability analysis, as described here, will normally suffice. However, if there is doubt about the foundation material in the region of the wall or the reliability of loading values, it may be necessary to perform a full slip-circle analysis, using techniques common to soil mechanics, or to use increased factors of safety.

(ii) Bearing pressure analysis

As with foundations, the bearing pressures underneath retaining walls are assessed on the basis of the serviceability limit state when determining the size of base that is required. The analysis will be similar to that discussed in section 10.1 with the foundation being subject to the combined effects of an eccentric vertical load, coupled with an overturning moment.

Considering a unit length of the cantilever wall (figure 11.14) the resultant moment about the centroidal axis of the base is

$$M = \gamma_{f1} H_k y + \gamma_{f2} G_k (D/2 - x) + \gamma_{f3} V_k (D/2 - q) \tag{11.10}$$

and the vertical load is

$$N = \gamma_{f2} G_k + \gamma_{f3} V_k \tag{11.11}$$

where in this case for the serviceability limit state the partial factors of safety are

$$\gamma_{f1} = \gamma_{f2} = \gamma_{f3} = 1.0$$

The distribution of bearing pressures will be as shown in the figure, provided the effective eccentricity lies within the 'middle third' of the base, that is

$$\frac{M}{N} \leq \frac{D}{6}$$

The maximum bearing pressure is then given by

$$p_1 = \frac{N}{D} + \frac{M}{I} \times \frac{D}{2}$$

where $I = D^3/12$. Therefore

$$p_1 = \frac{N}{D} + \frac{6M}{D^2} \tag{11.12}$$

and

$$p_2 = \frac{N}{D} - \frac{6M}{D^2} \tag{11.13}$$

(iii) Member design and detailing

As with foundations, the design of bending and shear reinforcement is based on an analysis of the loads for the ultimate limit state, with the corresponding bearing pressures. BS 8002 suggests that in some cases it may be appropriate to design on the basis of serviceability values of earth pressures ($\gamma_f = 1.0$) but BS 8110 recommends normal values of γ_f associated with the ultimate limit state. Gravity walls will seldom require bending or shear steel, while the walls in counterfort and cantilever construction will be designed as slabs. The design of counterforts will generally be similar to that of a cantilever beam unless they are massive.

With a cantilever-type retaining wall the stem is designed to resist the moment caused by the force $\gamma_f H_f$, with $\gamma_f = 1.4$ or larger, depending on how accurately the load may be predicted. For preliminary sizing, the thickness of the wall may be taken as 80 mm per metre depth of backfill.

The thickness of the base is usually of the same order as that of the stem. The heel and toe must be designed to resist the moments due to the upward earth bearing pressures and the downward weight of the soil and base. The soil-bearing pressures are calculated from equations 11.10 to 11.13, provided the resultant of the horizontal and vertical forces lies within the 'middle third'. Should the resultant lie outside the 'middle third', then the bearing pressures should be calculated using equation 10.4. The partial factors of safety γ_{f1}, γ_{f2} and γ_{f3} should be taken to provide a combination which gives the critical design condition.

Reinforcement detailing must follow the general rules for slabs and beams as appropriate. Particular care must be given to the detailing of reinforcement to limit shrinkage and thermal cracking. Gravity walls are particularly vulnerable because of the large concrete pours that are generally involved, and these should be treated in the manner described in section 11.1 for thick sections.

Restraints to thermal and shrinkage movement should be reduced to a minimum; however, this is counteracted in the construction of bases by the need for good friction between the base and soil; thus a sliding layer is not possible. Reinforcement in the bases must thus be adequate to control the cracking caused by a high degree of restraint. Long walls retained by the rigid bases are particularly susceptible to cracking during thermal movement due to loss of hydration heat, and detailing must attempt to distribute these cracks to ensure acceptable widths. Complete vertical movement joints must be provided, and the methods used for the design of joints for water-retaining structures can be used. These joints will often incorporate a shear key to prevent differential movement of adjacent sections of wall, and waterbars and sealers should be used as shown in figure 11.4a.

Figure 11.15
Drainage layer

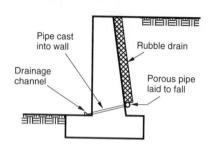

The back faces of retaining walls will usually be subject to hydrostatic forces from groundwater. This may be reduced by the provision of a drainage path at the face of the wall. It is usual practice to provide such a drain by a layer of rubble or porous blocks as shown in figure 11.15, with pipes to remove the water, often through to the front of the wall. In addition to reducing the hydrostatic pressure on the wall, the likelihood of leakage through the wall is reduced, and water is also less likely to reach and damage the soil beneath the foundations of the wall.

The following example illustrates typical procedures for one particular set of soil conditions. In practice it may be necessary to consider both drained and undrained conditions.

EXAMPLE 11.4

Design of a retaining wall

The cantilever retaining wall shown in figure 11.16 supports a granular material of bulk density 1700 kg/m^3, and the allowable bearing pressure is 110 kN/m^2. It is required to

1. check the stability of the wall
2. determine the actual bearing pressures, and
3. design the bending reinforcement using high-yield steel, $f_y = 460$ N/mm^2 and grade 35 concrete.

(a) Stability

Horizontal force: it is assumed that the coefficient of active pressure $K_a = 0.33$, for this granular material. So the earth pressure due to the retained material is given by

$$p_a = K_a \rho g h$$

where ρ is the density of the backfill and h is the depth considered. Thus at the underside of the base AB

$$p_a = 0.33 \times 1700 \times 10^{-3} \times 9.81 \times 4.9$$
$$= 27.0 \text{ kN/m}^2$$

Allowing for the minimum required surcharge of 10 kN/m^2, an additional horizontal pressure

$$p_s = K_a \times 10 \text{ kN/m}^2 = 3.3 \text{ kN/m}^2$$

acts uniformly over the whole depth h.

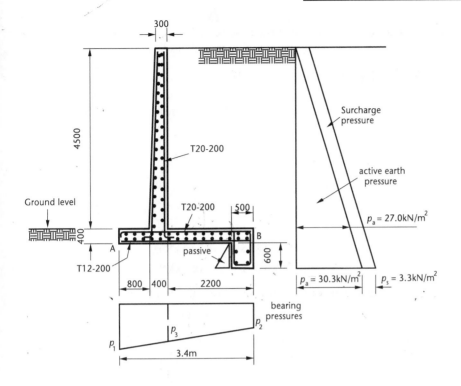

Therefore the horizontal force on 1 m length of wall is

$$H_k = 0.5p_a h + p_s h = 0.5 \times 27.0 \times 4.9 + 3.3 \times 4.9 = 82.3 \text{ kN}$$

Vertical loads

wall	$= \frac{1}{2}(0.4 + 0.3) \times 4.5 \times 24$	$= 37.8$ kN
base	$= 0.4 \times 3.4 \times 24$	$= 32.6$
earth	$= 2.2 \times 4.5 \times 1700 \times 10^{-3} \times 9.81$	$= 165.1$
surcharge	$= 2.2 \times 10$	$= 22$
	Total	$= 257.5$ kN

For stability calculations a partial factor of safety of 1.6 is used for the lateral loadings, while 1.4 will be used for strength calculations.

(i) Sliding

From equation 11.9 it is necessary that

$$\mu(1.0G_k + 1.0V_k) \geq \gamma_f H_k \text{ for no heel beam}$$

Assuming a value of coefficient of friction $\mu = 0.45$

frictional resisting force $= 0.45 \times 1.0 \times 257.5 = 115.8$ kN

sliding force $= 1.6 \times 82.3 = 131.7$ kN

Since the sliding force exceeds the frictional force, resistance must also be provided by the passive earth pressure acting against a heel beam and this force is given by

$$H_p = \gamma_f \times 0.5 K_p \rho g a^2$$

where K_p is the coefficient of passive pressure, assumed to be 3.0 for this granular material, and a is the depth of the heel below the 0.5 m 'trench' allowance in front of the base.

Therefore

$$H_p = 1.0 \times 0.5 \times 3.0 \times 1700 \times 10^{-3} \times 9.81 \times 0.5^2$$
$$= 6.3 \text{ kN}$$

Sliding must now be considered on a plane at the level of the underside of the heel beam. Thus

$$p_a = 0.33 \times 1700 \times 10^{-3} \times 9.81 \times 5.5 = 30.3 \text{ kN/m}^2$$

and $\quad H_k = 0.5 \times 30.3 \times 5.5 + 3.3 \times 5.5 \quad = 101.5 \text{ kN}$

Vertical loads are also increased by the weight of soil + heel beam

$$= 0.6 \times (1700 \times 10^{-3} \times 9.81 \times 2.9 + 24 \times 0.5) \text{ kN} = 36.2 \text{ kN}$$

Thus taking $\mu = 0.58$ at this level ($= \tan \phi$ where $\phi = 30°$)

$$\text{resisting force} \quad = 0.58(257.5 + 36.2) + 6.3 = 176.6 \text{ kN}$$

and $\quad$ sliding force $\quad = 1.6 \times 101.5 \quad\quad\quad\quad = 162.4 \text{ kN}$

thus the sliding requirement is satisfied.

(ii) Overturning

Taking moments about point A at the edge of the toe and ignoring the heel beam, at the ultimate limit state

$$\text{overturning moment} = \gamma_f(0.5 p_a h^2/3 + p_s h^2/2)$$
$$= 1.6(0.5 \times 27 \times 4.9^2/3 + 3.3 \times 4.9^2/2)$$
$$= 236.2 \text{ kN m}$$
$$\text{restraining moment} = 1.0(37.8 \times 1.0 + 32.6 \times 1.7 + 165.1 \times 2.3 + 10 \times 2.2 \times 2.3)$$
$$= 523.6 \text{ kN m}$$

Thus the criterion for overturning is comfortably satisfied.

(b) Bearing pressures

From equations 11.12 and 11.13 the bearing pressures are given by

$$p = \frac{N}{D} \pm \frac{6M}{D^2}$$

where M is the moment about the base centre-line. Therefore, ignoring the heel beam

$$M = 0.5 \times 27 \times 4.9 \times \frac{4.9}{3} + 3.3 \times 4.9 \times \frac{4.9}{2}$$
$$+ 37.8(1.7 - 1.0) + 165.1(1.7 - 2.3) + 22(1.7 - 2.3)$$
$$= 108 + 39.6 + 26.5 - 99.1 - 13.2 = 61.8 \text{ kN m}$$

Therefore

$$\text{maximum bearing pressure } p_1 = \frac{257.5}{3.4} + \frac{6 \times 61.8}{3.4^2}$$
$$= 75.7 + 32.1 = 107.8 \text{ kN/m}^2$$

which is less than the allowable.

(c) Bending reinforcement

(i) Wall

Horizontal force $= \gamma_f 0.5 K_a \rho g h^2 + \gamma_f p_s h$
$$= 1.4 \times 0.5 \times 0.33 \times 1700 \times 10^{-3} \times 9.81 \times 4.5^2 + 1.4 \times 3.3 \times 4.5$$
$$= 78.0 + 20.8 = 98.8 \text{ kN}$$

Considering the effective span, the maximum moment is

$$M = 78.0 \left(0.2 + \frac{4.5}{3} \right) + 20.8 \left(0.2 + \frac{4.5}{2} \right) = 184 \text{ kN m}$$

$$\frac{M}{bd^2 f_{cu}} = \frac{184 \times 10^6}{1000 \times 330^2 \times 35} = 0.05$$

for which $l_a = 0.94$ (figure 7.5). Therefore

$$A_s = \frac{184 \times 10^6}{0.94 \times 330 \times 0.95 \times 460} = 1357 \text{ mm}^2/\text{m}$$

Provide T20 bars at 200 mm centres.

(ii) Base

The bearing pressures are obtained from equations 11.10 to 11.13. The critical partial factors of safety are

$$\gamma_{f1} = 1.4 \text{ and } \gamma_{f2} = \gamma_{f3} = 1.0$$

Using the figures from part (b) of this example, the moment about the base centre-line is

$$M = \gamma_{f1} \times (108 + 39.6) + \gamma_{f2} \times 26.5 - \gamma_{f3.} \times (99.1 + 13.2)$$
$$= 120.8 \text{ kN m}$$

and

$$N = \gamma_{f2}(37.8 + 32.6) + \gamma_{f3} \times (165.1 + 22)$$
$$= 257.5 \text{ kN}$$

Therefore

$$\text{pressure } p_1 = \frac{257.5}{3.4} + \frac{6 \times 120.8}{3.4^2} = 76 + 63 = 139 \text{ kN/m}^2$$
$$p_2 = 76 - 63 = 13 \text{ kN/m}^2$$

and in figure 11.16

$$p_3 = 13 + (139 - 13)2.2/3.4 = 95 \text{ kN/m}^2$$

about the stem centre-line for the vertical loads and the bearing pressures

$$32.6 \times 1.3 \times \frac{2.2}{3.4} + \gamma_{f3} \times (165.1 + 22) \times 1.3$$

$$- 13 \times 2.2 \times 1.3 - (95 - 13) \times \frac{2.2}{2} \times 0.93 = 150 \text{ kN m}$$

ore

$$A_s = \frac{150 \times 10^6}{0.95 \times 460 \times 0.95 \times 330} = 1095 \text{ mm}^2/\text{m}$$

Provide T20 bars at 200 mm centres, top steel.

Toe

Taking moments about the stem centre-line

$$M \approx \gamma_{f2} \times 32.6 \times 0.6 \times \frac{0.8}{3.4} - \gamma_{f3} \times 139 \times 0.8 \times 0.6$$

$$= 62 \text{ kN m}$$

(In fact for this wall the design moment for the toe would be marginally higher with $\gamma_{f2} = 1.4$ and $\gamma_{f3} = 1.4$ throughout.)

$$A_s = \frac{62 \times 10^6}{0.95 \times 460 \times 0.95 \times 330} = 452 \text{ mm}^2/\text{m}$$

The minimum area for this, and for longitudinal distribution steel which is also required in the wall and the base is

$$A_s = 0.13 \times 1000 \times 400 = 520 \text{ mm}^2/\text{m}$$

Thus, provide T12 bars at 200 mm centres, bottom and distribution steel.

Also steel should be provided in the compression face of the wall in order to prevent cracking – say, T10 bars at 200 mm centres each way.

Bending reinforcement is required in the heel beam to resist the moment due to the passive earth pressure. This reinforcement would probably be in the form of closed links.

CHAPTER 12

Prestressed concrete

CHAPTER INTRODUCTION

The analysis and design of prestressed concrete is a specialised field which cannot possibly be covered comprehensively in one chapter. This chapter concentrates therefore on the basic principles of prestressing, and the analysis and design of statically determined members in bending for the serviceability and ultimate limit states.

A fundamental aim of prestressed concrete is to limit tensile stresses, and hence flexural cracking, in the concrete under working conditions. Design is therefore based initially on the requirements of the serviceability limit state. Subsequently considered are ultimate limit state criteria for bending and shear. In addition to the concrete stresses under working loads, deflections must be checked, and attention must also be paid to the construction stage when the prestress force is first applied to the immature concrete. This stage is known as the transfer condition.

Design of prestressed concrete may therefore be summarised as

1. design for serviceability – cracking
2. check stresses at transfer
3. check deflections
4. check ultimate limit state – bending
5. design shear reinforcement for ultimate limit state.

The stages are illustrated by the flow chart in figure 12.1.

When considering the basic design of a concrete section subject to prestress, the stress distribution due to the prestress must be combined with the stresses from the loading conditions to ensure that permissible stress limits are satisfied. Many analytical approaches have been developed to deal with this problem; however, it is considered that the method presented offers many advantages of simplicity and ease of manipulation in design.

Figure 12.1
Prestressed concrete design
flow chart

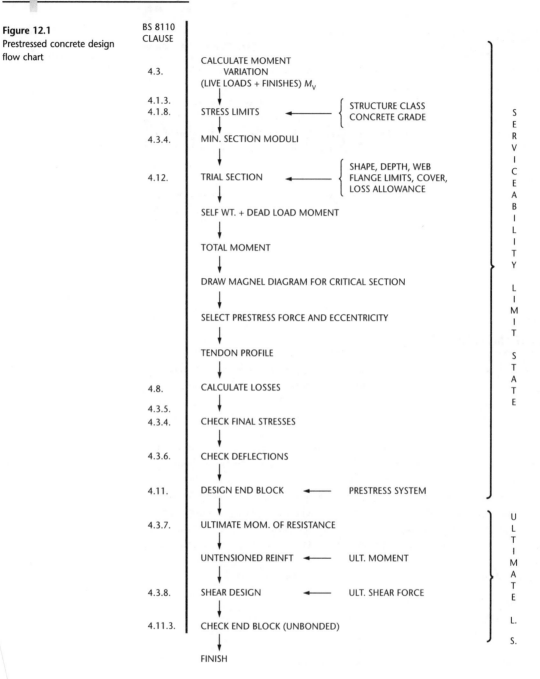

12.1 Principles of prestressing

In the design of a reinforced concrete beam subjected to bending it is accepted that the concrete in the tensile zone is cracked, and that all the tensile resistance is provided by the reinforcement. The stress that may be permitted in the reinforcement is limited by the need to keep the cracks in the concrete to acceptable widths under working conditions, thus there is no advantage to be gained from the use of very high strength steels which are available. The design is therefore uneconomic in two respects: (1) dead weight includes 'useless' concrete in the tensile zone, and (2) economic use of steel resources is not possible.

'Prestressing' means the artificial creation of stresses in a structure before loading, so that the stresses which then exist under load are more favourable than would otherwise be the case. Since concrete is strong in compression the material in a beam will be used most efficiently if it can be maintained in a state of compression throughout. Provision of a longitudinal compressive force acting on a concrete beam may therefore overcome both of the disadvantages of reinforced concrete cited above. Not only is the concrete fully utilised, but also the need for conventional tension reinforcement is removed. The compressive force is usually provided by tensioned steel wires or strands which are anchored against the concrete and, since the stress in this steel is not an important factor in the behaviour of the beam but merely a means of applying the appropriate force, full advantage may be taken of very high strength steels.

The way in which the stresses due to bending and an applied compressive force may be combined is demonstrated in figure 12.2 for the case of an axially applied force acting over the length of a beam. The stress distribution at any section will equal the sum of the compression and bending stresses if it is assumed that the concrete behaves elastically. Thus it is possible to determine the applied force so that the combined stresses are always compressive.

By applying the compressive force eccentrically on the concrete cross-section, a further stress distribution, due to the bending effects of the couple thus created, is added to those shown in figure 12.2. This effect is illustrated in figure 12.3 and offers further advantages when attempting to produce working stresses within required limits.

Early attempts to achieve this effect were hampered both by the limited steel strengths available and by shrinkage and creep of the concrete under sustained

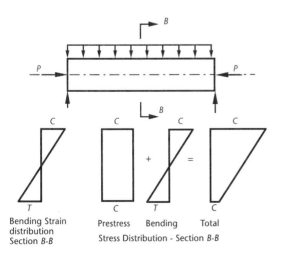

Bending Strain
distribution
Section *B-B*

Prestress   Bending   Total

Stress Distribution - Section *B-B*

Figure 12.2
Effects of axial prestress

Figure 12.3
Effects of eccentric prestress

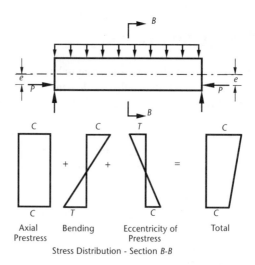

Stress Distribution - Section *B-B*

compression, coupled with relaxation of the steel. This meant that the steel lost a large part of its initial pretension and as a result residual stresses were so small as to be useless. It is now possible, however, to produce stronger concretes which have good creep properties, and very high strength steels which can be stressed up to a high percentage of their 0.2 per cent proof stress are also available. For example, hard-drawn wires may carry stresses up to about six times those possible in mild steel. This not only results in savings of steel quantity, but also the effects of shrinkage and creep become relatively smaller and may typically amount to the loss of only about 25 per cent of the initial applied force. Thus, modern materials mean that the prestressing of concrete is a practical proposition, with the forces being provided by steel passing through the beam and anchored at each end while under high tensile load.

12.2 Methods of prestressing

Two basic techniques are commonly employed in the construction of prestressed concrete, their chief difference being whether the steel tensioning process is performed before or after the hardening of the concrete. The choice of method will be governed largely by the type and size of member coupled with the need for precast or *in situ* construction.

12.2.1 Pretensioning

In this method the steel wires or strands are stretched to the required tension and anchored to the ends of the moulds for the concrete. The concrete is cast around the tensioned steel, and when it has reached sufficient strength, the anchors are released and the force in the steel is transferred to the concrete by bond. In addition to long-term losses due to creep, shrinkage and relaxation, an immediate drop in prestress force occurs due to elastic shortening of the concrete. These features are illustrated in figure 12.4.

Because of the dependence of bond, the tendons for this form of construction generally consist of small diameter wires or small strands which have good bond

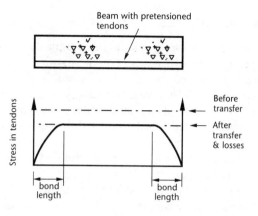

Figure 12.4
Tendon stresses –
pretensioning

characteristics. Anchorage near the ends of these wires is often enhanced by the provision of small indentations in the surface of the wire.

The method is ideally suited for factory production where large numbers of identical units can be economically made under controlled conditions, a development of this being the 'long line' system where several units can be cast at once – end to end – and the tendons merely cut between each unit after release of the anchorages. An advantage of factory production of prestressed units is that specialised curing techniques such as steam curing can be employed to increase the rate of hardening of the concrete and to enable earlier 'transfer' of the stress to the concrete. This is particularly important where re-use of moulds is required, but it is essential that under no circumstances must calcium chloride be used as an accelerator because of its severe corrosion action on small diameter steel wires.

One major limitation of this approach is that tendons must be straight, which may cause difficulties when attempting to produce acceptable final stress levels throughout the length of a member. It may therefore by necessary to reduce either the prestress or eccentricity of force near the ends of a member, in which case tendons must either be 'debonded' or 'deflected'.

1. Debonding consists of applying a wrapping or coating to the steel to prevent bond developing with the surrounding concrete. Treating some of the wires in this way over part of their length allows the magnitude of effective prestress force to be varied along the length of a member.

2. Deflecting tendons is a more complex operation and is usually restricted to large members, such as bridge beams, where the individual members may be required to form part of a continuous structure in conjunction with *in situ* concrete slabs and sill beams. A typical arrangement for deflecting tendons is shown in figure 12.5, but it must be appreciated that substantial ancillary equipment is required to provide the necessary reactions.

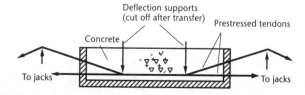

Figure 12.5
Tendon deflection

12.2.2 Post-tensioning

This method, which is the most suitable for *in situ* construction, involves the stressing against the hardened concrete of tendons or steel bars which are not bonded to the concrete. The tendons are passed through a flexible sheathing, which is cast into the concrete in the correct position. They are tensioned by jacking against the concrete, and anchored mechanically by means of steel thrust plates or anchorage blocks at each end of the member. Alternatively, steel bars threaded at their ends may be tensioned against bearing plates by means of tightening nuts. It is of course usually necessary to wait a considerable time between casting and stressing to permit the concrete to gain sufficient strength under *in situ* conditions.

The use of tendons consisting of a number of strands passing through flexible sheathing offers considerable advantages in that curved tendon profiles may be obtained. A post-tensioned structural member may be constructed from an assembly of separate pre-cast units which are constrained to act together by means of tensioned cables which are often curved as illustrated in figure 12.6. Alternatively, the member may be cast as one unit in the normal way but a light cage of untensioned reinforcing steel is necessary to hold the ducts in their correct position during concreting.

Figure 12.6
Post-tensioned segmental construction

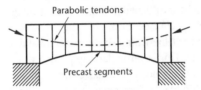

After stressing, the remaining space in the ducts may be left empty ('unbonded' construction), or more usually will be filled with grout under high pressure ('bonded' construction). Although this grout assists in transmitting forces between the steel and concrete under live loads, and improves the ultimate strength of the member, the principal use is to protect the highly stressed strands from corrosion. The quality of workmanship of grouting is thus critical to avoid air pockets which may permit corrosion. The bonding of the highly stressed steel with the surrounding concrete beam also greatly assists demolition, since the beam may then safely be 'chopped-up' into small lengths without releasing the energy stored in the steel.

12.3 | Analysis of concrete section under working loads

Since the object of prestressing is to maintain favourable stress conditions in a concrete member under load, the 'working load' for the member must be considered in terms of both maximum and minimum values. Thus at any section, the stresses produced by the prestress force must be considered in conjunction with the stresses caused by maximum and minimum values of applied moment.

Unlike reinforced concrete, the primary analysis of prestressed concrete is based on service conditions, and on the assumption that stresses in the concrete are limited to values which will correspond to elastic behaviour. In this section, the following assumptions are made in analysis.

1. Plane sections remain plane.
2. Stress–strain relationships are linear.

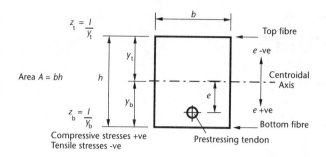

3. Bending occurs about a principal axis.

4. The prestressing force is the value remaining after all losses have occurred.

5. Changes in tendon stress due to applied loads on the member have negligible effect on the behaviour of the member.

6. Section properties are generally based on the gross concrete cross-section.

The stress in the steel is unimportant in the analysis of the concrete section under working conditions, it being the force provided by the steel that is considered in the analysis.

The sign conventions and notations used for the analysis are indicated in figure 12.7.

12.3.1 Member subjected to axial prestress force

In section BB of the member shown in figure 12.8 is subjected to moments ranging between M_{max} and M_{min}, the net stresses at the outer fibres of the beam are given by

under M_{max}
$$\begin{cases} f_t = \dfrac{P}{A} + \dfrac{M_{max}}{z_t} & \text{at the top} \qquad\qquad (12.1) \\[4mm] f_b = \dfrac{P}{A} - \dfrac{M_{max}}{z_b} & \text{at the bottom} \qquad (12.2) \end{cases}$$

under M_{min}
$$\begin{cases} f_t = \dfrac{P}{A} + \dfrac{M_{min}}{z_t} & \text{at the top} \qquad\qquad (12.3) \\[4mm] f_b = \dfrac{P}{A} - \dfrac{M_{min}}{z_b} & \text{at the bottom} \qquad (12.4) \end{cases}$$

where z_b and z_t are the elastic section moduli and P is the final prestress force.

The critical condition for tension in the beam is given by equation 12.2 which for no tension, that is $f_b = 0$, becomes

$$\frac{P}{A} = \frac{M_{max}}{z_b}$$

or

$$P = \frac{M_{max} A}{z_b} = \text{minimum prestress force required}$$

For this value of prestress force, substitution in the other equations will yield the stresses in the beam under maximum load and also under minimum load. Similarly the stresses immediately after prestressing, before losses have occurred, may be calculated if the value of losses is known.

Figure 12.8
Stresses in members with axial
prestress force

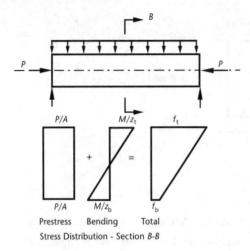

Prestress   Bending   Total

Stress Distribution - Section B-B

For example, the maximum stress in the top of the member is given by equation 12.1

$$f_t = \frac{P}{A} + \frac{M_{max}}{z_t}$$

where

$$P = \frac{M_{max}A}{z_b}$$

therefore

$$f_t = \frac{P}{A} + \frac{P}{A}\frac{z_b}{z_t} = \frac{P}{A}\frac{(z_b + z_t)}{z_t}$$

It can be seen from the stress distributions in figure 12.8 that the top fibre is generally in considerable compression, while the bottom fibre is generally at lower stresses. Much better use of the concrete could be made if the stresses at both top and bottom can be caused to vary over the full range of permissible stresses for the two extreme loading conditions. This may be achieved by providing the force at an eccentricity e from the centroid.

12.3.2 Member subjected to eccentric prestress force

The stress distributions will be similar to those in section 12.3.1 but with the addition of the term $\pm Pe/z$ due to the eccentricity e of the prestressing force. For the position shown in figure 12.9, e will have a positive value. So that

under M_{max}
$$f_t = \frac{P}{A} + \frac{M_{max}}{z_t} - \frac{Pe}{z_t} \quad \text{at the top} \tag{12.5}$$

$$f_b = \frac{P}{A} - \frac{M_{max}}{z_b} + \frac{Pe}{z_b} \quad \text{at the bottom} \tag{12.6}$$

under M_{min}
$$f_t = \frac{P}{A} + \frac{M_{min}}{z_t} - \frac{Pe}{z_t} \quad \text{at the top} \tag{12.7}$$

$$f_b = \frac{P}{A} - \frac{M_{min}}{z_b} + \frac{Pe}{z_b} \quad \text{at the bottom} \tag{12.8}$$

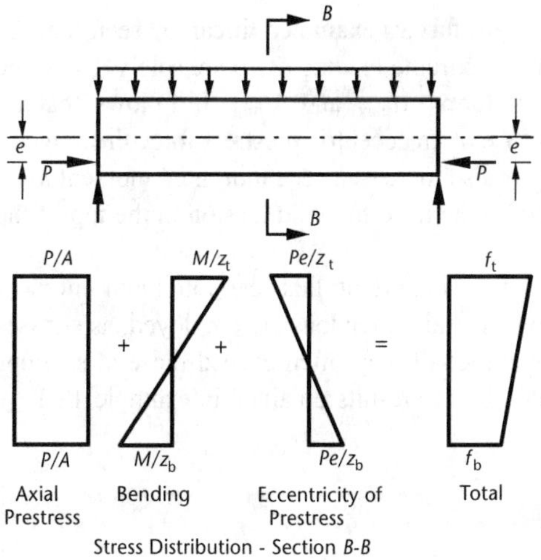

Figure 12.9
Stresses in member with
eccentric prestress

P/A   M/z_t   Pe/z_t   f_t

+   +   =

P/A   M/z_b   Pe/z_b   f_b

Axial   Bending   Eccentricity of Total
Prestress   Prestress

Stress Distribution - Section B-B

Note that, as the prestressing force lies below the neutral axis, it has the effect of causing hogging moments in the section.

The critical condition for no tension in the bottom of the beam is again given by equation 12.6, which becomes

$$\frac{P}{A} - \frac{M_{max}}{z_b} + \frac{Pe}{z_b} = 0$$

or

$$P = \frac{M_{max}}{\left(\frac{z_b}{A} + e\right)} = \text{minimum prestress force required for no tension in bottom fibre}$$

Thus for a given value of prestress force P, the beam may carry a maximum moment of

$$M_{max} = P\left(\frac{z_b}{A} + e\right)$$

When compared with $M_{max} = Pz_b/A$ for an axial prestress force it indicates an increase in moment carrying capacity of Pe.

The maximum stress in the top of the beam is given by equation 12.5 as

$$f_t = \frac{P}{A} + \frac{M_{max}}{z_t} - \frac{Pe}{z_t}$$

where

$$M_{max} = \frac{Pz_b}{A} + Pe$$

thus

$$f_t = \frac{P}{A} + \frac{Pz_b}{Az_t} + \frac{Pe}{z_t} - \frac{Pe}{z_t}$$

$$= \frac{P}{A}\left(\frac{z_b + z_t}{z_t}\right)$$

which is the same as that obtained in section 12.3.1 for an axially prestressed member. Thus the advantages of an eccentric prestress force with respect to the maximum moment-carrying capacity of a beam are apparent.

If the stress distributions of figure 12.9 are further examined, it can be seen that the differences in the net stress diagrams for the extreme loading cases are solely due to the differences between the applied moment terms M_{max} and M_{min}. It follows that by increasing the range of the stresses by the use of an eccentric prestress force the range of applied moments that the beam can carry is also increased. The minimum moment M_{min} that can be resisted is generally governed by the need to avoid tension in the top of the beam, as indicated in equation 12.7.

In the design of prestressed beams it is important that the minimum moment condition is not overlooked, especially when straight tendons are employed, as stresses near the ends of beams where moments are small may often exceed those at sections nearer mid-span. This feature is illustrated by the results obtained in example 12.1.

EXAMPLE 12.1

Calculation of prestress force and stresses

A rectangular beam 300×150 mm is simply supported over a 4 m span, and supports a live load of 10 kN/m. If a straight tendon is provided at an eccentricity of 65 mm below the centroid of the section, find the minimum prestress force necessary for no tension under live load at mid-span. Calculate the corresponding stresses under self-weight only at mid-span and at the ends of the member.

(a) Beam properties

$$\text{Self-weight} = 0.15 \times 0.3 \times 24 = 1.08 \text{ kN/m}$$

$$\text{Area} = 45 \times 10^3 \text{ mm}^2$$

$$\text{Section moduli } z_t = z_b = z = \frac{bh^2}{6} = \frac{150 \times 300^2}{6} = 2.25 \times 10^6 \text{ mm}^3$$

(b) Loadings (mid-span)

$$M_{max} = \frac{(10 + 1.08) \times 4^2}{8} = 22.2 \text{ kN m}$$

$$M_{min} = \frac{1.08 \times 4^2}{8} = 2.2 \text{ kN m}$$

(c) Calculate minimum prestress force

For no tension at the bottom under M_{max}

$$\frac{P}{A} - \frac{M_{max}}{z} + \frac{Pe}{z} = 0$$

where

$$e = 65 \text{ mm}$$

hence

$$P = \frac{M_{max}}{\left(\dfrac{z}{A} + e\right)} = \frac{22.2 \times 10^6 \times 10^{-3}}{\dfrac{2.25 \times 10^6}{45 \times 10^3} + 65}$$

$$= 193 \text{ kN}$$

(d) Calculate stresses at mid-span under $M_{\min}$

$$\text{stress at top } f_t = \frac{P}{A} + \frac{M_{\min}}{z} - \frac{Pe}{z}$$

where

$$\frac{P}{A} = \frac{193 \times 10^3}{45 \times 10^3} = 4.3 \text{ N/mm}^2$$

$$\frac{M_{\min}}{z} = \frac{2.2 \times 10^6}{2.25 \times 10^6} = 1.0 \text{ N/mm}^2$$

$$\frac{Pe}{z} = \frac{193 \times 10^3 \times 65}{2.25 \times 10^6} = 5.6 \text{ N/mm}^2$$

Hence

$$f_t = 4.3 + 1.0 - 5.6 = -0.3 \text{ N/mm}^2 \text{ (tension)}$$

and

$$\text{stress at bottom } f_b = \frac{P}{A} - \frac{M_{\min}}{z} + \frac{Pe}{z}$$
$$= 4.3 - 1.0 + 5.6 = +8.9 \text{ N/mm}^2$$

The calculation shows that with minimum load it is possible for the beam to hog with tensile stresses in the top fibres. This is particularly so at the initial transfer of the prestress force to the unloaded beam.

(e) Calculate stresses at ends

In this situation $M = 0$. Hence

$$f_t = \frac{P}{A} - \frac{Pe}{z} = 4.3 - 5.6 = -1.3 \text{ N/mm}^2$$

and

$$f_b = \frac{P}{A} + \frac{Pe}{z} = 4.3 + 5.6 = 9.9 \text{ N/mm}^2$$

12.4 | Design for the serviceability limit state

The design of a prestressed concrete member is based on maintaining the concrete stresses within specified limits at all stages in the life of the member. Hence the primary design is based on the serviceability limit state, with the concrete stress limits based on the acceptable degree of flexural cracking.

A prestressed member may be categorised into one of three basic groups depending on the allowable concrete tensile stress.

Class 1 – no tension permitted under working conditions.

Class 2 – tensile stresses are permitted, but these are limited to avoid flexural cracking.

Class 3 – cracking permitted, but tensile stresses limited on the basis of maximum permissible flexural crack widths.

Guidance regarding suitable tensile stress limits for class 2 and 3 members is given in BS 8110, but the maximum allowable concrete compressive stress in bending is generally the same for all three classes at one-third of the characteristic compressive cube strength, this value being determined by the dual requirements of avoidance of spalling in the compression zone, and the prevention of excessive loss in the prestress force due to creep.

At initial transfer to the concrete, the prestress force will be considerably higher than the 'long-term' value as a result of subsequent losses which are due to a number of causes including elastic shortening, creep and shrinkage of the concrete member. Estimation of losses is described in section 12.4.6. Since these losses commence immediately, the conditions at transfer represent a transitory stage in the life of the member and maximum permissible concrete stresses are related to the actual cube strength at transfer, usually by a factor of one-half. Concrete tensile stress limits may be increased where they are due to prestress alone, and for a class 1 structure 1.0 N/mm^2 is permitted.

The choice of class for a structure will depend upon a number of factors which include conditions of exposure and the nature of loading. If a member consists of precast segments with mortar joints, or if it is essential that cracking should not occur then design must be as a class 1 member, but otherwise class 2 would generally be used. This offers the most efficient use of materials, while still avoiding flexural cracking under normal circumstances. The design procedure for class 1 and class 2 members will be similar, with the basic cross-section and prestress force details being determined by the above serviceability requirements. Subsequent checks for adequacy at the ultimate limit state will generally be satisfied, although a class 2 member may sometimes require a small amount of additional reinforcing steel (see section 12.5.2).

Class 3, which is often known as partial prestressing, represents a form of construction which is intermediate between reinforced and prestressed concrete. While not offering the full advantages of prestressing, this technique allows high-strength steels to be used in situations where crack avoidance is not essential, and the otherwise excessive deflections are controlled by the prestressing. This form of construction is governed by the requirements of the ultimate limit state, thus the design procedure should consider this first, followed by the design of prestressing.

The design of prestressing requirements is based on the manipulation of the four basic expressions given in section 12.3.2 describing the stress distribution across the concrete section. These are used in conjunction with the permissible stresses appropriate to the class of member, coupled with the final prestress force after losses and the maximum and minimum loadings on the member. These loadings must encompass the full range that the member will encounter during its life, and the minimum value will

Figure 12.10
Prestressed beam at transfer and service

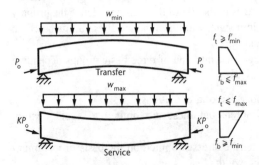

thus be governed by the construction techniques to be used. The partial factors of safety applied to these loads will be those for the serviceability limit state, that is 1.0 for both dead and live loads.

For a beam with a cantilever span or a continuous beam it is necessary to consider the loading patterns of the live loads at service in order to determine the minimum and maximum moments. For a single-span, simply supported beam it is usually the minimum moment at transfer and the maximum moment at service that will govern, as shown in figure 12.10. From figure 12.10 the governing equations for a single-span beam are:

At transfer

$$\frac{P_0}{A} - \frac{P_0 e}{z_t} + \frac{M_{min}}{z_t} = f'_t \geq f'_{min} \qquad (12.9)*$$

$$\frac{P_0}{A} + \frac{P_0 e}{z_b} - \frac{M_{min}}{z_b} = f'_b \leq f'_{max} \qquad (12.10)*$$

At service

$$\frac{KP_0}{A} - \frac{KP_0 e}{z_t} + \frac{M_{max}}{z_t} = f_t \leq f_{max} \qquad (12.11)*$$

$$\frac{KP_0}{A} + \frac{KP_0 e}{z_b} - \frac{M_{max}}{z_b} = f_b \geq f_{min} \qquad (12.12)*$$

where f'_{max}, f'_{min}, f_{max} and f_{min} are the appropriate permissible stresses at transfer and serviceability conditions. P_0 is the prestressing force at transfer and K is a loss factor that accounts for the prestress losses – for example, $K = 0.8$ for 20 per cent loss.

12.4.1 Determination of minimum section properties

The two pairs of expressions can be combined as follows:

12.9 and 12.11

$$(M_{max} - KM_{min}) \leq (f_{max} - Kf'_{min})z_t \qquad (12.13)$$

12.10 and 12.12

$$(M_{max} - KM_{min}) \leq (Kf'_{max} - f_{min})z_b \qquad (12.14)$$

Hence, if $(M_{max} - KM_{min})$ is written as M_v, the moment variation

$$z_t \geq \frac{M_v}{(f_{max} - Kf'_{min})} \qquad (12.15)*$$

and

$$z_b \geq \frac{M_v}{(Kf'_{max} - f_{min})} \qquad (12.16)*$$

In equations 12.15 and 12.16, for z_t and z_b it can be assumed with sufficient accuracy, for preliminary sizing that

$$M_v \approx M_{max} - M_{min}$$

M_{max} will depend on both the imposed and dead (self-weight) load and M_{min} will depend on the dead (self-weight) load only, so that in effect the calculations for M_v become independent of the self-weight of the beam.

These minimum values of section moduli must be satisfied by the chosen section in order that a prestress force and eccentricity exist which will permit the stress limits to be met; but to ensure that practical considerations are met the chosen section must have a margin above the minimum values of section moduli calculated above. The maximum moment on the section has not directly been included in these figures, thus it is possible that the resulting prestress force may not be economic or practicable. However, it is found in the majority of cases that if a section is chosen which satisfies these minimum requirements, coupled with any other specified requirements regarding the shape of the section, then a satisfactory design is usually possible. The ratio of acceptable span–depth for a prestressed beam cannot be categorised on the basis of deflections as easily as for reinforced concrete. In the absence of any other criteria, the following formulae may be used as a guide and will generally produce reasonably conservative designs for post-tensioned members.

$$\text{span} \leq 36 \text{ m} \quad h = \frac{\text{span}}{25} + 0.1 \text{ m}$$

$$\text{span} \geq 36 \text{ m} \quad h = \frac{\text{span}}{20} \text{ m}$$

In the case of short-span members it may be possible to use very much greater span–depth ratios quite satisfactorily, although the resulting prestress forces may become very high.

Other factors which must be considered at this stage include the slenderness ratio of beams, where the same criteria apply as for reinforced concrete, and the possibility of web and flange splitting in flanged members.

EXAMPLE 12.2

Selection of cross-section

Select a rectangular section for a post-tensioned beam to carry, in addition to its self-weight, a uniformly distributed load of 3 kN/m over a simply supported span of 10 m. The member is to be designed as class 1 with grade 40 concrete, without lateral support. Assume 20 per cent loss of prestress ($K = 0.8$).

Class 1 member, thus

At service

$f_{max} = f_{cu}/3 = 40/3 = 13.33 \text{ N/mm}^2$ $\qquad$ $f_{min} = 0.0 \text{ N/mm}^2$

At transfer

$f'_{max} = 16 \text{ N/mm}^2 \approx 0.5 \text{ strength at transfer}$ $\qquad$ $f'_{min} = -1.0 \text{ N/mm}^2$

$M_v = 3.0 \times 10^2/8 = 37.5 \text{ kN m}$

From equations 12.15 and 12.16

$$z_t \geq \frac{M_v}{(f_{max} - Kf'_{min})} = \frac{37.5 \times 10^6}{(13.33 - 0.8(-1))} = 2.65 \times 10^6 \text{ mm}^3$$

$$z_b \geq \frac{M_v}{(Kf'_{max} - f_{min})} = \frac{37.5 \times 10^6}{(0.8 \times 16 - 0.0)} = 2.93 \times 10^6 \text{ mm}^3$$

To prevent lateral buckling BS 8110 specifies maximum permissible span/breadth = 60.

Take $b = 200$ mm which meets the span/breadth requirement. Hence

$$z = 200h^2/6 \geq 2.93 \times 10^6$$

therefore

$$h \geq \sqrt{(2.93 \times 10^6 \times 6/200)} = 297 \text{ mm}$$

The minimum depth of beam is therefore 297 mm and to allow a margin in subsequent detailed design a depth of 350 mm would be appropriate as a first attempt.

12.4.2 Design of prestress force

The inequalities of equations 12.9 to 12.12 may be rearranged to give expressions for the minimum required prestress force for a given eccentricity:

$$P_0 \leq \frac{(z_t f_{max} - M_{max})}{K(z_t/A - e)} \tag{12.17}$$

$$P_0 \geq \frac{(z_t f'_{min} - M_{min})}{(z_t/A - e)} \tag{12.18}$$

$$P_0 \geq \frac{(z_b f_{min} + M_{max})}{K(z_b/A + e)} \tag{12.19}$$

$$P_0 \leq \frac{(z_b f'_{max} + M_{min})}{(z_b/A + e)} \tag{12.20}$$

Note that in equations 12.17 and 12.18 it is possible that the denominator term, $(z_t/A - e)$, might be negative if $e > z_t/A$. In this case, the sense of the inequality would have to change as the effect of dividing an inequality by a negative number is to change its sense.

These equations give a range within which the prestress force must lie to ensure that the allowable stress conditions are met at all stages in the life of the member. In the case of a simply supported beam, the design prestress force will generally be based on the minimum value which satisfies these equations at the critical section for bending in the member.

Although a range of values of permissible prestress force can be found, this makes no allowance for the fact that the corresponding eccentricity must lie within the beam. It is therefore necessary to consider the effect of limiting the eccentricity to a maximum practical value for the section under consideration. The effect of this limitation will be most severe when considering the maximum moments acting on the section, that is, the inequalities of equations 12.11 and 12.12.

If the limiting value for maximum eccentricity e_{max}, depends on cover requirements, equation 12.11 becomes

$$M_{max} \leq f_{max} z_t - KP_0 \left(\frac{z_t}{A} - e_{max} \right) \tag{12.21}$$

and equation 12.12 becomes

$$M_{max} \leq KP_0 \left(\frac{z_b}{A} + e_{max} \right) - f_{min} z_b \tag{12.22}$$

Figure 12.11
Maximum moment and
prestress force relationship

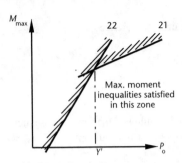

These represent linear relationships between M_{max} and P_0. For the case of a beam subject to sagging moments e_{max} will generally be positive in value, thus equation 12.22 is of positive slope and represents a lower limit to P_0. It can also be shown that for most practical cases $[(z_t/A) - e_{max}] < 0$, thus equation 12.21 is similarly a lower limit of positive, though smaller slope.

Figure 12.11 represents the general form of these expressions, and it can be seen clearly that providing a prestress force in excess of Y' produces only small benefits of additional moment capacity. The value of Y' is given by the intersection of these two expressions, when

$$KP_0\left(\frac{z_b}{A} + e_{max}\right) - f_{min}z_b = f_{max}z_t - KP_0\left(\frac{z_t}{A} - e_{max}\right)$$

thus

$$P_0 = \frac{f_{max}z_t + f_{min}z_b}{K\left(\dfrac{z_b + z_t}{A}\right)} \tag{12.23}$$

Thus the value of prestress force $P_0 = Y'$ may be conveniently considered as a maximum economic value beyond which any increase in prestress force would be matched by a diminishing rate of increase in moment-carrying capacity. If a force larger than this limit is required for a given section it may be more economic to increase the size of this section.

EXAMPLE 12.3

Calculation of prestress force

The 10 metre span beam in example 12.2 was determined to have a breadth of 200 mm and a depth of 350 mm ($z_b = z_t = 4.08 \times 10^6$ mm^3). Determine the minimum initial prestress force required for an assumed maximum eccentricity of 75 mm.

From example 12.2:

$$f'_{max} = 16 \text{ N/mm}^2 \qquad f_{max} = 13.33 \text{ N/mm}^2$$
$$f'_{min} = -1.0 \text{ N/mm}^2 \qquad f_{min} = 0.0 \text{ N/mm}^2$$

Self-weight of beam $= 0.2 \times 0.35 \times 24 = 1.68$ kN/m

$M_{min} = 1.68 \times 10^2/8 = 21$ kN m

$M_{max} = 3.0 \times 10^2/8 + 21 = 58.5$ kN m

(a) From equation 12.17

$$P_0 \leq \frac{(z_t f_{max} - M_{max})}{K(z_t/A - e_{max})}$$

$$\leq \frac{(4.08 \times 10^6 \times 13.33 - 58.5 \times 10^6)}{0.8(4.08 \times 10^6/70\,000 - 75)} \times 10^{-3}$$

and allowing for the division by the negative denominator

$$P_0 \geq -308 \text{ kN}$$

Similarly from equations 12.18 to 12.20:

$$P_0 \leq 1505 \text{ kN}$$
$$P_0 \geq 548 \text{ kN}$$
$$P_0 \leq 647 \text{ kN}$$

The minimum value of prestress force is therefore 548 kN with an upper limit of 647 kN.

(b) Check the upper economic limit to prestress force

From equation 12.23:

$$P_0 \leq \frac{f_{max}z_t + f_{min}z_b}{K\left(\frac{z_b + z_t}{A}\right)} = \frac{13.33zA}{2Kz}$$

$$\leq 6.67A/K \leq 6.67 \times (350 \times 200) \times 10^{-3}/0.8$$
$$\leq 584 \text{ kN}$$

Since this is lower than the upper limit already established from equation 12.20 a design with an initial prestressing force between 548 kN and 584 kN will be acceptable.

12.4.3 Magnel diagram construction

Equations 12.17 to 12.20 can be used to determine a range of possible values of prestress force for a given or assumed eccentricity. For different assumed values of eccentricity further limits on the prestress force can be determined in an identical manner although the calculations would be tedious and repetitive. In addition, it is possible to assume values of eccentricity for which there is no solution for the prestress force as the upper and lower limits could overlap.

A much more useful approach to design can be developed if the equations are treated graphically as follows. Equations 12.9 to 12.12 can be rearranged into the following form:

$$\frac{1}{P_0} \geq \frac{K(1/A - e/z_t)}{(f_{max} - M_{max}/z_t)} \tag{12.24}$$

$$\frac{1}{P_0} \geq \frac{(1/A - e/z_t)}{(f'_{min} - M_{min}/z_t)} \tag{12.25}$$

$$\frac{1}{P_0} \leq \frac{K(1/A + e/z_b)}{(f_{min} + M_{max}/z_b)} \tag{12.26}$$

$$\frac{1}{P_0} \geq \frac{(1/A + e/z_b)}{(f'_{max} + M_{min}/z_b)} \tag{12.27}$$

Figure 12.12
Magnel diagram construction

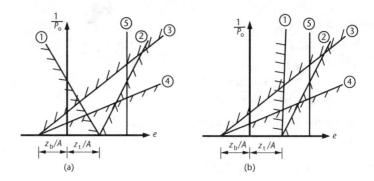

These equations now express linear relationships between $1/P_0$ and e. Note that in equation 12.25 the sense of the inequality has been reversed to account for the fact that the denominator is negative (f'_{min} is negative according to the chosen sign convention). The relationships can be plotted as shown in figure 12.12 a and b and the area of the graph to one side of each line, as defined by the inequality, can be eliminated, resulting in an area of graph within which any combination of force and eccentricity will simultaneously satisfy all four inequalities and hence will provide a satisfactory design. The lines marked ① to ④ correspond to equations 12.24 to 12.27 respectively. This form of construction is known as a *Magnel Diagram*.

The additional line, ⑤ shown on the diagram corresponds to a possible physical limitation of the maximum eccentricity allowing for the overall depth of section, cover to the prestressing tendons, provision of shear links and so on. Two separate figures are shown as it is possible for line ①, derived from equation 12.24, to have either a positive or a negative slope depending on whether f_{max} is greater or less than M_{max}/z_t.

The Magnel diagram is a powerful design tool as it covers all possible solutions of the inequality equations and enables a range of prestress force and eccentricity values to be investigated. Values of minimum and maximum prestress force can be readily read from the diagram as can intermediate values where the range of possible eccentricities for a chosen force can be easily determined. The diagram also shows that the minimum prestress force (largest value of $1/P_0$) corresponds to the maximum eccentricity, and as the eccentricity is reduced the prestress force must be increased to compensate.

EXAMPLE 12.4

Construction of magnel diagram

Construct the Magnel diagram for the beam give in example 12.2 and determine the minimum and maximum possible values of prestress force. Assume a maximum possible eccentricity of 125 mm allowing for cover etc. to the tendons.

From the previous examples:

$$f'_{max} = 16 \text{ N/mm}^2 \qquad\qquad f_{max} = 13.33 \text{ N/mm}^2$$
$$f'_{min} = -1.0 \text{ N/mm}^2 \qquad\qquad f_{min} = 0.0 \text{ N/mm}^2$$
$$M_{min} = 21 \text{ kN m} \qquad\qquad M_{max} = 58.5 \text{ kN m}$$
$$K = 0.8 \qquad\qquad z_b = z_t = 4.08 \times 10^6 \text{ mm}^3$$
$$A = 70\,000 \text{ mm}^2$$

From equation 12.24:

$$\frac{1}{P_0} \geq \frac{K(1/A - e/z_t)}{(f_{max} - M_{max}/z_t)}$$

$$\frac{1}{P_0} \geq 0.8\left(\frac{1}{70\,000} - \frac{e}{4.08 \times 10^6}\right) \times 10^3 / \left(13.33 - \frac{58.5 \times 10^6}{4.08 \times 10^6}\right)$$

which can be re-arranged to give:

$$\frac{10^6}{P_0} \leq -11\,335 + 194.5e$$

and similarly from the other three inequalities, equations 12.25 to 12.27:

$$\frac{10^6}{P_0} \geq -2324 + 39.9e$$

$$\frac{10^6}{P_0} \leq 797 + 13.7e$$

$$\frac{10^6}{P_0} \leq 676 + 11.6e$$

These inequalities are plotted on the Magnel diagram in figure 12.13 and the zone bounded by the four lines defines an area in which all possible design solutions lie. The line of maximum possible eccentricity is also plotted but, as it lies outside the zone bounded by the four inequalities, does not place any restriction on the possible solutions.

From figure 12.13 it can be seen that the maximum and minimum values of prestress force are given by:

Maximum $10^6/P_0 = 2430$; hence minimum $P_0 = 412$ kN ($e = 120$ mm)

Minimum $10^6/P_0 = 1430$; hence maximum $P_0 = 700$ kN ($e = 66$ mm)

The intersection of the two lines at position A on the diagram corresponds to a value of $P_0 = 584$ kN, established in example 12.3 as the maximum economical value of prestress force for this section (see equation 12.23). Hence the intersection of these two

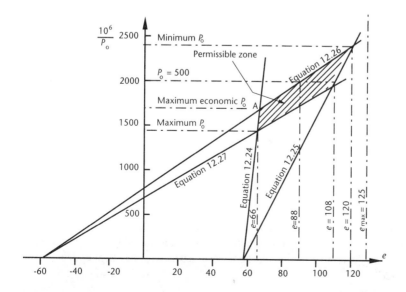

Figure 12.13
Magnel diagram for example 12.4

lines should be taken as the maximum prestress force and, as can be seen, this information can be readily determined from the diagram without the need for further calculation.

The Magnel diagram can now be used to investigate other possible solutions for the design prestressing force and eccentricity. For a fixed value of prestress force (and hence fixed value of $1/P_0$) the corresponding range of permissible eccentricity can be read directly from the diagram. Alternatively, if the eccentricity is fixed, the diagram can be used to investigate the range of possible prestress force for the given eccentricity.

12.4.4 Design of tendon profiles

Having obtained a value of prestress force which will permit all stress conditions to be satisfied at the critical section, it is necessary to determine the eccentricity at which this force must be provided not only at the critical section but also throughout the length of the member.

At any section along the member, e is the only unknown term in the four expressions 12.9 to 12.12 and these will yield two upper and two lower limits which must all be simultaneously satisfied. This requirement must be met at all sections throughout the member and will reflect both variations of moment, prestress force and section properties along the member.

The design expressions can be re-written as:

At transfer

$$e \leq \left[\frac{z_t}{A} - \frac{f'_{min}z_t}{P_0} \right] + \frac{M_{min}}{P_0} \tag{12.28}$$

$$e \leq \left[-\frac{z_b}{A} + \frac{f'_{max}z_b}{P_0} \right] + \frac{M_{min}}{P_0} \tag{12.29}$$

At service

$$e \geq \left[\frac{z_t}{A} - \frac{f_{max}z_t}{KP_0} \right] + \frac{M_{max}}{KP_0} \tag{12.30}$$

$$e \geq \left[-\frac{z_b}{A} + \frac{f_{min}z_b}{KP_0} \right] + \frac{M_{max}}{KP_0} \tag{12.31}$$

The above four equations can be evaluated at any section to determine the range of eccentricities within which the resultant force P_0 must lie. The moments M_{max} and M_{min} are those relating to the section being considered.

For a member of constant cross-section, if minor changes in prestress force along the length are neglected, the terms in brackets in the above expressions are constant. Therefore the zone within which the centroid must lie is governed by the shape of the bending moment envelopes, as shown in figure 12.14.

In the case of uniform loading these are parabolic, hence the usual practice is to provide parabolic tendon profiles if a straight profile will not fit within the zone. At the critical section, the zone is generally narrow and reduces to zero if the value of the prestress force is taken as the minimum value from the Magnel diagram. At sections away from the critical section, the zone becomes increasingly greater than the minimum required.

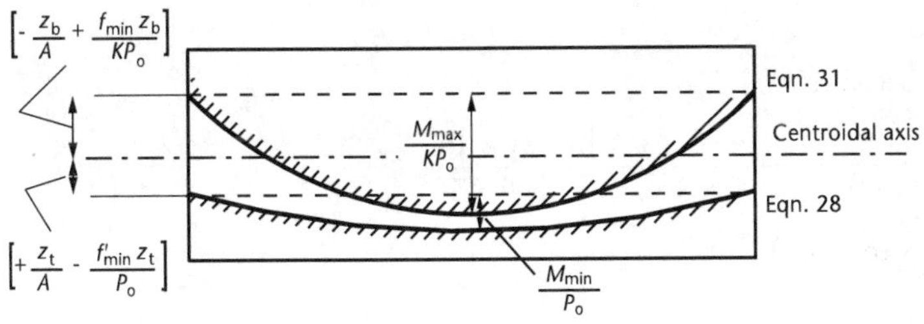

Figure 12.14
Cable zone limits

EXAMPLE 12.5

Calculation of cable zone

Determine the cable zone limits at mid-span and ends of the member designed in examples 12.2 to 12.4 for a constant initial prestress force of 500 kN. Data for this question are given in the previous examples.

(a) Ends of beam

Limits to cable eccentricity are given in equation 12.28 which, at the end section can be readily shown, for this example, to be more critical than equation 12.29:

$$e \leq \left[\frac{z_t}{A} - \frac{f'_{min}z_t}{P_0} \right] + \frac{M_{min}}{P_0}$$

Likewise equation 12.31 is more critical than equation 12.30:

$$e \geq \left[-\frac{z_b}{A} + \frac{f_{min}z_b}{KP_0} \right] + \frac{M_{max}}{KP_0}$$

As there are no moments due to external loading at the end of a simply supported beam, equation 12.28 becomes

$$e \leq \left[\frac{4.08 \times 10^6}{(350 \times 200)} + \frac{(-1) \times 4.08 \times 10^6}{500 \times 10^3} \right] + 0$$

$$\leq 58.29 + 8.16$$

$$\leq 66.5 \text{ mm}$$

Similarly equation 12.31 becomes

$$e \leq \left[-\frac{4.08 \times 10^6}{(350 \times 200)} + 0 \right] + 0$$

$$\geq -58.3 \text{ mm}$$

At the ends of the beam where the moments are zero, and for $z_t = z_b$ the inequality expressions can apply with the tendon eccentricities above or below the neutral axis (e positive or negative), so that e must lie within the range ± 58.3 mm.

(b) Mid-span

Equation 12.28 becomes

$$e \leq \left[\frac{4.08 \times 10^6}{(350 \times 200)} - \frac{(-1)4.08 \times 10^6}{500 \times 10^3} \right] + \frac{21 \times 10^6}{500 \times 10^3}$$

$$\leq 58.29 + 8.16 + 42.0$$

$$\leq 108.5 \text{ mm}$$

Equation 12.29 might be more critical than equation 12.28 and should be also checked. From equation 12.29:

$$e \leq \left[-\frac{4.08 \times 10^6}{(350 \times 200)} + \frac{16 \times 4.08 \times 10^6}{500 \times 10^3} \right] + \frac{21 \times 10^6}{500 \times 10^3}$$

$$\leq -58.27 + 130.56 + 42.0$$

$$\leq 114.3 \text{ mm}$$

Hence equation 12.28 is critical and the eccentricity must be less than 108.5 mm.
Equation 12.30 gives

$$e \geq \left[\frac{4.08 \times 10^6}{(350 \times 200)} - \frac{13.33 \times 4.08 \times 10^6}{0.8 \times 500 \times 10^3} \right] + \frac{58.8 \times 10^6}{0.8 \times 500 \times 10^3}$$

$$\geq 58.29 - 135.97 + 146.25$$

$$\geq 68.6 \text{ mm}$$

Equation 12.31 should also be checked:

$$e \geq \left[-\frac{4.08 \times 10^6}{(350 \times 200)} + 0 \right] + \frac{52.5 \times 10^6}{0.8 \times 500 \times 10^3}$$

$$\geq -58.29 + 146.25$$

$$\geq 88.0 \text{ mm}$$

Hence at mid-span the resultant of the tendon force must lie at an eccentricity in the range of 108.5 to 88.0 mm. Provided that the tendons can be arranged so that their resultant force lies within the calculated limits then the design will be acceptable.

If a Magnel diagram for the stress condition at mid-span had been drawn, as in example 12.4 then the eccentricity range could have been determined directly from the diagram without further calculation. For tendons with a combined prestress force at transfer of $P_0 = 500$ kN ($10^6/P_0 = 2000$), plotting this value on the diagram of figure 12.13 will give the range of possible eccentricity between 88 and 108 mm.

12.4.5 Width of cable zone

From the Magnel diagram of figure 12.13 it can be seen that for any chosen value of prestress force there is an eccentricity range within which the resultant tendon force must lie. As the force approaches a value, corresponding to the top and bottom limits of the diagram, the width of the available cable zone diminishes until at the very extremities the upper and lower limits of eccentricity coincide, giving zero width of cable zone.

Practically, therefore, a prestress force will be chosen which has a value inbetween the upper and lower limits of permissible prestress force whilst, at the same time, ensuring that, for the chosen force, a reasonable width of cable zone exists. The prestressing cables must also satisfy requirements of cover, minimum spacing between tendons, available size of tendons and so on. A number of alternative tendon combinations and configurations are likely to be tried so that all requirements are simultaneously met. The advantage of the Magnel diagram is that a range of alternatives can be quickly considered without the necessity for any further calculation, as illustrated at the end of example 12.5.

12.4.6   Prestress losses

From the moment that the prestressing force is first applied to the concrete member, losses of this force will take place because of the following causes

1. Elastic shortening of the concrete.
2. Creep of the concrete under sustained compression.
3. Relaxation of the prestressing steel under sustained tension.
4. Shrinkage of the concrete.

These losses will occur whichever form of construction is used, although the effects of elastic shortening will generally be much reduced when post-tensioning is used. This is because stressing is a sequential procedure, and not instantaneous as with pre-tensioning. Creep and shrinkage losses depend to a large extent on the properties of the concrete with particular reference to the maturity at the time of stressing. In pre-tensioning, where the concrete is usually relatively immature at transfer, these losses may therefore be expected to be higher than in post-tensioning.

In addition to losses from these causes, which will generally total between 20 to 30 per cent of the initial prestress force at transfer, further losses occur in post-tensioned concrete during the stressing procedure. These are due to friction between the strands and the duct, especially where curved profiles are used, and to mechanical anchorage slip during the stressing operation. Both these factors depend on the actual system of ducts, anchorages and stressing equipment that are used.

Thus although the basic losses are generally highest in pre-tensioned members, in some instances overall losses in post-tensioned members may be of similar magnitude.

Elastic shortening

The concrete will immediately shorten elastically when subjected to compression, and the steel will generally shorten by a similar amount (as in pre-tensioning) with a corresponding loss of prestress force. To calculate this it is necessary to obtain the compressive strain at the level of the steel.

If the transfer force is P_0 and the force after elastic losses is P' then

$$P' = P_0 - \text{loss in force}$$

and the corresponding stress in the concrete at the level of the tendon

$$f_c = \frac{P'}{A} + \frac{(P'e) \times e}{I} + f(w_d)$$

where $f(w_d)$ is the stress due to self-weight which will be relatively small when averaged over the length of the member and may thus be neglected. Hence

$$f_c = \frac{P'}{A}\left(1 + \frac{e^2 A}{I}\right)$$

and concrete strain $= f_c/E_c$, thus reduction in steel strain $= f_c/E_c$ and

$$\text{reduction in steel stress} = \left(\frac{f_c}{E_c}\right) E_s = \alpha_e f_c$$

thus

$$\text{loss in prestress force} = \alpha_e f_c A_{st}$$

where $A_{st} = $ area of tendons

$$= \alpha_e \frac{A_{st}}{A} P'\left(1 + \frac{e^2 A}{I}\right)$$

hence

$$P' = P_0 - \alpha_e \frac{A_{st}}{A} P'\left(1 + \frac{e^2 A}{I}\right)$$

so that

$$\text{remaining prestress force } P' = \frac{P_0}{1 + \alpha_e \dfrac{A_{st}}{A}\left(1 + \dfrac{e^2 A}{I}\right)}$$

In pre-tensioned construction this full loss will be present; however when post-tensioning the effect will only apply to previously tensioned cables and although a detailed calculation could be undertaken it is normally adequate to assume 50 per cent of the above losses. In this case the remaining prestress force is

$$P' = \frac{P_0}{1 + 0.5\alpha_e \dfrac{A_{st}}{A}\left(1 + \dfrac{e^2 A}{I}\right)}$$

and it is this value which applies to subsequent loss calculations.

Creep of concrete

The sustained compressive stress on the concrete will also cause a long-term shortening due to creep, which will similarly reduce the prestress force. As above, it is the stress in the concrete at the level of the steel which is important, that is

$$f_c = \frac{P'}{A}\left(1 + \frac{e^2 A}{I}\right)$$

and

$$\text{loss of stress} = E_s f_c \times \text{specific creep strain}$$

then

$$\text{loss of prestress force} = E_s \frac{A_{st}}{A} P'\left(1 + \frac{e^2 A}{I}\right) \times \text{specific creep strain}$$

The value of specific creep used in this calculation will be influenced by the factors discussed in section 6.3.2, and may be obtained from the values of creep coefficient ϕ given in figure 6.5 using the relationship

$$\text{specific creep strain} = \frac{\phi}{E_c} / \text{N/mm}^2$$

For most outdoor exposure purposes in the UK it will be adequate to use values of creep coefficient between 1.8 for transfer within 3 days and 1.4 for transfer after 28 days.

Relaxation of steel

Despite developments in prestressing steel manufacture which have taken place in recent years, relaxation of the wire or strand under sustained tension may still be expected to be a significant factor. The precise value will depend upon whether pre-tensioning or post-tensioning is used and the characteristics of the steel type defined in BS 5896. Factors allowing for method of construction are given in BS 8110 which should be applied to 1000 hour relaxation values provided by the manufacturer. The amount of relaxation will also depend upon the initial tendon load relative to its breaking load. In most practical situations the transfer steel stress is about 70 per cent of the characteristic strength and relaxation losses are likely to be approximately 8–10 per cent of the tendon load remaining after transfer. This loss decreases linearly to zero for a transfer stress of about 40 per cent characteristic.

Shrinkage of concrete

This is based on empirical figures for shrinkage/unit length of concrete (ε_{sh}) for particular curing conditions and transfer maturity as discussed in chapter 6. Typical values for pre-tensioned concrete (stressed at 3 to 5 days) range from 100×10^{-6} for UK outdoor exposure to 300×10^{-6} for indoor exposure. Corresponding values for post-tensioning (stressed at 7–14 days) are reduced to 70×10^{-6} and 200×10^{-6}. More detailed guidance in unusual circumstances may be obtained from section 6.3.2.

The loss in steel stress is thus given by $\varepsilon_{sh}E_s$, hence

$$\text{loss in prestress force} = \varepsilon_{sh}E_sA_{st}$$

Friction in ducts (post-tensioning only)

When a post-tensioned cable is stressed, it will move relative to the duct and other cables within the duct and friction will tend to resist this movement hence reducing the effective prestress force at positions remote from the jacking point. This effect may be divided into unintentional profile variations, and those due to designed curvature of ducts.

(a) 'Wobble' effects in straight ducts will usually be present. If $P_0 = $ jack force, and $P_x = $ cable force at distance x from jack then it is generally estimated that

$$P_x = P_0 e^{-kx}$$

where $e = $ base of napierian logs (2.718) and $k = $ constant, depending on duct characteristics and construction procedures, generally taken as $\not< 33 \times 10^{-4}$ but reducing to 17×10^{-4} in special cases.

(b) Duct curvature will generally cause greater prestress force losses, and is given by

$$P_x = P_0 e^{-\mu x/r_{ps}}$$

where μ = coefficient of friction (typically 0.55 steel on concrete, 0.3 steel on steel, 0.12 greased strand on plastic) and r_{ps} = radius of curvature of duct. If r_{ps} is not constant, the profile must be subdivided into sections, each assumed to have constant r_{ps}, in which case P_0 is taken as the force at the jacking end of the section and x the length of the segment P_x, the force at the end remote from the jack then becomes P_0 for the next section and so on.

The above effects may be combined to produce an effective prestress force diagram for a member. If friction losses are high, it may be worthwhile to jack simultaneously from both ends, in which case the two diagrams may be superimposed, maintaining symmetry of prestress force relative to the length of the member.

EXAMPLE 12.6

Estimation of prestress losses at mid-span

A post-tensioned beam shown in figure 12.15 is stressed by two tendons with a parabolic profile and having a total cross-sectional area $A_{st} = 7500$ mm^2. The total initial prestress force $P_0 = 10\,500$ kN and the total characteristic strength of the tendons is $14\,000$ kN.

Assume the following data for estimating losses: coefficient of friction $\mu = 0.20$; wobble factor $K = 17 \times 10^{-4}$/metre; elastic modulus E_c(transfer) 32 kN/mm^2; specific creep = 48×10^{-6}/ N/mm^2; shrinkage/unit length $\varepsilon_{sh} = 300 \times 10^{-6}$.

(1) Friction

The equation of the parabola is $y = Cx^2$ and with the origin at mid-span when $x = 15\,000$, $y = 640$, so that $C = 640/15\,000^2 = 2.844 \times 10^{-6}$.

The radius of curvature of the tendons is given by

$$r_{ps} \approx \frac{1}{d^2y/dx^2} = \frac{1}{2 \times C}$$

$$= \frac{1}{2 \times 2.844 \times 10^{-6}} \times 10^{-3} = 175.81 \text{ m}$$

At mid-span:

$$\text{Loss } \Delta P(x) = P_0 \left(1 - e^{-(\mu x/r_{ps} + Kx)}\right)$$

$$= P_0 \left(1 - e^{-(0.20 \times 15/175.81 + 17 \times 10^{-4} \times 15)}\right)$$

$$= 0.043 P_0 = 452 \text{ kN} = 4.3 \text{ per cent}$$

Figure 12.15
Post-tensioned beam

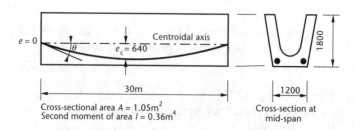

$e = 0$ θ Centroidal axis $e_c = 640$

30m

Cross-sectional area $A = 1.05$m^2
Second moment of area $I = 0.36$m^4

1800   1200

Cross-section at mid-span

(2) Elastic shortening for post-tensioned construction

Take the average eccentricity for the parabolic tendons as

$$\frac{5}{8}e_c = \frac{5}{8} \times 640 = 400 \text{ mm and } \alpha_e = \frac{E_s}{E_c} = \frac{205}{32} = 6.41$$

$$P' = \frac{P_0}{1 + 0.5\alpha_e\dfrac{A_{st}}{A}\left(1 + e^2\dfrac{A}{I}\right)}$$

$$= \frac{P_0}{1 + 0.5 \times 6.41 \times \dfrac{7.5 \times 10^3}{1.05 \times 10^6}\left(1 + 400^2\dfrac{1.05 \times 10^6}{0.36 \times 10^{12}}\right)}$$

$$= 0.968P_0 = 10160 \text{ kN}$$

$$\text{Loss } \Delta P = 10\,500 - 10\,160 = 340 \text{ kN} = 3.2 \text{ per cent}$$

$$\text{Total short-term losses} = 452 + 340 = 792 \text{ kN}$$

$$P' = P_0 - \text{short-term losses} = 10\,500 - 792 = 9708 \text{ kN}$$

(3) Creep

$$\text{Loss } \Delta P = \text{specific creep} \times E_s \times \frac{P'}{A}\left(1 + e^2\frac{A}{I}\right)A_{st}$$

$$= 48 \times 10^{-6} \times 205 \times 10^3 \times \frac{9708}{1.05 \times 10^6}\left(1 + 400^2\frac{1.05 \times 10^6}{0.36 \times 10^{12}}\right)7500$$

$$= 1001 \text{ kN}(= 9.5 \text{ per cent of } P_0)$$

(4) Shrinkage

$$\text{Loss } \Delta P = \varepsilon_{sh}E_sA_{st} = 300 \times 10^{-6} \times 205 \times 7500$$

$$= 461 \text{ kN } (= 4.4 \text{ per cent of } P_0)$$

(5) Relaxation

$P' \approx 70$ per cent of the characteristic strength P_0. Hence take relaxation losses as 8 per cent.

Hence loss in force $\approx \dfrac{8}{100} \times 9708 = 777$ kN (≈ 7.4 per cent of P_0)

Thus

$$\text{Total estimated losses} = 792 + 1001 + 461 + 777 = 3031\text{kN} = 29 \text{ per cent of } P_0$$

12.4.7 Calculation of deflections

The anticipated deflections of a prestressed member must always be checked since specific span–effective depth ratios are not met in the design procedure. The deflection due to the eccentric prestress force must be evaluated and added to that from the normal dead and applied loading on the member. In the case of class 1 and 2 structures, the member is designed to be uncracked, and a similar procedure is followed to that described in chapter 6. Although class 3 members are designed as cracked under full load, when evaluating deflections due to non-prestress loadings it has been found that little error is introduced if the uncracked case is again considered, thus simplifying calculations considerably. BS 8110 recommends that for class 3 members such as an assumption may be made if the stresses due to the design permanent loads are limited to values specified in the code. If this is not satisfied then the member deflections must be evaluated as cracked unless the basic span–effective depth ratios (section 6.2) are satisfied, in which case the deflections of the member may be assumed to be not excessive.

The basic requirement which should generally be satisfied in respect of deflections are similar to those for a reinforced beam (section 6.3), which are

1. Final deflection $\ngtr$ span/250 measured below the level of supports.
2. 20 mm or span/500 maximum movement after finishes applied.

Additionally in prestressed concrete

3. Total upward deflection $\ngtr$ span/350 or 20 mm where finishes are applied, unless uniformity of camber between adjacent units can be ensured.

The evaluation of deflections due to prestress loading can be obtained by double integration of the expression

$$M_x = Pe_x = \frac{EI d^2 y}{dx^2}$$

over the length of the member, although this calculation can prove tedious for complex tendon profiles.

The simple case of straight tendons in a uniform member however, yields $M = -Pe =$ a constant, which is the situation evaluated in section 6.3.3 to yield a maximum mid-span deflection of $ML^2/8EI = -PeL^2/8EI$. If the cables lie below the centroidal axis, e is positive, and the deflection due to prestress is then negative, that is upwards.

Another common case of a symmetrical parabolic tendon profile in a beam of constant section can also be evaluated quite simply by considering the bending-moment distribution in terms of an equivalent uniformly distributed load.

For the beam in figure 12.16 the moment due to prestress loading at any section is $M_x = -Pe_x$ but since e_x is parabolic, the prestress loading may be likened to a uniformly distributed load w_e on a simply supported beam; then mid-span moment

$$M = \frac{w_e L^2}{8} = -Pe_c$$

thus

$$w_e = -\frac{8Pe_c}{L^2}$$

Figure 12.16
Parabolic tendon profile

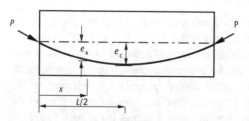

But since the mid-span deflection due to a uniformly distributed load w over a span L is given by

$$y = \frac{5}{384} \frac{wL^4}{EI}$$

the deflection due to w_e is

$$y = -\frac{5}{48} \frac{(Pe_c)L^2}{EI}$$

If the prestress force at the centroid of the section at the ends of the beam, but at an eccentricity e_0 as shown in figure 12.17, the expression for deflection must be modified. It can be shown that the deflection is the same as that caused by a force P acting at a constant eccentricity e_0 throughout the length of the member, plus a force P following a parabolic profile with mid-span eccentricity e_c' as shown in figure 12.17.

The mid-span deflection thus becomes

$$y = \frac{(Pe_0)L^2}{8EI} - \frac{5}{48} \frac{(Pe_c')L^2}{EI}$$

Deflections due to more complex tendon profiles are most conveniently estimated on the basis of coefficients which can be evaluated for commonly occuring arrangements. These are on the basis $y = (KL^2)/EI$ where K incorporates the variations of curvature due to prestress along the member length.

There are three principal stages in the life of a prestressed member at which deflections may be critical and may require to be assessed.

1. At transfer – a check of actual deflection at transfer for comparison with estimated values is a useful guide that a prestressed beam has been correctly constructed.

2. Under dead load, before application of finishes – deflections must be evaluated to permit subsequent movement and possible damage to be estimated.

3. Long term under full load – deflections are required, both to determine the subsequent movement and also to assess the appearance of the final structure.

Short-term deflections will be based on materials properties associated with characteristic strengths $(\gamma_m = 1)$ and with actual loading $(\gamma_f = 1)$. Long-term assessment however must not only take into account loss in prestress force, but also the effects of creep both on the applied loading and the prestress loading components of the deflection. Creep is allowed for by using an effective modulus of elasticity for the concrete, as discussed in section 6.3.2.

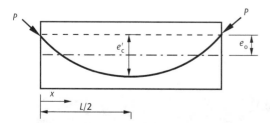

Figure 12.17
Parabolic tendon profile eccentric at ends of beam

Thus if E_c is the instantaneous value after creep is given by

$$E_{eff} = \frac{E_c}{1 + \phi}$$

where the value of ϕ, the creep coefficient can be obtained from figure 6.5.

It can be shown in some instances that when net upward deflections occur, these often increase because of creep, thus the most critical downward deflection may well be before creep losses occur, while the most critical upward deflection may be long term. This further complicates a procedure which already has many uncertainties as discussed in chapter 6; thus deflections must always be regarded as estimates only.

EXAMPLE 12.7

Calculation of deflection

Estimate transfer and long-term deflections for a 200×350 mm beam of 10 m span. The prestressing tendon has a parabolic profile with mid-span eccentricity $= 110$ mm and the end eccentricity $= 55$ mm at both ends, measured below the neutral axis. The initial prestress force at transfer P_0 is 525 kN and there are losses of 20 per cent. The load applied after transfer consists of 2.0 kN/m finishes and 1.0 kN/m imposed load. $E_c = 31$ kN/mm^2 and the creep coefficient $\phi = 2$.

Self-weight $= 0.2 \times 0.35 \times 24 = 1.68$ kN/m

$$I = \frac{bh^3}{12} = \frac{200 \times 350^3}{12} = 715 \times 10^6 \text{ mm}^4$$

(a) At transfer

$$
\begin{aligned}
\text{Deflection } y_a &= \frac{5}{384} \frac{w_{min}L^4}{E_cI} + \frac{(P_0e_0)L^2}{8E_cI} - \frac{5}{48} \frac{(P_0e_c)L^2}{E_cI} \\
&= \frac{5}{384} \times \frac{1.68 \times 10^4 \times 10^{12}}{31 \times 10^3 \times 715 \times 10^6} + \frac{525 \times 10^3 \times (-55) \times 10^2 \times 10^6}{8 \times 31 \times 10^3 \times 715 \times 10^6} \\
&\quad - \frac{5}{48} \times \frac{525 \times 10^3 \times (110 - 55) \times 10^2 \times 10^6}{31 \times 10^3 \times 715 \times 10^6} \\
&= 9.9 - 16.3 - 13.6 \\
&= -20 \text{ mm (upwards)}
\end{aligned}
$$

(b) At application of finishes

Assume that only a small proportion of prestress losses have occurred:

Weight of finishes $= 2.0$ kN/m, therefore

$$
\begin{aligned}
\text{Deflection } y_b &= y_a + \frac{5}{384} \frac{w_{min}L^4}{E_cI} \\
&= -20 + \frac{5}{384} \times \frac{2.00 \times 10^4 \times 10^{12}}{31 \times 10^3 \times 715 \times 10^6} \\
&= -20 + 11.7 \\
&= -8 \text{ mm (upwards)}
\end{aligned}
$$

(c) In the long-term

Prestress forces after losses $= 0.8P_0 = 0.8 \times 525 = 420$ kN

$$E_{\text{eff}} = \frac{E_c}{1 + \phi} = \frac{31}{1 + 2} = 10.3 \text{ kN/mm}^2$$

Thus deflection under sustained minimum loading of dead load plus finishes becomes

$$\text{Deflection } y_c = \frac{5}{384} \frac{w_{\min}L^4}{E_c I} + \frac{(KP_0 e_0)L^2}{8E_c I} - \frac{5}{48} \frac{(KP_0 e_c)L^2}{E_c I}$$

$$= \frac{5}{384} \times \frac{(1.68 + 2.0) \times 10^4 \times 10^{12}}{10.3 \times 10^3 \times 715 \times 10^6} + \frac{420 \times 10^3 \times (-55) \times 10^2 \times 10^6}{8 \times 10.3 \times 10^3 \times 715 \times 10^6}$$

$$- \frac{5}{48} \times \frac{420 \times 10^3 \times (110 - 55) \times 10^2 \times 10^6}{10.3 \times 10^3 \times 715 \times 10^6}$$

$$= 65.1 - 39.2 - 32.7$$

$$= -7 \text{ mm (upwards)}$$

The deflection under sustained maximum loading is given by

$$\text{Deflection } y_d = 65.1 \times \frac{4.68}{3.68} - 39.2 - 32.7$$

$$= 82.8 - 39.2 - 32.7$$

$$= 11 \text{ mm (downwards)}$$

(d) Deflection after application of finishes

y_e = maximum long-term deflection (y_d) – instantaneous deflection after application of finishes (y_b) = $11 - (-8) = 19$ mm

The criteria that should be satisfied are:

1. Maximum downward deflection = span/250 = 10 000/250 = 40 mm. This is satisfied (11 mm).

2. Maximum upward deflection = span/350 = 29 mm or 20 mm. This is satisfied (20 mm).

3. Maximum movement after application of finishes = span/500 = 20 mm. This is satisfied (19 mm).

12.4.8 End blocks

In pre-tensioned members, the prestress force is transferred to the concrete by bond over a definite length at each end of the member. The transfer of stress to the concrete is thus gradual. In post-tensioned members however, the force is concentrated over a small area at the end faces of the member, and this leads to high-tensile forces at right angles to the direction of the compression force. This effect will extend some distance from the end of the member until the compression has distributed itself across the full concrete cross-section. This region is known as the 'end block' and must be heavily reinforced by steel to resist the bursting tension forces. End block reinforcement will generally consist of closed links which surround the anchorages, and the quantities provided are usually obtained from empirical methods.

Figure 12.18
Stress distribution in end
blocks

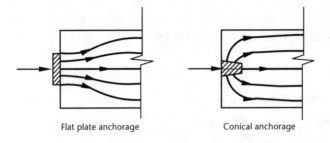

Flat plate anchorage   Conical anchorage

Figure 12.19
Bursting tensile stress in end
blocks

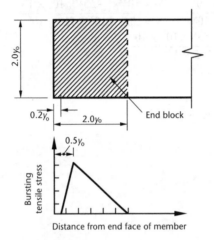

Typical 'flow lines' of compressive stress are shown in figure 12.18, from which it
can be seen that whatever type of anchorage is used, the required distribution can be
expected to have been attained at a distance from the loaded face equal to the lateral
dimension of the member. This is relatively independent of the anchorage type, and the
distribution of bursting tensile stress is generally as shown in figure 12.19.

The magnitude of these stresses depends on the ratio of the loaded area of the end
block. It will normally be necessary to establish the end-block dimensions both
horizontally and vertically based on the size of the face of the beam and the layout of the
anchorages. The end block for each individual anchorage will be symmetrical about the
centre-line of the anchorage and its total width ($2y_0$) will be limited by the distance (y_0)
to an edge of the concrete member or half the distance to an adjacent anchorage. Values
of bursting tensile force (F_{bst}) are given in table 12.1 related to the jacking force (P_0) for
a square end block of side $2y_0$ loaded through a square anchorage of side $2y_{p0}$. If a
circular anchorage is used, then $2y_{p0}$ is taken as the side of a square of equivalent area,
and if the block is not square, then separate values of F_{bst} must be evaluated for both
vertical and horizontal planes based on the largest symmetrical end block.

Table 12.1 Bursting forces in end blocks

$\dfrac{2y_{p0}}{2y_0}$	0.3	0.4	0.5	0.6	0.7
$\dfrac{F_{bst}}{P_0}$	0.23	0.20	0.17	0.14	0.11

Once F_{bst} has been obtained, reinforcement is provided to act at a stress of 200 N/mm^2 and is usually distributed evenly over the length of the end block. The calculation is thus based on serviceability conditions and will be adequate for bonded tendons. If tendons are unbonded, an ultimate limit state check with F_{bst} based on the tendon characteristic load and with reinforcement acting at its design strength of $0.95 f_y$ will be necessary.

High local stresses should also be controlled by limiting the maximum compressive bearing stress to $0.6 \times$ transfer cube strength, and extra helical reinforcement is often incorporated into 'wedge' type anchorages.

In situations where there is more than one anchorage, each should be treated individually and then combined as indicated in example 12.8.

EXAMPLE 12.8

Design of end block reinforcement (bonded)

The beam end in figure 12.20 is stressed by four identical 100 mm conical anchorages located as shown, with a jacking force of 400 kN applied to each.

The area may be subdivided into four equal zones of side 200×150 mm (figure 12.20a), that is

$2y_0 = 200$ mm vertically

$\quad\quad = 150$ mm horizontally

Equivalent square anchorage has side $2y_{p0} = \sqrt{(\pi \times 100^2/4)} = 88$ mm. Thus *vertically*

$$\frac{2y_{p0}}{2y_0} = \frac{88}{200} = 0.44$$

hence from table 12.1

$F_{bst} = 400 \times 0.188 = 75.2$ kN

to be resisted by horizontal steel within 200 mm of end face; and *horizontally*

$$\frac{2y_{p0}}{2y_0} = \frac{88}{150} = 0.59$$

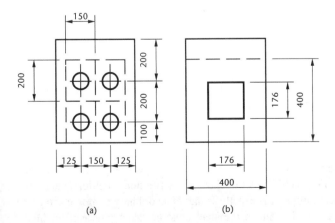

Figure 12.20
End block reinforcement
example

(a)   (b)

hence from table 12.1

$$F_{bst} = 400 \times 0.143 = 57.2 \text{ kN}$$

to be resisted by vertical steel within 150 mm of end face.

Then using high-yield steel with $f_y = 460$ N/mm^2 for bonded tendons

allowable stress $= 200$ N/mm^2

hence force of 75.2 kN requires

$$\frac{75.2 \times 10^3}{200} = 376 \text{ mm}^2$$

that is, three 10 mm closed links (471 mm^2) adequate, at say 50, 100 and 150 mm from end face.

Check horizontal plane: two links lie within 150 mm of end face, thus requirement satisfied.

Consider combined effects of anchorages, $P_k = 4 \times 400 = 1600$ kN

side of end block $= 400$ mm each way (figure 12.20b)

side of equivalent anchorage $= \sqrt{(88^2 \times 4)} = 176$ mm

hence

$$\frac{2y_{p0}}{2y_0} = \frac{176}{400} = 0.44$$

and

$$F_{bst} = 1600 \times 0.188 = 301 \text{ kN}$$

to be resisted by horizontal and vertical steel over 400 mm from end face needing

$$\frac{301}{200} \times 10^3 = 1505 \text{ mm}^2$$

provided as seven 12 mm links (1584 mm^2) at 50 mm centres commencing 50 mm from end face of the beam.

12.5 Analysis and design at the ultimate limit state

After a prestressed member has been designed to satisfy serviceability requirements, a check must be carried out to ensure that the ultimate moment of resistance and shear resistance are adequate to satisfy the requirements of the ultimate limit state. The partial factors of safety on loads and materials for this analysis are the normal values for the ultimate limit state which are given in chapter 2.

12.5.1 Analysis of section

As the loads on a prestressed member increase above the working values, cracking occurs and the prestressing steel begins to behave as conventional reinforcement. The behaviour of the member at ultimate is exactly as that of an ordinary reinforced concrete member except that the initial strain in the steel must be taken into account in the

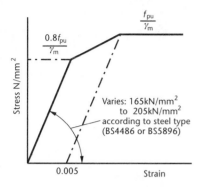

Figure 12.21
Stress–strain curve for
prestressing steel

calculations. The section may easily be analysed by the use of the equivalent rectangular stress block described in chapter 4. BS 8110 contains tables to permit the stress in the prestressing steel at ultimate, and the corresponding neutral-axis position to be obtained for rectangular sections. These are based on empirical results but alternatively the simplified method illustrated in example 12.9 may be adopted for bonded members.

Although illustrated by a simple example this method may be applied to a cross-section of any shape which may have an arrangement of prestressing wires or tendons. Use is made of the stress–strain curve for the prestressing steel as shown in figure 12.21, to calculate tension forces in each layer of steel. The total steel strain is that due to bending added to the initial strain in the steel resulting from prestress. For a series of assumed neutral axis positions, the total tension capacity is compared with the compressive force developed by a uniform stress of $0.45 f_{cu}$, and when reasonable agreement is obtained, the moment of resistance can be evaluated.

EXAMPLE 12.9

Calculation of ultimate moment of resistance

The section of a pretensioned beam shown in figure 12.22 is stressed by ten 5 mm wires of characteristic strength $f_{pu} = 1470$ N/mm^2. If these wires are initially stresses to 1000 N/mm^2 and 30 per cent losses are anticipated, estimate the ultimate moment of resistance of the section if grade 40 concrete is used. The stress–strain curve for prestressing wire is shown in figure 12.23.

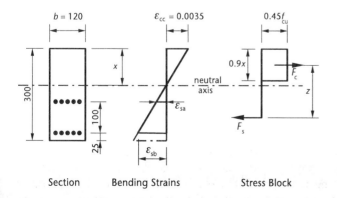

Figure 12.22
Ultimate moment of resistance
example

Section   Bending Strains   Stress Block

Figure 12.23
Stress–strain curve for wire

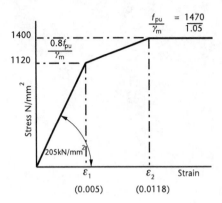

Area of 5 mm wire $\quad = \pi \times 5^2/4 \quad = 19.6 \ \text{mm}^2$

Stress in steel after losses $= 1000 \times 0.7 = 700 \ \text{N/mm}^2$

therefore

$$\text{strain in steel after losses} = \frac{f_s}{E_s} = \frac{700}{205 \times 10^3} = 0.0034$$

which is less than ε_1, the lower yield strain.

A depth x of neutral axis must be found for which the compressive force F_c in the concrete is balanced by the tensile force F_s in the steel. Then the ultimate moment of resistance is given by

$$M_u = F_c z = F_s z \tag{12.32}$$

where z is the lever arm between F_c and F_s.

As a first attempt try $x = 130$ mm, approximately equal to $0.5d$.

(a) Steel strains

Final steel strain ε_s = prestress strain + bending strain, ε'_s

(In calculating ε'_s the initial concrete strain due to prestress can be ignored without undue error).

Top layer

$$\varepsilon_{sa} = 0.0034 + \varepsilon'_{sa}$$

therefore

$$\varepsilon_{sa} = 0.0034 + \frac{(175 - x)}{x} \varepsilon_{cc} \tag{12.33}$$

$$= 0.0034 + \frac{(175 - 130)}{130} 0.0035 = 0.0046$$

Bottom layer

$$\varepsilon_{sb} = 0.0034 + \varepsilon'_{sb}$$

$$= 0.0034 + \frac{(275 - x)}{x} \varepsilon_{cc} \tag{12.34}$$

$$= 0.0034 + \frac{(275 - 130)}{130} 0.0035 = 0.0073$$

(b) Steel stresses

From the stress–strain curve the corresponding steel stresses are

Top layer

$$f_{sa} = \varepsilon_{sa} \times E_s = 0.0046 \times 205 \times 10^3 = 943 \text{ N/mm}^2 \tag{12.35}$$

and

$$f_{sb} = 1120 + \frac{(1400 - 1120)}{(0.0118 - 0.005)}(\varepsilon_{sb} - 0.005) \tag{12.36}$$

$$= 1120 + 41176(0.0073 - 0.005)$$

$$= 1215 \text{ N/mm}^2$$

(c) Forces in steel and concrete

Steel tensile force $F_s = \sum f_s A_s = (f_{sa} + f_{sb})5 \times 19.6 \tag{12.37}$

$$= (943 + 1215)98$$

$$= 212 \times 10^3 \text{ N}$$

With a rectangular stress block

concrete compressive force $F_c = 0.45 f_{cu} b \times 0.9x \tag{12.38}$

$$= 0.45 \times 40 \times 120 \times 0.9 \times 130$$

$$= 253 \times 10^3 \text{ N}$$

The force F_c in the concrete is larger than the force F_s in the steel, therefore a smaller depth of neutral axis must be tried.

Table 12.2 shows the results of calculations for further trial depths of neutral axis. For $x = 110$, F_c became smaller than F_s, therefore $x = 115$ and 120 were tried and it was then found that $F_s = F_c$.

Table 12.2

	Strains		Stresses		Forces	
x (mm)	ε_{sa}	ε_{sb}	f_{sa}	f_{sb}	F_s	F_c
	$(\times 10^{-3})$		(N/mm^2)		(kN)	
130	4.6	7.3	945	1215	212	253
110	5.5	8.7	1139	1270	236	214
115	5.2	8.3	1129	1255	234	224
120	5.0	7.9	1120	1240	231	233

In terms of the tensile force in the steel, the ultimate moment of resistance of the section is given by

$$M_u = F_s z = \sum [f_s A_s (d - 0.45x)] \tag{12.39}$$

$$= 5 \times 19.6[1120(175 - 0.45 \times 120) + 1240(275 - 0.45 \times 120)]$$

$$= 40.1 \times 10^6 \text{ N mm}$$

If x had been incorrectly chosen as 130 mm then using equation 12.39 M_u would equal 36.6 kN m, or in terms of the concrete

$$M_u = 0.45 f_{cu} b \times 0.9xz$$

$$\approx 0.45 \times 40 \times 120 \times 0.9 \times 130(225 - 0.45 \times 130) \times 10^{-6}$$

$$\approx 42.1 \text{ kN m}$$

Comparing the average of these two values of M_u ($=39.4$ kN m) with the correct answer, it can be seen that a slight error in the position of the neutral axis does not have any significant effect on the calculated moment of resistance.

12.5.2 Design of additional reinforcement

If it is found, as may be the case with class 2 or 3 members, that the ultimate limit state requirements are not met, additional untensioned or partially tensioned steel may be added to increase the ultimate moment of resistance.

EXAMPLE 12.10

Design of untensioned reinforcement

Design untensioned high yield reinforcement ($f_y = 460$ N/mm^2) for the rectangular beam section shown in figure 12.24 which is stressed by five 5 mm wires, if the ultimate moment of resistance is to exceed 45 kN m for grade 50 concrete. The characteristic strength of tensioned steel, $f_{pu} = 1470$ N/mm^2.

Figure 12.24
Ultimate moment of resistance example

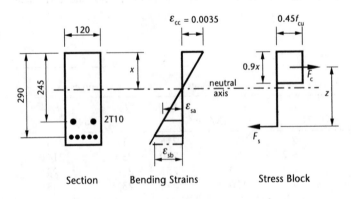

Section   Bending Strains   Stress Block

(a) Check ultimate moment of resistance

Maximum tensile force if prestressing steel yielded $= 5 \times 19.6 \times \dfrac{1470}{1.05} \times 10^{-3} = 137$ kN

Concrete compressive area to balance $= \dfrac{137 \times 10^3}{0.45 \times 50} = 0.9 \times 120x$

thus neutral-axis depth $x = 56$ mm.

Assuming prestrain as calculated in example 12.9

total steel strain = prestrain + bending strain

$$= 0.0034 + \frac{(d-x)}{x} \times 0.0035$$

$$= 0.0034 + \frac{234}{56} \times 0.0035 = 0.0180 \ (> \text{yield})$$

Lever arm $= 290 - 0.45 \times 56 = 265$ mm

Hence

ultimate moment of resistance $= 265 \times 137 \times 10^{-3} = 36.3$ kN m

Untensioned steel is therefore required to permit the beam to support an ultimate moment of 45 kN m.

Additional moment of capacity to be provided $= 45 - 36.3 = 8.7$ kN m

Effective depth of additional steel $= 245$ mm

then

lever arm to additional steel ≈ 220 mm

then

additional tension force required $= \dfrac{8700}{220} = 39.5$ kN

thus

estimated area of untensioned steel
required at its yield stress $= \dfrac{39\,500}{460 \times 0.95} = 90 \text{ mm}^2$

Try two 10 mm diameter bars (157 mm^2).

(b) Check steel strain

If additional steel has yielded, force in two T10 bars $= 157 \times 460 \times 10^{-3}/1.05$
$= 68.8$ kN, therefore

total tensile force if all the steel has yielded $= 137 + 68.8$

$$= 205.8 \text{ kN}$$

Thus

depth of neutral axis at ultimate $= \dfrac{205.8 \times 10^3}{0.45 \times 50 \times 0.9 \times 120}$

$$= 85 \text{ mm}$$

Therefore

prestressing steel strain $\varepsilon_{sb} = \dfrac{(290-85)}{85} \times 0.0035 + 0.0034$

$$= 0.0118 \ (= \text{yield})$$

and

untensioned steel strain $\varepsilon_{sa} = \dfrac{(245-85)}{85} \times 0.0035$

$$= 0.0066$$

This value is greater than the yield strain of 0.00219 from section 4.1.2.

(c) Check ultimate moment of resistance

Taking moments about the centre of compression

$$M_u = 137(290 - 0.45x) + 68.8(245 - 0.45x)$$
$$= [137(290 - 0.45 \times 85) + 68.8(245 - 0.45 \times 85)]10^{-3}$$
$$= 48.7 \text{ kN m}$$

If it had been found in (b) that either the prestressing steel or untensioned steel had not yielded, then a trial and error approach similar to example 12.9 would have been necessary.

12.5.3 Shear

Shear in prestressed concrete is considered at the ultimate limit state. Design for shear therefore involves the most severe loading conditions, with the usual partial factors for safety on loading for the ultimate limit state being incorporated.

The action of a member in resisting shear is similar to that for reinforced concrete, but with the additional effects on the compression due to the prestress force. This will increase the shear resistance considerably, since design is based on limiting the diagonal principal tensile stresses in the concrete.

Although most prestressed concrete members will be uncracked under working loads, when carrying the loads for the ultimate limit state they may well be cracked over part of their span. This will reduce the shear capacity, but fortunately the regions of cracking in simply supported members will generally be the centre part of the span where shear forces are relatively small.

Uncracked section

At an uncracked section, a Mohr's circle analysis of a beam element shown in figure 12.25 which is subjected to a longitudinal compressive stress f_c and a shear stress v_{co}, gives the principal tensile stress as

$$f_t = \sqrt{\left[\left(\frac{f_c}{2}\right)^2 + v_{co}^2\right]} - \left(\frac{f_c}{2}\right)$$

This can be rearranged to give the shear stress

$$v_{co} = \sqrt{(f_t^2 + f_c f_t)}$$

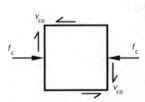

Figure 12.25
Stress in an uncracked section

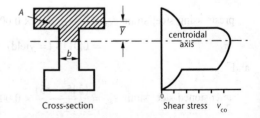

Figure 12.26
Shear stress distribution

The actual shear stress at any level of a beam subjected to a shear force, V, can be shown to be

$$\nu = \frac{V(A\bar{y})}{bI}$$

where $(A\bar{y})$ is the first moment of area of part of the section above the level considered about the centroidal axis of the beam, as shown in figure 12.26, b is the breadth of the section at the level considered and I is the second moment of area of the whole section about its centroidal axis.

Hence if f_t is the limiting value of principal tensile force, the ultimate shear resistance V_{co} of an uncracked section becomes

$$V_{co} = \frac{bI}{(A\bar{y})}\sqrt{(f_t^2 + f_c f_t)}$$

For a rectangular section the maximum shear stress occurs at the centroid, thus $A = bh/2$, $I = bh^3/12$, $\bar{y} = h/4$, then

$$\frac{Ib}{(A\bar{y})} = 0.67bh$$

and

$$\nu_{co} = \frac{3}{2}\frac{V_{co}}{bh}$$

giving

$$V_{co} = 0.67bh\sqrt{(f_t^2 + f_c f_t)}$$

This equation forms the basis of the design expression given in BS 8110. A partial factor of safety of 0.8 is applied to the centroidal compressive stress due to prestress f_{cp} hence $f_c = 0.8 f_{cp}$. f_t is taken as positive and is given a limiting value of $0.24\sqrt{f_{cu}}$ which may be regarded as being equivalent to $0.3\sqrt{(f_{cu}/\gamma_m)}$ with $\gamma_m = 1.5$.

The resulting expression

$$V_{co} = 0.67bh\sqrt{(f_t^2 + 0.8 f_{cp} f_t)}$$

may also be applied to I- and T-sections with sufficient accuracy for practical purposes, although the maximum principal tensile stress may not coincide with the centroid. If the centroid of the section lies within the flange however, the expression should be evaluated for the flange/web junction with b taken as the web width and f_{cp} being the compression due to prestress at that level.

If a duct lies in the web, then the value of b used in calculations should be reduced by the duct diameter if the tendons are unbonded or two-thirds of the diameter if bonded.

Additional shear resistance will be provided by the vertical component of the prestress force where curved cables are used, provided the section is uncracked. Near the ends of beams where shear forces are highest, and cable slopes generally greatest, a considerable increase in resistance can be obtained from this, and shear strength contribution should be a consideration when detailing tendon profiles.

The total shear resistance of an uncracked section may then be taken as $V_c = V_{co} + P\sin\beta$ where β is the cable slope.

Cracked section

BS 8110 gives an empirical expression for the calculation of shear resistance of a section which is cracked in flexure

$$V_{cr} = \left(1 - 0.55\frac{f_{pe}}{f_{pu}}\right)v_c bd + \frac{M_0}{M}V \not< 0.1bd\sqrt{f_{cu}}$$

where f_{pe} = prestressing steel stress after losses
  d = effective depth to centroid of tendons
  b = width of web for flanged beam
  v_c = allowable ultimate shear stress (as for reinforced concrete)
  V = ultimate shear force acting on section
  M = ultimate moment acting on section
  M_0 = 0.8 $f_{pt}I/y$ is the moment necessary to produce zero stress at the extreme tensile fibre which is a distance y from the centroid of the section, where f_{pt} is the concrete compressive stress at this level due to prestress and a factor of safety of 0.8 is applied to this value.

Thus if $M < M_0$ it follows that V_{cr} will always be greater than the applied ultimate shear force, and a check on cracking is thus incorporated. The vertical component of prestressing force should not be added to the value of V_{cr} obtained from this expression.

Upper limit to shear force

A further upper limit to shear force must be imposed to avoid web crushing and this is achieved by limiting the value of shear stress so that $V/bd < v_{max}$ in the same way as for reinforced concrete. v_{max} is the maximum allowable ultimate shear stress with a value which may be calculated as the lesser of $0.8\sqrt{f_{cu}}$ or 5 N/mm^2.

Design procedure

The usual design procedure consists of calculating the shear resistance of the cracked and uncracked sections at intervals along the length of the member for comparison with the applied ultimate shear force V. The lower of the two values obtained from the analyses must be taken as shear resistance at the point concerned. Thus

ultimate shear resistance V_c = lesser of V_{cr} or $V_{co} + P\sin\beta$

If V is less than $0.5V_c$ no shear reinforcement is required, but for values between $0.5V_c$ and $V_c + 0.4bd$ nominal links should be provided such that

$$\frac{A_{sv}}{s_v} \geq \frac{0.4b}{0.95 f_{yv}}$$

and where $V > V_c + 0.4bd$ designed steel is needed such that for links

$$\frac{A_{sv}}{s_v} \geq \frac{V - V_c}{0.95 f_{yv}d_t}$$

In this expression d_t is the greater of the depth to the centroid of the tendons or the corner longitudinal bars anchoring links.

As for reinforced concrete the usual design procedure will be to evaluate the shear resistances of the sections plus nominal steel to identify areas which require more detailed attention, as illustrated in example 12.11.

EXAMPLE 12.11

Design of shear reinforcement

The beam cross-section in figure 12.27 is constant over a 30 m span with a parabolic tendon profile and an eccentricity varying between 300 mm at the ends to 750 mm at midspan. The beam supports an ultimate uniformly distributed load of 43 kN/m and is of grade 40 concrete.

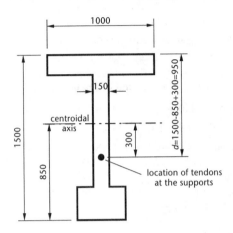

Figure 12.27
Shear reinforcement example

Prestress forces after losses $= 2590$ kN

$$I = 145\,106 \times 10^6 \text{ mm}^4$$

$$A = 500 \times 10^3 \text{ mm}^2$$

(a) Upper limit to shear force

$$\frac{V}{bd} = \frac{43 \times 15 \times 1000}{150 \times 950} = 4.5 \text{ N/mm}^2$$

$$< 0.8\sqrt{f_{cu}}(= 5.1 \text{ N/mm}^2) \text{ and } < 5 \text{ N/mm}^2 \text{ at end of beam}$$

(b) Uncracked resistance: since centroid lies within web

$$V_{co} = 0.67bh\sqrt{(f_t^2 + 0.8\,f_{cp}\,f_t)}$$

where $f_t = 0.24\sqrt{f_{cu}} = 0.24\sqrt{40} = 1.51 \text{ N/mm}^2$ and

$$f_{cp} = \frac{KP_0}{A} = \frac{2590 \times 10^3}{500 \times 10^3} = 5.18 \text{ N/mm}^2$$

hence

$$V_{co} = 0.67 \times 150 \times 1500\sqrt{(1.51^2 + 0.8 \times 5.18 \times 1.51)} \times 10^{-3}$$

$$= 440.4 \text{ kN}$$

The vertical component of prestress force is $P \sin \beta$, where $\beta =$ tendon slope.
Tendon profile is $y = Kx^2 + C$, and if origin is at mid-span $x = 0$, $y = 0$ and $C = 0$ hence at $x = 15\,000$, $y = 750 - 300 = 450$, and

$$450 = K \times 15\,000^2$$

$$K = 2.0 \times 10^{-6}$$

therefore tendon profile is $y = 2.0 \times 10^{-6}x^2$, therefore

$$\text{tendon slope} = \frac{dy}{dx} = 2Kx$$

$$\text{at end } \frac{dy}{dx} = 2 \times 2.0 \times 10^{-6} \times 15\,000 = 0.060 = \tan \beta$$

hence $\beta = 3.43°$ and $\sin \beta \approx \tan \beta = 0.06$. Therefore

vertical component of prestress force at end of beam $= 2590 \times 0.06 = 155$ kN

Hence

$$\text{maximum uncracked resistance} = 440 + 155$$
$$= 595 \text{ kN}$$

This value will decrease away from the end of the beam

at   2 m from support $= 440 + 134 = 574$ kN

5 m from support $= 440 + 103 = 543$ kN

10 m from support $= 440 + 51 = 491$ kN

(c) Cracked resistance

$$V_{cr}\left(1 - 0.55\frac{f_{pe}}{f_{pu}}\right)\nu_c bd + M_0\frac{V}{M}$$

This will vary along the beam. At mid-span, $V = 0$, $d = 1400$ mm. If tendons are stressed to 70 per cent characteristic strength at transfer and then subject to 30 per cent losses

$$\frac{f_{pe}}{f_{pu}} = 0.7 \times 0.7 = 0.49$$

If total area of tendons $= 3450$ mm^2, then

$$\frac{100A_s}{bd} = \frac{100 \times 3450}{150 \times 1400} = 1.64$$

therefore from table 5.1, $\nu_c = 0.86$ N/mm^2 for grade 40 concrete

$$V_{cr} = (1 - 0.55 \times 0.49)0.86 \times 150 \times 1400 \times 10^{-3} = 132 \text{ kN}$$

Also check minimum

$$V_{cr} \not< 0.1bd\sqrt{f_{cu}} \not< 0.1 \times 150 \times 1400 \times \sqrt{40} \times 10^{-3} = 133 \text{ kN}$$

At section 10 m from supports, $d = 1400 - 2.0 \times 10^{-6} \times 5000^2 = 1350$ mm, therefore

$$\frac{100A_s}{bd} = 1.70 \text{ and hence } \nu_c = 0.87$$

$$V = 43 \times 5 = 215 \text{ kN}$$

$$M = 15 \times 43 \times 10 - 10 \times 43 \times 5 = 4300 \text{ kN m}$$

$$M_0 = 0.8 f_{pt}\frac{I}{y}$$

where $y = y_1 = 850$ mm, and

$$f_{pt} = \frac{KP_0}{A} + \frac{KP_0 ey_1}{I} = 5.18 + \frac{2590 \times 700 \times 850 \times 10^3}{145\,106 \times 10^6}$$
$$= 15.8 \text{ N/mm}^2$$

hence

$$M_0 = \frac{0.8 \times 15.8 \times 145\,106}{850} = 2158 \text{ kN m}$$

and

$$V_{cr} = (1 - 0.55 \times 0.49)0.87 \times 150 \times 1350 + \frac{2158 \times 215 \times 10^3}{4300}$$
$$= (128.7 + 107.9) \times 10^3 \text{ N}$$
$$= 236.6 \text{ kN}$$

This calculation may be repeated from the other sections to give the resistance diagram shown in figure 12.28.

From this diagram it can be seen that all points except for about 3 m at midspan $V > \frac{1}{2}V_c$ and hence nominal reinforcement is required such that

$$\frac{A_{sv}}{s_v} = \frac{0.4b}{0.95\,f_{yv}}$$

therefore with mild-steel links $f_{yv} = 250$ N/mm², hence

$$\frac{A_{sv}}{s_v} = \frac{0.4 \times 150}{0.95 \times 250} = 0.253$$

which could be provided by 8 mm stirrups at 350 mm centres $(A_{sv}/s_v = 0.287)$.

Shear resistance provided by these links $= 0.95\,f_{yv}d_t\left(\dfrac{A_{sv}}{s_v}\right)$

$$= 0.95 \times 250 \times 1400 \times 0.287 \times 10^{-3}$$
$$= 95.4 \text{ kN}$$

hence at the ends of the beam

total shear resistance of section $+$ nominal steel $= 595 + 95.4 = 690.4$ kN

Since this is greater than the ultimate shear force of 645 kN, no additional reinforcement is required. Thus provide 8 mm mild-steel links at 350 mm centres throughout.

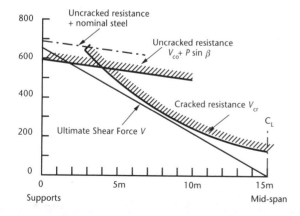

Figure 12.28
Shear resistance diagram

CHAPTER 13

Composite
construction

CHAPTER INTRODUCTION

Many buildings are constructed with a steel framework composed of steel beams and steel columns but mostly with a concrete floor slab. A much stiffer and stronger structure can be achieved by ensuring that the steel beams and concrete slabs act together as composite and so effectively monolithic units. This composite behaviour is obtained by providing shear connections at the interface between the steel beam and the concrete slab as shown in figure 13.1. These shear connections resist the horizontal shear at the interface and prevent slippage between the beam and the slab. The shear connectors are usually in the form of steel studs welded to the top flange of the beam and embedded in the concrete slab.

The steel beam will usually be a universal I-beam. Other alternatives are a castellated beam or a lattice girder as shown in figure 13.2. These alternative types of beams provide greater depth for the floor system and openings for the passage of service conduits such as for heating and air conditioning systems.

Two other types of composite floor systems are shown in figure 13.3. The stub girder system consists of a main beam with transverse secondary beams supported on the top flange. Short lengths of stub members similar in section to the secondary beams are also connected to the top flange of the main beam. The stub beams and the secondary beams are connected to the slab with steel studs as shown.

⟶

The Slimdec system shown is manufactured by British Steel. The special steel beams have a patterned tread on the top flange which provides an enhanced bond with the concrete slab so that a composite action can be developed without the use of shear studs. Deep ribbed profiled sheeting is used to support the slab with the deep ribs resting on the bottom flange of the beam. With this arrangement the steel beam is partially encased by the concrete which provides it with better fire resistance. Openings for services can be cut in the web of the beam between the concrete ribs.

The concrete slab itself can also be constructed as a composite member using the profiled steel decking on the soffit of the slab as shown in figure 13.4. The steel decking acts as the tension reinforcement for the slab and also as permanent shuttering capable of supporting the weight of the wet concrete. It is fabricated with ribs and slots to form a key and bond with the concrete. Properties of the steel decking and safe load tables for the decking and the composite floors are obtainable from the manufacturing companies.

The majority of composite beams are designed as simply supported non-continuous beams. Beams which are continuous require moment resisting connections at the columns and additional reinforcing bars in the slab over the support.

The method of construction may be either

- propped or
- unpropped.

With propped construction temporary props are placed under the steel beam during construction of the floor and the props carry all the construction loads. After the concrete has hardened the props are removed and then the loads are supported by the composite beam. The use of temporary props has the disadvantage of the lack of clear space under the floor during construction and the extra cost of longer construction times.

Unpropped construction entails that the steel beam itself must support the construction loads and the steel beam has to be designed for this condition which may govern the size of beam required. The beam can only act as a composite section when the concrete in the slab has hardened. This also means that the deflection at service is greater than that of a propped beam as the final deflection is the sum of the deflection of the steel beam during construction plus the deflection of the composite section due to the additional loading that takes place after construction. The calculations for this are shown in example 13.4 which sets out the serviceability checks for an unpropped beam.

As there are differences in the design procedures for these two types of construction it is important that the construction method should be established at the outset.

The design of the composite construction has to be according to a number of Codes of Practice, including those for reinforced concrete, steelwork and the sections of the steel code for composite beams and composite slabs as listed in Further Reading at the end of this book.

Figure 13.1
Composite beam sections

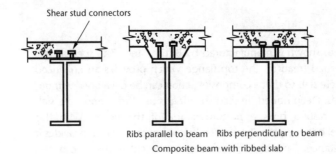

Shear stud connectors

Ribs parallel to beam   Ribs perpendicular to beam

Composite beam with ribbed slab

Figure 13.2
Composite floor beams

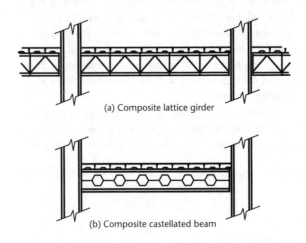

(a) Composite lattice girder

(b) Composite castellated beam

Figure 13.3
Composite floor systems

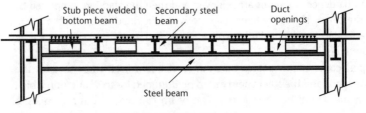

Stub piece welded to   Secondary steel   Duct
bottom beam   beam   openings

Steel beam

(a) Typical stub-girder system

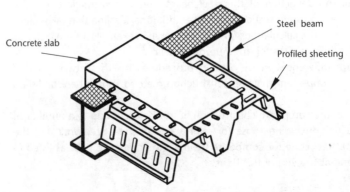

Concrete slab   Steel beam

                         Profiled sheeting

(b) Composite profiled slim deck system

13.1 | The design procedure

The design procedure for the beams is taken to follow the requirements of BS 5950: Part 1 and Part 3: Section 3.1.

An early step in the design of the composite beam section is to determine the effective breadth B_f of the concrete flange. This is taken as the smaller of

- Secondary beams: spacing of beams, or beam span/4
- Primary beams: $0.8 \times$ spacing of beams, or beam span/4.

For a preliminary sizing of the steel universal beam the depth may be taken as approximately the span/20 for a simply supported span.

The principal stages in the design are now listed with brief descriptions.

(1) During construction (for unpropped construction only)

The loading is taken as the self-weight of the steel beam with any shuttering or steel decking, the weight of the wet concrete and an imposed construction load of at least 0.5 kN/m^2. The following design checks are required:

(a) At the ultimate limit state

Check the strength of the steel section in bending and shear. The shear is taken by the area of the web of the section.

(b) At the serviceability limit state

Check the elastic stresses in the steel section and the deflection of the steel beam.

(2) Bending and shear of the composite section at the ultimate limit state

Check the ultimate moment of resistance of the composite section and compare it with the ultimate design moment. Check the shear strength of the web of the steel beam.

(3) Design of the shear connectors and the transverse steel at the ultimate limit state

The shear connectors are required to resist the horizontal shear at the interface of the steel and the concrete so that the steel beam and the concrete flange act as a composite unit. The shear connectors can be either a full shear connection or a partial shear connection depending on the design and detailing requirements.

Transverse reinforcement is required to resist the longitudinal shear in the concrete flange and to prevent cracking of the concrete in the region of the shear connectors.

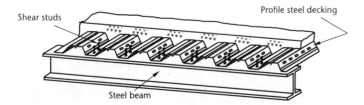

Shear studs

Profile steel decking

Steel beam

Figure 13.4
Composite slab with steel decking

(4) Bending and deflection at the serviceability limit state for the composite beam

It is necessary to check the bending stresses in the concrete flange and the steel beam to ensure they are within the elastic range. The deflection of the beam is checked to ensure it is not excessive and so causing cracking of the architectural finishes.

13.2 Design of the steel beam for conditions during construction (for unpropped beams only)

The steel beam must be designed to support a dead load of its estimated self weight, the weight of wet concrete and the weight of the profiled steel decking or the formwork, plus a construction live load of at least 0.5 kN/m^2 covering the floor area.

(a) At the ultimate limit state

The plastic section modulus S required for the steel beam may be calculated from

$$S = \frac{M_u}{p_y}$$

where M_u is the ultimate design moment
         p_y is the design strength of the steel as obtained from table 13.1.

This assumes that the compression flange of the steel beam is adequately restrained against buckling by the steel decking for the slab and the steel section used can be classified as a plastic or compact section as defined in clause 3.5 of BS 5950 Part 1.
The ultimate shear strength of a rolled I-beam based on the area of its web is

$$P_v = 0.6 p_y t D$$

where t is the thickness of the steel web
         D is the overall depth of the steel section.

Table 13.1 Values of steel design strengths, p_y, for steel to BS 4360

BS 4360 grade	Thickness, less than or equal to (mm)	Sections, plates and hollow sections p_y (N/mm^2)
43	16	275
A, B and C	40	265
	100	245
50	16	355
B and C	63	340
	100	325
55	16	450
C	25	430
	40	415

(b) At the serviceability limit state

The deflection δ at mid span for a uniformly distributed load is

$$\delta = \frac{5wL^4}{384EI}$$

where w is the serviceability load per metre at construction

L is the beam span

E is the elastic modulus of the steel

I is the second moment of area of the steel section.

The elastic bending stresses in the steel beam are

$$f = \frac{M}{Z}$$

where M is the design bending moment at the serviceability limit state

Z is the elastic section modulus of the steel section.

These deflections and elastic stresses are locked into the beam as the concrete hardens.

EXAMPLE 13.1

Design of steel beam for construction loads

Figure 13.5 shows the section of an unpropped composite beam. Check the strength of the universal $457 \times 191 \times 74$ steel beam for the loading at construction. The steel is grade 50 with $p_y = 355$ N/mm^2 and the plastic modulus for the steel section is $S = 1653$ cm^3. The beam spans 12.0 metres and the width of loading on the concrete flange is 3.0 metres. Assume the steel deck gives lateral support.

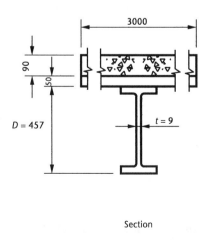

Section

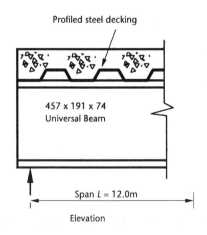

Elevation

Figure 13.5
Construction design example

Loading

Average depth of concrete slab and ribs $= 90 + 50/2 = 115$ mm

Weight of concrete $= 0.115 \times 24 = 2.76$ kN/m^2

Steel deck	0.15
Steel beam	0.24
Total dead load	3.15 kN/m^2
Imposed construction load	0.50 kN/m^2

Ultimate load $= 1.4g_k + 1.6q_k = (1.4 \times 3.15 + 1.6 \times 0.5) \times 3.0$
$$= 15.6 \text{ kN/m}$$

Bending

Maximum bending moment $= wL^2/8 = (15.6 \times 12^2)/8 = 281$ kN m

Moment of resistance of steel section $= Sp_y = 1653 \times 355 \times 10^{-3}$
$$= 587 \text{ kN m} > 281 \text{ kN m} \qquad \text{OK}$$

Shear

For the steel section the overall depth $D = 457$ mm and the web thickness $t = 9$ mm

Maximum shear force $V = wL/2 = 15.6 \times 12/2 = 93.6$ kN

Shear resistance of section $= 0.6p_ytD = 0.6 \times 355 \times 9 \times 457 \times 10^{-3}$
$$= 876 \text{ kN} > 93.6 \text{ kN} \qquad \text{OK}$$

13.3 | The composite section at the ultimate limit state

At the ultimate limit state it is necessary to check the composite section for its moment capacity and its shear strength and compare them against the maximum design ultimate moment and shear.

13.3.1 The moment capacity

The moment capacity M_c of the composite section is derived in terms of the tensile or compressive strengths of the various elements of the section as follows:

Resistance of the concrete flange	$R_c = 0.45 f_{cu} B_e (D_s - D_p)$
Resistance of the steel section	$R_s = p_y A$
Resistance of the steel flange	$R_{sf} = p_y B T$
Resistance of overall web depth	$R_w = R_s - 2R_{sf}$
Resistance of clear web depth	$R_v = dt p_y$
Resistance of the concrete above the neutral axis	$R_{cx} = 0.45 f_{cu} B_e x$
Resistance of the steel flange above the neutral axis	$R_{sx} = p_y B x_1$
Resistance of the web over distance x_2	$R_{wx} = p_y t x_2$

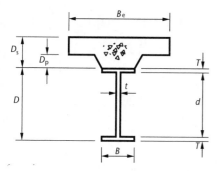

Figure 13.6
Composite section dimensions

The dimensions used in these expressions are defined in figures 13.6 and 13.7. It should be noted in the figures that the stress block for the concrete extends to the depth of the neutral axis as specified in the steel code for composite design.

There are three possible locations of the neutral axis as shown in figure 13.7. These are

(a)   the neutral axis in the concrete flange
(b)   the neutral axis in the steel flange
(c)   the neutral axis in the steel web.

The location of the neutral axis is determined from the equilibrium equation of the resistance forces R at the section, that is

$$\sum R = 0$$

The moment of resistance at the section is then obtained by taking moments about a convenient axis such as the centre-line of the steel section, so that

$$M = \sum Rz$$

where z is the lever arm for the resistance R.

For cases (b) and (c) the analysis is facilitated by considering an equivalent system of the resistance forces as shown in the relevant diagrams.

(a) Neutral axis in the concrete flange, $x < D_s$ (figure 13.7a)

This condition occurs when $R_c > R_s$. Then the depth x of the neutral axis is given by

$$R_{cx} = 0.45 f_{cu} B_e x = R_s$$

Therefore

$$x = \frac{R_s}{0.45 f_{cu} B_e} = \frac{R_s (D_s - D_p)}{R_c}$$

The moment of resistance is

$$M = R_s z$$

where the lever arm z taken to the centre-line of the universal beam is

$$z = (D/2 + D_s - x/2)$$

therefore

$$M_c = R_s \left\{ \frac{D}{2} + D_s - \frac{R_s}{R_c} \frac{(D_s - D_p)}{2} \right\} \tag{13.1}$$

Figure 13.7
Stress blocks at the ultimate
limit state

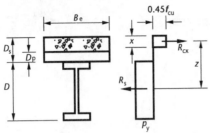

(a) Neutral axis in the concrete flange $x < D_s$: $R_c > R_s$

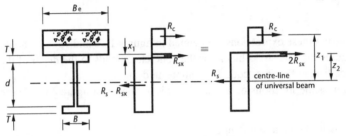

(b) Neutral axis in the steel flange $D < x_s < D_s + T$ and $R_s > R_c > R_w$

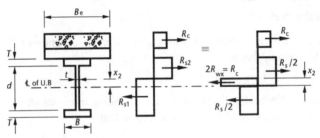

(c) Neutral axis in the steel web $x > D_s + T$: $R_c < R_w$

(b) Neutral axis in the steel flange, $D_s < x < D_s + T$ (figure 13.7b)

This condition occurs when $R_s > R_c > R_w$. For the equilibrium of the resistance forces

$$R_c + 2R_{sx} = R_s$$

that is

$$2R_{sx} = 2p_yBx_1 = R_s - R_c$$

and

$$x_1 = \frac{(R_s - R_c)}{2p_yB} = \frac{(R_s - R_c)T}{2R_{sf}}$$

where B is the breadth and T is the thickness of the steel flange.
    The moment of resistance is given by

$$M_c = R_c z_1 + 2R_{sx} z_2$$
$$= R_c z_1 + (R_s - R_c) z_2$$

where z_1 and z_2 are the lever arms as shown in figure 13.7b and

$$z_1 = (D + D_s + D_p)/2$$
$$z_2 = (D - x_1)/2$$

Therefore substituting for z_1, z_2 and x_1 and rearranging

$$M_c = \frac{R_s D}{2} + \frac{R_c(D_s + D_p)}{2} - \frac{(R_s - R_c)^2 T}{4R_{sf}}$$ (13.2)

(c) Neutral axis in the steel web, $x > D_s + T$ (figure 13.7c)

This condition occurs when $R_c < R_w$. This analysis only applies to beams with a compact web such that the ratio of the web dimensions are

$$\frac{d}{t} < 76\varepsilon \quad \text{or} \quad \frac{d}{t} < \frac{76\varepsilon}{1 - \dfrac{R_c}{R_v}}$$

where $\varepsilon = \left(\dfrac{275}{p_y}\right)^{1/2}$

For equilibrium of the equivalent arrangement of the resistance forces

$$2R_{wx} = 2p_y t x_2 = R_c$$

Therefore

$$x_2 = \frac{R_c}{2p_y t} = \frac{d R_c}{2R_v}$$

where x_2 is the distance between the neutral axis and the centre-line of the steel section.

The moment of resistance of the composite section is the moment of the two couples produced by R_s, and R_c with $2R_{wx}$ so that

$$M_c = M_s + \frac{R_c(D + D_s + D_p - x_2)}{2}$$

or $M_c = M_s + \dfrac{R_c(D + D_s + D_p)}{2} - \dfrac{R_c^2 d}{4R_v}$ (13.3)

EXAMPLE 13.2

Moment of resistance of a composite section

Determine the moment of resistance of the composite section shown in figure 13.8. The universal $457 \times 191 \times 74$ steel beam is of grade 50 steel with $p_y = 355$ N/mm^2 and its cross-sectional area is $A = 94.6$ cm^2. The characteristic concrete strength is $f_{cu} = 30$ N/mm^2.

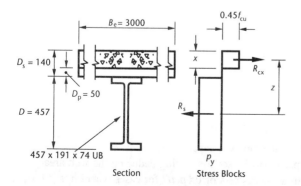

Figure 13.8
Moment of resistance example

(a) From first principles

Resistance of concrete flange $R_c = 0.45 f_{cu} B_e (D_s - D_p)$

$$= 0.45 \times 30 \times 3000 \times (140 - 50) \times 10^{-3}$$
$$= 3645 \text{ kN}$$

Resistance of steel beam $\quad R_s = A p_y = 9460 \times 355 \times 10^{-3} = 3358 \text{ kN}$

As $R_s < R_c$ the neutral axis is within the concrete flange.

Depth of neutral axis is derived from

$$0.45 f_{cu} B_e x = R_s = 3358 \text{ kN}$$

therefore

$$x = \frac{3358 \times 10^3}{0.45 \times 30 \times 3000} = 82.9 \text{ mm}$$

Moment of resistance:

Lever arm z to the centre of the steel section is

$$z = (D/2 + D_s - x/2) = 457/2 + 140 - 82.9/2 = 327 \text{ mm}$$
$$M_c = R_s z = 3358 \times 327 \times 10^{-3} = 1098 \text{ kN m}$$

(b) Using the design equations derived

From part (a) the neutral axis is within the concrete flange, therefore from equation 13.1 the moment of resistance of the section is given by

$$M_c = R_s \left\{ \frac{D}{2} + D_s - \frac{R_s}{R_c} \frac{(D_s - D_p)}{2} \right\}$$
$$= 3358 \left\{ \frac{457}{2} + 140 - \frac{3358}{3645} \frac{(140 - 50)}{2} \right\} = 1098 \text{ kN m}$$

13.3.2 The shear strength P_v of the composite section

The shear strength is based upon the web area of the steel beam and is given by

$$P_v = 0.6 p_y t D$$

When the depth to thickness ratio d/t of a web exceeds 63ε where $\varepsilon = (275/p_y)^{1/2}$ then it is necessary to check for web buckling as specified in BS 5950 *Structural use of steelwork in building, Part 1*.

For beams that support point loads high shear forces and moments can occur at the same section and in these cases it may be necessary to use a reduced moment capacity. If the design shear exceeds $0.5 P_v$ then the calculated moment capacity must be reduced to

$$M_{cv} = M_c - (M_c - M_f) \left\{ \frac{2 F_v}{P_v} - 1 \right\}^2$$

where M_c is the original calculated moment capacity

M_f is the moment capacity of the section having deducted the web area

P_v is determined from a shear stress of $0.6 p_y t D$ for cases where $d/t < 63\varepsilon$.

13.4 | Design of shear connectors

The shear connectors are required to prevent slippage between the concrete flange and the steel beam thus enabling the concrete and steel to act as a composite unit. Stud shear connectors welded to the steel flange are the most common type used. The head on the stud acts to prevent the vertical lifting or prising of the concrete away from the steel beam.

Figure 13.9a shows the slippage that occurs without shear connectors. The slippage is a maximum at the supported end of the beam where the shear V and the rate of change of moment dM/dx are a maximum. The slippage reduces to zero at mid-span where the the moment is a maximum and shear $V = 0$ for a uniformly distributed load.

The connectors restrain the slippage by resisting the horizontal shear at the interface of the concrete and the steel. The design is carried out for the conditions at the ultimate limit state.

The characteristic strengths Q_k of stud connectors in normal weight concrete as given by the code for composite beams are shown in table 13.2. These characteristic values are multiplied by the following reduction factors:

0.8 for positive bending moments i.e. sagging moments

0.6 for negative moments i.e. hogging moments

0.9 for lightweight concrete.

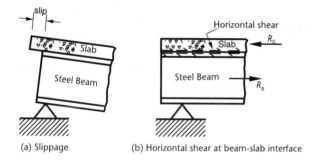

(a) Slippage   (b) Horizontal shear at beam-slab interface

Figure 13.9
Slippage and horizontal shear

Table 13.2 Characteristic resistance Q_k of headed studs in normal weight concrete

Dimensions of stud shear connectors			Characteristic strength of concrete (N/mm²)			
Nominal shank diameter (mm)	Nominal height (mm)	As-welded height (mm)	25 (kN)	30 (kN)	35 (kN)	40 (kN)
25	100	95	146	154	161	168
22	100	95	119	126	132	139
19	100	95	95	100	104	109
19	75	70	82	87	91	96
16	75	70	70	74	78	82
13	65	60	44	47	49	52

Note 1. For concrete of characteristic strength greater than 40 N/mm² use the values for 40 N/mm².
Note 2. For connectors of heights greater than tabulated use the values for the greatest height tabulated.

Further reduction factors for Q_k are specified in the code for when a composite slab with ribbed profile steel sheeting is used. These reduction factors depend on the dimensions of the profile sheeting, the direction of the sheeting and the number of studs per rib.

13.4.1 Full shear connection

The change in horizontal shear between zero and maximum moment is the lesser of the resistance R_s of the steel section and R_c the resistance of the concrete flange. Therefore to develop the full bending strength of the composite section, the number of shear connecters N_f required over half the span is the lesser of

$$N_f = \frac{R_c}{Q_e} \quad \text{or} \quad \frac{R_s}{Q_e} \quad \text{for a full shear connection}$$

where the effective strength of a shear stud $Q_e = kQ_k$, and k is the product of the reduction factors applied to the characteristic strength Q_k.

$$R_c = 0.45 f_{cu} B_e (D_s - D_p)$$
$$R_s = p_y A$$

Full-scale tests with uniformly distributed loading have shown that with plastic conditions during the ultimate limit state the shear studs can develop their full strength when spaced uniformly along the span of the beam.

13.4.2 Partial shear connection

In some cases it is not necessary to have a full shear connection in order to resist an ultimate design moment which is somewhat less than the moment capacity of the composite section. Also using fewer shear studs can often provide a simpler detail for the layout of the stud connectors. For partial shear connection the number of shear connectors N_p required over the half span is then

$$N_p = \frac{R_q}{Q_e}$$

where R_q is the shear resistance of the stud connectors provided over the half span.

The ultimate moment resistance of the composite section with partial shear connection is derived from the analysis of the stress block system shown in figure 13.10. In the analysis the depth of the concrete stress block s_q is

$$s_q = \frac{R_q}{0.45 f_{cu} B_e}$$

As previously shown in section 13.3, the depth of the section's neutral axis is obtained by considering the equilibrium of the material resistances R. The moment of resistance M_c is obtained by taking moments about a convenient axis such as the centre-line of the steel section, followed by some rearrangement of the equations. The diagrams for this analysis are shown in figure 13.10 for the two possible cases of

(a)   the neutral axis in the steel flange $R_q > R_w$

$$M_c = \frac{R_s D}{2} + R_q \left[D_s - \frac{R_q (D_s - D_p)}{2R_c} \right] - \frac{(R_s - R_q)^2 T}{4 R_{sf}} \qquad (13.4)$$

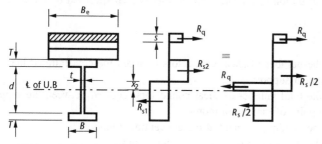

Figure 13.10
Stress blocks for partial shear connection

(a) Neutral axis in the steel flange $D_s < x < D_s + T$ and $R_s > R_q > R_w$

(b) Neutral axis in the steel web $x > D_s + T$: $R_c < R_w$

(b)   the neutral axis in the steel web $R_q < R_w$

$$M_c = M_s + R_q\left[\frac{D}{2} + D_s - \frac{R_q(D_s - D_p)}{2R_c}\right] - \frac{dR_q^2}{4R_v} \qquad (13.5)$$

Figure 13.11 shows the interaction diagram for the moment of resistance of the composite section against the degree of shear resistance K where

$$K = \frac{N_{partial}}{N_{full}}$$

The curved interaction line (a) is based on the stress block equations 13.4 or 13.5 and gives the more precise results. The straight interaction line (b) represents a linear relation between M_c and K which provides a simpler and safe, but less economic, solution.

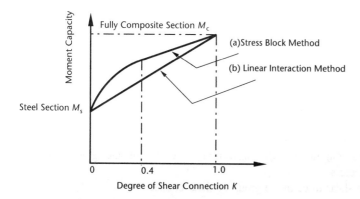

Figure 13.11
Interaction diagram for partial shear connection

A minimum degree of partial shear connection is specified as $K = 0.4$ for spans less than 10 m. For spans between 10 and 16 m the minimum value of K is specified by

$$K > (L - 6)/10$$

13.4.3   Shear connection for concentrated loads

When the beam supports concentrated loads the slope dM/dx of the bending moment diagram is greater and the shear is more intense. This means that the shear connectors have to be spaced closer together between the concentrated load and the adjacent support. The distribution of the shear connectors is then specified by the equation

$$N_i = \frac{N_t(M_i - M_s)}{(M_c - M_s)} \tag{13.6}$$

where N_i is the number of shear connectors between the concentrated load and the adjacent support
   N_t is the total number of shear connectors required between the support and the point of maximum moment
   M_i is the bending moment at the concentrated load
   M_s is the moment capacity of the steel member
   M_c is the moment capacity of the composite section.

Figure 13.12 shows a beam supporting concentrated loads and the distribution of the shear connectors.

Figure 13.12
Arrangement of shear connectors with concentrated load

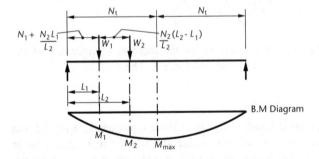

13.5   Transverse reinforcement

Transverse reinforcement is required to resist the longitudinal shear in the concrete flange. This shear acts on vertical planes either side of the shear connectors as shown in figure 13.13.

The shear force ν per unit length to be resisted is given in terms of the shear in the shear studs as

$$\nu = \frac{NQ}{s}$$

where N is the number of shear connectors in a group
   s is the longitudinal spacing centre to centre of the groups of shear connectors
   Q is the shear force in the group of shear connectors

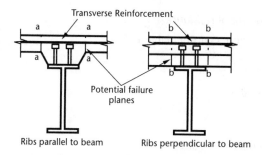

Transverse Reinforcement

a a b b

a a b b

Potential failure planes

Ribs parallel to beam   Ribs perpendicular to beam

Figure 13.13
Transverse reinforcement in
the concrete flanges

This shear is resisted by the sum of the shear strengths of the transverse steel, the concrete flange and the steel decking if present. The shear resistance of these three components is given by

$$\nu_r = 0.7A_{sv}f_y + 0.03\eta A_{cv}f_{cu} + \nu_p \qquad (13.7)$$

but

$$\nu_r < 0.8\eta A_{cv}(f_{cu})^{1/2} + \nu_p$$

where f_{cu} is the characteristic cube strength of the concrete but not greater than 40 N/mm^2

η is 1.0 for normal weight concrete and 0.8 for lightweight concrete

A_{cv} is the mean longitudinal sectional area per unit length of the concrete flange

A_{sv} is the cross-sectional area per unit length of the beam of the transverse steel crossing the shear planes

ν_p is the contribution of the steel decking

The contribution of the steel decking ν_p is

$$\nu_p = t_p p_{yp} \quad \text{for decking continuous over the steel beam}$$

or

$$\nu_p = N(4d_s t_p p_{yp})/s \quad \text{for decking which is non-continuous but is welded to the steel beam and studs}$$

where t_p is the thickness of the steel decking

p_{yp} is the design strength of the steel decking (usually taken as 280 N/mm^2)

d_s is the stud diameter.

EXAMPLE 13.3

Shear connectors and transverse reinforcement

The composite beam of example 13.2 and figure 13.8 spans 12 metres and is provided with shear stud connectors in pairs at 300 mm centres to suit the spacing of the ribs of the steel profiled decking. The studs are 19mm diameter and of 100mm height.

(a) Calculate the degree of shear resistance and the moment of resistance of the composite beam based upon the shear connectors provided.

(b) Design the transverse reinforcement required in the concrete slab.

(a) Degree of shear resistance and moment of resistance

The characteristic resistance q_k of each shear stud from table 13.2 is

$$q_k = 100 \text{ kN for grade 30 concrete}$$

The design shear capacity q_e of each stud is

$$q_e = k_1 k_2 q_k$$

where $k_1 = 0.8$ for positive moments (that is, sagging)
and k_2 is the factor determined from the dimensions of the profiled steel decking, given
               in BS 5950: Part 3, Section 3.1 as

$$k_2 = 0.6 \frac{b_r}{D_p}\left(\frac{h}{D_p} - 1\right) \quad \text{but not greater than 0.8}$$

where b_r is the breadth of the concrete rib (Take $b_r = 150$ mm)
               D_p is the depth of the profiled steel decking
               h is the height of the stud.

Therefore $k_2 = 0.6 \times \dfrac{150}{50} \times \left(\dfrac{100}{50} - 1\right) = 1.8 > 0.8$

Hence $q_e = 0.8 \times 0.8 \times 100 = 64$ kN

Number of studs N at 300 mm centres in pairs over half the 12 m span is

$$N = \frac{6000}{300} \times 2 = 40$$

For full shear connection

$$N_{full} = \frac{R_s}{Q_e} = \frac{3358}{64} = 52.5$$

($R_s = 3358$ is obtained from example 13.2.)
    The degree of shear connection K is

$$K = \frac{N}{N_f} = \frac{40}{52.5} = 0.762$$

The moment of the resistance M_p of the composite beam based on the partial shear resistance can be obtained using the linear action method of figure 13.11. From the proportions of the straight-line relationship

$$M_p = K(M_c - M_s) + M_s$$

where M_c is the moment capacity with full shear connection from example 13.2
               M_s is the moment capacity of the steel beam

$$M_s = S p_y = 1653 \times 355 \times 10^{-3} = 587 \text{ kN m}$$

Therefore

$$M_p = 0.762 \times (1098 - 587) + 587$$
$$= 976 \text{ kN m}$$

(b) Transverse reinforcement

Longitudinal shear force per unit length is given by

$$\nu = \frac{NQ}{s}$$

Studs are in pairs therefore $N = 2$ and spacing $s = 300$ mm, hence

$$\nu = \frac{2 \times 64}{300} = 0.472 \text{ kN/mm}$$

For each shear plane

$$\nu = 0.427 \times 10^3 / 2 = 214 \text{ N/mm}$$

Shear resistance ν_r is

$$\nu_r = 0.7 A_{sv} f_y + 0.03 \eta A_{cv} f_{cu} + \nu_p$$

For A_{sv} try the minimum steel area of 0.13 per-cent of the slabs longitudinal cross-section/mm

$$A_{sv} = 0.13 \times 1 \times 90/100 = 0.117 \text{ mm}^2/\text{mm}$$

Mean longitudinal area A_{cv} of the concrete flange per unit length is

$$A_{cv} = 0.5 \times (D_s + h) \times 1 = 0.5(140 + 90) = 115 \text{ mm}^2/\text{mm}$$

$$\nu_p = t_p p_{yp}$$

$$= 1 \times 280 = 280 \text{ N/mm for 1mm thickness of the profiled steel sheeting}$$

Hence

$$\nu_r = 0.7 \times 0.117 \times 460 + 0.03 \times 1.0 \times 115 \times 30 + 280$$
$$= 38 + 104 + 280$$
$$= 422 \text{ N/mm} > \nu = 214 \text{ N/mm} \qquad \text{OK}$$

The maximum value for ν_r is specified as

$$\nu_r = 0.8 \eta A_{cv} (f_{cu})^{\frac{1}{2}} + \nu_p$$
$$= 0.8 \times 1.0 \times 115 \times 30^{\frac{1}{2}} + 280$$
$$= 504 + 280$$
$$= 784 \text{ N/mm} > 422 \text{ N/mm} \qquad \text{OK}$$

Therefore minimum slab reinforcement is adequate.

Provide 8mm bars at 200 mm centres $A_{sv} = 252 \text{ mm}^2/\text{metre}$.

13.6 The composite section at the serviceability limit state

At the serviceability limit state it is necessary to check the elastic bending stresses in the concrete and the steel and also to calculate the maximum deflection of the composite beam.

13.6.1   The elastic bending stresses

The code of practice limits the elastic bending stresses to $0.5f_{cu}$ in the concrete and p_y (see table 13.1) in the steel beam for non-slender sections. This is to ensure the deflections are within the elastic range during service with no permanent deformation.

The composite section is converted into a transformed section so that the area of concrete in compression is transformed to an equivalent steel area with a flange width of B_e/α_e as shown in figure 13.14, where α_e is the modular ratio $= E_{steel}/E_{concrete}$.

The maximum bending stresses are calculated from the equation for elastic bending, that is

$$\text{For the concrete} \quad f_c = \frac{Mx_t}{I_T}$$

$$\text{For the steel} \quad f_s = \frac{Mx_b}{I_T}$$

where M is the serviceability moment due to the unfactored loads

         x_t is the distance of the neutral axis from the top of the concrete flange

         x_b is the distance of the neutral axis from the bottom of the steel section

and I_T is the second moment of area of the transformed cross-section.

For office buildings and ones with a similar loading the value of the modular ratio may be taken as 10 for normal weight concrete and 15 for light-weight concrete. Alternatively it can be calculated from the formula given in the code based on the proportion of loading that is long term.

For the case of unpropped construction the elasic stresses are the summation of two parts so that

$$f_{final} = f_{constr} + f_{composite}$$

The stresses f_{constr} are those caused by the dead loads during construction and are locked into the steel section as the concrete hardens. They are calculated on the basis of the elastic section modulus of the steel section. The stresses $f_{composite}$ are those caused by the live load and additional dead load at service and are calculated on the basis of the composite section. A summation of these patterns of stresses is shown in figure 13.16 of example 13.4.

In the analysis of the transformed section to determine x and I_T there are two cases to consider

(a)   the concrete uncracked with the neutral axis below the concrete flange

(b)   the concrete in the flange cracked with the neutral axis within the concrete flange.

Case (a) with the concrete uncracked is the one that most commonly occurs at the serviceability limit state.

Figure 13.14
The transformed section at service

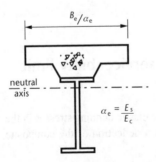

(a) The concrete flange uncracked $x_t > (D_s - D_p)$

For two areas A_1 and A_2 the position of their neutral axis may be found by taking area moments about the centroidal axis of A_1 such that

$$\bar{x} = \frac{A_2 s}{A_1 + A_2}$$

where x is the distance to the neutral axis from the centroid of A_1
   s is the distance between the centroids of A_1 and A_2.

The second moment of area of about the neutral axis of A_1 and A_2 combined can be calculated from

$$I_T = I_1 + I_2 + \frac{A_1 A_2 s^2}{A_1 + A_2}$$
$$= I_1 + I_2 + A_1 s \bar{x}$$

where I_1 and I_2 are the second moments of areas A_1 and A_2 respectively about their centroidal axes.

So for the transformed composite section

$$s = (D + D_s + D_p)/2$$

and the equations for x and I become

$$\bar{x} = \frac{A \alpha_e (D + D_s + D_p)}{2 \left[A \alpha_e + B_e (D_s - D_p) \right]} \tag{13.8}$$

$$I_T = I_s + \frac{B_e (D_s - D_p)^3}{12 \alpha_e} + \frac{B_e (D_s - D_p)(D + D_s + D_p) \bar{x}}{2 \alpha_e} \tag{13.9}$$

where I_s is the second moment of area of the steel section.

The depth of the neutral axis, x_t from the top of the concrete flange is

$$x_t = \bar{x} + \frac{D_s - D_p}{2}$$

If $x_t < (D_s - D_p)$ then the neutral axis is within the flange and the cracked condition applies as in case (b).

(b) The concrete flange cracked, $x_t < (D_s - D_p)$

Cracking of the concrete flange occurs when the centroid of the composite section as calculated from equation 13.8 is within the concrete flange.

For the cracked section the depth x_t of the neutral axis can be determined by taking area moments about the top of the concrete flange and then solving the resulting quadratic equation for x, so that

$$(A + B_e x / \alpha_e) x_t = A(D/2 + D_s) + B_e x_t^2 / 2 \alpha_e$$

The solution of this quadratic with some rearrangement gives

$$x_t = \frac{D + 2D_s}{1 + [1 + B_e(D + 2D_s)/A\alpha_e]^{1/2}} \tag{13.10}$$

The second moment of area about the neutral axis of the cracked composite section is

$$I_T = I_s + \frac{B_e x^3}{3\alpha_e} + A(D/2 + D_s - x_t)^2 \tag{13.11}$$

These equations for x_t and I_T are as shown in the appendix of BS 5950: Part 3.

13.6.2　The deflections at service due to the imposed loads

The deflections are calculated for the unfactored imposed loads and are limited to span/360 for a beam carrying plaster or other brittle finishes.

The second moment of area of the gross uncracked composite section as in section 13.6.1 part (a) is used in the calculations. For the unpropped case the total deflection is:

$$\delta_{total} = \delta_{constr} + \delta_{composite}$$

where　δ_{constr}　is the deflection at construction when the steel beam supports the wet concrete

　　　　δ_{comp}　is the deflection of the composite beam subject to the additional imposed load.

With partial shear connection the deflection is increased to

For propped construction
$$\delta = \delta_c + 0.5(1 - N_a/N_p)(\delta_s - \delta_c) \tag{13.12a}$$
For unpropped construction
$$\delta = \delta_c + 0.3(1 - N_a/N_p)(\delta_s - \delta_c) \tag{13.12b}$$

where　δ_s　is the deflection with the steel beam acting alone
and　　δ_c　is the deflection of a composite beam with full shear connection and the same loading.

EXAMPLE 13.4

Serviceability checks

For the composite beam of the previous examples calculate the elastic stresses and the deflections at service. The relevant sectional properties for the $457 \times 191 \times 74$ Universal Beam are

　Cross-sectional area $A = 94.6$ cm^2

　Elastic section modulus $Z = 1450$ cm^3

　Second moment of area $I_s = 33300$ cm^4

Assume the beam is unpropped during construction.
　The uniformly distributed characteristic loadings are

　　During construction – dead load　　9.5 kN/m,　live load　1.5 kN/m
　　During service – dead load　　10.5 kN/m,　live load　18　kN/m

Take the modular ratio $\alpha_e = 12$.

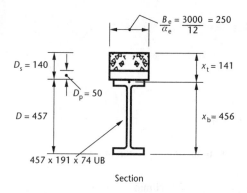

Figure 13.15
Transformed section –
example 13.4

Section

(a) At construction – the concrete has not hardened so that the steel beam supports the load

Due to the dead load:

$$\text{Moment } M = \frac{wL^2}{8} = \frac{9.5 \times 12^2}{8} = 171 \text{ kN m}$$

Maximum bending stresses f_{bc} in the steel beam are

$$f_{bc} = \frac{M}{Z} = \frac{171 \times 10^3}{1450} = 118 \text{ N/mm}^2$$

$$\text{Deflection } \delta_c = \frac{5wL^4}{384EI} = \frac{5 \times 9.5 \times 12^4 \times 10^5}{384 \times 205 \times 33\,300} = 38 \text{ mm}$$

These stresses and deflections at this stage are locked into the beam as the concrete hardens after construction.

(b) At service

The composite section is transformed into an equivalent steel section as shown in figure 13.15.

The position of the centroid of the transformed section is given by equation 13.8 as

$$\bar{x} = \frac{A\alpha_e(D + D_s + D_p)}{2\{A\alpha_e + B_e(D_s - D_p)\}}$$

$$= \frac{94.6 \times 10^2 \times 12 \times (457 + 140 + 50)}{2 \times \{94.6 \times 10^2 \times 12 + 3000 \times (140 - 50)\}} = 95.8 \text{ mm}$$

$$x_t = \bar{x} + (D_s - D_p)/2 = 96 + (140 - 50)/2 = 141 \text{ mm} > D_s - D_p$$

Therefore the concrete is not cracked.

$$x_b = D + D_s - x_t = 457 + 140 - 141 = 456 \text{ mm}$$

The second moment of area of the composite figure is given by equation 13.9 as

$$I_T = I_s + \frac{B_e(D_s - D_p)^3}{12\alpha_e} + \frac{B_e(D_s - D_p)(D + D_s + D_p)\bar{x}}{2\alpha_e}$$

$$= 333 \times 10^6 + \frac{3000 \times (140 - 50)^3}{12 \times 12} + \frac{3000 \times (140 - 50) \times (457 + 140 + 50)}{2 \times 12} \times 95.8$$

$$= (333 + 15 + 697) \times 10^6 \text{ mm}^4$$

$$= 1045 \times 10^6 \text{ mm}^4$$

At service the additional unfactored load is

$$w = (10.5 - 9.5) + 18 = 19.0 \text{ kN/m}$$

Maximum elastic stresses

$$\text{Moment } M = \frac{wL^2}{8} = \frac{19.0 \times 12^2}{8} = 342 \text{ kN m}$$

At service the additional elastic stresses in the transformed section are:

$$\text{In the concrete } \quad f_c = \frac{Mx_t}{\alpha_e I_T} = \frac{342 \times 10^6 \times 141}{12 \times 1045 \times 10^6} = 3.8 \text{ N/mm}^2$$

$$\text{In the steel } \quad f_s = \frac{Mx_b}{I_T} = \frac{342 \times 10^6 \times 456}{1045 \times 10^6} = 149 \text{ N/mm}^2$$

Final stresses at service are $f_{final} = f_{constr} + f_{addit}$

$$\text{In the concrete } \quad f_c = \quad 0 + 3.8 = 3.8 \text{ N/mm}^2 \quad < 0.5 f_{cu} = 15 \text{ N/mm}^2 \quad \text{OK}$$

$$\text{In the steel } \quad f_s = \quad 118 + 149 = 267 \text{ N/mm}^2 \quad < p_y = 355 \text{ N/mm}^2 \quad \text{OK}$$

The stresses are shown plotted in figure 13.16.

Deflections

The deflection for the composite beam at service is given by equation 13.12 for the unpropped beam as

$$\delta = \delta_c + 0.3(1 - N_a/N_p)(\delta_s - \delta_c)$$

The live load deflection for the transformed composite section and full shear connection is

$$\delta_c = \frac{5wL^4}{384 E_s I_T} = \frac{5 \times 18 \times 12^4 \times 10^5}{384 \times 205 \times 1045 \times 10^6} = 22.7 \text{ mm}$$

The corresponding deflection with the steel beam acting alone is

$$\delta_s = \frac{\delta_c I_{comp}}{I_s} = \frac{22.7 \times 104\,500}{33\,300} = 71.2 \text{ mm}$$

The degree of shear connection has been calculated in example 13.2 as

$$K = N_a/N_p = 0.762$$

Figure 13.16
Elastic stresses at service

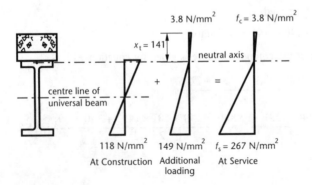

3.8 N/mm² $f_c = 3.8$ N/mm²

$x_t = 141$

neutral axis

centre line of universal beam

118 N/mm²   149 N/mm² $f_s = 267$ N/mm²

At Construction   Additional loading   At Service

Therefore substituting in equation 13.12b the live load deflection is

$$\delta = \delta_c + 0.3(1 - N_a/N_p)(\delta_s - \delta_c)$$
$$= 22.7 + 0.3 \times (1 - 0.762)(71.2 - 22.7)$$
$$= 26\text{mm} = \text{span}/461 < \text{span}/360 \qquad \text{OK}$$

At service the additional dead load above the construction dead load is 1.0 kN/m. Therefore due to this additional dead load and the 18 kN/m live load at service

$$\delta = 26 \times \frac{19.0}{18.0} = 27 \text{ mm}$$

Therefore due to the total dead load and live load

$$\delta = \delta_{\text{constr}} + 27 = 38 + 27 = 65 \text{ mm} = \text{span}/185$$

For this order of total deflection pre-cambering of the steel beam is probably advisable.

Appendix

Typical weights and live loads

$$1\ \text{lb} = 0.454\ \text{kg} \quad = 4.448\ \text{N force}$$
$$1\ \text{lb/ft}^2 = 4.88\ \text{kg/m}^2 \quad = 47.9\ \text{N/m}^2$$
$$1\ \text{lb/ft}^3 = 16.02\ \text{kg/m}^3 = 157\ \text{N/m}^3$$

Weights

	kN/m^3
Aluminium, cast	26
Asphalt paving	23
Bricks, common	19
Bricks, pressed	22
Clay, dry	19–22
Clay, wet	21–25
Concrete, reinforced	24
Glass, plate	27
Lead	112
Oak	9.5
Pine, white	5
Sand, dry	16–19
Sand, wet	18–21
Steel	77
Water	9.81

	kN/m^2
Brick wall, 115 mm thick	2.6
Gypsum plaster, 25 mm thick	0.5
Glazing, single	0.3

Floor and roof loads

	kN/m^2
Classrooms	3.0
Dance halls	5.0
Flats and houses	1.5
Garages, passenger cars	2.5
Gymnasiums	5.0
Hospital wards	2.0
Hotel bedrooms	2.0
Offices for general use	2.5
Flat roofs, with access	1.5
Flat roofs, no access	0.75

Bar areas and perimeters

Table A.1 Sectional areas of groups of bars (mm^2)

Bar size (mm)	Number of bars									
	1	2	3	4	5	6	7	8	9	10
6	28.3	56.6	84.9	113	142	170	198	226	255	283
8	50.3	101	151	201	252	302	352	402	453	503
10	78.5	157	236	314	393	471	550	628	707	785
12	113	226	339	452	566	679	792	905	1020	1130
16	201	402	603	804	1010	1210	1410	1610	1810	2010
20	314	628	943	1260	1570	1890	2200	2510	2830	3140
25	491	982	1470	1960	2450	2950	3440	3930	4420	4910
32	804	1610	2410	3220	4020	4830	5630	6430	7240	8040
40	1260	2510	3770	5030	6280	7540	8800	10100	11300	12600

Table A.2 Perimeters and weights of bars

Bar size (mm)	6	8	10	12	16	20	25	32	40
Perimeter (mm)	18.85	25.1	31.4	37.7	50.2	62.8	78.5	100.5	125.6
Weight (kg/m)	0.222	0.395	0.616	0.888	1.579	2.466	3.854	6.313	9.864

Bar weights based on density of 7850 kg/m^3.

Table A.3 Sectional areas per metre width for various bar spacings (mm^2)

Bar size (mm)	Spacing of bars								
	50	75	100	125	150	175	200	250	300
6	566	377	283	226	189	162	142	113	94
8	1010	671	503	402	335	287	252	201	168
10	1570	1050	785	628	523	449	393	314	262
12	2260	1510	1130	905	754	646	566	452	377
16	4020	2680	2010	1610	1340	1150	1010	804	670
20	6280	4190	3140	2510	2090	1800	1570	1260	1050
25	9820	6550	4910	3930	3270	2810	2450	1960	1640
32	16100	10700	8040	6430	5360	4600	4020	3220	2680
40	25100	16800	12600	10100	8380	7180	6280	5030	4190

Shear reinforcement

Table A.4 A_{sv}/s_v for varying stirrup diameter and spacing

Stirrup diameter (mm)	Stirrup spacing (mm)										
	85	*90*	*100*	*125*	*150*	*175*	*200*	*225*	*250*	*275*	*300*
8	1.183	1.118	1.006	0.805	0.671	0.575	0.503	0.447	0.402	0.366	0.335
10	1.847	1.744	1.57	1.256	1.047	0.897	0.785	0.698	0.628	0.571	0.523
12	2.659	2.511	2.26	1.808	1.507	1.291	1.13	1.004	0.904	0.822	0.753
16	4.729	4.467	4.02	3.216	2.68	2.297	2.01	1.787	1.608	1.462	1.34

Wire fabric

Table A.5 Sectional areas for different fabric types

Fabric reference	Longitudinal wires			Cross wires		
	Wire size (mm)	Pitch (mm)	Area (mm²/m)	Wire size (mm)	Pitch (mm)	Area (mm²/m)
Square mesh						
A393	10	200	393	10	200	393
A252	8	200	252	8	200	252
A193	7	200	193	7	200	193
A142	6	200	142	6	200	142
A98	5	200	98	5	200	98
Structural mesh						
B1131	12	100	1131	8	200	252
B785	10	100	785	8	200	252
B503	8	100	503	8	200	252
B385	7	100	385	7	200	193
B285	6	100	283	7	200	193
B196	5	100	196	7	200	193
Long mesh						
C785	10	100	785	6	400	70.8
C636	9	100	663	6	400	70.8
C503	8	100	503	5	400	49
C385	7	100	385	5	400	49
C283	6	100	503	5	400	49
Wrapping mesh						
D98	5	200	98	5	200	98
D49	2.5	100	49	2.5	100	49

Anchorage and lap requirements

Table A.6 Anchorage lengths (anchorage length $L = K_{A} \times$ bar size)

	K_A			
	$f_{cu} = 25$	30	35	40 or more
Plain (250)				
Tension	43	39	36	34
Compression	34	32	29	27
Deformed Type 1 (460)				
Tension	55	50	47	44
Compression	44	40	38	35
Deformed Type 2 (460)				
Tension	44	40	38	35
Compression	35	32	30	28

Basic lap lengths in tension and compression (lap length $= K_{L} \times$ bar size)

	K_L			
	$f_{cu} = 25$	30	35	40 or more
Plain (250)	43	39	36	34
Deformed Type 1 (460)	55	50	47	44
Deformed Type 2 (460)	44	40	38	35

Minimum lap lengths: 15 × bar size or 300 mm.
Refer to figure 5.8 for increased lap lengths at certain locations in a member section.
Type 1 and 2 bars are described in section 1.6.2.
Type 2 bars are most common.

Maximum and minimum areas of reinforcement

Table A.7 Maximum areas of reinforcement

For a slab or beam, tension or compression reinforcement

$100A_s/A_c \leq 4$ per cent other than at laps

For a column

$100A_s/A_c \leq 6$ per cent for vertically cast columns
≤ 8 per cent for horizontally cast columns
≤ 10 per cent at laps

For a wall, vertical reinforcement

$100A_s/A_c \leq 4$ per cent

Table A.8 Minimum areas of reinforcement

Tension reinforcement in beams: for grade 250 steel $A_{s,\,min}/bd > 0.24$ per cent
for grade 460 steel $A_{s,\,min}/bd > 0.13$ per cent

Tension reinforcement in slabs: for grade 250 steel $A_{s,\,min}/bd > 0.24$ per cent
for grade 460 steel $A_{s,\,min}/bd > 0.13$ per cent
This minimum applies in both directions.

Compression reinforcement in rectangular beams: $A_{s,\,min} > 0.2$ per cent of A_c

Longitudinal reinforcement in columns: $A_{s,\,min} > 0.4$ per cent of A_c

Vertical reinforcement in walls: $A_{s,\,min} > 0.4$ percent of A_c

Note: Consult table 6.5 for flanged beams.

Summary of basic design equations for the design of reinforced concrete

(a) Design for bending (see chapters 4 and 7)

For a singly reinforced section:

$$A_s = \frac{M}{0.95 f_y z}$$

$$z = d\left[0.5 + (0.25 - K/0.9)^{1/2}\right]$$

$$K = M/bd^2 f_{cu}$$

For a double reinforced section $(K > K')$ – see figure A.1:

$$A'_s = \frac{(K - K')f_{cu}bd^2}{0.95 f_y(d - d')}$$

$$A_s = \frac{K' f_{cu}bd^2}{0.95 f_y z} + A'_s$$

When moment redistribution has been applied then the above equations must be modified – see table 4.1.

(b) Design for shear (see chapters 5 and 7)

$$\nu = V/b_v d$$

Consult table 5.1 for values of ν_c.

For $0.5\nu_c < \nu < (\nu_c + 0.4)$: $A_{sv} \geq 0.4 b_v s_v/0.95 f_{yv}$

For $(\nu_c + 0.4) < \nu < 0.8\sqrt{f_{cu}}$ or 5 N/mm²: $A_{sv} \geq b_v s_v(\nu - \nu_c)/0.95 f_{yv}$

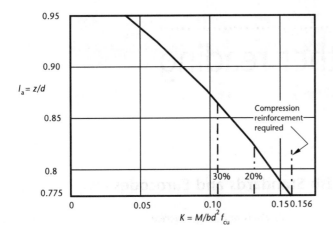

(c) Design for torsion (see chapters 5 and 7)

$$\nu_t = \frac{2T}{h_{min}^2(h_{max} - h_{min}/3)}$$

$$\frac{A_{sv}}{s_v} = \frac{T}{0.8x_1y_1(0.95f_{yv})}$$

$$A_s = \frac{A_{sv}}{s_v}\left(\frac{f_{yv}}{f_y}\right)(x_1 + y_1)$$

(d) Design for punching shear in slabs (see chapter 8)

$$\nu = V/ud$$

Consult table 5.1 for values of ν_c.

For $\nu_c < \nu \le 1.6\nu_c$: $\sum A_{sv} \ge (\nu - \nu_c)ud/0.95f_{yv}$

For $1.6\nu_c < \nu \le 2\nu_c$: $\sum A_{sv} \ge 5(0.7\nu - \nu_c)ud/0.95f_{yv}$

Further reading

(a) British Standards and Eurocodes

BS 1881	*Methods of testing concrete*
BS 4449	*Specification for carbon steel bars for the reinforcement of concrete*
BS 4466	*Specification for bending dimensions and scheduling of reinforcement for concrete*
BS 4482	*Cold reduced steel wire for the reinforcement of concrete*
BS 4483	*Steel fabric for the reinforcement of concrete*
BS 5057	*Concrete admixtures*
BS 5328	*Part 1: Guide to specifying concrete*
BS 5896	*Specification for high tensile steel wire and strand for the prestressing of concrete*
BS 5950	*Structural use of steelwork on buildings. Part 3: Design in composite construction*
BS 6399	*Design loading for buildings*
BS 8002	*Earth retaining structures*
BS 8004	*Foundations*
BS 8007	*Code of practice for the design of concrete structures for retaining aqueous liquids*
BS 8110	*Structural use of concrete, Parts 1, 2 and 3*
DD ENV 1992-1-1	*Eurocode 2; Design of concrete structures. Part 1*
DD ENV 206	*Concrete – performance, production, placing and compliance criteria*
Draft prEN 10080	*Steel for the reinforcement of concrete*

(b) Textbook and other publications

A. W. Beeby and R. S. Narayanan, *Designers Handbook to EuroCode 2*. Thomas Telford, London, 1995.

J. H. Bungey and S. G. Millard, *The Testing of Concrete in Structures*, 3rd edn. Chapman & Hall, London, 1995.

R. Hulse and W. H. Mosley, *Reinforced Concrete Design by Computer*. Macmillan, Basingstoke, 1986.

R. Hulse and W. H. Mosley, *Prestressed Concrete Design by Computer*. Macmillan, Basingstoke, 1987.

M. K. Hurst, *Prestressed Concrete Design*, 2nd edn. Chapman & Hall, London, 1998.

F. K. Kong and R. H. Evans, *Reinforced and Prestressed Concrete*. Chapman & Hall, London, 1988.

R. M. Lawson, *Commentary on BS 5950 Part 3 Section 3.1, Composite Beams*. The Steel Construction Institute, 1990.

T. Y. Lin and N. H. Burns, *Design of Prestressed Concrete Structures*. J. Wiley, Chichester, 1983.

T. J. MacGinley and B. S. Choo, *Reinforced Concrete Design Theory and Examples*. E & F N Spon, London, 1990.

W. H. Mosley, R. Hulse and J. H. Bungey, *Reinforced Concrete Design to Eurocode 2*. Macmillan, Basingstoke, 1996.

A. M. Neville, *Properties of Concrete*, 4th edn. Longman Scientific and Technical, Harlow, 1998.

A. M. Neville and J. J. Brooks, *Concrete Technology*. Longman Scientific and Technical, Harlow, 1987.

A. H. Nilson and G. Winter, *Design of Concrete Structures*. McGraw-Hill, Maidenhead, 1991.

C. E. Reynolds and J. C. Steedman, *Reinforced Concrete Designer's Handbook*, 10th edn. E & F N Spon, London, 1988.

Concise EuroCode for the Design of Concrete Buildings. British Cement Association, Crowthorne, Berks, 1993.

Worked Examples for the Design of Concrete Buildings. British Cement Association, Crowthorne, Berks, 1994.

Index

Foreword

The theory of multiple intelligences places value on a range of eight different learning intelligences—acknowledging individual differences. Teachers and children favour a particular learning style (or styles). This series aims to provide teaching and learning opportunities, using the eight multiple intelligences through a thematic approach in the classroom.

Titles in this series:
Multiple intelligences – Lower Primary
Multiple intelligences – Middle Primary
Multiple intelligences – Upper Primary

Contents

Teachers notes

What is 'multiple intelligences'?

The theory of multiple intelligences was developed by psychologist Dr Howard Gardner after years of biological and cultural research into human cognition.

In his 1983 book, *Frames of mind: the theory of multiple intelligences*, Gardner suggests that there are seven (later eight) different types of human intelligence or ways of understanding the world—and possibly even more yet to be identified. This idea is in contrast to the traditional view of intelligence, where it is thought of as a general characteristic that affects our skills and abilities. IQ tests are a perfect example of this latter belief.

Gardner believes that each person has one or two dominant intelligences, although it is possible to strengthen all eight. He points out that our intelligences aren't used in isolation; instead, one activity or task requires the use of a number of intelligences working together.

The eight intelligences identified by Gardner are verbal–linguistic, logical–mathematical, naturalist, visual–spatial, bodily–kinaesthetic, musical–rhythmic, interpersonal and intrapersonal. Typical characteristics of a child with a dominance in an intelligence and suitable activities for developing or assessing each intelligence are outlined below. Each of these intelligences is also described on the teacher page preceding each worksheet.

To make the terminology easier for the children to understand, the terms have been simplified with an accompanying icon for each intelligence.

Intelligence		Activities involving …
Verbal–Linguistic A child who thinks in words. He/She learns best through activities involving reading, writing and speaking.		verbal and written communication, vocabulary, word puzzles and games, spelling, listening to people speak or read aloud
Logical–Mathematical A child who thinks rationally and in abstractions. He/She learns best through activities involving numbers and patterns.		problem-solving, brainteasers, logical puzzles, questioning how things work, science experiments, number games or problems, complex ideas
Naturalist A child with an awareness of the patterns in nature. He/She learns best through activities involving animals, plants and the environment.		gardening, animals and plants, observing and identifying environmental features
Visual–Spatial A child who thinks in images, colours and shapes. He/She learns best through activities involving visualisation.		art, craft and design, watching films, interpreting images, visual puzzles or games
Bodily–Kinaesthetic A child with good physical awareness. He/She learns best through 'hands-on' activities.		craft, motor coordination, sports skills, acting, demonstrations, taking objects apart and putting them back together
Musical–Rhythmic A child with an awareness of rhythm and sound. He/She learns best through activities involving music or rhythms.		playing musical instruments, singing, rhythm, identification of sounds, interpreting music, chants
Interpersonal A child who enjoys being in groups and teams. He/She learns best through activities involving working with others.		friendship qualities, being a leader, playing team sports, group work and showing empathy for others
Intrapersonal A child who understands and analyses his/her thoughts and feelings. He/She learns best through individual activities.		identifying beliefs, expressing feelings, working alone, personal challenges, setting and reaching goals

Teachers notes

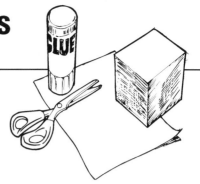

Implications of multiple intelligences for teaching

In the traditional western education system, a child's intelligence is largely measured by his/her linguistic and mathematical abilities. This undervalues abilities and achievements in other curriculum areas. The theory of multiple intelligences, in contrast, values equally a range of different intelligences and thereby acknowledges individual differences. If teachers accept Gardner's theory, it has implications for the way they plan, present and assess child work.

Setting up a multiple intelligences classroom

• Research schools that use a multiple intelligences approach by visiting their websites. Try:

  http://www.gardnerschool.org
  http://www.newcityschool.org/home.html
  http://cookps.act.edu.au/mi.htm

  More schools can be found by typing 'multiple intelligence school' into a search engine. (Please note that the above websites were in operation at the time of publication.)

• Create intelligence profiles for your class by identifying each child's dominant intelligence(s). This can be done formally or informally.
  Some formal tests can be found on the Internet. Try:

  http://www.mitest.com/omitest.htm
  http://cortland.edu/psych/mi/measure.html
  (will need adapting to a child's level)

  More tests can be found by typing 'multiple intelligence checklist' into a search engine. (Please note that the above websites were in operation at the time of publication.)

  Informal methods may include observing work habits, asking children about their interests and hobbies, holding parent–teacher conferences, talking to other teachers or reading a child's previous school records. A series of checklists to help identify a child's dominant intelligence(s) is also provided on pages x – xi.

• Identify your own dominant intelligence(s) (and, therefore, your teaching approach) by using the checklist on page ix. Use the results to help you decide on the most effective teaching/learning tools for you. You may also like to consider team teaching with other staff members who are dominant in different intelligences. Remember that although you don't have to teach/learn every concept in eight different ways, it is important to develop other teaching styles or intelligences to cater for children who may have different strengths from yours.

• Educate children about multiple intelligences and allow them to discover their own strengths and weaknesses. Discuss how everyone is 'wise' in a different way and encourage children to work on their weaknesses. During lessons, show that you value individual differences.

• Allow children to tutor other children using their strong intelligences.

• Encourage children to use their dominant intelligences to aid understanding of topics that would usually require using a weaker intelligence.

• Use a range of methods to assess child work; e.g. traditional tests, role-play, work samples, portfolios. The methods you choose should allow children to demonstrate their intelligence strengths. Some assessment proformas are found on pages xii – xiii.

Teachers notes

- Plan cross-curricular units of work that allow children to use all the intelligences. One suggested method of doing this is to brainstorm ideas for each intelligence on a particular topic. For example:

Verbal–Linguistic

- Write about a day in the life of a slave in an ancient city.
- Write a conversation between two children living in an ancient civilisation.

Logical–Mathematical

- Research the monetary system used in a specific ancient civilisation.
- Categorise information about two or three ancient civilisations under selected headings.

Naturalist

- Explain/Write the procedure for creating paper from papyrus in the same manner the Ancient Egyptians did.
- Compare the physical environment around an ancient civilisation to that of the same area in the present day.

Visual–Spatial

- Locate and colour-code ancient civilisations on a world map.
- Design a 'tourist brochure' for an ancient civilisation.

Bodily–Kinaesthetic

- Create a dance based on pictures of celebrations shown in ancient murals.
- Mime daily activities from a particular civilisation for class members to guess.

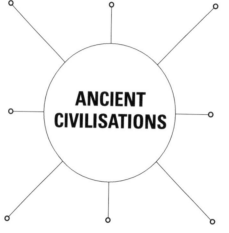

ANCIENT CIVILISATIONS

Musical–Rhythmic

- Research the musical instruments of an ancient civilisation
- Write a cinquain, haiku or rhythmic poem which relates to an ancient civilisation.

Interpersonal

- Work with a group to reconstruct an ancient village.
- Work in a group to write a daily menu for people living in an ancient civilisation.

Intrapersonal

- Research housing of a particular civilisation and time.
- Write a reflection comparing life then and now.

Remember that an activity or task is likely to involve more than one intelligence, but you can choose to focus on a particular intelligence.

Another form of planning an overview is illustrated below.

Ancient Civilisations

Verbal–Linguistic	Logical–Mathematical	Naturalist	Visual–Spatial	Bodily–Kinaesthetic	Musical–Rhythmic	Interpersonal	Intrapersonal
Write about a day in the life of a slave in an ancient city.	Research the monetary system used in a specific ancient civilisation.	Explain/Write the procedure for creating paper from papyrus in the same manner the Ancient Egyptians did.	Locate and colour-code ancient civilisations on a world map.	Create a dance based on pictures of celebrations shown on ancient murals.	Research the musical instruments of an ancient civilisation.	Work with a group to reconstruct an ancient village.	Research housing of a particular civilisation and time.
Write a conversation between two children living in an ancient civilisation.	Categorise information about two or three ancient civilisations under selected headings.	Compare the physical environment around an ancient civilisation to that of the same area today.	Design a 'tourist brochure' for an ancient civilisation.	Mime daily activities from a particular civilisation for class members to guess.	Write a cinquain, haiku or rhythmic poem which relates to an ancient civilisation.	Work in a group to write a daily menu for people living in an ancient civilisation.	Write a reflection comparing life then and now.

How to use this book

This book contains six units of work, each of which covers a single topic.
The topics are:

Endangered species	Disasters	Ancient civilisations	Environmental issues	Sport	Personal development

Each unit consists of the following pages:

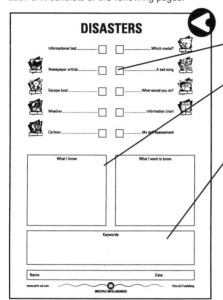

The first page of each unit is a **cover page** designed for the children. It can be glued into children's workbooks at the beginning of the unit. Children can fill in the tick boxes to indicate which worksheets and subsequent intelligences have been completed.

Before the children begin work on the unit, they should complete these sections individually. Teachers may ask children to brainstorm possible answers as a class or in small groups first.

A keyword section is provided for children to list words or phrases important to the subject. Children may begin by writing a few and adding to the list as they work through the unit. The words or phrases can be typed directly into the childrens' preferred Internet search engine to promote the most appropriate response to the topic.

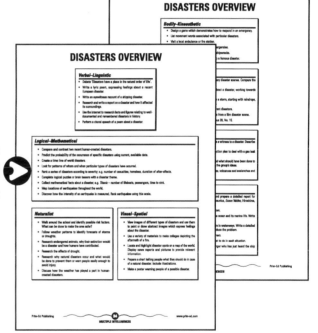

An **overview** for teachers has been included for each unit to provide ideas for activities that focus on each intelligence. Teachers could use these activities to further develop the unit topic with the class or as extension work for more able children.

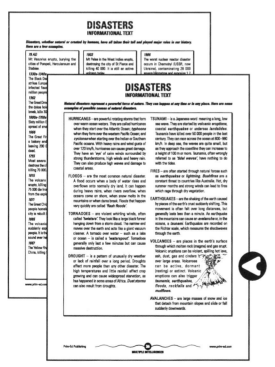

Two pages of general **informational text** about the topic have been provided, written at a child's level of understanding. This text could be used in variety of ways. For example:

- to provide information the children can use in the worksheets,
- for comprehension exercises,
- as a springboard for research projects,
- as a stimulus for class or group discussions.

How to use this book

Eight worksheets are contained in each unit. Each worksheet has been designed to focus on a single intelligence. However, as Gardner has pointed out, every activity we do requires the use of more than one intelligence. Therefore, teachers will be able to identify other intelligences operating as the children complete the worksheets.

It is advisable that teachers use each worksheet in the unit to ensure that all the intelligences have been covered.

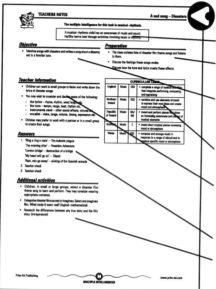

Each worksheet has an accompanying teachers page.

General information about the dominant intelligence is provided.

Preparation details what needs to be done before the teacher introduces the activity page to the children. Some materials and preparations are required, others are suggestions.

One or more objectives are given for each activity page, providing the teacher with the focus for the activity and the behaviours the children should be demonstrating by completing the activity.

Curriculum links appropriate to each country are provided across the main learning area that best represents the intelligence being explored.

Teacher information provides any information needed to use the worksheet most effectively. It may include background information or suggestions on how to organise the lesson.

Answers, if required, are included.

Additional activities are suggested to further develop the skills and/or concepts taught during the activity. Some of the additional activities will focus on a different intelligence than that of the worksheet—if so, this is indicated.

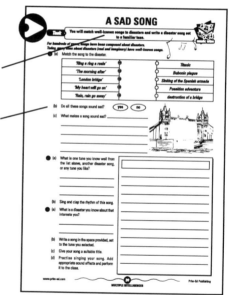

The task and multiple intelligence for each worksheet are provided at the top of the page for the child's information.

The activities have been selected to focus on the multiple intelligence indicated and cover a range of curriculum areas.

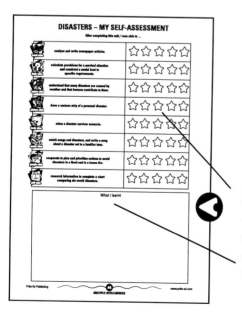

A child assessment page completes each unit. It should be given to the children when all the worksheets have been finished.

The children assess their work on the unit by colouring in the stars (with five stars being the best).

What I learnt can be completed after the children have brainstormed ideas in small groups or after a class discussion.

Teacher self-assessment proforma

Find out the intelligences in which you are strongest by ticking any statements that are true for you.

Verbal–Linguistic
I like to read during my leisure time. .... ❏
I enjoy teaching creative writing. .... ❏
I have strong verbal communication skills. .... ❏
I am skilled at teaching reading skills. .... ❏

Logical–Mathematical
I enjoy questioning how things work. .... ❏
I am an organised, logical person. .... ❏
I enjoy teaching number skills. .... ❏
I enjoy problem-solving activities. .... ❏

Naturalist
I enjoy caring for animals. .... ❏
I enjoy gardening. .... ❏
I am interested in environmental issues. .... ❏
I like teaching science lessons involving nature or natural forces. .... ❏

Visual–Spatial
I enjoy teaching art and craft. .... ❏
I am skilled in making or building things. .... ❏
I can easily picture creative ideas in my head. .... ❏
I am skilled at drawing or painting. .... ❏

Bodily–Kinaesthetic
I enjoy teaching physical education. .... ❏
I am skilled at dancing or acting. .... ❏
I enjoy activities that require fine or gross motor skills. .... ❏
I regularly play a sport for enjoyment. .... ❏

Musical–Rhythmic
I play a musical instrument or sing well. .... ❏
I regularly use music and rhythms in the classroom. .... ❏
I can successfully teach children musical concepts. .... ❏
I enjoy listening to music. .... ❏

Interpersonal
I have a wide circle of friends. .... ❏
I am skilled at teaching children how to develop good relationships with others. .... ❏
I am a natural leader. .... ❏
I enjoy working in a group or team. .... ❏

Intrapersonal
I regularly set and achieve personal goals. .... ❏
I like teaching lessons about feelings and emotions. .... ❏
I usually enjoy the time I spend alone. .... ❏
I have strong beliefs and opinions. .... ❏

Which intelligences did you score the most ticks in? _____
Use these results to reflect on how you teach and how you might change your teaching style to incorporate all of the intelligences.

Assessment of child learning styles proforma–1

Highlight any statements that describe the child's behaviours or skills.
Write any other appropriate behaviours or skills you have observed.

Child name:

Verbal–Linguistic

The child:

- achieves outstanding results in English.
- enjoys writing stories or poems.
- has an excellent vocabulary.
- enjoys reading.
- is skilled at word games.
- enjoys being read to.
- is skilled at verbal communication.

Other:

Naturalist

The child:

- likes to talk about his/her pets.
- enjoys natural science lessons.
- is fascinated with plants.
- brings natural objects to class to talk about.
- enjoys learning about animals.
- enjoys learning about the environment.

Other:

Logical–Mathematical

The child:

- has excellent number skills.
- enjoys logic puzzles and games.
- often questions how things work.
- is a competent problem-solver.
- enjoys science experiments.
- likes playing board games.
- can organise objects into logical groups.

Other:

Visual–Spatial

The child:

- enjoys art and craft lessons.
- interprets visual texts more easily than words.
- is a daydreamer.
- is skilled at making models.
- often doodles on work.
- enjoys viewing films or pictures.
- enjoys completing visual puzzles like mazes.

Other:

Assessment of child learning styles proforma–2

Highlight any statements that describe the child's behaviours or skills.
Write any other appropriate behaviours or skills you have observed.

Child name:

Bodily–Kinaesthetic

The child:

- enjoys physical education lessons.
- has excellent coordination skills.
- has a talent for acting.
- is skilled at craft activities.
- enjoys hands-on activities.
- moves or fidgets at his/her desk.
- enjoys taking objects apart and putting them back together.

Other:

Interpersonal

The child:

- is a natural leader.
- prefers to work in groups or teams.
- has a wide circle of friends.
- is empathetic to others.
- belongs to clubs or other groups.
- enjoys helping others.

Other:

Musical–Rhythmic

The child:

- can play a musical instrument.
- enjoys singing or chanting.
- likes listening to music.
- taps feet or fingers when working.
- demonstrates a good sense of rhythm.
- hums to himself/herself.
- creates his/her own songs.

Other:

Intrapersonal

The child:

- enjoys working on his/her own.
- likes to think about his/her feelings.
- shows independent thought or action.
- can easily express his/her feelings or opinions.
- has a good sense of his/her abilities.
- can set and reach personal goals.

Other:

Child self-assessment of learning styles proforma–1

What kind of learner are you? Tick the sentences that are true for you.

Am I word wise?

I love to read books. ☐

I like writing stories and poems. ☐

Word puzzles and games are fun. ☐

I am good at spelling. ☐

I enjoy telling news. ☐

I like learning new words. ☐

Am I body wise?

I like playing sport. ☐

I find it hard to sit still at my desk. ☐

Drama is lots of fun. ☐

I like to know what objects feel like. ☐

I like making things with my hands. ☐

I prefer to 'do' rather than watch. ☐

Am I logic wise?

I like to know how things work. ☐

I love board games like chess. ☐

I enjoy science experiments. ☐

I like puzzles that make me think. ☐

I like trying to solve problems. ☐

Number games are fun. ☐

Am I picture wise?

Art is my favourite subject. ☐

I like to do jigsaw puzzles. ☐

I am good at drawing. ☐

I can read maps easily. ☐

I enjoy making models. ☐

I often have vivid dreams. ☐

Am I nature wise?

I have a collection of shells, rocks or other natural objects. ☐

I like to care for animals. ☐

I enjoy gardening. ☐

I love to visit museums or zoos. ☐

I prefer to be outdoors rather than indoors. ☐

Looking after the environment is important to me. ☐

Child self-assessment of learning styles proforma–2

What kind of learner are you? Tick the sentences that are true for you.

Am I music wise?

I like to sing. .... ❑

I play, or would like to play, a musical instrument. .... ❑

When I work, I often tap my feet or my fingers. .... ❑

I enjoy listening to music. .... ❑

I know lots of songs off by heart. .... ❑

I enjoy listening to rhymes/raps. .... ❑

Am I people wise?

I enjoy team sports. .... ❑

I like to work in a group. .... ❑

I like sharing my ideas with others. .... ❑

I have more than three close friends. .... ❑

I find it interesting to meet new people. .... ❑

When people around me are happy it makes me feel happy too. .... ❑

Am I self wise?

I do my best schoolwork on my own. .... ❑

I often think about what I will do when I grow up. .... ❑

Staying home is usually more fun than being in a crowd of people. .... ❑

I have one or two close friends. .... ❑

I like to think about how I feel. .... ❑

I write in a diary in my free time. .... ❑

❷ Most of your ticks should be in one or two learning styles. Which learning style(s) has/have the most ticks? Circle the icon(s).

❸ Complete these sentences.

   (a)   I have found I am a _____ learner.

   (b)   Look at the learning styles which you ticked the least. Which of these learning styles would you most like to work on?

ENDANGERED SPECIES

Informational text........................ ☐   ☐ .... What would they say?

Status report............................... ☐   ☐ ....The hunted

Which species?............................ ☐   ☐ .... Can we fix it?

Introduced species – Australia ☐   ☐ .... Wildlife magazine

Cube vision.................................. ☐   ☐ ....My self-assessment

What I know	What I want to know

Keywords

Name:	Date:

ENDANGERED SPECIES OVERVIEW

Verbal–Linguistic

- Write articles or letters about threatened species to newspapers.
- Create a crossword puzzle using information about endangered species.
- Debate issues about the human impact on endangered species, such as logging and clearing land for development.
- Interview a conservation officer/park ranger about the dangers for local animals.
- Write a biography of an explorer hunting an elusive species.
- Write an acrostic poem using the name of an endangered animal.
- Write a playscript with endangered animal characters.
- Debate whether zoos or animals in captivity help or hinder endangered animals.

Logical–Mathematical

- Write an action plan, using logical steps, for saving an endangered plant species.
- Graph the numbers of endangered animals in Africa or Australia.
- Analyse similarities and differences among endangered species.
- Compare open model zoos to the enclosed zoos of the past.
- Organise data on the decline or increase of endangered species.
- Predict the numbers of certain species alive in specific areas in 20 years time if development continues at the same rate.
- Write word problems about specific endangered species.
- Draw a time line showing the decline of selected species which are now endangered.
- Rank the top ten animals considered endangered.

Naturalist

- Research to find out what sorts of environmental problems have led to endangered species.
- Research and discuss the possible reasons for dinosaurs becoming extinct.
- Research the effects of the introduction of the grey squirrel on the red squirrel.
- List reasons why some animals are/were hunted by humans (e.g. elephants–tusks, whales–oil).
- Investigate why some plants are endangered (e.g. green pitcher plant).
- Research to find if any local animals are endangered/threatened. Develop a plan to save the wildlife in the area.
- Develop a recovery plan to increase the numbers of the declining population of an endangered animal.

Visual–Spatial

- Make a TV advertisement advocating the preservation of a particular species. Record on videotape.
- Take pictures of endangered animals at a wildlife park or zoo. Arrange them on a display board.
- Create puppets of endangered species. Use them to perform a short play explaining why they are endangered.
- Design a poster that encourages people to join or support a conservation group.
- Make papier-mâché models of endangered species
- Design a set of postcards, stamps or a desktop calendar depicting endangered species.
- View the video *Mr Bear* to appreciate things from the viewpoint of an animal. Discuss characters, issues and human qualities.
- Create a diorama on a chosen endangered animal and its ideal habitat.
- On a map of the world, show where a chosen endangered animal was found 20 years ago and compare this to areas where it is found now.
- Make endangered animal masks to use in a class play.

ENDANGERED SPECIES OVERVIEW

Bodily–Kinaesthetic

- Create and perform movements to suit endangered species (e.g. giant panda, bilby, black rhinoceros).
- Dramatise a situation in which poachers are prevented from hunting an animal because they are confronted by a group of rangers.
- Children imagine they are a bear confined to a small cage. Mime the situation.
- Play charades using endangered species.
- Role-play scenes that show how humans destroy animal habitats.
- Create a board game to teach about the conservation of animals.

Interpersonal

- In a small group, create an advertising campaign to educate people about the plight of an endangered animal.
- Discuss the differences between 'endangered', 'threatened', and 'vulnerable' species.
- Survey the community to find out people's opinion on saving endangered species. Are people more inclined to want to save 'cute/cuddly' animals as opposed to a reptile?
- Compile a register of endangered animals in a particular country/continent.
- Work in a group to list reasons for species becoming endangered.
- Design a poster to show how we can help endangered animals.

Musical–Rhythmic

- Write a rap or poem where sound or movement can be added to tell the tale of an endangered animal (e.g. Tasmanian tiger, whaling, poaching elephants).
- Learn songs about the effect of people on animal species (e.g. 'Rip, rip, woodchip', 'Big yellow taxi').
- Create simple rhythms, chants or body percussion to show the different reasons that animals become endangered (e.g. logging, introduced species).
- Listen to background music used in animal films (e.g. *Free Willy*). Discuss how the music changes to suit the mood/action in the film.
- Tape or create animal noises for others to guess their origin.
- Create a scene with corresponding music to show an animal being hunted.
- Learn songs that have been written about the importance of helping endangered animals.
- Identify endangered animal sounds.

Intrapersonal

- Locate the WWF or similar websites to find out about endangered species.
- Consider what he/she can do to protect endangered species.
- Research why it is helpful to endangered animals to be a good pet owner.
- Children write about their feelings in regards to a specific endangered species.
- Write about the threats to 'water' and 'land' animals. Compare.
- Write a poem expressing personal views about endangered animals.
- Research the plight of bears in Asia.
- Write a procedure to make an 'endangered animal' craft.
- Write a letter inviting a local conservationist or ranger to speak to the class or to share information about threats to local animals and ways children can help.
- Watch TV programmes on endangered animals. Keep a 'feelings' diary about what was viewed.

ENDANGERED SPECIES
INFORMATIONAL TEXT

Each year, the number of plants and animals listed as threatened or endangered increases. In the past, species were affected by natural changes, such as the earth's climate in the Ice Age. Today, however, species are more likely to be affected by human interference, like the following:

Habitat destruction

People clear land to make way for farming, roads, buildings, houses or industry. Tropical rainforests have the largest variety of plant and animal life but are being destroyed worldwide, threatening many species. Most species adapt to living in specific areas and cannot survive when their habitat is damaged or destroyed.

Wildlife trade

Many animals are hunted (generally illegally) and killed for fur or body parts. Animals may also be caught as pets, for zoos or for research. The colourful Brazilian parrot —Spix's macaw— is now extinct in the wild as so many were caught for private collections.

Introduced species

Many places have had their native wildlife threatened because people have introduced species that compete with the native animals for survival. Australia has many introduced species, including rabbits, foxes, camels, cats and goats. These introduced species have become a threat to native animals, destroying their habitats, competing for the same food supply or even hunting the native animals.

Other factors

Disease and pollution are other factors that threaten various plant and animal species. Pollution, including the use of chemicals and fertilisers, factory wastes, litter and oils spills, has seriously affected a large number of aquatic and terrestrial species.

ENDANGERED SPECIES
INFORMATIONAL TEXT

All animals that are 'endangered' or 'vulnerable' are threatened because they are in danger of becoming extinct. The expression 'As dead as a dodo' means something that is lost or completely gone. The dodo was a flightless bird that inhabited the island of Mauritius in the Indian Ocean. It was wiped out by humans and their domestic animals when they moved onto the island in 1507. By 1861, dodos were extinct.

'Threatened species' means that their numbers have declined so far that their long-term survival is cause for concern. Once a species is listed as endangered, its survival chances are thought to be further reduced. At this point, not many individuals are left and most of their habitat has been destroyed.

The World Conservation Union (IUCN) lists status categories for threatened species as follows:

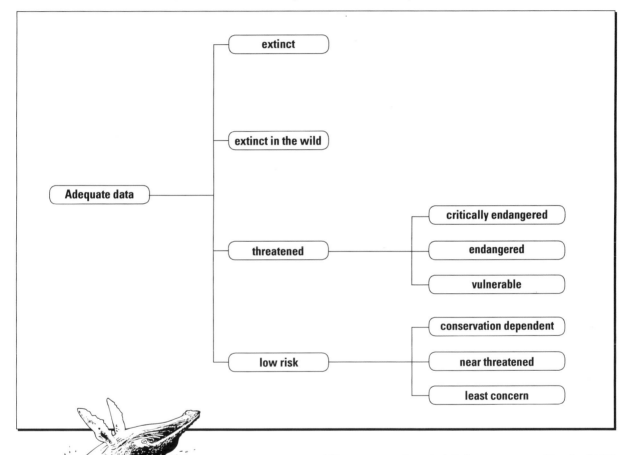

These categories allow for greater understanding of the urgency level and action required for threatened species.

People have become increasingly aware of the plight of endangered species and many groups and individuals are attempting to find solutions. Animals such as the tiger, orang-outang, giant panda, hairy-nosed wombat, dugong and African elephant are all well-known animals that are at great risk of eventual extinction if current human behaviours are allowed to continue.

What can we do to help? Contact groups like the IUCN about conservation programmes, as well as voicing your concern to government departments. Study the local fauna and flora in your area to build a better understanding of the wildlife and to find out the best way to recycle and reduce wastes. Limit the use of harmful chemicals in your home, conserve energy and water, help control introduced species into your area and educate the community about being responsible pet owners.

Groups like the the WWF and Greenpeace work hard to change community attitudes towards this and many other environmental issues.

The multiple intelligence focus for this task is verbal–linguistic.

A verbal–linguistic child thinks in words.
He/She learns best through activities involving reading, writing and speaking.

Objectives

- Finds the meanings of status terms related to species at risk.
- Researches endangered animals for selected categories.

Teacher information

- An 'extinct' animal is a species that is no longer living or has not been seen for 50 years or more; for example, Tasmanian tiger, dodo, stegosaurus (and other dinosaurs), the great auk, quagga, Steller's sea cow.

- 'Endangered' species are in immediate danger of disappearing altogether. Their numbers are low and they need protection to survive; for example, the green pitcher plant, the southern sea otter, numbat, Siberian tiger, snow leopard, Florida manatee, peregrine falcon and the Atlantic salmon.

- All animals that are 'vulnerable' or 'endangered' are 'threatened' because they are in danger. Threatened species are not yet low enough in numbers to be immediate danger, but any problems affecting the species need to be resolved to prevent a further decline.

- 'Vulnerable' species are those whose numbers (or range) have decreased. These species will become endangered over the next 25 years if nothing is done to help them.

Answers

- Teacher check

- See teacher information for meaning and species examples. Childrens' answers may vary for the research section of this worksheet.

Additional activities

- Make lists of species according to their status (e.g. endangered, extinct). (mathematical-logical)

- Label a world map with locations of endangered animals. Discuss which parts of the world/continents have the most/least. Why do they think this? (visual-spatial)

- Write a speech on 'Why should we worry about endangered animals?' Present your thoughts to a small group or the class. (verbal-linguistic)

Preparation

- Children will need materials for research; e.g. dictionaries, books, charts, videos, Internet, library access.

CURRICULUM LINKS			
England	Literacy	Yr 5	• locate information confidently and efficiently
Northern Ireland	English	KS2	• engage with a range of texts, e.g. non-fiction materials and read for information
Republic of Ireland	English	5th/ 6th	• explore appropriate non-fiction texts for various purposes
Scotland	English	C	• read for information, including developing the ability to scan
Wales	English	KS2	• read and use a wide range of sources of non-fiction information

STATUS REPORT

Explain the meaning of each word. Research, write and draw an animal to best suit each status. Give reasons for each animal's status (e.g. hunted, habitat loss).

1 (a) extinct _____

	⌐ animal _____
Draw your picture here	

(b) endangered _____

	⌐ animal _____
Draw your picture here	

(c) threatened _____

	⌐ animal _____
Draw your picture here	

(d) vulnerable _____

	⌐ animal _____
Draw your picture here	

The multiple intelligence focus for this task is logical–mathematical.

A logical–mathematical child thinks rationally and in abstractions.
He/She learns best through activities involving problem-solving, numbers and patterns.

Objectives

- Researches endangered animals from a chosen continent.
- Plans and writes a report on an endangered animal.
- Ranks endangered animals.
- Constructs a time line to show an animal's decline in numbers.

Teacher information

Some endangered animals for each continent include:

North America
- American bison, volcano rabbit, West Indian manatee, Eastern cougar, Californian condor, Kemp's Ridley turtle, rhinoceros iguana, spotted salamander

South America
- jaguar, vicuna, indigo macaw, emperor tamarin, giant armadillo, Chaco tortoise, spectacled bear, boto, pirarucu

Africa
- black rhinoceros, Indri, Nile crocodile, brown hyena, pygmy hippopotamus, chimpanzee, African elephant, aye-aye, addax, Grevy's zebra

Europe
- bowhead whale, loggerhead turtle, barn owl, red kite, European otter, olm, Mediterranean monk seal, common sturgeon

Asia
- Indian python, tiger, giant panda, Malayan tapir, orang-utan, pileated gibbon, Komodo dragon, snow leopard, greater bilby, tuatara, ghost bat, Kakapo, koala, dugong, Gouldian finch, takahe, kiwi

Oceanic Islands
- Giant clam, Galapagos giant tortoise, Abbott's booby, land iguana, robber crab, Hawaiian goose

Possible threats:
- Possible threats: habitat loss, illegal hunting, overfishing, introduced animals, capture, disease, extermination of prey, pollution

Possible solutions:
- Support wildlife conservation groups' laws to reduce hunting/ poaching, breeding programmes in captivity, relocation of animal groups, reintroduction to the wild, preservation of natural habitats, animal reserves.

Preparation

- Children will need access to a wide variety of resources for research (books, videos, charts, library access, Internet).

Answers

Teacher check (See Teacher information for possible answers.)

Additional activities

- Make time lines showing the decline of selected species which are now endangered. (logical–mathematical)
- Provide solutions to the declining populations of endangered species. (logical–mathematical)
- Write an action plan showing logical steps for saving an endangered plant species. (logical–mathematical)

CURRICULUM LINKS			
England	Science	KS2	• know about ways in which living things and the environment need protection
Northern Ireland	Geography	KS2	• know some of the ways in which people affect the environment and be aware of issues associated with conservation of the environment
Republic of Ireland	Science	5th/ 6th	• recognise and investigate aspects of human activities that may have had adverse effects on the environment
Scotland	Science	D	• describe examples of human impact on the environment that have brought about beneficial changes and examples that have detrimental effects
Wales	Geography	KS2	• identify ways in which people affect the environment

WHICH SPECIES?

You will research and report on endangered animals from a chosen continent.

1 Choose a continent and make a list of endangered species from that area.

Continent: _____

Endangered species: _____

_____

2 Choose one of these species to research further. Write notes below. Present your completed report on a separate sheet.

Species	Sketch
Found	
Interesting facts	
Threats	
Solutions	

3 Rank eight animals from this continent from most endangered to least endangered.

start			
			finish

4 Use the time line to show the decline of this animal over time (e.g. 1979 – 1.3 million, 1990 – 600000).

now

The multiple intelligence focus for this task is naturalist.

A naturalist child has an awareness of the patterns in nature.
He/She learns best through activities involving animals, plants and the environment.

Objectives

- Researches introduced species to Australia.
- Recognises the environmental impact of introducing species to a particular area.
- Identifies solutions on the problem of introduced species.

Teacher information

- Native species are those plants and animals that have been part of a particular geographic area for a lengthy period of time. They are well adapted and work in balance with the other native species within the same environment. Introduced species are brought into a new environment by humans, either accidentally or intentionally. They may cause no obvious problems, but most cause serious damage to the ecological balance of the environment, usually with direct consequences to the native species.

- Many were introduced to solve a problem but instead became an even greater problem. Australia has many introduced species, including rabbits, foxes, camels, cane toads, cats and goats. These introduced species have become a threat to native animals, destroying their habitats, competing for the same food supply or even hunting the native animals. In areas where introduced species have been released, they have caused the decline and vulnerability of many of the Australian native species.

Answers

1 (a) Rabbits – introduced for 'game' meat. Only 25 were released in the bush 200 years ago and today there are hundreds of millions! Damage – attack crops and eucalyptus plantations, damage fences and land. They dig under fences leaving holes for other animals like foxes to get in and do further damage.

   (b) Teacher check

   (c) Teacher check

2. Teacher check possible solutions:

   – Continued quarantine vigilance, education of environmental consequences, finding commercial use for introduced species.

   – Scientists study habitats and living needs of animals and plants so we can better understand how to help them.

   – Introduce laws to stop people within the country doing the wrong thing.

   – Restore degraded habitats.

Preparation

- Discuss the meanings of the terms 'native' and 'introduced'.
- Expose children to a variety of materials related to introduced species (books, videos, charts, Internet).
- Discuss the decisions made to introduce different species and the levels of their success/failure.
- Discuss possible solutions to these problems.

Additional activities

- Design a poster explaining the effects of introduced species and possible solutions. (visual–spatial)
- Compile reports on different introduced species from around the world. Display the reports for discussion. (verbal–linguistic)
- Show on a map of Australia where populations of introduced species such as rabbits, foxes and camels can be found. How are these areas different now from when the animals were first introduced? (visual–spatial)

CURRICULUM LINKS		
England	Science	KS2	• know about ways in which living things and the environment need protection
Northern Ireland	Geography	KS2	• know some of the ways in which people affect the environment and be aware of issues associated with conservation of the environment
Republic of Ireland	Science	5th/ 6th	• recognise and investigate aspects of human activities that may have had adverse effects on the environment
Scotland	Science	D	• describe examples of human impact on the environment that have brought about beneficial changes and examples that have detrimental effects
Wales	Geography	KS2	• identify ways in which people affect the environment

INTRODUCED SPECIES – AUSTRALIA

You will research and recognise problems caused to an
environment by introduced species.

An introduced species is a plant or animal that does not 'naturally' exist in a particular area. Australia
is a good example of how humans have introduced animals that have had a great influence on the
environment and endangered native flora and fauna species.

1 Research the effects that rabbits have had on the Australian environment. Select one introduced plant and
animal to complete the information boxes below.

Rabbits	draw your picture here	draw your picture here
How and why were they introduced?	How and why were they introduced?	How and why were they introduced?
Effect on the environment	Effect on the environment	Effect on the environment

2 List three possible solutions to this problem.

①

②

③

The multiple intelligence focus for this task is visual–spatial.

A visual–spatial child thinks in images, colours and shape.
He/She learns best through activities involving visualisation.

Objective

- Plans and constructs a 3-D informational cube on an endangered species.

Preparation

- Expose children to a wide variety of research materials on endangered species.
- Supply paper and card to construct the cube.
- Children should have prior knowledge of a cube net, how to make a pattern and construct 3-D shapes (about A3 in size).

Teacher information

- Direct children to construct a cube net (see illustration below) from card with glue tabs, based on a square between 10 and 15 cm.
- Try to guide children into choosing different species to widen their knowledge and enhance discussions.
- Children use the plan to write ideas and notes for each face of their cube.
- Good copies will need to be reproduced onto paper squares equivalent to the cube size.
- Encourage children to decorate and even hang additional labels from their completed cube. Display and discuss the childrens' work.

Answers

Teacher check

Additional activities

- Plan and construct a diorama about an endangered species and its environment. (bodily–kinaesthetic)
- Make papier-mâché models of endangered species.
- Design and construct animal masks to use in a play on endangered animals. (bodily–kinaesthetic)

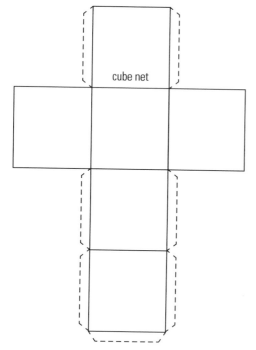

cube net

CURRICULUM LINKS			
England	Numeracy	Yr 6	• visualise 3–D shapes from 2–D drawings and identify different nets for a closed cube
Northern Ireland	Maths	KS2	• use nets to explore the relationship between 2–D and 3–D shapes
Republic of Ireland	Maths	5th/ 6th	• draw the nets of simple 3–D shapes and construct the shapes
Scotland	Maths	D	• make 3–D models of cubes using nets
Wales	Maths	KS2	• make 3–D shapes with increasing accuracy

CUBE VISION

① Construct a cube as directed by the teacher. Use the plan below to design and collect information on your endangered species.

Title	
Design ideas (e.g. colours, styles)	**Habitat/Food/Location**
Interesting facts	**Threats**
Drawing ideas/pictures	**Ways to help this endangered species**

② Complete each section on separate pieces of paper that will fit on your cube. Glue and decorate your cube. Discuss and display your finished work.

The multiple intelligence focus for this task is bodily–kinaesthetic.

> A bodily–kinaesthetic child has good physical awareness.
> He/She learns best through 'hands-on' activities.

Objective

- Writes and performs character conversations relating to endangered species.

Teacher information

- Direct children to find out the reasons why these animals are endangered and what is being done to help them.

- Use this information to consider the possible thoughts or conversations that might occur.

- Encourage children to share their answers with a partner.

- Together choose two (one from each sheet if possible) to practise and present to the class. The presentation should also include a brief explanation of the animal's plight or how it is being helped.

- Allow children to rate their performance and discuss ways to improve if necessary.

Answers

Teacher check

Additional activities

- Develop a cartoon strip using an endangered animal as the main character. (verbal–linguistic)

- Dramatise a situation in which poachers are prevented from hunting an animal as they are confronted by rangers. (bodily–kineasthetic)

- Create and perform skits to show the plight of some endangered animals (e.g. giant panda, blue whale, bilby, black rhinoceros. (bodily–kinaesthetic)

Preparation

- Children need access to research materials about the endangered animals (e.g. books, videos, charts, Internet).

CURRICULUM LINKS			
England	English	KS2	• create, adapt and sustain different roles
Northern Ireland	English	KS2	• engage in role-play
Republic of Ireland	English	5th/6th	• use improvisational drama
Scotland	English	C	• communicate through role-play
Wales	English	KS2	• participate in a wide range of drama activities, including improvisation and role-play

WHAT WOULD THEY SAY?

Task You will write and perform conversations related to endangered species.

1 Write what you think is being said between the characters below.

(a) One endangered animal talking to another.

(b) A poacher (illegal hunter) and an endangered animal.

(c) An endangered animal and a conservationist.

(d) A zoo keeper and an animal in captivity.

2 Share your work with a partner. Discuss the differences and explain your choices. Together, choose two of the best from your sheets. Practise and present these to the class with an explanation of why these animals are endangered or how they can be helped.

Rate your performance out of 10.

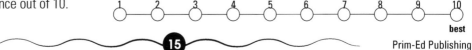

1   2   3   4   5   6   7   8   9   10

best

The multiple intelligence for this task is musical–rhythmic.

A musical–rhythmic child has an awareness of music and sound.
He/She learns best through activities involving music or rhythms.

Objectives

- Develops a storyboard with a simple musical accompaniment.
- Performs in a play with simple musical accompaniment.

Preparation

- Children will need prior knowledge of endangered animals, and practice working on a storyboard and working with simple musical instruments.
- Children will need access to a variety of simple musical instruments. Some sounds or beats can even be made using body parts (claps, clicks, slaps, vocal sounds, etc) to enhance the performance.
- Allow children adequate time to discuss, select and practise their plays before a final performance.
- Enlarge worksheet to A3 for individuals or group work. (optional)

Teacher information

- Discuss the idea of the story having a 'climax' and how the music should reflect this.
- Discuss how repeated beats, chants or verses can establish a character or story structure. Different instruments or sounds can represent a character; the intensity of that sound (dynamics), the duration, tempo (fast/slow) and texture (how many sounds are happening at the same time) should all be considered when creating the musical accompaniment to appeal to an audience.

Answers

Teacher check

Additional activities

- Make animal masks, simple costumes or props to use in the performance. (bodily–kinaesthetic)
- Write a report on an endangered animal that is hunted, explaining why it is pursued, its uses and how the process can be stopped. (verbal–linguistic)
- Create musical sounds to suit a variety of endangered animals, or use different beats for their names. (musical–rhythmic)

CURRICULUM LINKS			
England	Music	KS2	• engage in a range of musical activities that integrate performing, composing and appraising
Northern Ireland	Music	KS2	• create short stories and pictures told through sound
Republic of Ireland	Music	5th/ 6th	• select from a wide variety of sound sources for a range of musical purposes, e.g. to illustrate sequences of events
Scotland	Music	C	• stimulate musical imagination through inventing 'sound pictures'
Wales	Music	KS2	• improvise, compose and arrange music in response to a range of stimuli

THE HUNTED

Task ● **You will create and perform a short play with a simple musical accompaniment.**

❶ Use words or pictures to complete the storyboard about the hunting of an endangered animal.
Add musical beats, chants or instruments to best suit each stage of the story.

music			

music			

music	

❷ Share your ideas within the group.

♪ Select the story to be performed.

♪ Practise the music.

♪ Bring the two together. Practise.

♪ Give a performance.

♪ Rate your performance.

① ② ③ ④ ⑤
best

www.prim-ed.com 　　　　17　　　　Prim-Ed Publishing

MULTIPLE INTELLIGENCES

The multiple intelligence focus for this task is interpersonal.

An interpersonal child enjoys being in groups or teams.
He/She learns best through activities involving working with others.

Objectives

- Records group discussions on problems facing endangered species.
- Records solutions to problems facing endangered animals.

Teacher information

- Discuss with children the possible threats to species caused by human activity such as habitat loss, hunting/poaching, over-exploitation, overfishing, introduced animals, disease, capture, extermination of prey, pollution.
- Discuss why humans have pursued these activities and the damage they have caused.
- Discuss possible solutions to these problems.

Threats

Habitat loss
- city/housing development, farming, logging (Animals lose their homes.)

Hunting exploitation
- food, clothing, products (meat, oil, etc.)
- body parts (tusks, horns, paws)

Overfishing
- food, greed, industry, monetary gains
- fish, other animals caught in nets
- large fishing nets wipe out large populations at one time

Pollution
- oil spills, plastics in the ocean, water/air pollution

Introduced species
- for game (rabbits) but now pests
- usually failed to solve an environmental or human problem and are now pests (e.g. cane toads, camels, fox, Paterson's curse)

Disease
- introduced accidentally or intentionally
- killing animals, upsetting the balance in the environment

Capture
- for pets or sale (smuggling)

Extermination of prey
- for food, skins or to eliminate as pests. These animals may be a source of food for other animals.

Possible solutions

- Continued quarantine vigilance, education about environmental consequences, finding commercial use for introduced species.
- Scientists study habitats and living needs of animals and plants so we can better understand how to help them.
- Introduce laws (or enforce existing laws) to stop people within the country doing the wrong thing.
- Restore degraded habitats.
- Educate and make people more aware of their actions and the effects of human activities on our earth and endangered species.

Preparation

- Children will need access to a variety of resources for research (e.g. videos, books, charts, library, Internet).
- Select working groups.
- Select group leaders to report groups' findings, at the end of discussions, to the class.

Answers

Answers may vary. (For possible answers see Teacher information).

Additional activities

- Group endangered species by their main reason for decline (e.g. habitat loss, hunting). Create a chart in small groups to present or display. (logical–mathematical)
- Debate 'Human activities have no effect on animal populations!' (verbal–linguistic)
- Design a poster to show 'How we can help' endangered animals in small groups. Present the finished poster to the class. (visual–spatial)

CURRICULUM LINKS			
England	English	KS2	• talk effectively as members of a group by making contributions relevant to the topic and taking turns in discussion
Northern Ireland	English	KS2	• participate in informal discussions
Republic of Ireland	English	5th/ 6th	• converse freely and confidently on a range of topics, and discuss issues of major concern
Scotland	English	D	• work independently as a group and discuss tasks
Wales	English	KS2	• make a range of contributions in discussions

CAN WE FIX IT?

You will discuss and record problems facing endangered species and possible solutions.

people wise

1 Discuss with your group the impact the human activities listed could have on animal or plant species, why they were used, ways these problems can be addressed and, if possible, prevented.

Developing land	*Damage caused*	*Reasons why*
	Can we fix it?	

Introducing species	*Damage caused*	*Reasons why*
	Can we fix it?	

Logging forests	*Damage caused*	*Reasons why*
	Can we fix it?	

Hunting/Exploitation	*Damage caused*	*Reasons why*
	Can we fix it?	

Pollution	*Damage caused*	*Reasons why*
	Can we fix it?	

2 Discuss with the group other human activities that cause harm to the environment. List them on the back of the sheet.

TEACHERS NOTES

The multiple intelligence focus for this task is intrapersonal.

An intrapersonal child understands and analyses his/her thoughts and feelings.
He/She learns best through individual activities.

Objective

- Plans and writes an article for a wildlife magazine on endangered animals.

Preparation

- Children need access to resources for research information on endangered animals.
- A variety of magazines for viewing, discussion and analysis.

Teacher information

- Allow children to view magazines and discuss the layout of articles; e.g. colours, styles, headlines (size and wording), catchy phrases, visual effects on page, article length, photo/artwork, audience appeal, target audience.
- Discuss important parts of an article.
  - Headline: attention-grabbing, short; varies in print size according to article importance
  - Visuals: photographs, maps, diagram, artwork– to focus readers' attention and add story content
  - Introduction
  - Main details: who? what? where? when? how? why?
  - Incidental detail/Conclusion/Summary/Opinion

CURRICULUM LINKS			
England	Literacy	Yr 6	• use the styles and conventions of journalism to report on events
Northern Ireland	English	KS2	• write in different forms, e.g. reports, and develop control of the different conventions
Republic of Ireland	English	5th/6th	• write in a wide variety of genres, e.g. reports
Scotland	English	D	• produce a variety of different kinds of writing
Wales	English	KS2	• write in a range of non-fiction forms, e.g. reports

Answers

- Teacher check

Additional activities

- Make a class magazine with the completed articles. (interpersonal)
- Write a letter to a conservation group (e.g. WWF) to find out more about endangered animals and how their fund helps. (verbal–linguistic)
- Write a poem using the letters of 'endangered species', or haiku or shape poem to suit the topic. (verbal–linguistic)

WILDLIFE MAGAZINE

self wise

You have been chosen to write an article for a wildlife magazine on the plight of endangered species.

1 Use the boxes below to plan your article.

Catchy title/Headline

Introduction

Draw or glue picture here

Points of interest

Conclusion/Summary

Picture/Photo ideas

Layout/Style ideas

Present your finished story on a separate sheet so it looks like a magazine article.

ENDANGERED SPECIES – MY SELF-ASSESSMENT

After completing this unit, I was able to …

word wise	find meanings for suitable endangered species to represent environmental status terms.	☆ ☆ ☆ ☆ ☆
logic wise	research and report on an endangered species.	☆ ☆ ☆ ☆ ☆
nature wise	recognise and research the problems of introduced species in Australia.	☆ ☆ ☆ ☆ ☆
picture wise	construct a 3-D informational cube reporting on an endangered species.	☆ ☆ ☆ ☆ ☆
body wise	write and perform a short skit of conversations.	☆ ☆ ☆ ☆ ☆
music wise	work with a group to write and perform a short play with musical accompaniment.	☆ ☆ ☆ ☆ ☆
people wise	record group discussions on the impact of human activities on endangered species.	☆ ☆ ☆ ☆ ☆
self wise	plan and write an article for a wildlife magazine.	☆ ☆ ☆ ☆ ☆

What I learnt

DISASTERS

Informational text........................ ☐   ☐ .... Which medal?

Newspaper article .... ☐   ☐ ....A sad song

Escape boat .... ☐   ☐ .... What would you do?

Weather..................................... ☐   ☐ ....Information chart

Cartoon .... ☐   ☐ ....My self-assessment

What I know	What I want to know

Keywords

Name: Date:

DISASTERS OVERVIEW

Verbal–Linguistic

- Debate 'Disasters have a place in the natural order of life'.
- Write a lyric poem, expressing feelings about a recent European disaster.
- Write an eyewitness recount of a shipping disaster.
- Research and write a report on a disaster and how it affected its surroundings.
- Use the Internet to research facts and figures relating to well-documented and remembered disasters in history.
- Perform a choral speech of a poem about a disaster.

Logical–Mathematical

- Compare and contrast two recent human-created disasters.
- Predict the probability of the occurrence of specific disasters using current, available data.
- Create a time line of world disasters.
- Look for patterns of where and when particular types of disasters have occurred.
- Rank a series of disasters according to severity; e.g. number of casualties, homeless, duration of after-effects.
- Complete logical puzzles or brain teasers with a disaster theme.
- Collect mathematical facts about a disaster; e.g. *Titanic* – number of lifeboats, passengers, time to sink.
- Map locations of earthquakes throughout the world.
- Discover how the intensity of an earthquake is measured. Rank earthquakes using this scale.

Naturalist

- Walk around the school and identify possible risk factors. What can be done to make the area safer?
- Follow weather patterns to identify forecasts of storms or droughts.
- Research endangered animals, why their extinction would be a disaster and how humans have contributed.
- Research the effects of drought.
- Research why natural disasters occur and what could be done to prevent them or warn people easily enough to avoid injury.
- Discuss how the weather has played a part in human-created disasters.

Visual–Spatial

- View images of different types of disasters and use them to paint or draw abstract images which express feelings about the disaster.
- Use a variety of materials to make collages depicting the aftermath of a fire.
- Locate and highlight disaster spots on a map of the world. Display news reports and pictures to provide relevant information.
- Prepare a chart telling people what they should do in case of a natural disaster. Include illustrations.
- Make a poster warning people of a possible disaster.

DISASTERS OVERVIEW

Bodily–Kinaesthetic

- Design a game which demonstrates how to respond in an emergency.
- List movement words associated with particular disasters.
- Visit a local ambulance or fire station.
- Investigate procedures for different emergencies.
- Visit a museum to view artefacts from shipwrecks.
- Re-enact the probable events leading to a famous disaster.

Musical–Rhythmic

- Listen to film soundtracks that accompany disaster scenes. Compare the music and the types of disasters.
- Create a soundscape (voice + sound) about a disaster, working towards a climax and resolution.
- Use percussion instruments to simulate a storm, starting with raindrops, building to a roaring storm and abating.
- List sound words associated with different disasters.
- Create group movement pieces to music from a film disaster scene.
- Listen to Chopin's *Raindrop* prelude, Opus 28, No. 15.

Interpersonal

- Interview a partner for a TV news item as a witness to a disaster. Describe how he or she survived.
- Work in a small group to formulate an action plan to deal with a gas leak at a school.
- Discuss views on particular disasters and what should have been done to reduce the risks. Prepare a summary of the group's ideas.
- Research to find the cause of earthquakes, volcanoes and avalanches and discuss the effects they have.

Intrapersonal

- View documentaries about disasters and prepare a detailed report for other children to read; e.g. Krakatoa, Vesuvius, *Exxon Valdez*, Hiroshima, *Titanic*, *Hindenburg*.
- Research disasters in space. Compare two.
- Research the effects of an oil spill on the ocean and its marine life. Write a detailed report.
- Research the effects of garden fertilisers in waterways. Write a detailed summary and provide suggestions to reduce the problem.
- Research information about a disaster hero.
- Read disaster scenarios and decide what to do in each situation.
- Write their feelings as a *Titanic* passenger who has just heard the ship is about to sink.

DISASTERS
INFORMATIONAL TEXT

Natural disasters represent a powerful force of nature. They can happen at any time or in any place. Here are some examples of possible causes of natural disasters.

HURRICANES – are powerful rotating storms that form over warm ocean waters. They are called hurricanes when they start over the Atlantic Ocean; *typhoons* when they form over the western Pacific Ocean; and *cyclones* when starting over the Indian or Southern Pacific oceans. With heavy rains and wind gusts of over 120 km/h, hurricanes can cause great damage. They have an 'eye' of calm winds surrounded by strong thunderstorms, high winds and heavy rain. They can also produce high waves and damage to coastal areas.

FLOODS – are the most common natural disaster. A flood occurs when a body of water rises and overflows onto normally dry land. It can happen during heavy rains, when rivers overflow, when oceans come on shore, when snow melts in the mountains or when dams break. Floods that happen very quickly are called *'flash floods'*.

TORNADOES – are violent whirling winds, often called *'twisters'*. They look like a large black funnel hanging down from a storm cloud. The narrow end moves over the earth and acts like a giant vacuum cleaner. A tornado over water – such as a lake or ocean – is called a *'waterspout'*. Tornadoes generally only last a few minutes but can cause massive destruction.

DROUGHT – is a pattern of unusually dry weather or lack of rainfall over a long period. Droughts affect more people than any other disaster. The high temperatures and little rainfall affect crop growing and can cause widespread starvation, as has happened in some areas of Africa. *Dust storms* can also result from droughts.

TSUNAMI – is a Japanese word meaning a long, low sea wave. They are started by *volcanic eruptions*, coastal *earthquakes* or undersea *landslides*. Tsunamis have killed over 50 000 people in the last century. They can race across the ocean at 800–960 km/h. In deep sea, the waves are quite small, but as they approach the coastline they can increase to a height of 100 m or more. Tsunamis, often wrongly referred to as *'tidal waves'*, have nothing to do with the tides.

FIRES – are often started through natural forces such as *earthquakes* or *lightning*. *Bushfires* are a constant threat to countries like Australia. Hot, dry summer months and strong winds can lead to fires which rage through dry vegetation.

EARTHQUAKES – are the shaking of the earth caused by pieces of the earth's crust suddenly shifting. This movement is often felt over long distances, but generally lasts less than a minute. An earthquake in the mountains can cause an *avalanche* or, in the oceans, a *tsunami*. Earthquakes are recorded on the Richter scale, which measures the shockwaves through the earth.

VOLCANOES – are places in the earth's surface through which molten rock (magma) and gas erupt. Volcanic eruptions can be violent, spilling hot lava, ash, dust, gas and cinders over large areas. Volcanoes can be active, dormant (resting) or extinct. Volcanic eruptions can also trigger *tsunamis, earthquakes, floods, rockfalls* and *mudflows*.

AVALANCHES – are large masses of snow and ice that detach from mountain slopes and slide or fall suddenly downwards.

DISASTERS
INFORMATIONAL TEXT

Disasters, whether natural or created by humans, have all taken their toll and played major roles in our history. Here are a few examples.

79 AD
Mt Vesuvius erupts, burying the cities of Pompeii, Herculaneum and Stabiae.

1330s-1340s
The Black Death or bubonic plague strikes Europe and Asia. Spread by infected fleas and rats, it kills 75 million people over 12 years.

1362
The Great Drowning in Holland, when the dykes holding back floodwaters break, kills 30 000 people.

1600s-1700s
Sixty million Europeans die from the spread of smallpox.

1666
The Great Fire of London starts in a bakery and burns for five days, leaving 200 000 homeless and six dead.

1755
Most severe earthquake recorded destroys the city of Lisbon in Portugal, killing 70 000.

1815
The volcano Tambora near Java erupts, killing 12 000. A further 75 000 die from the famine resulting from the explosion.

1871
The Great Chicago Fire leaves 90 000 people homeless and 300 dead. The city is rebuilt by 1875.

1885
The volcanic island of Krakatoa suddenly explodes, killing 40 000 people. It is thought to be the loudest sound ever heard on earth.

1887
The Yellow River (Huang He) floods in China, killing 900 000 people.

1902
Mt Pelee in the West Indies erupts, destroying the city of St Pierce and killing 40 000. It is still an active volcano today.

1906
A violent typhoon hits Hong Kong with winds of more than 160 km/h, killing 10 000.

1912
The luxury ocean liner *Titanic* sinks on its maiden voyage from London to New York after it hits an iceberg. Fifteen hundred passengers and crew are lost.

1933
A tsunami caused by an earthquake kills 3000 people on the island of Honshu, Japan, and destroys 9000 homes.

1936
The *Hindenburg*—the largest airship built—explodes and crashes, killing 35.

1951
Two hundred and fifty people are killed and more than 45 000 trapped when a series of avalanches thunder through the Swiss, Austrian and Italian Alps.

1970
A cyclone-driven tsunami hits the Bay of Bengal, killing over 200 000 people. More than 100 000 are missing.

1974
Cyclone Tracy nearly destroys the city of Darwin in Australia, causing a mass evacuation and leaving 65 dead.

1984
Poisonous gases escape from a pesticide factory in Bhopal, India, killing 6300.

1986
The worst nuclear reactor disaster occurs in Chernobyl (USSR, now Ukraine), contaminating 28 000 square kilometres and exposing 1.7 million people to radiation.

The *Challenger* space shuttle explodes 73 seconds after lift-off, killing all seven on board.

1988
A terrorist bomb explodes aboard a plane over Lockerbie, Scotland, killing all 259 passengers and 11 people on the ground.

1989
The oil tanker *Exxon Valdez* runs aground in Prince William Sound, Alaska, spilling oil that pollutes 2400 km of coastline.

1991
A cyclone in south-east Bangladesh kills 131 000 and leaves nine million homeless. Many survivors die from hunger or waterborne diseases.

1995
Kobe, Japan, is hit by an earthquake, killing 5500 and leaving 300 000 homeless. The damage costs more than $100 billion.

1998
Many villages are wiped out in Papua New Guinea when three tsunamis kill over 2000 people and leave many more homeless.

2001
Terrorists fly two passenger jets into the twin towers of the World Trade Centre in New York on 11 September, killing 2752 people.

2003
An earthquake registering 6.6 hits the city of Bam in Iran. Despite the efforts of rescue teams from 21 countries, there are few survivors found in the rubble. Over 25 000 people die and tens of thousands are left homeless.

The multiple intelligence focus for this task is verbal–linguistic.

A verbal–linguistic child thinks in words.
He/She learns best through activities involving reading, writing and speaking.

Objective

- Analyses and writes newspaper articles about disasters.

Preparation

- Ensure that children have some understanding of disasters, both natural and those caused by human actions.
- Brainstorm different types of disasters and encourage children to research information about any of particular, personal interest.
- Children should collect, read and study newspaper articles about disasters before commencing this task.
- Analyse some disaster reports using questions from the frameworks provided.

Teacher Information

- Newspapers aim to attract the reader's attention and sell copies by:
  - attention-catching headlines,
  - presenting the most important and sensational information first,
  - the subtle use of some emotive instead of neutral language,
  - appealing to the reader's emotions to elicit a response,
  - using language that most readers will understand,
  - explaining technical terms.
- Childrens' understanding of the differences between newspaper reports and other reports (e.g. scientific, financial) will be enhanced by comparisons using the above features.

CURRICULUM LINKS			
England	Literacy	Yr 5/6	• identify the features of recounted texts and use the style and conventions of journalism to report
Northern Ireland	English	KS2	• be aware of how the media present information and write in different forms
Republic of Ireland	English	5th/6th	• learn about the structure and function of parts of a newspaper and write in a range of genres
Scotland	English	C/D	• adjust reading approaches to the different way that information is presented in newspapers and produce a variety of different kinds of writing
Wales	English	KS2	• read and use newspapers and write in a range of non-fiction forms

Answers

Teacher check

Additional activities

- Write a newspaper article and a factual report (using headings, subheadings etc.) about the same disasters. How do these forms of writing differ?
- Write an acrostic poem about disasters generally or a particular disaster, using the letters in the word DISASTER.
- Write six questions you would like to ask a hero who survived a disaster.

NEWSPAPER ARTICLE

Task ● You will analyse and write a newspaper article about a disaster.

❶ (a) Choose a newspaper report about a disaster.

(b) Analyse the article using the framework below.

NEWSPAPER ARTICLE

What is the headline?_____

Is it short and attention-grabbing? (**yes**) (**no**)

Where did it happen? _____

When did it happen? _____

Who did it happen to? _____

How many people were involved? _____

What happened?

1. _____

2. _____

3. _____

4. _____

Why did it happen? _____

Could it have been avoided? _____

Was anyone or anything responsible? _____

What does the article want people to feel, think or do? _____

_____

How did it make you feel and think? _____

_____

Why was it a good or bad newspaper article? Why? _____

_____

Research information and then ...

❷ Write a newspaper article about a disaster of your choice. Use the questions from the framework above to help in planning your article. Provide an illustration or map if you think it is appropriate.

❸ Work with a partner to discuss and analyse your disaster report using the questions from the framework above.

(a) Did your article provide enough information to answer most of the questions? _____

(b) How did it make your partner feel?_____

(c) How do you think you could have improved your article? _____

The multiple intelligence focus for this task is logical–mathematical.

A logical–mathematical child thinks rationally and in abstractions.
He/She learns best through activities involving problem-solving, numbers and patterns.

Objectives

- Plans and calculates quantities of provisions for survival.
- Constructs a model boat to meet specific requirements.

Preparation

- Children will need plasticine and a variety of materials, including glue, tape, scissors, paper and bathroom and kitchen scales.
- Children need an agreed understanding of the facilities available on the island—e.g. shelter and water—and the expected weather conditions.

Teacher information

- Children should work in small groups of 2–4 to complete these tasks.
- It will take considerable time for children to decide on what they need to take and the quantities needed. They should realise the difficulties in packing, transporting and storing supplies, and that there is no refrigeration available.
- It is suggested that the children brainstorm to make categories of provisions—e.g. food, drink utensils, clothing, toiletries—prior to commencing their lists.

CURRICULUM LINKS

England	D & T	KS2	• complete design and make assignments using a range of materials
Northern Ireland	Technology	KS2	• plan what they are going to make and develop manipulative skills using a range of materials and tools
Republic of Ireland	Science	5th/ 6th	• communicate a design plan using sketches and models
Scotland	Technology	C	• complete designing and making tasks, following a plan
Wales	D & T	KS2	• plan the making of their product

Answers

Teacher check

Additional activities

- Analyse the factors which contributed to a shipping disaster.
- Create a time line of shipping disasters.
- Classify materials into floating/non-floating and research why some heavier materials can float.

ESCAPE BOAT

Task You will plan and calculate quantities of provisions needed for survival and construct a model boat to meet specific requirements.

You have been marooned on a deserted island with:
(write the names of those in your group)

Discuss with your group the things you will need to survive this disaster.

❶ Write your list in the space provided. Calculate the quantities of each item. For example, calculate how many litres of water you'll need if there isn't any available.

item	quantity	item	quantity	item	quantity

After three days, the boat you have been expecting doesn't arrive. You will need to build a boat, but first you need to make a model and test its capacity to carry you.

❷ Calculate the total weight of the people in your group and then estimate the weight of anything you decide to take with you. Divide your total by 1000 to get the weight your model must carry.

What weight will your model need to carry?

❸ Make a plasticine ball weighing the same number of grams.

❹ Build a seaworthy vessel capable of carrying your plasticine ball without sinking. Use any materials available.

❺ Draw and label a diagram of your boat below.

The multiple intelligence focus for this task is naturalist.

A naturalist child has an awareness of the patterns in nature.
He/She learns best through activities involving animals, plants and the environment.

Objective

- Understands that many disasters are caused by weather and that humans contribute to them.

Preparation

- Discuss what is meant by weather and the factors affecting it; e.g. latitude, altitude, distance from ocean, global warming.
- Discuss the term 'precipitation' and the different forms; e.g. rain, hail, snow.

Teacher information

- Natural disasters are caused by a contributing factor or a combination of factors associated with wind, precipitation or temperature.
- They include:
  - floods, tidal waves, tsunamis, snowstorms, hail, black ice, avalanches, rock falls, mud slides, landslides, hurricanes, cyclones, tornadoes, blizzards, dust storms, twisters, willy-willies, droughts, forest fires, lightning, electrical storms.
- Children need to consider the human costs associated with these disasters and to what degree humans contribute to natural disasters.
- Refer children to the informational text on page 26.

Answers

Teacher check

Additional activities

- List possible disasters on a car trip through a desert area. Plan a survival kit to assist in preventing or coping with these disasters.
- Research and list ways of keeping safe if caught outside in a thunder storm.
- What are some of the disasters that could threaten local flora and fauna? How could they be protected?

CURRICULUM LINKS			
England	Geography	KS2	• study environmental issues, caused by changes in the environment, e.g. drought
Northern Ireland	Geography	KS2	• learn about the effects of extreme weather upon the lives of people
Republic of Ireland	Geography	5th/ 6th	• develop simple understanding of some atmospheric features, e.g. weather disasters
Scotland	Society	D	• describe how extremes of weather and climate can disastrously affect people and places
Wales	Geography	KS2	• investigate ways in which people attempt to look after the present and safeguard the future environment through sustainable development, e.g. seeking to prevent floods

WEATHER

1 (a) List disasters caused by weather in the appropriate boxes.
(Note. Some disasters will need to be listed in more than one box.)

Water/Snow/Ice	Wind	Temperature

(b) Choose one disaster from each category listed above. What damage is caused and are there any ways it could be prevented? Record your ideas below.

Disaster	Damage caused	Prevention
_____ (water, snow, ice)		
_____ (wind)		
_____ (temperature)		

2 (a) Explain some of the ways humans are contributing to climatic change.

_____

_____

_____

(b) What do you think should be done about climate change?

_____

_____

_____

The multiple intelligence focus for this task is visual–spatial.

A visual–spatial child thinks in images, colours and shape.
He/She learns best through activities involving visualisation

Objective

- Draws a cartoon strip of a personal disaster.

Preparation

- Children should collect different examples of cartoons.
- Discuss the features of cartoons. What do they have in common? How do they vary? Are they all humorous?
- Do some have a serious message or comment?

Teacher information

- Cartoons are visual representations of situations or events. They can be political, humorous or make social comments. Some are purely visual, some have written text (direct speech). Cartoons often employ exaggeration and caricatures.
- Some children may choose not to include written tasks.
- Children may like to sign their cartoons and/or give them titles.
- Cartoon strips could be displayed or incorporated into a class disaster book.

CURRICULUM LINKS

England	English	KS2	• write in a range of forms
Northern Ireland	English	KS2	• write in different forms, e.g. comic strips
Republic of Ireland	English	5th/ 6th	• write in a wide variety of genres
Scotland	English	C	• use different forms of personal writing
Wales	English	KS2	• write in a range of forms, in response to a wide range of stimuli

Answers

Teacher check

Additional activities

- Use a wash of gold or sienna and black ink to portray a drought-stricken or burnt landscape.
- Watch and review a disaster film.
- Make a collage using various materials to depict the aftermath of a hurricane.

CARTOON

1 Think of a disaster that has involved you.

  (a) When did it happen? _____

  (b) Where were you? _____

  (c) Who else was involved? _____
_____

  (d) What was the initiating event? _____
_____

  (e) What happened? List the events.
_____
_____
_____
_____

  (f) How did it end? _____
_____
_____
_____

  (g) Could this disaster have been avoided?
_____

  (h) How do you feel about it now?
_____
_____
_____
_____
_____

2 Plan your cartoon strip by sketching your ideas below, then draw your cartoon on a separate sheet of paper.

The multiple intelligence focus for this task is bodily–kinaesthetic.

> A bodily–kinaesthetic child has good physical awareness.
> He/She learns best through 'hands-on' activities.

Objective

- Mimes a disaster survivor scenario.

Teacher information

- Encourage children to plan the scenario that precedes their disaster and to include this context in their mimes.
- The emphasis needs to be on clarifying where they are, who they are and what happens to them and their feelings. They need to focus on making the audience aware of what happened by **showing**, not **telling**.

Answers

None required

Additional activities

- Make a volcano model that explodes.
  You need ...

  - modelling clay, vinegar, baking soda, red food colouring, flat tray, toilet tissue/cardboard tube.

- Use modelling clay to build a solid volcano on the tray. Make an opening at the top for the tube. Fill the tube with baking soda and add a few drops of colouring. Pour vinegar into tube slowly and move away. Watch the volcano erupt!

- Use body language and facial expressions to show reactions and feelings during a disaster.

- Investigate the causes of volcanoes. (verbal–linguistic)

Preparation

- Children need to be aware of the need to use different parts of their bodies in a mime and the importance of facial expressions.
- Provide opportunities for children to practise miming different feelings.

CURRICULUM LINKS			
England	Literacy	Yr 6	• create, adapt and sustain different roles in groups
Northern Ireland	English	KS2	• improvise a scene based on imagination
Republic of Ireland	English	5th/ 6th	• use mime to convey ideas, reactions and emotions
Scotland	Drama	D	• decide, from their knowledge of their role, how the character would react non-verbally in varying situations and build appropriate gesture and movement into the situation
Wales	English	KS2	• participate in a wide range of drama activities

WHICH MEDAL?

Task ● You will work in small groups to mime disaster survivor scenarios for others to identify.

1 (a) In small groups, plan then mime one of the survivor scenarios engraved on the medals.

(b) Ask your audience (another small group or the whole class) to award your group the appropriate medal.

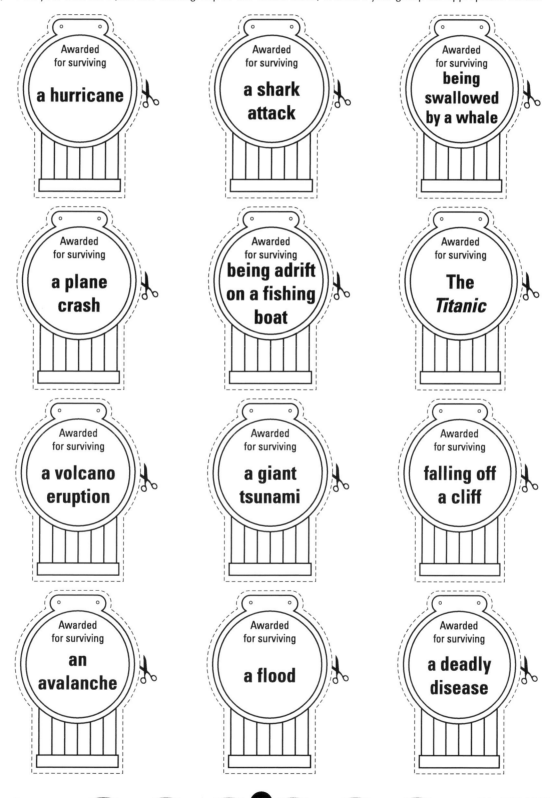

Awarded for surviving **a hurricane**

Awarded for surviving **a shark attack**

Awarded for surviving **being swallowed by a whale**

Awarded for surviving **a plane crash**

Awarded for surviving **being adrift on a fishing boat**

Awarded for surviving **The *Titanic***

Awarded for surviving **a volcano eruption**

Awarded for surviving **a giant tsunami**

Awarded for surviving **falling off a cliff**

Awarded for surviving **an avalanche**

Awarded for surviving **a flood**

Awarded for surviving **a deadly disease**

The multiple intelligence for this task is musical–rhythmic.

> A musical–rhythmic child has an awareness of music and sound.
> He/She learns best through activities involving music or rhythms.

Objective

- Matches songs with disasters and writes a song about a disaster, set to a familiar tune.

Preparation

- The class collates lists of disaster film theme songs and listens to them.
- Discuss the feelings these songs evoke.
- Discuss how the tune and lyrics create these effects.

Teacher information

- Children can work in small groups to listen and write down the lyrics of disaster songs.
- You may wish to consider and discuss some of the following:
  - ~ **the lyrics** – rhyme, rhythm, word length etc.
  - ~ **the tune** – tempo, range, beat, rhythm etc.
  - ~ **instruments used** – other sound effects, volume etc.
  - ~ **vocalist** – voice, range, volume, timing, expression etc.
- Children may prefer to work with a partner or in a small group to create their songs.

CURRICULUM LINKS			
England	Music	KS2	• complete a range of musical activities that integrate performing, composing and appraising
Northern Ireland	Music	KS2	• combine and use elements of music to express their own ideas and create mood and atmosphere
Republic of Ireland	Music	5th/6th	• invent and perform pieces that show an increasing awareness and control of musical elements
Scotland	Music	C	• invent short musical pieces conveying mood or atmosphere
Wales	Music	KS2	• compose and arrange music in response to a range of stimuli and to produce specific mood or atmosphere

Answers

1. 'Ring a ring a rosie' – The bubonic plague

   'The morning after' – *Poseidon Adventure*

   'London bridge' – destruction of a bridge

   'My heart will go on' – *Titanic*

   'Rain, rain go away' – sinking of the Spanish armada
2. Teacher check
3. Teacher check

Additional activities

- Children, in small or large groups, select a disaster film theme song to learn and perform. They may consider wearing appropriate costumes.
- Categorise disaster films as real or imaginary. Select one imaginary film. What made it seem real? (logical–mathematical)
- Research the differences between any true story and the film story. (intrapersonal)

A SAD SONG

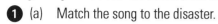

Task You will match well-known songs to disasters and write a disaster song set to a familiar tune.

For hundreds of years, songs have been composed about disasters.
Today, many films about disasters (real and imaginary) have well-known songs.

1 (a) Match the song to the disaster.

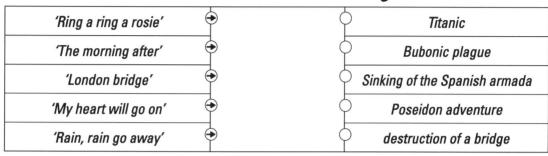

'Ring a ring a rosie'		Titanic
'The morning after'		Bubonic plague
'London bridge'		Sinking of the Spanish armada
'My heart will go on'		Poseidon adventure
'Rain, rain go away'		destruction of a bridge

(b) Do all these songs sound sad?   **yes**   **no**

(c) What makes a song sound sad? _____

_____

_____

_____

_____

2 (a) What is one tune you know well from the list above, another disaster song, or any tune you like?

_____

_____

_____

(b) Sing and clap the rhythm of this song.

3 (a) What is a disaster you know about that interests you?

_____

_____

(b) Write a song in the space provided, set to the tune you selected.

(c) Give your song a suitable title.

(d) Practise singing your song. Add appropriate sound effects and perform it to the class.

The multiple intelligence focus of this task is interpersonal.

An interpersonal child enjoys being in groups or teams.
He/She learns best through activities involving working with others.

Objective

- Cooperates to plan and prioritise actions to avoid disaster in a flood and a house fire.

Preparation

- Discuss ways of working cooperatively to complete tasks; for example: listening to others, taking turns, valuing all opinions, reaching consensus, delegating specific tasks, managing disputes, conflict resolution.

- Advise children of the different research resources available to them.

Teacher information

- The process is equally as important as the product in this activity and children should be aware of this. A group evaluation sheet can be used to emphasis the importance of working well collaboratively.

For example:

How well did we work together?				
Name	listened to others	spoke politely	good ideas	worked hard

CURRICULUM LINKS			
England	PSHE	KS2	• know basic emergency aid procedures and where to get help
Northern Ireland	Personal development*	KS2	• have a pro-active and responsible approach to safety, know basic emergency procedures and where and how to seek help (* proposed curriculum)
Republic of Ireland	SPHE	5th/ 6th	• develop an awareness of health and safety and know what to do in the event of an accident
Scotland	Health	C	• demonstrate safe ways of responding to risks to health and personal safety
Wales	PSE	KS2	• recognise how to be safe and what to do when feeling unsafe

- Refer children to the informational text on pages 26 – 27.

Answers

Teacher check

Additional activities

- Work in a small group to develop an action plan to deal with a fire caused by a frying pan.

- Formulate a list of potential dangers in a home. Work cooperatively in small groups to suggest ways to avoid a disaster.

- Research which electrical appliances should be switched off during a storm and why.

WHAT WOULD YOU DO?

Task • You will work in a small group to decide on priorities and actions to avoid disaster in a flood and a house fire.

Your group has been stranded by floodwater which is still rising slowly.
The power is off, it is cold and the water supply may soon become contaminated.

1 Discuss each problem and decide what you will do about it.

(a)	drinking water
(b)	food
(c)	keeping warm
(d)	keeping dry
(e)	lighting
(f)	seeking help
(g)	being scared

2 Discuss and decide the five most important things to tell a child who wakes up with a strong smell of smoke in his or her bedroom. Start each list with the most important instruction.

House fire	
Do	*Don't*
1.	1.
2.	2.
3.	3.
4.	4.
5.	5.

3 Share and discuss your ideas with other groups.

The multiple intelligence focus for this task is intrapersonal.

> An intrapersonal child understands and analyses his/her thoughts and feelings.
> He/She learns best through individual activities.

Objective

- Researches information to complete a chart comparing six world disasters.

Teacher information

- Refer children to the information text on page 27 as one possible source to use in completing the chart.
- Suggest that children formulate some inferential questions instead of only literal ones, requiring their partners to 'read and think', instead of just reading to find answers.

Answers

1. Teacher check
2. Teacher check

Additional activities

- Read books about children's lives during the disaster of war, then write a personal account expressing thoughts and feelings.
- Which world disaster was the worst? Why?
- Write an eyewitness report of a flood.

Preparation

- Discuss the factors about disasters that interest individual children; for example; cause(s), nature, casualties, time, place.

CURRICULUM LINKS			
England	Literacy	Yr 5	• locate information confidently and efficiently
Northern Ireland	English	KS2	• engage with a range of texts, e.g. non-fiction materials and read for information
Republic of Ireland	English	5th/6th	• explore appropriate non-fiction texts for various purposes
Scotland	English	C	• read for information, including developing the ability to scan
Wales	English	KS2	• read and use a wide range of sources of non-fiction information

INFORMATION CHART

1 Research facts about six disasters to complete this chart.

Disaster	*Natural*	*Human*	*When*	*Where*	*Loss of life*	*Damage*	*Interesting facts*

2 (a) Write five questions about the information on your chart on a separate sheet of paper.

   (b) Ask a partner to answer your questions, using your chart as a reference.

DISASTERS – MY SELF-ASSESSMENT

After completing this unit, I was able to …

word wise	analyse and write newspaper articles.	☆ ☆ ☆ ☆ ☆
logic wise	calculate provisions for a survival situation and construct a model boat to specific requirements.	☆ ☆ ☆ ☆ ☆
nature wise	understand that many disasters are caused by weather and that humans contribute to them.	☆ ☆ ☆ ☆ ☆
picture wise	draw a cartoon strip of a personal disaster.	☆ ☆ ☆ ☆ ☆
Body wise	mime a disaster survivor scenario.	☆ ☆ ☆ ☆ ☆
music wise	match songs and disasters, and write a song about a disaster set to a familiar tune.	☆ ☆ ☆ ☆ ☆
people wise	cooperate to plan and prioritise actions to avoid disasters in a flood and in a house fire.	☆ ☆ ☆ ☆ ☆
self wise	research information to complete a chart comparing six world disasters.	☆ ☆ ☆ ☆ ☆

What I learnt

ANCIENT CIVILISATIONS

Informational text........................ ☐   ☐ ....Mayan household

Terrifying Titans........................ ☐   ☐ .... The rhythm of a dead city

Mayan mathematicians .... ☐   ☐ ....Atlantis—myth or reality?

Slash and burn! .... ☐   ☐ .... Daily life in Atlantis

Great glyphs! .... ☐   ☐ ....My self-assessment

What I know	What I want to know

Keywords

Name:	Date:

ANCIENT CIVILISATIONS OVERVIEW

Verbal–Linguistic

- Learn words from ancient languages such as Latin.
- Write about a day in the life of a slave in an ancient city.
- Investigate the origins of words.
- Create a quiz about one or more ancient civilisations for other children to complete.
- Research a legend or myth to retell in written or spoken form.
- Write the biography of an ancient hero.
- Create a crossword puzzle consisting of words relevant to an information text about an ancient civilisation.
- Conduct an interview with a child from an ancient civilisation.
- Write a recipe for a meal from an ancient civilisation.
- Write a conversation between two children living in an ancient civilisation.
- Research lesser-known ancient civilisations, such as that of Ancient Japan.
- Write a poem about a special event in ancient history.

Visual–Spatial

- Children imagine they have travelled in time to Ancient Greece. What do they see?
- Make replicas of toys that would have been played with by children in ancient times, such as clay animals and spinning tops.
- Locate and colour-code ancient civilisations on a world map.
- Design a 'tourist brochure' for an ancient civilisation.
- View Ancient Egyptian hieroglyphics. Design their own hieroglyphics and make an alphabet.
- Research and draw the clothing worn by people living in an ancient civilisation.
- Research and illustrate cooking utensils or artefacts from an ancient civilisation.
- Draw or recreate jewellery worn in a specific ancient civilisation.
- Create a visual representation as a report about an ancient civilisation.
- Create a map of a typical town or village in an ancient civilisation.
- Watch films representing ancient times, for example *Troy* and *Ben Hur* (Caution: check classifications.)

Logical–Mathematical

- Given a key, interpret lines of hieroglyphics.
- Compare the structure of an ancient calendar to the one currently in use.
- Compare and contrast ancient civilisations using a semantic grid.
- Study Roman numerals.
- Research the monetary system used in a specific ancient civilisation.
- Categorise information about two or three ancient civilisations under selected headings.
- Investigate the use of the abacus or Roman numerals and their influence on modern civilisations.
- Create a time line showing the development of a civilisation from ancient to modern times.

Naturalist

- Research to find out the importance of the cat to the Ancient Egyptians.
- Write facts about animals and plants in ancient times; e.g. 'Which animals were kept as pets? What fruits and vegetables were eaten?'
- Explain/Write the procedure for creating paper from papyrus in the same manner that the Ancient Egyptians did.
- Compare the physical environment around an ancient civilisation to that of the same area in the present day.
- Investigate the role played by domestic animals in an ancient civilisation.
- Research food production in an ancient civilisation.
- Discuss how water, landforms and climate influenced aspects of civilisations, such as buildings, food production and trade.
- Record how natural phenomena, such as earthquakes, tidal waves and volcanic eruptions, affected specific ancient civilisations.

ANCIENT CIVILISATIONS OVERVIEW

Bodily–Kinaesthetic

- Create a dance based on pictures of celebrations shown on ancient murals.
- Set up and participate in some of the ancient sports that are still included in the modern Olympics, such as discus and the javelin.
- Participate in games the American Plains Indians took part in, such as archery contests, hoop and ball rolling and lacrosse.
- Study and learn dance movements used in Aboriginal Australian culture.
- Construct a pyramid or other significant ancient building or monument.
- Research sports and games from an ancient civilisation and select one to learn or teach to class members.
- Mime daily activities from a particular civilisation for class members to guess.

Musical–Rhythmic

- Invite guest musicians to play instruments that would have been used in ancient times; e.g. harps, pipes, lutes, lyres.
- Create music involving drumbeats as used by native American Indian tribes.
- Research the musical instruments of an ancient civilisation.
- Write a cinquain, haiku or rhythmic poem which relates to an ancient civilisation.
- Compare and contrast music used in particular civilisations.
- Create sound to add to a presentation about life in a particular civilisation.

Interpersonal

- Create a detailed presentation of a chosen ancient civilisation, using written and graphic methods decided by the group.
- Work with a group to reconstruct an ancient village.
- Work in a group to write a daily menu for people living in an ancient civilisation.
- Present a research project about an ancient civilisation, with each group member selecting and reporting about a different aspect of everyday life.
- Write a cooperative story about a child living in an ancient civilisation. Each group member contributes a page or chapter to the story.

Intrapersonal

- Research to find out what your life would have been like as a child living in ancient Rome.
- Research various theories about how the pyramids were built. Present a written and graphic exploration for the class to study.
- Research the role of women in particular civilisations.
- Research housing of a particular civilisation and time.
- Write a personal diary for a child living in an ancient civilisation.
- Write a reflection comparing life then and now.
- Select a different civilisation from those given to research and report about.

ANCIENT CIVILISATIONS
INFORMATIONAL TEXT

The Mayan civilisation

The Mayan people lived around 250 AD in an area of land covering Mexico, Guatemala, Belize, Honduras and El Salvador. This land was called *Mesoamerica*.

The Maya were skilled farmers who produced a variety of *crops,* including maize, squash, beans, chilli peppers, amaranth, manioc, cacao, tobacco, cotton and sisal for rope and heavy cloth. Precious gems and minerals such as obsidian, jade, cinnabar and haematite were found in the volcanic highlands and used for trading. The rivers were vital to transport goods and people.

As well as building large reservoirs for storing rainwater underground, the Maya built temple-pyramids and palaces. The Maya were proficient *weavers* and *potters*. They also cleared routes through swamps and jungles to encourage trade.

Because of the geographical spread of the Mayan civilisation, many *languages* evolved which were related but also distinctive.

The Maya believed in many *gods* — more than 166! There was also thought to be one supreme deity, called Itzamna, who invented writing, and was the patron of the arts and sciences. His wife was called Ix Chel. She was the goddess of weaving, medicine and childbirth and the ancient goddess of the moon. Often, religious ceremonies were accompanied by bloodletting, animal or human sacrifice or burning of incense.

The Maya developed a complicated *writing* system consisting of 800 individual signs or *glyphs*. Their *counting system* was also very intricate, consisting of three symbols: a dot (which had a value of one), a bar (representing five) and a shell, representing zero. Some number signs were also depicted in the form of glyphs.

Mayan *art* depicted the lifestyle and culture. The art consisted of sketches, tracings, charts, diagrams and painting on paper or plaster, carvings in wood and stone, clay and stucco models and terracotta figurines from moulds. They also created ornaments from metal, although this was not common as resources were rare. Many of the artworks were commissioned by kings and rulers to ensure their place in history.

Weavers embroidered diamond motifs, which represented cosmological patterns, on their wares .

Many other *interesting facts* are known about the Maya civilisation:

The Maya calendar system was extremely accurate and complicated.

Astronomy played an important part in the Mayan culture.

Crossed-eyes were highly prized, so to encourage this trait, parents hung beads over the noses of their children.

Parents liked to shape the skulls of their children into a cone shape. It is thought that this was to represent the shape of an ear of corn. This was done either incidentally, as a result of strapping babies to a cradle board, or by squeezing their heads into a cone shape.

The Maya filed their teeth into a T shape or point, or inlaid them with small, round pieces of jade or pyrite.

It is unclear why the Mayan civilisation *died out,* but a number of reasons have been suggested, including excessive warfare, food and water shortages and overpopulation.

ANCIENT CIVILISATIONS
INFORMATIONAL TEXT

The lost city of Atlantis

This powerful, ancient civilisation, considered by many to be a *myth*, is alleged to have been submerged by a devastating *earthquake* and *tsunami* thousands of years ago.

Many rumours exist about its destruction, including the belief that it was destroyed in the biblical flood of Noah. Others believe that Atlantis was a powerful nation whose people became so corrupted by greed that Zeus destroyed it.

The capital city of Atlantis is believed to have consisted of a series of concentric walls and canals. At the centre was a hill on which a temple to *Poseidon* was built, with a gold statue of the god driving six winged horses.

Some sources state that Poseidon, the god of the sea, entrusted the rule of this island domain to his eldest son, *Atlas the Titan*, who became the personification of the mountains or pillars which held up the sky.

Cities, large *pyramid-shaped* buildings, larger than any in the known world, and a complex system of streets, are alleged to have been found during archaeological expeditions. Many statues are believed to have been used. *Domes*, columns, canals, rectangular buildings, unidentified metal objects and artefacts are also alleged to have been found. A statue holding a 'mysterious' *crystal* is rumoured to have been discovered, as well as a harbour-like complex. These all contribute to the speculation about the existence of Atlantis.

Rumours vary about the actual location and description of Atlantis.

The exact *location* of Atlantis is hard to determine, because the continent is believed to have split into many sections which moved in many directions.

Some people think that Atlantis existed at least 6000 years ago. Cyprus is thought to be a mountain top region of Atlantis or, according to *Plato* (an ancient philosopher), a continent in the Atlantic Ocean near the Straits of Gibraltar.

Some allege that Atlantis was part of the *Minoan* culture. The Minoans were a peaceful race, although they enjoyed bullfighting. This involved unarmed bullfighters wrestling and jumping over bulls. This ritual can be seen in Minoan artwork.

Atlanteans are believed to have been wealthy from commerce and advanced in scientific knowledge.

It is rumoured that the ancient Atlanteans used *crystals* extensively in their daily lives. The crystals were believed to amplify the energy which passed through them.

Other speculations suggest that Atlantis was really Crete—now a part of modern Greece. The island of *Santorinas*, located to the north of Crete, had a volcano at its centre, which blew apart around 1500 BC. When the volcano erupted, it is thought to have been four times as powerful as that of Krakatoa, causing a tsunami which destroyed all shipping and coastal towns within almost a kilometre.

If Atlantis existed as a part of Crete, then other aspects of life are known: women held important political positions, the culture was peaceful and ritualistic bullfighting was a popular sport.

Many *ancient writings* translated from the Aztecs and Maya, as well as from ancient Greece, mention Atlantis.

Ancient *maps* and Greek *documents* show the location of a large unknown island.

Perhaps we will never know for certain about the existence of the ancient civilisation of Atlantis. Nevertheless, archaeologists will continue to search for clues to the answer to this *ancient mystery*!

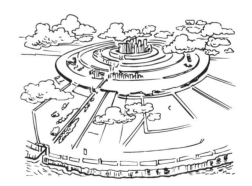

The multiple intelligence focus for this task is verbal–linguistic.

> A verbal–linguistic child thinks in words.
> He/She learns best through activities involving reading, writing and speaking.

Objective

- Researches and records information about Atlas.

Preparation

- Children should have read the background information about Atlas on the child information pages before commencing this activity.

- Children should have competent research skills to undertake this task.

Teacher information

- Children should use a variety of different sources to find their background information, including encyclopaedias, the Internet and library books. Different sources of information may give slightly different accounts about Atlas. Children should be aware that both Roman and Greek mythology have varying accounts. Teachers should accept both versions as valid research solutions.

- In Roman mythology, Atlas was a giant who led the Titans against the gods, including Jupiter. Jupiter was trying to take control of the world from his father, the Titan, Saturn. They fought for 10 years, after which Jupiter defeated his father and took over the world. Jupiter punished the Titans harshly. Atlas, as the leader, was forced to carry the sky on his shoulders. Atlas was married to Pleione. He was the father of Pleiades, Hyades and the Hesperides. The Hesperides were the guardians of a tree of golden apples that the Earth goddess Gaea gave to Juno, Jupiter's wife, as a wedding present. The location of the tree was a secret. Atlas was told by an oracle that a son of Jupiter would one day steal the apples. For this reason, Atlas did not welcome visitors. Because he was so inhospitable, Perseus showed him the Medusa's head, which turned Atlas to stone.

- In Greek mythology, Atlas was the son of Iapetus and Clymene, who were two of the 12 Titans. One day, Zeus fought against his father, Cronus, in order to rule the gods. Atlas joined Cronus and the Titans. They fought for 10 years (the Titanomachy) until finally Zeus defeated Cronus and took control. Zeus imprisoned the Titans in Tartarus and punished Atlas by giving him the task of holding up the sky. One myth involves Hercules. In his desire to be immortal, Hercules had to perform 12 labours. One labour was to pick the golden apples from a tree guarded by the Hesperides and the serpent, Laden. Hercules, with the help of Athena, held up the sky while Atlas picked the apples. Atlas thought he had been freed from his task of holding up the sky, but Hercules tricked him and Atlas returned to his task.

Answers

- Teacher check.

- Some Internet information may be found on:

  http://ancienthistory.about.com
  http://www.windows.ucar.edu

Additional activities

- Select another god from an ancient civilisation to write a biography on.

- Research to find out what trick Hercules played on Atlas to make him return to his task of holding up the sky.

- Research other gods found in Greek or Roman mythology and compare them.

CURRICULUM LINKS			
England	Literacy	Yr 5	• locate information confidently and efficiently and plan, compose, edit and refine non-chronological reports
Northern Ireland	English	KS2	• engage with a range of texts, e.g. non-fiction materials, read for information and write in different forms
Republic of Ireland	English	5th/6th	• explore appropriate non-fiction texts for various purposes and write in a wide range of genres
Scotland	English	C/D	• read for information, including developing the ability to scan and produce a variety of different kinds of writing
Wales	English	KS2	• read and use a wide range of sources of non-fiction information and write in a range of forms

TERRIFYING TITANS

Atlantis is believed to have been named after Atlas, a Greek god. Some sources state that Atlas, the Titan, was the son of the Titans Iapetus and Clymene, two of the 12 Titans. It is believed that Zeus waged a war against his father, Cronus, in order to rule the gods. Atlas fought on the side of the Titans and Cronus. After Zeus defeated Cronus, following a long 10-year war, he imprisoned the Titans and punished Atlas by making him hold up the sky.

1 Use a variety of resources to find information about Atlas. You may use the library, the Internet, class, home or community resources.

(a) List the sources of your information, including website addresses and specific book titles.

- _____
  _____

- _____
  _____

- _____
  _____

- _____
  _____

- _____
  _____

- _____
  _____

You will need to select a number of headings to categorise your information. These may include things such as parentage, background and interesting feats.

(b) The headings I have selected to record my information are:

- _____

- _____

- _____

- _____

- _____

- _____

(c) Write these headings on a sheet of paper and record your information under the relevant headings.

(d) Write a final copy of your report, using your information.

(e) Draw, copy or print from the computer any illustrations to enhance your report. Attach to the final copy of your report.

Often Greek and Roman mythology have similar gods with a slightly different version of their lives.

2 During your research you may have found slightly different forms of information about Atlas. List some of these.

_____

_____

_____

_____

_____

_____

The multiple intelligence focus for this task is logical–mathematical.

A logical–mathematical child thinks rationally and in abstractions.
He/She learns best through activities involving problem-solving, numbers and patterns.

Objective

- Solves number problems based on the Mayan number system and creates a number system of his/her own.

Preparation

- Children should have read the information about the Mayan mathematical system on page 48 before commencing this task.

- Children should be familiar with the word 'glyph' and, if possible, view pictures of some.

Teacher information

- The Mayan number system was very complicated. It consisted of three symbols: a dot representing a value of one, a bar representing five and a shell representing zero. These could be used in various combinations. Numbers were written from top to bottom, instead of horizontally.

- Head glyphs were also used as number signs. For example, the number one was often depicted as a young earth goddess, while two was represented by a god of sacrifice.

- To make numbering more complicated, numerical head glyphs were combined with dots, bars or shells.

CURRICULUM LINKS

England	Numeracy	Yr 5/6	• solve mathematical problems or puzzles, recognise and explain patterns
Northern Ireland	Maths	KS2	• recognise general patterns and relationships
Republic of Ireland	Maths	5th/6th	• identify relationships in number patterns
Scotland	Maths	C	• work with patterns and relationships
Wales	Maths	KS2	• interpret patterns which arise in numerical or practical situations

Answers

1. (a) 3   (b) 17   (c) 6   (d) 11   (e) 20   (f) 26
   (g) 38   (h) 60   (i) 31   (j) 22

2. Teacher check

3. Teacher check

4. Teacher check

5. Teacher check

Additional activities

- Categorise information about two ancient civilisations, using the same headings.

- Investigate the Mayan calendar and compare it to the one currently in use. Discuss the advantages and disadvantages of each.

- Investigate numbers which the Maya considered sacred and the reason for this.

MAYAN MATHEMATICIANS

In the Mayan numerical system

 = zero   ● = 1

—— = 5   = 18

 = 20

Numbers larger than 19 were represented in the same sequence, with a dot above for each group of 20. For example, 32 was represented as:

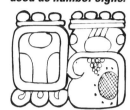

Head glyphs were also used as number signs.

1 Use this information to decipher the numbers below.

(a) ● ● ● _____   (b)  _____

(c) ● —— _____   (d) (two dots) _____

(e) _____   (f) ● —— _____

(g) _____   (h) _____

(i) _____   (j) _____

2 Write five more of your own and ask a class member to solve them.

(a) ☐ _____

(b) ☐ _____

(c) ☐ _____

(d) ☐ _____

(e) ☐ _____

3 Choose and draw three simple symbols to use in your number system. Give each of them a value.

4 Write some numbers in your numerical system below and ask a class member to decipher them.

(a) ☐ _____

(b) ☐ _____

(c) ☐ _____

(d) ☐ _____

(e) ☐ _____

5 Discuss how easy or difficult your number system was to decipher. How could it have been improved?

The multiple intelligence focus for this task is naturalist.

> A naturalist child has an awareness of the patterns in nature.
> He/She learns best through activities involving animals, plants and the environment.

Objective

- Identifies environmental problems and provides solutions.

Preparation

- Read and discuss the background information about the farming methods of the Maya to the children before commencing this activity.

Teacher information

- The Maya cleared forests to make more room for farming by using a method called *'slash and burn'*. This farming technique was also called 'milpa'. This meant that they cleared the land by cutting down and burning all the foliage in spring before the summer rains came. They poked sticks in the ground and planted seeds in the holes. They planted crops such as maize (corn), beans, squash, avocado pear, sweet potato, guava, chilli peppers, cocoa beans, vanilla beans, papaya, tomatoes and tobacco. They *terraced* slopes using stone walls and cleared the jungle for planting. Every two years, they moved their fields to new locations and allowed the old fields to lie fallow for 10 years before using them again *(crop rotation)*.

- It is thought that the destruction of the rainforest ecosystem was one possible reason for the disappearance of the Mayan civilisation. It is also a possible reason for the disappearance of some animals which depend on the rainforest for their existence.

CURRICULUM LINKS			
England	Geography	KS2	• study environmental issues, caused by changes in the environment and attempts to manage the environment sustainably
Northern Ireland	Geography	KS2	• know some of the ways in which people affect the environment, e.g. deforestation
Republic of Ireland	Geography	5th/ 6th	• recognise and investigate aspects of human activities which may have positive or adverse effects on environments, e.g. deforestation
Scotland	Society	D	• for a selected land use, describe possible effects, good and bad, on the environment, e.g. tropical forest clearance
Wales	Geography	KS2	• identify ways in which people affect the environment

Answers

1. Teacher check
2. Terracing; crop rotation; Teacher check
3. Teacher check
4. Teacher check
5. Teacher check

Additional activities

- List and research unusual animals found in the area where the Maya lived. These may include peccaries, tapirs, the peca, the agouti and quetzal.

- Create a typical Mayan menu involving tortillas or tamales with hot chocolate or atole. Write the procedures for creating the food. (verbal-linguistic)

- The Maya believed that the earth was flat and four-cornered, with each corner located at a cardinal point and having a different colour. East was red, north was white, west was black and south was yellow. The centre was green. Some Maya believed that the sky was multilayered and supported at the corners by four gods called 'Bacabs'. Others believed that the sky was supported by four trees of different colours and species. The green ceiba, or silk-cotton, was in the centre. Earth was thought to be the back of a giant crocodile, resting in a pool of lilies. Use this information to make a series of visual representations of the universe according to the Maya. (visual–spatial)

SLASH AND BURN!

Mayan farmers used a technique called 'slash and burn' to provide fields for farming.

1 Explain what 'slash and burn means'. _____

_____

_____

Is this a good method to gain farming land? (**yes**) (**no**)

Explain your reasons. _____

_____

_____

2 Describe two other methods the Maya used to create more farmland.

State your opinion of each farming technique.

(i) _____

_____

_____

_____

_____

(ii) _____

_____

_____

_____

_____

3 Complete the boxes. You may discuss these with a partner.

(a) Some ways to improve farmland that has been overused are:

(b) Some methods of gaining more farmland without damaging the environment are:

4 How can the environment be affected by the removal of areas of the rainforest?

_____

_____

_____

5 Some species of animals are disappearing due to the destruction of rainforest. The ozone layer is being affected as well. Can anything be done about this? Discuss in a group.

The multiple intelligence focus for this task is visual–spatial.

A visual-spatial child thinks in images, colours and shape.
He/She learns best through activities involving visualisation.

Objective

- Understands and creates glyphs to write his/her name.

Preparation

- Read and discuss the background information about glyphs to the children before commencing this activity. They also should understand the concept 'syllable' and be able to identify syllables in words or phrases.

Teacher information

- A glyph is a pictograph or hieroglyph. The Mayan hieroglyphs were very elaborate. Many were found as inscriptions in ruins and helped to explain the history and customs of the Maya.

- Epigraphers (people who decipher glyphs) have discovered that Mayan writing is constructed of symbols that represent whole words (logographs) or syllables consisting of consonant-vowel pairs or vowels. When writing in syllables, words are spelled out by signs ordered within glyph blocks. Within blocks, the symbols were ordered from top to bottom and left to right.

- A syllable is one segment of speech or sound in a word. For example, 'dog' has one syllable, while 'hous/es' has two, and 'un/der/stand' has three.

CURRICULUM LINKS			
England	History	KS2	• study the Maya, including their pictures, words and communication
Northern Ireland	History	KS2	• be aware of life in early times in the wider world
Republic of Ireland	History	5th/ 6th	• study Central and South American peoples, including their language
Scotland	Society	D	• study features of people from the ancient world
Wales	Art	KS2	• make images for a variety of purposes

Answers

- Teacher check

Additional activities

- View the glyphs created by other children to see if they are a correct indication of that person. Offer other suggestions.

- Draw a toy used by a Mayan child or a child from another ancient civilisation.

- View some ancient Egyptian hieroglyphics and design some of your own.

GREAT GLYPHS!

Task You will write and decipher names in glyphs.

 Mayan hieroglyphic writing was made up of symbols which represented whole words or syllables. These were drawn inside glyph blocks. Quite often there was more than one way to write a particular word or sentence. Mostly heads of objects were used.

1 List some characteristics which represent you. For example, if you are an animal lover, your symbol may be a cat or a dog. If you love to read stories, you may choose a book as your symbol.

_____

_____

_____

_____

2 Choose one of these characteristics and draw a symbol to represent you. (Don't forget that glyphs were often heads only!)

3 Write your name in the box and divide it by drawing a line between the syllables.

There are ☐ syllables, so you will need ☐ symbols to represent your name.

4 Draw symbols to represent each syllable. You may select other characteristics from Question 1 to use as your symbols or you may invent a new symbol of your own.

5 Look at these glyphs. They represent a person's name. Write words or sentences to tell about the person.

_____

_____

_____

_____

_____

6 Write possible names for this person based on the number of syllables in the name.

_____   _____

_____   _____

The multiple intelligence focus for this task is bodily–kinaesthetic.

> A bodily-kinaesthetic child has good physical awareness.
> He/She learns best through 'hands-on' activities.

Objective

- Creates a plan for a Mayan household from a description.

Preparation

- Allow children to plan and construct other models in other learning areas.
- Children should be familiar with a variety of construction techniques before commencing this task.
- Children may bring materials from home.

Teacher information

- Children may wish to draft a number of copies of their model before deciding on one to be drawn on the worksheet.
- Children should feel confident to use construction materials and equipment.
- Allow children time to collect materials from the playground or home to use in the model.

Answers

- Teacher check

Additional activities

- Join all models to create a Mayan village.
- Use the same format to create pyramid-temples or palaces to add to the village scene.
- Mime daily activities of the Maya for class members to guess.

CURRICULUM LINKS			
England	D & T	KS2	• complete design and make assignments using a range of materials
Northern Ireland	Technology	KS2	• plan what they are going to make, talking about materials they could use
Republic of Ireland	Science	5th/ 6th	• communicate a design plan and make objects using a range of tools and materials
Scotland	Technology	D	• develop and communicate a sequenced plan
Wales	D & T	KS2	• plan the making of their product

MAYAN HOUSEHOLD

Task • You will plan and construct a model of a Mayan household from a description.

A typical Mayan family consisted of between five and seven members. The day began before dawn with a breakfast of hot chocolate or atole (a thick, hot corn drink) and tortillas or tamales. The house was a hut constructed of poles woven together and plastered with dried mud. There was usually only one room. The men spent most of the day in the fields, while the women stayed at home weaving or sewing or preparing the food. The children helped the mothers with the chores and did not go to school unless they were from noble families. Prayers were said at the end of the day by the head of the household. This was accompanied by bloodletting and chants. Sometimes, the men spent their time building pyramids and temples.

1 Plan your model using the headings below. Label your designs. Include some people in or near your household to make it look authentic, as well as some fields.

Materials required

House design

Model of Mayan person

2 Briefly explain how you will construct your model. _____

_____

_____

_____

_____

_____

3 Construct your model using your materials and display it in the room.

4 Evaluate your model. Does it fit the description above? (**yes**) (**no**)
Discuss how it could be improved.

The multiple intelligence focus for this task is musical–rhythmic.

> A musical-rhythmical child has an awareness of music and sound.
> He/She learns best through activities involving music or rhythms.

Objective

- Identifies musical elements in a poem and creates percussion to accompany the poem.

Teacher information

- Important musical concepts found in poetry include pulse (the regular beat), duration (how long or short a sound is), tempo (how fast or slow a piece is), dynamics (how loud or soft a piece is), timbre (the sound that different instruments or voices have), texture (how many different sounds are occurring at the same time) and structure (plan of a piece).

- Voices and environmental materials may be used to explore sounds which create percussion.

Answers

- Teacher check

Additional activities

- Write a cinquain or haiku which relates to an ancient civilisation.

- View a film set in ancient times, focusing on the background music used to add suspense or drama.

Preparation

- Listen to and read poetry of various forms, including narrative poetry and recordings of poems which have background music or sounds.

CURRICULUM LINKS			
England	Music	KS2	• show how the combined musical elements of duration, dynamics, tempo, timbre and texture can be organised and used to communicate different effects
Northern Ireland	Music	KS2	• show an increasing ability to combine and use the elements of music to express their ideas and create effects
Republic of Ireland	Music	5th/6th	• invent and perform pieces that show an increasing awareness and control of musical elements
Scotland	Music	C	• invent short musical pieces to convey atmosphere
Wales	Music	KS2	• create, select and organise sounds to produce a specific atmosphere

THE RHYTHM OF THE DEAD CITY

Task • You will identify musical elements in a poem and create percussion to accompany the poem.

Poetry exhibits musical elements, including pulse, duration, tempo, dynamics, timbre, texture and structure.

1 Read the poem and mark the strong beats (pulse) in each line with a coloured pencil. You may need to tap the beat with your hand or foot. There are four strong beats in each line.

> *A mystery remains in the depths of the sea*
> *A city of temples; people forced to flee*
> *A disaster so vast that all was destroyed*
> *Only the memory stays in the modern world.*

Poetry usually has a structure. Poems could take the form of a haiku, cinquain, limerick, narrative, shape poem or may have a rhyming pattern within the poem.

2 Read the poem again to yourself and write a sentence or two to describe the structure.

_____

_____

_____

3 (a) In pairs, take turns to read the poem in expressive voices. Decide whether to:

- add eerie or sad sounds to create effect in the background (texture)
- speak quickly or slowly (tempo) or to vary speeds in certain places
- make some words shorter or longer to add emphasis or drama (durations)
- speak in a quiet voice (dynamics) or a loud voice
- change your voices so that they sound different (timbre)

(b) Colour the ones above that you used.

4 Choose a structure of your own to write another verse for the poem.

_____

_____

_____

_____

_____

_____

_____

_____

_____

_____

_____

5 Add percussion using other materials such as paper, stringed sounds or body percussion to add background music to your poem. Perform your poem in pairs, individually or in small groups.

The multiple intelligence focus for this task is interpersonal.

> An interpersonal child enjoys being in groups or teams.
> He/She learns best through activities involving working with others.

Objective

- Forms groups to carry out a debate.

Preparation

- Children should be able to complete research into various topics using the library, the Internet or other resources.
- Children should be familiar with the format of a debate.

Teacher information

- A debate is an organised argument between two teams. One team argues for the topic. This is called the affirmative team. The other team, called the negative team, argues against the topic. There are nine people involved in a debate: a chairperson, three affirmative team members, three negative team members, an adjudicator (judge) and a timekeeper.

- Before the debate begins, the chairperson states the topic and introduces the members of each team.

  Team members speak in the following order:

  (i) *first member of the affirmative team;*
  (ii) *first member of the negative team;*
  (iii) *second member of the affirmative team;*
  (iv) *second member of the negative team;*
  (v) *third member of the affirmative team;*
  (vi) *third member of the negative team.*

- The timekeeper allows each speaker a set time to speak, after which he/she rings three sets of bells. The first bell warns the speaker that time is almost finished; a double bell tells the speaker that time is up, and a continuous bell tells the speaker that the time is completed and that the judge will take no notice of any further arguments put forward.

- The chairperson deals with comments or interjections from the audience. He/She will also announce the winner, after consulting with the adjudicator.

- The jobs of each team member are as follows:

  - the first member for the affirmative team defines the topic, outlines the argument and allocates jobs to specific team members;
  - the first member for the negative team either accepts the definition of the topic or shows why it is wrong and changes it;
  - the second member for the affirmative team restates the case, then deals with the arguments presented by the first negative speaker. He/She may add new arguments to the affirmative's case;
  - the second member for the negative team argues against the points brought forward by the two affirmative speakers, then develops his/her own argument;
  - the third member for the affirmative team tries to persuade the audience that the arguments of the negative team are worthless;
  - the third member for the negative team performs the same role as the third speaker for the affirmative, but places emphasis on the negative aspects of the topic.

- The adjudicator assesses the performance of both teams in relation to the matter (the content of the debate – definition of the topic, the outline, explanation of the team's argument and examples to support the argument); the manner (the way a speech is presented); and the method (how the content is planned and organised). Usually, 40 marks are given for matter and manner and 20 for the method.

Answers

- Teacher check

Additional activities

- Form small groups to debate the topic 'Atlantis was a very advanced civilisation'.
- Using research from the Internet or library, form groups to create a model of Atlantis as it may have appeared before its destruction.
- In groups, role-play daily life as it may have been as a member of a family in Atlantis.

CURRICULUM LINKS			
England	English	KS2	• take up and sustain different roles, adapting them to suit the situation, including chair and spokesperson
Northern Ireland	English	KS2	• participate in formal discussions
Republic of Ireland	English	5th/ 6th	• argue points of view from the perspective of agreement and disagreement in the context of formal debates
Scotland	English	C	• argue points and assess their own performance in discussion
Wales	English	KS2	• make a range of contributions in discussions

ATLANTIS—MYTH OR REALITY?

Task | **You will form groups to debate the topic 'Atlantis is nothing more than a myth'.**

There are nine people involved in a debate: a chairperson, three affirmative team members, three negative team members, an adjudicator (judge) and a timekeeper.

1 Form groups of nine and allocate responsibilities for the debate. Complete the boxes to show who has been chosen for each job.

chairperson	timekeeper	adjudicator
affirmative speaker 1	affirmative speaker 2	affirmative speaker 3
negative speaker 1	negative speaker 2	negative speaker 3

2 Does each person understand his/her role? (**yes**) (**no**)

(If people are uncertain, let them reread the teacher information.)

3 Complete the sentences below.

(a) My job is to be _____

(b) I have to _____ .

_____

_____

4 Use the space below to make notes or reminders about your job. You may also use this space to make notes about your arguments if you are a speaker.

5 Hold your debate and evaluate how well you carried out your job by colouring the stars. (Colouring five stars indicates that you think you performed your responsibility well.)

6 List the things that you would change if you were to take on the same role again.

_____

_____

The multiple intelligence focus for this task is intrapersonal.

An intrapersonal child understands and analyses his/her thoughts and feelings.
He/She learns best through individual activities.

Objective

- Writes a personal diary for a child living in Atlantis.

Preparation

- Children read or research information about life in Atlantis before commencing this task.

Teacher information

- Children may use their background research to gain an impression of life in ancient Atlantis. Child research and opinions about Atlantis will vary; however, children will need to accept the existence of Atlantis for this task.

- Children must write their diary entry from a personal point of view and include the use of personal pronouns such as 'I' and 'We'.

- A record is kept each day of what happens, as well as a comment about feelings. Children may also write the actual words spoken by themselves and others.

- A diary entry is a form of recount.

- A recount needs to meet the following criteria:

  - tells what happened and is sequential;
  - begins with an introduction to the scene (setting or orientation);
  - important events are written in detail in chronological order;
  - connectives are included to suggest time passing (first, next, finally etc.);
  - has a conclusion, often with a comment reflecting the person's feelings.

- Many diaries other than *The diary of Anne Frank* have been published which may interest children. Another is *One man's war* by Stan Arneil. Stan was an Australian soldier kept prisoner by the Japanese.

CURRICULUM LINKS			
England	Literacy	Yr 5	• write recounts
Northern Ireland	English	KS2	• write in different forms, e.g. diaries
Republic of Ireland	English	5th/6th	• write in a wide variety of genres, e.g. diaries
Scotland	English	D	• produce a variety of different kinds of writing
Wales	English	KS2	• write in different forms, e.g. diaries

Answers

- Teacher check

Additional activities

- Children use their diary story to illustrate a picture book for a younger child. (visual–spatial)

- Select another ancient civilisation to repeat the activity. Compare the accounts.

- Role-play aspects of life in Atlantis. (bodily–kinaesthetic)

DAILY LIFE IN ATLANTIS

Task • **You will write a personal diary for a child living in Atlantis.**

Some diaries of ordinary people have become famous. **The diary of Anne Frank** *tells the story of a Jewish girl living in Holland during World War II. She kept her diary to tell what happened to her while she was hiding from German soldiers.*

1 Use your research information to write diary entries for a child living in Atlantis. Try to include possible dates for seven days. (You may use an extra sheet of paper if you need to.)

Date

Date

Date

Date

Date

Date

Date

2 Evaluate your diary writing by ticking the elements you were able to use:

personal pronouns   sequential events   feelings

3 Investigate other well-known diaries.

ANCIENT CIVILISATIONS – MY SELF–ASSESSMENT

After completing this unit, I was able to ...

word wise	research and record information about Atlas.
logic wise	solve number problems based on the Mayan number system and create a number system of my own.
nature wise	identify environmental problems and provide solutions.
picture wise	understand and create glyphs to write my name.
body wise	create a plan for a Mayan household from a description.
music wise	identify musical elements in a poem and create percussion to accompany the poem.
people wise	form groups to carry out a debate.
self wise	write a personal diary story for a child living in Atlantis.

What I learnt

ENVIRONMENTAL ISSUES

Informational text........................ ☐   ☐ .... What's the problem?

Environmental disaster recount ☐   ☐ .... Environmental soundscape

Save energy! .... ☐   ☐ ....Lights! Camera! Action!

Garden guru .... ☐   ☐ .... The 'Clean-up' man

Poster design brief .... ☐   ☐ ....My self-assessment

What I know	What I want to know

Keywords

Name: **Date:**

ENVIRONMENTAL ISSUES OVERVIEW

Verbal–Linguistic

- Create a 'press kit' for a conservation group.
- Listen to a guest speaker from an environmental association.
- Write a recount of the *Exxon Valdez* oil spill disaster and the effects it had on the environment.
- Participate in debates on environmental issues such as 'Dolphins should not be kept in captivity' or 'Plastic bags should be banned'.
- Write a letter to a newspaper about an environmental issue of personal concern.
- Use the words 'environment' or 'pollution' to write an acrostic poem.
- Write a biography about a person who has influenced views or participation in environmental issues; e.g. Ian Kiernan– Clean Up Australia Day.
- Create a crossword, with clues, covering environmental issues.
- Write a narrative on a water conservation or pollution theme with imaginary characters such as the frogs 'Lester' and 'Clyde' from the book of the same name.
- Investigate natural herbicides and explain how they can be used in the garden.
- Compare the heat/energy differences between fluorescent and incandescent light bulbs. Write a report about which is more energy efficient and would be better to use.
- Design an energy quiz.

Logical–Mathematical

- Make a chart showing the environmental problems in the local area.
- Graph the results of a survey about how people in the local community recycle.
- Collect and display data about the amount of rubbish children throw away at school over a week.
- Categorise resources as 'renewable' and 'non-renewable'.
- Devise a game to be played which highlights environmental issues and provides possible solutions.
- Make a scientific model to show the effect of excess fertiliser run-off into lakes and rivers.
- Collect data about the amount of water in a dam if rain continues at a low rate over a given time.
- Formulate and test a hypothesis on the amount of pollution in the air around the school at a given time.
- Investigate and record the number of different appliances used in the home/school. How can these be reduced to save energy?
- Research why insulation is a sound energy-saving device. Run tests to decide the most efficient materials.

Naturalist

- Write a report about a plant or animal species native to the local area.
- Research to find out facts about the problems introduced species have caused.
- Visit a landfill facility or rubbish treatment plant.
- Identify environmental issues in the community and develop a strategy to deal with the problem as a community.
- Take part in community recycling programmes.
- Follow a procedure to make a compost bin.
- Participate in tree-planting activities at school and in the community.
- Participate in a Clean Up School Day, Walk to School Day etc.
- Take digital photographs of areas in the school that highlight environmental concerns; e.g. an area where more rubbish bins are needed, a tree branch overhanging a building, or soil building up on a pathway.
- Design an experiment to make clean water from muddy water.

Visual–Spatial

- Design signs that inform tourists how they should behave in public areas to conserve the environment.
- Map different environmental zones in the British Isles and the problems found in each.
- Design a poster to promote alternatives to the use of plastic bags or how to save energy or conserve water.
- Locate water, soil or air pollution articles in newspapers or magazines to display on a 'clippings' board.
- Make 'trash art' using clean recycled materials brought in by children.
- Create a model of a machine that is an alternative to electricity for power.
- Create a board game about the environment; e.g. move ahead 2 if rubbish is picked up, back 3 if forget to turn off tap.
- Design a poster to show how we can aid the environment by reducing, reusing, refusing and recycling.
- Design a' recycling guide' to be sent to community members about what can be recycled and how to do it.

ENVIRONMENTAL ISSUES OVERVIEW

Musical–Rhythmic

- In a group, write and perform a radio commercial, with appropriate background music, about an environmental issue.
- Write lyrics to a song that illustrate the facts about an environmental issue.
- Make a list of song titles concerning environmental issues and choose one to learn. Add musical instruments.
- Write and record a catchy jingle to encourage the local community to help solve an environmental issue.
- Write a haiku, cinquain or chant about an environmental issue.
- Study the background of a musician who or band which composes songs about environmental issues; e.g. Midnight Oil.
- Mime or create music to suit different types of environmental dangers, such as floods, earthquakes, fire, droughts or tornadoes.

Bodily–Kinaesthetic

- Role-play a protest march about an environmental problem.
- Role-play scenarios of environmental issues in the community; e.g. constantly finding broken bottles at the local beach. Plan a solution for each scenario.
- Mime an energy-saving idea for the rest of the class to guess.
- Write and perform a play about a group of animals, trees and/or plants that are about to lose their home to development.
- Create puppets and a script for a group of animals or plants to teach about an environmental issue.
- Create body movements for a drama which depicts the loss of an animal, plant or other resource.
- Hold a scavenger hunt around the school grounds to collect rubbish.
- Make a simple electromagnet using batteries, thin wire, paper clips and a long nail. Explain how this concept is used as an energy-saving device in industry.
- Build a terrarium to create a healthy, self-sufficient environment.
- Build a model to show how the water cycle works.

Intrapersonal

- Reflect on which environmental issues you think are the most urgent for the world to focus on.
- Research to write a detailed report on the effects that clearing of rainforest in the Amazon Basin has on the environment.
- Select an environmental issue of personal interest, such as water pollution, to research and present to the class.
- Make an action plan for an environmental problem to be dealt with in the home, school or local area; for example, invasive weeds from grass clippings going into natural land, trail bikes destroying an open space.
- Use the Internet to discover websites of environmental groups and organisations.
- Relate a personal incident which may have influenced children on an environmental issue.
- Write a narrative about being caught in a power failure for a long time and its consequences.
- What is the sun's job? Create a booklet that explains what the sun's energy provides.

Interpersonal

- In groups, discuss the harmful effects human activities such as logging or mining have on the environment. Discuss how/if the problem can be solved.
- In a group, plan a community environmental meeting.
- In groups, make a list of the most important ways children can help the environment.
- Organise for a 'car-free' trip to school day; i.e. children and teachers find alternative means of transport or car pool if possible.
- In groups, devise a list of the top 10 environmental mistakes made by people and how the damage caused was treated.
- Give a team presentation of an environmental disaster. Include a solution. The presentation could be in the form of a skit, drama, play, movements story or choral work.
- In groups, design a chart to show what renewable energy and non-renewable energy are and how each is used.
- Investigate how some energy-driven devices work, such as fridge, toaster or airconditioner. Present the group's findings to the class.

ENVIRONMENTAL ISSUES
INFORMATIONAL TEXT

In defining the 'environment', it is important to understand that it is not just the physical conditions or surroundings of a place, such as the vegetation, water and weather. The environment also includes all those conditions and influences that exist and affect it.

Factors affecting the environment

Many factors influence the environment and the effects can vary from positive to negative. For example, a good spell of rain in a particular area can mean plants will flourish and animals survive. The same amount of rain elsewhere could result in flooding that will destroy crops, erode soil and kill animals.

Natural occurrences can affect the environment to varying degrees– natural disasters are a powerful force of nature. Examples of these include earthquakes, floods, drought, hurricanes, tornadoes, volcanoes, tsunami and fires.

Human behaviour is responsible for many changes in the environment—human influences have caused great damage.

Some damage is beyond repair; other damage may require hundreds of years before the environment returns to its natural state. The main destructive causes have been:

(a) *Pollution of the air, water and soil.* Humans dispose of many industrial waste products directly into the environment, damaging plant and animal species in the process.

(b) *The clearing of large areas of old growth forests, destroying the natural habitats of animals.* This has led to a number of plant and animal species becoming endangered or even extinct.

(c) *Clearing huge areas of land of all trees for farming,* which has led to 'dust bowls' or increased salt in the soil. This makes the land useless for plants, animals or humans.

(d) *Commercial hunting* of animals for meat, body parts, or as pests has also threatened many species.

Since the Industrial Age began in the 18th century, accidents with dangerous chemicals have greatly increased. Many industrial accidents involve an explosion, killing people directly, or leaking poisonous chemicals and gases that can spread for thousands of kilometres, affecting people and the environment for many years afterwards.

Examples of those human-created disasters include the Chernobyl nuclear explosion in 1986 and the *Exxon Valdez* oil spill in 1989.

ENVIRONMENTAL ISSUES
INFORMATIONAL TEXT

Pollution

The three main areas of pollution are:

1. *air pollution*;
2. *water pollution*; and
3. *soil pollution*.

Air pollution

This is the pollution of the earth's atmosphere. It is caused mainly by emissions from machinery and factories in the form of smoke or gases such as carbon dioxide. By far the greatest amount of pollution is caused when fossil fuels—such as petrol, gas or coal—are burned to produce energy. This applies especially to motor vehicle engines.

Water pollution

This is the pollution of the earth's oceans, seas and waterways. It is caused in much the same way as air pollution. When unclean or dangerous wastes—chemical or other materials find their way into the water, great damage is caused to the animals and plants living there. It also often makes the water unfit for drinking.

Soil pollution

This is where waste or hazardous products are stored or released on land and quickly, or over a period of time, mix with the soil, reducing its fertility and creating a build-up of dangerous products. Materials released into the soil can also find their way into the underground water supplies and pollute them.

Conserving the environment

Conservation is the careful use and protection of our natural resources. Our environment is our most valuable resource as it holds the key to our survival. All people should be aware that not only do we need to keep our environment healthy, we also need to minimise the damage caused by our activities. We are all aware that our everyday actions can have a big impact on the environment. It is not the responsibility of just the government, or environmental organisations, to clean up the earth, but ours, too– and there are many ways that we can help.

We can change our lifestyle, so that the things we do have a lessened detrimental impact on the environment. We can also undertake activities to improve the environment. Simple things—such as using the car less, walking, cycling, using public transport, being more energy conscious and recycling waste—can all make the environment a cleaner place for the future.

For young people, getting involved with tree planting, cleaning up rubbish and fundraising for threatened species are just a few ways they can learn how to care responsibly for their natural world.

Renewable and non-renewable resources

Natural resources come from the air, soil, water and living organisms as well as the sun. These are called 'renewable resources'. They include such things as wind, solar power and trees. Non-renewable resources generally come from the subterranean areas of the earth and include fossil fuels, such as coal, oil and gas. Humans are on the verge of using all the non-renewable resources, and polluting many of those areas such as the soil, air and water, where their renewable resources come from.

The multiple intelligence focus for this task is verbal–linguistic.

> A verbal–linguistic child thinks in words.
> He/She learns best through activities involving reading, writing and speaking.

Objectives

- Develops awareness of the problems caused by the release of pollutants in the environment.

- Writes a recount about an environmental disaster caused by humans.

Teacher information

- Discuss the difference between environmental disasters caused by natural and human means. Refer to the informational text on pages 70–71.

- Children will need to use the Internet, encyclopedias or other nonfiction materials to research an *environmental disaster* caused by humans. They could type the bold words into a search engine to discover one of their own, or choose one of the examples mentioned.

- The *Exxon Valdez* oil spill occurred on 24 March 1989 when an American oil tanker ran aground on Bligh Reef in Prince William Sound in Alaska. Over 30 000 tonnes of oil leaked into the Sound, with 3840 kilometres of coastline polluted. This was disastrous for the terrestrial and marine plants and animals of the area, some of which have still not recovered.

- The Chernobyl nuclear disaster occurred on 26 April 1986 in the then Soviet Union. An explosion and fire at the Chernobyl nuclear power plant released large amounts of radioactive material into the atmosphere. Thousands of people were exposed to dangerous levels of radiation. Everything from health to agriculture was affected by the radiation.

- Revise the elements of a recount with children.

- A recount needs to meet the following criteria:

  - tells what happened and is sequential,
  - begins with an introduction to the scene (setting or orientation),
  - important events are written in detail in chronological order,
  - connectives are included to suggest time passing (first, next, finally etc.),
  - the past tense should be maintained,
  - has a conclusion, often with a comment reflecting the person's feelings.

- At this level, children should be able to use these criteria to help them define the paragraphs in the text.

Preparation

- Collect samples of recounts written previously by children or taken from magazine articles to view and discuss with the class.

Answers

- Teacher check

Additional activities

- Write a newspaper report on an environmental disaster caused by humans—real or imaginary.

- Compare and contrast the *Exxon Valdez* oil spill with a hypothetical 'local' oil spill. Include lessons learnt from the spill and how these can be applied to the 'local' spill. (logical–mathematical)

- Write a poem or song about the tragedy of Chernobyl, *Exxon Valdez* oil spill or other environmental disaster. (musical–rhythmic)

CURRICULUM LINKS		
England	Literacy	Yr 5 • write recounts
Northern Ireland	English	KS2 • engage with a range of texts, e.g. non-fiction materials, read for information and write in different forms
Republic of Ireland	English	5th/6th • explore appropriate non-fiction texts for various purposes and write in a wide range of genres
Scotland	English	C/D • read for information, including developing the ability to scan and produce a variety of different kinds of writing
Wales	English	KS2 • read and use a wide range of sources of non-fiction information and write in a range of forms

ENVIRONMENTAL DISASTER RECOUNT

You will write a recount about an environmental disaster caused by humans.

Environmental disasters can be natural, such as floods and earthquakes, or caused by humans, such as oil spills and nuclear explosions.

1 Choose an environmental disaster caused by humans to research and write a recount. Two well-known examples are the *Exxon Valdez* oil spill and the Chernobyl nuclear explosion. Use the framework below to plan your recount.

Title

Opening statement *(what, when, who, why)*

_____

_____

_____

_____

Events in chronological order

_____

_____

_____

_____

_____

_____

_____

_____

_____

_____

Ending statement

_____

_____

_____

_____

2 Use the plan to write a draft copy, then edit and publish your recount to share with the class.

The multiple intelligence focus for this task is logical–mathematical.

> A logical–mathematical child thinks rationally and in abstractions.
> He/She learns best through activities involving problem-solving, numbers and patterns.

Objectives

- Identifies sources of energy used by home appliances.
- Identifies practical ways of conserving the energy used by these appliances.

Preparation

- Collect four or five portable household appliances as examples to use in discussion with children. Suggestions: toaster, hairdryer, iron, CD player or electric blanket.

Teacher information

- The main source of energy in our homes is electricity. Other sources of energy are natural gas, solid fuel (wood and coal) and solar energy. We use these energy sources to produce heating, cooling, motion (fans, saws etc.), light, sound, images and other requirements in our daily lives.

- Children can refer to the informational text on pages 70-71 concerning renewable and non-renewable energy sources and the importance of conserving energy.

- Use the examples of the household appliances above for children to identify what is meant by an appliance that needs 'external energy' to operate.

- Direct children to suggest ways each appliance could be used to conserve energy. For example, the electric blanket should be turned off when not in use/turned to a low setting/turned off once the bed is warmed, or extra blankets used rather than the electric blanket.

- Children could complete part of this activity at home if necessary to accurately identify the energy source used by a particular appliance.

- Note: Some appliances may be used for more than reason; e.g. reverse cycle airconditioner.

CURRICULUM LINKS			
England	Geography	KS2	• recognise how and why people may seek to manage environments sustainably and to identify opportunities for their own involvement
Northern Ireland	Science/ Geography	KS2	• find out about the range of energy sources used at home and be aware of issues associated with conservation of the environment, e.g. efficient use of energy
Republic of Ireland	Science	5th/ 6th	• come to appreciate the need to conserve resources
Scotland	Society	D	• describe some methods used and reasons for conserving major resources
Wales	Geography	KS2	• understand the individual's responsibility for the environment

Answers

- Teacher check

Additional activities

- Collate the energy-saving hints suggested by the children to form a class book or display chart.
- Class tallies the total number of appliances, taken from each child's worksheet, according to the energy source or what each is used for. These results can be displayed in a bar graph or pie graph.

SAVE ENERGY!

List 10 appliances in your home which need external energy to operate (i.e. not hand-operated) and complete the table below.

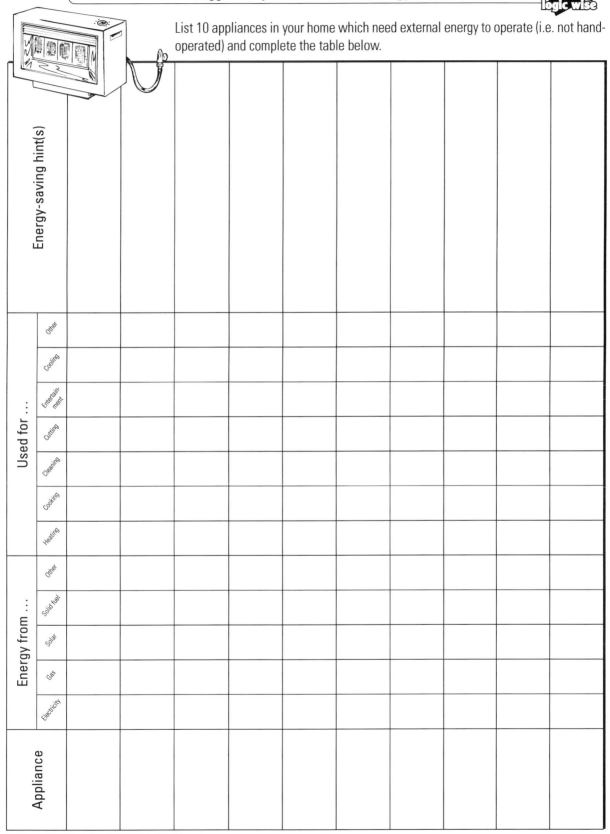

Energy-saving hint(s)											
Used for …	Other										
	Cooling										
	Entertain-ment										
	Cutting										
	Cleaning										
	Cooking										
	Heating										
Energy from …	Other										
	Solid fuel										
	Solar										
	Gas										
	Electricity										
Appliance											

The multiple intelligence focus for this task is naturalist.

A naturalist child has an awareness of the patterns in nature.
He/She learns best through activities involving animals, plants and the environment.

Objectives

- Identifies the importance of using environmentally-friendly products.

- Evaluates the effectiveness of using environmentally-friendly methods to control pests.

Teacher information

- Children may work with a partner or in a small group for this activity.

- Discuss the following information with the children as a starting point.

  Herbicide – a chemical or biological agent which kills plants or inhibits their growth.

  Pesticide – a chemical substance which destroys pests.

  Pesticides by design are toxic. Many have been associated with birth defects, mutations, cancers, liver and kidney damage and short-term health effects.

  Humans can ingest herbicides and pesticides in a number of ways, including through the air, through the skin, by drinking contaminated water or eating contaminated food.

- Discuss how many natural (environmentally-friendly) remedies are quite old and were used before chemical herbicides and pesticides were developed.

- Children investigate the effectiveness of each remedy, giving it a rating and noting any positive or negative observations.

Answers

- Teacher check

Additional activities

- Create a 'Garden guru' guide to using environmentally-friendly remedies by collating the given methods and those discovered by the child in the activity.

- Discuss the positive and negative comments made by the children. These could be added to the remedy as an improvement. For example, children may discover that the containers with beer to catch slugs and snails should not be dug in so the rim is flush with the soil, or else ground beetles may fall in accidentally. When the container is put on top of the ground, slugs and snails will climb up the sides, but ground beetles will go around.

Preparation

- Collect the ingredients needed for children to make each remedy. Refer to the worksheet.

- Items such as buckets, watering cans, spray bottles and wooden spoons for stirring will also be required.

CURRICULUM LINKS			
England	Science	KS2	• use simple equipment and materials, make systematic observations and draw conclusions
Northern Ireland	Science	KS2	• make observations, record findings and draw conclusions
Republic of Ireland	Science	5th/ 6th	• carry out simple experiments
Scotland	Science	C	• make appropriate observations and record findings
Wales	Science	KS2	• use equipment correctly, make careful observations and draw conclusions

GARDEN GURU

We are all aware of the health problems the overuse of chemical herbicides and pesticides can cause. The suggestions below provide environmentally-friendly alternatives to control or eradicate pests.

1 (a) Identify places in the school, or at home, where each of the remedies below can be used. Rate each remedy's effectiveness after you have trialled it. (5 being extremely effective)

Make brief positive or negative comments.

(b) Research or ask a parent, neighbour or relative about two more remedies to complete the two blank boxes.

Weeds in the brick paving

(Not for use in the garden as the plants will be killed!)

PROBLEM

- $^1/_2$ *cup salt*
- *1 tsp liquid detergent*
- *2 L vinegar*

1. Combine the ingredients in a bucket.
2. Stir to mix.
3. Sprinkle or spray over weeds.

Comment   1   2   3   4   5

Ants in the kitchen

PROBLEM

- $^1/_2$ *tsp boric acid*
- *1 tsp honey*

1. Add a very small amount of water to the boric acid to make a thin paste.
2. Mix in the honey.
3. Set out on pieces of greaseproof paper.

Comment   1   2   3   4   5

Powdery mildew and blackspot

PROBLEM

- *milk* (low fat milk produces less odour)
- *water*

1. Mix the milk and water at a ratio of 1 part milk to 9 parts water.
2. Spray on affected plants.
3. Apply every 5–7 days for three applications.

Comment   1   2   3   4   5

Snails and slugs eating seedlings

PROBLEM

- *several small plastic containers* (e.g. margarine containers)
- *beer*

1. Fill each container with 3–5 cm of beer.
2. Place the containers in the garden.
3. Remove the drowned slugs and snails daily.

Comment   1   2   3   4   5

PROBLEM

Comment   1   2   3   4   5

PROBLEM

Comment   1   2   3   4   5

The multiple intelligence focus for this task is visual–spatial.

> A visual–spatial child thinks in images, colours and shape.
> He/She learns best through activities involving visualisation.

Objectives

- Designs and creates a poster to develop awareness about an environmental issue.
- Employs visual appeal and design elements to construct a poster.

Preparation

- Make materials available for creating the posters, such as drawing equipment, large sheets of plain and coloured card, scissors and glue.

Teacher information

- Children could work individually, with a partner or in small groups for this activity.
- Discuss the types of issues children might present; e.g. alternatives to plastic bags, the dangers to sea animals of discarded plastic bags and fishing lines/hooks, procedure for making a homemade compost bin, or advice on conserving energy or water.
- Children will need to do some research to help them design their poster.
- Points to consider for a successful poster:
  - overall attractiveness
  - attention-grabbing titles, captions and slogans
  - clear, simple, bold design that gives the viewer a quick overview of the topic without a lot of reading
  - colour (clear, bright to draw attention)
  - the use of humour if applicable
  - consideration given to art style/design; for example, art style (media), type of graphics, placement of pictures/ graphics.

CURRICULUM LINKS			
England	Art & design	KS2	• collect visual and other information to help them develop their ideas and work on projects in two dimensions
Northern Ireland	Art & design	KS2	• express and represent their ideas through a range of materials and techniques
Republic of Ireland	Science	5th/ 6th	• communicate design plan using sketches
Scotland	Art & design	D	• use visual elements studied to enhance art and design work
Wales	Art	KS2	• plan and make images using various materials for various purposes

Answers

- Teacher check

Additional activities

- Display completed posters for other children in the school to read the environmental messages. For example, the school noticeboard, library, on a wall or window along a thoroughfare or in actual classrooms may be suitable locations.
- Survey children and teachers about the posters after they have been displayed for a while. Did they learn something from the posters? Are they aware of a problem they didn't know existed? Have they changed their behaviour? (logical–mathematical)

POSTER DESIGN BRIEF

You will design and create a poster to develop awareness of an environmental issue.

1 Choose an environmental issue you wish to create awareness of.

Research the topic and record notes for your poster in the sections below.

Design brief/purpose

Key research points

Who is the target audience?

Poster layout/design plan

Catchy titles

Pictures/graphics to include

2 Use your ideas to complete your poster on a large sheet of card or heavy paper.

The multiple intelligence focus for this task is bodily–kinaesthetic.

> A bodily–kinaesthetic child has good physical awareness.
> He/She learns best through 'hands-on' activities.

Objective

- Uses role-play to explore environmental issues.

Preparation

- Photocopy the role-play cards on page 81 onto stiff card and laminate them for durability.

Teacher information

- Children work in small groups for this activity. Distribute the role-play cards to the groups, ensuring at least two groups will be using each scenario. In this way, children will experience different solutions to the problem when the role-plays are performed.

- Children plan their given role-play, creating characters, movements and script. As a group, they work out a solution to the environmental issue to conclude their role-play.

- Allow two or more sessions for practising the role-plays, out of sight of other groups.

- Discuss each role-play after each performance. Was the solution practical/viable? Compare and contrast the solutions to the same scenario.

- Teachers may wish to devise a checklist to record the scenarios each child has taken part in.

Answers

- Teacher check

Additional activities

- Change group members and scenarios so children have the opportunity to explore the same/different scenarios and problems with varying approaches.

- Brainstorm to list other environmental issues in the school, community and beyond. Consider possible solutions. (Children should come to the realisation that political and monetary aspects have an impact on environmental solutions.) (verbal–linguistic)

CURRICULUM LINKS			
England	English	KS2	• create, adapt and sustain different roles in group drama
Northern Ireland	English	KS2	• engage in role-play and drama
Republic of Ireland	English	5th/ 6th	• explore and express conflicts of opinion through improvisational drama
Scotland	Drama	C	• cooperate with others and sustain and develop roles
Wales	English	KS2	• participate in a wide range of drama activities, including role-play

WHAT'S THE PROBLEM?

1
SCENARIO

Broken bottles are constantly found at the local beach.

2
SCENARIO

A vacant block of land in the area has become a dumping ground for lawn clippings, pruned branches and unwanted household items.

3
SCENARIO

Used syringes are regularly discovered in the sandpit of the community playground.

4
SCENARIO

Several childrens' neighbours are using hose pipes during a water shortage.

5
SCENARIO

Grass and soil are being eroded in an area of the school due to children walking across the lawn on the way to the library.

6
SCENARIO

After a recycling activity, some children have become concerned about the reluctance of parents to recycle at home.

7
SCENARIO

After a transport survey activity, it was noticed that some neighbours of various children drove their cars into the city to work each day with only the driver (no passengers).

8
SCENARIO

The community newspaper has reported on findings about a particular species of frog that is declining in numbers from the local lake.

9
SCENARIO

Several childrens' neighbours have wood fires which emit foul-smelling smoke due to them burning green timber.

10
SCENARIO

The amount of rubbish littering the school is steadily increasing.

11
SCENARIO

After a water use activity, children have become concerned about family members leaving taps running when cleaning teeth, leaving sprinklers on too long etc.

12
SCENARIO

Off-road motorbikes have become a problem on the school field and local park.

The multiple intelligence focus for this task is musical–rhythmic.

A musical–rhythmic child has an awareness of music and sound.
He/She learns best through activities involving music or rhythms.

Objectives

- Creates and performs a soundscape in a group.
- Demonstrates an awareness of how human intervention can disturb the natural harmony of an environment.

Preparation

- Children can assist in collecting items suitable for sound effects, according to the particular environment their group chooses. Suggestions are cardboard, shakers, paper, water in jugs, buckets, watering cans, musical instruments. Encourage children to also use items from the environment such as whistles made from leaves, sticks for clicking, shakers made from nuts in containers or drums made by banging wood on a rock or log. Vocal sound effects could also be used.
- Organise children into groups of four.
- Tape recorder(s) will be needed for each group to record its presentations.

Teacher information

- Discuss various types of environments with children—tropical rainforest, hot desert, a pond, running brook surrounded by trees, alpine area and so on.
- Discuss what sounds might be heard in each environment; e.g. jungle—birds chirping, animals walking over leaves, monkeys screeching, elephants trumpeting, gentle breeze/strong wind, light/heavy/no rain.
- Discuss how the sounds will change when humans intervene; e.g. poachers creep up to shoot an elephant, loggers come to saw trees or bulldozers approach to clear land.
- Children plan their soundscape on the worksheet, adding some kind of human intervention and how the sounds of the environment will change accordingly.
- Two or three 20-minute rehearsal sessions will be needed by the groups (separated from each other as it will be noisy!).
- Each group performs its soundscape to the class or records it for playing back later. The class has to guess the type of environment and the sequence of events.
- A discussion of the performances should follow, where the children can give their opinions of how easy the soundscapes were to follow and what objects made the most effective noises.

CURRICULUM LINKS			
England	Music	KS2	• complete a range of musical activities that integrate performing, composing and appraising
Northern Ireland	Music	KS2	• create short stories and pictures told through sound
Republic of Ireland	Music	5th/6th	• select from a wide range of sound sources for a range of musical purposes
Scotland	Music	C	• invent 'sound pictures'
Wales	Music	KS2	• compose and arrange music in response to a range of stimuli, using a range of sound sources

Answers

Teacher check

Additional activities

- Discuss the short-term and long-term consequences the types of human intervention used in each soundscape may have on the environment; e.g. how much land can be cleared before certain animals will have no shelter? (naturalist)
- Use the soundscapes as a stimulus for creative writing. (verbal–linguistic)

ENVIRONMENTAL SOUNDSCAPE

Task — You will create and perform a soundscape about a particular environment, demonstrating the effects of human intervention.

1 Choose an environment your group would like to create a soundscape for. (A soundscape is a story told by sound.) List the sounds you might hear in this environment.

> *Environment:* _____

2 Think of human activity that would disturb the harmony of this environment.

3 Plan your soundscape below. Briefly describe the sequence of events, the sounds that will be heard, the materials used to make them and which member(s) of your group will be in charge of each sound effect.

Sequence of events	Sound(s)	Materials	Who

4 Present your soundscape to the class. It can be recorded or performed live. The audience members should close their eyes when they are listening.

The multiple intelligence focus for this task is interpersonal.

> An interpersonal child enjoys being in groups or teams.
> He/She learns best through activities involving working with others.

Objectives

- Plans a TV commercial about an environmental issue.
- Performs and rates the effectiveness of the commercial.

Teacher information

- Discuss the types of issues children might use; e.g. saving a native animal from extinction, encouraging people to keep waterways free of pollution, encouraging recycling or taking part in a tree-planting activity.

- Children will need to consider the target audience and the purpose of their commercial. Children will also need to do some research to help them present their commercials; e.g. watching similar commercials to imitate style and language and researching facts to present in their commercials.

- Children use the headings on the worksheet to plan their commercial.

- Children will need time out of sight of other groups to rehearse their commercial.

- People who represent the target audience—e.g. parents, preschoolers—could be invited to view the commercial.

Answers

- Teacher check

Additional activities

- Create an ongoing list of commercials on television and radio, or advertisements in magazines, newspapers and billboards, about environmental issues. Add comments about people's opinions. (intrapersonal)

- Create posters or information charts about the environmental issues chosen by other groups for their commercial. (visual–spatial)

Preparation

- Organise children into groups of three to five.

CURRICULUM LINKS			
England	English	KS2	• use character, action and narrative to convey themes in drama
Northern Ireland	English	KS2	• engage in drama
Republic of Ireland	Drama	5th/ 6th	• co-operate and communicate with others in helping to shape the drama
Scotland	Drama	D	• improve collaborative group work in contexts which reflect issues
Wales	English	KS2	• participate in a wide range of drama activities

LIGHTS! CAMERA! ACTION!

people wise

Task You will work in a small group to plan and present a 'television' commercial about an environmental issue.

TV commercial plan
by

---

1 Issue or topic of commercial _____

2 Purpose of commercial _____

_____

_____

3 Target audience _____

4 How will we make the commercial appeal to the target audience?

Language	Music
Sound effects	**Visual images**

5 Rate the effectiveness of your television commercial and explain your reasoning.

freezing	*chilly*	*warm*	*hot*	*sizzling*

_____

_____

6 What improvements could your group make?

_____

_____

_____

The multiple intelligence focus for this task is intrapersonal.

> An intrapersonal child understands and analyses his/her thoughts and feelings.
> He/She learns best through individual activities.

Objectives

- Researches the life of a significant environmentalist.
- Identifies the impact made by this person on environmental protection.
- Writes a short biography.

Teacher information

- There are many websites offering information about Ian Kiernan's life and his contributions to environmental protection. Children will find keywords such as 'Ian Kiernan' or 'Clean Up Australia Day' will lead them to suitable sites.
- Children should record the sources of the information they have collected.
- Display or distribute the biographies children write about Ian Kiernan.

Answers

Some answers may vary slightly according to the source.
1. 1940, Sydney
2. Fishing, swimming and sailing in Sydney Harbour
3. Builder's labourer
4. Made a fortune as a developer, owning or part-owning hundreds of houses, many restaurants and several developments.
5. His business empire collapsed when interest rates rose sharply in 1974.
6. While participating in a solo round-the-world yacht race, he was disgusted at the appalling amount of pollution and rubbish he encountered, particularly in the Sargasso Sea—a place he had always wanted to visit.
7. He organised a Clean Up Sydney Harbour Day on Sunday 8 January 1989
8. This led to Clean Up Australia Day in 1990 and Clean Up the World in 1993.
9. 1940 – Ian Kiernan was born
   1974 – his business collapsed
   1987 – participated in a solo-round-the-world yacht race
   1989 – launched Clean Up Sydney Harbour Day
   1990 – launched Clean Up Australia Day
   1993 – won Australian of the year
   1995 – received an Order of Australia
   1998 – Won United Nations Sasakawa Environment Prize
10. Answers will vary

Preparation

- Children will need library and Internet resources to complete this activity.

Additional activities

- Children can organise events in their school for a 'Clean Up School Day'. (naturalist)
- Research to write a biography of another person who has made significant achievements in environmental issues; for example, Peter Garrett (ex-lead singer for Midnight Oil and environmental campaigner).

CURRICULUM LINKS			
England	Literacy	Yr 5	• locate information confidently and efficiently
Northern Ireland	English	KS2	• engage with a range of texts, e.g. non-fiction materials and read for information
Republic of Ireland	English	5th/6th	• explore appropriate non-fiction texts for various purposes
Scotland	English	C	• read for information, including developing the ability to scan
Wales	English	KS2	• read and use a wide range of sources of non-fiction information

THE 'CLEAN-UP' MAN

Task ● You will understand through research the worldwide impact
Ian Kiernan has had on environmental protection.

Australian, Ian Kiernan, is one of the most influential environmentalists in the world. His passion for environmental protection led him to become the founder and force behind the Clean Up Australia and Clean Up the World organisations.

How did he manage to achieve these things? What inspired him? You will discover the answers by researching into his life. Use the questions below as a guide to getting to know what makes Ian Kiernan 'tick'. You are sure to be inspired!

---

❶ When and where was he born?

❷ What pastimes did he enjoy as a youngster?

❸ What was his first job?

❹ What were his business achievements up until the 1970s?

❺ What happened in 1974?

❻ What experience in 1986–87 changed his life?

❼ What did he decide to do as a result of this experience?

❽ What did he do after that?

❾ Complete this time line of Ian Kiernan's life.

❿ List qualities that enabled Ian Kiernan to achieve his dreams.

⓫ Use the information you have found to write a short biography about Ian Kiernan.

ENVIRONMENTAL ISSUES – MY SELF-ASSESSMENT

After completing this unit, I was able to ...

word wise	write a recount about an environmental disaster caused by humans.	☆ ☆ ☆ ☆ ☆
logic wise	identify the source of energy used by appliances in my home and suggest ways to conserve this energy.	☆ ☆ ☆ ☆ ☆
nature wise	evaluate the effectiveness of environmentally-friendly methods to control pests and other garden problems.	☆ ☆ ☆ ☆ ☆
picture wise	design and create a poster to develop awareness of an environmental issue.	☆ ☆ ☆ ☆ ☆
body wise	role-play scenarios of given environmental issues, concluding with a solution.	☆ ☆ ☆ ☆ ☆
music wise	create and perform a soundscape about a particular environment, demonstrating the effects of human intervention.	☆ ☆ ☆ ☆ ☆
people wise	work in a group to plan and present a 'television' commercial about an environmental issue.	☆ ☆ ☆ ☆ ☆
self wise	understand through research the worldwide impact Ian Kiernan has had on environmental protection.	☆ ☆ ☆ ☆ ☆

What I learnt

SPORT

Informational text....................... ☐   ☐ ....Invent a new game

Read all about it! .... ☐   ☐ ....Team song

Sport participation..................... ☐   ☐ ....Sports day

Sporting activities...................... ☐   ☐ ....My greatest athlete

Design a uniform........................ ☐   ☐ ....My self-assessment

What I know	What I want to know

Keywords

Name: Date:

SPORT OVERVIEW

Verbal–Linguistic

- Children choose a physical skill they know how to do and explain it to the class; e.g. performing a swimming stroke, hitting a cricket ball or doing the splits.
- Write an appropriate commentary for a sports match.
- Write a newspaper report on a sporting event.
- Read autobiographies of famous sporting personalities.
- Write a biography of a famous sporting personality.
- Write a letter to their sporting hero.
- Prepare a list of 10 questions they would like to ask about a particular sport.
- Plan and present a 10-minute talk about their favourite sport/sporting personality.
- Debate: 'Sporting heroes are good role models,' OR 'Dancers are not as fit as sportspeople'.
- Write a report about a particular sportsperson's progress during the Olympics or world championship competition.
- Research and write the rules of your favourite sport.
- Write a diary entry for 'A day in the life of your favourite sporting hero'. Consider diet, training and media events that may need to be attended.

Logical–Mathematical

- Using the statistics of a famous sportsperson, make some predictions about his/her future performance; e.g. How many goals will he/she score in the next match?
- Conduct experiments that show how the heart rate changes during exercise.
- Create puzzles using sporting heroes, equipment, sport etc.
- Record/Interpret data about sporting information using a variety of graphs; e.g. record darts scores and attempts in a bar graph or work out the percentage of children playing a particular sport from a pie graph.
- Record and graph class members' participation in different physical activities.
- Calculate the percentage of each day spent being physically active.
- Calculate the cost of the equipment needed in a particular sport.
- Calculate the money spent over a year for dance, taekwondo or cricket lessons.
- Collect information about two or three sporting people of the immediate past or the present. Predict the length of their sporting career.

Naturalist

- Compare the movements made by a range of four-legged animals used in sporting events. Suggest reasons for any differences.
- Research to find out how different environmental conditions affect athletes.
- Identify and consider potential problems to the environment a sporting event may cause and suggest ways these problems could be solved.
- Research different animals involved with sport.
- Identify sporting activities requiring fresh and/or salt water.
- Identify and categorise 'outdoor' venues for sporting events.
- Select a lake/park/river and list activities suitable to be played which do not interfere with the natural features or wildlife.
- Research to find out how sporting fields are maintained for events.
- What happens to all the rubbish produced by spectators at large sporting events?

Visual–Spatial

- Using a model of the human body, explain which bones and muscles are involved in simple movements.
- Design a poster/billboard advertising a major sporting event.
- Collect pictures of famous sports people or dancers. Create a collage and decorate with uplifting words such as 'determination', 'perseverance', 'strength', 'endurance'.
- Watch films such as *D2—The Mighty Ducks*, *Field of Dreams* and *Cool Runnings* and evaluate realism, spirit evoked, characters etc. (Caution: Check classifications)
- Design and create a programme of events for a sporting event.
- Draw a plan of a stadium for a favourite event. Include the sports field, any markings required, seating, change rooms, entry and exit points, toilets, food outlets, a first aid post and parking.
- Design a new uniform, including shoes, for a favourite team. Incorporate colours, logos and sponsorship.
- Design a new logo for a favourite sporting organisation.

SPORT OVERVIEW

Bodily–Kinaesthetic

- Mime a slow-motion game of football, cricket or basketball.
- Devise an aerobic routine using current Top 40 hits.
- Dramatise a sporting incident involving an umpire.
- Create a daily fitness activity of about 10 minutes. Practise and teach the class—carry out over one week.
- Create a game to play indoors or outdoors to promote specified physical skills.
- Children 'do' and record their daily fitness routine.
- Role-play unusual sports from other countries. Children guess which sport from background information given.
- Create 'equipment' for indoor games; e.g. newspaper (rolls) hockey, ten-pin bowling etc.
- Design and build a 3-D stadium for a favourite sport.
- Create a new celebratory dance which can be used by players when they score a goal or reach a milestone.
- Children imagine their favourite sport is played by robots. Dramatise a game or match using robot-type movements to play.

Musical–Rhythmic

- In a group, compose a 'body percussion' piece.
- Listen to the musical themes from past Olympic Games and decide which are the most inspiring and why.
- Create a jingle/chant for members of their sporting faction to use at a sporting event.
- Research the songs of different sporting clubs and choose one to learn and perform.
- Create a 'health hustle' to a popular tune.
- Listen to/view songs/anthems/performances from a sporting event. Evaluate performances.
- Select songs which identify sporting achievements; e.g. *We are the champions* by Queen.
- Devise a chant/team song for a favourite sporting team.

Interpersonal

- Compete in teams to complete a series of movements as fast as possible.
- In a group, discuss how men's sport is given more media coverage than women's. Is this fair?
- Plan a new game with a partner using specified sporting equipment such as a ball and a rope.
- Working in a small group, compile a list of the five best reasons for and against playing football.
- In a group, create a 'round robin' of physical activities for the class to participate in. Carry out over a term or two.
- Plan a Year-level 'games day' as a group.

Intrapersonal

- Research to find which are the most popular sports in the world.
- Ask children, 'If you could try any sport in the world, what would it be? Why?'
- Use the Internet to find the answer to a sporting question, noting the search engine(s), search words and website used to find the answer.
- Write an account of feelings experienced when winning and losing.
- Research information about a sport they would like to try; e.g. equipment, venues, costs.
- Children report about a special physical activity they participate in. Include training times, skills, levels, achievements, equipment, uniform/costume etc.
- Create a personal time line for a sporting/physical achievement for the near future.
- Make an action plan for a sporting goal.
- Reflect upon sports or activities they have participated in throughout their life. Which is their favourite? Why?
- Research to find the greatest athlete to date in their favourite sport.

SPORT
INFORMATIONAL TEXT

The definition of sport is:
something done for pleasure or exercise, usually needing some bodily skill.

Highest women's heptathlon score:

7291 points by Jacqueline Joyner-Kersee of USA

Men's long jump record:

Mike Powell of USA at 8.95 m
How far can you jump?

Fastest female runner over 1000 m:

Svetlana Masterkova of Russia at 2 min 28.98 sec

Fastest bicycle rider:

Fred Rompelberg from Utah, USA has ridden
at 268.831 km/h

Fastest skateboarder:

Gary Hardwick of USA has skateboarded at 100.66
km/h

Fastest cricket bowler:

Shoaib Akhtar of Pakistan has bowled a cricket ball
at 161.3 km/h

World's fastest man (over 100 m):

Tim Montgomery of South Carolina, USA has run
100 m in 9.78 sec.
How long does it take you to run 100 m?

Longest ocean swim:

Susie Maroney, 197 km, Mexico to Cuba

Fastest 400 m freestyle swimmer:

Ian Thorpe of Australia can swim the 400 m
freestyle in 3 min 40.66 sec
What can you do in 3 min 40 sec?

Most goals in a football career:

Pelé, from 1956–1977, 1279 goals

World's largest enclosed dome:

Louisiana Superdome, New Orleans

World's oldest football player:

Enrique Alcocer, born 28 August 1924

World's oldest sport:

possibly running or wresting—this is disputed

Largest football arena in the world:

Maracana Stadium, Rio de Janeiro, Brazil

Test cricket's highest individual score:

400 by Brian Lara of the West Indies in 2004

World's oldest hockey club:

Teddington Hockey Club, London, UK

World's most popular sport (by audience):

football

Youngest female Wimbledon champion:

Martina Hingis, 15 years old, 1996

World's fastest ball in sport:

Jai-Alai, approx. 302 km/h

(Note: Records correct at
time of publication.)

SPORT

INFORMATIONAL TEXT

How many of these sports or recreations have you heard of?

acrobatics	dog racing	marathon	skindiving
aerobatics	dogsled racing	martial arts	ski orienteering
aerobics	drag racing	modern pentathlon	skittles
aikido	duckpin bowling	motocross	skydiving
air racing	equestrian	motorboat racing	skysurfing
archery	extreme sports	motorcycling racing	sled dog racing
arm wrestling	fencing	mountain biking	snowboarding
athletics	field hockey	moutaineering	snowmobiling
auto racing	figure skating	netball	snowshoe racing
badminton	fishing	off-road racing	soap box derby
ballooning	five-pin bowling	orienteering	soaring
bandy	flying discs	paddle tennis	soccer
barefoot water skiing	footbag	paddleball	softball
barrel jumping	football	paintball	speedball
baseball	formula one racing	parachuting	squash
basketball	freestyle skiing	paragliding	steamboat racing
baton twirling	frisbee	petanque	steeplechase
beach volleyball	Gaelic football	pickleball	street luge
biathlon	gliding	platform tennis	sumo wrestling
bicycle polo	golf	polo	surfing
bicycle stunt riding	greyhound racing	powerboat racing	swimming
bicycle racing	gymnastics	powerlifting	synchronised diving
billiards	hackeysack	quarter horse racing	synchronised swimming
BMX racing	handball	quoits	table tennis
boardsailing	hang gliding	race walking	tae kwon do
boat racing	harness racing	racquetball	tennis
bobsledding	hockey	rafting	
bocce	horse racing	rhythmic gymnastics	
bodybuilding	horseshoe pitching	rifle shooting	
boomeranging	hurling	ringette	
bowling	ice boating	rock climbing	
boxball	ice dancing	rodeo	toboganning
boxing	ice hockey	roller derby	touch football
broomball	ice skating	rollerskating	track and field
bullfighting	ice yachting	rounders	trampoline/tumbling
bungee jumping	in-line skating	rowing	trapshooting
candlepin bowling	jai alai	rugby	triathlon
canoe polo	jet ski boating	sailboarding	tug-of-war
canoeing and kayaking	jogging/running	sailing	underwater hockey
climbing	jousting	sandboarding	unicycle hockey
cricket	judo	scuba diving	vaulting
croquet	karate	sepak takraw	volleyball
cross-country running	karting	shinty	wakeboarding
cross-country skiing	kendo	shooting	walking
curling	kite flying	shuffleboard	water polo
cycling	korfball	skateboarding	water skiing
danball	lacrosse	skating	weightlifting
darts	lawn bowls	skeet shooting	windsurfing
discus	luge	skiboarding	wrestling
diving	lumberjack sports	skiing	yachting

/50	/50	/50	/45

TOTAL

/195

The multiple intelligence focus for this task is verbal–linguistic.

A verbal–linguistic child thinks in words.
He/She learns best through activities involving reading, writing and speaking.

Objective

- Selects a major sporting event and writes a newspaper report about it.

Teacher information

- Allow children time to read and review the articles.

- Discuss and list the features of a newspaper article.

- Children need time to think about a recent sporting event they may like to write about.

- Children may need to research the details and facts relating to the event. Children may use newspaper articles or the Internet to research.

- Children should be encouraged to write brief notes before starting to write their article.

Answers

- Teacher check

Additional activities

- Collect all articles and display in a class newspaper. (interpersonal)

- Children work in groups or pairs to record a television or radio interview to support the newspaper article. (interpersonal)

Preparation

- Collect various newspaper articles displaying sporting news.

CURRICULUM LINKS			
England	Literacy	Yr 5/6	• identify the features of recounted texts and use the style and conventions of journalism to report
Northern Ireland	English	KS2	• be aware of how the media present information and write in different forms
Republic of Ireland	English	5th/ 6th	• learn about the structure and function of parts of a newspaper and write in a range of genres
Scotland	English	C/D	• adjust reading approaches to the different way that information is presented in newspapers and produce a variety of different kinds of writing
Wales	English	KS2	• read and use newspapers and write in a range of non-fiction forms

READ ALL ABOUT IT!

word wise

Task • You will select a major sporting event and write a newspaper report about it.

THE TIMES WEEKLY *SPORT REPORT*

_____

headline

_____

reporter's name

_____

_____

_____

_____

opening paragraph (briefly outlines the article)

photograph in box and caption below

caption

main body of the article (gives detailed information)

conclusion of article

The multiple intelligence focus for this task is logical–mathematical.

A logical–mathematical child thinks rationally and in abstractions.
He/She learns best through activities involving problem-solving, numbers and patterns.

Objective

- Graphs the types of sports in which children in the class participate throughout the year.

Teacher information

- Ask the children one-by-one what sports they play through the year and record on the board for the class to see. Do not record repeated sports, only the new ones.

- Children can then record the sports played in the class in the tally table provided.

- Once the sports are recorded, ask for a show of hands for each sport and allow children to record the numbers in their tally.

- Once all sports have been tallied, children can independently graph the results. Remind children that graphs need a title and each axis must also be titled.

Answers

Teacher check

Additional activities

- What could this information be used for? Discuss in small groups. (interpersonal)

- Record data to show which sports are played at different times of the year. (logical–mathematical)

CURRICULUM LINKS			
England	Numeracy	Yr 5	• represent data in tables and graphs
Northern Ireland	Maths	KS2	• represent data using graphs and tables
Republic of Ireland	Maths	5th/ 6th	• represent data using bar charts
Scotland	Maths	C	• use a tally sheet with grouped tallies and construct a bar graph
Wales	Maths	KS2	• represent data using graphs

SPORT PARTICIPATION

Task — You will graph the types of sports in which children in your class participate throughout the year.

1. List all the sporting activities in which children in your class participate throughout the year.

2. Record how many children participate in each sport in the form of a tally.

Sport	Tally	Total

3. Graph the results on the axes below. Remember to give your graph a title and label each axis.

_____
title

The multiple intelligence focus for this task is naturalist.

A naturalistic child has an awareness of the patterns in nature.
He/She learns best through activities involving animals, plants and the environment.

Objective

- Plans a sporting activity at the local park which does not affect the natural environment or wildlife in any way.

Teacher information

- Children need to identify the features of the park and highlight a suitable and safe playing area away from dangers. Children must demonstrate an awareness of safety issues, such as the lake. Games should be played a safe distance from the water to prevent any accidents. This may need to be discussed in groups.

- Consideration needs to be shown for the habitat and wildlife already in the park. Would you play a game of cricket in the middle of the geese?

Answers

Answers will vary

Additional activities

- Design a nature park that is suitable for sporting and recreational activities.

- Discuss the impact clearing land to make sporting fields has on the environment.

CURRICULUM LINKS			
England	PSHE	KS2	• face new challenges by making responsible choices
Northern Ireland	Personal development*	KS2	• have a pro-active and responsible approach to safety (* curriculum proposals)
Republic of Ireland	SPHE	5th/ 6th	• recognise places where it is safer to play and how to behave in a responsible manner when playing
Scotland	Health	C	• demonstrate safe ways of responding to risks to safety in their community
Wales	PSE	KS2	• recognise how to be safe and take increasing responsibility for their actions

SPORTING ACTIVITIES

1 Look at the picture of the park below.

2 What type of sporting activity could be played in this park? _____

Why did you choose this activity? _____

_____

3 What considerations will need to be made to ensure the animals are safe and the habitat undamaged?

_____

_____

_____

_____

_____

_____

_____

4 What considerations will need to be made to ensure the participants are safe?

_____

_____

_____

_____

_____

_____

_____

5 What equipment will you need to take with you to the park?

_____

_____

_____

_____

_____

_____

_____

The multiple intelligence focus for this task is visual–spatial.

A visual–spatial child thinks in images, colours and shape.
He/She learns best through activities involving visualisation.

Objective

- Designs a new uniform for a favourite sport.

Teacher information

- Direct children to the worksheet. Children can work through the questions in any order but must answer them all. This will ensure they have considered all aspects of the design of the uniform.

- Encourage children to notice that the colours on a uniform are often restricted to two or three. Discuss why this might be.

- The final design should incorporate all the design ideas in the previous questions, including the colours, logos and type of fabric.

Answers

- Answers will vary

Additional activities

- Use a paper doll-style cut-out and make the uniform to be displayed on the doll.

- Design a mascot for their favourite team.

Preparation

- Ask children to bring in a picture of the uniform their favourite sports team currently wears.

CURRICULUM LINKS			
England	D & T	KS2	• communicate design ideas, bearing in mind aesthetic qualities and the uses and purposes for which the product is intended
Northern Ireland	Technology	KS2	• plan what they are going to make, talking about materials they could use
Republic of Ireland	Science	5th/6th	• present design proposal on a 'design sheet'
Scotland	Technology	C	• communicate a design plan and select possible resources
Wales	D & T	KS2	• develop and communicate aspects of their design ideas in a variety of ways, considering appearance, function and safety

DESIGN A UNIFORM

1 What is your favourite sport?

_____

2 What components does your uniform have? List them.

_____

_____

_____

_____

_____

_____

3 Consider the colours of your uniform. Show them below.

4 Every sport has some type of sponsorship to support the team or individual financially. This means the logo of the sponsor needs to be displayed prominently on the uniform.

What company will be your sponsor?

_____

Draw the company's logo here.

5 What type of fabric will you use? Consider weather conditions, comfort, flexibility and durability.

_____

_____

_____

_____

6 Draw your uniform design here. Show front and back views. Remember to include the team name, logos, participant's name and number if necessary.

The multiple intelligence focus for this task is bodily–kinaesthetic.

> A bodily–kinaesthetic child has a good physical awareness.
> He/She learns best through 'hands-on' activities.

Objective

- Invents a new game which can be played indoors or outdoors.

Teacher information

- Note: In order for this activity to be truly bodily–kinaesthetic, once children have completed the worksheet they must be given the opportunity to teach the class how to play the game and to participate in it. A different game could be chosen every few days to play.

- When creating a new game, children need to consider all aspects. This worksheet will help to guide children through the thought process of developing a new game.

- Those children who do not participate in a great deal of sport may need assistance with timing, players, scoring and so on. Some discussion about existing sports may give children the ideas they need to complete the worksheet.

Answers

- Answers will vary

Additional activities

- Invent and make new equipment to go with their new game.

- Design a uniform that could be worn when playing their new game. (visual–spatial)

- Create a song or chant that could be sung or chanted during their new game. (musical–rhythmic)

CURRICULUM LINKS			
England	PE	KS2	• play and make up small-sided and modified competitive games
Northern Ireland	PE	KS2	• make up, play and refine their own games and explain the rules and scoring
Republic of Ireland	PE	5th/6th	• create and develop games with a partner or with a small group
Scotland	PE	C	• understand and use some features of different forms of physical activity in planning solutions, e.g. inventing simple games
Wales	PE	KS2	• respond imaginatively to different activities and put forward their ideas about what to include in a game

INVENT A NEW GAME

body wise

1 What will your game be called?

_____

2 Where will your game be played?

indoors	outdoors

3 When will your game be played?

summer	autumn
winter	spring

4 How will your game be played?

in teams	in pairs
by individuals	

5 How many people will be able to play your game at any time?

_____

6 Briefly explain the aim of your game.

_____

_____

_____

_____

_____

7 How will people play your game?

_____

_____

_____

_____

_____

_____

8 What rules will your game have?

_____

_____

_____

_____

_____

_____

_____

_____

9 How long will your game last?

_____

10 What equipment and playing area will be needed to play your game?

11 How will you score the game?

_____

12 Will players need to wear any special clothing?

yes	no

Explain. _____

_____

The multiple intelligence focus for this task is musical–rhythmic.

A musical–rhythmic child has an awareness of music and sound.
He/She learns best through activities involving music or rhythms.

Objective

- Creates a new song or chant for a favourite sporting team.

Preparation

- Collect the song or chant currently being used by the sporting team. Listen to it carefully.
- Provide various musical instruments in the class; e.g. drums, tapping sticks, guitars, recorders, cymbals.
- Provide tape recorders.

Teacher information

- Children may need to complete some of this activity at home or in a quiet place away from others in order to be able to listen to music and to record their ideas onto tape. The recording process may take a number of attempts before a child is happy with his/her final piece.
- Children need to be aware of the types of instruments or sound effects they have at their disposal in order to plan what they are going to use in their song or chant.
- Children may also find the use of a thesaurus helpful when brainstorming the types of words they would like to include in their song or chant.

Answers

Answers will vary

Additional activities

- Create a dance or movements that would complement their song or chant. (bodily–kinaesthetic)
- Create banners and pompoms in team colours for team members and supporters to wave. (visual–spatial)

CURRICULUM LINKS			
England	Music	KS2	• complete a range of musical activities that integrate performing, composing and appraising
Northern Ireland	Music	KS2	• create short musical pieces
Republic of Ireland	Music	5th/6th	• select from a wide range of sound sources for a range of musical purposes
Scotland	Music	D	• provide opportunities for musical invention
Wales	Music	KS2	• compose and arrange music in response to a range of stimuli

TEAM SONG

Task ○   **You will create a new song or chant for your favourite sporting team.**

1   Listen to the song or chant currently being used by your favourite sporting team.
Note the main theme behind it and the feelings being evoked by the song or chant.

Theme	Feelings

2   The team song or chant is often used to encourage a positive team spirit. The words are usually strong and positive. When the team sings the song or chant together, it is a powerful tool to present a united front to the opposition.

Brainstorm some words you would like to use in your song or chant.

3   (a)   What type of music will you use?

_____

_____

_____

(b)   What mood do you want to get across?

_____

_____

_____

(c)   What instruments will you use?

4   Write the words to your song or chant.

_____

_____

_____

_____

_____

_____

_____

_____

_____

_____

_____

5   Record your song or chant complete with music and share with the class.

The multiple intelligence focus for this task is interpersonal.

An interpersonal child enjoys being in groups or teams.
He/She learns best through activities involving working with others.

Objective

- Works in a small group to plan a sports day for the school.

Teacher information

- Children work in groups of four or five for this activity.
- Children work together to complete the activities on the worksheet and record their final answers on the worksheet.
- Children may wish to use the computer to design and create the programme of events for Question 4.

Answers

Answers will vary

Additional activities

- Design and make the medals or ribbons which will be given to participants of the events who receive a place. (visual–spatial)
- Plan a nutritious menu for the sports day. (intrapersonal)

Preparation

- Children may need sheets of scrap paper to plan their ideas before recording them on the worksheet.
- Presentation card will be needed for the programme of events.

CURRICULUM LINKS			
England	English	KS2	• talk effectively as a member of a group, making contributions relevant to the topic
Northern Ireland	English	KS2	• take part in group discussions for a variety of purposes
Republic of Ireland	English	5th/ 6th	• discuss ideas and concepts encountered in other areas of the curriculum
Scotland	English	D	• work in groups to discuss tasks and how to deal with them
Wales	English	KS2	• make a range of contributions in discussions

SPORTS DAY

1 List the events your group would like to include in the sports day. Remember to include all Year levels in the events.

2 On the sports field below, show where the main events will be held and where the teams will spend the day, as well as any other features (e.g. judges announcers, start/finish, food stalls, first aid).

150 m

150 m

3 Discuss and list issues which will need to be considered on the day; for example, weather, shade or shelter, toilet breaks, organising teams and so on.

Issue	Solution

4 Prepare and present a programme of events. Remember to include the time of the event, the event and the location of the event.

The multiple intelligence focus for this task is intrapersonal.

An intrapersonal child understands and analyses his/her thoughts and feelings.
He/She learns best through individual activities.

Objective

- Researches and records information about an athlete he/she considers to be the greatest in a particular field.

Teacher information

- Children use the worksheet to record, in note form, details about their chosen athlete. Children should use keywords and phrases when recording information.

- Children will also need to record the source of the information they have collected.

Answers

- Answers will vary

Additional activities

- Children write a biography of their chosen athlete, using their research notes. (verbal–linguistic)

- Create a collage using various textures to make a portrait of their chosen athlete. (visual–spatial)

- Write a series of interview questions children would like to ask their chosen athlete. (verbal–linguistic)

Preparation

- Children may need to use library or Internet resources to complete this activity.

CURRICULUM LINKS			
England	Literacy	Yr 5	• locate information confidently and efficiently
Northern Ireland	English	KS2	• engage with a range of texts, e.g. non-fiction materials and read for information
Republic of Ireland	English	5th/6th	• explore appropriate non-fiction texts for various purposes
Scotland	English	C	• read for information, including developing the ability to scan
Wales	English	KS2	• read and use a wide range of sources of non-fiction information

MY GREATEST ATHLETE

Task You will research and record information about an athlete you consider to be the greatest in his/her field.

Name:	
Date of birth:	Death:
Where born:	Lived:
Sport:	

How it all began:

Achievements:

Most famous for:

Why does this person inspire you?	Where did you get your information?

SPORT – MY SELF–ASSESSMENT

After completing this unit, I was able to ...

word wise	select a major sporting event and write a newspaper report about it.	☆ ☆ ☆ ☆ ☆
logic wise	graph the types of sports in which children in my class participate throughout the year.	☆ ☆ ☆ ☆ ☆
nature wise	plan a sporting activity at the local park which will not affect the natural environment or wildlife in any way.	☆ ☆ ☆ ☆ ☆
picture wise	design a new uniform for my favourite sport.	☆ ☆ ☆ ☆ ☆
body wise	invent a new game which can be played indoors or outdoors.	☆ ☆ ☆ ☆ ☆
music wise	create a new song or chant for my favourite sporting team.	☆ ☆ ☆ ☆ ☆
people wise	work in a small group to plan a sports day for our school.	☆ ☆ ☆ ☆ ☆
self wise	research and record information about an athlete I consider to be the greatest in his/her field.	☆ ☆ ☆ ☆ ☆

What I learnt

MULTIPLE INTELLIGENCES

PERSONAL DEVELOPMENT

Informational text......................... ☐   ☐ .... Bullying role-plays

word wise

Relationships .... ☐   ☐ ....Right behaviour raps

music wise

logic wise

Time line of changes .... ☐   ☐ .... Difficult situations

people wise

nature wise

Survey .... ☐   ☐ ....Puberty

self wise

picture wise

Magazine stereotypes .... ☐   ☐ ....My self-assessment

What I know	What I want to know

Keywords

Name:	Date:

PERSONAL DEVELOPMENT OVERVIEW

Verbal-Linguistic

- Invite a child health expert to talk about newborn babies and what they can and can't do.
- Complete a questionnaire on how they think their life will change at 16, 21, 30, 50 etc.
- Write a record about themselves that states their name, address, family members, hobbies, best features, achievements etc.
- Write a poem that explores the feelings they have about puberty or growing up.
- Present a report about a partner after interviewing him/her about his/her life. Find out if it reflects the person's own opinions about himself/herself.
- Write a report about how the school has changed since they started going there.
- Write an autobiography of their life so far.
- Discuss and describe special friendships experienced at different stages of their life.
- Discuss and describe changes in relationships with parents, teachers, friends and siblings at different stages of their life.

Logical-Mathematical

- Find out the average height of children in the class and compare them to the average heights of younger classes.
- Draw a time line showing their life and changes from birth to now.
- Investigate what children of different ages in the school think about different social issues.
- Survey the class about the brands or types of different products they use and why. The products chosen might include shampoo, soft drink, toothpaste or clothing. Collate the results and present the data as a graph, a table etc.
- List and organise facts about the childrens' favourite CDs, clothing brands, television shows, singers/bands, books etc.
- Research and create a time line of an older person's life.
- Calculate the age in years and months of class members and graph the numbers of children in each category.
- Calculate how many more months to wait before getting a driver's licence, leaving school, turning 21 etc.

Naturalist

- Compare human growth to that of other mammals; e.g. how long it takes to reach adulthood.
- Take photographs of people of various ages to create a mural. Write the similarities and differences noted.
- Compare physical changes in children from one Year level to the next.
- Consider how the next generation's environment will differ from the environment they live in.

Visual-Spatial

- View magazine or television advertisements that contain stereotypes and discuss them in a group.
- Look at pictures of different everyday scenes and decide which make them angry and why.
- Draw detailed pictures of what they think particular types of people look like; e.g. punks, rock stars, drunks, superheroes. Compare 'stereotypical' pictures.
- Create a visual diary of themselves from birth to now, using photographs and written descriptions of achievements for each stage of life.
- Create a 'slide show' of the children in the class from the start of school to now.
- Create a collage which shows the major changes that have happened in their life over the last 12 months.
- View some scenes from television soap operas that involve people of their age. How realistic do they feel the problems are that the characters face?

PERSONAL DEVELOPMENT OVERVIEW

Bodily-Kinaesthetic

- Role-play peer pressure scenes.
- Play some of the games their grandparents used to play at school. Compare them to the ones they might play now.
- Learn dances that were popular when their parents were young and perform them. Compare them to the way people their age dance now.
- Show how humans at different ages might move; e.g. a baby crawling, a child taking its first steps, an older person with stiff joints etc.
- Play charades based on a list of happy or sad life events.
- Role-play scenarios that show the way children might react when a new child begins his/her first day in the class. The new child could be academic, sporty, have learning difficulties, be from a culture that is different from that of the other children in the class etc.
- Show how they think a 'typical' teenager might move. Discuss the similarities between his/her mime and other people's mimes. How stereotypical are they?

Musical-Rhythmic

- Change the words to songs about growing up or life changes; e.g. *It was a very good year, Cat's in the cradle* and *Que sera.*
- Write a new advertising jingle for the most popular food or drinks among the children in the class.
- Conduct a survey to find out the most popular musical video clips among children of different ages. View the video clips and compare the similarities and differences.
- In a group, create a jingle or a chant that encourages people not to bully.

Interpersonal

- Discuss health issues, such as smoking, in small groups.
- In a group, devise and role-play problem-solving scenarios involving peer pressure or bullying.
- Participate in teamwork activities requiring cooperation and communication.
- As a group, discuss issues such as why peer pressure can be such a strong influence; the qualities of a good friend; how we can show respect for people; how we can be good team members etc. Create motivational posters to display in the classroom using the ideas generated from these discussions.

Intrapersonal

- Complete report cards about themselves, giving scores out of 10 for areas like attitude, effort, confidence, empathy, cooperation, decision-making and other attributes. Write some comments that describe how they could improve their scores.
- Choose a goal for the future and write steps to show how they could achieve it.
- Describe what their 'perfect' future life would be like. Write which features of this life they think are achievable and why.
- Write about their greatest achievement.
- Think 10 years into the future. Describe how they expect their life will have changed and what things they expect will be the same.
- Write positive affirmations that can be used to enhance self-image or self-esteem and also aid the achievement of goals.
- Write what they would do in different 'moral dilemma' situations.

PERSONAL DEVELOPMENT
INFORMATIONAL TEXT

What does 'personal development' mean?

Personal development concerns a person's physical, social and emotional growth, particularly as he/she changes from a young child to an adult. As you get older, you will find that your relationships, values, attitudes and interests will develop and change. Your body will also go through many changes. In addition, you may have to deal with issues like bullying, divorce, moving house or going to a new school.

Values

As we get older, we are often faced with situations where it can be difficult to know what to do. When we have confidence in ourselves and strong values (ideals we believe strongly in), it is easier to do things that are right for us. Some of the things people commonly value include honesty, generosity and perseverance.

If people are unsure of what they value, they can be led easily by others and may end up doing things they don't want to do. Sometimes, people your own age (your 'peers') can influence your thoughts and actions—often negatively. This is called 'peer pressure'.

Relationships

The relationships you have with your family, friends and other people will change and grow throughout your life. Sometimes, this is simply due to your age – for example, the dependence you had on your parents when you were a baby had changed dramatically by the time you began school.

Relationships can also start, end or develop for social and emotional reasons. For example, changes in your expectations, interests or values may cause you to end some friendships and find new friends who are on a similar 'wavelength' to you.

It is important to remember that however your relationships change, all worthwhile relationships rely on mutual respect, effective communication and trust.

Life changes and choices

It is part of life to have to deal with important changes or choices that affect our emotions or cause us stress. Dealing with events such as the birth of a new brother or sister, the death of a relative or starting at a new school can be challenging, but can also help us to grow emotionally. It is important to remember that everyone goes through difficult times, but some people cope better with change than others. Some things you can do to help you cope with 'big' changes in your life include getting regular exercise, eating healthy food, taking time to relax and talking to someone you trust about your problems.

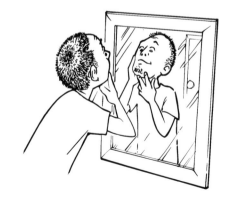

PERSONAL DEVELOPMENT
INFORMATIONAL TEXT

Puberty

Puberty, the period where a child develops to sexual maturity, is a major life change for everyone. Puberty usually happens between the ages of 10 and 16. During this time, girls and boys go through certain stages of development. These stages will happen at different times for every individual.

Both physical and emotional changes will happen during puberty. Physical changes for boys include weight and height gain, growing pubic hair, growing hair under the arms and on the face, getting a deeper voice, oilier skin and the penis growing longer and wider. Physical changes for girls include weight and height gain, growing breasts, the beginning of menstruation, growing pubic hair and oilier skin.

Emotional changes will also occur for both boys and girls. This is due to the rapid release of hormones or chemicals during puberty. It is perfectly normal during puberty to feel moody – sometimes for no reason at all!

When people go through puberty, they usually feel they want more independence. They also start to form their own ideas and values. Sometimes, they may feel closer to their friends than to their parents or siblings because their friends are going through the same changes. These feelings can often cause conflict with family, especially with parents.

Bullying and stereotyping

Most people will have to deal with being bullied or stereotyped at some stage in their lives.

Bullying is deliberate, hurtful treatment that is repeated over time. Some strategies that can be used to deal with bullying include acting confidently, avoiding bullying situations and asking an adult for help. If bullying is not stopped, it can lead to emotional and physical effects, such as low self-esteem and illness.

Stereotyping is a very simple, and often incorrect, picture people have of a person, based on elements like gender, age, religion or culture. Making unfair assumptions about a person can affect his/her self-worth. It is important to remember that everyone is an individual. You should also try to accept yourself as you are – you are special!

The multiple intelligence focus for this activity is verbal–linguistic.

> A verbal–linguistic child thinks in words.
> He/She learns best through activities involving reading, writing and speaking.

Objective

- Considers how relationships change over time.

Preparation

- The children will need to work with a partner for Question 5.

Teacher information

- Before the children begin the worksheet, discuss the different types of relationships they may have had over a period of at least five years. These will probably be mostly family and friends. Discuss how the relationships might have changed, including elements like dependence, shared activities and feelings between the people in the relationship. The children should then complete Questions 1 to 4 individually and Question 5 with a partner. The similarities they find should be orally reported to the class. The children from each pair should share the report as equally as possible.

Answers

Teacher check

Additional activities

- Children write poems about aspects of their favourite relationships.
- Create a flow chart that shows the steps they could use to maintain a positive relationship with someone. (logical–mathematical)

CURRICULUM LINKS			
England	PSHE	KS2	• be aware of different types of relationship and develop the skills to be effective in relationships
Northern Ireland	Personal development*	KS2	investigate relationships with family, friends and in school (* curriculum proposals)
Republic of Ireland	SPHE	5th/ 6th	• discuss possible changes in family relationships and realise that making and changing friends is part of the natural process of growing
Scotland	Health	D	• recognise the ways in which behaviour can influence people's relationships
Wales	PSE	KS2	• understand the benefits of friends and families and the challenges and issues that can arise

RELATIONSHIPS

Task ● You will consider how relationships can change over time.

Our relationships with people change over time. For example, as you get older you may become less dependent on a parent or enjoy different activities with a friend.

1 Choose two people you have had a relationship with for at least the past five years. They should be two different types of relationships; e.g. a family member and a friend.

2 In the table below, write notes about how each relationship has changed over the years. You might consider:

(a)   what you and each person did together or talked about when you were younger and what you do/talk about now,

(b)   how you treated the other person when you were younger and how you treat him/her now,

(c)   what the person did for you when you were younger and what he/she does for you now.

Relationship (e.g. mother, friend)	In the past	Now
Person 1:		
Person 2:		

3 Circle the relationship where the most dramatic changes occurred. Write some reasons why you think things changed.

_____

_____

_____

_____

_____

_____

4 Write how you think the other relationship you wrote about might change in the future.

_____

_____

_____

_____

_____

5 Discuss your answers with a partner. Highlight any similarities between your answers. Report these to the class.

MULTIPLE INTELLIGENCES

The multiple intelligence focus for this activity is logical–mathematical.

A logical–mathematical child thinks rationally and in abstractions.
He/She learns best through activities involving problem-solving, numbers and patterns.

Objectives

- Constructs a time line based on important events in his/her life.
- Correctly interprets a time line.

Teacher information

- Before the children are given the worksheet, hold a class discussion about some important events that have happened in their lives. Teachers may like to list on the board some of the answers given that are not suggested on the worksheet; e.g. parents getting divorced, a family wedding. Teachers will need to be aware that some important events will evoke emotional memories for some children.

Answers

- Answers will vary

Additional activities

- Write a diary entry about an important day in their life. (verbal–linguistic)
- Make a collage using a range of different materials to show their emotions about an important event in their life. (visual–spatial)

Preparation

- Depending on the class's experience, the teacher may like to show examples of the format of time lines before the children begin the worksheet.

CURRICULUM LINKS			
England	History	KS2	• place events into correct periods of time
Northern Ireland	History	KS2	• show chronological awareness by sequencing events
Republic of Ireland	History	5th/6th	• record events using simple time lines
Scotland	Society	C	• put a series of events with their dates in chronological order
Wales	History	KS2	• use chronological frameworks

TIME LINE OF CHANGES

Task You will construct a time line based on important events in your life and interpret a time line.

1 What important changes have happened in your life so far? Perhaps some are the events listed below. Tick any that have happened to you.

- [ ] *moved house*
- [ ] *changed schools*
- [ ] *went on an overseas holiday*
- [ ] *achieved important goal*
- [ ] *relative/friend/pet died*
- [ ] *new brother/sister was born*

2 List any other important changes that have happened to you.

3 Circle six events you ticked or wrote about that happened in six different years of your life.

4 Write these events on the time line below. Begin by writing the year in which you were born (e.g. '1995'). Then write each of the following years on the lines given until you reach this year. Write each event next to the year in which it happened.

Year I was born:	

5 Answer these questions about your time line.

(a) Which was the earliest event you wrote about? _____

(b) How many events happened after you turned five? _____

(c) How many years were between the earliest event and the most recent event? _____

(d) How old were you when the most recent event occurred? _____

The multiple intelligence focus for this activity is naturalist.

A naturalist child has an awareness of the patterns in nature.
He/She learns best through activities involving animals, plants and the environment.

Objective

- Conducts a survey to find out some differences among children of different ages.

Preparation

- Contact teachers of two younger classes in the school and ask them to pair their children with children from your class. The two children from the younger classes must be between the ages of 5 and 6 and 7 and 8. The survey should take only a few minutes to complete.

- Height charts and scales will be needed to answer the first two survey questions. Teachers should be aware that some children of this age will be sensitive about their weight; therefore, they may like to write some weight ranges on the board and ask the children to select the correct one; e.g. '40 – 50 kilograms').

Teacher information

- Read the survey with the class and ask the children to complete the questions. If necessary, teachers can explain that the children are being asked to spell 'dinosaur' for the second last question. Teachers should also instruct the children to provide a full answer for the last question, rather than just 'yes' or 'no'. This question is provided to give an insight into the development of reasoning in children. Studies have shown that children about the age of 12 will give more complex answers (e.g. 'It is against the law to steal, but the boy would have died if the woman didn't take the tablets, so I think she probably made the right decision'), whereas for a younger child, the answer will usually be black or white (e.g. 'She should not have taken the tablets because stealing is wrong').

- The children should now ask the survey questions of the two younger children allocated to them. When asking the questions, they should follow the rules below, which may be copied and handed out to each class member. Teachers may also like to emphasise to their class that the children being surveyed should under no circumstances be made to feel uncomfortable.

- Speak clearly when you ask each question and allow the child time to think about each answer. Don't comment on any answers given. The answers should be written in note form.

- Some children will be sensitive about their height or weight. Don't show your results to other children in their class.

- If the child indicates that he/she can count to 50, ask him/her to do so. If he/she cannot, do not comment, but write 'no' in the box provided.

- If the child does not understand the question starting with 'Spell the …', you may ask him/her instead to spell 'dinosaur'. Write the word exactly the way he/she spells it.

- For the last question, encourage the child to give a full answer.

- Ask a spokesperson from each small group to report for Question 3. The class can then discuss the changes that occur as children age.

Answers

Teacher check

Additional activities

- Compare a simple format of a mathematics or English syllabus for children of different ages. (intrapersonal)

- Compile and conduct surveys among children of their own age.

CURRICULUM LINKS			
England	English	KS2	• speak with confidence in a range of contexts, adapting their speech for a range of purposes and audiences
Northern Ireland	English	KS2	• use questionnaires to seek information
Republic of Ireland	English	5th/ 6th	• use questions as a means of extending knowledge
Scotland	English	C	• organise research and obtain necessary information
Wales	English	KS2	• express themselves confidently and listen to others, questioning them to clarify what they mean

SURVEY

Task • You will conduct a survey to find some differences among children of different ages.

1 Complete the questions in the survey below, then ask two younger children at your school the same questions.

	You	Younger child (7–8 years old)	Youngest child (5–6 years old)
How old are you?			
How tall are you?			
What do you weigh?			
Are your friends a mix of boys and girls?			
What are your hobbies or interests?			
Name two things that make you worry.			
What do you want to do when you are an adult?			
What do you like to do with your friends?			
Can you count to 50?			
Spell the name of the type of animal a *Tyrannosaurus rex* is.			
A poor woman's son is very ill. The tablets she needs to cure him cost a lot of money. The woman tries everything but she cannot get enough money to buy the tablets, so she steals them. Should she have done this? Say why/why not.			

2 Discuss the answers you have for each age group with a small group. Tick any similarities.

3 Report the similarities to the class and discuss.

The multiple intelligence focus for this activity is visual–spatial.

A visual–spatial child thinks in images, colours and shape.
He/She learns best through activities involving visualisation.

Objective

- Understands how magazines use stereotypes.

Preparation

- The children will require drawing materials such as crayons or pencils and scrap paper.

Teacher information

- Before the children begin the worksheet, teachers may like to read the information at the top of the page to the class and discuss the concept of stereotypes further, particularly stereotypical ideas based on gender.

- After the answers to Questions 1 and 2 have been completed individually, teachers may like to ask some children to volunteer their answers to the class.

- When the children have completed Question 3, they may like to enlarge their designs to A4 size to display in the classroom.

Answers

Teacher check

Additional activities

- Children find examples of magazine advertisements they think are stereotypical and explain their reasons to the class.

CURRICULUM LINKS			
England	PSHE	KS2	• recognise and challenge stereotypes
Northern Ireland	Personal development*	KS2	• recognise the pressure and influences from various sources to behave in certain ways (* curriculum proposals)
Republic of Ireland	SPHE	5th/ 6th	• recognise unequal treatment of sexual roles and other issues in magazines
Scotland	Health	D	• recognise that media influences can affect choices they make
Wales	PSE	KS2	• recognise and understand the power of (peer) influence and pressure

MAGAZINE STEREOTYPES

picture wise

A stereotype is a fixed idea people have of a particular type of person. Many stereotypes can be found in the media. Imagine you have just started work at a new publishing company. Here are the cover designs for the next issue of two of the company's magazines.

1 What are the magazines assuming boys and girls like or want to be like? (for example, 'Girls like pink'.)

Girls

Boys

2 Do you think all girl or all boys would like to read the magazine aimed at them? Explain.

_____

_____

_____

_____

_____

_____

_____

3 In the space provided, design a magazine cover you think would appeal to both boys and girls your age. Plan your cover on a separate sheet of paper first.

The multiple intelligence focus for this activity is bodily–kinaesthetic.

> A bodily–kinaesthetic child has good physical awareness.
> He/She learns best through 'hands-on' activities.

Objectives

- Role-plays bullying scenarios with a partner.
- Uses voice and body effectively in role-plays.

Preparation

- Each child will need a partner to complete this worksheet.
- The children will need appropriate rehearsal space to practise their role-plays. It is suggested that approximately 15 – 20 minutes total time is given for practising.

Teacher information

- When the children are given the worksheet, teachers should read the information at the top of the page to the class and then read each of the scenarios. With the teacher's guidance, the children can suggest some positive ways that each scenario could end. Encourage the children to use such positive endings when creating their role-plays.

- Before children begin practising their role-plays, the teacher should discuss how voice and body can be used to indicate feelings and moods; e.g. a character's lack of confidence can be shown by speaking in a low voice, while looking at the ground.

- The children can present their role-plays to a small group or the whole class. A class discussion about the endings chosen by each pair could follow.

- The scales at the bottom of the page should be completed individually.

CURRICULUM LINKS

England	English	KS2	• create, adapt and sustain different roles in group drama
Northern Ireland	English	KS2	• engage in role-play and drama
Republic of Ireland	English	5th/6th	• explore and express conflicts of opinion through improvisational drama
Scotland	Drama	C	• cooperate with others and sustain and develop roles
Wales	English	KS2	• participate in a wide range of drama activities, including role-play

Answers

Teacher check

Additional activities

- Write about a bullying situation they have witnessed. Was the situation resolved? If so, how? What else could have been done? (verbal–linguistic)

- Write scripts of bullying scenes and perform them to the class with a partner or in a small group.

BULLYING ROLE-PLAYS

Task ● You will role-play bullying scenarios, concentrating on your voice and body.

Bullying is deliberately hurting other people with words or actions that are repeated over a period of time. Bullying can be physical (e.g. hitting someone), verbal (e.g. teasing someone) or social (e.g. leaving someone out of a group).

1 Find a partner to role-play these bullying scenarios, creating your own endings. Write notes on how you will use your voice and body to perform your best in each scenario.

A waits until B is alone and then demands that B gives up his/her lunch money. B is frightened of A and gives the money. This has been happening for many weeks.	*A deliberately trips B over in the playground. B is hurt and starts to cry. A teases B for being a cry-baby.*
B hears A talking to a group of children in the class about his/her birthday party. B asks when it is. A tells B that he/she is not invited and should go away.	*A is new to the school. A asks B, a child from the class, if he/she can sit with B at lunchtime. B pretends not to hear A.*
B walks past A's desk and knocks everything off, then walks away laughing. A is sick of B always doing this.	*A is tired of B boasting about all the expensive presents B's parents give him/her. One day, A has had enough. He/She takes one of the presents and holds it up out of B's reach, then hides it.*

2 Rehearse your two best scenarios and present them to the class.

3 Show how well you thought you performed in your scenarios by colouring each scale.

Use of voice	sizzling!	hot	warm	freezing
Use of body	sky high!	ceiling level	knee high	ground level

The multiple intelligence focus for this activity is musical–rhythmic.

> A musical–rhythmic child has an awareness of music and sound.
> He/She learns best through activities involving music or rhythms.

Objectives

- Composes a performance poem with a given number of beats in each line.
- Presents a performance poem to the class.

Teacher information

- Teachers should introduce the worksheet by reading the information at the top of the page to the class. Some examples of appropriate raps may be brainstormed by the class before the groups begin work, depending on the ability of the class.

Answers

Teacher check

Additional activities

- Perform favourite raps for a younger class of children.

Preparation

- Organise the children into groups of four.
- The children will need appropriate rehearsal space to practise their raps. It is suggested that approximately 15 – 20 minutes is allowed.
- Percussion instruments may be provided.

CURRICULUM LINKS			
England	Music	KS2	• complete a range of musical activities that integrate composing and performing
Northern Ireland	Music	KS2	• create short pieces of music which explore and combine elements of music
Republic of Ireland	Music	5th/ 6th	• invent and perform pieces that show an increasing awareness and control of musical elements
Scotland	Music	D	• invent a rap, adding simple rhythms and sounds
Wales	Music	KS2	• improvise, compose and arrange music in response to a range of stimuli

RIGHT BEHAVIOUR RAPS

Task • You will compose a rap with a given number of beats in each line and perform a rap with a group.

Find a group of four people. Imagine you are television presenters on a weekly programme for young children. The programme promotes values and attitudes. For your next show, your producer wants you to present a series of raps using simple language that remind children how to treat other people nicely. She hands you the following information.

Please create four raps that promote the following:

- *using good manners*
- *taking turns*
- *sharing*
- *not hurting others when playing*
- *being tolerant with others*

Each rap will have the same number of beats or syllables in each line. Here is an example of the form each rap should take:

I like biscuits	(4 beats)
I like cheese.	(3 beats)
I remember	(4 beats)
To say please!	(3 beats)

As in the example above, the first two lines of each rap may start with the same words; e.g. ' I like', 'I can', 'It is'.

---

1 With your group, try composing four raps using the rules given above. To help you begin, write some rhyming pairs with words you think you might use in your raps; for example, good – should, could; share – care; kind – find, mind etc.

_____

_____

_____

2 Compose your four raps and then write them in the spaces below. You might like to write drafts on a scrap sheet of paper first. Remember to check the number of beats in each line.

RAP 1 _____

_____

_____

RAP 2 _____

_____

_____

RAP 3 _____

_____

_____

RAP 4 _____

_____

_____

3 Practise performing your raps with your group. You can add movement, percussion or vocal sounds to your performance. When you are ready, perform your raps for the class.

The multiple intelligence focus for this activity is interpersonal.

An interpersonal child enjoys being in groups or teams.
He/She learns best through activities involving working with others.

Objectives

- Participates in group discussions.
- Prepares and presents a group report.

Preparation

- Organise the children into groups of five.

Teacher information

- Depending on the ability of the class, teachers may like to read the scenarios aloud before the groups start work.
- Teachers should emphasise that there are no right or wrong answers to the scenarios and that each group will need to reach a majority decision.
- For Question 2, the children could also discuss how well their groups worked and what problems in reaching decisions were encountered. The group members should share the presentation of the report as equally as possible.

Answers

Teacher check

Additional activities

- Create role-plays based on some of the scenarios. (bodily–kinaesthetic)
- Write about some difficult decisions they have had to make. (verbal–linguistic)

CURRICULUM LINKS			
England	PSHE	KS2	• resolve differences by looking at alternatives, making decisions and explaining choices
Northern Ireland	Personal development*	KS2	• investigate situations they and others have faced and how this made them feel (* curriculum proposals)
Republic of Ireland	SPHE	5th/6th	• recognise that decisions have consequences and that not all people will make the same decisions all of the time
Scotland	Health	C/D	• show ways of dealing with a range of situations and recognise that peer influences can affect choices they make
Wales	PSE	KS2	• understand that actions have consequences and that people differ in what they believe is right or wrong

DIFFICULT SITUATIONS

Task • You will work in a group to discuss some difficult situations and present a group report to the class.

As we get older, we often face situations where it can be difficult to know what to do.

1 In a group of five, discuss each of the situations below. Write what you think each person should do, considering the consequences of his/her actions.

Jessica's younger brother, Adam, tells her he has a secret. Jessica promises not to tell anyone. Then Adam tells her that the group of friends he hangs around with have started shoplifting.
They have told Adam that if he doesn't start doing it, they no longer want to be friends with him. Adam is very shy and finds it difficult to make friends.

What should Jessica do?

_____
_____
_____
_____
_____

Danielle wants to be a writer. One day, her teacher announces a school writing competition that Danielle wants to enter. However, the day before the competition closes, she is still struggling to write something suitable. Then one of her friends from another school offers to let Danielle copy one of his stories to enter in the competition. He says he doesn't care. The story is excellent and Danielle thinks it would have a good chance of winning.

What should Danielle do?

_____
_____
_____
_____
_____

Chris has been learning the guitar for five years. He wants to play professionally one day. For months, he has been practising hard for an important music exam. Two weeks before the exam, Chris's friend David invites him to go on holiday with his family. Chris is excited until he realises the date of his exam falls in the middle of the holiday. It is too late to change the exam date. If Chris goes on the holiday, he will have to wait until next year to do the exam. He also knows his teacher will be disappointed.

What should Chris do?

_____
_____
_____
_____
_____

Scott has been saving up his pocket money for months to buy a computer game. When he goes to pay for it at the shop, the shop assistant mistakenly charges Scott half of the real cost of the game. Scott takes the game, but feels bad and asks his friends who are with him if they think he should point out the mistake.
His friends tell him not to be stupid. They suggest that Scott buy another game he really wants with the money he has left.

What should Scott do?

_____
_____
_____
_____
_____

2 As a group, report your solutions to the class.

The multiple intelligence focus for this task is intrapersonal.

An intrapersonal child understands and analyses his/her thoughts and feelings.
He/She learns best through individual activities.

Objective

- Understands how changes at puberty might affect him/her.

Teacher information

- It is important to create a warm, caring and honest classroom environment to alleviate any embarrassment or pressure the children may feel about this topic. Begin by holding a class discussion about the changes that may occur during puberty. This should include emotional as well as physical changes. The children can then help to create a list of changes before completing the questions on the worksheet individually.

- After completing the worksheet, teachers may ask the children to volunteer their answers to Questions 2 – 4, but they should not be forced to do this. If some children are willing to volunteer answers, a class discussion may follow.

CURRICULUM LINKS			
England	PSHE	KS2	• know about how the body changes as they approach puberty
Northern Ireland	Personal development*	KS2	• investigate what changes the body experiences both physically and emotionally during puberty (* curriculum proposals)
Republic of Ireland	SPHE	5th/ 6th	• identify and discuss the physical and other changes that occur in boys and girls with the onset of puberty
Scotland	Health	C	• identify the different ways in which people grow and change, e.g. in puberty
Wales	PSE	KS2	• understand the physical and emotional changes which take place at puberty

Answers

- Answers will vary

Additional activities

- Role-play some of the situations described in Question 2. Other situations could also be devised and role-played. (bodily-kinaesthetic)

- Write 'feelings' poems based on the words or phrases written for Questions 3 and 4. (verbal–linguistic)

PUBERTY

You will understand how the physical and emotional changes of puberty might affect you.

Puberty begins when your brain sends messages to your body to start releasing chemicals called hormones. Hormones cause changes to your body as well as to your emotions and moods. Dealing with the changes at puberty can affect the way you feel about yourself and other people.

1 What changes do you know happen to boys and girls during puberty?

Boys	Girls

2 How do you think you would deal with these issues that might occur during puberty?

You have always shared a room with your younger sister, but now you want some privacy.	You suddenly grow a lot taller than your friends and you feel awkward.	You are getting ready to go to a big party when you discover that you have pimples on your chin.

3 List some words that describe how you feel about the changes that occur at puberty.

4 What do you think the best things about puberty and growing up will be for you?

PERSONAL DEVELOPMENT –
MY SELF-ASSESSMENT

After completing this unit, I was able to …

word wise	consider how relationships can change over time.	☆ ☆ ☆ ☆ ☆
logic wise	construct a time line based on important events in my life and interpret a time line.	☆ ☆ ☆ ☆ ☆
nature wise	conduct a survey to find some differences among children of different ages.	☆ ☆ ☆ ☆ ☆
picture wise	understand how magazine covers use stereotyping.	☆ ☆ ☆ ☆ ☆
body wise	role-play bullying scenarios, concentrating on my voice and body.	☆ ☆ ☆ ☆ ☆
music wise	compose a rap with a given number of beats in a line and perform it with a group.	☆ ☆ ☆ ☆ ☆
people wise	work in a group to discuss some difficult situations and present a group report to the class.	☆ ☆ ☆ ☆ ☆
self wise	understand how the physical and emotional changes of puberty might affect me.	☆ ☆ ☆ ☆ ☆

What I learnt